THE RESTORATION
AND 18th-CENTURY

ST. JAMES REFERENCE GUIDE TO ENGLISH LITERATURE

Editor: James Vinson
Associate Editor: D. L. Kirkpatrick

THE RESTORATION AND 18th-CENTURY

INTRODUCTIONS BY

PAT ROGERS

ARTHUR H. SCOUTEN

ST. JAMES PRESS
CHICAGO AND LONDON

St. James Press, Inc.
425 North Michigan Avenue
Chicago 60611

First published by St. James/Macmillan in the
UK in 1983
First published in the USA in 1985

ISBN 0-912289-20-1

Printed in the U.S.A.

CONTENTS

EDITOR'S NOTE

The entry for each writer consists of a biography, a complete list of his published books, a selected list of published bibliographies and critical studies on the writer, and a signed critical essay on his work.

In the biographies, details of education, military service, and marriage(s) are generally given before the usual chronological summary of the life of the writer; awards and honours are given last.

The Publications section is meant to include all book publications, though as a rule broadsheets, single sermons and lectures, minor pamphlets, exhibition catalogues, etc. are omitted. Under the heading Collections, we have listed the most recent collections of the complete works and those of individual genres (verse, plays, novels, stories, and letters); only those collections which have some editorial authority and were issued after the writer's death are listed; on-going editions are indicated by a dash after the date of publication; often a general selection from the writer's works or a selection from the works in the individual genres listed above is included.

Titles are given in modern spelling, though the essayists were allowed to use original spelling for titles and quotations; often the titles are "short." The date given is that of the first book publication, which often followed the first periodical or anthology publication by some time; we have listed the actual year of publication, often different from that given on the title-page. No attempt has been made to indicate which works were published anonymously or pseudonymously, or which works of fiction were published in more than one volume. We have listed plays which were produced but not published, but only since 1700; librettos and musical plays are listed along with the other plays; no attempt has been made to list lost or unverified plays. Reprints of books (including facsimile editions) and revivals of plays are not listed unless a revision or change of title is involved. The most recent edited version of individual works is included if it supersedes the collected edition cited.

In the essays, short references to critical remarks refer to items cited in the Publications section or in the Reading List. Introductions, memoirs, editorial matter, etc. in works cited in the Publications section are not repeated in the Reading List.

PROSE AND POETRY

INTRODUCTION

To understand the past requires more than the exercise of intellect: it means an act of imagination, as well. For hindsight, in the very process of clarifying historical issues, serves all too easily to rob them of their urgency, their "open" quality to contemporaries, their shock-value. It is not hard to come up with an account of literary history between the Restoration of Charles II and the publication of *Lyrical Ballads* which will chart a smooth and explicable course of events. Prose and poetry fall into convenient patterns of evolution rather than revolution. Even the Romantic movement itself can be assimilated into this graceful progression: scholars who seek (wrongheadedly, as we may think) to find a "conventional side" in the *Lyrical Ballads*, and to show that they conformed to existing taste, can achieve some disconcerting success. But it is surely right to press in the other direction, to look for discontinuities and to emphasise novelty where it appears. In this introduction I shall hope to take proper account of the fluidity of the period, not because it makes better copy for the literary historian, but because the dynamics were generally more apparent than the statics to people alive at the time. After all, the common reader does not have a research library at his or her finger-tips, so as to check out possible sources and analogues. If a theme or style *looks* new, then it will reasonably be taken as such by most of the reading public. By rooting out the rare exception, scholars falsify the experience of encountering the new: and in blurring the transitions we make the story duller than it really was – something pedants mistake for accuracy.

Conventionally the period covered here has been divided into three clearcut stages. First, the Restoration period itself, that is, running from the King's return to the throne in 1660, through his own reign and that of his brother James, and then extending either to the death of William III in 1702 or to the close of the Stuart dynasty in 1714. The second phase begins either at the start or the close of Anne's reign (1702 or 1714) and reaches to about 1742 (the fall of Walpole). The last proceeds from this point to about 1789, a year inconveniently hazy in English history, or 1798, when Wordsworth and Coleridge produced their epoch-making volume.

By that reckoning the phases are determined in relation to external events in church or state. Those who object to using political dividing-lines still tend to place the watersheds around the same date. The major figure of the Restoration literature, beyond any question, is John Dryden. His centrality is such that the looming presence of Milton (whose masterpiece did not appear until 1667) is never allowed to affect decisions in this area. Dryden's earliest significant poetry dates from 1659–60; his first major play was produced in 1663, and his first critical essay of any substance appeared in 1668. His career proceeded tidily until the end of the century: it is not merely that he died on May Day 1700, but the fact that he went on through the 1690's developing and refining the manner of his earlier writing, which prompts us to see his *oeuvre* as precisely delimiting "Restoration" modes. Drama is not my concern here, but since it bears on the choices made by literary historians a word or two is in place. It happens that the greatest of later Restoration playwrights, William Congreve, abandoned the stage in 1700, although he was to live for another 30 years. His rival Vanbrugh was soon to be sidetracked into architecture, at Castle Howard and Blenheim; while Farquhar died, aged no more than thirty, in 1707. So a juncture around 1700 or 1702 makes sense, if we are looking for a *terminus ad quem*.

But equally, if we desire a *terminus a quo*, Defoe and Swift, slow to get into their stride, were in their thirties when the new century dawned. Nevertheless, they were only just beginning to produce significant work: Defoe, with *An Essay upon Projects* (1697) and *The True-Born Englishman* (1701), and Swift, with *A Tale of a Tub* and *The Battle of the Books* (published 1704). The first decade of the century saw the emergence of Addison and Steele, who were to pioneer one of the most influential forms of writing between 1709 and 1711. Pope, more precocious, was already establishing his name by this time. It could be said that

3

none of the masters of what is sometimes called the "high" Augustan style (a notion to which I shall return) had produced work of lasting value in 1700. All of them had done so by 1715 — unless we extend the term to cover figures such as Fielding and Thomson, men who have one foot in the third phase, and who were incidentally born in the new century. Consequently it takes no wrenching of the time-scale to identify this phase with a "generation" of important writers — actually men born over a period of some 25 years, but all reaching maturity as artists around the time of Queen Anne. Older cultural historians would have been inclined to attribute this phenomenon to the existence of a flood-tide of patronage, sponsored by Kit-Cat Club aristocrats such as Somers and Halifax. Modern accounts have displayed a more sceptical attitude towards these benefactors of literature, but it may well be (as often) that Macaulay had it right on fundamentals. Certainly the immediately succeeding generations felt that they had missed something: Goldsmith was not alone in deploring the passing of the noble patron.

Throughout the 1720's, and to a lesser extent the 1730's, the same stars shone on the literary firmament. One by one they depart — Addison, Steele, Defoe, Gay, and finally Pope and Swift. If Pope had lived beyond middle age, he might have prolonged the active life of the Augustan mode; but *The New Dunciad* was his last bitter prophecy of social and cultural breakdown. Ironically, the chief instrument of this collapse, as Pope saw it, was the prime minister Robert Walpole: and his long ascendancy came to a close in the very year of *The New Dunciad*. It is true that political life went on along an essentially similar course under the Pelhams, and that George II showed no respect for these tidy dividing-lines by surviving until 1760, when he must have seemed a creature from another continent to the young. But it is hard to think of an author who had achieved anything before 1740 enhancing his reputation in the later period. James Thomson, whose *Seasons* (1726–30) had marked one point of growth in imaginative vocabulary, contracted rather than expanded his vision; while Henry Fielding turned his back on the stage, where he had made his early mark, and from 1742 forged a new — in my belief, largely unrelated — expressive idiom in his novels. The fact is that the 1740's left a clear field to new talents; the old guard died off as briskly as the mock-heroic Noodles and Doodles in the *dénouement* of Fielding's own *Tom Thumb*.

Samuel Johnson, it is true, had taken his first insecure steps as a man of letters: his satire *London* dates from 1738, and he was already established in the capital, in the shabby circumstances from which he was never altogether to escape. But — slow rises worth — and despite his graphic *Life of Savage* (1744), it was a decade and more before Johnson attained full prominence, above all with *The Rambler* and the *Dictionary*. Perhaps when we assign "the age of Johnson" to the second half of the century, we are unduly influenced by Boswell — who did not know his future subject for biography until much later, and who was actually born in 1740. Nevertheless these reflexes generally have some underlying logic about them, and while Johnson has intellectual roots spreading back into the age of Pope and Swift he remains undeniably a product of a later generation. For Samuel Johnson, to take a few cases at random, the continental enlightenment was a fact of life, little store as he set by Voltaire and Rousseau: the novel was a dominant form of literature, mixed though his assessment of mid-century novelists was: and Jacobitism was a vanishing dream, sympathetic as he may possibly have been to its aspirations. None of these things could have been said of Dryden, of Swift, or of Defoe. To put it another way — the nature of Johnson's conservatism depends on social and cultural developments which were only fully under way in the middle of the century. There is nothing anachronistic about Johnson's stance as a thinker. When he takes what might seem in the light of history to be the "losing" side (over Wilkes, the American Revolution, the afflatus of sensibility literature), he uses the argumentative procedures and the illustrations which spoke to contemporaries. The canon of English literature to which he supplied his "Prefaces" (what we now call *The Lives of the Poets*) was all the more representative because it stopped short of living poets. So did, and does, the taste of a large section of the reading public. To bring matters up to date in 1780 would only have involved smuggling into the collection some early Cowper (no *Task*, as yet), perhaps the juvenilia of Crabbe, more likely James Beattie or William Mason — for neither Burns nor Blake had yet been heard. Let no-one suppose that the *Lives of the Poets* exhibits antediluvian attitudes. They are saved, indeed, from the strictest orthodoxy only by their author's rugged independence of outlook, and his total reluctance to borrow opinions at second hand.

But Johnson's was a long life, and his career does span some major shifts in taste. At the beginning, he was to witness the half-delayed "rise of the novel," with Richardson, Fielding, Smollett, and Sterne. By the end of the period he had seen the success of his *protégée* Fanny Burney, and perhaps less congenially of Henry Mackenzie's *Man of Feeling*. Within a few years of his death came the decadent novel in the shape of *Vathek*, the gothic tale as practised by Ann Radcliffe, and the political fable exemplified by the Godwins. (In a sense *Frankenstein* merges all three: but that is another story.)

In non-fictional prose, the 1730's had seen important works of philosophy by George Berkeley, including *Alciphron* (1732), and the highly influential *Analogy of Religion* (1736) by Joseph Butler. By the time of Johnson's death, 50 years later, the sheltered calm of Anglican theology had been invaded by the Wesleyan movement, and was beginning to experience another challenge to its attitudes from within – the rise of Evangelicalism, where the first clear literary imprint can be traced in the works of Cowper. In wide philosophic or metaphysical speculation, the crucial figure had been David Hume, whom Dr. Johnson ranked (along with other "sceptical innovators") as "vain" in his denial of miracles and ironic treatment of religious belief. A work of this present kind will not easily provide a home for such men as Hume, Berkeley, and Locke, since they operated outside the strict limits of creative literature: none of them could be termed in any real sense a poet, a dramatist, or a novelist. It is just worth recalling, however, that Hume was as famous in his own day in the role of historian (and more commercially successful, one might add). The novel still occupied a somewhat uncertain position in the literary scheme of things, and the hunger for prose narrative was partly satisfied by massive works of historiography. Some dealt with the topical or close at hand, as for example Bishop Burnet's *History of His Own Times* (1724–34). Others concerned matters more remote in time or space, such as William Robertson's *History of America* (1777). The obvious consummation of this trend is to be found in Gibbon's *Decline and Fall of the Roman Empire* (1776–88), although from a different point of view these magisterial volumes could be seen as the legacy of moral and philosophic debate.

One of the literary forms which Johnson mastered in middle life was the periodical essay. *The Rambler* (1750–52) and *The Idler* (1758–60) were among his most esteemed works during his own lifetime. It is hard for us to take proper account of these essays today, just as we commonly accord too little regard to the great *Dictionary* (1755). The modern reader is disqualified by taste and education from fully appreciating such modes of literary endeavour. It is worth stressing the fact that, over the course of several generations, moral essays stood at the centre of almost everyone's reading experience. After Johnson came Lamb, Hazlitt, and De Quincey; right through the Victorian era to Stevenson and beyond, essays were among the best-known "gems" of English literature – and not just for the unsophisticated reader. It happens, too, that the essay made an important contribution to the rhetorical equipment of the emerging novel. This is obvious enough when we find Fielding halting the course of *Tom Jones* to instruct and cajole us, on topics such as love, critics, or the marvellous. It may be less obvious in a novel such as *The Vicar of Wakefield*, but here too the author's way of moving from particular to general, or his use of anecdotal support, owes much to the essay tradition. (One side-issue, not often considered, is the absence of a short story tradition: the form scarcely existed, outside the essayists that is, in the period under review.) It was to Addison, Steele, and their successors that the earliest practitioners of fiction went, for models of style, for techniques of characterisation, and for a definition of literary good manners. English literature would have been unimaginably different from 1710 up to 1914 if this immensely popular genre had not existed.

The relatively insecure hold on literary esteem which novelists enjoyed during the period was not strengthened until the appearance of Scott's Waverley novels early in the 19th century. Even then, one could argue that the first great writer to learn the right lessons from Scott was not engaged in fiction at all: it was Macaulay, whose *History of England* outsold the best-known novelists at the very height of (as we think) the Victorian hegemony of the novel. And of course poets like Byron and Tennyson more than once achieved greater impact with verse narratives than their contemporaries in prose. It is therefore natural that 18th-century critics should have gone on regarding the novel as an upstart form, long after its first great masters had opened out some high expressive potentiality in the form, and that the average educated reader in 1780 should continue to look elsewhere for major imaginative statements. Our own sense of the past has been warped by the survival of *Moll Flanders*, *Tom Jones*, and *Tristram Shandy* as living classics. Poetry remained the centre of literary consciousness.

Yet, paradoxically, the finest poetic talents of the middle of the 18th century were all in some degree blighted or deflected. There was Johnson himself, a sonorous exponent of one mode in decline (high Augustan satire), and an occasional versifier of surprisingly light-footed charm. There was Thomas Gray, with his mixture of calm, ruminative grandeur and excitable, almost neurotic intensities. A close contemporary is William Collins, sunk into an incurable depressive state by the age of thirty, having produced a tantalisingly small body of original and intriguing poems. In one way or another the pattern is repeated in Christopher Smart (mental breakdown and a clutch of seminal, if little understood, poems), Thomas Chatterton (an even earlier death, with a posture of alienation in life breaking out into creative indiscretions in poetry), and William Cowper (a wounded spirit who became a poet largely in response to personal crisis). Even the more robust writers of this generation reflect this sense of frustration and unfulfilled aspirations. Mark Akenside produced before he was twenty-five one outstanding poem, *The Pleasures of Imagination* (1744); his later career traces a decline, through a period of poverty, into graceful inutility as a fashionable physician. George Crabbe moved from dependence and indigence to comparative popularity, without seemingly achieving real peace of mind.

All these men, except perhaps Akenside, suffered from unmistakable symptoms of nervous illness. Their energies are fitful; their domestic crises assume grandiose proportions; their will is paralysed, and their talent thwarted by lack of an appreciative audience. Much of their best work manages to turn these psychodramas into genuine poetry: Cowper, for example, *uses* – as well as staves off – his neurasthenia in *The Task*. He claims to "peep" at the world "through the loopholes of retreat," and "to see the stir/Of the great Babel, and not feel the crowd" ("The Winter Evening"); the poem makes a virtue of its own indirection and acts out the feelings of attraction and repulsion towards society which Cowper harboured. Similarly, in Collins, the role of the poet is perceived as both noble and threatening, condemned as he is to pursue faint glimpses of an imaginative world "curtained" by the intellect, maturity, or advancing civilisation. In each case poetry ceases to be a way of affirming a vision; it describes the conditions in which wholeness of vision, now unavailable, might be achieved. Instead of the completed statements of Dryden and Pope, we tend to get fragments or aborted projects; instead of the confident topicality of the Augustans, we have medieval themes and Celtic landscapes. Instead of the urban tumult of satire, we encounter a retreat into the private, the concealed, the crepuscular. The most significant difference, however, lies in the area of poetic idiom. Where writers earlier in the century had triumphed in the power of words to master experience, and had relished their own control, clarity, and sequential flow –

> Dim, as the borrow'd beams of Moon and Stars
> To *lonely, weary, wandring* Travellers,
> Is *Reason* to the *Soul*: And as on high,
> Those rowling Fires *discover* but the Sky
> Not light us *here*; So *Reason's* glimmering Ray
> Was lent, not to *assure* our *doubtfull* way,
> But *guide* us upward to a *better Day* ...

– now the later generation are apt to glory in their own irresolutions –

> As one who, long in thickets and in brakes
> Entangled, winds now this way and now that
> His devious course uncertain, seeking home;
> Or, having long in miry ways been foil'd
> And sore discomfited, from slough to slough
> Plunging, and half despairing of escape;
> If chance at length he finds a greensward smooth
> And faithful to the foot, his spirits rise,
> He chirrups brisk his ear-erecting steed,
> And winds his way with pleasure and with ease;
> So I, designing other themes, and call'd
> T'adorn the Sofa with eulogium due,
> To tell its slumbers and to paint its dreams,
> Have rambled wide.

Dryden runs on freely from line to line; but his syntax propels us steadily forwards, and the triplet closes all further development for the moment. Cowper, on the other hand, flops about, into one more clause and then one more. The simile in Dryden is abetted by a strong iambic beat, by successive antitheses in the shape "not ... but," and by typographic emphases. With Cowper, the simile trails along across several mini-statements, the movement of the lines "plunging" us into fresh areas of experience: the syntax straggles into a mass of subsidiary clauses governed by hazy present participles. The difference is not just that between organised couplets and loose blank verse, or between heroic defining and Miltonic alluding. A crucial fact is that Cowper allows each new idea to subvert the expected movement, to alter the centre of rhythmic and syntactic gravity. The effect is all the more marked because of the incursion of formulaic mock-heroic at the end of the passage. In Dryden, this would have been tonally inappropriate, but linguistically in register. When Cowper comes to the sofa, his Augustan antithesis ("To tell its slumbers, and to paint its dreams") derives comic energy from its placing in the middle of a cumbrous periphrasis. Dryden might have written such a line, but he would made it occupy a resonant place in the sentence, probably at the end of a statement. Cowper allows it to drift off into a flaccid cadence ("have rambled wide"), a suspended construction reaching back somewhere into the undergrowth of the preceding lines. Dryden dramatises the untangling capacity of reason; Cowper's style gets entangled for us, to show us what it feels like.

This rapid survey has been conducted in terms of individuals for the most part. That is appropriate for a reference guide which is made up of entries detailing the biographic and bibliographic facts with regard to a given writer. But in addition, this line of approach is a useful corrective to the sort of sweeping generalisation which brevity can often induce. Books are written by men and women, not by movements and tendencies. Even the threefold division of the period may appear dangerous to some, and certainly we should be risking distortion of the real events if we accepted too uncritically the favourite labels, such as "neo-classic," "Augustan," "pre-romantic," or "sensibility."

Nobody is very concerned about the term "Restoration literature," as it appears to be simply a descriptive historical phrase. There is *some* oddity about it, insofar as we generally extend the compass of this expression to include the whole of Charles II's reign (not just the moment of his return to England); and even to include the reigns of James II and William III. This is reasonably logical in the case of his brother James, but when we come to the time of William and Mary a certain poetic license creeps into the terminology. Mary, it is true, was the niece of Charles II; but she had married a more distant relative of the Stuarts, who belonged to a strongly protestant Dutch house, and who had been more of a professional soldier and diplomat than a prince until he was offered the English throne in 1688. More seriously, the epithet as used in "Restoration literature" has acquired distinct overtones which are not entirely self-evident. We usually have in the back of mind the notion of an aristocratic culture revolving around the court. When used in this way, the phrase points to Dryden rather than to Milton; to Clarendon rather than to Bunyan; to Wycherley rather than to Aphra Behn. This does not make it a wholly misleading expression, but we should take care lest its apparent "objectivity" masks a subtle emphasis towards one particular aspect of the age. In speaking of Restoration literature I shall have the whole period in view, so far as possible. The dominant modes in poetry and prose were those practised by the court circle, but there are fainter voices and fugitive songs to be heard: Charles Cotton, say, or Tom Brown, men variously ill-fitted to court life.

"Neo-classic" is today an unfashionable term, and perhaps rightly so. It risks confusion with the quite different usage employed by art historians, which relates to a mainly Hellenic influence on taste at the very end of the 18th century. As once favoured by literary critics, the phrase referred to a code of propriety imported from France, and a body of ideas more Roman than Greek in their ultimate inspiration. Another problem with this way of looking at things was that it always proved easier to see divagations from the letter of "neo-classicism" than any firm adherence to the code in England. The expression has some limited utility if we do not strain it too far. It reminds us that the Restoration and early 18th century witnessed the rise of what might be called the "professional critic," exemplified in the person of Thomas Rymer or John Dennis. And it serves to bring into focus the lively intellectual debates of the age: notably the *querelle des anciens et des modernes*. This fierce controversy involved some important figures on both sides of the Channel: Perrault, Madame Dacier, La Motte, Boileau, Bentley, Temple, and many others. It ranged over critical issues of enduring significance: primitivism and progress, imitation and originality. Its muffled echoes can be detected in 18th-century writers of the highest distinction: Voltaire, Vico, Rousseau, Gibbon, Burke. Since Macaulay's time the tendency in England has been to downgrade the whole affair into a parochial squabble, but that is a mistake. We cannot begin to understand Swift's intellectual bearings until we take stock of the impact which the Ancient and Moderns debate had on his formative years as a writer. By this, I do mean simply to recall that *A Tale of a Tub* and *The Battle of the Books* make direct capital of the affair. As late as *Gulliver*, Swift is still rehearsing the issues which had come to the forefront of his mind when he was under the tutelage of Sir William Temple: the relationship between political and cultural development, and the clash between Spartan and Corinthian attitudes to life. Swift could be called, in quite a deep sense, a "neo-classic" writer: the sense is not, of course, that he subscribed to a rigid set of antiquated notions, but that his moral and psychological outlook was informed by a pervading ideal drawing heavily on the ancient civilisations. His poetry is chock-a-block with allusions to Ovid, Horace, Virgil, and Plutarch − often so fleeting that they escape our attention.

The second and third divisions of the period have attached to them more questionable labels. Of these, it is the term often applied to that central phase, from 1700 or 1714 to 1740 or 1745, which occasions most discussion at present: the so-called "Augustan," or sometimes "high Augustan" era. The usage grew up contemporaneously, and survived more or less intact until the last 20 years. Recently there has been a fairly concerted movement to put the expression out of serious use. An important book by Howard Weinbrot, entitled *Augustus Caesar in "Augustan" England* (1978), seeks to undermine our confidence in the term in a variety of ways. The essence of Weinbrot's case is that the Emperor Augustus suffered a considerable loss of reputation during the 18th century at the hands of historians and political writers. It would therefore be inappropriate to appeal to his reign as an embodiment of enlightened patronage, cultural advance, or anything positive along these lines. Weinbrot believes that the irony of Pope's *Epistle to Augustus* (1737) has been misread. The point of it, he argues, is not that George II fails to live up to the Horatian ideal of a noble ruler: the English king is, on the contrary, all too like his despotic and insensitive predecessor in Rome. My own opinion is that Weinbrot can only reach the conclusion which he does by means of tailoring the facts and suppressing a good deal of the evidence. Do we have to go back to the Augustan age for a high point of patronage, asks Charles Churchill in his poem *Independence* (1764): "must I seek Maecenas in a tomb?" The general answer in the period is yes, except that later writers can find an approximate British equivalent in the reign of Queen Anne. Soame Jenyns, all the more typical for his mediocrity, writes characteristic lines in the Earl of Oxford's library (1729):

> See how, in fam'd Augustus' golden days,
> Wit triumphs, crown'd with universal praise!
> Approaches thrones with a majestic air,
> The prince's mistress, and the statesman's care.
> Maecenas shines in every classic page,
> Maecenas, once the glory of his age.
> Not with less glory she her charms display'd,
> In Albion once when royal Anna sway'd.

In such routine attempts at flattering, the received ideas of the age are shamelessly revealed. Weinbrot ignores the bulk of this material, and chooses to emphasise some distinctly atypical figures, such as the freethinker John Toland. Consequently he minimises the aspiration towards "Augustan" values which is spread so thickly in minor writing throughout the century.

This may seem a fuss about very little. There is, however, a significant question at issue. If Weinbrot is right, then we must do more than abandon the use of "Augustan" as a shorthand phrase. We must regard the whole appeal to the ancient world as fundamentally bogus, and we must award centrality to those writers who cherish "modern" ideals. We necessarily realign the course of literary development so as to place at the heart of things those books and authors who can be defined as "anti-Augustan." On Weinbrot's showing, these will be the camp which is "libertarian, and philosophe in spirit." This would certainly have surprised Johnson and most of his contemporaries. What is at stake is not the merit of men like Owen Ruffhead or Jabez Hughes, whom Weinbrot calls in support of his case: it is their degree of influence or typicality. What is here defined as the "anti-Augustan" trend seems to me marginal, eccentric, and spasmodic. The main highroad of letters was thronged by less radical spirits.

I do not mean to suggest that we should throw around the expression "Augustan" with careless abandon. It is a term to be employed with due caution. Its semantic range should not be extended to cover anything much beyond 1750; it does not illuminate very much when applied to certain writers (notably Defoe, most of whose career was an aberration from "Augustan" expectations); and it should not be taken lazily to indicate some monolithic "peace" or torpor stretching from Dryden to Cowper. If we apply the word "Augustan" sensibly, within the sort of constraints I have suggested, then it points to something real and coherent. It isolates a quality common to *The Rape of the Lock* and *The Beggar's Opera*, to *The Way of the World* and *Shamela*, to *The Spectator* and *Gulliver's Travels*, to *Annus Mirabilis* and Prior's *Alma*. It serves to identify a learned and sophisticated literary craftsmanship, allied to clarity and "ease" of manner; a faith in the ordinary as opposed in the transcendental, and a suspicion of elaborate metaphysical flights; an affection for wholeness, and a recoil from exorbitant emotionalism. None of these statements would fit heroic drama at the start of the period: none of them would fit *Clarissa* or the odes of Collins. There are of course marginal cases, where the definition may partially fit: much of Johnson's work (say, the *Journey to the Western Islands*); Gray's *Elegy*; in some respects *Tom Jones*. But the concept remains clear, despite some blurring at the fringe.

The last section of our period used often to be dignified with the term "pre-romantic." This has been found impossibly whiggish, in that it seems to rely on later developments to make sense of an earlier stage in history. At present the word is scarcely ever used without irony; and its rival "post-Augustan" is open to *almost* the same objections – though the logic is not quite identical in that case.

Instead of these unacceptable descriptions, the current fashion is to speak of "the age of sensibility." This phrase goes back to a seminal essay by Northrop Frye, published in 1956, and widely reprinted. Frye is an eloquent and powerful critic, with a taste for categorisation, and it is understandable that his enticing models should have laid the ground for subsequent critical reassessment, both of terms and of individuals. The need to make sense of some confused and abortive developments around the mid-century added to the appeal of Frye's nomenclature.

Frye begins by combatting what now seems an unlikely caricature, the "vague notion that the age of sensibility was the time when poetry moved from a reptilian Classicism, all cold and dry reason, to a mammalian Romanticism, all warm and wet feeling." He goes on to contrast two opposing varieties of expression, "literature as product" and "literature as process." The former is exemplified by writers with "a strong sense of literature as a finished product," and here Frye uses a novel such as *Tom Jones* as representative. The latter presents instead the spectacle of the author at work on his own composition, and here *Tristram Shandy* is the case in point. Similarly with verse: the regular metre of *The Dunciad* provides "a sense of continually fulfilled expectation," whereas in "sensibility" poetry the effects will be "hypnotically repetitive, oracular, incantatory, dreamlike, and in the original sense of the word charming." Another distinction is drawn as follows:

> Where there is a strong sense of literature as aesthetic product, there is also a sense of its detachment from the spectator. Aristotle's theory of catharsis describes how this works for tragedy: pity and fear are detached from the beholder by being directed towards objects. Where there is a sense of literature as process, pity and fear become states of mind without objects, moods which are common to the work of art and the reader, and which binds them together psychologically instead of separating them aesthetically.

Frye concludes by showing a special use of metaphor is central to what he calls the age of sensibility, and by emphasising the "oracular" quality it displays. One of the most interesting features of the discussion is the way Frye is able to effect a disjunction not just with the Augustans but also with the Romantics: indeed, for the purposes of his argument he aligns both schools as concerned with "literature as product." The essay has a sharp, bright texture which gives it unusual intellectual force and clarity.

Naturally it is possible to pick holes in the case. No such brief survey (it runs only to about 4000 words) can deal comprehensively with such a complex period of literature. Many important writers of the period figure intermittently in the discussion, or not at all. There is scarcely any mention of Johnson, the greatest English author active throughout the key period: although Boswell, significantly, appears as a practitioner of the new mode. Drama is totally absent, and so the potential difficulties occasioned by Goldsmith and Sheridan elude observation. The novel appears in the shape of Richardson and Sterne, but the forms of fiction most popular in the heyday of "sensibility" poetry – barring a cursory reference to the Gothic novel – play no part in the argument. However, the chief value of the essay has lain in the purchase it offers a critic with regard to poetry: it is in relation to Collins, Smart, Chatterton, Cowper, and Blake that Frye's concept has proved most fruitful. Essentially, then, the notion of an "age of sensibility" stands or falls by its ability to explain or illuminate the poetic history of our final phase, c. 1740 to 1790.

As such, the model works well in practice. I should prefer to say that Augustan poetic ministers to something a little different from "continually fulfilled expectation." We might suggest that the poem will tend sometimes to fulfil, and sometimes to contradict, the reader's expectations – very much as is the case with a listener to the music of Haydn or Mozart. Consider a familiar passage from Pope:

> This Day, black Omens threat the brightest Fair
> That e'er deserv'd a watchful Spirit's Care;
> Some dire Disaster, or by Force, or Slight,
> But what, or where, the Fates have wrapt in Night.

> Whether the Nymph shall break *Diana*'s Law,
> Or some frail *China* Jar receive a Flaw,
> Or stain her Honour, or her new Brocade,
> Forget her Pray'rs, or miss a Masquerade,
> Or lose her Heart, or Necklace, at a Ball;
> Or whether Heav'n has doom'd that *Shock* must fall.

The surprises here all assume a set pattern of predictable elements, against which the successive ironical adjustments make their point. These are not examples of the "deliberate discord" which Frye grants to be a possible refinement of the Augustan style. Our certainty that rhyme and rhythm will bring a conclusive alternative to "*Diana*'s Law" does not prepare us for a phrase "receive a Flaw," which works back on to the sexual meaning of the previous line. Our *un*certainty as we move from *or* to *or* (Pope can do more here, because this formula covered our present-day use of *either ... or*) leads us to anticipate a "serious" alternative coming first in the final line. We get only the truncated, implicit seriousness of "Heav'n has doom'd." Earlier on, Pope has taken up a phrase from Spenser ("whether by force, or sleight") and made it hang puzzlingly in the air. Spenser, as a matter of fact, has a further possibility to tag on the end: "Or their owne guilt." If we pick up the reference, we are asked to speculate as to the culpability of the heroine. Pope's is a poetry full of pseudo-alternatives, seemingly unequal choices that prove to mean much the same thing, apparently similar fates that turn out to be very different. In a way, we could detect in this the "continuous present" created, according to Frye, by the incantatory rhythms of sensibility verse. Our anticipations are subverted, not line-by-line as in a Donne song or a romantic ode, but almost word by word. When we come to the line "Or lose her Heart, or Necklace, at a Ball" we have just encountered "*miss* a Masquerade" – therefore our immediate impulse is to expect "losing" to be a trivial inadvertence. But go on as far as "lose her Heart," and the emotional possibilities are deepened. Promptly the qualification "or Necklace" reinforces the slighter sense. But "at a Ball" applies to the love-affair scenario quite as well as to the necklace, and completes the logic of a sentence that might *primarily* concern young love. It is altogether subtler than simply "using" the figure of zeugma for deflatory purposes. We do not have the pattern: potentially serious statement + zeugma = deflation. Rather, we have a movement in and out of the more serious sense, towards and against predictability: a second-by-second adjustment which is highly characteristic of Augustan satire, in Dryden and Swift as well as Pope.

Frye's argument is at its strongest when he deals with the "associative" properties of sensibility writing, and when he stresses the urge towards "the brief and even fragmentary utterance" – a formulation which paradoxically can accommodate such sustained works as Blake's prophetic poems, Cowper's *Task*, or Ossian's epics. As Frye puts it, the poet "is attracted by the ruinous ... the primeval and 'unspoiled.' " The finest moments in the poetry of sensibility often register a failure of vision or an incomplete apprehension: in the last strophe of Gray's "Progress of Poesy" (1757), for example, or in the crushed hopes that suffuse Collins's "Ode on the Poetical Character" (1746). Poetry finds itself more and more drawn to the mantic, the impenetrable, the inaccessible, as in Christopher Smart's *Song to David* (1763):

> The world – the clustring spheres he made,
> The glorious light, the soothing shade,
>   Dale, champaign, grove, and hill;
> The multitudinous abyss,
> Where secrecy remains in bliss,
>   And wisdom hides her skill.

It was left for Blake, in "Auguries of Innocence," to decipher these secrets. The earlier generation of poets share with Blake a sense of numinous and privileged moments, but they have not gone so far in rejecting all systems of interpretation, or in radically remaking poetic forms. Another way of putting this would be to say that the sensibility poets seek the intensity of primitive scenes and child-like states of feeling, but they have not had the artistic courage to break down Augustan poetic, root and branch. Even Smart's most impassioned verse works through symmetry, antithesis, and parallelism. Sensibility deals not so much in organic form as in fractured versions of synthetic form.

Two caveats are in order. The first is simply to remind ourselves that one very considerable poet, Robert Burns, lies at a tangent to these broad developments. Frye's analysis does not account for his peculiar importance, and I am conscious that my own argument has been no more helpful. The personal chemistry of Burns's poetry has to do with his native inheritance (songs, oral tales, the strength of the Scottish language as a storehouse of living speech) and, superimposed rather awkwardly at times, his "education" – in "polite" literature. This last was mostly English, generally Augustan in the normal acceptation of that term, much of it in prose. His early reading included Shakespeare, Pope, Locke, the *Spectator*, Hervey's *Meditations among the Tombs* (1746), and Jethro Tull on agriculture. The semi-anglicised poetry of Allan Ramsay was one influence: another was the *Pantheon* of classical mythology compiled by Andrew Tooke – Keats was another to draw heavily on this work. Direct assessment of Burns appears in the text below: my aim here is simply to indicate the slightly skewed relation of Burns to literary history in England.

The second caveat is this. I have deliberately chosen clear-cut examples to make the point: as, indeed, Frye does. It would be possible to select more problematic instances: Thomson, Goldsmith, Akenside, Edward Young, and so on. Some of the prose writers raise equally complex issues: Hume, the dramatist Lillo, Burke. The important thing is not to allocate each individual to a tidy slot, but to see individuals in relation to a dynamic and constantly evolving cultural situation.

At this point, something might be said about the milieu in which authors lived and wrote. The literary profession scarcely existed at the start of the period, and even at the end of what we have been calling the Restoration phase there were few men and women of letters who were not, socially speaking, ladies and gentlemen. The lapse of the Licensing Act in 1695 made for greater opportunities in a number of fields – journalism, preeminently, with the rise of the first regular newspapers inside the next decade, but also in political and controversial pamphleteering. It should not be forgotten that all books, not just topical tracts, needed an official government *imprimatur*; it is odd to think that even *Paradise Lost* had to endure this censorship. But printers bore the brunt of the danger, as more easily located, and might even face the threat of being hanged for producing heretical works. Two years after the Licensing Act was passed, that is in 1664, this fate actually overtook a printer named Twyn, who had disseminated a book justifying the execution of Charles I. In the same year a dissenting divine was prosecuted for libel on account of remarks concerning infant baptism. He got off comparatively lightly: the pillory, a fine of £20, and 14 days in prison. Throughout the remainder of the Stuart rule, such little discouragements to authorship survived. After 1695, and more particularly after 1714, they died away. The point was not that censorship acquired a bad name, but that it seemed ineffectual in its efforts to stem a rising tide of openly expressed public opinion. By the time of Walpole, official policy had changed, and the state had organised its own publicity machine. Writers and booksellers (i.e., publishers) who went beyond the accepted limits could still find themselves in trouble. A hapless youth named Matthews was hauled off to the gallows at Tyburn in 1719, after printing an exceptionable pamphlet; the Jacobite journalist Mist was driven abroad a decade later; and the rascally Edmund Curll was prosecuted for obscenity and breach of parliamentary privilege. If Swift had not had good friends around him, he would have been arrested more than once. But as time went on, things improved for the writer. Gradually the obstacles were dismantled: it became legal to report parliamentary proceedings, copyright was secured on an established legal basis, and the activities of government spies became much more restricted.

In the first phase of our period, then, professional authors were all but unknown. In the middle "Augustan" era, gentility continued to be a prime qualification for writers. But the thrusting new men, journalists and pamphleteers, made extensive inroads into this conservative way of literary life. One has only to think of Daniel Defoe: he may not have made any huge fortune – indeed he certainly did not – but he was able to transform his identity from "Mr. Daniel Foe," of the City of London, to "Daniel De Foe, Esq.," of Stoke Newington, an agreeable suburb set amid bosky countryside. More important, perhaps, he was able to get more than 500 separate books and pamphlets published, and to write for a steady succession of daily and weekly newspapers. Even if Defoe had never written *Robinson Crusoe* and *Moll Flanders*, to secure his immortality, he would have been a significant figure in social history. He took advantages of the expanding market and enlisted new polemical strategies to get his message before the public. He wrote as clearly as Dryden, and with more of the flavour of the street. On every imaginable topic he contrived to turn out the kind of book which people wanted to read: on politics, warfare, economics, insubordinate servants and "conjugal lewdness," on the devil and on saintly clergymen, on pirates and highwaymen, on shipping and imaginary voyages to the moon. He advanced the cause of authorship, not by sitting on committees or sponsoring awards, but by showing its practical possibilities in his own career.

Meanwhile, Alexander Pope had made almost as sharp a break with the past. Where Dryden had stuck to the court in good times and bad, clinging to office as poet laureate and historiographer royal, Pope made a proud gesture out of his own independent status. There is a consequent difference in subject-matter, closely allied though the two men were in literary temperament. Dryden operates almost entirely in a public mode: even when he writes about more remote matters, he cannot help reverting to national issues – his verses to his relative John Driden, a country squire, soon leave the crops and the hunting-field for international conflict and analogies with Hannibal. Pope, on the other hand, infuses every public theme with private sentiment: he uses his own boyhood retreat of Windsor Forest as the basis of a political poem on the Treaty of Utrecht. Where Dryden had been content to style himself "Servant" to Charles II, Pope proclaimed himself "Un-plac'd, un-pension'd, no Man's Heir, or Slave." A "place" in society has become an encumbrance to the writer, no longer a secure point of vision from which to review the spectacle of life.

The difference between these two crucial figures has been well expressed by Ian Jack:

> During the central part of Dryden's career, from the Restoration to the Whig Revolution, the audience for which Dryden wrote was the Court, "the best and surest judge of writing," with the King at its centre as the sun to which all writers and other men of wit naturally inclined.... As Laureate, Dryden did not so much regard it as his task to create the taste by which he was to be enjoyed ... as to write in a manner that would please the taste of the audience provided for him by circumstances.... The brilliant rapport which he established with his audience, after a decade and more in the theatre, may be studied in *Absalom and Achitophel*, a poem written by royal command which is a supreme masterpiece of tone in the sense defined by I. A. Richards, "the perfect recognition of the writer's relation to the reader in view of what is being said and their joint feelings about it."

For Pope, as Jack explains, things were quite otherwise:

> One reason why Pope's career could not follow a similar course was that England had changed so radically. Another was that he was born (as Dryden had died) a Roman Catholic – and it is one of the more attractive traits of his complicated character that he refused to render himself eligible for a "place" which he viewed (at best) with philosophical detachment.... Instead of protesting or yielding to self-pity, he early devoted himself to the problem of finding an audience for his poetry with the same astonishing capacity for taking pains which he devoted to the writing of it.

One of the most celebrated ways in which Pope solved the "problem of finding an audience" was his use of the subscription system to publish his versions of Homer and his edition of Shakespeare. He was not the first writer to take this path. In 1688 Jacob Tonson had issued a new edition of *Paradise Lost* (for which Milton had been paid £10, two decades earlier): he had the support of some notable patrons, including the influential politician, lawyer, and collector John – later Lord – Somers. Over 500 subscribers were obtained, and the bookseller made a good profit. In 1697 Dryden completed a translation of Virgil for Tonson, and again it was decided to use the subscription method. The negotiations surrounding this transaction were described a century ago by Alexandre Beljame, and in outline his account remains valid. There was a *de luxe* edition at five guineas a set, and a plainer text at two guineas. In all some 350 subscribers were enrolled. Dryden's rewards have been variously estimated, but seem to have reached approximately £1,250. "Tonson meantime," as Beljame puts it, was "laying the foundations of his fortune."

These were two of the major literary ventures into the subscription market when Pope began his career, although the same mode of publication had been used for religious, historical, and scientific works. Pope's first project concerned his translation into English verse of *The Iliad*, issued in annual instalments between 1715 and 1720. Detailed analysis of the subscription lists reveals that the 575 names were impressive in social range and influence, although not overwhelmingly distinguished in comparison with other contemporary lists – Prior's *Poems* of 1718, Gay's *Poems* (1720) and Addison's posthumous *Works* (1721). In 1725–26 Pope again utilised the services of the bookseller Bernard Lintot to issue his translation of *The Odyssey*. This time there were about 610 subscribers: slightly older, slightly more worldly, slightly more meritocratic in composition. One astonishing finding is that about 120 among those listed were current members of parliament – this is quite apart from 20 or more who were later to enter parliament. That figure represents a fifth of the total subscribers, and it constitutes a remarkable 22% of the sitting members in 1725. At the same time Tonson was issuing, for his benefit, an edition of Shakespeare somewhat laxly put together by Pope. The poet took much less interest in this project, and it was not promoted with anything like the same success.

Subscriptions went on throughout the 18th century, and it was the means by which Fielding, for example, chose to publish his *Miscellanies* in 1743. For this work 425 names were collected, and Fielding managed to make something like £800, at a time when he badly needed funds. But that was a slender return compared with Pope's. *He* had carried away £9,000, according to the general estimate, from his two Homeric ventures. Nevertheless, it is important not to jump to wrong conclusions about this huge success. The detailed analysis to which I have referred (see "Pope and his Subscribers", *Publishing History*, vol. 3, 1978) prompted some more restrained conclusions:

> Pope's triumph was largely financial rather than social. The terms he extracted from Lintot meant that he took all the subscription money, without the deductions for printing, paper, distribution etc. which normally came off the author's share.... Fortunately, in the end Lintot did well enough out of his own edition not to regret his generosity. But publishers in the future would be more cagey. Subscription ventures went on unabated, but few – if any – authors could demand Pope's terms. The whole episode was less typical than historians of literature and of the book trade have chosen to believe.

For our present purposes, the main point is this: it may be true that Pope achieved unprecedented independence and "genteel" status as a professional writer, initially as a result of his Homeric works. (Later he was to make some equally advantageous business deals with regard to the *Essay on Man*, and was to act virtually as his own publisher during the 1730's.) But nobody else could quite manage to repeat this victory over the book trade, and as time went on it became harder and harder to outwit the shrewd and often well-capitalised publishers, like Andrew Millar, Thomas Cadell, and William Strahan. It was all very well for writers to become gentlemen, but that was not going to interfere with the progress of booksellers in *their* climb to social respectability. Strahan even became an MP, which is more than his friend Samuel Johnson could aspire to.

The social standing of authorship in this period is too complex an issue to consider fully here. As a rough guide, I have carried out a simple survey with respect to the poets represented in this collection. Out of 70 individuals under scrutiny, five were women and thus debarred from serious educational opportunities, other than what governesses and home-instruction could provide. Among the men, only two were full-blown aristocrats, though others like Lyttelton and Blackmore achieved a peerage or a knighthood. (Two of the women fall into this category: Lady Mary Wortley Montagu, daughter of a great Whig dynast, and the Countess of Winchilsea, married to an earl.) The men attended universities as follows: Oxford, 21; Cambridge, 13; Edinburgh, 8; Trinity College, Dublin, 3; Aberdeen, 2; St. Andrews, 1. That is not an unfair picture of the degree of influence throughout the period, as commanded by these particular institutions: although Edinburgh climbed in prestige, even in England, during the later years, and its reputation for medicine always stood high. Schools represented include Winchester, 7; Westminster, 6; Eton, 2. One might have expected the first two placings to be reversed, but again the broad picture is accurate. Fewer writers went on to study at the inns of court than in previous generations. The learned professions are represented more strongly by doctors, where we find no fewer than seven men with some medical training – allowing for the moment Goldsmith's claims to some *locus standi* as a physician. As for clergymen, there are 16 men in orders, mostly in the Anglican church: this is slightly fewer than one would have expected on a random sample, where clergy often account for about a third of all poets at this date. The dissenting interest is not well represented, even if we include Scottish writers: Isaac Watts and, dubiously, Charles Wesley are about the only English nonconformists in the sample. Mrs. Barbauld was essentially a Unitarian. Equally, there are very few Roman Catholics: apart from Dryden and Pope, not a single member of this persecuted community figures in the group.

The sample is too restricted to provide a basis for establishing high statistical significance. It could be pointed out that the first phase of the period is under-represented in this group: of the 70 authors, only about twelve were fully active before 1700. It could also be argued that to include the non-poets covered in this volume, including men like Addison, Boswell, Bunyan, Burke, Defoe, Gibbon, and Steele, would fill out the picture. For example, it would add at a stroke three names to the slender tally of MPs (four) among the poets. Nevertheless, it is possible to make certain deductions from the figures, particularly if we compare them with those provided by control groups.

It is worth noting that an arbitrary selection of 19th-century poets in *Great Writers of the English Language*, and of 20th-century poets in the same category, yielded distinctly different results. (In both cases the count was limited to British poets, and excluded writers from America or the Commonwealth.) A sample of 15 poets with surnames beginning from F to K was assembled for each period. One immediately observes the wider range of universities open to writers (undergraduate studies at London, Belfast, University College, Dublin; postgraduate work at Stanford). The medical element has all but disappeared, apart from Oliver St. John Gogarty (and unless we include Keats); there is only one MP in the 19th-century group, and none at all in the 20th-century sample. One must apply such small-scale comparisons with caution; the proportion of women poets has actually declined on these samples – one in the 19th century, none in the 20th. All the same, the comparison does bring out the more homogeneous background and education of the earlier poets, and their greater involvement in worldly activities. A small point which may be significant is the lower proportion of Cambridge to Oxford products in the later periods. For the 1660–1800 era, the ratio is 1.62: 1 in favour of Oxford. For the 19th century, it is 2.5: 1, and since 1900 it is exactly the same. One might not reproduce these proportions exactly with a larger sample, but I think the general slant may be accurately portrayed. The great public schools are far more scantily represented in the post-1800 groups.

A different mode of control is to set the poets against some prominent men of their own time. A sample was taken of MPs who sat in parliament at the centre of our period: 50 were chosen at random, whose surname began with L, with birth-dates ranging between 1657 and 1721. Out of these 50 men, 21 studied at Oxford, the same figure reached by the 70 poets – although the latter included five "ineligible" women. Of the MPs, only nine were at Cambridge, a slightly lower percentage than for the poets, but not markedly out of line. What is different is the number of MPs who had proceeded to the Inns of Court – exactly one half, 25 of the group. This is clearly a differentiating factor. It is also worth noting that Westminster and Eton dominate the schooling of the MPs, with Winchester more or less out of sight. More of the control group had aristocratic connections, more served in the armed forces, and more of them (naturally) held official posts. But there is some overlap with the poets in all these categories, and it is equally the case that more men with a mercantile background (about a sixth of the present sample) reached parliament than scaled Parnassus. With these qualifications, it would be fair to say that most writers of the period came from the dominant social group; their origins were not markedly different from those who achieved political and economic power, and their education equipped them for success in worldly pursuits, when they chose to exercise this opportunity. In the sample, only Stephen Duck could be regarded as a truly proletarian writer in origin, although others on the list, such as Blake, Burns, Cunningham, and Allan Ramsay (none of them English apart from Blake), sprang from an untypical social background.

So much for the standing of the writer in society. It would raise too many complex issues to try to assess the size and composition of the reading public over so long a period. However, it is just worth saying that Beljame's notion of an audience of "debauchees" for Restoration drama has recently come under fire: see for example articles by Harold Love and by A. H. Scouten and R. D. Hume in the *Yearbook of English Studies*, vol. 10 (1980). Much of this argument applies equally to the audience for poetry in the age of Dryden, and we should be very imprudent to make easy assumptions about the court as an agent of pure licentiousness and triviality. Throughout the period, the audience for literature was stratified, heterogeneous, and diverse. It is certainly true that few ordinary working people would have been able to afford even the sum of five shillings charged for a book like *Moll Flanders*, and would need to wait for chapbook abridgements at a penny or twopence. *Absalom and Achitophel*, at sixpence or so, and *The Rape of the Lock* (a shilling) were more within range; but of course the taste for such works implied a certain sophistication in literary response. We know that adult literacy was on the increase, more especially perhaps among men than women. The position has been summarised by W. A. Speck:

> By and large [illiteracy] around 1760 was higher in the country than in the urban areas, and certainly lowest of all in London. It also varied from rung to rung down the social ladder. There was virtually no illiteracy among the gentry and professions, including government officials; among tradesmen and craftsmen it varied between five and forty per cent, while husbandmen, servants and labourers were the most illiterate sections of the population, between forty-five and sixty per cent being unable to sign marriage registers for the years 1754–84. Since substantially more women were illiterate than men, then female servants were probably among the least literate people in eighteenth-century England.

This last injustice was only beginning to be rectified at the end of our period. Until it was less marked a phenomenon, the contribution of women as creators of literature, and as shapers of taste as readers, was inevitably restricted. In a good many respects England between 1660 and 1800 made advances in social provision, in limiting arbitrary actions by the executive, and in toleration of deviant groups. It cannot be said that sexual equality was one of the spheres where rapid progress was evident.

If the period under review is defined as extending from 1660 to 1789, then the exact centre will lie around 1724/25. If the terminal date is set instead at 1800, then the mid-point will fall in 1730. Both junctures are apt for our purposes, for each saw the appearance of one of the most characteristic works of the "Augustan" era. Between 1724 and 1726 Daniel Defoe issued his *Tour thro' the Whole Island of Great Britain*, with the second volume (1725) hinging round a famous description of the metropolis which stood at the heart of British culture – the city which Dryden had lauded in *Annus Mirabilis* (1667) and which was to provide a classic ground on which the heroic exploits of Samuel Johnson were acted out in Boswell's *Life*. Later in the decade, James Thomson was to chart contemporary experience in time rather than place, with his poem *The Seasons*: the first part, *Winter*, appeared in 1726, and the work evolved in stages until it reached its complete form in 1730 – when, by the way, it was issued in a subscription edition.

I have isolated these productions, appearing right at the arithmetic centre of the period, for a specific reason. They possess a Janus face: sinking deep tentacles into the literature of the past, they yet point forwards to an unrealised vision – political, economic, literary. In the case of Defoe, we can see how his busy survey of topical reality is nourished by a haunting Virgilian sense of the rise and fall of civilisations: equally, his aim is constantly to outdo the great Renaissance expression of nationhood, embodied in Camden's *Britannia*. On the other hand, his sense of a country on the verge of "take-off" into modern industrialism is amazingly prescient and profound. In the case of Thomson, we have an art again reaching back to Virgil, along with Milton and others, to establish its perspective on contemporary life. At the same time, it stretches the regular vocabulary of formal epic towards a new, more inward and expressive mode of writing: an idiom of subjectivity rather than objectivity, of feeling rather than pure reason, of sentiment rather than judgment. Both works can be said to mark a unique moment in the course of literary history when, briefly, both the Renaissance and the Romantic movement were (metaphorically if not literally) within range together.

It could indeed be argued that the period constitutes a point of equilibrium in English Literature, poised between Milton and Wordsworth. This is of course not the orthodox way of reading our poetic history, but it may be as productive an approach as that which requires us to look back from Blake over the head of the Augustans to the early 17th century. In support of the alternative reading, we might adduce the metaphysical elements in Butler and Rochester, for example, or the "Restoration" quality in some of Marvell. Equally, at the other end, the superannuated term "pre-romantic" has its value if we use it as a technical or descriptive instrument rather than as a vague qualitative expression. Viewed in this light, the years between 1660 and 1798 no longer seem a divagation, but emerge as a time of consolidation and creation, rich in innovative energy, and permanently significant for the new aspects of experience explored in prose and verse. An era which saw poetry ranging from Sedley's "Not, Celia, that I juster am" and Rochester's "Phillis, be gentler" to *An Essay on Criticism*, and beyond that to Cowper's *Castaway* and Crabbe's *Village* was plainly no static lapse of years. Equally, the new ideas expressed in the periodical essay, in historiography and in travel-writing vastly increased the compass of prose literature. One has only to think of a writer like Hume, whose more technical works of philosophy and psychology were complemented by history, essays on taste, political tracts, and a stream of absorbing private letters (another favourite Augustan kind). There is also a wide array of distinguished criticism: Dryden's vivid dramatisation of ideas in *An Essay of Dramatic Poesy*, in the first phase; Addison's pioneering articles on Milton and on the imagination in *The Spectator*, during the central phase; and Johnson's unequalled *Lives of the Poets*, near the end of the final phase. Such achievements endure, and repay our attention. The makers, both great and small, of so worthy a tradition are the men and women whose careers are charted in the pages that follow.

READING LIST

1. Bibliographies, handbooks, etc.

Draper, John W., *Eighteenth-Century Aesthetics: A Bibliography*, 1931.

Dyson, H. V. D., and John Butt, *Augustans and Romantics 1689–1830*, 1940; revised edition, 1961.

Crane, R. S., editor, *English Literature 1660–1800: A Bibliography of Modern Studies 1926–50*, 2 vols., 1950–52; *1950–60*, 2 vols., 1962; *1961–70*, edited by Curt A. Zimansky and others, 2 vols., 1972.

Wikelund, P., *Restoration Literature: An Annotated Bibliography*, 1954.

Dobrée, Bonamy, *English Literature in the Early Eighteenth Century 1700–1740*, 1959.

Renwick, W. L., *English Literature 1789–1815*, 1963.

Sutherland, James, *English Literature of the Late Seventeenth Century*, 1969.

Sena, John F., *A Bibliography of Melancholy 1660–1800*, 1970.

Bond, Donald F., *The Eighteenth Century*, 1975.

Foxon, D. F., *English Verse 1701–1750: A Catalogue of Separately Printed Poems with Notes on Contemporary Collected Editions*, 2 vols., 1975.

Butt, John, and Geoffrey Carnall, *The Mid-Eighteenth Century*, 1979.

2. General Histories

Elton, Oliver, *A Survey of English Literature 1780–1830*, 2 vols., 1912; *A Survey of English Literature 1730–80*, 2 vols., 1928.

Dyson, H. V. D., and John Butt, *Augustans and Romantics 1689–1830*, 1940; revised edition, 1961.

McKillop, Alan D., *English Literature from Dryden to Burns*, 1948.

Butt, John, *The Augustan Age*, 1948.

McCutcheon, R. P., *Eighteenth-Century English Literature*, 1950.

Wedgwood, C. V., *Seventeenth-Century English Literature*, 1950.

Humphreys, A. R., *The Augustan World*, 1954.

Burton, K. M. P., *Restoration Literature*, 1958.

Dobrée, Bonamy, *English Literature in the Early Eighteenth Century 1700–1740*, 1959.

Renwick, W. L., *English Literature 1789–1815*, 1963.

Korninger, S., *English Literature and Its Background: The Restoration Period and the Eighteenth Century 1660–1780*, 1964.

Sutherland, James, *English Literature of the Late Seventeenth Century*, 1969.

Lonsdale, Roger, editor, *Dryden to Johnson*, 1971.

Butt, John, and Geoffrey Carnall, *The Mid-Eighteenth Century*, 1979.

3. Themes, topics, short periods, etc.

Tinker, Chauncey B., *Nature's Simple Plan*, 1922.

Havens, R. D., *The Influence of Milton on English Poetry*, 1922.

Doughty, O., *English Lyric in the Age of Reason*, 1922.

Snyder, E. D., *The Celtic Revival in English Literature 1760–1800*, 1923.

Hussey, Christopher, *The Picturesque: Studies in a Point of View*, 1927.

Fairchild, Hoxie, *The Noble Savage: A Study in Romantic Naturalism*, 1928.

Stauffer, Donald A., *English Biography Before 1700*, 1930.

Bond, R. P., *English Burlesque Poetry 1700–1750*, 1932.

Willey, Basil, *The Seventeenth-Century Background: Studies in the Thought of the Age in Relation to Poetry and Religion*, 1934.

Monk, Samuel Holt, *The Sublime: A Study of Critical Theories in Eighteenth-Century England*, 1935.

Deene, C. V., *Aspects of Eighteenth-Century Nature Poetry*, 1935.
Bredvold, L. I., *The Intellectual Milieu of John Dryden: Studies in Some Aspects of Seventeenth-Century Thought*, 1935.
Lovejoy, A. O., *The Great Chain of Being: A Study of the History of an Idea*, 1936.
Aubin, R. A., *Topographical Poetry in Eighteenth-Century England*, 1936.
Richards, E. A., *Hudibras in the Burlesque Tradition*, 1937.
Smith, David Nicol, *Some Observations on Eighteenth-Century Poetry*, 1937.
Shuster, G. N., *The English Ode from Milton to Keats*, 1940.
Willey, Basil, *The Eighteenth-Century Background: Studies on the Idea of Nature*, 1940.
Galloway, Francis, *Reason, Rule, and Revolt in English Classicism*, 1940.
Stauffer, Donald A., *The Art of Biography in Eighteenth-Century England*, 2 vols., 1941.
Fairchild, Hoxie, *Religious Trends in English Poetry*, vol. 2: *1740–80*, 1942; vol. 3: *1780–1830*, 1949.
Swedenberg, H. T., Jr., *The Theory of the Epic in England 1650–1800*, 1944.
Bate, Walter Jackson, *From Classic to Romantic: Premises of Taste in Eighteenth-Century England*, 1946.
Nicolson, Marjorie Hope, *Newton Demands the Muse: Newton's Opticks and the Eighteenth-Century Poets*, 1946.
Wasserman, E. R., *Elizabethan Poetry in the Eighteenth Century*, 1947.
Fitzgerald, M. M., *First Follow Nature: Primitivism in English Poetry 1725–50*, 1947.
Brown, W. C., *The Triumph of Form: A Study of the Later Masters of the Heroic Couplet*, 1948.
Wilson, J. H., *The Court Wits of the Restoration: An Introduction*, 1948.
Sutherland, James, *A Preface to Eighteenth-Century Poetry*, 1948.
Arthos, J., *The Language of Natural Description in Eighteenth-Century Poetry*, 1949.
The Age of Johnson: Essays Presented to Chauncey B. Tinker, 1949.
Pope and His Contemporaries: Essays Presented to George Sherburn, 1949.
Atkins, J. W. H., *English Literary Criticism: Seventeenth and Eighteenth Centuries*, 1951.
Jones, R. F., and others, *The Seventeenth Century: Studies in the History of English Thought and Literature from Bacon to Pope*, 1951.
Davie, Donald, *Purity of Diction in English Verse*, 1952; revised edition, 1967.
Jack, Ian, *Augustan Satire: Intention and Idiom in English Poetry 1660–1750*, 1952.
Congleton, J. E., *Theories of Pastoral Poetry in England 1684–1798*, 1952.
Studies in the Literature of the Augustan Age: Essays in Honour of A. E. Case, 1952.
Bosker, A., *Literary Criticism in the Age of Johnson*, 1953; revised edition, 1971.
Abrams, M. H., *The Mirror and the Lamp: Romantic Theory and the Critical Tradition*, 1953.
Moore, C. A., *Backgrounds of English Literature 1700–60*, 1953.
Unwin, R., *The Rural Muse: Studies in Peasant Poetry of England*, 1954.
Fussell, P., Jr., *Theory of Prosody in Eighteenth-Century England*, 1954.
Chapin, C. F., *Personification in Eighteenth-Century English Poetry*, 1955.
Wellek, René, *A History of Modern Criticism 1750–1950*: vol. 1: *The Later Eighteenth Century*, 1955.
Walton, G., *Metaphysical to Augustan: Studies in Tone and Sensibility in the Seventeenth Century*, 1955.
Marks, E. R., *Relativist and Absolutist: The Early Neo-Classical Debate in England*, 1955.
Leyburn, E. D., *Satiric Allegory: Mirror of Man*, 1956.
Watson, W. R., *Magazine Serials and the Essay Tradition 1746–1820*, 1956.
Sutherland, James, and Ian Watt, *Restoration and Augustan Prose*, 1957.
Hagstrum, Jean H., *The Sister Arts: The Tradition of Literary Pictorialism and English Poetry from Dryden to Gray*, 1958.
Nicolson, Marjorie Hope, *Mountain Gloom and Mountain Glory: The Development of the Aesthetics of the Infinite*, 1959.
George, M. D., *English Political Caricature to 1792*, 1959.

Wasserman, E. R., *The Subtler Language: Critical Readings of Neoclassic and Romantic Poems*, 1959.

Bald, R. C., *Seventeenth-Century English Poetry*, 1959.

Clifford, James L., editor, *Eighteenth-Century English Literature: Modern Essays in Criticism*, 1959.

Wedgwood, C. V., *Poetry and Politics under the Stuarts*, 1960.

Leach, M., and T. P. Coffin, editors, *The Critics and the Ballad*, 1961.

Friedman, A. B., *The Ballad Revival: Studies in the Influence of Popular on Sophisticated Poetry*, 1961.

Schilling, B. N., editor, *Essential Articles for the Study of English Augustan Backgrounds*, 1961.

Tillotson, Geoffrey, *Augustan Studies*, 1961.

Bredvold, L. I., *The Brave New World of the Englightenment*, 1961.

Reason and the Imagination: Studies in the History of Ideas 1600–1800: Essays in Honor of Marjorie Hope Nicolson, 1962.

Nevo, R., *The Dial of Virtue: A Study of Poems on Affairs of State in the Seventeenth Century*, 1963.

Restoration and Eighteenth-Century Essays in Honor of Alan D. McKillop, 1963.

Davie, Donald, *The Language of Science and the Language of Literature 1700–40*, 1963.

Boulton, James T., *The Language of Politics in the Age of Wilkes and Burke*, 1963.

Price, Martin, *To the Palace of Wisdom: Studies in Order and Energy from Dryden to Blake*, 1964.

Fussell, P., Jr., *The Rhetorical World of Augustan Humanism: Ethics and Imagery from Swift to Burke*, 1965.

Sutherland, W. O. S., *The Art of the Satirist: Essays on the Satire of Augustan England*, 1965.

Pinto, V. de S., *The Restoration Court Poets*, 1965.

Marsh, R., *Four Dialectical Theories of Poetry: An Aspect of English Neoclassical Criticism*, 1965.

Wasserman, E. R., editor, *Aspects of the Eighteenth Century*, 1965.

Johnson, Boswell, and Their Circle: Essays Presented to Lawrence Fitzroy Powell, 1965.

From Sensibility to Romanticism: Essays Presented to Frederick A. Pottle, 1965.

Malins, E. G., *English Landscaping and Literature 1660–1840*, 1966.

Marks, E. R., *The Poetics of Reason: English Neoclassical Criticism*, 1966.

Spacks, Patricia M., *The Poetry of Vision: Five Eighteenth-Century Poets*, 1967.

Trickett, Rachel, *The Honest Muses: A Study in Augustan Verse*, 1967.

Johnson, J. W., *The Formation of English Neo-Classical Thought*, 1967.

Stone, P. W. K., *The Art of Poetry 1750–1820: Theories of Poetic Composition and Style*, 1967.

Fowler, D. C., *A Literary History of the Popular Ballad*, 1968.

Bronson, B. H., *Facets of the Enlightenment: Studies in English Literature and Its Contexts*, 1968.

Watt, Ian, editor, *The Augustan Age: Approaches to Literature, Life, and Thought*, 1968.

Clifford, James L., editor, *Man Versus Society in Eighteenth-Century Britain: Six Points of View*, 1968.

Daghlian, P. B., editor, *Essays in Eighteenth-Century Biography*, 1968.

Weinbrot, Howard, *The Formal Strain: Studies in Augustan Imitation and Satire*, 1969.

Piper, W. B., *The Heroic Couplet*, 1969.

Downey, James, *The Eighteenth-Century Pulpit*, 1969.

Chalker, John, *The English Georgic*, 1969.

Delany, P., *British Autobiography in the Seventeenth Century*, 1969.

Miller, Henry Knight, E. Rothstein, and G. S. Rousseau, editors, *The Augustan Milieu: Essays Presented to Louis A. Landa*, 1970.

Kallich, Martin, *The Association of Ideas and Critical Theory in Eighteenth-Century England*, 1970.

Braudy, L., *Narrative Form in History and Fiction*, 1970.
Fish, Stanley E., editor, *Seventeenth-Century Prose*, 1971.
Bate, Walter Jackson, *The Burden of the Past and the English Poet*, 1971.
Hughes, P., and D. Williams, editors, *The Varied Pattern: Studies in the Eighteenth Century*, 1971.
Miner, Earl, *The Cavalier Mode from Jonson to Cotton*, 1971.
Lipking, Lawrence, *The Ordering of the Arts in Eighteenth-Century England*, 1971.
Love, Harold, editor, *Restoration Literature: Critical Approaches*, 1972.
Edwards, Thomas R., *Imagination and Power: A Study of Poetry on Public Themes*, 1972.
Rogers, Pat, *Grub Street: Studies in a Subculture*, 1972.
Morris, David B., *The Religious Sublime: Christian Poetry and Critical Tradition in Eighteenth-Century England*, 1972.
Korshin, Paul J., *From Concord to Dissent: Major Themes in English Poetic Theory 1640–1700*, 1973.
Spencer, Jeffry B., *Heroic Nature: Ideal Landscape in English Poetry from Marvell to Thomson*, 1973.
Elkin, P. K., *The Augustan Defence of Satire*, 1973.
Rivers, Isabel, *The Poetry of Conservatism 1600–1745: A Study of Poetry and Public Affairs from Jonson to Pope*, 1973.
Miner, Earl, *The Restoration Mode from Milton to Dryden*, 1974.
Farley-Hills, David, *The Benevolence of Laughter*, 1974.
Byrd, Max, *Visits to Bedlam: Madness and Literature in the Eighteenth Century*, 1974.
DePorte, Michael V., *Nightmares and Hobbyhorses: Swift, Sterne, and Augustan Ideas of Madness*, 1974.
Rogers, Pat, *The Augustan Vision*, 1974.
Battestin, Martin C., *The Providence of Wit: Aspects of Form in Augustan Literature and the Arts*, 1974.
Ehrenpreis, Irvin, *Literary Meaning and Augustan Values*, 1974.
Malek, James S., *The Arts Compared: An Aspect of Eighteenth-Century British Aesthetics*, 1974.
Mell, Donald C., *A Poetics of the Augustan Elegy*, 1974.
Goldgar, Bertrand A., *Walpole and the Wits; The Relation of Politics to Literature 1722–42*, 1976.
Hunt, John Dixon, *The Figure in the Landscape: Poetry, Painting, and Gardening During the Eighteenth Century*, 1976.
Carnochan, W. B., *Confinement and Flight*, 1977.
Byrd, Max, *London Transformed*, 1978.
Rogers, Pat, editor, *The Eighteenth Century*, 1978.
Weinbrot, Howard, *Augustus Caesar in "Augustan" England*, 1978.
Evidence in Literary Scholarship: Essays in Memory of J. M. Osborn, 1979.

4. Anthologies of primary material

Spingarn, J. E., editor, *Critical Essays of the Seventeenth Century*, 3 vols., 1908–09.
Doughty, O., editor, *Forgotten Lyrics of the Eighteenth Century*, 1924.
Smith, David Nicol, editor, *The Oxford Book of Eighteenth-Century Verse*, 1926.
Bredvold, L. I., Alan D. McKillop, and L. Whitney, editors, *Eighteenth-Century Poetry and Prose*, 1939; revised edition, 1956.
Stead, P. J., editor, *Songs of the Restoration Theatre*, 1948.
Hanford, James Holly, editor, *A Restoration Reader*, 1954.
Brinton, Crane, editor, *The Portable Age of Reason Reader*, 1956.
Davie, Donald, editor, *The Late Augustans: Longer Poems of the Later Eighteenth Century*, 1958.
Elledge, Scott, editor, *Eighteenth-Century Critical Essays*, 2 vols., 1961.
Brady, F., and Martin Price, editors, *English Prose and Poetry 1660–1800*, 1961.

Quintana, Ricardo, and A. Whitley, editors, *English Poetry of the Mid and Late Eighteenth Century: An Historical Anthology,* 1963.

Lord, G. de F., and others, editors, *Poems on Affairs of State: Augustan Satirical Verse 1660–1714,* 7 vols., 1963–75; selection, 1975.

Spacks, Patricia M., editor, *Eighteenth-Century Poetry,* 1964.

Sutherland, James, editor, *Early Eighteenth-Century Poetry,* 1965.

Chapman, G. W., editor, *Literary Criticism in England 1660–1800,* 1966.

Pinto, G. de S., editor, *Poetry of the Restoration 1653–1700,* 1966.

Starkman, M. K., editor, *Seventeenth-Century Poetry,* 2·vols., 1967.

Jarrell, M. L., and W. Meredith, *Eighteenth-Century English Minor Poets,* 1969.

Tillotson, Geoffrey, P. Fussell, Jr., and M. Waingrow, editors, *Eighteenth-Century English Literature,* 1969.

Love, Harold, editor, *The Penguin Book of Restoration Verse,* 1969.

Simon, Irene, editor, *Neo-Classical Criticism 1660–1800,* 1971.

Gilmore, Thomas B., editor, *Early Eighteenth-Century Essays on Taste,* 1972.

Davison, Dennis, editor, *The Penguin Book of Eighteenth-Century Verse,* 1973.

Spacks, Patricia M., editor, *Late Augustan Poetry,* 1973.

Barlough, J. E., *Minor British Poetry 1680–1800,* 1973.

Davie, Donald, editor, *Augustan Lyric,* 1974.

Lindsay, David W., editor, *English Poetry 1700–80,* 1974.

Holloway, John, and Joan Black, editors, *Later English Broadside Ballads,* 1975.

Wilson, J. H., editor, *Court Satires of the Restoration,* 1976.

Crawford, Thomas, editor, *Love, Labour, and Liberty: The Eighteenth-Century Scottish Lyric,* 1976.

Sisson, C. H., editor, *The English Sermon,* vol. 2: *1650–1750,* 1976.

ADDISON, Joseph. English. Born in Milston, Wiltshire, 1 May 1672. Educated at schools in Amesbury, Salisbury, and Lichfield; Charterhouse, London, where he met Richard Steele; Queen's College, Oxford, 1687–89, and Magdalen College, Oxford, 1689–93, M.A. 1693. Married Charlotte, Dowager Countess of Warwick, 1716. Fellow of Magdalen College, 1698–1711; received government pension, 1699, and travelled in France, Italy, Germany, and Holland, 1699–1704: served under Prince Eugene in Italy as a "Secretary from the King," 1702; settled in London; member of the Kit-Cat Club, and embarked on a political career in the service of the Whigs: Commissioner of Appeal in Excise, 1704–08; Under-Secretary of State, 1705; Secretary to Lord Halifax on his mission to Hanover, 1707; Member of Parliament for Lostwithiel, 1708–10, and for Malmesbury, 1710 until the end of his life; Secretary to Lord Wharton, Lord Lieutenant of Ireland, 1708–10; Editor, *Whig Examiner*, 1710; contributor to Steele's *Tatler*, 1709–11, and Co-Editor, with Steele, and major contributor to *Spectator*, 1711–12, then sole Editor of the revived *Spectator*, 1714; contributor to Steele's *Guardian*, 1713; purchased the estate of Bilton, near Rugby, 1713; after accession of George I, Secretary to Earl of Sunderland, as Lord Lieutenant of Ireland, 1714–15; appointed a commissioner for trade and the colonies, 1715; Editor, *The Freeholder*, London, 1715–16; Secretary of State in the Sunderland cabinet, 1717–18. *Died 17 June 1719.*

PUBLICATIONS

Collections

> *Miscellaneous Works,* edited by Adolph C. Guthkelch.   2 vols., 1914.
> *Letters*, edited by Walter Graham.   1941.

Essays and Prose Works

> *Remarks on Several Parts of Italy.*   1705; revised edition, 1718.
> *The Present State of the War and the Necessity of an Augmentation Considered.*   1708.
> *The Tatler,* with Steele.   4 vols., 1710–11; edited by G. A. Aitken, 4 vols., 1898–99; selections edited by L. Gibbs, 1953.
> *The Spectator,* with Steele.   8 vols., 1712–15; edited by D. F. Bond, 5 vols., 1965; selections edited by R. J. Allen, 1957.
> *The Late Trial and Conviction of Count Tariff.*   1713.
> *The Guardian,* with others.   2 vols., 1714; edited by Alexander Chalmers, 1802.
> *The Free-Holder; or, Political Essays.*   1716.
> *A Dissertation upon the Most Celebrated Roman Poets.*   1718.
> *The Old Whig.*   1720.
> *Miscellanies in Verse and Prose.*   1725.
> *A Discourse on Ancient and Modern Learning.*   1734.
> *Critical Essays from The Spectator,* edited by D. F. Bond.   1970.

Plays

> *Rosamond,* music by Thomas Clayton (produced 1707).   1707.
> *Cato* (produced 1713).   1713.
> *The Drummer; or, The Haunted House* (produced 1716).   1716.

Verse

A Poem to His Majesty.   1695.
The Campaign.   1705.
Poems on Several Occasions.   1719.
The Christian Poet: A Miscellany of Divine Poems.   1728.

Other Works

Works, edited by Thomas Tickell.   4 vols., 1721.

Editor, *Musarum Anglicanarum,* vol. 2.   1699.

Reading List: *The Life of Addison* by Peter Smithers, 1954, revised edition, 1968; *Steele, Addison, and Their Periodical Essays* by Arthur R. Humphreys, 1959; *The Cultural Milieu of Addison's Literary Criticism* by Lee A. Elioseff, 1963; *Natur und Landschaft bei Addison* by Hans J. Possin, 1965; *Addison's Sociable Animal* by Edward A. and Lillian D. Bloom, 1971.

*   *   *

Joseph Addison's high reputation in the eighteenth and nineteenth centuries was based upon his essays for *The Spectator* (1711–12), a daily periodical edited in conjunction with Richard Steele, but to which Addison was the major contributor. It was revived in 1714 entirely under Addison's control (nos. 556–635). *The Spectator* derived from Steele's *The Tatler* (1709–11), for which Addison wrote, and led on to *The Guardian* (1713). It is an invidious task to distinguish between the two writers, especially in their application of wit to the reform of manners, and in the sharp particularity with which they describe the contemporary scene.

Addison, however, was the more philosophical moralist. The lay sermons which distinguish the Saturday papers in *The Spectator* were his. So too were the major series of critical essays. The character of Sir Roger de Coverley, although invented by Steele, was especially developed by Addison (nos. 106–31), and the limpid elegance of Addison's studied but easy style has generally been preferred to Steele's more careless manner.

Their relationship began at Charterhouse School, and continued at Oxford and in the Kit-Cat Club where many of the leading wits and Whigs gathered under the auspices of Jacob Tonson the publisher. Addison's pretentions to a serious career, however, were weightier than Steele's. He spent twelve years at Oxford where he had achieved considerable distinction, becoming a fellow of Magdalen. Thereafter his political career in the service of the Whig party led him to high office as Secretary of State (and to his marriage with the Dowager Countess of Warwick). Thus many of his works, for instance, "The Dialogues upon Ancient Medals" and *Remarks on Italy,* have a strong scholarly bias, and the most famous of his plays, the tragedy *Cato,* combines classical learning with a strong political bias, for the celebration of the Roman Republic was taken by his friends as an indictment of the tyrannical pretentions of the Tory Jacobites and praise of the Whig hero, the Duke of Marlborough (also the subject of Addison's best known poem *The Campaign*). At the end of his life it was politics which led to his estrangement from Steele (see *The Old Whig*) and may even have prompted Pope's long-delayed satiric portrait of Addison as Atticus in *An Epistle to Dr. Arbuthnot* (1735), although the original cause of that quarrel probably derived from Pope's belief that Addison was sponsoring a rival translation of Homer. Addison's last major venture into periodical journalism, *The Freeholder* (1715–16) is Party propaganda, and even in *The Spectator,* where the editors deliberately avoided political controversy, the de Coverley papers contain a political barb fleshed with humour. Although the rustic squire is almost always amiable and charms the reader, the sentimental comedy only partially conceals the fact that Sir Roger is of the wrong political persuasion, and is a man to whom no one would entrust public affairs, or private business.

The main stream of Addison's career, therefore, was not literary, and his major creative work as an essayist may be viewed as merely the cultural embellishment of a man of affairs. *The Spectator* essays especially were written in the enforced idleness subsequent on the Whigs' fall from power in 1710. Whereas in the eighteenth and nineteenth centuries Addison was frequently invoked as a model of style, and his advice as a moralist was consciously pursued, more recently his easy-going lightness of touch has encouraged the view that his is merely the dilettante manner of the school of *belles lettres*.

Addison's declared aim, however, was to digest substantial learning into simple form, to clarify complex arguments, and, while sustaining that firm moral tone which earned him the sobriquet of "the parson in a tie-wig," to relate moral concerns to the everyday business of society with good humour and wit. He saw himself in the tradition of Horatian satire – a humanistic tradition in which the man of affairs and the man of letters were familiar companions, and in which even the most important philosophical matters were handled without pedantry: "I have brought Philosophy out of Closets and Libraries, Schools and Colleges, to dwell in Clubs and Assemblies, at Tea-Tables, and in Coffee-Houses" (*Spectator* 10). His papers on "The Pleasures of the Imagination" provide the clearest and most pregnant account available of a major aesthetic and psychological concern of the time, and the elaborated criticism of *Paradise Lost* is not only one of the most important early assessments of Milton's poem, but shows also Addison's deep concern with the relation between ethical and literary matters. Such serious preoccupations are matched with a lively and detailed presentation of the everyday scene in his social and satiric essays which challenge comparison with any of the novelists of the time.

Bacon, Montaigne, and Temple are among Addison's models, and periodicals like the *Mercure Galant* in France and Motteux's *Gentleman's Journal* in England suggest earlier analogies to *The Spectator*, but it was Addison especially who established the periodical essay as one of the major artistic genres of the century. Among numerous imitations were Johnson's *The Idler* and *The Rambler*, Hawkesworth's *The Adventurer*, and Dodsley's and Moore's *The World*.

—Malcolm Kelsall

AKENSIDE, Mark. English. Born in Newcastle upon Tyne, 9 November 1721. Educated at a dissenting minister's school, Newcastle; studied theology in Edinburgh, 1739, then medicine at the University of Edinburgh (elected Member of the Medical Society of Edinburgh, 1740), and at the University of Leyden, Dr. of Physic 1744; awarded M.D., Cambridge, 1753. Practised medicine in Newcastle, 1741–43, Northampton, 1744–45, and in Hampstead, London, 1745–47; Editor, *The Museum; or, The Literary and Historical Register*, London, 1746–47; granted a pension by Jeremiah Dyson, 1747; resumed practice of medicine, 1748; appointed Assistant Physician, then Principal Physician, St. Thomas's Hospital, London, and Principal Physician, Christ's Hospital, London, 1759; created Physician to the Queen, 1761. Fellow, 1754, and gave the Gulstonian Lectures, 1755, Croonian Lectures, 1756, and the Harveian Oration, 1759, College of Physicians, London. Fellow of the Royal Society, 1753. *Died 23 June 1770.*

PUBLICATIONS

Collections

Poetical Works, edited by George Gilfillan.   1857.

Verse

A British Philippic: A Poem in Miltonic Verse.   1738; as The Voice of Liberty, 1738.
The Pleasures of Imagination.   1744; revised edition, in Poems, 1772.
An Epistle to Curio.   1744.
Odes on Several Subjects.   1745; revised edition, 1760.
Friendship and Love: A Dialogue, to Which Is Added A Song.   1745.
An Ode to the Earl of Huntingdon.   1748.
An Ode to the Country Gentlemen of England.   1758.
An Ode to the Late Thomas Edwards.   1766.
Poems, edited by Jeremiah Dyson.   1772.

Other

Dissertatio Medica Inauguralis, de Ortu et Encremento Foetus Humani.   1744.
De Dysenteria Commentarius.   1764.

Editor, The Works of William Harvey.   1766.

Bibliography: in Seven 18th Century Bibliographies by Iolo A. Williams, 1924.

Reading List: Akenside: A Biographical and Critical Study by C. T. Houpt, 1944 (includes bibliography); Four Dialectial Theories of Poetry by R. Marsh, 1965; The Rhetoric of Science by W. P. Jones, 1966.

*   *   *

Mark Akenside's most important poem is The Pleasures of Imagination, a didactic poem in blank verse. Whereas other eighteenth-century poets, such as Thomson and Young, when they attempted blank verse might be accused of writing heroic couplets without the rhymes, Akenside showed a far better grasp of the metonic style, and could weld together a blank verse paragraph by the construction of long periodic sentences and the skilful use of enjambement. Sometimes indeed his sentences are too long and involved, and this tends to obscure his argument. The matter of the poem derives partly from Addison's Essays on the Imagination, partly from Shaftesbury's Characteristics. It has something of a Platonic tinge, foreshadowing the idealistic philosophy of Coleridge and the other Romantics:

> Mind, mind alone (bear witness earth and heaven!)
> The living fountains in itself contains
> Of beauteous and sublime.

Some other passages in which Akenside describes the mountainous scenery of his native Northumberland have often been noted as anticipating Wordsworth. But Akenside's relation is less to Romanticism than to the development of a line of Neo-Classical writing which began in the mid-eighteenth century and ran on into the Romantic period, finding its fullest expression in the work of Landor. There are elements of it in the Odes of Keats, and such poems as Wordsworth's *Laodamia*. In the earlier period this eighteenth-century Neo-Classicism, which manifested itself most clearly in the fields of painting and architecture, should be distinguished from the dominant Augustan style, based on Roman models, by its orientation towards the Greek ideal. In poetry, the Odes of Gray and Collins belong here, as do those of Akenside. These last do not deserve their almost total dismissal by Johnson. They are rather stiff, have less musical quality than Gray's, and have much less imaginative and formal originality than those of Collins. Nevertheless some of them, such as the "Ode to the Evening Star," have considerable merit and deserve to be better known.

Akenside's "Hymn to the Naiad" is an extended blank verse lyric modelled on the Hymns of the Alexandrine Greek poet Callimachus. It represents another aspect of Neo-Classicism, the reviving feeling for Greek mythology. Of his other pieces, "The Virtuoso" is a youthful exercise in the Spenserian manner, which like many eighteenth-century poems in this vein is as much a parody as an imitation. *An Epistle to Curio* (later remodelled as an ode) is addressed to William Pulteney who deserted Walpole for the Tory side. It is a notable piece of political invective, illustrating the Radical stance which, at least in his early Nonconformist years, Akenside evinced. The short "Inscriptions" show his lapidary style at perhaps its most effective.

—John Heath-Stubbs

ANSTEY, Christopher. English. Born in Brinkley, Cambridgeshire, 31 October 1724. Educated at school in Bury St. Edmunds, Suffolk; Eton College; King's College, Cambridge, 1742–46, B.A. 1746. Married Ann Calvert in 1756; several children, including the poet John Anstey. Fellow, King's College, 1745 until he succeeded to his family estates, 1754. Moved to Bath, 1770. *Died 3 August 1805.*

PUBLICATIONS

Collections

Poetical Works, edited by John Anstey. 1808.

Verse

Elegia Scripta in Coemeterio Rustico Latine Reditta, from Gray's poem, with W. H. Roberts. 1762.
On the Death of the Marquis of Tavistock. 1767.
The New Bath Guide; or, Memoirs of the B--r--d Family in a Series of Poetical Epistles. 1766; edited by P. Sainsbury, 1927.
The Patriot: A Pindaric Address to Lord Buckhorse. 1767; *Appendix,* 1768.
Ode on an Evening View of the Cresent at Bath. 1773.
The Priest Dissected. 1774.

An Election Ball in Poetical Letters in the Zommerzetshire Dialect from Mr. Inkle of Bath to His Wife in Gloucester.   1776; revised edition, 1776.
Ad C. W. Bampfylde, Arm: Epistola Poetica Familiaris.   1776; translated as *A Familiar Epistle,* 1777.
Fabulae Selectae (in Latin), from Gay's poems.   1777(?).
Envy.   1778.
Winter Amusements: An Ode.   1778.
A Paraphrase or Poetical Exposition of the Thirteenth Chapter of First Corinthians.   1779.
Speculation; or, A Defence of Mankind.   1780.
Liberality; or, The Decayed Macaroni: A Sentimental Piece.   1788.
The Farmer's Daughter: A Poetical Tale.   1795.
The Monopolist: A Poetical Tale.   1795.
Britain's Genius: A Song Occasioned by the Late Mutiny at the Nore.   1797.
Contentment; or, Hints to Servants on the Present Scarcity: A Poetical Epistle.   1800.
Ad Edvardum Jenner: Carmen Alcaicum.   1803.

Bibliography: "A Bibliography of Anstey's First Editions" by Iolo A. Williams, in *London Mercury,* January-July 1925.

Reading List: *Anstey, Bath Laureate* by William C. Powell, 1944; *Portraits in Satire* by Kenneth Hopkins, 1958.

*   *   *

Christopher Anstey's son John, in the preface to his father's *Poetical Works,* praises his "power of originating by the natural force of his genius, new and unexpected images, with the admirable talent of combining, varying, and multiplying them at pleasure." *The New Bath Guide,* however, remains the only poem of this skillful dilettante's small but varied English output – he also wrote Latin verse – in which he used his power and talent with real success. A comfortable country squire who enjoyed the wit and learning of acquaintances in Cambridge and Bath, Anstey specialized in verse of gentle mockery. His unpretentious, graceful, sprightly style won him admiration from the other fashionable amateurs who frequented Lady Anne Miller's salon near Bath, where the guests met to hear read and to judge their own verse, dropped by each (so as to preserve anonymity) into an allegedly antique urn upon entering. With this sort of audience, Anstey aspired to little and achieved it. His elegy for the Marquis of Tavistock, his burlesque ode to the boxer Buckhorse, and his *Election Ball,* and imitation of his *New Bath Guide,* are sporadically effective; the shorter light verse is pleasant.

The New Bath Guide, a series of verse letters supposedly written from Bath by members of the visiting Blunderhead family, achieved a great vogue and stimulated such parodies and imitations as *Tunbridge Epistles* and *Poetical Epistles to the Author of the New Bath Guide.* Anstey spoofs various kinds of modern verse (odes, hymns, songs, religious stanzas) while he offers comic accounts of Bath customs and habitués (bell-ringing, medical consultations, the baths themselves; gouty lords, amorous "beaux garçons"). He also satirizes pedantry and zeal, particularly evangelistic Methodism in Letter VII and the ribald Letter XIV, where Prudence Blunderhead describes her seduction by young Roger as a visit from a divine spirit come to "fill [her] full of Love." Most of the letters use a tripping anapaestic tetrameter which, in Anstey's hands, serves well for medical jargon, colloquialism, and ironic poetic cliché, sometimes with rhymes ("her toe" / "concerto," "takes here" / "Shakespeare") that recall Butler's *Hudibras.* The metre kept its popularity for light verse through the nineteenth century. Gilbert used it for the Nightmare song of the Lord Chancellor in *Iolanthe* (1882) and, more recently, T. S. Eliot, for several poems in *Old Possum's Book of Practical Cats* (1939).

—Eric Rothstein

ARMSTRONG, John. Scottish. Born in Castleton, Liddesdale, Roxburghshire, c. 1709. Educated at the University of Edinburgh, M.D. 1732. Practised in London from 1735: Physician to the London Soldiers' Hospital, 1746–60; Physician to the Army in Germany, 1760–63; returned to London on half-pay and resumed his medical practice, 1763; toured Europe with the painter Fuseli, 1770. *Died 7 September 1779.*

PUBLICATIONS

Collections

   Poetical Works, with Dyer and Green, edited by George Gilfillan.   1858.

Verse

   The Oeconomy of Love: A Poetical Essay.   1736; expurgated edition, 1768.
   The Art of Preserving Health.   1744.
   Of Benevolence: An Epistle to Eumenes.   1751.
   Taste: An Epistle to a Young Critic.   1753.
   A Day: An Epistle to John Wilkes.   1761.

Play

   The Forced Marriage, in *Miscellanies.*   1770.

Other

   Dissertation Medica Inauguralis de Tabe Purulenta.   1732.
   An Essay for Abridging the Study of Physick.   1735.
   The Muncher's and Guzzler's Diary.   1749.
   Sketches; or, Essays on Various Subjects.   1758.
   Miscellanies.   2 vols., 1770.
   A Short Ramble Through Some Parts of France and Italy.   1771.
   Medical Essays.   1773.

   Translator, *A Synopsis of the History and Cure of Venereal Diseases,* by L. Luisini.   1737.

Bibliography: in *Seven 18th-Century Bibliographies* by Iolo A. Williams, 1924.

Reading List: "Armstrong: Littérateur and Associate of Smollett, Thomson, Wilkes, and Other Celebrities" by L. M. Knapp in *Publications of the Modern Language Association,* 1944; *George and John Armstrong of Castleton* by William J. M. A. Maloney, 1954.

*   *   *

The oldest function of poetry may indeed have been to convey information, particularly of battles or other historic events. It was, however, used notably by Ovid in *The Art of Love* for instruction in the ways of love, and by Virgil in his *Georgics* for information on horticulture, though in neither case was the conveying of information the only purpose achieved.

John Armstrong, the son of a Roxburghshire clergyman, inherited the gift of homily and had the good fortune to be a friend and fellow student at Edinburgh University of James Thomson. Armstrong thus became one of the "vast assembly moving to and fro" portrayed in the lotus-land of Thomson's *Castle of Indolence*. Himself reputedly an extremely lazy man, Thomson got Armstrong to write the last four stanzas of the first canto of *The Castle of Indolence*; those in which human diseases born of laziness are delineated. Here is how Armstrong delineates what he might nowadays term psychosomatic depression – from *The Art of Preserving Health*:

> Sour melancholy, night and day provokes
> Her own eternal wound....
> Then various shapes of curs'd illusion rise:
> Whate'er the wretched fears, creating fear
> Forms out of nothing....
>   The prostrate soul beneath
> A load of huge imagination heaves;
> And all the horrors that the murderer feels
> Will anxious flutterings wake the guiltless breast.

Armstrong was a doctor through and through. His professional skills were put to informative literary use in his poem in four books, *The Art of Preserving Health* a surprisingly lively compendium of common sense cast in blank verse, dividing the four books of his subject into air, diet, exercise and the passions. Doubtless he was aware of the difficulties of reaching the higher flights with such a theme, for of diet he remarks: "A barren waste, where not a garland grows / To bind the Muse's brow."

Armstrong's *Taste: An Epistle to a Young Critic* is in some respects a fairly conventional satire in the manner of Pope and Swift; *A Day: An Epistle to John Wilkes Esq.* provoked the virulence of Churchill, who described Armstrong's work as a repository "Where all but barren labour was forgot, / And the vain stiffness of a lettered Scot."

The "lettered Scot," however, turned his verse to a use neither vain nor stiff in his poem *The Economy of Love*, which led an apothecary, having read it, to inquire rhetorically: "How, in the name of heaven, could he ever expect that a woman would let him enter her house again, after that?" "That" was, in fact, a practical sex manual intended for the helpful instruction of newly married couples who might otherwise have been forced to rely upon the antique circumlocutions of Aristotle. Banned from reprints of Armstrong's work throughout the 19th century, with its Thomsonian periphrasis it may make us smile in the 20th. But there is vigour in the writing, and the practical doctor was no prude. One sample must suffice. Having for the first time removed his new wife's clothes, the young husband is told:

> Then when her lovely limbs,
> Oft lovely deem'd, far lovlier now beheld,
> Thro' all your trembling joints increase the flame;
> Forthwith discover to her dazzled sight
> The stately novelty, and to her hand
> Usher the new acquaintance. She perhaps
> Averse, will coldly chide, and half afraid,
> Blushing, half pleas'd, the tumid wonder view.

Dr. Armstrong could not of course foresee that a later generation of women would be taught to suffer sex and "think of England," or that many of the representatives of a still later age would not have waited until after marriage to become acquainted with each other's bodies.

In his day his work won the admiration of such divers critics as Goldsmith, Lord

Monboddo, Hume and Boswell, who found it "impossible to translate into French his force of style a force remarkable even in English." He inspired Dr. Theobald to produce an Ode, "Ad Ingenuum Virum, tum Medicis, tum Poeticis, Facultatibus Praestantum, Johannum Armstrong, M.D."

—Maurice Lindsay

BARBAULD, Anna (Laetitia, née Aikin). English.   Born   in   Kibworth-Harcourt, Northamptonshire, 20 June 1743. Educated at her father's school in Kibworth, and at Warrington Academy, Lancashire. Married the Rev. Rochemont Barbauld in 1774 (died, 1808). With husband, kept a boarding school in Palgrave, Suffolk, 1774– 87. Lived in London after 1787. *Died 9 March 1825.*

PUBLICATIONS

Collections

> *A Memoir, Letters, and a Selection,* by Grace A. Ellis.   2 vols., 1874.
> *Tales, Poems, and Essays.*   1884.

Verse

> *Corsica: An Ode.*   1768.
> *Poems.*   1773; revised edition, 1792.
> *Epistle to William Wilberforce.*   1791.
> *Eighteen Hundred and Eleven.*   1812.

Other

> *Miscellaneous Pieces in Prose,* with John Aikin.   1773.
> *Lessons for Children.*   1778.
> *Hymns in Prose for Children.*   1781; revised edition, 1814.
> *Civic Sermons to the People.*   1792.
> *Evenings at Home; or, The Juvenile Budget Opened,* with John Aikin.   6 vols., 1792–96.
> *Remarks on Wakefield's Enquiry.*   1792.
> *Sins of Government, Sins of the Nation.*   1793.
> *Works.*   2 vols., 1825.
> *A Discourse on Being Born Again.*   1830. ·
> *Letters of Maria Edgeworth and Barbauld,* edited by Walter Sidney Scott.   1953.

Editor, *Devotional Pieces from the Psalms and the Book of Job.*   1775.
Editor, *The Pleasures of the Imagination,* by Akenside.   1794.
Editor, *Poetical Works,* by Collins.   1797.
Editor, *Selections from the Spectator, Tatler, Guardian, Freeholder.*   3 vols., 1804.
Editor, *Correspondence of Samuel Richardson.*   6 vols., 1804.
Editor, *The British Novelists.*   50 vols., 1810.
Editor, *The Female Speaker.*   1811.

Reading List: *A Memoir of Mrs. Barbauld, Including Letters* by Anna L. LeBreton, 1874; *Georgian Chronicle : Mrs. Barbauld and Her Family* by Betsy Rodgers, 1958.

*   *   *

Mrs. Barbauld remains a valuable writer if only because her work serves so well as a compendium of late eighteenth-century taste. Her *Poems* are representative of the themes, genres, and styles of late neoclassicism. *Corsica,* for example, is a meditative-descriptive poem in blank verse which echoes Milton by way of Thomson and which espouses the rights of man in the Corsica discovered by Boswell. Her two major satires, *Epistle to William Wilberforce* and *Eighteen Hundred and Eleven,* are stately, declamatory, public rather than personal, written in heroic couplets. Her couplets, like all her verses, are competent, somewhat mechanical, yet pleasing, as these lines from *Eighteen Hundred and Eleven* illustrate:

> And think'st thou, Britain, still to sit at ease,
> An island queen amidst thy subject seas,
> While the vext billows, in their distant war,
> But soothe thy slumbers, and but kiss thy shore?

As essayist, also, she followed eighteenth-century models, usually striving for the dignity and grandeur of Johnson's balanced style, most often choosing serious subjects such as "Education" and "Inconsistency in Our Expectations."

But Mrs. Barbauld was more than a pale survivor of a fading culture. If she merited the gibes of young Romantic poets, she also deserved the popular respect which lasted throughout her life. For she was a courageous woman who accepted the duty of writing for the radical dissent to which her family adhered. In political pamphlets, she wrote with tough vitality against the Corporation and Test Acts, against "Sins of Government, Sins of the Nation," or for the rights of common men in "Civic Sermons to the People." Generally free of neoclassic convention in these pamphlets, she is the plain-speaker as well as the voice of reason, the angry prophet as well as the patient teacher.

By temperament conventional, as a woman uneasy about being a published author, Mrs. Barbauld nonetheless ventured into new directions if the need were sufficient. She became a pioneer in juvenile literature because as a teacher she found no books suitable for children under six. Despite Charles Lamb's accusation that the "accursed band of Barbaulds" stifled imagination with "geography and natural history," she created in *Lessons for Children* and *Hymns in Prose for Children* a small world which still evokes the freshness and delight of a child's view of country life.

Similarly, when required to turn editor-critic for Samuel Richardson's *Correspondence* and for a collection of novels, *British Novelists,* Mrs. Barbauld wrote a group of essays which dealt seriously and perceptively with a genre not then entirely respectable, arguing always that "this species of composition is entitled to a higher rank than has generally been assigned to it."

No single work of Mrs. Barbauld's stands above the rest, except perhaps the charming *Hymns* with their rhythmical prose or, for an earlier generation, an ode entitled "Life."

Rather, her importance is based upon the whole of her work: poems, essays, pamphlets, pieces for children, and critical prefaces. Taken as a whole, they not only reveal a gifted, highly intelligent, serious woman who was motivated to write by respect for reason and duty to an idealistic yet practical religion, Unitarian Christianity, but they also illuminate the literary and social milieu of that highly significant transitional period which her life spanned.

—Catherine E. Moore

BEATTIE, James. Scottish. Born in Laurencekirk, Kincardineshire, 25 October 1735. Educated at Marischal College, Aberdeen, 1749–53, M.A. 1753. Married Mary Dunn in 1767; two sons. Schoolmaster and Parish Clerk, Fardoun, near Laurencekirk, 1753–58; Master, Aberdeen Grammar School, 1758–60; Professor of Moral Philosophy and Logic, Marischal College, 1760–93, and lectured occasionally until 1797. LL.D.: Oxford University, 1770. Granted pension from the king, 1773. *Died 18 August 1803.*

PUBLICATIONS

Collections

Poetical Works, edited by Alexander Dyce. 1831.

Verse

Original Poems and Translations. 1760.
The Judgement of Paris. 1765.
Verses Occasioned by the Death of Charles Churchill. 1765.
Poems on Several Subjects. 1766.
The Minstrel; or, The Progress of Genius. 2 vols., 1771–74.
The Minstrel, with Some Other Poems. 1775; revised editon, 1799.
Poems on Several Occasions. 1776.

Other

An Essay on the Nature and Immutability of Truth. 1770.
Essays. 1776.
Scoticisms, Arranged in Alphabetical Order. 1779.
Dissertations Moral and Critical. 1783.
Evidences of the Christian Religion. 2 vols., 1786.
The Theory of Language. 1788.
Elements of Moral Science. 2 vols., 1790–93.
Some Unpublished Letters, edited by A. Mackie. 1908.
London Diary 1773, edited by Ralph S. Walker. 1946.
Day-Book 1773–98, edited by Ralph S. Walker. 1948.

Editor, *Poems,* by Gray.   1768.
Editor, *Essays and Fragments,* by James Hay Beattie.   1794.

Reading List: *An Account of the Life and Writings, Including Many Letters* by W. Forbes, 2 vols., 1806; *Beattie's Theory of Rhetoric* by V. M. Bevilacqua, 1967; *Beattie* by Everard H. King, 1978.

*   *   *

When James Beattie's name comes to mind today, it is less likely to be because of his poetry than for Dr. Johnson's remark: "We all love Beattie. Mrs. Thrale says if ever she has another husband she will have him." As a metaphysician, although hailed by the devout for his *Essay on Truth,* he failed to demolish Hume, whose scepticism his work was designed to combat. As a critic, he was taken in by the alleged genuineness of the verses of James "Ossian" Macpherson. As a Scottish man of letters, he was one of that to us now slightly absurd company who anxiously compiled and compared lists of Scoticisms which should be eradicated from their speech. However, when Christians in England excitedly hailed his attack on Hume, Beattie was offered, but refused, English clerical preferment. His lines "On the Proposed Monument to Churchill" do not spare a versifier whose antipathy to Scots and Scotland made him unloved north of the Border. An isolated Scots poem by Beattie in the epistle style – encouragement to his fellow poet in Scots, Alexander Ross, to keep writing – suggests that Beattie could have achieved work of substance in his native tongue had he been sure of his literary aims.

But he never was. For the most part, he modelled himself on his English contemporaries and produced the once-popular poem which traces the progress of the poet from a "rude age" to a period in which he could earn a loftier title. *The Minstrel,* widely hailed and much reprinted during the 18th century, purls along pleasantly, its nature painting still acceptable. Unfortunately, like most other later handlers of the Spenserian stanza, Beattie is apt to achieve an unintentional comic effect when applying the form to topics concerned with daily life.

A frequently anthologised stanza from *The Minstrel* give a flavour of Beattie's scene painting at its best:

> But who the melodies of morn can tell? –
>   The wild brook babbling down the mountain side;
> The lowing herd; the sheepfold's simple bell;
>   The pipe of early shepherd dim descried
>   In the lone valley; echoing far and wide,
> The clamorous horn along the cliffs above;
>   The hollow murmur of the ocean-tide;
>   The hum of bees; the linnet's lay of love;
> And the full choir that wakes the universal grove.

—Maurice Lindsay

BLACKMORE, Sir Richard.   English.   Born in Corsham, Wiltshire, in 1653. Educated at Westminster School, London; St. Edmund Hall, Oxford, B.A. 1674, M.A. 1676; University of Padua, M.D.; Fellow of the Royal College of Physicians, 1687. Married Mary Blackmore. Schoolmaster after leaving Oxford; then travelled and studied on the Continent; appointed Physician to William III, 1697, and later to Queen Anne. Censor, 1716, and Elect, 1716–22, Royal College of Physicians. Knighted, 1697. *Died 9 October 1729.*

PUBLICATIONS

Verse

Prince Arthur.   1695.
King Arthur.   1697.
A Satire Against Wit.   1700; edited by F. H. Ellis, in *Poems on Affairs of State 6,* 1971.
A Paraphrase on the Book of Job.   1700.
Discommendatory Verses.   1700; edited by R. C. Boys, in *Blackmore and the Wits,* 1949.
A Hymn to the Light of the World.   1703.
Eliza.   1705.
Advice to the Poets.   1706.
The Kit-cats.   1708.
Instructions to Vander Bank: A Sequel to the Advice to the Poets.   1709.
The Nature of Man.   1711.
Creation: A Philosophical Poem.   1712.
A Collection of Poems on Various Subjects.   1718.
A New Version of the Psalms of David.   1721.
Redemption: A Divine Poem.   1722.
Alfred.   1723.

Other

A Short History of the Last Parliament.   1699.
The Report of the Physicians and Surgeons Dissecting the Body of His Late Majesty (William III), with Thomas Millington and Edward Hannes.   1702.
The Lay-Monastery, Consisting of Essays, Discourses, etc., with John Hughes.   1714.
Essays upon Several Subjects.   2 vols., 1716–17.
Just Prejudices Against the Arian Hypothesis.   1721.
Modern Arians Unmasked.   1721.
A Discourse upon the Plague.   1721.
A True and Impartial History of the Conspiracy Against King William in 1695.   1723.
A Treatise upon the Small-Pox.   1723.
A Treatise of Consumptions and Other Distempers.   1724.
A Critical Dissertation upon Spleen.   1725.
A Treatise of the Spleen and Vapours.   1725.
Discourses on the Gout, Rheumatism, and the King's Evil.   1726.
Dissertations on a Dropsy, a Tympany, the Jaundice, the Stone, and a Diabetes.   1727.
Natural Theology; or, Moral Duties Considered Apart from Positive.   1728.
The Accomplished Preacher; or, An Essay on Divine Eloquence, edited by J. White.   1731.

Reading List: *Blackmore and the Wits* by R. C. Boys, 1949; *Blackmore* by Albert Rosenberg, 1953.

*   *   *

In the preface to *Prince Arthur* Richard Blackmore confesses, "Poetry has been so far from being my business ... that it has employed but a small part of my time ... as the entertainment of my idle hours...." No English writer better illustrates the sad fact that integrity, loyalty, diligence, and information do not in themselves make a poet. Blackmore has all these, yet his neglect by all save scholars picking over the debris of Augustan literary battlefields is perfectly understandable.

Even among his contemporaries his reputation was unsure. He was unfortunate in his choice of enemies, antagonising Dryden, Swift, and Pope, as well as lesser men like Garth who had more wit if not vastly more talent than himself. Hence he comes to us as pure buffoon; a figure from a Molière satire, scribbling in his coach as he goes from one consultation to another; or pontificating in Will's coffee-house amidst his heavy, Whiggish, city friends.

Blackmore's great defect is the unexciting quality of his language: he was said to be equally cautious in his medical practice (sound enough, however, to be Royal Physician to William and to Anne). He often preaches rather than teaches, and is entirely bound by those rules which the great writers of epic understand but often break or extend. His work is undramatic: never once does he create a character like Milton's Adam, let alone his Satan. Exactly where he should rise – in the set-piece descriptions of battle, journey, and debate – Blackmore falls. The following (from *Eliza*) is typical of the physician-poet:

> He raised his reeking sword with slaughter red,
> And aimed his blow between the breast and head,
> Which did the pipe, that breath conveys, divide,
> And cut the Jugulars from side to side.
> And had it met the juncture of the bone
> The Spaniard's head had from his shoulders flown.

His epic similes too often slide into this dismal world of eighteenth-century McGonagall-ism. The *Essays* are equally heavy-handed and ungracious: dissent at its most gawky. Yet his claim that "I have impartially pursued the interests of truth and virtue, without a design of pleasing or provoking any" is honestly meant. But it remains Blackmore's misfortune that he cannot "sing," and that his sense of "wonder" remains uncommunicated through his inert language.

Yet his first epic, *Prince Arthur*, was not ill received, and Johnson and Addison both praised *Creation*, his lengthy rhymed answer to the Aristotelian and Lucretian origins of the universe. As a document in the history of ideas, *Creation* does have interest, and its total sincerity can be engaging:

> I would th'Eternal from his works assert,
> And sing the wonders of creating art.

—T. Bareham

BLAIR, Robert. Scottish. Born in Edinburgh in 1699. Educated at the University of Edinburgh: also studied in Holland, took a degree there. Married Isabella Law in 1738; five sons, one daughter. Lived in Edinburgh, on an independent income, 1718–30; licensed to preach, 1729; ordained, Presbyterian Church, 1731; Minister of Athelstaneford, Haddingtonshire, 1731 until his death. *Died 4 February 1746.*

PUBLICATIONS

Collections

Poetical Works, with Beattie and Falconer, edited by George Gilfillan. 1854.

Verse

A Poem Dedicated to the Memory of William Law. 1728.
The Grave. 1743; revised edition, 1747.

Reading List: *The Background of Gray's Elegy: A Study in the Taste for Melancholy Poetry 1700–1760* by A. L. Read, 1953.

*   *   *

Robert Blair, though a minister of the episcopal Church of Scotland, has strong Evangelical, and even somewhat Calvinistic, leanings. His published verse consists only of the unremarkable *A Poem Dedicated to the Memory of William Law* and his famous blank-verse meditation *The Grave,* which was contemporaneous with Edward Young's *Night Thoughts,* and has commonly been associated with Parnell's *A Night-Piece on Death* and with Gray's *Elegy,* as a production of "the Graveyard School." Blair's avowed purpose is to recall men to an awareness of their own sinfulness by fixing their attention upon the facts of death and judgement; but his self-indulgent relish in describing cadaverous horrors goes well beyond the requirements of mere didacticism; so the poem becomes largely a succession of picturesque descriptions of such objects as mouldy damps, ropy slime and high-fed worms lazily coiled as they feed upon damask cheeks. The free movement of Blair's lines, as well as his occasional dry humour and macabre images, owes more to Jacobean dramatists and early seventeenth-century mortuary verse than they do to the eighteenth-century tradition of writing in blank verse. Most modern readers will find Blair grotesque, and perhaps even silly, where he seeks to be sublime; but in the heyday of the early nineteenth-century Evangelical Movement *The Grave* was immensely popular. One incidental consequence of this popularity was that Blake's magnificent designs to illustrate an edition of Blair's poem in 1808 were, in Blake's lifetime, his best-known work. Now *The Grave* is remembered more in connection with Blake than with Blair.

—A. J. Sambrook

BLAKE, William. English. Born in London, 28 November 1757. Studied at Pars' Drawing School, Strand, London, 1767; apprentice to the engraver James Basire, 1772–79; subsequently studied at the Royal Academy of Arts, London. Married Catharine Boucher in 1782. Worked as an illustrator and graphic designer, and gave drawing lessons, London, after 1778; moved to Felpham, Sussex, under the patronage of William Hayley, 1800; returned to London, 1803; after unsuccessful one-man show of his works in 1809 retreated into obscurity; in the 1820's attracted a group of young painters. *Died 12 August 1827.*

PUBLICATIONS

Collections

> *Writings*, edited by Geoffrey Keynes.   3 vols., 1925; revised edition, as *Poetry and Prose*, 1927, 1939; as *Complete Writings*, 1957, 1966.
> *Letters*, edited by Geoffrey Keynes.   1956; revised edition, 1968.
> *Poetry and Prose*, edited by David Erdman.   1965.
> *Complete Poems*, edited by W. H. Stevenson.   1973.
> *The Illuminated Blake*, edited by David Erdman.   1974.
> *Complete Poems*, edited by A. Ostriker.   1977.
> *Writings*, edited by G. E. Bentley, Jr.   2 vols., 1978.

Verse

> *Poetical Sketches.*   1783.
> *The Book of Thel.*   1789.
> *Songs of Innocence.*   1789; expanded edition, as *Songs of Innocence and of Experience, Shewing the Two Contrary States of the Human Soul*, 1794.
> *The French Revolution.*   1791.
> *The Marriage of Heaven and Hell.*   1793.
> *For Children: The Gates of Paradise.*   1793; revised edition, as *For the Sexes*, 1818(?).
> *Visions of the Daughters of Albion.*   1793.
> *America: A Prophecy.*   1793.
> *Europe: A Prophecy.*   1794.
> *The First Book of Urizen.*   1794.
> *The Book of Ahania.*   1795.
> *The Book of Los.*   1795.
> *The Song of Los.*   1795.
> *Milton.*   1804–09(?).
> *Jerusalem: The Emanation of the Giant Albion.*   1804–20(?).
> *The Ghost of Abel: A Revelation in the Visions of Jehovah Seen by William Blake.*   1822.
> *Tiriel.*   1874; edited by G. E. Bentley, Jr., 1967.
> *Vala*, edited by H. M. Margoliouth.   1956; as *The Four Zoas*, edited by G. E. Bentley, Jr., 1963.

Other

> *Notebook*, edited by Geoffrey Keynes.   1935; edited by David Erdman, 1973.
> *Engravings*, edited by Geoffrey Keynes.   1950.
> *The Blake-Varley Sketchbook of 1819*, edited by Martin Butlin.   1969.
> *The Complete Graphic Works*, edited by David Bindman.   1977.

Bibliography: *A Blake Bibliography: Annotated Lists of Works, Studies, and Blakeana* by G. E. Bentley, Jr., and M. K. Nurmi, 1964, revised by Bentley, as *Blake Books*, 1977.

Reading List: *The Life of Blake* by Mona Wilson, 1927, revised editon, 1948, edited by Geoffrey Keynes, 1971; *Fearful Symmetry* by Northrop Frye, 1947; *Infinity on the Anvil: A Critical Study of Blake's Poetry*, 1954, and *Blake*, 1968, both by Stanley Gardner; *Blake, Prophet Against Empire* by David Erdman, 1954, revised edition, 1969; *The Everlasting Gospel: A Study in the Sources of Blake* by Arthur L. Morton, 1958; *The Valley of Vision: Blake as Prophet and Revolutionary* by Peter F. Fisher, edited by Northrop Frye, 1961; *Blake's Apocalypse: A Study in Poetic Argument* by Harold Bloom, 1963; *Innocence and Experience: An Introduction to Blake* by E. D. Hirsch, Jr., 1964; *Blake's Humanism*, 1968, and *Blake's Visionary Universe*, 1969, both by John B. Beer; *Blake: The Lyric Poetry* by John Holloway, 1968; *Blake and Tradition* by Kathleen Raine, 2 vols., 1969; *A Blake Dictionary: The Ideas and Symbols of Blake* by S. Foster Damon, 1973; *Blake: The Critical Heritage* edited by G. E. Bentley, Jr., 1976.

*   *   *

It is hardly too much to say that William Blake achieved greatness in several different fields. He was not merely one of the best lyrical poets of the last five hundred years. His engravings for *Job*, and the unfinished series for Dante's *Divine Comedy*, are generally recognised as one of the peaks of English art. As a painter his quality is still a matter of controversy: he was in violent reaction against the fashionable portraits by Sir Joshua Reynolds, his own visionary pictures being regarded as crazy. In his old age, however, he acquired several disciples, including Richmond and Palmer. He was, finally, a prophet, convinced that he had rediscovered the truth of Christianity, which had become perverted by the Churches.

Blake was a radical who supported the French Revolution before the Reign of Terror. He was horrified by the results of the Industrial Revolution and he was almost alone in his outright condemnation of the age, in which he saw "A pretence of Art to destroy art; a pretence of liberty/To destroy liberty; a pretence of religion to destroy religion." He believed that "the arts of life had been changed into the arts of death"; that a world had been created "In which Man is by his nature the enemy of man," a world in which the poor were mercilessly exploited. But although Blake was a passionate critic of social evils, he was also a mystic. This can be illustrated by the experience related in a letter to Thomas Butts (22 November 1802) or by the opening quatrain of "Auguries of Innocence":

> To see a World in a Grain of Sand,
>   And heaven in a Wild Flower,
> To hold Infinity in the palm of your hand,
>   And Eternity in an hour.

Blake had many brilliant insights which he expressed in marginalia, in note-books, in letters, and most incisively in *The Marriage of Heaven and Hell*, but he also picked up a number of eccentric ideas. He believed, for example, that the English were the lost Ten Tribes, and he had curious notions about Druids. But the silliness is often transformed by the poetry. Not many who sing his most famous verses really believe that Jesus visited Britain, but they rightly accept that the building of Jerusalem in "England's green and pleasant land" is a powerful symbol of their social aspirations.

For two reasons it is impossible to consider Blake's poetry in isolation from his work as an artist and from his social and political ideas. First, because nearly all his verse was printed by himself from engraved copper plates, with hand-coloured illustrations, and these often give a necessary clue to the meaning; and, secondly, because even some of his simple songs embody his religious and political views.

Blake's first book, *Poetical Sketches*, written in his nonage, shows him imitating the precursors of romanticism – Gray, Collins, Ossian – and, inspired by Percy's *Reliques*, producing songs in the Elizabethan style. But the finest poem in the book, and arguably the best poem of the second half of the eighteenth century, is an address "To the Muses," lamenting their departure from England, and unconsciously proving their return. It might serve as a model of pure classical style.

Songs of Innocence, Blake's first illustrated poems, are simple without being naive, childlike without being childish, innocent without being insipid. Their subject is childhood as a symbolic representation of the Kingdom of Heaven; but, as we can see from the illustrations to "Infant Joy" and "The Blossom," several of the poems are concerned with sex and procreation. *Songs of Experience*, published five years later, are written in deliberate contrast. There love is treated as a crime; religion is mere hypocrisy; society is in the grip of a tyrannical class system; instead of the Divine Image of Mercy, Pity, Peace, and Love, we have Cruelty, Jealousy, Terror, and Secrecy; instead of sexual freedom there is enforced virginity; instead of the Lamb there is the Tyger.

Blake published no more lyrical verse, although he continued to write it for another ten years. A few of these later poems are as lucid as the *Songs*, but "The Mental Traveller" is as difficult as any of the prophetic books, and "The Everlasting Gospel," in which Blake gives his plainest statement of his disagreements with the Churches, was left unfinished. He probably came to feel that the propagation of his gospel could best be accomplished by means of the prophetic books.

It is characteristic of Blake's dialectical method that after the contrast in the *Songs* between the two contrary states of the human soul – good and bad – he should declare in *The Marriage of Heaven and Hell* that without contraries there is no progression. The marriage is that of energy and reason. Satan symbolises energy, and Blake's famous epigram that Milton "was a true Poet and of the Devil's party without knowing it" means in its context almost what Wordsworth meant when he said that poetry was "the spontaneous overflow of powerful feelings." The book, apart from prefatory and concluding poems in free verse, is written in witty and humorous prose: it is the most entertaining of Blake's writings. It was followed soon afterwards by *Visions of the Daughters of Albion*, a plea for the sexual emancipation of women, written in vigorous and eloquent verse. Blake rejected the use of blank verse, "derived from the modern bondage of rhyming," and he claimed later that in *Jerusalem* "Every word and every letter is studied and put into its fit place; the terrific numbers are reserved for the terrific parts, the mild & gentle for the mild & gentle parts, and the prosaic for inferior parts." This seems to conflict with his other statement that the poem was dictated to him, he being merely the secretary. Some critics have suspected that the verse of the prophetic books is really prose cut up into length. This may be true of the prosaic parts: Blake's chief model was the King James Bible. But it is important to recognize that there are many passages where rhythm, alliteration, and assonance bear out Blake's claims.

A more serious obstacle to enjoyment is the mythology, invented by Blake to avoid the misleading associations of classical mythology. (Keats, it will be remembered, found some discrepancy between the story of Hyperion and the meaning he wished to convey in his poem.) Blake's names, such as Urizen, Oothoon, Theotormon, Bromion, need a key; and the need is increased by the fact that the significance of the characters varies from poem to poem. Yet the difficulties can easily be exaggerated. Years ago, a recital of the last part of *Jerusalem* in Masefield's private theatre was enthusiastically received by an audience who did not know the difference between Enitharmon and Palamabron.

Although their strictly poetical qualities have usually been undervalued, the greatness of *Milton* and *Jerusalem* depends largely on their prophetic message. *Milton* originated in Blake's difficulties with Hayley and in his wish to correct the "errors" of *Paradise Lost*. On these foundations Blake constructed a metaphysical drama of great profundity, in which the religion, the art, the morality, and the literature of his time were tried and found wanting. The climax of his attack comes in the splendid speech beginning "Obey thou the words of the Inspired Man" (Plate 40), in which he goes on to protest at "the aspersion of Madness/Cast on the Inspired" by the poetasters of the day.

In *Jerusalem* Blake introduces Scofield, the soldier who had accused him of sedition, but he is mainly concerned with the necessity of mutual forgiveness and of self-annihilation, which to him were the essentials of Christ's teaching, and the conditions for the establishment of the Kingdom of Heaven on earth, and specifically in England. In *Milton* Bacon, Locke, and Newton were treated as symbols of barren rationalism, but towards the end of *Jerusalem*, no longer enemies of the imagination, they are welcomed alongside Chaucer, Shakespeare, and Milton as part of the English tradition.

Bronowski argued in *The Man Without a Mask* that Blake turned from political to religious subjects because he was afraid of prosecution, and that he adopted the obscure style of the prophetic books for the same reason. But, despite the repressive age in which he lived, Blake did not become obscure for this reason. He continued to advertise two of his most radical works (*America* and *Europe*); some of his earlier prophecies are much more obscure than *Milton*; and his move away from politics was more likely due to his disappointment with the course of the French Revolution. We should remember, too, that Blake's politics and religion are inseparable: art, poetry, and politics are all part of his religion. It is significant that in *America* he uses the resurrection as a symbol of political emancipation, and in *Jerusalem* he asks: "Are not Religion & Politics the same Thing? Brotherhood is Religion." Jesus in the same poem declares that Man cannot "exist but by Brotherhood."

Blake's message fell on deaf ears. The one coloured copy of *Jerusalem* – artistically his most beautiful book – was unsold at his death; and it was not until the present century that critics and readers began to understand him.

—Kenneth Muir

BOSWELL, James. Scottish. Born in Edinburgh, 29 October 1740. Educated at Edinburgh High School, and the University of Edinburgh; studied law at the University of Glasgow, and at the University of Utrecht, 1764; admitted an advocate, 1765; admitted to the Scottish Bar, 1766. Married Margaret Montgomerie in 1769 (died, 1789); seven children. Met Samuel Johnson in London, 1763; made a tour of the Continent, and visited Voltaire and Rousseau, 1764–66; practised law in Edinburgh from 1769; frequent visitor to London: a member of Dr. Johnson's Literary Club, 1773; escorted Johnson on a tour of the Highlands and Hebrides, 1773; Contributor (as "The Hypochondriack") to *London Magazine*, 1777–83; abandoned his Scottish practice, moved his family to London, entered the Middle Temple, and was admitted to the English Bar, 1788, but never practised: thereafter worked on his biography of Johnson. *Died 19 May 1795.*

PUBLICATIONS

Collections

> *Letters,* edited by C. B. Tinker.   2 vols., 1924.
> *Private Papers from Malahide Castle,* edited by Geoffrey Scott and Frederick A. Pottle.   18 vols., 1928–34.
> *Yale Edition of the Private Papers,* edited by F. W. Hilles and others.   1951–; research edition, 1966–.

Fiction and Prose

A View of the Edinburgh Theatre During the Summer Season 1759.   1760.
Oberservations on Foote's The Minor.   1760.
Critical Strictures on Elvira by David Malloch, with Andrew Erskine and George
    Dempster.   1763; edited by Frederick A. Pottle, 1952.
The Essence of the Douglas Cause.   1767.
Dorando: A Spanish Tale.   1767.
*An Account of Corsica: The Journal of a Tour to That Island, and Memoirs of Pascal
    Paoli.*   1768; in Yale Edition, 1955.
Reflections on the Late Alarming Bankruptcies in Scotland.   1772.
A Letter to the People of Scotland on the Present State of the Nation.   1784.
*A Letter to the People of Scotland on the Attempt to Infringe the Articles of the
    Union.*   1785.
The Journal of a Tour to the Hebrides with Samuel Johnson.   1785; in Yale Edition,
    1961.
The Life of Samuel Johnson.   2 vols., 1791; revised edition, 1793, 1799; edited by R.
    W. Chapman, 1953.
Letters to W. J. Temple, edited by Philip Francis.   1857; edited by T. Seccombe, 1908.
Boswelliana: The Commonplace Book, edited by C. Rogers.   1874.
Boswell's Consultation Book.   1922.
Notebook 1776–77, edited by R. W. Chapman.   1923.

Editor, *British Essays in Favour of the Brave Corsicans.*   1768.

Verse

*An Elegy on the Death of an Amiable Young Lady, with an Epistle from Menalcus to
    Lycidas.*   1761.
An Ode to Tragedy.   1761.
The Cub at Newmarket: A Tale.   1762.
*Ode by Dr. Samuel Johnson to Mrs. Thrale upon Their Supposed Approaching
    Nuptials.*   1784.
No Abolition of Slavery; or, The Universal Empire of Love.   1791.
Boswell's Book of Bad Verse (A Verse Self-Portrait); or, Love Poems and Other Verses,
    edited by Jack Werner.   1974.

Bibliography: *The Literary Career of Boswell* by Frederick A. Pottle, 1929; *The Private
Papers of Boswell from Malahide Castle: A Catalogue* by Frederick A. and M. S. Pottle, 1931.

Reading List: *The Highland Jaunt,* 1954, and *Corsica Boswell,* 1966, both by Moray
McLaren; *Boswell* by P. A. W. Collins, 1956; *Boswell's Political Career* by Frank Brady,
1965; *Boswell* by Alfred R. Brooks, 1972; *Boswell and His World* by David Daiches, 1975.

*   *   *

The appreciation of James Boswell as a figure of independent literary status has been
considerably advanced in this century by the publication of a remarkable collection of his
personal papers, following the discovery of them at Malahide Castle near Dublin and at
Fettercairn House in Kincardineshire. We now know that Boswell kept, from 1758, and
elaborately from 1762, a journal of his personal life, recording his experiences in London in
1762–63, his studies in Holland in 1763–64, his travels in Germany, Switzerland, Italy, and

France in 1764–66, and his later life in Scotland. It was Boswell's usual practice to make brief daily memoranda of events and reflections; these were the raw materials out of which he would make, some few days later, his journals. As a consequence the journals are not merely accidental aggregations of material, but the products of a conscious process of composition. They were generally written with an audience of some kind in mind. The particularly lively London journal was written for Boswell's friend John Johnston and sent to him in weekly parcels. The journals of Boswell's continental travels show at many points Boswell's intention to make out of them a travel-book, and indeed he published, in 1768, his *Account of Corsica*, which both describes his experiences on the island and is a work of propaganda in the cause of Pasquale de Paoli's independent Corsica.

The journals are a colourful and intimate first-hand account of England, Scotland, and continental Europe in the late eighteenth century, covering a remarkable spectrum of life, from the courts of European rulers (Boswell earned the personal friendship of the Margrave of Baden-Durlach, for example) to encounters with street girls. They are also a spiritual autobiography of one of the period's most remarkable personalities, showing Boswell searching for religious truth, attempting with the most partial success to lead a moral life, fighting his melancholia, and finding in his meetings, and friendships, with such great men of his time as Johnson, Voltaire, and Rousseau models of thought and action. If the journals resemble the mid-eighteenth century novel in their explorations of individual experience (Boswell is of kin perhaps to Sterne's half-fictional Yorick), they resemble fiction too in their shaping and heightening of experience. Boswell's accounts of his interviews with Rousseau in Môtiers, and of his affair with "Louisa" in London, for example, are fully-realised actions. The recriminatory scene of parting with Louisa is a marvellous moment of comic drama, presented in animated and polished dialogue. There is in Boswell a pervading sense of the identity of life and literature: "I should live no more than I can record."

The most important experience in Boswell's life was his friendship with Samuel Johnson, and from that friendship his most important literary work arose. Boswell was only twenty-two when he first met Johnson in London in May 1763, and he lived in Johnson's company only intermittently in the twenty-one years before Johnson's death in 1784, but in the *Journal of a Tour to the Hebrides*, published as an account of the journey he had persuaded Johnson to take with him in 1773, and in the monumental *Life* of Johnson itself, he produced a biographical record which is not only scholarly and complete, but also a considerable imaginative achievement. Boswell's writings on Johnson put into practice his belief, shared with Johnson himself, that biography must include all available details: "Every thing relative to so great a man is worth observing." The *Life* and Hebridean *Journal* are together a storehouse of the opinions of Johnson on all subjects, and a portrait of the man down to the fit of his clothes and his method of eating fish. The portrait is drawn both from a variety of documentary materials, and from an ordered shaping and selection of memoranda taken at the time of the events they describe, a method essentially the same as that of the journals, though the *Life* and Hebridean narrative, as published works, are at a further stage of refinement. The Johnson here presented, though a true image of the intellect and personality of the real man, is, like the Boswell of the journals, to some extent a created persona. Shorthand notes of Johnson's conversations are reconstructed, in Boswell's version of a consistent Johnsonian style. Episodes are made dramatic, notably the meeting of Johnson with the politician John Wilkes on the 15th of May 1776, an occasion of which Boswell was himself in real life the playwright. Boswell found in Johnson a subject as interesting as himself, and, as in the journals, turned personality into art.

—Marcus Walsh

BOWLES, William Lisle. English. Born in King's Sutton, Northamptonshire, 24 September 1762. Educated at Winchester College, (scholar), 1775–81; Trinity College, Oxford (Chancellor's Prize for Latin Verse, 1783; Cobden Exhibitioner, 1785–89), B.A. 1786, M.A. 1792. Married Madgaden Wake in 1797 (died, 1844). Ordained deacon, 1788: Curate, Knoyle, now Bishop's Knoyle, Wiltshire, 1788; Rector, Chicklade, 1795–97, Dumbleton, 1797, and Bremhill, Wiltshire, 1804–45; Prebendary, 1804, and Canon Residentiary, 1828, Salisbury. *Died 7 April 1850.*

PUBLICATIONS

Collections

> *Poetical Works,* with Lamb and Hartley Coleridge, edited by William Tirebuck. 1887.
> *A Wiltshire Parson and His Friends: Correspondence,* edited by Garland Greever. 1926.

Verse

> *Fourteen Sonnets, Elegiac and Descriptive.* 1789; revised edition, as *Sonnets Written Chiefly on Picturesque Spots,* 1789; as *Sonnets, with Other Poems,* 1794, 1796.
> *Verses to John Howard.* 1789.
> *The Grave of Howard.* 1790.
> *Verses on the Benevolent Institution of the Philanthropic Society.* 1790.
> *A Poetical Address to Edmund Burke.* 1791.
> *Elegy Written at the Hot-Wells, Bristol.* 1791.
> *Monody, Written at Matlock.* 1791.
> *Elegiac Stanzas, Written During Sickness at Bath.* 1796.
> *Hope: An Allegorical Sketch.* 1796.
> *St. Michael's Mount.* 1798.
> *Coombe Ellen.* 1798.
> *Song of the Battle of the Nile.* 1799.
> *Poems.* 1801.
> *The Sorrows of Switzerland.* 1801.
> *The Picture: Verses Suggested by a Landscape of Rubens.* 1803.
> *The Spirit of Discovery; or, The Conquest of Ocean.* 1804.
> *Bowden Hill.* 1806.
> *Poems, Written Chiefly at Bremhill.* 1809.
> *The Missionary.* 1813; revised edition, 1815; as *The Ancient Missionary of Chile,* 1835.
> *The Grave of the Last Saxon; or, The Legend of the Curfew.* 1822.
> *Ellen Gray; or, The Dead Maiden's Curse.* 1823.
> *Charity.* 1823.
> *Days Departed; or, Banwell Hill: A Lay of the Severn Sea.* 1828.
> *St. John in Patmos.* 1832.
> *The Little Villager's Verse Book.* 1837.

Play

> *The Ark: A Dramatic Oratorio.* 1824(?).

Other

A Few Plain Words for the Bible.   N.d.
Sermons.   1815.
Thoughts on the Increase of Crimes, The Education of the Poor, and the National Schools.   1818.
Vindiciae Wykehamicae; or, A Vindication of Winchester College.   1818.
The Invariable Principles of Poetry in a Letter to Thomas Campbell.   1819.
A Reply to the Reviewer.   1820.
A Vindication of the Editor of Pope's Works.   1821.
Two Letters to Lord Byron.   1821.
A Voice from St. Peter's and St. Paul's.   1823.
A Final Appeal Relative to Pope.   1825.
Lessons in Criticism to William Roscoe.   1826.
Paulus Parochialis (sermons).   1826.
Hermes Britannicus.   1828.
The Parochial History of Bremhill.   1828.
The Life of Thomas Ken.   2 vols., 1830.
A Word on Cathedral-Oratorios and Clergy-Magistrates.   1830.
A Few Words on the Cathedral Clergy.   1831.
A Last and Summary Answer to the Question "Of What Use Have Been, and Are, the English Cathedral Establishments" with a Vindication of Anthems and Cathedral Services.   1833.
Annals and Antiquities of Lacock Abbey.   1835.
Scenes and Shadows of Days Departed (includes verse).   1835.
The Patronage of the English Bishops.   1836.
The Cartoons of Raphael (sermons).   1838.
A Final Defence of the Rights of Patronage in Deans and Chapters.   1838.

Editor, *The Works of Pope.*   10 vols., 1806.

Bibliography: "Some Uncollected Authors XVIII: Bowles" by Cecil Woolf, in *Book Collector* 7, 1958.

Reading List: *Bowles, Byron, and the Pope-Controversy* by J. J. van Rennes, 1927; *Bowles: A Lecture* by A. J. A. Waldock, 1928; *Bowles* by Oskar Rietmann, 1940.

*   *   *

Coleridge acknowledged a debt to the *Fourteen Sonnets* of William Lisle Bowles, speaking of "their mild and manliest melancholy" as giving impetus to his own youthful feelings. Looking back from his mid-Victorian vantage point, Gilfillan, perhaps influenced by Coleridge's praise, hailed Bowles as "the father of modern poetry." Both accolades now seem surprising. Bowles is the epitome of the second rank of writing which prevailed below the "Romantic" surface between 1780 and 1830, and his place, historically, is fixed by this representative quality. It is difficult to discern much individuality in him.

The *Fourteen Sonnets*, first published in 1789, proved very popular and certainly had the merit of restoring dignity to a verse form which had been neglected by the two previous generations. In them Bowles seems the natural successor to the refined, almost debilitated, sensitivity of Gray or Shenstone. In "A Garden-Seat at Home," he speaks of himself as

> ... scarce wishing to emerge
> Into the troubled ocean of that life,
> Where all is turbulence, and toil, and strife.
> Calm roll the seasons o'er my shaded niche;
> I dip the brush or touch the tuneful string....

His work is full of such aspirations for rural retirement, but he lacks the slow, dignified reflection which allowed Cowper to make major statements from within such isolation. Nor was Bowles' life as a busy cleric and magistrate consistent with his adopted poetic persona. There is not enough human passion in his writing to persuade the reader that his claim to have been spiritually wounded by an early unhappy love affair is necessary to an understanding of his work.

He never sinks below a mellifluous and careful competence, but seldom rises to anything fresh or startling. In reading a public poem like *The Battle of the Nile* one could forget that there had been any prosody in the previous hundred years other than that written by imitators of Dryden. Though in the preface to *The Grave of the Last Saxon* he speaks of "that which alone can give dignity to poetry – the cause of moral and religious truth," there is no urgent sense of an impassioned moral crusade in his work. *St. John in Patmos* describes the visionary experience of the disciple from outside rather than probing for an empathy with it.

It is the more surprising that such a poet could have been a vigorous and racy controversialist, yet there is no lack of energy about his war with Byron and the *Quarterly Review* over the merits of Alexander Pope. In 1806 Bowles published an edition of Pope in which he claimed that Pope was the leader only of a second rank of poets since he directed his attention to "artificial" life rather than to nature. This began a war of words in which Bowles maintained his standpoint, against powerful opposition, and with vigour and wit. The literature of this controversy is still of interest.

Bowles is a poet for dipping into. His minute care for detail, his eye for landscape, and his evocations of a mild nostalgia can be pleasing. He sometimes demonstrates a technical competence in handling narrative which makes, for instance, *The Grave of the Last Saxon* still readable, and even a poem like *The Spirit of Discovery* can convey a sense of the dignity with which the second flight of poets in the Regency period gave utterance to their personal accounts of common emotions.

—T. Bareham

BROWN, Tom (Thomas Brown). English. Born in Shifnal, Shropshire, in 1663. Educated at Newport School, Shropshire; Christ Church, Oxford, 1678–85, left without taking a degree. Usher in a school in Kingston-upon-Thames, and subsequently Headmaster of Kingston Grammar School, for three years; settled in London, and supported himself as a hack writer and translator; started the *Lacedaemonian Mercury* c. 1691; notorious for his licentious life and for the animosity of his feuds with, among others, Sir Richard Blackmore and John Dryden. *Died 16 June 1704.*

PUBLICATIONS

Fiction, Sketches, and Dialogues

The Reason of Mr. Bays Changing his Religion, Considered in a Dialogue Between Crites,
    Eugenius, and Mr. Bays.   1688; part 2, 1690; part 3, 1690.
The Reasons of the New Convert's Taking the Oaths to the Present Government.   1691.
Wit for Money; or, Poet Stutter.   1691.
Novus Reformator Vapulans; or, The Welsh Levite Tossed in a Blanket.   1691.
Physic Lies a Bleeding; or, The Apothecary Turned Doctor.   1697.
Amusements Serious and Comical, Calculated for the Meridian of London.   1700; edited
    by A. L. Hayward, 1927.
Laconics; or, New Maxims of State and Conversation, with others.   1701.
Advice to the Kentish Long-Tails, by the Wise Men of Gotham.   1701.
Letters from the Dead to the Living, with others.   3 vols., 1702–03.
The Dying Thoughts and Last Reflections, in a Letter to a Friend.   1704.
A Collection of All the Dialogues.   1704.
A Legacy for the Ladies; or, Characters of the Women of the Age, with *A Comical View of*
    London and Westminster, by Ned Ward.   1705.
Azarias: A Sermon Held Forth in a Quakers Meeting.   1710.
Twenty-Two Select Colloquies by Erasmus, to Which Are Added Seven More
    Dialogues.   1711.

Play

The Stage-Beaux Tossed in a Blanket; or, Hypocrisy Alamode, Exposed in a True Picture
    of Jerry.   1704.

Verse

The Weasels: A Satrical Fable.   1691.
The Moralist; or, A Satire upon the Sects.   1691.
Commendatory Verses on the Author of The Two Arthurs, and The Satire Against Wit,
    with others.   1700; revised edition, 1702.
A Description of Mr. D[ryden]n's Funeral.   1700.
The Mourning Poet.   1703.

Other

A Collection of Miscellany Poems, Letters, etc.   1699; revised edition, 1700.
Works.   2 vols., 1707; revised edition, 3 vols., 1708; 4 vols., 1711–12; 5 vols.,
    1719–20.

Editor, *The Lives of All the Princes of Orange,* by L. Aubery du Maurier.   1693.
Editor, with Charles Gildon, *Familiar Letters,* by Rochester, Otway, and Katherine
    Philips.   2 vols., 1697.
Editor, *Miscellanea Aulica; or, A Collection of State Treatises.*   1702.
Editor, *The Adventures of Lindamira.*   1702; as *The Lover's Secretary,* 1713.
Editor, *The Miscellaneous Works of the Duke of Buckingham.*   2 vols., 1704.

Translator, *Memoirs of the Court of Spain*, by Marie d'Aulnoy. 1692.
Translator, *The Life of Cardinal Richelieu*, by A. J. Du Plessis. 1695.
Translator, *A New and Easy Method to Understand the Roman History*, by Abbé de Fourcroy. 1695.
Translator, *Twelve Dissertations Out of Jean Le Clerc's Genesis.* 1696.
Translator, *Seven New Colloquies*, by Erasmus. 1699.
Translator, *Select Epistles Out of Cicero.* 1702.
Translator, *The Circe*, by G. B. Gelli. 1702.
Translator, *Justin's History of the World, Being an Abridgement of Trogus Pompeius' Phillipic History.* 1702.
Translator, *France and Spain Naturally Enemies*, by Carlos García. 1704.
Translator, *A Looking-Glass for Married People*, by L. de Gaya. 1704.

Reading List: *Brown of Facetious Memory* by Benjamin Boyce, 1939; *Brown e le Origini del Saggio di Costume* by Edrige Schulte, 1969.

*   *   *

While living, Tom Brown was considered a "*Pestilence* of Wit"; once dead, his was a "facetious Memory." One detractor, in the *Discommendatory Verses* (1700), went so far as to insist: "But this I dare affirm, without a Lie,/His *Epigrams* are only *born* to *die*." Curiously enough, this anonymous slanderer was dead wrong, for Brown is best remembered for his supposedly spontaneous epigram (see Martial, I, 32) against Dr. John Fell, Dean of Christ Church while Brown was at Oxford:

> I do not love thee, Dr. Fell,
> The reason why I cannot tell;
> But this I know, and know full well,
> I do not love thee, Dr. Fell.

To be sure, Brown was a prolific, scurrilous, witty and brash minor writer, but he was nonetheless a writer of considerable significance. In an era witnessing the decline of the nobility's patronage, and the corresponding rise of a middle-class reading audience, Tom Brown is a pure specimen of the hackney writer, an educated multifarious scribbler, offering himself and almost any subject to virtually every bidder – for hire. The genteel and the squeamish might label such efforts "prostitution," but they will have, somewhat uncomfortably, to admit Dryden, Defoe, Addison, Swift, Fielding, and Johnson among that company.

If most often unsteady and impecunious throughout his London-based life, Brown was nevertheless imaginative, diligent, and workmanlike. His voluminous productions include Tory and Anglican pamphlets, catches and lampoons, pieces for the magazines (*The Gentleman's Journal* and *The London Mercury*), translations (of Lucian, Lucretius, Cicero, Cervantes, Gelli, Scarron, Le Clerc, Mme. d'Aulnoy, Fontenelle, and Saint-Evremond), historical and biographical works (on Richelieu, on Roman history, on the ancient Druids), a satire upon Louis XIV, and contributions to the highly popular poetical miscellanies of his day (including the *Poems on Affairs of State*). Almost single-handedly, he roused the wits to war against that duncical physician and epical poet, Sir Richard Blackmore, producing the caustic *Commendatory Verses on the Author of the Two Arthurs.*

Most importantly, Tom Brown should be remembered for his share (Part III) of the *Laconics; or, New Maxims of State and Conversation*, where his terse reflections on the nature of politics and life are insightful and occasionally profound; for his hand in the epistolary novel (long before Richardson), *The Adventures of Lindamira*; for his *Letters from the Dead to the Living* – in the tradition of Lucian, Rabelais, Quevedo, Erasmus, Fontenelle (see

Frederick Keener, *English Dialogues of the Dead*, 1973). Above all stands his *Amusements Serious and Comical*, presenting in pert and gusty documentary prose a tour with an hypothetical Indian of the sights and lurid alleyways of old London. Utilizing the traditions of satire, the polemic, the epistle, the "Character," and the jest-book, Brown forges a rough and ready journalism that was destined to help play a role in shaping subsequent prose and the English novel as well. For the rest, he views the world, *cum grano salis*, as being no better than it should be (*Letters from the Dead*):

> We have nothing new here, because we are under the sun. Wise men keep company with one another; fools write and fools read; the booksellers have the advantage ...; some pragmatical fellows set up for politicians; others think they have merit because they have money. Cheats prosper, drunkenness is a little rebuked in the pulpit ...; people marry that don't love one the other, and your old mistress Melisinda goes to church constantly, prays devoutly, sings psalms gravely, hears sermons attentively, receives the sacrament monthly, lies with her footman nightly, and rails against lewdness and hypocrisy from morning till night.

—John R. Clark

BUNYAN, John. English. Born in Elstow, Bedfordshire, baptized 30 November 1628. Educated in the village school in Elstow and, possibly, at Bedford Grammar School. Served in the Parliamentary Army, 1644–46. Married 1) c. 1648 (his wife died, 1656), two sons and two daughters; 2) Elizabeth Bunyan in 1659, one son and one daughter. Practised the family trade of tinker, in Elstow and the surrounding area, from 1646; joined a nonconformist church in Bedford, 1653; moved to Bedford, 1655, and began preaching, 1656; ordained, 1657, and quickly became famous as a travelling preacher; indicted for preaching at Eaton Socon, 1658; imprisoned in Bedford Gaol for preaching without a license, 1660–66, 1666–72; licensed to preach, 1672; pastor of the nonconformist congregation in Bedford, 1678 until his death; also preached throughout Bedfordshire and beyond; Chaplain to the Lord Mayor of London, 1688. *Died 31 August 1688.*

PUBLICATIONS

Collections

> *Complete Works,* edited by George Offor.   3 vols., 1860–62.
> *Miscellaneous Works,* edited by Roger Sharrock.   2 vols. (of 13), 1976–78.

Fiction

The Pilgrim's Progress from This World to That Which Is to Come.   1678; revised
edition, 1679; part 2, 1684; edited by Roger Sharrock, with *Grace Abounding,* 1966.
The Life and Death of Mr. Badman.   1680; edited by G. B. Harrison, 1928.
The Holy War Made by Shaddai upon Diabolus.   1682; edited by Thomas Patrick
Murphy, 1975.
The Heavenly Footman.   1698; edited by Henri A. Talon, in *God's Knotty Log,* 1961.

Verse

Profitable Meditations Fitted to Man's Different Condition.   1661(?).
A Discourse of the Building of the House of God.   1688.

Other

Some Gospel Truths Opened According to the Scriptures.   1656.
A Vindication of Some Gospel Truths Opened.   1657.
A Few Sighs from Hell; or, The Groans of a Damned Soul.   1658.
The Doctrine of the Law and Grace Unfolded.   1659; edited by Richard L. Greaves, in
Miscellaneous Works 2, 1976.
I Will Pray with the Spirit and I Will Pray with the Understanding Also.   1663; edited by
Richard L. Greaves, in *Miscellaneous Works 2,* 1976.
Christian Behaviour; or, The Fruits of True Christianity.   1663.
A Map Showing the Order and Causes of Salvation and Damnation.   1664(?).
One Thing Is Needful; or, Serious Meditations upon the Four Last Things.   1665(?).
The Holy City; or, The New Jerusalem.   1665.
The Resurrection of the Dead.   1665(?).
*Grace Abounding to the Chief of Sinners; or, A Brief and Faithful Relation of the Mercy of
God to His Poor Servant John Bunyan.*   1666; revised edition, 1772(?); edited by
Roger Sharrock, with *Pilgrim's Progress,* 1966.
A Confession of My Faith and a Reason for My Practice.   1672.
A Defence of the Doctrine of Justification by Faith in Jesus Christ.   1672.
Differences in Judgment about Water Baptism.   1673.
The Barren Fig Tree; or, The Doom and Downfall of the Fruitless Professor.   1673.
*Reprobation Asserted; or, The Doctrine of Eternal Election and Reprobation
Promiscuously Handled.*   1674(?).
Light for Them That Sit in Darkness.   1675.
Instruction for the Ignorant.   1675.
The Strait Gate; or, Great Difficulty in Going to Heaven.   1676.
Come and Welcome, to Jesus Christ.   1678.
A Treatise of the Fear of God.   1679.
The Greatness of the Soul and Unspeakableness of the Loss Thereof.   1683.
A Case of Conscience Resolved.   1683.
A Holy Life, The Beauty of Christianity.   1684.
Seasonable Counsel; or, Advice to Sufferers.   1684.
A Discourse upon the Pharisee and the Publican.   1685.
Questions about the Nature and Perpetuity of the Seventh-Day Sabbath.   1685.
A Book for Boys and Girls; or, Country Rhymes for Children.   1686; as *Divine Emblems,*
1724; edited by E. S. Buchanan, 1928.
Good News for the Vilest of Men (includes verse).   1688; as *The Jerusalem Sinner Saved,*
1697.

The Advocateship of Jesus Christ Clearly Explained and Largely Improved.   1688; as
    The Work of Jesus Christ as an Advocate, 1688.
The Water of Life.   1688.
Solomon's Temple Spiritualized; or, Gospel Light Fetched Out of the Temple at
    Jerusalem.   1688.
The Acceptable Sacrifice.   1689.
Works, edited by Ebenezer Chandler and John Wilson.   1692.
A Relation of the Imprisonment of Bunyan.   1765.

Bibliography: *A Bibliography of the Works of Bunyan* by F. M. Harrison, 1932.

Reading List: *Bunyan: His Life, Times, and Work* by John Brown, 1885, revised by F. M.
Harrison, 1928; *Bunyan: A Study in Personality* by F. M. Harrison, 1928; *Bunyan,
Mechanick, Preacher* by William York Tindall, 1934; *Bunyan: L'Homme et l'Oeuvre* by
Henri A. Talon, 1948; *Bunyan* by Roger Sharrock, 1954; *Bunyan: A Study in Narrative
Technique* by Charles Baird, 1977.

*   *   *

It was once widely believed that John Bunyan was an ignorant rustic whose crude
allegories and meditations were inspired by evangelical tracts, the Authorized Version, and
the Holy Spirit. This misconception may have resulted in part from the calculated pose of
Bunyan himself, who, like Robert Burns, was inclined to dramatize himself as the egalitarian
spokesman of the common man. In reality, in spite of his humble origins, lack of formal
education, and unexalted occupations of tinker, soldier, and "mechanic" Baptist preacher,
Bunyan was an accomplished student of medieval pulpit literature, patristic writings, emblem
books, Spenser's *Faerie Queene*, Milton's poetry, and the whole range of Reformation
theological works by Luther, Zwingli, Calvin, and many others. Whether by self-training or
instinct, moreover, he was an astute logician and masterful prose stylist, as is evidenced by
his first two polemical tracts, *Some Gospel Truths Opened* and *A Vindication of Some Gospel
Truths Opened*, both composed in refutation of Bunyan's Quaker neighbors in Bedford. Both
tracts set forth the Reformation tenets he was to flesh out in allegory and characterizations in
his later writings for ordinary readers – the priesthood of all believers, the autonomy of
Scripture, predestination, total depravity, and salvation by faith alone. These were
commonplace Protestant doctrines, hardly original with Bunyan, who was not an innovative
theologian or even a very original religious thinker, but they were simple ideas he was able to
render in powerfully affective narratives, and in a time when such ideas, fired in the crucible
of widespread religious persecutions, struck Bunyan's readers with great emotional force.
Essentially a preacher, he knew how to reach out from his pulpit and touch the nerves and
hearts of a vast congregation of simple, uneducated listeners.

His disarming directness and candor are apparent in his extraordinary and immensely
popular autobiography *Grace Abounding to the Chief of Sinners* written during the twelve
years he spent in prison for unlicensed preaching. Like St. Augustine's *Confessions*, it charts
the progress of the author through despair and alienation to joyous reconciliation, and its one
abiding message is deceptively simple: "Take hope, my readers, because I, chief among
sinners, have experienced God's light." In the first part he describes his arduous, faltering trek
to conversion; in the second his equally agonizing decision to enter the ministry. The first
part is populated by characters as vivid and lively as any in Fielding or Dickens – his
uncomprehending, tawdry parents; village toughs and roisterers; rough companions among
Cromwell's pikemen; and his saintly wife, who read to him from soul-awakening evangelical
tracts like *The Plain Man's Pathway to Happiness*. Compelling for its graphic literary
qualities, *Grace Abounding*, is equally fascinating as a study in the psychopathology of guilt.
Behind the visible characters and events looms the vacillating spirit, lurching from despair to

ecstasy, from sinful bondage to the sudden release of vindication, from feelings of depravity to glowing transcendence. After an inspiring Sunday sermon, Bunyan joys in the conviction that he is surely among the Elect; at the next moment the sight of a pretty ankle or the tantalizing scent from a tavern door sends his spirit plummeting to Satan's carnal regions. Can he truly be predestined for Election if his weak flesh responds so easily to worldly temptations? Frail men long for a sign to end their doubts, but Scripture tells them there will be no sign, only the agony of pursuit that tests a wavering faith. Thus *Grace Abounding* is a poignant account of all the cruel afflictions of the Puritan experience.

Bunyan's next classic, *The Pilgrim's Progress*, is in the same direct, unpretentious style, but employs allegorical characterizations and narrative. If Spenser had fashioned his *Faerie Queene* for the edification of Queen Elizabeth's courtly gentlemen, Bunyan composed his *Pilgrim's Progress* for the spiritual inspiration of God's humblest Christians, and the amazing popularity of the work attests to Bunyan's keen awareness of the emotional needs of his readers. Not content with Milton's "fit audience, though few," Bunyan strives to reach the masses with a plain allegory devoid of theological complexities. His myth, based on the age-old device of the journey, describes his hero Christian's struggle to achieve salvation (the Celestial City) amid a world filled with such easily recognized threats to the soul as Vanity Fair and Giant Despair. Obviously Bunyan had read Book I of the *Faerie Queene* and stripped Spenser's allegory of its courtly equipage and philosophical complexities. The plain truth plainly told is Bunyan's guiding principle, embellished artistically by his sure sense of drama and talent for concrete, evocative description. *Pilgrim's Progress* is replete with what in modern parlance is called subliminal communication; through massing of associative images, Bunyan, to an extent even greater than that of Spenser, can make his readers *feel* the ugliness of vice and the beauties of virtue. Bunyan's deceptively simple style, consisting of a sonorous, rhythmic syntax clothed in images from folklore and the Bible, endured with the masses until the decline of religious sentiment in the twentieth century, when his *Pilgrim's Progress* was forgotten by the masses and first appreciated by the literati.

In his *Life and Death of Mr. Badman* Bunyan combines medieval exemplum, allegory, and dialogue, the last much favored for theological disputation. The work was intended as a companion-piece to *Pilgrim's Progress*. Whereas the story of Christian and his wife is a success tale depicting the various stages on the ascent to salvation, the narrative of Mr. Badman shows all the sordid steps in the descent to damnation. Bunyan's preface "To the Courteous Reader" makes clear that his story is intended to illustrate the awesome universality of human depravity, the terrifying finality of original sin. The dialogue that follows is between Mr. Wiseman, who relates Mr. Badman's sinful life, and Mr. Attentive, who provides questions enabling Wiseman to expand into details and interpretations at various points of the narrative. *The Life and Death of Mr. Badman* is patently less effective as literature than *Pilgrim's Progress* because, first, the dialogue form in the service of narration appears forced and artificial, always lapsing into sermonizing; and second, the fact that Mr. Badman is totally depraved from birth, totally beyond any possibility of redemption, gives the story a static, repetitious effect. Mr. Badman has none of Faustus's capacity for virtue; indeed, Bunyan's obligation to prove the ineluctible power of original sin prevents him from portraying a flexible, multi-dimensional anti-hero responding to experience. Hence Mr. Badman is not shaped by experience but doomed by hereditary curse; his actions are narrowly restricted to a somewhat tedious repetition of the Seven Deadly Sins. It would appear that in this work, at least, Bunyan's role as Baptist preacher wholly committed to expounding the doctrine of original sin prevented him from exercising his natural genius as a writer.

Bunyan's voluminous works include not only autobiography and allegorical fiction but children's verse, sermons, meditations, and theological tracts. A self-educated evangelist with an astonishing range of interests, he saw his religious faith as applicable to every human activity, and his one abiding goal as a writer was to communicate his clear vision of God.

—James E. Ruoff

BURKE, Edmund. Irish.   Born in Dublin, 12 January 1729. Educated at Abraham Shackleton's school in Ballitore, County Kildare, 1741–43; Trinity College, Dublin, 1744–48, B.A. 1748; entered the Middle Temple, London, 1750; left the law for literary work, 1755. Married Jane Nugent in 1756; two sons. Settled in London: Editor, *Annual Register*, 1759–66, and contributor to it until 1788; Private Secretary to William Gerard Hamilton, 1759–64: accompanied him to Ireland, 1763–64, and received a pension on Hamilton's retirement, 1764; Whig Member of Parliament for Wendover, 1765–74, Bristol, 1774–80, and for Malton, Yorkshire, 1781–94: Private Secretary to the Marquis of Rockingham, 1765; attacked administrations of Chatham and Grafton, especially their handling of the American question, 1767; vigorously opposed policies of the Tory government, 1769; succeeded in convincing Parliament to publicize its proceedings, 1771; attacked the North ministry's handling of affairs, 1774–75, and strongly advocated peace with the American colonies, 1775–76; advocated economic reform in the public services and limitations on the slave trade, 1780; by his attacks on the conduct of the American war, forced North to resign, 1781–82; in new Whig government served as Paymaster-General of the Forces, under Rockingham, 1782, and Portland, 1783, but was never given a Cabinet post; advocated self-government for Ireland, 1782; drafted the government's East India bill, 1783; involved in the impeachment of Warren Hastings of the East India Company, 1786–95; passed over by Fox ministry in forming a new Cabinet, but supported Fox in upholding the right of the Prince of Wales to regency, 1788; supported Wilberforce in advocating abolition of the slave trade, 1788–89; spoke against French democracy, 1790; quarrelled with Fox and the Whigs, 1791, and advised support for Pitt and the Tories, 1792; retired from Parliament, 1794. Lord Rector, University of Glasgow, 1784, 1785; encouraged foundation of Maynooth College, 1795; established school for sons of French refugees at Penn, Buckinghamshire, 1796. LL.D.: Dublin University, 1891. Granted government pension, 1794. *Died 9 July 1797.*

PUBLICATIONS

Collections

> *Works*, edited by French Laurence and Walker King.   8 vols., 1792–1827.
> *Select Works*, edited by E. J. Payne.   3 vols., 1874–78.
> *Correspondence*, edited by T. W. Copeland.   10 vols., 1958–77.
> *Selected Writings and Speeches*, edited by P. J. Stanlis.   1963.

Prose

> *A Vindication of Natural Society in a Letter.*   1756.
> *An Account of the European Settlements in America*, by William Burke, revised by Edmund Burke.   2 vols., 1757.
> *A Philosophical Enquiry into the Origin of Our Ideas of the Sublime and Beautiful.*   1757.
> *An Essay Towards an Abridgement of the English History.*   1757.
> *A Short Account of a Late Short Administration.*   1766.
> *Observations on a Late State of the Nation.*   1769.
> *Thoughts on the Cause of the Present Discontents.*   1770.
> *Reflections on the Revolution in France.*   1790; edited by Conor Cruise O'Brien, 1969.
> *Two Letters on the French Revolution.*   1791.
> *An Appeal from the New to the Old Whigs.*   1791.
> *Report from the Committee of the House of Commons on the Trial of Warren Hastings.*   1794.

Thoughts on the Prospect of a Regicide Peace. 1796.
Three Memorials on French Affairs Written 1791, 1792, and 1793. 1797.
Thoughts and Details on Scarcity. 1800.
The Catholic Claims. 1807.
Speeches in the House of Commons and in Westminster Hall. 4 vols., 1816.
Epistolary Correspondence of Burke and French Laurence. 1827.
Letters, Speeches, and Tracts on Irish Affairs, edited by Matthew Arnold. 1881.
Burke's Politics: Selected Writings and Speeches on Reform, Revolution, and War, edited by R. J. S. Hoffman and P. Levack. 1949.
A Note-Book, edited by W. V. F. Somerset. 1957.
The Philosophy of Burke: A Selection, edited by Louis I. Bredvold and R. G. Ross. 1960.

Editor, *The Annual Register.* 8 vols., 1759–66.
Editor, *J. P. Brissot to His Constituents,* translated by William Burke. 1794.

Bibliography: *A Bibliography of Burke 1748–1968* by P. J. Stanlis, 1972.

Reading List: *Burke and His Literary Friends* by Donald C. Bryant, 1939; *Burke* by Harold Laski, 1947; *Our Eminent Friend Burke: Six Essays* by T. W. Copeland, 1949; *The Moral Basis of Burke's Political Thought* by Charles Parkin, 1956; *Burke* by T. E. Utley, 1957; *Burke and the Natural Law* by P. J. Stanlis, 1958; *Burke: The Practical Imagination* by G. W. Chapman, 1967; *Burke* edited by Isaac Kramnick, 1974; *The Rage of Burke: Portrait of an Ambivalent Conservative* by Isaac Kramnick, 1977.

*   *   *

Edmund Burke's achievement in literature and thought may be considered under three rubrics: criticism, politics, and rhetorical style. His *Philosophical Enquiry into the Origin of Our Ideas of the Sublime and Beautiful,* an apparently anomalous work in the canon of one so deeply committed to Parliamentary affairs, is the product of his early intellectual endeavours before he sought to make his political fortune. Burke never again wrote so substantially about critical problems, although he did continue to show a lively interest in literature, as demonstrated, for example, by his reviews in the *Annual Register,* his connections with Samuel Johnson and other members of the Literary Club, and his patronage of George Crabbe.

In the *Enquiry,* Burke distinguishes between the two esthetic states, the sublime and the beautiful, on the basis of their psychological origins, particularly in sensation. Burke grounds the sublime upon the complex feeling of "delight," which, unlike ordinary or simple pleasure, results from the removal of pain or danger; and, unlike pleasure, is characterized by feelings of awe, surprise, and a tranquillity tinged with a sense of horror. Whatever excites a kind of "delightful horror," those ideas of pain and danger which permit, as it were, an esthetic distance, not the actual circumstances themselves, is an "efficient" cause of the sublime. Ideas, then, that generate the sublime effect are all terrifying, for terror is its ruling principle: vacuity, obscurity, darkness, solitude, silence, infinity, vastness, difficulty, negligent ruggedness, magnificence, massive solidity, and power.

For his theory of the beautiful, Burke grounds this esthetic state upon the pleasure of love, some quality in beautiful objects, he believes, causing love. The specific qualities of beauty, relative to those of sublimity, are smallness, smoothness, gradual variation, delicacy, and clear bright colors. Burke denies, however, that proportion, perfection, and fitness are ingredients of the beautiful. In the history of criticism, Burke's theory of the beautiful is less significant than that of the sublime – and much less original.

Burke's originality in this treatise consists in his elaborating a distinction between sublimity and beauty, a contrast that was significant to the development of the complex of ideas and qualities constituting Romanticism. But his esthetics, like affective and romantic theory, raises more questions than it settles, for it does not explore meaningfully normative problems of value.

In political thought and practice, Burke is significant for two great contributions to our time – for establishing the concept, structure, and function of modern political parties and, in this connection, developing the possibility of a continuing loyal Opposition; and for systematically illuminating the principles of modern conservatism. The first, the idea of open parties as legitimate vehicles of constitutional government, is proposed in *Thoughts on the Cause of the Present Discontents*. Here Burke argues for the need of a political party to counteract the King's influence in Parliament, as he raises serious objections to attempts to fortify and extend the royal prerogative, theorizes over a court cabal or secret "double cabinet," and criticizes the "King's friends" who constituted it. From 1770 to 1782, through the period of the American troubles, Burke was the party whip of the Rockingham Whigs in the House of Commons, and kept its members from abandoning their role as Opposition to the King.

Burke's conservative social and political philosphy remained the same from his first work, *A Vindication of Natural Society*, to his last group of publications on French affairs, including the celebrated *Reflections on the Revolution in France* and the essay in which he summarizes and defends his career in politics, *A Letter to a Noble Lord*. In the *Vindication*, Burke ironically demonstrates the absurdity of Bolingbroke's principles of natural religion by showing that if they were applied to civilized government as they had been to religion they would justify the destruction of civilized society and a return to "natural society" with as much validity as they had justified the adoption of natural religion.

Burke detested the deists for the unrelenting rigor in which they pursued nature as an ideal norm of value without considering the practical effect upon the structure of society. Believing that it is equally natural for man to live in accordance with tradition and law, to form social groups and develop a civilized and hierarchal order, Burke attacked those abstract perfectionists who wished to reform society by returning romantically to what he thought was an unreal state of nature. On the contrary, he asserted in his polemical *Appeal from the New to the Old Whigs*, "Art is man's nature." Therefore he passionately attacked not only deists and rationalists in his *Reflections* and his other writings on French Revolutionary ideals, but all levellers who wished to destroy long-established traditions and institutions made venerable by continued use in the course of time, while they asserted their hopes for equality and natural rights. Moreover, Burke was consistently sceptical of metaphysical reason when it pretended to be exact and conclusive in social affairs. He preferred to abide by the norms of prudence and moderation, guided by natural law, established precedents and patterns of behavior. Even in his great speeches on American Taxation (1774) and Conciliation with the Colonies (1775), Burke took a stand against the Parliamentary majority on prudential grounds.

As he responded to the controversial issues and events at the end of the eighteenth century, Burke hammered out a philosophy of political conservatism, the basic principles being the doctrine of aristocratic trusteeship – that is, civil authority must be restricted to men "of permanent property"; the sacredness of prescriptive rights – the hereditary principle of succession is necessary for social stability and order, and tradition and precedent are more significant than innovation; the utility of an established church – an alliance of civil government and the church is necessary for maintaining social order; and the positive value of a hereditary monarchy – monarchy protects liberty from the tyranny of the majority or democracy. With some modification, these principles have proved to be adaptable to nineteenth- and twentieth-century conservatism, thereby demonstrating their durability.

Finally, Burke is notable for the Baroque pomp and splendor of his oratory. In Parliamentary affairs, Burke was an experienced and skilful speaker who, if not always persuasive, was always fascinating for the sublimity of his discourse. Impassioned, rich in imagery and literary allusion, learned, and thoughtful, many of his speeches have become oratorical classics, those on America and on India and the impeachment of Warren Hastings being particularly outstanding. Similarly, the style of his written essays meant for the eye rather than the ear, like the *Reflections*, is characterized by a splendid manly vigor, a rhetorical audacity appropriate to the challenges presented by his compelling argument.

—Martin Kallich

BURNS, Robert.   Scottish.   Born at Alloway, near Ayr, 25 January 1759. Educated at a school in Alloway Mill, and at home. Married Jean Armour in 1788; nine children, and three other illegitimate children. Farmer at Mossgiel, near Mauchline, 1784; commissioned as excise officer (i.e., tax inspector), 1788, and settled at Ellisland, near Dumfries, combining official duties with farming; when farm failed moved with his family to the town of Dumfries. Honorary Member, Royal Company of Archers, 1792. *Died 21 July 1796.*

PUBLICATIONS

Collections

Works.   4 vols., 1800–04.
Letters, edited by J. Delancey Ferguson.   2 vols., 1931; *Selected Letters, 1953.*
Poems and Songs, edited by James Kinsley,   3 vols., 1968

Verse

Poems, Chiefly in the Scottish Dialect.   1786; revised edition, 1787; 2 vols., 1793; 1794; 1801.
The Scots Musical Museum, with others, edited by James Johnson.   6 vols., 1787–1803.
A Select Collection of Original Scottish Airs, with others, edited by G. Thomson.   4 vols., 1793–99.
Merry Muses of Caledonia.   1800(?).

Other

Notes on Scottish Song, edited by James C. Dick.   1908.
Journal of a Tour in the Highlands Made in 1787, edited by J. C. Ewing.   1927; edited by Raymond Lamont Brown, 2 vols., 1972–73.
Journal of the Border Tour, edited by J. Delancey Ferguson, in *Burns, His Associates and Contemporaries,* edited by Robert T. Fitzhugh.   1943.

Bibliography: *A Bibliography of Burns* by J. W. Egerer, 1964; *Burns* by G. R. Roy, 1966.

Reading List: *Burns* by David Daiches, 1950, revised edition, 1966; *The Burns Encyclopedia* by Maurice Lindsay, 1959, revised edition, 1970; *Burns Today and Tomorrow* by Hugh MacDiarmid, 1959; *Burns: His Life and Tradition in Words and Sounds* by Ian A. Nimmo, 1965; *Burns in His Time* by Alan H. Dent, 1966; *Burns, The Man and the Poet: A Round, Unvarnished Account* by Robert T. Fitzhugh, 1970; *Burns: The Critical Heritage* edited by Donald A. Low, 1974; *Burns: A Life* by Hugh Douglas, 1976.

* * *

Like many artists whose achievement is regarded as the crowning glory of a particular school or movement, Robert Burns was not an innovator. He took existing stanza forms and the Scots tongue as shaped for the purposes of colloquial poetry by his predecessors, notably Allan Ramsay and Robert Fergusson, and applied them with sharpened awareness to his own situations.

The fact that, unlike Ramsay and Fergusson, Burns was born a farmer, ensured that his upbringing would bring him into contact with rural Scotland where, before the triumph of the Industrial Revolution, agriculture was still the mainstay of the Scottish economy. The rural way of life, like the speech of the countryside, had changed comparatively little since mediaeval times. Yet changes which were stirring during Burns's lifetime had, by the end of the 18th century, transformed the very basis of Scottish life, and begun to alter the physical appearance of the environment, particularly of the countryside around Glasgow. Burns caught and fixed in poetry the essential quality of that old agrarian way of life just before it finally gave place to the new industrial emphasis.

He did so by making use of the images and particular situations he found around him in the rural life of Ayrshire, projecting the universal from the merely local. Thus "Holy Willie's Prayer," using for its prototype a petty, arid and dishonest old elder of the Church of Scotland, William Fisher, becomes what is probably the most effective denunciation of the sin of hypocrisy to be found in European literature. The picture of oozing unctuousness, of deadly self-revelation, unfolds as Holy Willie, on his knees, before his God, rationalises his catalogue of sins:

> O L ——d! yestreen, Thou kens, wi' Meg –
> Thy pardon I sincerely beg,
> O! may't ne'er be a livin' plague
>   To my dishonour,
> An' I'll ne'er lift a lawless leg
>   Again upon her ...

> Maybe Thou lets this fleshly thorn
> Buffet Thy servant e'en and morn,
> Lest he owre proud and high shou'd turn,
>   That he's sae gifted:
> If sae, Thy han' maun e'en be borne,
>   Until Thou lift it.

The main target of the young Burns's satirical anger was the Church of Scotland, which in his day still endeavoured to exercise a depressing and restrictive influence over even the most private aspects of everyday life. It was especially vigorous in its unmasking of sexual offences. As Burns was highly sexed, and already the father of an illegitimate daughter by one of his father's servants before he attained his majority, the poet and the Church came into vigorous conflict. Hypocrisy, usually rife in narrow sectarian forms of religious worship, was also flayed in the "Address to the Unco Guid," in which Burns's glancing ironic contrasts have a lasting deadliness:

> Ye high, exalted, virtuous dames
>   Tied up in godly laces,
> Before ye gie poor Frailty names,
>   Suppose a change o' cases;
> A dear-lov'd lad, convenience snug,
>   A treach'rous inclination;
> But, let me whisper i' your lug,
>   Ye're aiblins* nae temptation.   * perhaps

Moving into English for his serious conclusion, Burns pronounces proverb-like wisdom in language which has proved memorable even to the less literate:

> Then gently scan your brother man,
>   Still gentler sister woman:
> Tho' they may gang a kennin wrang,
>   To step aside is human,
> One point must still be greatly dark,
>   The moving *Why* they do it;
> An just as lamely can ye mark,
>   How far perhaps they rue it.

Whether he is celebrating family religious observance in the old style, as in "The Cottar's Saturday Night," or, as in "The Twa Dogs," using the old Scots animal tradition in poetry (best exemplified by the "Fables" of Henryson) to set the burden of the poor against the wasteful ease of the rich, Burns is throughout the spokesman for ordinary men and women. This radical quality was immediately recognised when *Poems, Chiefly in the Scottish Dialect*, was first published in Kilmarnock in 1786.

The most important poem left out of that collection, probably for political reasons, was his unbuttoned celebration of common humanity, "The Jolly Beggars," a "cantata," the songs of which were written to specified Scots airs. In the overheated atmosphere of a Mauchline tavern, a crowd of drop-outs meet together to celebrate the kind of total freedom which rejects any social organisation, though paradoxically such "freedom" can only flourish as a protected minority in a socially adjusted society. They sing:

> Life is all a variorum
>   We regard not how it goes;
> Let them cant about decorum,
>   Who have character to lose.
>
> A fig for those by law protected!
>   Liberty's a glorious feast!
> Courts for cowards were erected,
>   Churches built to please the priest.

This concept of liberty echoes through Burns's poems, songs, and letters, just as it concerned him practically, and sometimes indiscretely, throughout his life. It is one of many ways in which he anticipated early 19th-century European Romanticism, when poets and composers, notably Schiller and Beethoven, hymned Freedom as an end in itself.

Up to 1786, Burns's achievement was mainly that of a social satirist, using the "Standard Habbie" stanzas. This, a variation of *rime couée*, was so-called because it seems to have been first employed before the beginning of the 18th-century Scots revival by Robert Sempill in a poem "The Life and Death of Habbie Simson, the Piper of Kilbarchan" (about 1640), although it had also been used colloquially by Sir David Lyndsay a hundred years earlier in *The Thrie Estatis*, and stems from an early form employed by the French troubadours and in some mediaeval English miracle plays. It is the stanza of "Holy Willie" and many other Burns poems. He was no less successful with more elaborate stanza forms derived from the Scots Makars (or Scottish Chaucerians as they are sometimes rather unfairly described). During the remaining years of his short life he added to his already considerable corpus of songs, and composed his solitary narrative poem, "Tam o' Shanter," with its modulations of pace, subtlety of movement, and sustained dramatic implication, an effortless masterpiece.

Burns's song output began with a love song addressed to a girl with whom he shared the task of harvesting. Almost his last love song was addressed to the woman who was helping his wife nurse him in his final illness. In between came songs celebrating every aspect of the relationship between man and woman, from the first bashful stirrings of "I'm owre young to marry yet" through the rich satisfaction of "Corn Riggs" to the calm content near the end of married life in "John Anderson, My Jo." His best songs differ from those of all other Scottish and English poets of the period in that they infer physical realities and are infused with the same directness and sincerity that in his young manhood fired the flames of his social satire.

Burns's main strengths lay in his firm commitment to the Scots tongue at a time when the higher social classes were abandoning it in favour of English, and to his radical alignment with the common-sense interests of the ordinary man at a time when the justification of privilege was being questioned increasingly throughout Europe. (It is not without significance that Burns's Kilmarnock *Poems* and Mozart's *The Marriage of Figaro* appeared in the same year.) His weakness lay in the fact that he had to try to come to terms with a linguistic dichotomy first brought about by the haste of the Reformers of 1560, who introduced the vernacular Bible in English rather than in Scots, and furthered by the political effects of the Unions of 1603 and 1707. If a late 18th-century man wanted to succeed in the power-world of England, he had to eradicate all traces of Scoticisms from his speech, as Boswell, Hume, Beattie, and others so ridiculously strove to do. The traditional culture of the old Scotland thus fell under siege from within.

In an attempt to achieve the best of both worlds, besides writing in Scots Burns also copied the "bosom-melting throes" of Shenstone, Gray, and others. But their Augustan habit sat poorly on him, and encouraged him to adopt poetic postures, both in verse and in his letters, otherwise usually couched in a clear and balanced prose. The man whose warm sincerity has endeared him for more than two centuries even to those of his countrymen who never otherwise read poetry, could on occasion be guilty of achieving fatuities like "though something like moisture conglobes in my eye" when describing a tear.

Whenever he attempted the "high style," the 18th-century equivalent of the aureate manner of Dunbar and the other Scots Makars, Burns used English, and was at his least successful. The tone of the whole of the 18th-century Scots revival was colloquial, a reflection of fast-moving daily Scots speech. Burns excelled all other Scots poets in harnessing this aspect of this age to worthy poetic purpose. He achieved his wider fame through the warmth and emotional universality of his songs.

He is Scotland's "National Bard," celebrated by suppers every 25th January, on his birthday, wherever Scots are gathered together, for yet another reason. He shares with Sir Walter Scott the distinction of rescuing the Scottish sense of nationhood from the oblivion which under gathering English pressure threatened it. Scott, through the best six or so of the Waverley Novels, made the Scots more aware of the significant moments of historic confrontation in their past (and, incidentally, confirmed the interest of Romantic Europe, aroused by Macpherson's "Ossian," in Scotland). Burns, through his poems and songs, similarly established and consolidated lasting awareness of nothing less than the sense of being Scots, of Scottishness. This may perhaps seem an unimportant non-literary factor to readers outside Scotland, yet it explains the unique position of popular reverence and celebration that Burns, alone among world poets, enjoys from his own countrymen.

—Maurice Lindsay

BUTLER, Samuel. English. Born in Stevensham, Worcestershire, baptized 14 February 1613. Educated at King's School, Worcester; possibly at Oxford or Cambridge university; may have been a member of Gray's Inn, London. Married. As a young man, in the service of the Countess of Kent; thereafter held posts as clerk/secretary to Leonard Jeffrey, justice of the peace of Earls-Croome, Worcestershire, or his son Thomas, and as steward to Richard Vaughan, Earl of Carbery; by 1670 in the service of the Duke of Buckingham. Granted an annual pension of £100 from King Charles II for *Hudibras*. After initial success, ignored by the court, and thereafter lived and died in poverty. *Died 25 September 1680.*

PUBLICATIONS

Collections

Complete Works, edited by A. R. Waller and René Lamar. 3 vols., 1905–28.

Verse

Mola Asinaria. 1659.
The Lord Roos His Answer to the Marquess of Dorchester's Letter. 1660.
Hudibras, part 1. 1662; part 2, 1663; revised edition, 1678; part 3, 1678; complete edition, 1684; edited by John Wilders, 1967.
To the Memory of the Most Renowned Du-Vall; A Pindaric Ode. 1671.

Other

Two Letters. 1672.
Mercurius Menippeus: The Loyal Satirist; or, Hudibras in Prose. 1682.
The Plagiary Exposed. 1691.
Posthumous Works in Prose and Verse. 3 vols., 1715–17; revised edition, 1732.
Genuine Remains, edited by R. Thyer. 2 vols., 1759; revised edition (vol. 1 only), 1822.
Characters, edited by Charles W. Daves. 1970.

Bibliography: In Complete Works 3, 1928.

Reading List: Hudibras in the Burlesque Tradition by E. A. Richards, 1937; Augustan Satire by Ian Jack, 1952; "The Last of the Epics: The Rejection of the Heroic in Paradise Lost and Hudibras" by Michael Wilding, in Restoration Literature: Critical Approaches edited by Harold Love, 1972; The Restoration Mode from Milton to Dryden by Earl Miner, 1974.

*   *   *

Hudibras seems to have been composed in three stages: ca. 1658–60, 1660–63, and 1663–74. Its popularity is beyond question. Charles II memorized long portions and, in Zachary Grey's lavish two-volume edition in 1774, Butler received a seriously executed edition before his greater contemporaries, Milton and Dryden. So popular was *The First Part* that it ran through nine editions in its first year, four of them pirated, and a spurious second part also appeared in 1663. The bang-about tetrameter couplets with odd rhymes and other jocularities have been known thereafter as hudibrastics, and their inventor was sometimes called Hudibras, which would have angered him the more. Contrary to most modern tastes, the third part was better liked than the second. The only other important poem published by Butler was the mock heroic pindaric to Du-Vall, a lady-killer highwayman hanged at Tyburn on 21 January 1670. He left behind numerous manuscripts in verse and prose, including nearly 190 prose characters, random notes of caustic character, satires, parodies, and a couple of positive pieces.

Hudibras swallows up the importance of the other writings. It is the worst great poem in the language, a degraded mockery of *Don Quixote*. Each of the three parts has three cantos. Much is promised and nothing happens in I.i., except maddening argument between the Presbyterian anti-hero and Ralpho, his Independent Sancho Panza. In I. ii Hudibras routs bearbaiters by falling on their animal with all his gross bulk. In I. iii he is defeated in combat by a woman, Trulla (that is, trull, whore) who, unlike him, fights fairly. Put in the stocks with Ralpho, Hudibras is eventually let out by the Lady, a widow, whose property he seeks. Laughing over his plight, she rejects his suit unless he meets her condition:

> That never shall be done (Quoth she)
> To one that wants a *Tayl*, by me:
> For *Tayls* by Nature sure were meant
> As well as *Beards*, for ornament:
> And though the *Vulgar* count them homely,
> In *man* or *beast* they are so comely,
> So *Gentee*, *Allamode*, and handsom
> I'l never marry *man* that wants one.

She releases him from the stocks on promise that he will whip himself.

The two men next (II. ii) argue over who should whip himself until they are interrupted by a Skimmington, a folk procession mocking a henpecked husband and his shrewish wife. Hudibras's sally is beaten off. Having decided not to whip himself, Hudibras betakes himself and Ralpho to an Astrologer, Sidrophel, whom Hudibras attacks and knocks down senseless. (II. iii). Meanwhile, Ralpho has gone off to acquaint the Lady with Hudibras's deceit. When he arrives (III. i) she tortures him in the dark with "devils" to make him confess his misdeeds. In III. ii the plot merges with history, as the Interregnum ends. In the last canto (iii), Hudibras consults a lawyer about his suit.

Two other elements extend the stupid plot. Throughout there is argument, or harangue, on matters religious, political, and logical. And there are three "heroical epistles" nailed on: one from Hudibras to Sidrophel at the end of II. iii; one from Hudibras to the Lady at the end of III. iii; and one as her reply. A "heroical epistle" was properly a woman's address to her faithless lover. Butler spoils that of course, and has the Lady declare that women really hold power in the world. In the poem's last lines, she rejects Hudibras and male supremacy: just let them dare: "Let men usurp Th'unjust Dominion,/As if they were *the Better Women*."

All this is excuse and means for learned nonsense and unremitting degradation of truly awesome power. The poem does have some design in treating three days of action and three decades:

Parts − Cantos	Day	Decade
I. i-II. i	first	1640's
II. ii-III. i	second	1650's
(III. ii	transition	transition)
III. iii	third	1660's

Days correspond to decades but are of little importance otherwise; neither days nor decades correspond to Parts. The most important fact is that the satire moves into the 1660's, including the strange metamorphosis of Sidrophel from an Interregnum astrologer into a Royal Society virtuoso.

Given the topics of debate, the decades covered, and Butler's Tory Anglicanism, it is strange but crucial that he does not mention God, the Church, or the King. His refusal to allow decency into the poem is clearer still from the perverted misogyny represented by female victories (Trulla, the Skimmington shrew, the Lady). Nothing of redeeming value is allowed. The poem delivers us into noise, degradation, and nonsense. The humor grows ever more cruel and less funny; the joke is on the characters, the reader, and the poetry, which is steadily spoilt. Butler so skillfully evokes our worst passions and strongest fears of insanity and irrelevance as to make *Hudibras* one of the most powerfully moving and objectionable poems in English.

—Earl Miner

BYROM, John. English. Born in Broughton, near Manchester, 29 February 1692. Educated at Merchant Taylors' School, London; Trinity College, Cambridge, 1708–15 (Scholar, 1709), B.A. 1712, M.A. 1715; studied medicine briefly at Montpellier, 1716. Married a cousin in 1721. Fellow of Trinity College, 1714; after his travels on the Continent returned to England, 1718; copyrighted and taught his new system of shorthand in Manchester, London, and Cambridge; succeeded to the family estate, 1740. Fellow of the Royal Society, 1724. *Died 26 September 1763.*

PUBLICATIONS

Collections

Poems, edited by A. W. Ward.   3 vols., 1894–95.

Verse

An Epistle to a Gentleman of the Temple.   1749.
Enthusiasm: A Poetical Essay.   1751.
Miscellaneous Poems.   2 vols., 1773.
Seasonably Alarming and Humiliating Truths in a Metrical Version of Some Passages from the Works of William Law, edited by F. Okely.   1774.

Other

A Review of the Proceedings Against Dr. Bentley.   1719.
Letter to Mr. Comberbach in Defence of Rhyme.   1755.
The Universal English Short-Hand.   1767.
Private Journal and Literary Remains, edited by Richard Parkington.   4 vols., 1854–57.
Selections from His Journals and Papers, edited by Henri Talon.   1950.

Reading List: *Byrom and the Wesleys* by Elijah Hoole, 1864; *William Law and Eighteenth-Century Quakerism* by Stephen H. Hobhouse, 1927; *The Story of Christians Awake,* 1948, and *Previously Unpublished Bryomiana,* 1954, both by W. H. Thomson; *The Edges of Augustanism: The Aesthetics of Spirituality in Thomas Ken, Byrom, and William Law* by John Hoyles, 1972.

*   *   *

Those who sing the Christmas hymn "Christians, awake, salute the happy morn" may not realise its authorship. It appears among John Byrom's poems, the greater part of which are, however, devoted to the versification of the views of the non-juring mystic, William Law.

With Law Byrom rejects the Augustan regard for external evidence and ratiocinative method in matters religious. For him reason confirms the facts of experience, but does no more, while literal adherence to Scripture as objective record and submission to the Church as outward authority are equally valueless. Byrom looks rather to the direct enlightenment of the Holy Spirit. Not surprisingly therefore and in a very non-eighteenth-century fashion Bryom extols "enthusiasm." Indeed, he has a poem with that title, in the course of which he renders Law's idea that "in will, imagination and desire consists the life or fiery driving of every intelligent creature. And so every intelligent creature is its own *self-mover*." This view of imagination takes us forward from Hobbes, Dryden, and even Addison, reflecting Young and foreshadowing Blake and Coleridge.

Byrom, following Law, interpreted grace as love from God, exciting love for God, and this Abelardian cast resulted in their rejection of Calvinistic Evangelical soteriologies of penal satisfaction, associated chiefly with Whitefield. Their soteriology, however, tended to by-pass justification in making a short cut towards sanctification.

There is little to be said about Byrom's verse as such. It is a plain, workmanlike versifying of his master's ideas.

—Arthur Pollard

CHATTERTON, Thomas.   English.   Born in Bristol, 20 November 1752. Educated at Colston's Bluecoat School, Bristol, 1760–67; apprenticed to John Lambert, an attorney, Bristol, 1767–70. Produced Rowleie (Rowley) manuscript, 1768–69, and was encouraged by Horace Walpole, until he became convinced the Rowleyan works were modern. Went to London in 1770 and produced a great variety of work. *Died* (perhaps a suicide, but more probably the victim of an overdose of drugs) *25 August 1770.*

PUBLICATIONS

Collections

Complete Works, edited by Donald S. Taylor and Benjamin B. Hoover.   2 vols., 1971.

Verse

The Execution of Sir Charles Badwin. 1772.
Poems, Supposed to Have Been Written at Bristol by Thomas Rowley and Others in the Fifteenth Century, edited by Thomas Tyrwhitt. 1777.

Other

Miscellanies in Prose and Verse, edited by John Broughton.   1778; *Supplement*, 1784.

Reading List: *A Life of Chatterton* by E. H. W. Meyerstein, 1930; *Chatterton* by Basil Cottle, 1963; *The Marvelous Boy: The Life and Myth of Chatterton* by Linda Kelly, 1971; *Chatterton's Art: Experiments in Imagined History* by Donald S. Taylor,   1978.

*   *   *

Thomas Chatterton was an instinctive imitator of and innovator with forms and modes, and so his two-hundred-odd extant works are at first bewildering in their variety. His literary creditors range from Chaucer, Shakespeare, and the historian William Camden, through major 17th- and 18th-century writers – Dryden, Pope, Swift, Gay, Collins, Churchill – to contemporary periodicals with their evanescent spectrum of sub-literary genres. A clearer picture emerges if we view his works in four chronological groups – the hymns and verse fables of his tenth and eleventh years, the supposedly medieval Rowleyan works of his seventeenth year, the verse satires and journalistic prose of his last (eighteenth) year, and a miscellaneous group of four modes worked through both of his last two years – descriptive lyrics, pastorals, satiric epistles, and Ossianic prose poems. Nothing is extant from his twelfth through sixteenth years, though there is evidence that he then wrote a good deal of insipid, conventional amatory verse, some of it to order.

The early hymns are formally and prosodically precocious but conventional. The early fables, however, show – in diction, character portrayal, and prosody – skillful adaptation of the quietly ironic manner of John Gay. The best of these – "Apostate Will" and "The Churchwarden and the Apparition" – are succinct moral anatomies of Bristolians who mask consuming greed with complacent religious respectability. The prose "Letter from Fullford, The Grave-digger," probably Chatterton's, pursues the same theme with Swiftian ironies in the mock-pastoral mode.

In the Rowleyan year (summer 1768 through spring 1769), stimulated by heraldry, old books, architectural remains, and Bristol place names, Chatterton invented a rich history of his native city from pre-Roman origins through the late fifteenth century. He presented this history in an invented fifteenth-century English which is never *pure* invention. All but a few of its words can be traced to glossaries, dictionaries, and old books, all of which he took as equally reliable evidence for an English whose essence was grammatic and spelling lawlessness. His basic Rowleyan vocabulary of about 1800 words was enlarged by applying this posited lawlessness to current English. The sequence of the Rowleyan works can be fairly accurately fixed by calculating the percentages of Rowleyan words, for the language constantly grew as Chatterton used it. Efforts to translate the Rowley poems into modern English – those of Walter Skeat, for example – seem invariably to strip them of their expressive power.

The Rowleyan works consist of "documents" and drawings which "prove" the existence of Chatterton's historical Bristol and the literary works proper. Of the scores of documents, the elaborate "Discorse on Brystowe" gives the clearest sense of how Chatterton's imagination worked. His model for Rowley as historian is William Camden, especially Edmund Gibson's 1695 translated and emended *Camden's Britannia*. The Rowleyan literary works grow from a search for heroes and heroic modes that could express what Chatterton felt about his invented history, his poet-priest-connoisseur-historian Rowley, and that poet's generous, witty, warm-hearted patron, the merchant prince and builder of Redcliff Church William Canynge. Chatterton's own father died before the poet was born, and both Bertrand Bronson and Phyllis Greenacre have convincingly suggested that searches for patrons, beneficent paternal figures, catalyze much of the Rowleyan effort and much also of Chatterton's later satire, though here the filial stance emerges through acts of rebellion against authority figures in church and state. Pope is his major *poetic* father: Rowley is regularly shown as bringing a Popean correctness and polish to a coarse fifteenth-century poetry (this too invented in detail). Rowley regularly borrows and reworks imagery, ideas, and stances from Pope's translations and satires, and Rowley, Canynge, and their cozy circle of wits are seen as a fifteenth-century Scriblerus Club whose Pope is Rowley.

The strong Rowley poems begin with "Bristowe Tragedie," an English epic influenced by Percy's *Reliques* but gaining its major power from visual, almost cinematographic contrasts. The heroic odes "Songe of Sayncte Baldwyn" and "Songe toe Ella" are perfect in their kind – constructionally and prosodically brilliant. The major work is the "discoorseynge tragedie" *AElla*, an operatic Anglo-Saxon reworking of *Othello*. Though AElla's concluding suicide is unmotivated, the action is urgent and compelling, its characters are vividly evoked, and the striking and flexible rhetoric and prosody are nicely contrasted to fine intermittent pastoral songs which quietly reinforce the theme of thwarted love. Another heroic ode – "On Richard I" – effectively drew Horace Walpole's interest and, almost, his patronage. In "Englysh Metamorphosis" Chatterton builds an effective Ovidian narrative, with brilliant empathic strokes, from the Trojan Brutus tradition. "The Gouler's Requiem" is a flawless sympathetic-comic return to Chatterton's early interest in consuming greed; this and the intimately comic "Acconte of W. Canynges Feast" are attributed to Canynge. The best of Rowley's poems conclude with three eclogues which rework Collins' *Persian Eclogues* in medieval English tones and "An Excelente Balade of Charitie," the Good Samaritan parable in expressive medieval dress.

Two Popean satiric epistles effectively introduce *AElla*. Thence, in Chatterton's last year, various satiric modes develop, with help both poetical and in his religious and political radicalism from Charles Churchill. "Intrest" [sic], "Conversation," the freethinking "Epistle to Catcott," Chatterton's teasing "Will," a sexual mock-epic "The Exhibition," and his burletta "The Revenge" are the most artistically interesting and expressive of the longer satires. "To Miss Lydia Cotton" and "A New Song" bring freethinking vigor to tired amatory conventions. With the exception of "Kew Gardens," in which a central metaphor of an enforced state religion almost metaphysically organizes lengthy, slashing political and religious satire, most of the Churchillean political satires, the Junius-aping political letters, and the journalistic fiction of his last year demonstrate more a drive for Grub Street survival than for literary expression.

But Chatterton's final year was not entirely given over to Grub Street. After the Rowleyan pastorals, he writes both effective mock pastoral ("Hobbinol and Thyrsis") and the brilliantly colored African eclogues, which begin in the mode of Collins but move toward supposed ritualistic and mythic roots of the pastoral impulse. Chatterton's interestingly allusive and elaborate Ossianic writings are an attempt to imagine for pre-Norman Britain a pre-Rowleyan heroic mode. In Rowley, in these two modes, and in his better descriptive poetry (influenced most strongly by Gray and Collins) Chatterton partially justifies the Romantic legend which made him the proto-martyr of the new poetic faith. What the Romantics and the Victorians failed to see was that, to the end, the roots of his best poetry cling to eighteenth-century soil: Chatterton embodies in the writing of his last two years the course of English poetry from Pope through Keats. It is probable, however, that he will continue to be read primarily for the intensity, color, prosodic strength, and verbal richness by which his Rowleyan works bring his imagined medieval Bristol to life.

—Donald S. Taylor

CHURCHILL, Charles. English. Born in Westminster, London, February 1732. Educated at Westminster School, 1741–48; St. John's College, Cambridge, 1748. Married Martha Scott in 1749 (separated, c. 1760); one daughter, two sons. Ordained deacon, 1754: Curate of South Cadbury and Sparkford, Somerset, 1754–56, and of Rainham, Essex (to his father), 1756–58; Curate (and lectureship), St. John's, Westminster, 1758–63. Tutor at Mrs. Dennis's School for Girls, London, 1758. Bankrupt, c. 1760. Resigned Orders in the Church, 1763. Associated with John Wilkes and the *North Briton*, 1762–63; with Wilkes, member of the "Hell-Fire Club." *Died 4 November 1764.*

PUBLICATIONS

Collections

> *Poetical Works*, edited by Douglas Grant.   1956.
> *Poems*, edited by James Laver.   1970.

Verse

> *The Rosciad.*   1761; revised edition, 1763.
> *The Apology.*   1761.
> *Night: An Epistle to Robert Lloyd.*   1761.
> *The Ghost.*   3 vols., 1761–63.
> *The Conference.*   1763.
> *The Author.*   1763.
> *An Epistle to William Hogarth.*   1763.
> *The Prophecy of Famine: A Scots Pastoral.*   1763.
> *Poems.*   2 vols., 1763–65.
> *The Duellist.*   1764.
> *The Candidate.*   1764.
> *Gotham.*   3 vols., 1764.
> *Independence.*   1764.
> *The Times.*   1764.
> *The Farewell.*   1764.
> *The Journey: A Fragment.*   1765.

Other

> *The North Briton*, with John Wilkes and others.   3 vols., 1763.
> *Sermons.*   1765.
> *Correspondence of Wilkes and Churchill*, edited by E. H. Weatherley.   1954.

Bibliography: in *Seven 18th-Century Bibliographies* by Iolo A. Williams, 1924.

Reading List: *The North Briton* by G. Nobbe, 1939; *Churchill, Poet, Rake, and Rebel* by Wallace Cable Brown, 1953; *Portraits in Satire* by Kenneth Hopkins, 1958; *Forms of Discovery* by Yvor Winters, 1967.

*   *   *

Charles Churchill, in Byron's phrase, "blazed the comet of a season." His poetic career in fact lasted for about three years, and his admirers hailed him as "the British Juvenal." Subsequently his verse has been largely neglected, though not wholly with desert. It is true that the subjects of his satire are to a considerable degree ephemeral, and that he failed to give them that universality which would have made them enduring. His first poem, *The Rosciad*, gained him much acclaim, and is still of interest to those concerned with eighteenth-century theatrical history. *The Ghost*, in octosyllabic couplets, dealing with the episode of the "Cock Lane Ghost," is remembered for its unsympathetic portrait of Samuel Johnson as "pomposo, insolent and loud." Most of Churchill's other satires were written in the hurly-burly of party politics – clearly hastily – and are unequal in quality. But they possess remarkable energy and, at times, power.

The tradition of classical Augustan satire in Dryden, Swift, Pope, Johnson, and Goldsmith is a Tory one. The writer is able to criticise society as a moralist, from the point of view of a set of traditional values which are assumed to be universal and permanent. With Churchill, associated as he was with the Radicalism of Wilkes, the stance is necessarily somewhat different, and his work ought perhaps to be judged by rather different criteria. He abandoned the polished epigrammatic couplet, as it had been perfected by Pope, for a style marked by some of the original vigour of Dryden. Like Dryden, he tends to make the paragraph rather than the couplet the unit of his thought; but wanting Dryden's supreme technical mastery, he arrives too often at an effect of breathlessness. His language is strong and masculine, but he lacks alike the harmony and the memorability of Dryden. Cowper, who admired Churchill's work, learnt from him a certain conversational and colloquial ease (less rigid than the Popean model), though modulating it from the Juvenalian to the Horatian manner.

We have already mentioned Byron in connection with Churchill. When Byron visited the earlier poet's grave at Boulogne, he saw in him in some sense a forerunner. There are confessional passages in parts of Churchill's work, for example in *The Candidate*, which do partly make him the harbinger of Romanticism. The final line of his last poem *The Journey* – "I on my journey all alone proceed" – has this kind of resonance.

—John Heath-Stubbs

COLLINS, William.   English.   Born in Chichester, Sussex, 25 December 1721. Educated at Winchester College, 1733–40; Queen's College, Oxford, 1740–41, and Magdalen College, Oxford, 1741–43, B.A. 1743. Lived in London, attempting to support himself by his writing; befriended by Samuel Johnson; in ill-health after c. 1754, chronic fits of depression leading, finally, to insanity. *Died 12 June 1759.*

PUBLICATIONS

Collections

Poems, edited by C. Stone and R. L. Poole.   1914.
Poems, with Gray and Goldsmith, edited by R. H. Lonsdale.   1969.

Verse

Persian Eclogues.   1742; as *Oriental Eclogues,* 1757.
Verses Humbly Addressed to Sir Thomas Hanmer on His Edition of Shakespeare's Works.   1743; as *An Epistle,* 1744.
Odes on Several Descriptive and Allegoric Subjects.   1746.
Ode Occasioned by the Death of Mr. Thomson.   1749.
The Passions: An Ode.   1750.
Poetical Works, edited by John Langhorne.   1765.
Drafts and Fragments of Verse, edited by J. S. Cunningham.   1956.

Bibliography: in *Seven 18th-Century Bibliographies* by Iolo A. Williams, 1924.

Reading List: "The Romanticism of Collins" by Alan D. McKillop, in *Studies in Philology 20,* 1923; *Collins* by H. W. Garrod, 1928; *Poor Collins: His Life, His Art, and His Influence* by Edward G. Ainsworth, 1937; *Collins* by Oswald Doughty, 1964; *Collins* by Oliver F. Sigworth, 1965; "The Poetry of Collins Reconsidered" by A. S. P. Woodhouse, in *From Sensibility to Romanticism,* 1965; *The Poetry of Vision: Five Eighteenth Century Poets* by P. M. Spacks, 1967; *The Life of a Poet: A Biographical Sketch of Collins* by P. L. Carver, 1967; *Precious Bane: Collins and the Miltonic Legacy* by Paul S. Sherwin, 1977.

*   *   *

William Collins and Thomas Gray are often linked, not only because the corpus of each is small and can be usefully published in a joint volume, but because both display a tendency for nervous depression (a melancholia popularly associated with the "romantic" artist), controlled by a strong classical tradition in verse. This finds its ideal poetic realization in the Pindaric Ode and the short lyric where there is freedom within formal structure, while the aesthetic tension common to both poets is expressed through dramatic personification that distances emotion, making the subjective experience an objective reality.

Collins' lyrical facility marks him as an important contributor to the English tradition of verse. There is a simplicity of diction and rhythm in his "Young Damon of the Vale Is Dead" which prefigures the *Lyrical Ballads,* for instance. In contrast, his poetry can plumb the depths of the dark and irrational mind. The "Ode to Fear," as an example, breaks down into intense "psychomachia" where emotion becomes oppressively and obsessively present:

> Ah *Fear!* Ah frantic *Fear!*
> I see, I see Thee near.
> I know they hurried Step, thy haggard Eye!
> Like Thee I start, like Thee disorder'd fly,
> For lo what *Monsters* in thy Train appear!

The literary influences are Shakespeare, Spenser, and, of course, Milton whose "Gothic classicism" was akin to that of Collins.

The pastoral is Collins' natural forte, lending its classical mantle to natural imagery or Oriental and exotic subject-matter as in the *Persian Eclogues.* He moves towards the emotive and the sublime in description, while remaining within the pale of classical convention. The *Odes* also display an emotional range and dramatic realization beneath allegorical pictorialism (reminiscent of the painting of Thornhill or La Guerre). The odes to Pity, Fear, and Simplicity, for example, illustrate the poet's vacillating moods, always invoking a quiet, Horatian solitude, while aware of the "Gobblins" haunting his imagination and the "Fear" which tells him that true art can only be born out of divine fury, those "shad'wy Tribes of *Mind*" found in the "Ode on the Poetical Character."

Such sensitivity finds its most tranquil expression in the "Ode to Evening" with its impressionistic evocation of darkening day "where the Beetle winds/His small but sullen Horn." This midsummer night's dream (and there are clear echoes of Shakespeare) is marred only by a clumsy retreat into personification at the close. This must be set against the terrible Teutonic vision of Fiends in the "Ode to Fear" who "O'er Nature's Wounds, and Wrecks preside." Nature, for his tortured imagination, had a keen and double edge.

New ground is broken in Collins' "Ode on the Popular Superstitions of the Highlands," leaving conventional, celebratory verse like the "Ode to Liberty" to embrace a northern culture poles apart from classical norms. Here he follows the "Old RUNIC bards" to accept "Fancy" as his guide over landscapes haunted by supernatural shadows. In this poem, Collins' desire to pursue the "grandeur of wildness, and the novelty of extravagance" (Dr. Johnson) finds its fulfilment, creating a precedent for the Ossianic fantasies and Gothic terror of the later decades of the century.

Collins takes his place as a so-called pre-romantic poet alongside Gray, the Wartons, and Thomson, bridging the early neo-classic world and that of romantic revolution, very much as, in his own mind, he struggled to reconcile the rational, formal experience with the disorder and derangement of his inner life.

—B. C. Oliver-Morden

COMBE, William. English.   Born in London, 25 March 1742. Educated at Eton College, 1752–56; Inner Temple, London, 1760–63. Married 1) Maria Foster in 1777; 2) Charlotte Hadfield in 1795. Journalist, editor, ghost-writer, political pamphleteer, in London, from 1775: Editor and writer for John Walter, book and newspaper publisher, 1786–92; Editor, *The Pic Nic*, later *The Cabinet*, newspaper, 1803; Editor, *The Times*, 1803–08. Jailed for debt, King's Bench Prison, London, 1785–86, 1799–1823, with limited freedom from 1800. *Died 19 June 1823.*

PUBLICATIONS

Verse

   Clifton: A Poem in Imitation of Spenser.   1775.
   The Diaboliad, Dedicated to the Worst Man in His Majesty's Dominions.   2 vols.,
      1777–78; vol. 1 revised, 1777; *Additions,* 1777.
   The First of April; or, The Triumphs of Folly.   1777.
   An Heroic Epistle to the Noble Author of The Duchess of Devonshire's Cow.   1777.
   The Justification.   1777.
   A Poetical Epistle to Sir Joshua Reynolds.   1777.
   The Auction: A Town Eclogue.   1778.
   An Heroic Epistle to Sir James Wright.   1779.
   The World As It Goes.   1779.
   The Fast-Day: A Lambeth Eclogue.   1780.
   The Traitor: A Poetical Rhapsody.   1781.
   The Royal Dream; or, The P[rince] in a Panic: An Eclogue.   1785.

The Tour of Doctor Syntax, in Search of the Picturesque, illustrated by Thomas Rowlandson. 1812; *Second Tour, in Search of Consolation*, 1820; *Third Tour, in Search of a Wife*, 1821; *Three Tours*, 3 vols., 1826; edited by J. C. Hotten, 1868.
Six Poems Illustrative of the Engravings by the Princess Elizabeth. 1813.
The English Dance of Death, illustrated by Thomas Rowlandson. 2 vols., 1815–16.
The Dance of Life, illustrated by Thomas Rowlandson. 1817.
The History of Johnny Quae Genus, The Little Foundling of the Late Doctor Syntax, illustrated by Thomas Rowlandson. 1822.
Forget Me Not: A Christmas and New Year's Present for 1823. 1823.

Play

The Flattering Milliner; or, A Modern Half Hour (produced 1775).

Fiction

The Philosopher in Bristol. 1775.
Letters Between Two Lovers and Their Friends. 1781.
Letters of an Italian Nun and an English Gentleman. 1781.
Original Love-Letters Between a Lady of Quality and a Person of Inferior Station. 1784.
The Devil upon Two Sticks in England. 6 vols., 1790–91.
Letters Between Amelia in London and Her Mother in the Country. 1824.

Other

Letters to His Friends on Various Occasions, by Laurence Sterne. 1775 (six letters by Combe).
A Dialogue in the Shades. 1777.
A Letter to the Duchess of Devonshire. 1777; *Second Letter*, 1777; *Interesting Letter*, 1778.
The R[oya]l Register. 9 vols., 1778–84.
Letters Supposed to Have Been Written by Yorick and Eliza. 2 vols., 1779.
Letters of the Late Lord Lyttelton. 2 vols., 1780–82.
Original Letters of Laurence Sterne. 1788.
An History of the Late Important Period. 1789.
A Letter from a Country Gentleman to a Member of Parliament. 1789.
The Royal Interview: A Fragment. 1789.
Observations on the Present State of the Royal Academy. 1790.
Considerations on the Approaching Dissolution of Parliament. 1790.
A Word in Season to the Traders and Manufacturers of Great Britain. 1792.
An History of the River Thames. 2 vols., 1794.
Two Words of Counsel and One of Comfort, to the Prince of Wales. 1795.
Letter to a Retired Officer. 1796.
Plain Thoughts of a Plain Man. 1797.
Brief Observations on a Letter to Pitt by W. Boyd. 1801.
The Letters of Valerius. 1804.
The Thames; or, Graphic Illustrations. 2 vols., 1811; revised edition, as *Views on the Thames*, 1822.
Microcosm of London, vol. 3. 1811.
The History of the Abbey Church of St. Peter's Westminster. 2 vols., 1812.
Antiquities of York. 1813.

A History of the University of Oxford.   2 vols., 1814.
A History of the University of Cambridge.   2 vols., 1815.
The History of the Colleges.   1816.
Swiss Scenery.   1820.
A History of Madeira.   1821.
Letters to Marianne.   1823.

Editor and Contributor, *The Pic Nic.*   2 vols., 1803.

Translator, *History of the Campaigns of Count Alexander Suworow Rymniski,* by Friedrich Anthing.   2 vols., 1799.
Translator, *Memoir of the Operations of the Army of the Danube,* by Count Jean-Baptiste Jourdan.   1799.
Translator, *Report to the First Consul Bonaparte on the Antiquities of Egypt,* by Louis-Medeleine Ripault.   1800.
Translator, *Travels in Upper and Lower Egypt,* by C. N. S. Sonnini de Manoncourt.   1800.

Ghost-Writer or editor of the following: *A Description of Patagonia* by Thomas Falkner, 1774; *The Oeconomy of Health* by the School of Salerno, 1776; *A Practical Treatise on the Diseases of the Teeth* by John Hunter, 1778; *An Historical and Chronological Deduction of the Origin of Commerce* by Adam Anderson, 4 vols., 1787–89; *Voyages Made in the Years 1788 and 1789 from China to the North West Coast of America* by John Meares, 1790; *Alf von Deulman; or, The History of the Emperor Philip and His Daughters* by C. B. E. Naubert, translated by A. E. Booth, 2 vols., 1794; *A Letter to Uvedale Price,* 1794, and *Sketches and Hints on Landscape Gardening,* n.d., both by Humphry Repton; *A Narrative of the British Embassy to China 1792–94,* 1795, and *A Journal of the Forces Which Sailed in 1800,* 1802, both by Aeneas Anderson; *Voyage to the South Atlantic and round Cape Horn into the Pacific Ocean* by James Colnett, 1798; *Official Correspondence Containing the Whole of the State Papers from 1797 to 1799,* of the Congress of Rastadt, 1800; *The History of Mauritius* by Charles Grant, Viscount de Vaux, 1801; *The Life, Adventures, and Opinions of Col. George Hanger, Written by Himself,* 2 vols., 1801; *Voyages from Montreal Through the Continent of North America* by Alexander Mackenzie, 1802; *Fashionable Follies,* vol. 3, by Thomas Vaughan, 1810; *The Life of Arthur Murphy* by Jesse Foot, 1811; *Pompeii* by T. L. Donaldson, 1827.

Reading List: "Combe and the Original Letters of Sterne," in *Publications of the Modern Language Association,* 1967, and *Doctor Syntax: A Silhouette of Combe* (includes bibliography), 1969, both by Harlan W. Hamilton.

*   *   *

By his lifelong insistence upon anonymity William Combe avoided contemporary recognition and almost succeeded in excluding himself from literary history. He was, to be sure, a hack-writer, but hack-writers are part of literary history, and Combe was a very good one. In several respects his work has lasting literary importance.

He achieved sensational success in 1777 with a verse satire, *The Diaboliad,* a highly personal and scathing attack upon scandalous figures in London Society. Going into many editions and prompting a host of imitations, it attracted much attention and was remembered for many years. By April 1778 the *Monthly Review* was calling the author a "distinguished master of the poetical tomahawk and scalping knife." Though uneven in execution and concerned with long-forgotten personalities, Combe's satires are often imaginative and witty, his couplets neatly turned and sharply edged. He also wrote prose satires of which the longest and best are *The R[oya]l Register*, filled with scandals concerning 300 thinly veiled personalities, and *The Devil upon Two Sticks in England*, a bitter comment on London life at the turn of the century and, being more generalized, still a readable work.

Combe's friendship with Laurence Sterne gave rise to his equivocal "imitations" of Sterne's letters. These have muddied the waters of Sterne scholarship because they are not wholly devoid of authentic material; a few of them may be substantially Sterne's. This mixture of the fabricated and the authentic, now exasperating, was common at that time. Combe himself had published the highly successful but fabricated *Letters of the Late Lord Lyttelton*.

From 1788 to 1806 Combe was employed as propagandist for the Pitt Ministry and produced pamphlets on the controversies of those tortured years. Students of the period will find him an able polemicist writing in yet another of his many manners. As virtual editor of *The Times* from 1803 to 1808 he assisted John Walter II in establishing the independence of that newspaper.

Throughout his career Combe was busily producing journeyman work to order: editing, ghost-writing, translating, or simply filling blank space. It was for the last of these talents that he was employed by Rudolph Ackermann who wished him to provide letterpress to accompany those prints which were Ackermann's stock in trade. It was thus that he came to write the octosyllabic couplets describing the travels of Doctor Syntax. These achieved book form in 1812 as the *Tour of Doctor Syntax in Search of the Picturesque*, followed by second and third tours. These three *Tours*, reprinted again and again for nearly a century, were family favorites in Britain and America. They are, perhaps unjustly, the only work of Combe's still known. Doubtless the famous Rowlandson caricatures were a major reason for this popularity, but the *Tours* continued to sell even after the quality of the prints deteriorated, and there were editions with no illustrations at all. From his first appearance the good Doctor Syntax found a warm place in the hearts of thousands. He was a nostalgic, old-fashioned figure, an amalgam of Parson Adams, Parson Primrose, and Parson Yorick. The verses are often genuinely comic and are by no means to be held in contempt by the hypercritical.

—Harlan W. Hamilton

COTTON, Charles. English. Born at Beresford Hall, Staffordshire, 28 April 1630. Educated privately; travelled on the Continent as a boy. Married 1) Isabella Hutchinson in 1656 (died, 1669), three sons, five daughters; 2) Mary Russell, Dowager Countess of Ardglass in 1675. Landowner: Revenue Commissioner for Derbyshire and Staffordshire, 1660; Magistrate, 1665; commissioned Captain in Lord Chesterfield's regiment, 1667. *Died in February 1687.*

PUBLICATIONS

Collections

Poems, edited by John Buxton.   1958.
Selected Poems, edited by Geoffrey Grigson.   1975.

Verse

A Panegyric to the King's Most Excellent Majesty. 1660.
*Scarronides; or, Virgil Travestie: A Mock Poem on the First and Fourth Books of Virgil's
    Aeneis.* 2 vols., 1664–65; revised edition, 1667.
*Burlesque upon Burlesque; or, The Scoffer Scoft, Being Some of Lucian's Dialogues
    Newly Put into English Fustian.* 1675.
The Wonders of the Peak. 1681.
Poems on Several Occasions. 1689.

Plays

Horace, from the play by Corneille. 1671.
The Fair One of Tunis, from a French play. 1674.

Other

The Nicker Nickt; or, The Cheats of Being Discovered. 1669.
The Complete Gamester. 1674; as *How to Play at Billiards, Trucks, Bowls, and Chess,*
    1687; revised edition, 1709.
The Planter's Manual. 1675.
The Compleat Angler, part 2. 1676; edited by R. B. Marston, with Walton's *Compleat
    Angler,* 1888.

Translator, *The Moral Philosophy of the Stoics,* by G. du Vair. 1664.
Translator, *The History of the Life of the Duke of Espernon.* 1670.
Translator, *The Commentaries of Blaize de Montluc.* 1674.
Translator, *Essays of Montaigne.* 3 vols., 1685–86; edited by W. C. Hazlitt, 1877.
Translator, *Memoirs of de Pontis.* 1694.

Reading List: *The Life and Poetry of Cotton* by Charles J. Sembower, 1911; *Cotton and His
River* by Gerald G. P. Heywood, 1928; *The Cavalier Mode from Jonson to Cotton* by Earl
Miner, 1971.

*   *   *

Few facts have survived about the life of Charles Cotton the younger, poet, translator,
ardent royalist, and bon vivant, capacities hidden from readers who identify him solely as
author of a second part of *The Compleat Angler.* He was born at Beresford in Staffordshire,
which he never left without becoming homesick. He was tutored there; tradition, rather than
certain knowledge, holds that he went to Cambridge. From some quarter, including
continental travel in 1655, he learned French and Italian as well as Greek and Latin. He was
born to a good estate, but he was generous to others as well as himself and often writes of his
creditors.

Cotton's first known published work appeared with Dryden's in the collection of elegies,
Lachrymae Musarum (1649), mourning the Lord Hastings. His most popular poems during
his lifetime were burlesques: of Virgil in *Scarronides* and of Lucian in *Burlesque upon
Burlesque.*

The Wonders of the Peake was also popular. It is a redoing of Hobbes' *De Mirabilibus
Pecci,* reversing the order of sites visited in the Peak district of Derbyshire. The poems
contributed to the nascent interest in the sublime. This poem, the burlesques, and *The*

Planter's Manual were published in *The Genuine Works* (1715, often reprinted), but Cotton's finest poetry appeared in *Poems on Several Occasions.*

Among his descriptive poems, the quatrain poetry of "Winter" ("Morning," "Noon," and "Evening") ring the freshest note of nature poetry heard in the seventeenth century, as the Romantics understood. Coleridge discovered "every excellence of thought, images, and passions" in natural language. Another group of excellent poems includes those addressed to Izaak Walton, including "Contentation" and "The Retirement" as well as others with Walton's name in their main title. A poem "To the Countess of Chesterfield" must be included among his best occasional poems, as "Day Break" and "To Chloris. Stanzes Irreguliers" represent his best love poems, and "On Christmas-day" his best religious. His most extraordinary poem is the "Epitaph on M. H.," a prostitute of beauty and charm long remembered "With such a superstitious Lust/That I could fumble with her dust." With that we must poise lines from "The Retirement": "Good God! how sweet are all things here!/ How beautiful the Fields appear!" along with praise of his "beloved Nymph! fair Dove,/ Princess of Rivers" and even the rocky hills of the area.

The same sensibility is reflected in Cotton's addition to *The Compleat Angler* and *The Planter's Manual.* His clear, lively prose will also be found in his translations, whose addresses to the reader sparkle with humor. The greatest of his translations, *Essays of Montaigne* appeared in three volumes (1685–86). Other works have been attributed to Cotton, of which the most important is *The Compleat Gamester.* His translations also include one play, the *Horace* of Pierre Corneille and dozens of poems in *Poems on Several Occasions,* which closes with his one narrative, "The Battail of Yvry" (963 11.).

—Earl Miner

COWPER, William. English. Born in Great Berkhamsted, Hertfordshire, 15 November 1731. Educated at Dr. Pittman's School, Markyate Street, Hertfordshire, 1738–40, and at Mrs. Disney's (oculist), London, 1740–42; Westminster School, London, 1742–49; articled to Mr. Chapman, a London solicitor, 1750–52; took chambers in the Middle Temple, London, 1752; called to the Bar, 1754. A commissioner of bankrupts, 1759–64; Clerk of the Journals, House of Lords, 1763. Abandoned career after an attack of madness, 1763; periodically insane for the remainder of his life. Lived with the Evangelical clergyman Morley Unwin from 1765, and after Unwin's death in 1767 with Unwin's wife Mary until her death, 1796: lived in Olney, Buckinghamshire, 1767–95, and in East Dereham, Norfolk, 1795–1800. *Died 25 April 1800.*

PUBLICATIONS

Collections

> *Works: Poems, Correspondence and Translations,* edited by Robert Southey.   15 vols., 1835–37.
> *Correspondence,* edited by Thomas Wright.   4 vols., 1904.
> *Complete Poetical Works,* edited by H. S. Milford, 1905; revised edition, edited by Norma Russell, 1967.
> *Selected Poems and Letters,* edited by A. Norman Jeffares.   1963.
> *Poetry and Prose,* edited by Brian Spiller.   1968.

Verse

> *Olney Hymns,* with John Newton.   1779.
> *Anti-Thelyphthora: A Tale in Verse.*   1781.
> *Poems.*   1782; revised edition, 1794–95, 1797, 1800, 1806, 1808.
> *The Task,* vol. 2 of *Poems.*   1785.
> *The History of John Gilpin.*   1785.
> *Poems: On the Receipt of My Mother's Picture, The Dog and the Water-Lily.*   1798.
> *Adelphi,* edited by John Newton.   1802.
> *Posthumous Poetry,* edited by John Johnson.   1815.
> *Poems Now First Published,* edited by James Croft.   1825.
> *Unpublished and Uncollected Poems,* edited by Thomas Wright.   1900.
> *New Poems,* edited by Falconer Madan.   1931.

Other

> *Memoir of the Early Life of Cowper Written by Himself.*   1816; as *Autobiography,* 1835; edited by Maurice Quinlan, in *Proceedings of the American Philosophical Society 97,* 1953.
> *Unpublished and Uncollected Letters,* edited by Thomas Wright.   1925.

> Editor, *The Force of Truth,* by T. Scott.   1779 (or 1789 edition?).
> Editor, *Original Poems by a Lady* [Maria F. C. Cowper].   1792.
> Editor, *Sir Thomas More,* by James Hurdis.   1792.

> Translator, with others, *Works,* by Horace.   2 vols., 1757–59.
> Translator, with others, *The Henriade,* by Voltaire.   1762.
> Translator, *The Iliad and Odyssey,* by Homer.   2 vols., 1791.
> Translator, *The Power of Grace,* by H. R. Van Lier.   1792.
> Translator, *Poems,* by Jeanne Marie Guyon, edited by W. Bull.   1801.
> Translator, *Latin and Italian Poems of Milton,* edited by William Hayley.   1808; revised edition, as *Cowper's Milton,* 1810.

Bibliography: *Cowper: The Continuing Revaluation: Bibliography of Cowperian Studies from 1895 to 1960* by Lodwick Hartley, 1960; *A Bibliography of Cowper to 1837* by Norma Russell, 1963.

Reading List: *The Stricken Deer; or, The Life of Cowper* by David Cecil, 1929; *Cowper* by Norman Nicholson, 1951; *Cowper: A Critical Life* by Maurice Quinlan, 1953; *Cowper, Nature Poet* byRoderick Huang, 1957; *Cowper of the Inner Temple, Esq.: A Study of His Life and Work to 1768* by Charles Ryskamp, 1959; *In Search of Stability: The Poetry of Cowper* by Morris Golden, 1960; *The Life of Cowper* by John S. Memes, 1972.

*   *   *

William Cowper's early volume, the *Poems* of 1782, contained Augustan poetry with a dash of Evangelicism. But Cowper was not successful as a general satirist of society; in these poems – apart from a few passages on country life and some particular pieces of satire, notably on bores, the press, and Lord Chesterfield – he had not found his own voice. His friendship with Lady Austen helped him to find it. She suggested less abstract subjects which were part of his actual life – notably the sofa of *The Task,* where blank verse allowed him to be discursive, to indulge himself in what Coleridge called his "divine chit-chat." And Lady

Austen told him the story of an actual London draper one evening in 1782 when he was in a depressed mood. The result of his night's work was "The Diverting History of John Gilpin." In writing to his friend the Rev. William Unwin about it Cowper revealed his aim, of laughing himself and making two or three others laugh too. And while he enjoyed hearing the world laugh, he remarked that he was reduced to trifling "by necessity – a melancholy, that nothing else so effectually disposes, engages me sometimes in the arduous task of being merry by force.... To say truth, it would be but a shocking vagary, should the mariners on board a ship buffeted by a terrible storm, employ themselves in fiddling and dancing; yet sometimes much such a part act I...."

The underlying melancholia of the poet is there in *The Task.* In Book III he describes himself as a stricken deer that left the herd; and the whole poem is itself part of his cure, a quiet life in the countryside. To this he brought sharp, close, detailed observation, as in Book VI, "The Winter Walk at Noon," or else witty application of Augustan elegance of diction as in his mock heroic description of the ways of cultivating the cucumber, with the "stercoraceous heap" yielded by the stable, of dispersing the "gross fog Boeotian" from the drenched conservatory, or again of comfortable contemplation, in Book IV's "The Winter Evening," with its memorable description of the arrival of the post and its reception:

> Now stir the fire, and close the shutters fast
> Let fall the curtains, wheel the sofa round,
> And, while the bubbling and loud-hissing urn
> Throws up a steamy column, and the cups,
> That cheer but not inebriate, wait on each,
> So let us welcome peaceful evening in.

There were less cheerful poems, the despairing "Lines Written During a Period of Insanity" for example, with their disturbed rhythm, "The Shrubbery," and, a poignant poem, "The Castaway" with the sea imagery Cowper used to such effect. More general reflections were captured in the poem "On the Loss of the Royal George," which matches the obviousness – and the truth – of Gray's Elegy.

The Olney Hymns, written mostly during 1771 and 1772, drew upon Biblical imagery; they paraphrase Biblical texts, and they catch some of the ecstasy that Evangelicism gave Cowper briefly. They are honest hymns which record his own occasional delight and doubt, and yet express universal religious experience. "Light Shining Out of Darkness," written before Cowper's attack of madness in 1773, is perhaps the best known, its simplicity highly effective:

> God moves in a mysterious way,
>   His wonders to perform;
> He plants his footsteps in the sea,
>   And rides upon the storm

"Walking with God" and "Lively Hope and Gracious Fear" also capture general attitudes, but "Lovest Thou Me" and "Temptation" are filled with Cowper's own intense contemplation of existence.

Mrs. Unwin's friendship with Cowper was recorded in a notable sonnet of 1793, a year in which he also wrote "To Mary" to her. His directness of utterance (he thought the poetry of his own time artificial: "over-refined and delicate to exception") suited his recording of domestic drama: "The Retired Cat" lost in a drawer, "The Dog and the Water-Lily," and the magnificent "Epitaph on a Hare." Cowper, in short, was a master of the familiar style. He could express easily profound reflections upon life's progress in "Yardley Oak"; he could also translate Homer's "majestic plainess" effectively, and his two volume translation of Homer was a commercial success. And his translations of Milton's Latin and Italian poems are still immensely readable.

Cowper, one of the twelve most quoted writers in the *Oxford Dictionary of Quotations*, is attractive because of his blending of public speech and private emotion, his profound seriousness illuminated by his urbane wit, his religious enthusiasm matched by classical restraint, his melancholia mellowed by his "constant enjoyment of country air and retirement." And the *Letters* show us the kind of conversation we might have had with him; a man of moods – of demonic dreams at the horror of hell balanced by carefully ordered days creating peace and ease – sensitive, ruminative, ironic, and unfailingly courteous.

—A. Norman Jeffares

CRABBE, George.   English.   Born in Aldeburgh, Suffolk, 24 December 1754. Educated at schools in Bungay and Stowmarket, Suffolk; apprenticed to a village doctor at Wickham Brook, near Bury St. Edmunds, Suffolk, 1768–71, and to Mr. Page, a surgeon, at Woodbridge, Suffolk, 1771–75. Married Sarah Elmy in 1783 (died, 1813); two sons. Practised medicine in Aldeburgh, 1775–80, but found it difficult to make a living; settled in London, 1780, and attracted the patronage of Edmund Burke, who persuaded him to enter the church: ordained deacon, 1781, priest, 1782: Curate in Aldeburgh, 1781–82; Chaplain to the Duke of Rutland at Belvoir, 1782–85; Curate of Stathern, Leicestershire, 1785–89; Rector of Muston, Leicestershire, 1789; Curate of Sweffling and Great Glemham, 1792; returned to Muston, 1805; Vicar of Trowbridge, Wiltshire, 1814–32. *Died 3 February 1832.*

PUBLICATIONS

Collections

    Tales, 1812, and Other Selected Poems, edited by Howard Mills.   1967.
    Poems, edited by Norma Russell and Arthur Pollard.   1973.

Verse

    Inebriety.   1775.
    The Candidate.   1780.
    The Library.   1781.
    The Village.   1783.
    The News-Paper.   1785.
    Poems.   1807.
    The Borough: A Poem in Twenty-Four Letters.   1810.
    Tales in Verse.   1812.
    Poetical Works.   4 vols., 1816; revised edition, 7 vols., 1820; 8 vols., 1834.
    Tales of the Hall.   2 vols., 1819.
    New Poems, edited by Arthur Pollard.   1960.

Other

    Posthumous Sermons, edited by John D. Hastings.   1850.

Bibliography: *A Bibliography of Crabbe* by T. Bareham and S. Gattrell, 1978.

Reading List: *The Life of Crabbe* by his son, 1834; *Crabbe* by Alfred Ainger, 1903; *The Poetry of Crabbe* by Lilian Haddakin, 1955; *Crabbe* by Raymond L. Brett, 1956; *Nature's Sternest Painter: Five Essays on the Poetry of Crabbe* by Oliver F. Sigworth, 1965; *Crabbe* by Robert L. Chamberlain, 1965; *Crabbe: The Critical Heritage* edited by Arthur Pollard, 1972; *Crabbe's Poetry* by Peter New, 1976; *Crabbe's Arabesque: Social Drama in the Poetry of Crabbe* by Ronald B. Hatch, 1977; *Crabbe: A Critical Study* by T. Bareham, 1977.

*   *   *

George Crabbe is usually remembered as the author of *The Village* (written early in his career) or of "Peter Grimes," which is better known in the much altered operatic version. Neither work is really characteristic of his enormous and protean output. His creative life was long – from magazine poems in 1772 to the posthumous tales of 1834. This lengthy career, from the age of Johnson to the age of Byron, is divided into three parts.

His early works – *The Library*, *The Village*, and *The News-Paper* – seem content not only with the heroic couplet which he had inherited from the Augustans, but with the subject matter and moral attitudes of an earlier generation. These early poems seek general topics upon which Crabbe can weave moral comments and social aphorisms. He is never completely at home in this genre. Though *The Library* has patches of sombre brooding power, and *The Village* is shot through with a savage indignation at the unpleasantness of rustic life, there is no steady guiding principle in these works, no sustained intellectual thesis which will carry the sometimes lame couplets to a memorable conclusion. It is not even clear what is being attacked in *The Village* – for all that it is quoted *ad nauseam* by social historians of the period. The descriptions of rural hardship are strongly written, and the denunciation of pastoral poetry which glosses over them is warmly felt. Yet the blame for rustic ills is never squarely laid at any social or political door and the poem is void of any proper suggestions for the amelioration of the suffering it describes.

This phase of his work was followed by a twenty-two year silence, until the publication of *Poems* in 1807. The new volume showed a fresh side of Crabbe. His trenchant eye for detail, and his interest in human character made themselves manifest in poems like "The Parish Register," "Sir Eustace Grey" and "The Hall of Justice." Though many of his poems are character studies of his parishioners, observed in their daily lives by the parson, Crabbe also reveals a strong curiosity about the workings of aberrant minds – madness, thwarted love, disappointed ambition. In these dual concerns for humble life and for deranged states of mind he is as much a member of the Romantic avant-garde as, in his pontifical generalities, he can seem the last upholder of the post-Augustan order. His contemporaries found him difficult to "place," though he had the admiration of both liberal and conservative critics, and commanded an enormous readership. The tendency of his poetry to insist upon the graphic details of painful reality sometimes offended. Yet to people as divergent as Scott, Byron, Wordsworth, and Jane Austen he provided a unique fusion of the painful, the original, and the moral views of the world around him.

In *The Borough* his interest in shaping his material towards complete narratives is developed. It commences as a genre poem, describing the topography and life of an east coast seaport, gradually becoming a series of narratives linked only loosely to the central theme. Some of the twenty-four letters which comprise the poem are satiric descriptions of phenomena such as the borough election, lawyers and other professions, and the Church. These frequently have a vigour and saltiness which were absent from his earlier work, but they still require a capacity for compendious generalisation and methodical summation which was never Crabbe's forte. The best of the letters are those where he analyses individual characters – "The Parish Clerk," "Peter Grimes," "Abel Keene," and the loathsome scapegrace "Blaney." In this vein Crabbe is a totally original poet, reminding the reader of Chaucer in his handling of material, while often managing a manly concentration in his couplets, which he acknowledged he owed to a lifelong love for Dryden.

The last two volumes published in his lifetime – *Tales in Verse* and *Tales of the Hall* – carry his progress in narrative method to its conclusion. Character analysis is now avowedly the object of his art, and he develops a capacity for correlating the people in his tales with the objects, furniture, and backgrounds with which they choose to live. Dickens and Hardy admired him for this quality and learned much from him. *Tales in Verse* does not provide a linking narrative. Each story is complete in itself, a compressed account of the crisis in a man's life encompassed in about 750 terse, graphic lines. *Tales of the Hall* provides a somewhat sentimental frame-narrative, and for some critics this detracts from the power of the individual tales. Old age had possibly mellowed Crabbe's picture of the world. Certainly this is his most benign volume, though in tales like "Ellen" and "Smuggler and Poachers" he can still touch the genuine heights of tragedy.

Crabbe must not be seen as exclusively or even predominantly a gloomy writer, however. His humour, evident on many occasions, is quiet, wry, and trenchant, and his pity for men's follies and self-delusions always tempers his judgement. Pieces like "The Lovers' Journey," "The Dumb Orators," and "The Frank Courtship" are richly humorous, both verbally and situationally. Perhaps because of the length at which he wrote, Crabbe's technical skill has been undervalued. He can be prosaic to the point of banality, and his verbal wit is often arch; yet both these qualities are usually dramatic factors in controlling overall tone in a poem. He learned a great deal about control of atmosphere from Shakespeare, whom he had read in great depth. Shakespeare also provided the sanction for Crabbe's interest in the disturbed psyche. Crabbe is a moral poet, and there is a close link between his primary role as a dedicated teacher of practical morality, his poetic integrity, and his function as an Anglican priest. The degree to which he enlivens and gives permanent life to this fusion is what makes him a memorable and valuable contributor to the Enical heritage.

—T. Bareham

CUNNINGHAM, John. Scottish. Born in Dublin, Ireland in 1729. Educated at Drogheda. Appeared on the stage in Dublin, 1747, and thereafter travelled throughout the British Isles as a strolling actor. *Died 18 September 1773.*

PUBLICATIONS

Verse

A Poetical Essay in Manner of Elegy on the Death of His Majesty.   1760.
An Elegy on a Pile of Ruins.   1761.
Day and Other Pastorals.   1761.
The Contemplatist: A Night Piece.   1762.
Fortune: An Apologue.   1765.
Poems, Chiefly Pastoral.   1766; revised edition, 1771.
Poetical Works.   1781.

Play

Love in a Mist (produced 1747).   1747.

Reading List: *Poets of Ireland* by D. J. O'Donoghue, 1912; "Cunningham" by E. J. Morley, in *Essays by Divers Hands,* 1942.

*   *   *

After the early success of his farce *Love in a Mist,* acted in Dublin in 1747, Cunningham lived the precarious life of a strolling player and occasional poet. He was favoured in youth with a letter or two from Shenstone, who advised him to "proceed in the pastoral manner." This Cunningham duly did in the short pieces eventually collected into *Poems, Chiefly Pastoral.* His conventional pastoral dialogues between Damon, Phillis, Phoebe, etc., his pastoral love-songs to Phillis, Delia, etc., and his pastoral elegy on Corydon (i.e., Shenstone), are all conventional exercises in an exhausted tradition. There is little originality either in his jog-trot pastoral ballads about contented millers, pretty country lasses, and general rural contentment, though his songs "Kate of Aberdeen" and "Kitty Fell" have some simple charm. Best, and best known, is the little series of well-observed landscape vignettes which make up his "Day: A Pastoral" in three parts – "Morning," "Noon," and "Evening."

His longest poem, *An Elegy on a Pile of Ruins* is an avowed imitation of Gray's *Elegy,* but has more extravagant and stagey Gothick romantic effects than Gray's. The manner may be adequately illustrated by one stanza:

> Where the mild sun, through saint-encyphered glass,
>   Illum'd with mellow light yon dusky aisle,
> Many rapt hours might Meditation pass,
>   Slow moving 'twixt the pillars of the pile.

Cunningham wrote two other moral, reflective pieces – *The Contemplatist: A Night Piece* and *Fortune: An Apologue* – and wrote prologues, epilogues, fables, anacreontics, and occasional lyrics, but nearly all his work is derivative and factitious. There is, perhaps, most vigour and originality in his song in praise of Newcastle Beer, a "liquor so lively, so potent and clear."

—A. J. Sambrook

DARWIN, Erasmus. English.   Born in Elston, Nottinghamshire, 12 December 1731. Educated at Chesterfield School, 1741–50; St. John's College, Cambridge (Exeter Scholar), B.A. 1754, M.B. 1755; studied medicine in Edinburgh, 1754–55. Married 1) Mary Howard in 1757 (died, 1770), three sons; 2) Mrs. Chandos Pole in 1781, four sons, three daughters. Physician: settled in Lichfield, 1756, Derby, 1781, and afterwards at Breadsall Priory. Founder, Philosophical Society, Derby, 1784; Founder, Lichfield Dispensary, 1784; formed a botanical garden near Lichfield, 1778. *Died 18 April 1802.*

PUBLICATIONS

Collections

Essential Writings, edited by Desmond King-Hele. 1968.

Verse

The Loves of the Plants. 1789.
The Botanic Garden. 2 vols., 1791.
The Golden Age: A Poetical Epistle to T. Beddoes. 1794.
The Temple of Nature; or, The Origin of Society. 1803.
Poetical Works. 3 vols., 1806.

Other

Zoonomia; or, The Laws of Organic Life. 2 vols., 1794–96.
A Plan for the Conduct of Female Education in Boarding School. 1797.
Phytologia; or, The Philosophy of Agriculture and Gardening. 1800.

Editor, *Experiments Establishing a Criterion*, by Charles Darwin. 1780.

Translator, *The Families of Plants*, by Carolus Linnaeus. 1787.

Reading List: *Doctor Darwin* by Hesketh Pearson, 1930; *The Poetry and Aesthetics of Darwin* by James V. Logan, 1936; *Darwin*, 1963, and *Doctor of Revolution: The Life and Genius of Darwin*, 1977, both by Desmond King-Hele; *The Comedian as the Letter D: Darwin's Comic Materialism* by Donald M. Hassler, 1973.

*   *   *

Erasmus Darwin was a renowned medical doctor and the grandfather of Charles Darwin. His own early theories of biological evolution and other daring scientific speculations have been overshadowed by the work of his grandson, but his imaginative expressions of these speculations in ornate and comic Popean couplets and vigorous prose notes remain an interesting example of the late 18th-century Age of Sensibility. The literary effects in his verse, in particular, are deliberately contrived both to raise and to evade the notion of limitless fecundity in nature. Darwin was closely associated with other materialists, natural philosophers, and inventors such as Joseph Priestley, Josiah Wedgwood, and James Watt, with whom he founded the famous Lunar Society of Birmingham. His influence on the British romantic poets was considerable, and Coleridge coined the word "Darwinizing" to refer to his imaginative and wide-ranging speculations.

His long poems and prose treatises, world famous in his time but now available only in facsimile, were originally published by the radical London bookseller Joseph Johnson. Most notable among them are the poems *The Botanic Garden* and *The Temple of Nature* and the medical treatise containing evolutionary theory *Zoonomia*. Darwin's influences as a speculator and enthusiast of causes ranging from the French Revolution to the anti-slavery movement also extended to the circle of radicals such as William Godwin; and Godwin's daughter, Mary Shelley, mentions Darwin in her account of the intellectual origins of *Frankenstein*. William Blake illustrated some of Darwin's poems and delighted in his wide-ranging speculations, although he abominated the compressed and rational poetic form. Finally, Darwin should be remembered for his energy, his inventiveness, and his subtle expression of many ideas of the Enlightenment.

—Donald M. Hassler

DIAPER, William. English. Born in Bridgewater, Somerset, in 1685. Educated at Balliol College, Oxford, B.A. 1710. Ordained deacon at Wells Cathedral, 1709; Curate, Brent, Somerset, c. 1711, and probably at Crick, Northamptonshire, and Dean, Northamptonshire, 1713–14. Associated for a time with Swift and the Tory Wits. *Died in 1717.*

PUBLICATIONS

Collections

Complete Works, edited by Dorothy Broughton. 1952.

Verse

Nereides; or, Sea-Eclogues. 1712.
Dryades; or, The Nymph's Prophecy. 1713.
An Imitation of the Seventeenth Epistle of the First Book of Horace, Addressed to Dr. Swift. 1714.

Other

Translator, with others, *Callipaedia,* by Claudius Quillet. 1712.
Translator, with others, *Oppian's Halieuticks of the Nature of Fishes and Fishing of the Ancients.* 1722.

Reading List: "Faery Lore and The Rape of the Lock" by Pat Rogers, in *Review of English Studies,* 1974.

*   *   *

William Diaper reached the summit of his brief career in 1712, when he was taken up for a time by Swift and the Tory wits. His trajectory as a poet bears a close similarity to that of John Philips. Both came from the West of England; studied at Oxford (where Philips lingered sufficiently to allow Diaper to join him as a contemporary), attracted the attention of Henry St. John, later Lord Bolingbroke, and died at the age of thirty-two. Each constructed variations on the existing pastoral forms, and each extended the compass of descriptive writing to include a wider range of philosophic and political themes.

Diaper's topographic poem "Brent" (probably written c. 1711) is an amusing complaint regarding his exile in the damp alluvial countryside of coastal Somerset, where he was briefly a curate. Viewing himself as a second Ovid, cast away to the Scythian shores, he manages some pleasant turns of wit in the manner which Prior had evolved from seventeenth-century models. It has been much debated, he asserts, at what time of year the earth was created, but the scenery near bleak Brent Knoll "and all the marshes round," termed "a sort of chaos, and unfinish'd ground," leaves no room for doubt – the places round about "Were made in winter, one may safely swear,/For winter is the only season there." The imitation of Horace, addressed to Swift and published in 1714, is less assured in tone, but it handles the octosyllabic couplet with reasonable fluency, and achieves a certain bite in places: as when Diaper slyly pictures "the well-bred Dean" going about town "Drest up as spruce, as th'Author looks/When plac'd by *Gucht* before his Books." The two extended translations, from Oppian and Quillet, display a talent for leisurely paraphrase along with tactful amplification of the original.

Diaper's major achievement appears in the poems he produced in 1712, *Nereides* and *Dryades*. The former sticks closely to the traditional Theocritan eclogue-structures, but adds a vein of fantasy and bizarre occultism in transferring the setting to mysterious submarine regions: "Happy are those who know the secret Cause/Of strange Effects, and Nature's hidden Laws." Diaper's picturesque imagination is even more evident in *Dryades*, a kind of displaced Georgic where practical instruction is supplanted by detailed observation of nature (insects, particularly) and half-whimsical applications of native faery lore to patriotic and political ends. Its delicate imagery and minute observation produce some sensitive verbal effects which may well have influenced Pope in his revisions of *The Rape of the Lock*. There is a slightly archaic note in the phrasing here and there, as though Dryden were still a live and indeed contemporary force. But the closeness to natural phenomena and the freshness of the writing give *Dryades* a lasting charm which lifts it above the ruck of topographico-political poetry:

> Men Nature in her secret Work behold,
> Untwist her Fibres, and her Coats unfold;
> With Pleasure trace the Threds of stringy Roots,
> The various Textures of the ripening Fruits;
> And Animals, that careless live at ease,
> To whom the Leaves are Worlds, the Drops are Seas.

—Pat Rogers

DORSET, Earl of; Charles Sackville, 6th Earl of Dorset and Earl of Middlesex. English. Born in England, 24 January 1638. Privately educated. Married 1) Mary Berkeley (died); 2) Mary Compton in 1685 (died, 1691); 3) Anne Roche in 1704; one son. Known for excesses in his youth, in company with Sir Charles Sedley and others; a courtier of Charles II; elected to the first Parliament after the Restoration as Member for East Grinstead, Sussex, 1660; indicted for murder, 1662, but released; involved in the naval battle with the Dutch, 1665; sent on a diplomatic mission to France, 1668; withdrew from court during the reign of James II; returned to serve King William as Lord Chamberlain of the Household, 1689–97, and served as one of the regents during the king's absences. Inherited considerable estates on accession as Earl of Middlesex, 1675, and Earl of Dorset, 1677; known for his patronage of writers and artists, particularly Dryden. Knight of the Garter, 1691. *Died 29 January 1706.*

PUBLICATIONS

Collections

The Works of the Earls of Rochester, Roscommon, Dorset, etc.   2 vols., 1714.

Play

Pompey the Great, with others, from a play by Corneille (produced 1664).   1664.

Reading List: *Charles Sackville, Patron and Poet* by Brice Harris, 1940; *The Restoration Court Poets* by V. de Sola Pinto, 1965.

*   *   *

"... your lyric poems ... are the delight and wonder of this age, and will be the envy of the next.... There is more of salt in all your verses than I have seen in any.... Donne alone, of all our countrymen, had your talent ... this age and the last ... have excelled the Ancients in both [tragedy and satire] ... Shakespeare of the former ... your Lordship in the latter sort." The Earl of Dorset is the recipient of this extravagant praise from Dryden (in "A Discourse Concerning Satire," 1693). Early in Dryden's career, he had designated Dorset an elegant and gentlemanly defender of the Moderns, naming him Eugenius ("well-born") in the *Essay of Dramatick Poesie* (1668). And, because he displayed many of the cavalier features of the gentleman and courtier that Dryden extolled (wit; easy, natural language), Dorset was highly-regarded by his peers and by several succeeding generations. Addison found him one "who had the greatest Wit tempered with the greatest Candour, and ... one of the finest Criticks as well as the best Poets of his Age" (*Spectator 85*). At court, he held high office under three monarchs, and was a generous patron of authors (including Dryden). For such reasons, unlike the dissolute Rochester, he is remembered as a polished aristocrat, an exemplar of an ideal that the Restoration too seldom attained.

Yet, for all that, as concerns the praise for his poetry, we must remain with Dr. Johnson, incredulous. For the truth is that Dorset published nothing under his own name during his lifetime; a few poems crept into the numerous poetical miscellanies of the period, but that was all.

Doubtless his most well-known Song is the eleven-stanza poem that Johnson alluded to in his *Life*, "To all you ladies now at land":

> Then, if we write not by each post,
>   Think not we are unkind;
> Nor yet conclude our ships are lost
>   By Dutchmen, or by wind:
> Our tears we'll send a speedier way,
> The tide shall bring 'em twice a day.

A number of his songs are love lyrics, with a certain virility and facility in their expression, to numbers of Phillises and Chlorises; they are marked by relaxed and easy delivery:

> My love is full of noble pride,
>   Nor can it e'er submit,
> To let that fop, discretion, ride
>   In triumph over it.

Dorset could be, upon occasion, satiric – though many would find such poems mere scurrilous *ad hominem* lampoons ("To Mr. Edward Howard, On His Plays" and "On Mr. Edward Howard upon his *British Princes*"). Dorset was doubtless at his best in writing little biting, acerbic "songs," such as "Dorinda's sparkling wit, and eyes." Here, the flashy beauty overwhelms her would-be suitors: "Her Cupid is a black-guard boy,/That runs his link full in your face."

James Sutherland has aptly summed up Dorset's performance: "the satirical song is his special contribution to English poetry," and his shaped argumentation in verse "gives to the Restoration lyric its characteristic form: what is said, no matter how trivial or specious, is said with grace and control and finality" (*English Literature of the Late Seventeenth Century*). For a minor poet, that is a fairly impressive achievement.

—John R. Clark

DRYDEN, John.   English.   Born in Aldwinckle All Saints, Northamptonshire, 19 August 1631. Educated at Westminster School, London (King's Scholar), 1646–50; Trinity College, Cambridge (pensioner), 1650–54, B.A. 1654. Married Lady Elizabeth Howard in 1663. Remained in Cambridge, 1654–57; settled in London, 1657, and possibly held a minor post in Cromwell's government; thereafter supported himself mainly by writing plays. Appointed Poet Laureate, 1668, and Historiographer Royal, 1669: converted to Roman Catholicism, c. 1685, and lost his royal offices at the accession of William and Mary, 1689. Member, Royal Society, 1660. *Died 1 May 1700.*

PUBLICATIONS

Collections

> *The Works,* edited by Sir Walter Scott.   18 vols., 1808; revised edition edited by George Saintsbury, 1882–92.
> *Dramatic Works,* edited by Montague Summers.   6 vols., 1931–32.
> *Letters,* edited by Charles E. Ward.   1942.
> *Works,* edited by Edward N. Hooker and G. T. Swedenberg, Jr.   1956–
> *Poems,* edited by James Kinsley.   4 vols., 1958.
> *Four Comedies, Four Tragedies* (includes *Secret Love, Sir Martin Mar-All, An Evening's Love, Marriage A-la-Mode, The Indian Emperor, Aureng-Zebe, All for Love, Don Sebastian*), edited by L. A. Beaurline and Fredson Bowers.   2 vols., 1967.
> *A Selection,* edited by John Conaghan.   1978.

Verse

> *Heroic Stanzas to the Memory of Oliver, Late Lord Protector,* in *Three Poems upon the Death of His Late Highness Oliver, Lord Protector,* with Waller and Sprat.   1659.
> *Astraea Redux: A Poem on the Happy Restoration and Return of His Sacred Majesty Charles the Second.*   1660.

To His Sacred Majesty: A Panegyric on His Coronation. 1661.
To My Lord Chancellor, Presented on New Year's Day. 1662.
Annus Mirabilis, The Year of Wonders 1666: An Historical Poem. 1667.
Ovid's Epistles, with others. 1680.
Absalom and Achitophel. 1681; *Second Part,* with Nahum Tate, 1682; edited by James and Helen Kinsley, 1961.
The Medal: A Satire Against Sedition. 1682.
Mac Flecknoe; or, A Satire upon the True-Blue-Protestant Poet T[homas] S[hadwell]. 1682.
Religio Laici; or, A Layman's Faith. 1682.
Miscellany Poems. 1684; *Sylvae; or, The Second Part,* 1685; *Examen Poeticum, Being the Third Part,* 1693; *The Annual Miscellany, Being the Fourth Part,* 1694; *Fifth Part,* 1704; *Sixth Part,* 1709.
Threnodia Augustalis: A Funeral-Pindaric Poem Sacred to the Happy Memory of King Charles II. 1685.
The Hind and the Panther. 1687.
A Song for St. Cecilia's Day 1687. 1687.
Britannia Rediviva: A Poem on the Birth of the Prince. 1688.
Eleonora: A Panegyrical Poem Dedicated to the Memory of the Late Countess of Abingdon. 1692.
The Satires of Juvenal, with others, *Together with the Satires of Persius.* 1693.
An Ode on the Death of Henry Purcell. 1696.
The Works of Virgil, Containing His Pastorals, Georgics, and Aeneis. 1697; edited by James Kinsley, 1961.
Alexander's Feast; or, The Power of Music: An Ode in Honour of St. Cecilia's Day. 1697.
Fables Ancient and Modern. 1700.
Ovid's Art of Love, Book 1, translated. 1709.
Hymns Attributed to Dryden, edited by George Rapall and George Reuben Potter. 1937.
Prologues and Epilogues, edited by William B. Gardner. 1951.

Plays

The Wild Gallant (produced 1663). 1669; in *Works 8,* 1962.
The Indian Queen, with Sir Robert Howard (produced 1664). In *Four New Plays,* by Howard, 1665.
The Rival Ladies (produced 1664). 1664; in *Works 8,* 1962.
The Indian Emperor; or, The Conquest of Mexico by the Spaniards, Being the Sequel of The Indian Queen (produced 1665). 1667; in *Works 9,* 1966.
Secret Love; or, The Maiden Queen (produced 1667). 1668; in *Works 9,* 1966.
Sir Martin Mar-All; or, The Feigned Innocence, from a translation by William Cavendish of a play by Molière (produced 1667). 1668; in *Works 9,* 1966.
The Tempest; or, The Enchanted Island, with William Davenant, from the play by Shakespeare (produced 1667). 1670; edited by Vivian Summers, 1974.
An Evening's Love; or, The Mock Astrologer (produced 1668). 1671; in *Works 10,* 1970.
Tyrannic Love; or, The Royal Martyr (produced 1669). 1670; in *Works 10,* 1970.
The Conquest of Granada by the Spaniards, 2 parts (produced 1670, 1671). 1672; in *Works 2,* 1978.
Marriage A-la-Mode (produced 1672). 1673; in *Works 2,* 1978.
The Assignation; or, Love in a Nunnery (produced 1672). 1673; in *Works 2,* 1978.
Amboyna (produced 1673). 1673.
Aureng-Zebe (produced 1675). 1676; edited by Frederick M. Link, 1971.
The State of Innocence and Fall of Man. 1677.

All for Love; or, The World Well Lost, from the play *Antony and Cleopatra* by Shakespeare (produced 1677). 1678; edited by David M. Vieth, 1974.
The Kind Keeper; or, Mr. Limberham (produced 1678). 1680; edited by A. Norman Jeffares, in *Restoration Comedy,* 1974.
Oedipus, with Nathaniel Lee (produced 1678). 1679.
Troilus and Cressida; or, Truth Found Too Late, from the play by Shakespeare (produced 1679). 1679.
The Spanish Friar; or, The Double Discovery (produced 1680). 1681.
The Duke of Guise, with Nathaniel Lee (produced 1682). 1683.
Albion and Albanius, music by Lewis Grabu (produced 1685). 1685.
Don Sebastian, King of Portugal (produced 1689). 1690; in *Four Tragedies,* 1967.
Amphitryon; or, The Two Socias (produced 1690). 1690.
King Arthur; or, The British Worthy, music by Henry Purcell (produced 1691). 1691.
Cleomenes, The Spartan Hero (produced 1692). 1692.
Love Triumphant; or, Nature Will Prevail (produced 1694). 1694.
The Secular Masque, in *The Pilgrim,* by Vanbrugh (produced 1700). 1700.
Comedies, Tragedies, and Operas. 2 vols., 1701.

Other

Of Dramatic Poesy: An Essay. 1668; revised edition, 1684; edited by George Watson, in *Of Dramatic Poesy and Other Critical Essays,* 1962.
Notes and Observations on The Express of Morocco, with John Crowne and Thomas Shadwell. 1674.
His Majesty's Declaration Defended. 1681.
The Vindication. 1683.
A Defence of An Essay of Dramatic Poesy. 1688.
Works. 4 vols., 1695.
Critical and Miscellaneous Prose Works, edited by Edmond Malone. 4 vols., 1800.
Essays, edited by W. P. Ker. 2 vols., 1900.
Literary Criticism, edited by A. C. Kirsch. 1966.

Editor, *The Art of Poetry,* by Nicolas Boileau, translated by William Soames, revised edition. 1683.

Translator, *The History of the League,* by Louis Maimbourg. 1684.
Translator, *The Life of St. Francis Xavier,* by Dominique Bouhours. 1688.
Translator, with Knightly Chetwood, *Miscellaneous Essays,* by St. Evremond, 1692.
Translator, with others, *The Annals and History of Tacitus.* 3 vols., 1698.

Bibliography: *Dryden: A Bibliography of Early Editions and of Drydeniana* by Hugh Macdonald, 1939; *Dryden: A Survey and Bibliography of Critical Studies 1895–1974* by David J. Latt and Samuel J. Monk, 1976.

Reading List: *The Poetry of Dryden* by Mark van Doren, 1920, revised edition, 1931; *Dryden: Some Biographical Facts and Problems* by J. M. Osborn, 1940, revised edition, 1965; *Dryden and the Conservative Myth* by B. N. Schilling, 1961; *Life of Dryden* by Charles E. Ward, 1961; *Dryden's Imagery* by Arthur W. Hoffman, 1962; *Essential Articles for the Study of Dryden* edited by H. T. Swedenberg, Jr., 1966; *Dryden's Major Plays* by Bruce King, 1966; *Dryden's Poetry* by Earl Miner, 1967; *Contexts of Dryden's Thought* by Philip Harth, 1968; *Dryden: The Critical Heritage* edited by James and Helen Kinsley, 1971; *Dryden* by William Myers, 1973; *Dryden and the Development of Panegyric* by James Dale Garrison, 1975; *Dryden, The Public Writer 1660–1685* by George McFadden, 1978.

*   *   *

John Dryden's life is largely obscure until he commences as author. He was born on 19 August 1631 at Aldwinckle All Saints in Northamptonshire, and about 1646 he entered, as a King's Scholar, Westminster School under the famous master Richard Busby. Much later he recalled that about 1648 he had translated Persius's third satire as a Thursday night exercise for the school. His first published poem, "Upon the Lord Hastings," appeared in 1649; on 18 May of the following year he was admitted as pensioner to Trinity College, Cambridge, proceeding B.A. in 1654. The next years are yet more obscure. Some color is given to the tradition he served the Protectorate by the publication in 1659 of the *Heroique Stanza's* on Cromwell's death.

His career may be said to begin, however, with the Restoration, and its first period to run from 1660–1680. Early in these years he published poems on the new order, bringing together historical, political, religious, and heroic elements. Although such a poem as *Astraea Redux* is inferior to the poem on Cromwell, it is more ambitious. Somewhat of the new effort succeeds in *Annus Mirabilis*, whose year of wonders (1666) included the second naval war with Holland and the Great Fire of London. Dryden seeks too hard to connect these diverse events, and his execution is uneven. But it has bounding energy and is his sole fully narrative poem till far later. His talents were being recognized – in 1668 he succeeded Davenant as poet laureate, and in 1669 Howell as historiographer royal. By the end of this period he had completed but not published his first poetic masterpiece, *Mac Flecknoe*. If Elkanah Settle was its first dunce hero, Thomas Shadwell finally gained the honor. The poem assesses good and bad art, using a mock coronation skit. Father Flecknoe abdicates for his son (Shadwell). Art, politics, and religious matters combine with paternal love to assess both the dunces and true drama. Flecknoe is "King by Office" and "Priest by Trade." He passes to his son *Love's Kingdom*, his own dull play, as "Sceptre." From "this righteous Lore" comes Shadwell's soul, his opera *Psyche*. Humor and allusion combine to establish the true canons of drama and to fix Shadwell immemorially.

Mac Flecknoe shows that Dryden's chief interest in these decades is the stage. After a first comedy, he turned to the rhymed heroic play, rising to the high astounding terms of the two-part *Conquest of Granada*. He approached earth thereafter. *Marriage A-la-mode* consists of a mingling of serious and comic plots especially congenial to him, and a favorite still. In the Prologue to his heroic play *Aureng-Zebe*, he professes himself "weary" of rhyme, and in *All for Love* he wrote a blank verse tragedy on Antony and Cleopatra, thought by many his finest play. His collaboration with Nathaniel Lee for *Oedipus* altered his smooth earlier blank verse style to a harsher, more various medium that appears again in his adaptation of *Troilus and Cressida*. After his enormously popular *Spanish Fryar* (1680), he wrote no plays single-handedly till 1689.

The next period, 1680–1685, is dominated by engagement with the tumultuous times. In the state of near revolution over the Popish Plot and efforts to seize power from Charles II, Dryden published *Absalom and Achitophel*, his poem most admired today. Using the biblical parallel of the plot against David (Charles), Dryden creates an epic-historic-satiric blend for the machinations of Achitophel (Earl of Shaftesbury) and his dupe Absalom (Duke of Monmouth). The Chaucer-like portraits of individuals and the personal statement on government (ll. 751–810) show Dryden in full command of a public poetry.

1682 brought Dryden further attention. *Mac Flecknoe* now first appeared in print, pirated. When Shaftesbury was released from prison by a Whig jury in November 1681, a triumphant medal was struck. Next March Dryden's one bitter poem, *The Medall*, appeared. Perhaps his anger was feigned. His usual composure is evident in *Religio Laici*, his first religious poem, which curiously begins with rich imagery and progresses to a direct, non-metaphorical style unique in his poetry. In 1684 he published one of his poems most popular today, "To the Memory of Mr. Oldham," on a young poet recently dead. In that year and the next he joined the bookseller Jacob Tonson in putting out the first two of a series of "Dryden miscellanies," collections of poetry by various hands. Charles II died, and James acceded, in 1685. Dryden celebrated these events in *Threnodia Augustalis*, his first pindaric ode after one of his finest poems, the translation of Horace, *Odes*, III, xxix.

The next period, 1685–1688, coincides with the brief rule by James II. Probably about the summer of 1685 Dryden became a Roman Catholic, and in 1687 published his second religious poem, *The Hind and the Panther*, whose 2592 lines make it his longest poem apart from translations. Its style is as complex as that of *Religio Laici* had been simple. Using sacred zoögraphy (the Hind represents Catholicism, the Panther Anglicanism, etc.), fables, myth, allusion, allegory, and the slightest of plots, Dryden sets forth a timeless version of the times, including the recent and distant past (Part I), present contentions (II), and the ecclesiastical as well as national future (III). Each part has a moving personal passage and those who have most opposed Dryden's doctrine or his fable have often called the style of this poem his finest. The poetic and personal confidence thereby implied finds expression in the ode, so praised by Dr. Johnson, on Anne Killigrew, whose small poetic abilities nonetheless may represent the artist's high vocation. Music is an equally confidently used metaphor in *A Song for Cecilia's Day*, which enacts history from Creation to Judgment.

When James fled late in 1688, and when William and Mary were invited as sovereigns by Parliament, Dryden entered into the most difficult period of his career, 1688–1694. Stripped of offices and denied full engagement with his times, he turned again to "the ungrateful stage." Two plays that now seem his greatest resulted: *Don Sebastian*, concerned with tragic fate, and *Amphitryon*, a very bleak comedy. Both deal with human identity in a hostile world. In 1691 he enjoyed a fortunate collaboration with Henry Purcell on *King Arthur*, an opera. In 1694, his last play, *Love Triumphant*, featured a happy ending engineered by an unconvincing change of heart. Such doubts and sputters in these years had fullest exercise in the *Satires* of 1693 (translating Juvenal and Persius) and the Preface to *Examen Poeticum*, the third miscellany.

In the last period, 1694–1700, Dryden worked through his problems. If he could not address all his contemporaries, he could focus on individuals. In 1694 two of his finest poetic addresses appear: "To my Dear Friend Mr. Congreve" and "To Sir Godfrey Kneller." Gloom remains in both, but the gloomier "Kneller" shows chastened faith even in "these Inferiour Times." The "Congreve" bears uncanny resemblance in motif to *Mac Flecknoe*. Drama is again the topic, with comparisons again settling values. Now Dryden must abdicate and Congreve have legitimate succession, even if a usurper should sneak in for a time. The "son" merits, however, and the "father" loves.

Addresses lacked the capaciousness to adjust new strains to old hopes. Such scale was achieved in the 1697 *Virgil*. Although it and his comedies most require re-assessment, it does seem that he darkens the second half of his *Aeneis* (as if the military and the public worlds do not quite merge), and that he renders the *Georgics* even more heroically and sympathetically than Virgil to show the terms on which hope remained. His real epic was to come in cento, *Fables Ancient and Modern* (1700). It combines seventeen poems made over from Ovid, Boccaccio, Chaucer, and Homer with four solely Dryden's: those two handsome ones to the Duchess of Ormonde and to John Dryden of Chesterton toward the beginning, as also *Alexander's Feast* and "The Monument of a Fair Maiden Lady" toward the end. In redoing the *Metamorphoses* as Milton had redone the *Aeneid* in *Paradise Lost*, Dryden relates his poems by links, themes, motifs, and central subject – the human search for the good life. A serene wisdom shows that such a life can finally be gained only on Christian terms. Yet the vain and sinful race continues to endear itself to the old poet. *Fables* is once again becoming a favorite of readers as it had been for the Romantics and Dryden's own contemporaries. He died on May Day 1700 of degenerative diseases, yet calm of mind to the end.

The limitations of such periodizing are represented by its failure to allow for his constant writing in "the other harmony of prose" (Preface to *Fables*). He was by no means the modern stylist some claim. He writes in numerous styles and sometimes shows no more knowledge than Milton of modern paragraph and sentence writing. In his styles, however, he established English criticism, struggling like others before him to create the critical essay. As early as *The Rival Ladies* (1664) he found his way in use of the preface, employing a method inquisitive, devoted to current issues, and yet enough assured to deal with general principles. *Of Dramatick Poesy. An Essay* is really a dialogue, his most elaborate criticism, a semi-fiction, offering heroic debate on the proper character of drama. In the "Parallel Betwixt Poetry and Painting" (a preface to *De Arte Graphica* in 1695) we see most clearly his attempt to unite neo-Aristotelian mimesis with neo-Horatian affectivism. Once more he asserted the poet's right to heighten – to take a better or worse "likeness" and remain true, or to deal with the best "nature," unlike the scientist. In a way prescient for his career, the "Account" prefixed to *Annus Mirabilis* (1667) had placed historical poetry and panegyric (by implication satire also) under the aegis of epic. These prefaces, the *Dramatick Poesy*, and his poems as well dealt with the concept of hope for human progress, which was relatively new in England, and also introduced critical and historical principles. The element most neglected by historians of criticism was his historical understanding, which permitted him to compare and differentiate and evolve a historical relativism that would later undermine mimetic presumptions. To him we owe the concept of a historical age or period possessing its own temper or Zeitgeist, with all that such assumptions have meant to subsequent thought about literature.

Such diversity – there are over thirty plays, operas, and cantatas alone – yields to no easy summary. We can observe what joins him to, or differentiates him from, his great contemporaries – or the next century. Like Marvell, Dryden was a gifted lyric poet, although in odes rather than ruminative lyrics. Like Butler, he was a learned satirist, but where Butler degrades Dryden exalts. Like Milton, he excelled in varieties of narrative and drama, just as both also overcame crises toward the end of their lives. Dryden had what Milton lacked – wit, humor, and generosity. But his extraordinary intellectual power to liken and assimilate was incapable of Milton's higher fusion of all into a single intense reality. And where Milton, like Spenser, created an artistic language spoken by no one, Dryden like Donne and Jonson created a more natural language founded on actual speech. Born early enough to remember the outbreak of civil war (1642) and to live through four different national constitutions, Dryden wrote of subjects that no longer treat directly – the most momentous of their times. For all that, his powers took on greatness only in the second half of his life, developing to the end. He practiced every literary kind except the novel, never repeating himself except in songs for plays. He is a rare example of a writer whose finest work comes at the end of his lifetime, of a century, and of a distinct period of literature. The next equivalent of *Fables* is not heroic poetry but the novel.

—Earl Miner

DUCK, Stephen. English.   Born in Charlton, Wiltshire, in 1705. Agricultural labourer after age 14. Married in 1724 (first wife died in 1730), three children; 2) Sarah Big, the Queen's housekeeper, in 1733. His literary efforts were encouraged by Queen Caroline, who gave him money and made him a Yeoman of the Guard, 1733, and Keeper of the Queen's Library at Richmond. Ordained in 1746: preacher at Kew Chapel, 1751; Rector of Byfleet, Surrey after 1752. *Died* (by suicide) *21 March 1756.*

PUBLICATIONS

Verse

Royal Benevolence; A Poem on Providence.   1730.
Poems on Several Subjects.   1730.
To the Duke of Cumberland on His Birthday.   1732.
A Poem on the Marriage of the Prince of Orange; Verses to the Author by a Divine, with the Author's Answer; and His Poem on Truth and Falsehood.   1734.

Poems on Several Occasions.   1736; as *The Beautiful Works of Duck,* 1753.
The Vision: A Poem on the Death of Queen Caroline.   1737.
The Year of Wonders.   1737.
Curious Poems on Several Occasions (revised versions of *On Poverty, The Thresher's Labour, The Shunammite*).   1738.
Alrick and Isabel; or, The Unhappy Marriage.   1740.
Every Man in His Own Way: An Epistle to a Friend.   1743.
An Ode to the Battle of Dettingen.   1743.
Caesar's Camp; or, St. George's Hill.   1755.

Reading List: *Duck, The Thresher-Poet* by Rose M. Davis, 1926; "Duck, The Wiltshire Phenomenon" by R. G. Furnival, in *Cambridge Journal,* May 1953; "Duck, The Thresher Poet" by A. Warner, in *Review of English Literature 8,* 1967.

*   *   *

The Thresher's Labour is among the first of those poems describing rural activities and written from first-hand experience by untutored peasant-poets which gained some currency in the later eighteenth century. Stephen Duck had virtually no formal education; he taught himself to write verses by reading Milton with the aid of a dictionary, and formed his style and taste according to the precepts of Addison, whose *Spectator* papers he read avidly. He was eventually taken up and patronised by Queen Caroline (a little to the chagrin of Pope and the other literary giants of the day), was made Royal Librarian, and took holy orders. Duck's sad death — he drowned himself in a fit of depression — may reflect the pressures that this unnatural existence had brought to bear upon him.

Those pressures are equally apparent in his verse. He is rarely able to escape from the straitjacket of the Augustan couplet, and he lacks the wit or the crispness of phrase to make that measure rise above the pedestrian. Yet *The Thresher's Labour* has moments of charm and authenticity. Its rueful account of harvest-time toils, of the unavailing attempts to find some mitigation or relief, still strike true:

> When sooty pease we thresh, you scarce can know
> Our native colour, as from work we go:
> The sweat and dust, and suffocating smoke,
> Make us so much like Etheopians look,
> We scare our wives when evening brings us home;
> And frightened infants think the Bugbear come.
> Week after week we this dull task pursue,
> Unless when winnowing days produce a new:
> A new, indeed, but frequently a worse!
> The threshal yields but to the master's curse.
> He counts the bushels, counts how much a day:
> Then swears we've idled half our time away ...

In this vein Duck is attractive and readable. All too often he allows himself to fall prey to the temptation of writing society verse, panegyric, and compliment. He has neither the poise nor the authority to make anything of such forms. Some of his verse tales are unjustly neglected, though. In "Felix and Constance" and in "Avaro and Amanda" he shows an ability to conduct narrative and the heavy diction adds a period charm to his tales. And in *The Shunammite* (a redaction of the Biblical story from 2 Kings iv) his simple faith lends a credibility and directness to the story and makes it very readable. Hence, while it may be fair to say that Duck's real importance is as a historical curiosity – the peasant poet in an age of great erudition – there is enough of his work which rises above mere curiosity value and makes him worthy of inclusion among the English poets.

—T. Bareham

DYER, John. Welsh. Born in Llanfynydd, Caermarthenshire, 13 August 1699. Educated at Westminster School, London; studied painting with Jonathan Richardson. Married Miss Ensor; one son and three daughters. After a brief period in his father's solicitor's office in Aberglasney, traveled in Italy and studied painting: practiced as an itinerant painter in South Wales. Ordained: vicar of Calthorpe, Leicestershire, 1741–51; held livings of Belchford, 1751–55, Coningsby, 1752, and Kirkby-on-Bane, 1755, all in Lincolnshire. LL.B.: Cambridge University, 1751. *Died in 1758.*

PUBLICATIONS

Collections

Poems, edited by Edward Thomas.   1903.
Minor Poets of the Eighteenth Century, edited by Hugh I'A. Fausset.   1930.

Verse

A New Miscellany, Being a Collection of Pieces of Poetry from Bath, Tunbridge, Oxford, Epsom, and Other Places in 1725.   1726; *Grongar Hill* edited by Richard C. Boys, 1941.
The Ruins of Rome.   1740.
The Fleece.   1757.
Poems.   1761.

Reading List: *Poet, Painter, and Parson: The Life of Dyer* by R. M. Williams, 1956.

*   *   *

Before he was a poet John Dyer was a painter, studying with Jonathan Richardson, and visiting Italy, and especially Rome, in 1724–25. His first considerable poem, *Grongar Hill* (most familiar in the final octosyllabic version which appeared in D. Lewis's *Miscellaneous Poems by Several Hands*, 1726), shows a painterly and sympathetic response to the scenery of the vale of Towy, and draws on the contemplative tradition of Milton's *Il Penseroso*. The poet narrates in his own person, relishing the various beauty of the opening landscape and meditating and moralising upon it. To a modern reader it may seem that the poem's sententious morality is at least as notable as its appreciation of a visualised natural scene, but it was as a picturesque nature-poem that *Grongar Hill* was chiefly appreciated in the eighteenth century, and by such romantics as Wordsworth and Southey.

Dyer's later, and longer, poems, *The Ruins of Rome* and *The Fleece*, have been less well known. *The Ruins of Rome* describes the decaying remains of ancient Rome as an English traveller, such as Dyer himself, might have seen them in his time. In this melancholy scene Dyer gives an account of the loss of Roman virtue and liberty in the luxury of empire, and infers a warning lesson for Britain. Written on the model of Virgil's *Georgics*, *The Fleece* is a didactic poem about the British wool trade, describing the progress of the wool from the sheep on the hillside to the sale of the cloth. Most English georgic poems of the eighteenth century tread an uneasy path on the frontiers of burlesque, but *The Fleece* is entirely serious, written on a subject capable of bearing some at least of the Miltonic grandeur with which Dyer loads it. Wool was the commercial basis of British empire, and *The Fleece* is, especially in its climactic fourth book, a remarkable work in an English tradition of patriotic poetry.

—Marcus Walsh

FALCONER, William. Scottish. Born in Edinburgh, 11 February 1732. Self-taught. Married Miss Hicks in 1763. Merchant seaman: served as a second mate on a ship that was wrecked on a voyage from Alexandria to Venice; entered the Royal Navy, 1762: midshipman on the *Royal George*, 1762–63; purser on the frigate *Glory*, 1763–67, and of the *Swiftsure*, 1767–68; purser on the *Aurora*, 1769, which went down with all hands near Capetown. *Died in December 1769.*

PUBLICATIONS

Collections

Poetical Works, with Blair and Beattie, edited by George Gilfillan.   1854.

Verse

A Poem on the Death of Frederick Prince of Wales.   1751.
The Shipwreck.   1762; revised edition, 1764, 1769.
Ode on the Duke of York's Departure.   1763.
The Demagogue.   1766.

Other

An Universal Dictionary of the Marine.   1769; abridged by Claude S. Gill, as *The Old Wooden Walls*, 1930.

Reading List: *Falconer: The Shipwreck* by J. Friedrich, 1901; "Falconer" by M. K. Joseph, in *Studies in Philology*, 1950.

*　　*　　*

A self-educated writer, William Falconer spent most of his short life at sea as a merchant-seaman and later as a half-pay purser, and was mysteriously lost at sea. Leaving aside some magazine-verse of little merit, his reputation rests on two main works, the *Universal Dictionary of the Marine* and the poem *The Shipwreck*.

The *Dictionary*, a distinguished product of its encyclopaedic age, is of great authority in its own field, thorough, well-organised, and written in plain, vigorous prose.

The Shipwreck is the story, presumably autobiographical, of a trading-ship, the *Britannia*, which sails from Crete about 1750, is caught in a violent storm, and driven on to the rocks of Cape Sounion (near Athens) where nearly the whole crew perish. In three successive editions Falconer carefully reworked the poem, doubling its length. The many nineteenth-century editions are all based on a conflated text; for anyone who wishes to read the original, the third is Falconer's considered and final version, but a reader might prefer what one early reviewer called the "copious simplicity" of the first.

Falconer's revisions turned this originally simple narrative, rather heavily loaded with nautical technicalities, into a short neo-classical epic with fictitious characters and set episodes, modelled on Virgil, Milton, Dryden, and Pope. Whether or not he consciously intended it, the revised poem contains a judicious mixture of elements which appealed to contemporary taste. The "social horrors" of the stormy sea are right in the tradition of the sublime, while the hard fates of the sailors and their interspersed stories, "the tides of social woe," appeal to "sensibility" and humanitarianism. There is an element of the descriptive picturesque, and a long survey passage (in Canto III) is a landmark in the growing appreciation of Grecian antiquities.

But what makes it an original work is its combination of the heroic couplet and other standard elements of late Augustan poetry with first-hand, matter-of-fact detail. Its basic reality is the *Britannia* itself, every part of which Falconer knows and can use, even though in revision he smoothes out the use of the technical vocabulary, the "terms of art." The prevailing emotion reflects his own experience of "the faithless sea." And the poem is animated by his ambition, which is also the force behind the *Dictionary*, to instruct his fellow-seamen, in this case through a didactic poem (a kind of graphic treatise on how to handle a ship in a storm), then to dignify their craft by a narrative with distinct epic overtones, and further to arouse in the British public a proper sympathy for the brave and dangerous lives of their "faithful sailors." It won the admiration of the nineteenth-century public and of poets as different as Blake and Byron, and (like the *Dictionary*) maintained its reputation until the end of the great sailing-ships.

—M. K. Joseph

FERGUSSON, Robert. Scottish. Born in Edinburgh, 5 September 1750. Educated at Edinburgh High School; Dundee High School; University of St. Andrews, 1765–68. Lawyer's Clerk, Edinburgh, 1769–73; Contributor, Ruddiman's *Weekly Magazine*, Edinburgh, 1771–73. Died insane from effects of a fall down stairs. *Died 16 October 1774.*

Publications

Collections

Poetical Works, edited by Matthew P. McDiarmid.   2 vols., 1954–56.
Poems of Allan Ramsay and Fergusson, edited by Alexander M. Kinghorn and Alexander Law.   1974.

Verse

Auld Reikie. 1773.
A Poem to the Memory of John Cunningham.   1773.
Poems.   1773; revised edition, as *Poems on Various Subjects,* 1779.

Bibliography: *Bibliography of Fergusson* by John A. Fairley, 1915.

Reading List: *Fergusson: Essays by Various Hands* edited by Sydney Goodsir Smith, 1952; *Fergusson* by Allan H. MacLaine, 1965; *Fergusson and the Edinburgh of His Time* by Alexander Law, 1974.

*   *   *

Robert Fergusson is, above all, the poet of Edinburgh. The bulk of his significant work consists of brilliant satiric portraits of his beloved city in the 1770's, of the teeming, dramatic life of the streets and taverns. In depicting this world of the Old Town more vividly perhaps than any other writer has done, he uses traditional Scots poetic forms such as the 6-line *Habbie Simson* stanza (or "Burns stanza"), the stanza of "Christis Kirk on the Green," and tetrameter couplets; but he adapts these metres to new and modern purposes, thereby setting vital technical precedents for the work of Burns a few years later.

Fergusson's most characteristic genre is the poem of humorous social description, usually good-natured in tone, but occasionally marked by sharp satiric thrusts at sham or corruption. Among his more genial treatments of Edinburgh life are such pieces as "The Daft-Days," "The King's Birth-Day in Edinburgh," "Mutual Complaint of Plainstanes and Causey," "Caller Oysters," "Hallow-fair," and "Leith Races." In "The King's Birth-Day," for example, he makes fun of the custom of stilted, ceremonial "birthday odes," and opens with a hilarious burlesque invocation to the Muse (addressed as though she were a barmaid being warmed up with whisky for the task at hand); he then goes on to depict the livelier social aspects of the annual celebration. "Plainstanes and Causey" is a highly original fantasy, a kind of "flyting eclogue" between the sidewalk and roadway of the High Street which, by a clever twist, turns into a light-hearted social satire on Edinburgh street life. Similarly, in "Caller Oysters" the sea food serves only as a springboard for a humorous commentary on Edinburgh drinking habits.

In others of his town poems Fergusson cuts a little deeper. "Braid Claith," a small gem of a poem, is pure satire on a universal theme – pride in dress, symbolizing a whole social attitude. Here Fergusson clinches his theme with remarkable economy of expression:

> Braid Claith lends fock an unco heese,*   *Lift
> Makes mony kail-worms butter-flies,
> Gies mony a doctor his degrees
>   For little skaith:
> In short, you may be what you please
>   Wi' gude Braid Claith.

Again, in "The Election" and especially in "The Ghaists" he introduces pointed attacks on political corruption. The latter is informed by a strong spirit of Scottish nationalism, deploring the Union with England, a theme which Fergusson voiced repeatedly in such poems as "Hame Content" and "A Drink Eclogue."

The most ambitious of Fergusson's Edinburgh sketches, however, is *Auld Reikie*, a panoramic poem with morning, afternoon, and evening scenes, in which he attempts to capture the essence of the whole city. His method here is one of dramatic contrast, and it works extremely well. Fergusson perceives that the unique atmosphere of old Edinburgh lies in the startling contrasts, both physical and social, which the city presents. Thus, he juxtaposes images of beauty and squalor − a picture of the fleeting loveliness of sunrise over the ancient spire of St. Giles followed by a passage on the foul morning smell of sewage, a scene of drunkenness and bestiality followed by one of wholesome merriment and friendship. The total effect is cumulative and powerfully evocative, one of the finest treatments of city life in British poetry.

Apart from the Edinburgh poems, Fergusson achieved notable work in other directions. He wrote well in special traditional Scottish genres such as the verse epistle and the comic elegy, for example. In the latter form his "Elegy on John Hogg" has been judged the most brilliant specimen in Scots poetry. Even more important, however, was his development of Scottish pastoralism. In this realm, especially in the piece entitled "An Eclogue," he far surpassed his predecessor Allan Ramsay in the direction of convincing realism. More ambitious is the remarkable poem in modified Spenserian stanzas called "The Farmer's Ingle," which became the obvious model for Burns's more pretentious "Cotter's Saturday Night." Here Fergusson, in his most important serious poem, gives us a slightly idealized picture of Scottish rural life built upon the cumulative impression of simple, homely details. The effect, in its modest, well-wrought fashion, is strangely moving and impressive.

Because of his catalytic impact upon Burns, Fergusson has too often been considered a mere "forerunner," a lucky poet who is important only because he happened to have influenced Burns, rather than as a creative artist in his own right. Yet Fergusson's work has a perennial freshness, an enduring appeal. Though he seldom goes deeply below the surface of life, he has a bold yet sensitive imagination, a finished artistry of style, and a genial, s '8. - . His significant poetic career was pitifully brief (about two years); consequently his work is small in bulk and relatively narrow in scope; but within its special range it is unquestionably the finest body of Scots poetry of the eighteenth century before Burns.

—Allan H. MacLaine

GARTH, Sir Samuel. English. Born in Bowland Forest, Yorkshire, in 1661. Educated at Peterhouse, Cambridge, B.A. 1679, M.A. 1684, M.D. 1691; also studied medicine in Leyden, 1687; Fellow of the Royal College of Physicians, 1693. Married Martha Beaufoy (died, 1717); one daughter. Practised as a physician in London from 1693 until the end of his life: delivered the Gulstonian lecture, 1694, Harveian oration, 1697, and the funeral oration for Dryden, 1700, at the Royal College of Physicians, London; member of the Kit-Cat Club, London, 1702; knighted and appointed Physician-in-Ordinary to King George I and Physician-General to the Army, 1714. *Died 18 January 1719.*

PUBLICATIONS

Collections

Works, edited by A. Chalmers.   1810.

Verse

The Dispensary.   1699; revised edition, 1700, 1706; edited by F. H. Ellis, in *Poems on Affairs of State 6,* 1971.
A Poem to the Earl of Godolphin.   1710.
Claremont.   1715.

Other

Translator, with others, *Ovid's Metamorphoses.*   1717.

Reading List: *Garth und Seine Stellung zum Komischen Epos* by T. Schenk, 1900.

*   *   *

The Dispensary is the only poem of Sir Samuel Garth's we now remember. This mock-heroic account of the squabble between the College of Physicians and the apothecaries over the charitable dispensing of medicines to the poor of London was written by Garth (a member of the College) "to rally some of our disaffected members into a sense of their duty." The poem influenced Pope's *Rape of the Lock,* but it is wrong to remember *The Dispensary* only for this.

Garth has dexterity with words and a robust wit: he lacks the exquisite tact with which Pope can juxtapose the trivial and the serious, or the sustained grandiloquence with which Dryden annihilates his adversaries. Garth's Whiggish insistence on flattery of William III can also be tedious, and his personal involvement in the quarrel makes the dispassionate rallying tone difficult to sustain; nevertheless, his rumbustious fun deserves to be better known, offering an English counterpart to Boileau's *Le Lutrin,* with which *The Dispensary* has affinities. Lee, the warden of Apothecaries Hall, is thus described:

> In trifling show his tinsel talent lies;
> And form the want of intellect supplies....
> Hourly his learn'd impertinence affords
> A barren superfluity of words;
> The patient's ears remorseless he assails,
> Murders with jargon where his medicine fails.

Garth's own lazy colleagues are epigramatised: "Each faculty in blandishment they lull/ Aspiring to be venerably dull." The action of the poem includes mock-heroic debates, visions, a battle, a descent to the underworld – all garnished with solemn epic similes. Garth was probably the first Englishman to employ all of these devices in one satirical-comic poem. Here he describes the rumpus at its height:

> Whole heaps of warriors welter on the ground,
> With gally-pots and broken phials crowned;
> Whilst empty jars the dire defeat resound.
> Thus when some storm its crystal quarry rends,
> And Jove in rattling showers of ice descends;
> Mount Athos shakes the forests on his brow,
> Whilst down his wounded sides fresh torrents flow,
> And leaves and limbs of trees o'erspread the vale below.

This is predictable, if nicely contrived. Less expected is Garth's sense of wonderment at Nature:

> Eternal Spring with smiling verdure here
> Warms the mild air, and crowns the youthful year.
> The vine undress'd her swelling clusters bears,
> The labouring hind the mellow olive cheers;
> Blossoms and fruit at once the citron shews,
> And, as she pays, discovers still she owes.
> The orange to her sun her pride displays,
> And gilds her fragrant apples with his rays.

A similar view runs through *Claremont*, Garth's pastoral panygyric based on Denham's *Cooper's Hill*, where it is accompanied by some shrewd social commentary. This poem never gained the popularity which *The Dispensary* rightly achieved in Garth's lifetime. It is a loss to modern readers that the responses required in the reading of mock-heroic are no longer readily accessible.

—T. Bareham

GAY, John. English.   Born in Barnstaple, Devon, baptized 16 September 1685. Educated at the free grammar school in Barnstaple; apprenticed to a silk mercer in London. Secretary to the household of the Duchess of Monmouth, 1712–14; Secretary to the Earl of Clarendon on his diplomatic mission to Hanover, 1714; accompanied William Pulteney, later Earl of Bath, to Aix, 1717; lived at Lord Harcourt's estate in Oxfordshire, 1718; earned considerable income from publication of his collected poems, 1720, and made and lost a fortune in South Sea funds speculation; Commissioner for the Public Lottery, 1722–31; recovered much of his fortune from the success of the *Beggar's Opera*, 1728; lived with his patrons the Duke and Duchess of Queensberry, 1728–32. *Died 4 December 1732.*

PUBLICATIONS

Collections

Poetical, Dramatic, and Miscellaneous Works.   6 vols., 1795.
Plays.   2 vols., 1923.

Poetical Works, edited by G. C. Faber. 1926.
Letters, edited by Chester F. Burgess. 1966.
Poetry and Prose, edited by Vinton A. Dearing and Charles Beckwith. 2 vols., 1974.
Selected Works, edited by Samuel Joseloff. 1976.

Verse

Wine. 1708.
Rural Sports. 1713; revised edition, 1720; edited by O. Culbertson, 1930.
The Fan. 1714.
The Shepherd's Week. 1714.
A Letter to a Lady. 1714.
Two Epistles, One to the Earl of Burlington, The Other to a Lady. 1715(?).
Trivia; or, The Art of Walking the Streets of London. 1716.
Horace, epode iv, Imitated. 1717(?).
The Poor Shepherd. 1720(?).
Poems on Several Occasions. 2 vols., 1720.
A Panegyrical Epistle to Mr. Thomas Snow. 1721.
An Epistle to Her Grace Henrietta Duchess of Marlborough. 1722.
A Poem Addressed to the Quidnunc's. 1724.
Blueskin's Ballad. 1725.
To a Lady on Her Passion for Old China. 1725.
Daphnis and Cloe. 1725(?).
Molly Mog. 1726.
Fables. 2 vols., 1727–38; edited by Vinton A. Dearing, 1967.
Some Unpublished Translations from Ariosto, edited by J. D. Bruce. 1910.

Plays

The Mohocks. 1712.
The Wife of Bath (produced 1713). 1713; revised version (produced 1730), 1730.
The What D'ye Call It (produced 1715). 1715.
Three Hours after Marriage, with Pope and Arbuthnot (produced 1717). 1717; revised
    version, in *Supplement to the Works of Pope,* 1757; 1717 edition edited by Richard
    Morton and William Peterson, 1961.
Acis and Galatea, music by Handel (produced 1719). 1732.
Dione, in *Poems on Several Occasions.* 1720.
The Captives (produced 1724). 1724.
The Beggar's Opera (produced 1728). 1728; edited by Peter Lewis, 1973.
Polly, Being the 2nd Part of The Beggar's Opera (version revised by Colman the Elder
    produced 1777). 1729; in *Poetical Works,* 1926.
Achilles (produced 1733). 1733.
The Distressed Wife (produced 1743). 1743; as *The Modern Wife* (produced 1771).
The Rehearsal at Goatham. 1754.

Other

The Present State of Wit. 1711.
*An Argument Proving That the Present Mohocks and Hawkubites Are the Gog and Magog
    Mentioned in the Revelations.* 1712.

Bibliography: in *Poetical Works*, 1926; *Gay: An Annotated Checklist of Criticism* by Julie T. Klein, 1973.

Reading List: *Gay, Favorite of the Wits* by William H. Irving, 1940; *Gay, Social Critic* by Sven M. Armens, 1954; *Gay* by Oliver Warner, 1964; *Gay* by Patricia M. Spacks, 1965.

*   *   *

Although John Gay was one of the most talented English writers in the first third of the eighteenth century, he is overshadowed by his two close friends and fellow-members of the Scriblerus Club, Swift and Pope. Comparisons with the two literary giants of the period are therefore inevitable and usually to Gay's detriment, which is unfortunate since his gifts are significantly different from theirs. It is unfair to think of Gay as a lesser Swift or a lesser Pope. Gay certainly lacks the emotional intensity, intellectual power, and penetrating insight of Swift's great satires, and rarely equals Pope in refined verbal wit, imaginative inventiveness, and incisive irony. The all-embracing cultural survey of *Gulliver's Travels* or even the moral breadth of Pope's *Moral Essays* and *Imitations of Horace* were beyond Gay, as were the gloomy visionary quality and sustained mock-heroic elaboration of *The Dunciad*. Gay's mature work does not seem to stem from a firm ideological foundation of inter-connected philosophical ideas, political convictions and moral values in the way that Swift's and Pope's do. Nevertheless Swift and Pope are not the measure of all Augustan writers as they are sometimes thought to be, and Gay, although influenced by his two friends, usually followed his own creative impulses and did not attempt to do what they were doing. As a result he acquired a distinctive literary voice, less relentless and angry than Swift's, less acerbic and barbed than Pope's, more genial, warm-hearted and gentle than both. His satirical and burlesque works, for example, are less single-minded than theirs, so that his ridicule is often tempered with sentiment, producing a bitter-sweet amalgam that is very much Gay's own and that is particularly evident in his masterpiece, *The Beggar's Opera*. Furthermore Gay, with his less fixed intellectual commitment, was much more chameleon-like than his friends, which helps to explain the extraordinary diversity of his output.

In addition to being a versatile poet, he was a fairly prolific playwright in both verse and prose, and the only member of the Scriblerus Club to devote himself to drama. Indeed it is as the author of *The Beggar's Opera* that he is best remembered today. As a dramatist he did not restrict himself to the "regular" and neoclassically respectable genres of tragedy and comedy but attempted most of the theatrical forms of the period; and with *The Beggar's Opera* he actually invented the ballad opera, which became very popular in the eighteenth century and is the precursor of English comic opera and of the modern musical, as well as being an important influence on Brecht. Gay began his dramatic career with a short farce, *The Mohocks*, and followed this with an undistinguished comedy based on Chaucer, *The Wife of Bath*, before turning his hand to two very different satirical plays. The popular *The What D'Ye Call It* is a fine burlesque of contemporary tragedy, especially "pathetic" plays, that succeeds in transcending burlesque, while the controversial *Three Hours after Marriage*, written as a Scriblerian enterprise with Pope and Arbuthnot, is a lively and frequently farcical dramatic satire attacking a number of well-known contemporary intellectuals and artists. Not long after this he provided Handel with a libretto for his pastoral opera *Acis and Galatea* and then made two not particularly successful attempts at tragedy, *Dione*, written in couplets and in a pastoral and sentimental vein, and *The Captives*, a blank-verse tragedy in a more heroic manner that ends happily with virtue rewarded and poetic justice established. Next came by far his greatest theatrical success, *The Beggar's Opera*, a truly original work of genius and one of the very few eighteenth-century plays to hold the stage until the present day. By using a mixture of speech and song and by providing his own words for well-known tunes, Gay created a new kind of music theatre, the ballad opera, while simultaneously burlesquing Italian opera, which was enjoying a vogue in England. In addition *The Beggar's Opera*, set in the London underworld, is a most unusual love-story, both romantic and anti-romantic, as well as a pungently ironic social and political satire. Amazingly enough, Gay was able to weld these diverse elements together into a unified work of art that manages to be both highly topical and universal. After the unprecedented commercial success of *The Beggar's Opera*, Gay wrote an inferior sequel, *Polly*, which was banned from the stage by the Government, offended by the scathing political ridicule of its predecessor. None of his three posthumous plays, *Achilles*, a farcical treatment of a classical legend in ballad-opera form, and the two satirical comedies, *The Distress'd Wife* and *The Rehearsal at Goatham*, adds much to his dramatic achievement.

The range and variety of his dramatic work is matched by that of his poetry, although the quality is again decidedly uneven. He wrote mock-heroic poetry, notably *The Fan*, which is indebted to *The Rape of the Lock*, an extended georgic in the manner of Virgil, *Rural Sports*, a group of pastoral poems, *The Shepherd's Week*, which burlesque Ambrose Philips's *Pastorals* yet are much more than burlesque; a long mock-georgic about London life, laced with acute social observations, guide-book advice and moral precepts, *Trivia; or, The Art of Walking the Streets of London*; a number of urbane verse *Epistles* to friends on various topics; a set of ironic *Eclogues*, mainly Town Eclogues about fashionable women and love; two series of *Fables* in the manner of Aesop and La Fontaine; various narrative poems, including bawdy tales inspired by Chaucer's *fabliaux*; a few meditative poems such as "A Contemplation on Night" (1714); some lyrics and ballads including the well-known "Sweet William's Farewell to Black-ey'd Susan" (1720); and translations of Ovid and Ariosto. Although much of his poetry is written in decasyllabic couplets, the standard form of the time, Gay is again more varied than many of his contemporaries since he uses the lighter and racier octosyllabic couplets for the *Fables* and some of the tales, blank verse for his early mock-heroic *Wine*, ottava rima for one of his best Epistles, "Mr. Pope's Welcome from Greece," and a variety of stanza forms for his songs and ballads. His finest poetic achievement is the first series of *Fables*, ostensibly written to entertain a young member of the Royal Family but, as in the case of earlier fable literature, having a much wider moral, social, and political significance than the apparently innocuous subject-matter suggests. Gay's *Fables* are not of the supreme quality of La Fontaine's but they remain the best examples of their kind in English since Henryson's admirable adaptations of Aesop into Middle Scots. *Trivia*, which has been claimed to be the finest poem about London in the language, is also a genuinely individual work revealing some of his best qualities: his observant eye for detail, his great sympathy for ordinary humanity, his down-to-earth good sense, his sturdy versification, and plain, unfussy diction. *The Shepherd's Week* is probably the most important Augustan contribution to the genre of pastoral. Much of Gay's work is now of interest only to the specialist, but in a few cases, notably the *Fables* and above all *The Beggar's Opera*, he transcends his own time and must therefore rank as a major Augustan writer.

—Peter Lewis

GIBBON, Edward. English. Born in Putney, London, 27 April 1737. Educated at a day school in Putney; Dr. Wooddeson's school in Kingston-on-Thames, Surrey, 1746; Westminster ool, London, 1749–50; Magdalen College, Oxford (gentleman commoner), 1752–53; with Reverend M. Pavillard in Lausanne, 1753–58. Served in the Hampshire Militia, 1759–70: Major and Colonel Commandant. Toured Italy, 1764–65; settled in London, 1772, and began to write his history; joined Dr. Johnson's Literary Club, 1774; became Professor of Ancient History at the Royal Academy, 1774; Member of Parliament for Liskeard, 1774–80, and for Lymington, 1781–83: Commissioner of Trade and Plantations, 1779–82; lived in Lausanne, 1783–93, then returned to London. *Died 16 January 1794.*

Collections

Letters, edited by J. E. Norton.   3 vols., 1956.

Prose

Essai sur l'Etude de la Littérature.   1761; translated, as *An Essay on the Study of Literature,* 1764; revised edition, in *Miscellaneous Works,* 1837.
Mémoires Littéraires de la Grand Bretagne pour l'An 1767, with Jacques Georges Deyverdun.   1768.
Critical Observations on the Sixth Book of the Aeneid.   1770.
The History of the Decline and Fall of the Roman Empire.   6 vols., 1776–88; edited by J. B. Bury, 7 vols., 1926–29.
A Vindication of Some Passages in the Decline and Fall of the Roman Empire.   1779; revised edition, 1779.
Miscellaneous Works.   2 vols., 1796; revised edition, 1814, 1837.
Memoirs.   2 vols., 1827; edited by Georges A. Bonnard, 1966.
Journal to January 28th 1763, My Journal 1, 2, and 3, and Ephemerides.   1929.
Le Journal à Lausanne 17 Août 1763–19 Avril 1764, edited by Georges A. Bonnard.   1945.
Miscellanea Gibboniana, edited by G. R. de Beer, Georges A. Bonnard, and L. Junod.   1952.
Gibbon's Journey from Geneva to Rome: His Journal from 20 April to 2 October 1764, edited by Georges A. Bonnard.   1961.
Autobiography, edited by M. M. Reese.   1970.
The English Essays, edited by Patricia Craddock.   1972.

Bibliography: *A Bibliography of the Works of Gibbon* by Jane E. Norton, 1940; *Gibbon: A Handlist of Critical Notices and Studies* by F. Cordasco, 1950.

Reading List: *Gibbon* by Michael Joyce, 1953; *Gibbon* by C. V. Wedgwood, 1955; *The Literary Art of Gibbon* by H. L. Bond, 1960; *Gibbon the Historian* by Joseph W. Swain, 1966; *Gibbon and His World* by G. R. de Beer, 1968; *Narrative Form in History and Fiction* by Leo Braudy, 1970.

*   *   *

The last great English tragedy, according to E. M. W. Tillyard, was Edward Gibbon's *Decline and Fall.* It is a tragedy without a hero, though there are several candidates, and without even a villain. But it portrays the destruction of something great and beautiful, doomed more by its own fatal flaws than by the efforts of its enemies. And it is embellished by three qualities of great literature: brilliantly clear and exciting narrative, ironic wit, and majestically beautiful prose.

To sustain the intensity of a tragic drama for six volumes would of course be impossible for writer or reader. Instead, Gibbon divided the story into a number of discrete episodes, each with its own tragic action, its temporary relief, its finally inadequate heroes. After a three-chapter prologue describing the Roman Empire in the age of the Antonines, "the period in the history of the world in which the condition of the human race was most happy," the first three volumes are devoted to the successive stages of decline before the capture of Italy by the barbarians that marks the end of the Roman Empire in the West. The three volumes end with an epilogue, the "General Observations on the Fall of the Roman Empire in the West." The theme here discovered and pronounced is certainly worthy of tragedy: "the decline of Rome was the natural and inevitable effect of immoderate greatness."

The last three volumes, the account of the Eastern Empire, have a similar structure. Introductory chapters describe transient hopes and achievements, a Gothic king in Italy "who might have deserved a statue among the best and bravest of the ancient Romans," and the achievements of Justinian, Emperor of the East for nearly forty years, and his great general Belisarius. A final chapter again completes the frame, this time with a chronicle of the fortunes and decay of the city of Rome itself, a vast metonymy for Roman civilization. Although this latter half of the *Decline and Fall* suffered most from Gibbon's ignorance and biasses and has therefore been most fully superseded for historians by subsequent histories, its presentation of the theme that the rise of new cultural syntheses is experienced as the loss and destruction of the old is timeless. "I have described the triumphs of barbarism and religion," says Gibbon in the final chapter. In the glaring irony of the coupled causes, it is sometimes overlooked that he confesses to having described triumphs.

Though the *Decline and Fall* far outshines his other work, Gibbon is not a one-book author. Of the two other English works he published in his lifetime, the *Vindication* is a masterpiece of polemic. More important, however, is Gibbon's posthumous masterpiece, his history of himself. This work, which André Maurois called one of the few "perfect examples" of autobiography, gives the reader the literary pleasures of relating character and fate to experience, of the wit and elegance of Gibbon's prose, together with the interest of honest historical testimony. It is unmatched as an account of the growth of a great scholar's mind. Thus the *Memoirs*, like the *Decline and Fall*, is not merely a contribution to our knowledge of the past, but permanently valuable literature.

—Patricia Craddock

GOLDSMITH, Oliver. Irish. Born in Pallas, near Ballymahon, Longford. 10 November 1728. Educated at the village school in Lissoy, West Meath, 1734–37; Elphin School, 1738; a school in Athlone, 1739–41, and in Edgeworthstown, Longford, 1741–44; Trinity College, Dublin (sizar), 1745–49 (Smyth exhibitioner, 1747), B.A. 1749; studied medicine at the University of Edinburgh, 1752–53; travelled on the Continent, in Switzerland, Italy and France, 1753–56, and may have obtained a medical degree. Settled in London, 1756; tried unsuccessfully to support himself as a physician in Southwark; worked as an usher in Dr. Milner's classical academy in Peckham, 1756, and as a writer for Ralph Griffiths, proprietor of the *Monthly Review*, 1757–58; Editor, *The Bee*, 1759; contributed to the *British Magazine*, 1760; Editor, *The Lady's Magazine*, 1761; also worked for the publisher Edward Newbery: worked as a proof-reader and preface writer, contributed to the *Public Ledger*, 1760, and prepared a *Compendium of Biography*, 7 volumes, 1762; after 1763 earned increasingly substantial sums from his own writing; one of the founder members of Samuel Johnson's Literary Club, 1764. *Died 4 April 1774.*

PUBLICATIONS

Collections

Collected Letters, edited by Katharine C. Balderston.   1928.
Collected Works, edited by Arthur Friedman.   5 vols., 1966.
Poems and Plays, edited by Tom Davis.   1975.

Plays

The Good Natured Man (produced 1768).   1768.
The Grumbler, from a translation by Charles Sedley of a work by Brueys (produced
    1773).   Edited by Alice I. P. Wood, 1931.
She Stoops to Conquer; or, The Mistakes of a Night (produced 1773).   1773; edited by
    Arthur Friedman, 1968.
Threnodia Augustalis, Sacred to the Memory of the Princess Dowager of Wales, music by
    Mattia Vento (produced 1772).   1772.
The Captivity (oratorio), in *Miscellaneous Works*.   1820.

Fiction

The Vicar of Wakefield.   1766; edited by Arthur Friedman, 1974.

Verse

The Traveller; or, A Prospect of Society.   1764.
Poems for Young Ladies in Three Parts, Devotional, Moral, and Entertaining.   1767.
The Deserted Village.   1770.
Retaliation.   1774.
The Haunch of Venison: A Poetical Epistle to Lord Clare.   1776.

Other

An Enquiry into the Present State of Polite Learning in Europe.   1759.
The Bee.   1759.
The Mystery Revealed.   1762.
*The Citizen of the World; or, Letters from a Chinese Philosopher Residing in London to
    His Friends in the East*.   2 vols., 1762.
The Life of Richard Nash of Bath.   1762.
An History of England in a Series of Letters from a Nobleman to His Son.   2 vols., 1764.
An History of the Martyrs and Primitive Fathers of the Church.   1764.
Essays.   1765; revised edition, 1766.
The Present State of the British Empire in Europe, America, Africa and Asia.   1768.
*The Roman History, from the Foundation of the City of Rome to the Destruction of the
    Western Empire*.   2 vols., 1769; abridged edition, 1772.
The Life of Thomas Parnell.   1770.
The Life of Henry St. John, Lord Viscount Bolingbroke.   1770.
The History of England, from the Earliest Times to the Death of George II.   4 vols.,
    1771; abridged edition, 1774.

The Grecian History, from the Earliest State to the Death of Alexander the Great. 2 vols., 1774.
An History of the Earth and Animated Nature. 8 vols., 1774.
A Survey of Experimental Philosophy, Considered in Its Present State of Improvement. 2 vols., 1776.

Editor, *The Beauties of English Poesy.* 2 vols., 1767.

Translator, *The Memoirs of a Protestant,* by J. Marteilhe. 2 vols., 1758; edited by A. Dobson, 1895.
Translator, *Plutarch's Lives.* 4 vols., 1762.
Translator, *A Concise History of Philosophy and Philosophers,* by M. Formey. 1766.
Translator, *The Comic Romance of Scarron.* 2 vols., 1775.

Bibliography: *Goldsmith Bibliographically and Biographically Considered* by Temple Scott, 1928.

Reading List: *Goldsmith* by Ralph Wardle, 1957; *Goldsmith* by Clara M. Kirk, 1967; *Goldsmith: A Georgian Study* by Ricardo Quintana, 1967; *Life of Goldsmith* by Henry A. Dobson, 1972; *Goldsmith* by A. Lytton Sells, 1974; *Goldsmith: The Critical Heritage,* edited by George S. Rousseau, 1974; *The Notable Man: The Life and Times of Goldsmith* by John Ginger, 1977.

*   *   *

Oliver Goldsmith's reputation is made up of paradox. His blundering, improvident nature nevertheless won him the loyalty and friendship of figures like Dr. Johnson, Sir Joshua Reynolds, and Edmund Burke. While in society he was a buffoon, his writing testifies to personal charm and an ironic awareness of his own and others' absurdity. Critical opinion of his work similarly varies from acceptance of Goldsmith as the sensitive apologist for past values to appraisal of him as an accomplished social and literary satirist. Indeed, his work can operate on both levels, a fact perhaps recognised by the young Jane Austen in her *Juvenilia* when she took Goldsmith's abridgements of history for young persons as a model for her own exercise in irony.

Drifting into authorship after a mis-spent youth (as Macaulay notes in his disapproving *Life*), Goldsmith turned to hack writing, contributing articles to the *Monthly* and *Critical Reviews* from 1757. His more ambitious *Inquiry into the Present State of Polite Learning* of 1759 won him the reputation of a man of learning and elegant expression. In this last essay he reveals his fundamental dislike of the contemporary cult of sensibility which was to generate not only his own "laughing" form of comedy in the drama but also *The Vicar of Wakefield*. Meeting Smollett, then editor of the *British Magazine*, Goldsmith was encouraged to expand his contributions to literary journalism. He produced the weekly periodical *The Bee*; many papers collected and published in 1765 and 1766 as *Essays*; and, most important, the "Chinese Letters" of 1760–61 collected as *The Citizen of the World*.

The "citizen" is, of course, an Oriental traveller, observing the fashions and foibles of the *bon ton* in London with wide-eyed innocence that carries within it implicit comment and criticism not unmixed with humour. The device was borrowed from the French, notably Montesquieu's *Lettres Persanes* (1721). In each essay the absurdities of behaviour are marked, the whole inter-woven by continuing narratives around the Man in Black, Beau Tibbs, the story of Hingo and Zelis, for instance. In many ways the ironies, improbabilities, and apparent innocence of the Chinese letters prefigure the extended prose romance of *The Vicar of Wakefield*.

This could be seen as Goldsmith's answer to Sterne's *Tristram Shandy* (1759). He had attacked Sterne's sentimental fiction as "obscene and pert" in *The Citizen*; in many ways *The Vicar* parodies Sterne's novel but with such a light hand that it has been taken on face value for many generations as the tale indeed of a family "generous, credulous, simple, and inoffensive." However, Goldsmith early establishes for the observant the manifest danger of complacency in such apparent virtues. His Yorkshire parson displays the moral duplicity of a feeling heart, for Goldsmith's approach to life and art is the opposite of Sterne's relativism and dilettante values.

Oliver Goldsmith's moral seriousness (while softened by genial good humour) dominates that other work now considered "classic," *The Deserted Village*. His earlier sortie in the genre of topographical/philosophical verse, *The Traveller*, did much to establish his reputation. It is an accomplished use of convention, where the poet climbs an eminence only to have his mind expanded into contemplation of universal questions. In *The Deserted Village*, however, the poet comes to terms with a particular social problem in a particular landscape as opposed to former abstract musings above imaginary solitudes. "Sweet Auburn" can be identified closely with the village of Nuneham Courtenay, where the local land-owner had recently moved the whole community out in order to extend and improve his landscape park. The fact becomes a catalyst for Goldsmith in a consideration of where aesthetic values and irresponsible wealth lead: a symbol taken from life and not from poetic convention.

Goldsmith's rhymed couplets have grace and ease, particularly when his verse is unlaboured, as in the prologues and epilogues to his own and others' plays. The charm and humour of these can be observed in his later poem *Retaliation*, which has a pointed raciness born out of the settling of personal scores. Always the butt of jokes in the group known as The Club, here he gets his own back with a series of comic epitaphs for the other members. Notable is that for Garrick – "On the stage he was natural, simple, affecting; Twas only that when he was off he was acting" – but he labels himself the "gooseberry fool."

As a dramatist, Goldsmith exploited both verbal dexterity and the comedy of situation, looking back to Shakespeare in the rejection of the so-called genteel comedy of Hugh Kelly or Richard Cumberland. Affected and strained in tone and action, the drama of sentiment offered to Goldsmith nothing of the "nature and humour" that he saw as the first principle of theatre. However he might despise the sentimental school, he cannot avoid using some of its conventions, the good-natured hero, of course, and the device of paired lovers, but the way these are treated is particular to himself. Together with Sheridan, Goldsmith exploits the theatrical unreality of comedy, using the stage as a separate world of experience with its own laws and therefore demanding the suspension of disbelief in order that farcical unreality might unmask farcical reality. His character Honeydew in *The Good Natured Man* has something in common with Charles Surface in *School for Scandal*, but the tone of Goldsmith's comedy is less brittle than that of Sheridan. This mellow tone, a fundamental wholesomeness, is magnificently encapsulated in *She Stoops to Conquer*.

Oliver Goldsmith's first play met with a poor response, as being too "low" in its matter (especially the bailiffs scene), and, though *She Stoops to Conquer* was open to similar criticism, its riotous humour overcame prejudice. In short, it was good theatre and this is testified by its continuing popularity in production. Characters like Tony Lumpkin, Mrs. Hardcastle, and the old Squire have become literary personalities, while the pivot of the plot, Marlow's loss of diffidence in apparently more relaxed circumstances, holds true to human nature. The character of Kate is a liberated heroine in the Shakespearean style, contrasted as in the older comedy with a foil. One is able to relate Goldsmith's "laughing" comedy to that of Shakespeare in many ways, for the Lord of Misrule dominates both.

The range of Goldsmith's work is touched by this same humour and sensitivity, the good heart that is so easily squandered as he himself acknowledged in *The Good Natured Man*, but is just as easily extended with purpose to the reader. As Walter Scott observed, no man contrived "so well to reconcile us to human nature."

—B. C. Oliver-Morden

GRAINGER, James.   Scottish.   Born in Duns, Berwickshire, c. 1721. Educated at a school in North Berwick; studied medicine at the University of Edinburgh, M.D. 1753; Licentiate of the Royal College of Physicians, 1758. Served as an Army Surgeon, 1745–48. Married Miss Daniel Mathew Burt in 1759; two daughters. Practised medicine in London from 1753, but was more successful as a writer than as a physician; a friend of Dr. Johnson, Bishop Percy, and Smollett; contributor to the *Monthly Review*, London, 1756–58; lived and practised medicine in St. Christopher in the West Indies, 1759–66. *Died 16 December 1766.*

PUBLICATIONS

Collections

Poetical Works, edited by R. Anderson.   2 vols., 1836.

Verse

A Poetical Translation of Tibullus and Sulpicia.   2 vols., 1759.
The Sugar-Cane.   1764.

Other

Historia Febris Anomalae Batavae.   1753.
An Essay on the More Common West Indian Diseases.   1764.

Translator, *Cyclops,* by Euripides, in *The Greek Theatre of Father Brumoy.*   3 vols., 1759.

*   *   *

Though Johnson said that his "Ode on Solitude" (Dodsley's *Collection*, iv, 1755) was "very noble," and Percy considered his ballad "Bryan and Pereene" worth including in the first volume of the *Reliques* (1765), James Grainger's only notable poem is his 2,500 lines-long didactic blank-verse poem in four books, *The Sugar-Cane*. This poem describes with appropriate narrative and descriptive digressions the cultivation of sugar cane in the West Indies, the manufacture of sugar, and the management of negro slaves. It is avowedly an imitation of Virgil's *Georgics*, and thus claims a place alongside John Philips's *Cyder*, Somerville's *The Chace*, Smart's *The Hop-Garden* and Dyer's *The Fleece*, all of which are mentioned in Grainger's poem. *The Sugar-Cane* is more remorselessly didactic than any of those earlier eighteenth-century English georgics (for Grainger's botanical, etymological, geographical, historical, medical, zoological, and other notes to his text are as bulky as the poem itself), and deals with a novel, exotic subject which, according to Grainger's Preface, "could not fail to enrich poetry with many new and picturesque images"; but Grainger contrives only to be turgid where he tries to be sublime, and silly where he tries to be sentimental. There is a saving touch of the mock-heroic from time to time, but even here the poet is clumsy and his effects laboured. *The Sugar-Cane* fails absolutely to recapture anything approaching Virgil's perfect blend of the epical and the mundane; and so, perhaps, it is not unjust that the poem is best remembered in literary history on account of the mirth occasioned when Grainger read his manuscript to Sir Joshua Reynolds and his friends, and, after much blank-verse pomp, began a new paragraph with the words: "Now, Muse, let's sing of Rats."

—A. J. Sambrook

GRAY, Thomas. English. Born in Cornhill, London, 26 December 1716. Educated at Eton College, 1727–34; Peterhouse, Cambridge, 1734–39, 1742–43, LL.B. 1743; also studied law in London, 1741. Accompanied Horace Walpole on a grand tour of France and Italy, in 1739–41. Lived in Cambridge, as a don, at Peterhouse, 1741–56, and Pembroke Hall, 1756–71; Professor of Modern History, Cambridge University, 1768. *Died 30 July 1771.*

PUBLICATIONS

Collections

   Works in Prose and Verse, edited by Edmund Gosse.   4 vols., 1884.
   Correspondence, edited by Paget Toynbee and Leonard Whibley.   3 vols., 1935.
   Complete Poems, English, Latin, and Greek, edited by H. W. Starr and J. R. Hendrickson.   1966.
   Complete English Poems, edited by James Reeves.   1973.
   Poetical Works, with Collins, edited by R. H. Lonsdale.   1977.

Verse

   Ode on a Distant Prospect of Eton College.   1747.
   An Elegy Wrote in a Country Church Yard.   1751.
   Designs by Mr. R. Bentley for Six Poems by Gray.   1753.
   Odes.   1757.
   Poems.   1768.
   Ode Performed in the Senate House at Cambridge.   1769.

Other

   Walpole's Correspondence with Gray, West, and Ashton, edited by W. S. Lewis and others, in *Walpole's Correspondence,* vols. 13–14.   1948.

Bibliography: *A Bibliography of Gray* by Clark S. Northrup, 1917, supplement by H. W. Starr, 1953.

Reading List: *Gray as a Literary Critic* by H. W. Starr, 1941; *Gray: A Biography* by Robert R. Ketton-Cremer, 1955; *Gray* by Morris Golden, 1964; *Gray and the Bard* by A. Johnston, 1966.

*   *   *

Thomas Gray is generally and rightly regarded as a transitional figure in eighteenth-century poetry, providing a bridge between the poetic sensibility of his own generation and the Romantic revolution of the future. He combines in a unique way a classic perfection of form typical of the Augustan era with subject matters and attitudes which are clearly Romantic and anticipate later developments.

Nowhere is this fusion more obvious than in Gray's most famous poem, the "Elegy Written in a Country Churchyard." Here he works within the rigid limitations of a four-line iambic pentameter stanza, rhymed A B A B, constructing stately and memorable poetic locutions while remaining strictly conventional in his rhythms, rhymes, and diction. The very regularity of his heavy iambic beat helps to create a sense of the timeless, changeless routine of country life. In style the "Elegy" is traditional and neoclassical. But in ideas and attitudes, Gray breaks new ground. He celebrates the worth and humanity of the common man in a way that foreshadows Burns and Wordsworth; he ruminates with Romantic melancholy over "the short and simple annals of the poor." Moreover, in the later part of the poem where the focus shifts from the nameless dead to the poet himself we get a strong subjective and introspective emphasis that is startlingly new. For modern readers the poem is so familiar, so much a part of our cultural heritage, that we tend to lose the sense of its freshness for readers in 1751.

A large part of the elegy's appeal and greatness lies, of course, in its smoothly and meticulously wrought phrasing, its many unforgettable lines: "The paths of glory lead but to the grave," "Full many a flower is born to flush unseen,/And waste its sweetness on the desert air," "For from the madding crowd's ignoble strife," etc. Perhaps, after all, Dr. Johnson's is still the best distillation of the elegy's perennial power: it "abounds with images which find a mirror in every mind, and with sentiments to which every bosom returns an echo."

The same combination of classic form and emotional attitudes is observable in Gray's fine odes. The "Ode on a Distant Prospect of Eton College" evokes a nostalgic picture of the carefree life of college boys and grim forebodings of their adult futures. The poem suffers somewhat, at least for modern readers, from excessively "poetic" diction and rather wooden abstractions, but is redeemed (though to a lesser extent than the "Elegy") by some unforgettable phrasing. Lines such as the following, on schoolboys escaping on adventurous rambles, "They hear a voice in every wind,/And snatch a fearful joy," or the famous closing thought, "where ignorance is bliss,/'Tis folly to be wise," distill the special magic of Gray's style at its best. The longer ode on "The Progress of Poesy" is, on the whole, poetically superior, as Gray traces the evolution of the power of verbal harmony from Greece to Rome to England, with eloquent passages on Shakespeare, Milton, and Dryden. As in the "Elegy," the focus shifts significantly at the end to Gray himself, closing with a graceful definition of his own view of himself as poet and recluse who shall "keep his distant way/Beyond the limits of a vulgar fate." Here again Gray's gift for rich, memorable language is often evident, as in "O'er her warm cheek and rising bosom move/The bloom of young desire and purple light of love," or "The unconquerable mind, and Freedom's holy flame," or (on Milton) "He saw; but blasted with excess of light,/Closed his eyes in endless night."

The most ambitious of Gray's Pindaric odes is "The Bard," one fruit of his long and keen study of Celtic and Norse mythology and poetic antiquities. The speaker in this monologue is a Welsh bard pronouncing a terrible curse on Edward I and his invading English army, foretelling disaster for Edward's descendants. This device enables Gray to present an eloquent, impassioned summary of English history, climaxing in the ascent of a Welsh royal family (the Tudors) to usher in a golden age in the distant future. Opening with the strong lines, "Ruin seize thee, ruthless King!/Confusion on thy banners wait," the ode is Gray's most exuberant and Romantic poem, full of extravagantly emotional rhetoric, yet classic in form and impressive in its power. He followed this up with a few further experiments of the same antiquarian kind, notably two fine re-creations of Norse legends in "The Fatal Sisters" and "The Descent of Odin."

Despite the fact that Gray's work is small in bulk (Matthew Arnold called him "the scantiest" of classics), it is nevertheless remarkably varied and versatile. His achievements include poetry wholly different from the Romantic odes and elegies, such as attempts in purely neoclassical types of *vers de société* like the charming and clever "Ode on the Death of a Favourite Cat." As a letter writer, too, he is remarkable. Gray's letters are, in fact, the most humanly endearing part of his surviving writings – always interesting, full of keen observation, beautifully phrased, they give a new dimension to a personality that in the poetry often seems aloof and austere. They reveal much that is warm, witty, and sensitive in the man in the course of his daily life, as well as the fastidious elitism of his many intellectual pursuits and the obsessive enthusiasm for wild "Gothic" landscapes in his travels.

During a quiet, studious lifetime Gray immersed himself in many subjects – he was a fine scholar, historian, antiquarian, and folklorist, as well as a poet – and he achieved distinction in all of them. In poetry, however, he achieved greatness. His special power lies in the gift of precise and memorable language, the result of rigid discipline from long years of study of Greek and Roman literature combined with a soaring original imagination. Steeped as he was in the past, in his ideas and emotions Gray looked to the future.

—Allan H. MacLaine

GREEN, Matthew.   English.   Born in 1696. Little is known about his life, except that he held an appointment in the Customs House, London. *Died in 1737.*

PUBLICATIONS

Collections

> *Poetical Works*, with Armstrong and Dyer, edited by George Gilfillan.   1859.
> *Minor Poets of the Eighteenth Century*, edited by Hugh I'A. Fausset.   1930.

Verse

> *The Grotto.*   1733.
> *The Spleen*, edited by Richard Glover.   1737; edited by W. H. Williams, 1936.
> *Poems.*   1796.

*   *   *

Matthew Green is one of a number of minor eighteenth-century poets who are remembered for one poem. (Dyer and Goldsmith are others who quickly spring to mind.) *The Spleen* was published posthumously in 1737, soon became popular, and was much imitated during the later years of the century. Perhaps the most absurd imitation of Green's minor masterpiece is William Thompson's *The Sickness* of 1757, while the finest poem to owe something to it is undoubtedly William Cowper's *Retirement.*

We do not know how much poetry Green wrote, but we do know that very little ever saw the light of day. *The Grotto* was privately printed, several other poems found their way into Dodsley's various collections, and a necessarily slender edition of the poems was finally published in 1796. A reader dipping into that edition would soon identify *The Grotto* as one of those charming exercises in moralised landscape which eighteenth-century poets delighted to produce. Ultimately derived from Virgil's *Georgics*, the first example in English of this kind of poem is Denham's *Cooper's Hill*, which was written as early as 1643. "The Grotto" owes much to *Cooper's Hill*, but Green's verse form, the octosyllabic couplet – it is also the form of *The Spleen* – derives from Marvell, Butler, and, perhaps, the Dyer of *Grongar Hill*. Green's poem is a charming if slight addition to a line of English poetry which is at its clearest and firmest in Pope's *Windsor Forest*. *The Grotto*, that is to say, is a derivative poem.

The Spleen, on the other hand, is much more original. It is also a well-nigh flawless performance: witty, unfailingly well written, and very exactly able to match the deftness of argument to smooth handling of the verse. Green appears in the poem as a spokesman for moderation: he counsels caution, self-discipline, an unforced withdrawal from the stresses of social and imaginative life, and avoidance of the follies and excesses of enthusiasm and "self-consuming spleen." Yet the poem is not a weightily moral exercise. Green knows the Augustan arguments against excess, but he does not write in didactic vein. He is less interested in homily than in adroit turns of phrase. The enthusiast's "springy soul dilates like air,/When free from weight of ambient care." "Springy soul" looks at first glance to be an unqualified compliment, but on reflection we realise that Green is inviting us to see the enthusiast's soul as a gassy compound. The compliment is subtly undermined. And "care" has just the right double-edged feel about it. On the one hand it implies those sad, massy weights of earthly cares from which we rightly seek escape; on the other, it means prudence, caution, that which we renounce at our peril. Such urbanity of tone – for the wit of the couplet I have quoted is poised, civilised, isn't at all clumsy or "butchering" – runs through *The Spleen*, and gives it its distinction.

Green's tone always seems to me to aim for and achieve such urbanity, whether he is writing with the comparative seriousness that he employs in *The Spleen*, or whether he is writing such ephemeral but delightful pieces as "The Seeker" or "The Sparrow and Diamond." In short, it may be said that Green belongs to that "line of wit" which has properly been identified as running from the Cavalier poets through to Pope and the eighteenth century.

—John Lucas

JOHNSON, Samuel. English. Born in Lichfield, Staffordshire, 18 September 1709. Educated at Lichfield Grammar School, and at the Stourbridge School, to age 16; Pembroke College, Oxford, 1728–29, left without taking a degree. Married Elizabeth Porter in 1735 (died, 1752). Usher in a grammar school in Market Bosworth, Leicestershire; worked for the publisher of the *Birmingham Journal*, 1732; took pupils at Edial, Staffordshire, among them David Garrick, 1736–37; travelled with Garrick to London, and settled there, 1737; supported himself by writing for Cave's *Gentleman's Magazine*, 1738–44, for which he wrote reports on debates in Parliament, 1740–43; catalogued the library of the second Earl of Oxford, 1742; worked on his *Dictionary*, 1747–55; formed the Ivy Lane Club, 1749; Author/Editor, *The Rambler*, 1750–52; contributed to *The Adventurer*, 1753–54; arrested for debt, but released on a loan from Samuel Richardson, 1756; contributed to the *Literary*

Magazine, 1756–57; wrote "The Idler" for the *Universal Chronicle*, 1758–60; moved to Inner Temple Lane, now Johnson's Buildings, 1759; pensioned by the crown, 1762; founded The Literary Club, 1764; wrote pamphlets against Wilkes, 1770, a defense of government policy in the Falkland Islands, 1771, and in America, 1775; toured Scotland with James Boswell, subsequently his biographer, 1773; travelled to Wales, 1774, and Paris, 1775; formed the Essex Head Club, 1783. M.A.: Oxford University, 1775; LL.D.: Trinity College, Dublin, 1765; Oxford University, 1775. *Died 13 December 1784.*

PUBLICATIONS

Collections

Works. 16 vols., 1903.
Letters, edited by R. W. Chapman. 3 vols., 1952.
Works, edited by A. T. Hazen and others. 1958–
Complete English Poems, edited by J. D. Fleeman. 1971.
Selected Poetry and Prose, edited by Frank Brady and William K. Wimsatt. 1977.

Verse

London: A Poem in Imitation of the Third Satire of Juvenal. 1738.
The Vanity of Human Wishes: The Tenth Satire of Juvenal Imitated. 1749.

Play

Irene (produced 1749). 1749; as *Mohamet and Irene* (produced 1749).

Fiction

The Prince of Abyssinia: A Tale. 1759; revised edition, 1759; as *The History of Rasselas, Prince of Abyssinia: An Asian Tale*, 1768; edited by Geoffrey Tillotson and Brian Jenkins, 1971.

Other

A Complete Vindication of the Licensers of the Stage. 1739.
The Life of Admiral Blake. 1740.
An Account of the Life of Mr. Richard Savage, Son of the Earl Rivers. 1744; edited by Clarence Tracy, 1971.
An Account of the Life of John Philip Barretier. 1744.
Miscellaneous Observations on the Tragedy of Macbeth. 1745.
The Plan of a Dictionary of the English Language, Addressed to the Earl of Chesterfield. 1747.
The Rambler. 8 vols., 1750–52; edited by A. B. Strauss and Walter Jackson Bate, in *Works*, 1969.
The Adventurer, with others. 2 vols., 1753–54; in *Works*, 1963.
A Dictionary of the English Language. 2 vols., 1755; revised edition, 1773.

The Idler.   2 vols., 1761; edited by Walter Jackson Bate and J. M. Bullitt, in *Works,* 1963.
Preface to His Edition of Shakespeare's Plays.   1765.
The False Alarm.   1770.
Thoughts on the Late Transactions Respecting Falkland's Islands.   1771.
The Patriot, Addressed to the Electors of Great Britain.   1774.
Taxation No Tyranny: An Answer to the Resolutions and Address of the American Congress.   1775.
A Journey to the Western Islands of Scotland.   1775; edited by D. L. Murray, 1931.
Prefaces, Biographical and Critical, to the Works of the English Poets.   10 vols., 1779–81; as *The Lives of the English Poets,* 1781; revised edition, 1783; edited by G. B. Hill, 3 vols., 1905; selection edited by J. P. Hardy, 1972.
Prayers and Meditations, edited by George Strahan.   1785; revised edition, 1785, 1796; edited by D. and M. Hyde, in *Works,* 1958.
Debates in Parliament, edited by George Chalmers.   2 vols., 1787.
Letters to and from Johnson, by Hester Lynch Piozzo.   2 vols., 1788.
The Celebrated Letter to the Earl of Chesterfield, edited by James Boswell.   1790.
An Account of the Life of Johnson to His Eleventh Year, Written by Himself, edited by Richard Wright.   1805.
A Diary of a Journey into North Wales in the Year 1774, edited by R. Duppa.   1816; in *Works,* 1958.
Johnson: His Life in Letters, edited by David Littlejohn.   1965.
Literary Criticism, edited by R. D. Stock.   1974.

Editor, *The Works of Richard Savage, with an Account of the Author.*   1775.
Editor, *The Plays of Shakespeare.*   8 vols., 1765.

Translator, *A Voyage to Abyssinia,* by Father Jerome Lobo.   1735.
Translator, *A Commentary on Pope's Principles of Morality; or, An Essay on Man,* by Crousaz.   1739.

Bibliography: *A Bibliography of Johnson* by W. P. Courtney and D. N. Smith, 1915; *Johnsonian Studies 1887–1950: A Survey and Bibliography* by James L. Clifford, 1951, supplement by M. Wahba, in *Johnsonian Studies 1950–60,* 1962.

Reading List: *Life of Johnson* by James Boswell, 1791, edited by R. W. Chapman, 1953; *Passionate Intelligence: Imagination and Reason in the Work of Johnson* by Arieh Sachs, 1967; *Johnson as Critic,* 1973, and *Johnson* (biography), 1974, both by John Wain; *The Ascent of Parnassus* by Arthur Bryant, 1975; *Johnson and Poetic Style* by William Edinger, 1977; *The Stylistic Life of Johnson* by William Vesterman, 1977; *Johnson* by Walter Jackson Bate, 1978.

*   *   *

Johnson was regarded in his own time as the dominant figure of the English literary world; his achievement covers an extraordinary range: he was scholar and critic, moralist and essayist, poet and prose stylist, all in the first degree of merit.
With his verse-tragedy *Irene* in his pocket, and David Garrick as travelling companion, Johnson walked from Lichfield to London in 1737. *Irene* was not published and produced until 1749, and was no great success, but Johnson's heroic couplet satire *London,* based on Juvenal's third satire, appeared in 1738, on the same day as Pope's *Epilogue to the Satires. London* criticises the values of the city in general, and of Whig London in particular; here Johnson wears Pope's mantle of the conservative (and Tory) satirist. Johnson's first London

years were spent partly in the company of such Grub Street inhabitants as Richard Savage; the *Account of the Life of Richard Savage* is a product of this friendship, and is an important early essay by Johnson in the art of biography.

Johnson turned again to verse satire in *The Vanity of Human Wishes* based on Juvenal's tenth satire. This poem, Johnson's greatest, states a favourite theme: the inevitable unhappiness of human existence whatever choice in life is made. In turn Johnson considers mankind's yearnings for the various gifts of power, learning, military fame, long life, beauty, even virtue, and gives a melancholy account, with individual examples, of the misfortunes attendant upon each. This is not, however, mere pessimism. Johnson's Christian modification of Juvenal's stoic "mens sana in corpore sano" finds in religious faith a hard-fought-for consolation: "Still raise for good the supplicating voice,/But leave to heav'n the measure and the choice."

The theme of *Rasselas*, a moral tale set in Abyssinia and Egypt which has some similarities with Voltaire's *Candide*, is again the choice of life. Johnson's princely young hero escapes, with his sister and the poet Imlac, from the secluded innocence of the Happy Valley, and makes trial of various schemes of life. One after another the delusions and inconveniences of the pastoral life and the hermit's life, the life of the stoic and the life "according to nature," the family life and the scholar's life, are exposed. Life is found to be "every where a state in which much is to be endured, and little to be enjoyed"; the moral enforced is that no choice can be happy, but a choice must be made. Johnson may perhaps be seen returning to this theme with greater hope in his moving brief elegy "On the Death of Dr. Robert Levet" (1783), whose central message is that man finds fulfilment in the steady daily application of his particular talent: "The modest wants of ev'ry day/The toil of ev'ry day supplied."

It was with the 208 issues of *The Rambler* (1750–52), periodical essays on the pattern established earlier in the century by *The Spectator* and *The Tatler*, though more serious in tone and content, that Johnson became a major literary figure in contemporary estimation. In *The Rambler*, explicitly, it was Johnson's intention "to inculcate wisdom or piety," to teach both a reasonable and a religious attitude to life, dealing with topics as fundamental to human experience as youth and old age, marriage and death, grief and sorrow. In a small number of the *Rambler* essays Johnson is a literary critic, considering notably the topics of the novel (issue 4), biography (60), prejudice and the rules in criticism (93, 156, 158), and tragedy and comedy (125). Johnson's essays in *The Adventurer* and *The Idler* are in a rather lighter vein.

In the periodical essays and *Rasselas* may already be found the characteristic Johnsonian prose style, legislative and authoritative, often imitated, though far more flexible and exact than facile imitation would suggest. Careful judgements of life are crystallised in a precisely chosen diction, and ideas are given their relations by the balanced rhythms of clause echoing clause within the sentence. To this Johnson's weighty and pointed heroic couplets in *The Vanity of Human Wishes* and *London* are a poetic equivalent.

The reputation begun by *The Rambler* was established, in a different field, by the *Dictionary*, a triumph of individual scholarship and labour. Johnson as a lexicographer is distinguished by his accurate definitions of the meanings of words, and by his use of the historical principle. Words are illustrated by passages chosen not only for their semantic aptness, but also for their literary and moral qualities. The choice of passages reveals the enormous range of Johnson's reading, and, strikingly, his admiration for and knowledge of Elizabethan literature. The *Dictionary* is more descriptive than prescriptive; though he acknowledged that "there is in constancy and stability a general and lasting advantage," Johnson was too realistic to believe (with Swift, for example), that it is possible to fix and enforce linguistic usage.

Johnson's next major project was his edition of Shakespeare, remarkable for a commentary which shows Johnson's response to have been not only informed but also sometimes intensely personal, and for the theoretically and historically important preface. In the preface Johnson judges Shakespeare in a partly conservative light, approving of his "just representations of general nature" (a neo-classical position Johnson had already enunciated in the tenth chapter of *Rasselas*), and disapproving of his failure to provide a consistent and complete moral vision. Johnson shows a robust open-mindedness in defending Shakespeare against accusations that he mixes dramatic kinds and fails to observe the unities. Shakespeare's plays "are not in the rigorous and critical sense either tragedies or comedies" because they depict the mingled conditions of real life. The unities of time and place need not be observed because "the spectators are always in their senses and know ... that the stage is only a stage, and that the players are only players." Johnson rejects arbitrary prescription, steadily insisting that the primary aim of literature is a moral one, to be secured through delighting the reader: "there is always an appeal open from criticism to nature. The end of writing is to instruct; the end of poetry is to instruct by pleasing."

Johnson's literary output decreased in the late 1760's and 1770's. This is the period of gladiatorial conversation and literary dictatorship portrayed by James Boswell, whom Johnson had met in 1763. Johnson's main arena was the Club, founded at Joshua Reynolds's suggestion in 1764 and including, at its inception or in later years, many of the most eminent literary men of the time, among them Goldsmith and Garrick, Boswell and Burke, Edward Gibbon and Adam Smith.

To these years belong Johnson's most significant political writings, eloquent expressions of a personally consistent and conscientious conservatism. In *The False Alarm* Johnson defends Parliament's refusal to seat the radical John Wilkes. In *Taxation No Tyranny* he asserts the right of the British government to impose taxes upon the American colonists.

The *Journey to the Western Islands of Scotland* is a record of the tour, dangerous and adventurous for so old a man, that Johnson undertook with Boswell in 1773. If Johnson's account lacks the anecdotal vividness of Boswell's, there is here nonetheless the accustomed Johnsonian nobility of general moral reflection, in a social and physical landscape new to his experience.

Perhaps Johnson's greatest literary achievement came towards the end of his life, when he was commissioned by a group of London booksellers to provide a set of introductory essays for a collection of the works of the English poets. Each of the *Lives* consists of a detailed biography and brief character sketch, and a critical account of the poet. These critical passages are the fruition of a lifetime's reading and hard thought, providing a judicial assessment of the English poetic tradition against the twin standards of delight and truth to nature. Not surprisingly, Johnson's "great tradition" (though he has a wide range of interest and liking) is the line of satirical and ethical heroic couplet verse originating with Denham and Waller and perfected by Dryden and Pope, clear in expression and moral in intent. His aversion is poetry, whether by John Donne or Thomas Gray, which in his opinion fails to promote truth or express its meanings perspicuously. Though Johnson admired Milton's verse, and especially *Paradise Lost*, even so great a poem as *Lycidas* is attacked for what Johnson considered its harsh and unpleasing diction and metre, and its submergence of true feeling in an artificial pastoral allegory. Though the modern critical consensus does not accept all of Johnson's valuations, his criticism has the crucial virtues of exact and generally sympathetic understanding of what he reads, and the constant application of a systematic literary judgement. Johnson may seem to us sometimes too unwilling to compromise with historical relativism, or apparently insensitive to such of our favourite literary values as irony, ambiguity, imagination, and metaphor; yet his criticism is the work of a great and superbly stocked mind, always identifying the major questions, and the modern who takes issue with him needs to be armed with reasons.

—Marcus Walsh

KING, William. English. Born in London in 1662. Educated at Westminster School, London, 1678–81; Christ Church, Oxford, matriculated 1681, B.A. 1685, M.A. 1688, B.C.L. and D.C.L. 1692; admitted advocate at the Doctors' Commons, 1692. Secretary to Princess Anne; Judge of the Admiralty Court in Ireland, 1701–07; appointed Vicar-General of Armagh, 1703; Keeper of the Records, Birmingham Tower, Dublin Castle, 1707; returned to London, 1707, and succeeded Steele as gazetteer, 1711–12. *Died 25 December 1712.*

PUBLICATIONS

Collections

    Original Works, edited by John Nichols.   3 vols., 1776.
    Poetical Works.   2 vols., 1781.

Verse

    The Furmetary: A Very Innocent and Harmless Poem.   1699.
    Mully of Mountown.   1704.
    The Fairy Feast.   1704.
    Some Remarks on the Tale of a Tub.   1704.
    The Art of Cookery, in Imitation of Horace's Art of Poetry.   1708.
    The Art of Love, in Imitation of Ovid.   1709.

Other

    Reflections upon Monsieur Varillas's History of Heresy, with Edward Hannes.   1688.
    An Answer to a Book, in Vindication of the Trinity.   1693.
    Animadversions on a Pretended Account of Denmark.   1694.
    A Journey to London in the Year 1698.   1698; edited by K. N. Colvile, in *A Miscellany of the Wits,* 1920.
    Dialogues of the Dead.   1699; edited by K. N. Colvile, in *A Miscellany of the Wits,* 1920.
    The Transactioneer, with Some of His Philosophical Fancies, in Two Dialogues.   1700.
    Miscellanies in Prose and Verse.   2 vols., 1707(?).
    Useful Transactions in Philosophy and Other Sorts of Learning.   3 vols., 1709.
    The Present State of Physic in the Island of Cajamai.   1709(?).
    A Friendly Letter from Honest Tom Bobby to Mr. G[oddar]d.   1710; *Second Letter,* 1710.
    A Vindication of the Rev. Dr. Henry Sacheverell, with Charles Lambe.   1711.
    Mr. B[isse]t's Recantation.   1711.
    An Answer to a Second Scandalous Book That Mr. B[isse]t Is Now Writing.   1711.
    An Historical Account of the Heathen Gods and Heroes.   1711.
    Rufinus; or, An Historical Essay on the Favourite Ministry under Theodosius the Great and His Son Arcadius.   1712.
    Britain's Palladium; or, My Lord Bolingbroke's Welcome from France.   1712.
    Useful Miscellanies.   1712.
    Remains, edited by Joseph Browne.   1732; as *Posthumous Works,* 1734.

    Translator, *New Memoirs and Characters of the Two Great Brothers, the Duke of Bouillon and Mareschal Turenne,* by J. de Langlade, Baron de Saumières.   1693.

Translator, *Political Considerations upon Refined Politics*, by G. Naudé.   1711.
Translator, with others, *The Persian and Turkish Tales.*   1714.

Reading List: *King · Eine Interpretation seiner Gedichte* by Balthasar Kuebler, 1974.

*   *   *

William King is one of a very small number of English authors who, buried in undeserved obscurity, merit full resurrection. His robust originality invigorated several comic genres at the beginning of the eighteenth century. His special penchant was for burlesque, in which mode he pillories all varieties of dullness. *A Journey to London* mocks by imitation the tiresome scientific trivialities of physician and naturalist Martin Lister's record of *A Journey to Paris*. Similarly, the *Transactioneer* and *Useful Transactions in Philosophy and other Sorts of Learning* nip at the heels of Sir Hans Sloane's *Transactions of the Royal Society* in a Scriblerian vein, objecting to what King perceived as a myopic scientism. He opposed Richard Bentley's "minute" scholarship in clever *Dialogues of the Dead*. In a typical dialogue, the poetaster Richard Flecknoe contends to dramatist Thomas Dekker that his own poor epigrams would be as highly valued as the trivia Bentley perpetuates "were they sufficiently obscured by translation into Greek."

The mock-heroic method and the comic petition of Hunger to Famine in King's "very innocent and harmless poem" *The Furmetary* suggest the *Dunciad* almost as clearly as its use of gritty, concrete details anticipates Swift's "Description of the Morning." From the mock-pastoral *Mully of Mountown* to his surprisingly chaste Ovidian *Art of Love*, King reinvigorates forms that flourish later in the century. Nor is his energy undisciplined. At his best he handles the octosyllabic couplet with the delicacy of Prior and the surprise of Swift. A portion of the meal in miniature offered by the fairies in his popular tale "Orpheus and Eurydice" suggests King's grace:

> A roasted ant, that's nicely done,
> By one small atom of the sun....
> This is a dish entirely new,
> Butterflies' brains dissolved in dew;
> These lover's vows, these courtiers' hopes,
> Things to be eat by microscopes.

King draws on his adeptness in both harmonies of poetry and prose for his wittiest and most enjoyable work – *The Art of Cookery*. His old enemy Lister's outrageously pedantic edition of an obscure Latin work *Concerning the Soups and Sauces of the Ancients* elicited the facetious series of letters which precede King's Horatian treatment of that "learned, industrious, moral, upright, and warlike profession of cookery." Pretending interest only in "such parts of learning as lay remote and are fit only for the closets of the curious," King begs Lister "to communicate your remarks from the ancients concerning *dentiscalps*, vulgarly called *tooth-picks*." In return, King promises to let the world have his treatise of forks and napkins.

Despite a constitution given to sloth, of which his friend Swift complained, King produced an amazing variety of works, and whatever he attempted was infused with a unique energy and originality which survive today. However, still one of the most consistently readable of the minor writers of his time, King anticipates and thereby suffers in comparison with the best of his contemporaries. It is one of the injustices of literary history that King has been almost totally obscured by blooms of which his works were the bud.

—Harry M. Solomon

LANGHORNE, John.   English.   Born in Winton, Westmorland, in March 1735; younger brother of the poet and translator William Langhorne. Educated at schools in Winton and Appleby. Married 1) Ann Cracroft in 1767 (died, 1768), one son; 2) Miss Thompson in 1772 (died, 1776), one daughter. Tutor to a family near Ripon, 1753; subsequently an usher in a free school in Wakefield; took deacon's orders; tutor to the sons of Robert Cracroft at Hackthorn, near Lincoln, 1759–61; matriculated at Clare Hall, Cambridge, 1760, but left without taking a degree; Curate, Dagenham, Essex, 1761–64; Curate and Lecturer at St. John's, Camberwell, London, 1764–65; Assistant Preacher at Lincoln's Inn, London, 1765; Rector, Blagdon, Somerset, from 1766; Prebendary of Wells Cathedral, 1777. *Died 1 April 1779.*

PUBLICATIONS

Collections

   Poetical Works, edited by J. T. Langhorne.   2 vols., 1804.

Verse

   The Death of Adonis, from Bion.   1759.
   Job.   1760.
   The Tears of Music: A Poem to Handel, with an Ode to the River Eden.   1760.
   Poems on Several Occasions.   1760.
   A Hymn to Hope.   1761.
   The Viceroy.   1762.
   The Visions of Fancy, in Four Elegies.   1762.
   The Enlargement of the Mind.   2 vols., 1763–65.
   Genius and Valour: A Scotch Pastoral.   1764.
   The Fatal Prophecy: A Dramatic Poem.   1766.
   Poetical Works.   2 vols., 1766.
   Precepts of Conjugal Happiness.   1767.
   Verses in Memory of a Lady Written at Sandgate Castle.   1768.
   The Fables of Flora.   1771.
   The Origin of the Veil.   1773.
   The Country Justice.   3 vols., 1774; edited by Donald Davie, in *The Late Augustans,*
      1958.
   Owen of Carron.   1778.

Fiction

   Solyman and Almena: An Oriental Tale.   1762.
   The Letters Between Theodosius and Constantia, after She Had Taken the Veil.   1763;
      revised edition, 1765.
   Frederic and Pharamond; or, The Consolations of Human Life.   1769.

Others

   Letters on Religious Retirement, Melancholy, and Enthusiasm.   1762.

The Effusions of Friendship and Fancy, in Several Letters.   2 vols., 1763; revised
  edition, 1766.
Letters on the Eloquence of the Pulpit.   1765.
Sermons Preached Before the Society of Lincoln's-Inn.   2 vols., 1767.
Letters Supposed to Have Passed Between St. Evremond and Waller.   2 vols., 1769.
A Dialogue of the Dead Betwixt Lord Eglinton and Mungo Campbell.   1770.
Letters to Eleonora.   2 vols., 1770.
Editor, *The Poetical Works of Collins.*   1765.

Translator, with William Langhorne, *Plutarch's Lives.*   6 vols., 1770.
Translator, *A Dissertation on the Ancient Republics of Italy,* by C. G. M. Denina.   1773.
Translator, *Milton's Italian Poems.*   1776.

Reading List: "Langhorne" by H. Macdonald, in *Essays Presented to David Nichol Smith,*
1945.

*   *   *   *

John Langhorne is a minor poet of limited output, yet of various modes. His best poems
are *The Country Justice, Owen of Carron,* and *The Fables of Flora.* Besides his poems, he also
translated Plutarch in collaboration with his brother and contributed to *The Monthly Review.*
It is, however, as a poet that he principally matters.

Writing in the mid-eighteenth century he produced work, such as the Hymns to Plutus and
to Humanity, that is reminiscent of Collins, whose poems he edited. Langhorne's work,
however, looks backward and forward. A poem like *The Enlargement of the Mind* reminds us
by its subject of Prior's much more ambitious "Alma" and by its form and optimistic view of
human capacity and existence of Pope's *Essay on Man.*

Here Langhorne was philosophical and didactic. In *Owen of Carron,* his last work, he
produces a harrowing tale of blighted love and bloody vengeance in a mode of the four-line
stanza that he favoured increasingly in his later work. The primitive passions of this poem, set
though they are a little too neatly in the regular rhythms of the chosen verse-form, remind us
that we are in the era of Percy's *Reliques* and on the verge of that reviving medievalism that
includes Chatterton and, a little later, Scott and other Romantic poets.

The proximity of Gothic horror is the reminder behind the picture of the "bloody druid"
committing ghastly infanticide in "The Mistletoe and the Passion-Flower" (*Fables of Flora,*
XI): "Behold his crimson-streaming hand/Erect! – his dark, fix'd murderous eye!" By
contrast, there is the occasional very direct visual awareness of natural beauty, as of the
"gaily-painted Tulip" (VIII), seen and more vividly described as "crimson fading into gold/In
streaks of fairest symmetry."

This exact observation may foreshadow a Coleridge or a Clare; the moral tone, though all
too wordy, has at least some relationship with what Blake would do inimitably better in
Songs of Innocence and Experience. The link, however, is closer in "To a Redbreast":

> Little bird, with bosom red,
> Welcome to my humble shed!
> Courtly domes of high degree
> Have no room for thee and me....
>
> Daily near my table steal
> While I pick my scanty meal.
> Doubt not, little though there be,
> But I'll cast a crumb to thee

The second part of this poem is a counterpointing song of experience.

Finally, however, the resemblance is with Crabbe or Wordsworth as poet of low and rustic life. *The Country Justice*, with its vagrant, poor widow, unmarried mother, shepherd and his wife, gives us a first glimpse of types with which writers not much later make us more and better familiar. Wordsworth indeed said of this poem that, with the possible exception of Shenstone's *The School Mistress*, it was "the first poem ... that fairly brought the Muse into the company of common life." Langhorne's own achievement may be limited, but he is a quite remarkable precursor of better things.

—Arthur Pollard

LYTTELTON, George; 1st Baron Lyttelton.   English.   Born in Hagley, Worcestershire, 17 January 1709. Educated at Eton College; Christ Church, Oxford, matriculated 1726, left without taking a degree. Married 1) Lucy Fortescue in 1742 (died, 1747), one son, two daughters; 2) Elizabeth Rich in 1749 (separated). Toured the Continent, 1728–31; Equerry, 1731–37, then Secretary, 1737–44, to the Prince of Wales; Member of Parliament for Okehampton, Devonshire, 1735–56: opposed Walpole, and with Pitt and the Grenvilles formed party known as the Cobhamites; a Lord of the Treasury, 1744–54; Member of the Privy Council, 1754; Chancellor of the Exchequer, 1755–56; created Baron Lyttelton, 1756, and thereafter sat in the House of Lords: opposed repeal of the Stamp Act, 1766. *Died 22 August 1773.*

PUBLICATIONS

Collections

> *Works*, edited by G. E. Ayscough.   1774.
> *Poetical Works.*   1785.

Verse

> *Blenheim.*   1728.
> *An Epistle to Mr. Pope, from a Young Gentleman at Rome.*   1730.
> *The Progress of Love, in Four Eclogues.*   1732.
> *Advice to a Lady.*   1733.
> *To the Memory of a Lady Lately Deceased: A Monody.*   1747.
> *The Fourth Ode of the Fourth Book of Horace.*   1749.
> *Poems.*   1773.

Other

> *Letters from a Persian in England to His Friend at Ispahan,* vol. 1.   1735.
> *Considerations upon the Present State of Our Affairs at Home and Abroad.*   1739; *Farther Considerations,* 1739.
> *Obersations on the Life of Cicero.*   1741.

The Court Secret: A Melancholy Truth.   1742; as *The New Court Secret,* 1746.
Observations on the Conversion and Apostleship of St. Paul, in a Letter to Gilbert West.   1747.
A Modest Apology for My Own Conduct.   1748.
Dialogues of the Dead.   1760; *An Additional Dialogue,* 1760; *Four New Dialogues,* 1765.
The History of the Life of King Henry the Second and of the Age in Which He Lived.   4 vols., 1767–71.

Editor, *Works of James Thomson.*   4 vols., 1750.

Reading List: *An Eighteenth-Century Gentleman* by Sydney C. Roberts, 1930; *A Minor Augustan: The Life and Works of Lyttelton* by A. V. Rao, 1934; *The Good Lord Lyttelton* by Rose M. Davis, 1939.

*   *   *

George Lyttelton is known more for his literary patronage than as a poet. He is essentially a minor Augustan versifier, following the lead of his friend Pope, and a prose-writer in the tradition of Fénelon and Montesquieu. His poetry follows conventional forms, generally pastoral and in low key. The "Monody" written in praise of "The Conjugal and the maternal love" on the death of his wife Lucy has a particular beauty, however, as he adapts the Miltonic pastoral elegy to the expression of private grief.

Lyttelton's dexterity with the rhymed couplet never achieves the pungency of Pope, despite the attempt to exploit Augustan antitheses in a similar manner. He does reconcile the urbane and the pastoral in his realized vision of a rural retreat at his estate, Hagley Park. Here he entertained Fielding, Pope, Shenstone, and Thomson, and was celebrated by the last as the epitome of friend, patron, and host. *The Seasons* bear the unmistakable mark of editorial interference by Lyttelton in the later revisions. Thomson's idiosyncratic style is muffled by heavy general moralizing. However, Lyttelton remains as an archetype of the man of "taste."

—B. C. Oliver-Morden

MACPHERSON, James.   Scottish.   Born in Ruthven, Inverness-shire, 27 October 1736. Educated at the University of Aberdeen and the University of Edinburgh, but did not take a degree; studied for the ministry, but did not take holy orders. Had 4 illegitimate children. Taught in the village school in Ruthven; tutor at Moffat, 1759; at the instigation of John Home, and later Lord Bute, published his "translations" of ancient Highland poetry, 1760, and of the two epic poems of "Ossian," 1762–63, all of which were generally believed by literary men, particularly Samuel Johnson, to be his own inventions; Secretary to the Governor of Florida, 1764–66; settled in London and worked for the government as a political writer; employed by Lord North's ministry to defend its American policy and to supervise ministerial newspapers, 1776–80; Member of Parliament for Camelford, Cornwall, 1780–96; Agent in London to the Nabob of Arcot, from 1781. *Died 17 February 1796.*

PUBLICATIONS

Collections

The Poems of Ossian and Macpherson, edited by Malcolm Laing.   2 vols., 1805.

Verse

The Highlander: An Heroic Poem in Six Cantos.   1758.
Fragments of Ancient Poetry Collected in the Highlands of Scotland.   1760; edited by J. J. Dunn, 1966.
Fingal: An Ancient Epic Poem, with Several Other Poems Translated from the Gaelic Language.   1762.
Temora: An Ancient Epic Poem, with Several Other Poems Translated from the Gaelic Language.   1763.
The Works of Ossian, translated by James Macpherson.   2 vols., 1765; as *Ossian*, edited by O. L. Jiriczek, 3 vols., 1940.

Other

An Introduction to the History of Great Britain and Ireland.   1771; revised edition, 1772.
The History of Great Britain from the Restoration to the Accession of the House of Hanover.   2 vols., 1775.
Original Papers, Containing the Secret History of Great Britain.   2 vols., 1775.
The Rights of Great Britain Asserted Against the Claims of America.   1776.
A Short History of the Opposition During the Last Session of Parliament.   1779.
The History and Management of the East India Company.   1779.

Translator, *The Iliad Translated into Prose*, by Homer.   2 vols., 1773.

Reading List: *A Critical Dissertation on the Poems of Ossian* by H. Blair, 1763; *The Gaelic Sources of Macpherson's Ossian* by Derick S. Thomson, 1952.

*   *   *

The *Ossian* controversy dominated the literary world from the 1760's until in 1805 a committee of enquiry proved beyond doubt that the supposed translations were in large part the original work of James Macpherson. The nationalistic tone of the poems appealed to the Scottish *literati* of the time (Fingal the Scottish hero is constantly represented as being superior to the Irish and to the Romans) who defended their provenance against such sceptics as Dr. Johnson. The appeal of *Fingal* and *Temora* was widespread, creating a European phenomenon that helped set the tone for a "romantic" movement.

Macpherson's major work describing wild, northern landscapes and heroes lost in a Celtic twilight embodies that form of stylistic "sublimity" which Burke had advocated in 1757, appealing to the emotions rather than the reason. Rather than harmony and number in poetry, Macpherson exploits the "fragmented" nature of the supposed translations, allowing gaps in comprehension to work for him in the creation of atmosphere. The bardic tone is borrowed from Miltonic and Biblical sources; applied to ancient northern mythology it created in its time a cult for the remote past, the mysterious, and the irrational.

—B. C. Oliver-Morden

MALLET, David.   Scottish.   Born David Malloch in Crieff, Perthshire, c. 1705; changed name to Mallet, 1726. Educated in the parish school in Crieff, and at the University of Edinburgh, 1721–22, 1722–23; St. Mary Hall, Oxford, 1731–34, B.A. and M.A. 1734. Married 1) Susanna c. 1734 (died, 1741), one son, one daughter; 2) Lucy Elstob in 1742, two daughters. Janitor in the high school of Edinburgh, 1717; resident tutor to the sons of Mr. Home of Dreghorn, 1720–23; tutor to the sons of the Duke of Montrose, in London and at Shawford, near Winchester, 1723–31; tutor to the stepson of John Knight, whom he accompanied to Oxford, 1731–34; appointed Under-Secretary to the Prince of Wales, 1742, and received a pension from him until 1748; also enjoyed the patronage of Bolingbroke through whose influence he was appointed Inspector of the Exchequer-Book in the Outports of London, 1763 until his death. *Died 21 April 1765.*

PUBLICATIONS

Collections

Works of the English Poets 14, edited by A. Chalmers.   1810.

Plays

Eurydice (produced 1731).   1731.
Mustapha (produced 1739).   1739.
Alfred: A Masque, with James Thomson, music by Thomas Arne (produced 1740).   1740; revised version (produced 1751), 1751; as *Alfred the Great,* 1753.
Britannia: A Masque, music by Thomas Arne (produced 1755).   1755.
Elvira (produced 1763).   1763.

Verse

William and Margaret: An Old Ballad.   1723.
A Poem in Imitation of Donaides.   1725.
The Excursion.   1728.
Of Verbal Criticism: An Epistle to Mr. Pope.   1733.
Verses Presented to the Prince of Orange on His Visiting Oxford, with Walter Harte.   1734.
Poems on Several Occasions.   1743.

Amyntor and Theodora; or, The Hermit.   1747.
Edwin and Emma.   1760; edited by F. T. Dinsdale, 1849.
Verses on the Death of Lady Anson.   1760.
Poems on Several Occasions.   1762.
Ballads and Songs, edited by F. T. Dinsdale.   1857.

Other

The Life of Francis Bacon.   1740.
Works.   4 vols., 1743; revised edition, 3 vols., 1759.
A Congratulatory Letter to Selim on the Three Letters to the Whigs.   1748.
Observations on the Twelfth Article of War.   1757.

Editor, *Letters on the Spirit of Patriotism, On the Idea of a Patriot King,* by Lord
    Bolingbroke.   1749.
Editor, *Works of Lord Bolingbroke.*   5 vols., 1754.

Reading List: "The Early History of *Alfred*" by Alan D. McKillop, in *Philological Quarterly*
41, 1962.

*   *   *

David Mallet's earliest work was his most famous and best. His *William and Margaret,*
which is so free an adaptation of the authentic traditional ballad of Fair Margaret and Sweet
William (F. J. Child's Ballad number 74) as to rank as an original work, was often printed in
periodicals and miscellanies in the 1720's, then reprinted, often with revisions by the author,
in many other collections, including Percy's *Reliques* (1765), until it came to be regarded as
one of the most significant contributions to the eighteenth-century ballad revival, and so, in
its small way, a contribution to the romantic revival. Another ballad, *Edwin and Emma,*
wholly of Mallet's conception and composition, was published in 1760, but deservedly failed
to match the success of *William and Margaret.*

The Excursion, in Miltonic blank verse, was influenced by his friend Thomson's *Winter*
and *Summer.* In it Mallet makes "a short excursive survey of the Earth and Heavens," aiming
at a sublime effect with his somewhat turgid descriptions of earthquakes, volcanos,
thunderstorms, the vast spaces of the stellar universe, and other such natural wonders. One of
the poem's more interesting romantic features is the address to the imagination as a creative
principle. Mallet showed his virtuosity by then imitating his patron, Pope, in *Of Verbal
Criticism,* a satire in heroic couplets, against Pope's enemies Bentley and Theobald; but in his
longest poem, *Amyntor and Theodora,* Mallet returns to his romantic vein. This sentimental
love story is set in an idealized primitive setting upon the remote Hebridean island of St.
Kilda, and takes a hermit for its central character.

Mallet wrote part of *Alfred; A Masque,* though its one memorable song, "Rule Britannia,"
was the work of his co-author, Thomson. A revised version of *Alfred,* containing more work
by Mallet, was acted in 1751; and Mallet was sole author of another patriotic masque,
Britannia. His three heroic tragedies, *Eurydice, Mustapha,* and *Elvira,* are as vapid and stiff as
Thomson's tragedies, after which they were to some extent modelled.

—A. J. Sambrook

MASON, William. English. Born in Hull, Yorkshire, 12 February 1724. Educated at St. John's College, Cambridge, matriculated 1743, scholar 1744, B.A. 1745, M.A. 1749. Appointed Fellow of Pembroke Hall, Cambridge, through the influence of Thomas Gray, 1749–54 (maintained friendship with Gray and became his literary executor). Ordained: Vicar of Aston, Yorkshire, 1754–97; one of the king's chaplains, 1757–73; Canon Residentiary of York, 1762; Precentor and Prebendary of Driffield, Yorkshire, 1763–97. *Died 7 April 1797.*

PUBLICATIONS

Collections

Works. 4 vols., 1811.

Verse

Musaeus: A Monody to the Memory of Pope, in Imitation of Lycidas. 1747.
Isis: An Elegy. 1749.
Ode Performed in the Senate House at Cambridge. 1749.
Odes. 1756.
Elegies. 1763.
Poems. 1764; revised edition, 1764; 3 vols., 1796–97.
A Supplement to Watts' Psalms and Hymns. 1769.
The English Garden. 4 vols., 1772–81.
An Heroic Epistle to Sir William Chambers. 1773.
An Heroic Postscript to the Public. 1774.
Ode to Mr. Pinchbeck upon His Newly Invented Patent Candle-Snuffers. 1776.
An Epistle to Dr. Shebbeare, An ode to Sir Fletcher Norton in Imitation of Horace Ode VIII Book IV. 1777.
Ode to the Naval Officers of Great Britain. 1779.
An Archaeological Epistle to Jeremiah Milles. 1782.
The Dean and the 'Squire: A Political Eclogue. 1782.
King Stephen's Watch: A Tale Founded on Fact. 1782.
Ode to William Pitt. 1782.
Secular Ode in Commemoration of the Glorious Revolution. 1788.
Religio Clerici. 1810.
Satiric Poems Published Anonymously, edited by Paget Toynbee. 1926.

Plays

Elfrida. 1752.
Caractacus: A Dramatic Poem. 1759; revised version (produced 1764), 1777.
Sappho and *Argentile and Curran,* in *Poems.* 1796–97.

Other

A Copious Collection of Portions of the Psalms, A Critical and Historical Essay on Cathedral Music. 1782.

Animadversions on the Present Government of the York Lunatic Asylum.   1788.
An Occasional Discourse on the Slave Trade.   1788.
Essays on English Church Music.   1795.
Anecdotes of Reynolds.   1859.
The Correspondence of Richard Hurd and Mason, edited by E. H. Pearce and Leonard
     Whibley.   1932.
Gray's Correspondence with Mason, edited by Paget Toynbee and Leonard Whibley, in
     Gray's Correspondence.   3 vols., 1935.
Walpole's Correspondence with Mason, edited by W. S. Lewis and others, in *Walpole's
     Correspondence,* vols. 28–29.   1955.

Editor, *A Catalogue of the Antiquities, Houses, Parks, Plantations, Scenes, and Situations
     in England and Wales.*   1773.
Editor, *The Poems of Gray* (with a memoir).   1775.

Translator, *The Art of Painting of du Fresnoy.*   1783.

Bibliography: *First Editions of Mason* by P. Gaskell, 1951.

Reading List: *Mason: A Study in Eighteenth-Century Culture* by J. W. Draper, 1924; in
Portraits in Satire by Kenneth Hopkins, 1958.

*   *   *

William Mason is probably best remembered for his *Memoir of Thomas Gray,* which
Edmund Gosse magisterially dismissed as a "timid and imperfect work." Mason had been
befriended by Gray, but he has found favour with few other writers. Thomas Seccombe, in
his *The Age of Johnson,* describes Mason's tragedies as "negligible," and that is a kinder
remark than most. And where commentators have not been abusive they have passed over
poor Mason in stony silence. There is, indeed, a very real sense in which he can be regarded
as the Enoch Soames of the eighteenth century.

How fair is this assessment? Unfairly fair, one has to admit. For it does seem unfair that
someone who tried so hard to be a poet and man of letters should have had so little success.
But so it is. Perhaps under the influence of Gray, Mason wrote a number of odes which at
best are mediocre. George Colman published some parodies of them in his *Odes to Obscurity
and Oblivion,* and yet in a sense Mason had already done the job for him. Certainly there is
nothing as funny in Colman's volume as Mason's own "To a Water-Nymph" ("Thy wanton
waters, volatile and free,/Shall wildly warble, as they please,/Their soft loquacious
harmony").

Mason seems to have tried his hand at most kinds of poetry. Quite apart from the verse
tragedies and odes, there are epistles, elegies, satires, and imitations, especially of Milton. For
example, "Ill Bellicoso" is meant to be a comic, sprightly poem in the manner of early Milton
(and in particular of "L'Allegro" and "Il Penseroso"). In fact, it achieves little more than a
leaden buffoonery. As for the monody *Musaeus: To the Memory of Mr. Pope,* with which,
according to Seccombe, Mason "began his pseudo-poetical career," the best that can be said
for it is that at least Pope was out of harm's way by then. The poem is clearly indebted to
Milton's great elegy "Lycidas," but unfortunately *Musaeus* is too bankrupt to be able to repay
the smallest part of the debt. In fact, it has to be said that the poem is an anthology of every
conceivable fault and absurdity, a lesson in how not to do it.

Yet the story is not entirely one of abject failure. For we have to accept that Mason's
readiness to rush into poetic forms where better and wiser poets feared to tread helped give
those forms a currency without which his great successors might have had to struggle harder
than in fact was necessary to break out of what Blake called "the great cage" of the Augustan

heroic couplet. Mason's attempts to write in the Spenserian stanza form are not successful. But those attempts made it that much more possible for Wordsworth and Keats to invade the form like monarchs. Mason deserves our thanks for that, if for no other reason.

—John Lucas

MICKLE, William (Julius).   Scottish.   Born in Langholm, Dumfriesshire, 28 September 1735. Educated at Langholm Grammar School and Edinburgh High School. Married Mary Tomkins in 1781. Clerk in his father's brewery in Edinburgh, 1750–56, and subsequently Chief Partner, 1756–57, and, on his father's death, Owner, 1757 until the business failed, 1763; moved to London; Corrector, Clarendon Press, Oxford, 1765–71; worked on his translation of Camoës at Forest Hill, Oxford, 1772–75; appointed Secretary to Commodore Johnston, sailing with a squadron to Portugal, 1779–80, and on his return to London appointed joint agent for disposal of the squadron's prizes; settled at Wheatley, near Oxford, 1781. Member, Royal Academy of Portugal, 1779. *Died 28 October 1788.*

PUBLICATIONS

Collections

    Poetical Works, edited by J. Sim.   1806.

Verse

    Providence; or, Arandus and Emilee.   1762.
    Pollio: An Elegiac Ode.   1766.
    The Concubine: A Poem in the Manner of Spenser.   1767; as *Syr Martyn*, 1778.
    Almada Hill: An Epistle from Lisbon.   1781.
    The Prophecy of Queen Emma by Turgotus, Prior of Durham in the Reign of William Rufus.   1782.
    Poems, and a Tragedy.   1794.

Play

    The Siege of Marseilles, in *Poems and a Tragedy*.   1794.

Other

    A Letter to Dr. Harwood.   1768.
    Voltaire in the Shades.   1770.
    A Candid Examination of the Reasons for Depriving the East India Company of Its Charter.   1779.

Translator, *The Lusiads; or, The Discovery of India* (in verse), by Camoës.   1776.

Reading List: *Mickle* by Mary E. Taylor, 1937 (includes bibliography).

*   *   *

William Mickle's poems include *The Concubine* (later retitled *Syr Martyn*), a romantic narrative in Spenserian stanzas and pseudo-archaic English, and the ballad "Cumnor Hall." Both may be considered as exercises in the sentimental "Gothic" style of the late eighteenth century. "Cumnor Hall" deals with the story of Amy Robsart, the unfortunate first wife of Robert Dudley, Earl of Leicester, favourite of Queen Elizabeth I. It is said to have influenced Scott's treatment of the same story in *Kenilworth*. Of much more enduring merit than these pieces is "The Mariner's Wife" ("There's nae luck about the house"). This is surely one of the best and best-loved Scottish songs outside the works of Burns. The picture of a sailor's wife awaiting the return of her husband is brought to life by some vivid touches of detail, and without undue sentimentality. (But Mickle's authorship of this poem is doubtful; it has been attributed to Jean Adam, 1710–1765.)

Mickle's most ambitious literary venture was his translation, into herioc couplets, of the *Lusiads*, by the sixteenth-century Portuguese epic poet Luis de Camoës. He accompanied this with a life of Camoës, a dissertation upon the *Lusiads* and on epic poetry, and a sketch of the Portuguese discovery of India. Mickle sometimes expands or paraphrases his original, but his version is vigorous and readable, in the same way that Pope's Homer is readable. The subject – Vasco da Gama's voyage to India via the Cape Route – doubtless appealed to readers in the period when Britain was in the process of founding her own Indian Empire.

—John Heath-Stubbs

MONTAGU, Lady Mary Wortley.   English.   Born in London, baptized 26 May 1689; eldest daughter of the Earl, later Duke, of Kingston. Educated privately. Married Edward Wortley-Montagu in 1712 (separated, 1739; died, 1761); one son and one daughter, Countess of Bute. After her marriage lived in London, a friend of Addison, Pope, and others; lived in Constantinople (while her husband was Ambassador there), 1716–18; thereafter lived in Twickenham; after leaving her husband, 1739, lived in Italy; returned to England after his death, 1761. *Died 21 August 1762.*

PUBLICATIONS

Collections

Complete Letters, edited by Robert Halsband.   3 vols., 1965–67.
Essays, Poems, and Simplicity: A Comedy, edited by Robert Halsband and Isobel Grundy.   1977.

Verse

Court Poems. 1716.
Verses Addressed to the Imitator of Horace. 1733.
An Elegy to a Young Lady in the Manner of Ovid, with an Answer (James Hammond
    wrote the Elegy). 1733.
The Dean's Provocation for Writing the Lady's Dressing-Room. 1734.
Six Town Eclogues, with Some Other Poems. 1747.
Poetical Works, edited by I. Reed. 1768.

Play

Simplicity, from a play by Marivaux, in Essays, Poems, and Simplicity. 1977.

Other

Letters Written During Her Travels. 3 vols., 1763.
The Nonsense of Common-Sense (periodical), edited by Robert Halsband. 1947.

Reading List: The Life of Lady Mary Wortley Montagu by Robert Halsband, 1956.

*   *   *

Lady Mary Wortley Montagu's earliest appearances in print were anonymous or
clandestine. It is believed that she wrote Spectator 573 (28 July 1714) where, under the
character of the president of a club of widows, a kind of latter-day Wife of Bath, she argues
wittily and feelingly the cause of women's rights. Her most considerable venture into
journalism was the nine issues of The Nonsense of Common-Sense (1737–38) which she
wrote to defend Walpole's ministry against an opposition journal entitled Common-Sense,
and where she returned, in passing, to the theme of feminism. A penetrating critique of
Addison's Cato, written in 1713, furnished the playwright with many hints for his revisions
and, perhaps for that reason, was "suppressed at the desire of Mr. Addison" during Lady
Mary's lifetime, but it is difficult to understand why her own play, Simplicity: A Comedy (a
lively adaptation of Le Jeu de l'Amour et du Hasard by Marivaux) remained unacted and
unprinted until the twentieth century.

In her day she was known as a poet, though most of her verses circulated in manuscript
and what was printed appeared usually without her authority. Six burlesque-pastoral "Town
Eclogues," satirizing specific, easily recognizable members of court society, were written in
1715 with some help from Gay and Pope, and this, perhaps, is why they are more
concentrated, vigorous, and polished than any of her other verse. There is more feeling,
however, in her graver feminist poems: for instance, the "Epistle from Mrs. Y. to her
Husband, 1724" which comments on a contemporary divorce case from the viewpoint of a
wronged wife who has committed justifiable adultery (see Review of English Studies, 1972).
The rest of her facile and sometimes extempore occasional verse includes imitations,
translations, love-lyrics, comic squibs (some quite indecent) on contemporary scandals, and
lampoons (mostly against Pope with whom she quarrelled violently in the 1720's).

Her fame now rests mainly upon her letters. Those written from Turkey (where her
husband was ambassador from 1716 to 1718) were edited by her for posthumous publication
and make up one of the outstanding travel books of the eighteenth century – for she was an
alert, sympathetic, inquisitive, articulate, and impressionable traveller. Many of her later
letters retail gossip and London scandals with the racy vigour of a witty, tough-minded

woman of the world; others describe Italian scenes with the clarity and colour of a Canaletto; while others, addressed to a Venetian lover half her age, display, in extraordinary and touching contrast, girlish infatuation and timidity.

—A. J. Sambrook

OLDHAM, John.   English.   Born in Shipton-Moyne, Gloucestershire, 9 August 1653. Educated at Tetbury Grammar School; St. Edmund Hall, Oxford, 1670–74, B.A. 1674. Usher in Archbishop Whitgift's free school at Croydon, Surrey, 1675–78; tutor to the grandsons of Sir Edward Thurland, Reigate, Surrey, 1678–81, and to the son of Sir William Hickes, London, 1681–82; may have briefly studied medicine, 1682; befriended by Lord Kingston, 1682–83. *Died 9 December 1683.*

PUBLICATIONS

Collections

> *Compositions in Prose and Verse,* edited by E. Thompson.   3 vols., 1770.
> *Poetical Works,* edited by R. Bell.   1854.

Verse

> *Upon the Marriage of the Prince of Orange.*   1677.
> *A Satire Against Virtue.*   1679.
> *Garnet's Ghost.*   1679.
> *Satires upon the Jesuits and Some Other Pieces.*   1681.
> *Some New Pieces.*   1681.
> *Poems and Translations.*   1683.
> *Remains in Verse and Prose.*   1684.
> *A Second Musical Entertainment Performed on St. Cecilia's Day.*   1685.

Bibliography: by H.F. Brooks, in *Oxford Bibliographical Society Proceedings 5,* 1936.

Reading List: Introduction by Bonamy Dobrée to *Poetical Works,* 1960.

*   *   *

The Civil War in England divided the country against itself and fostered a taste for political satire. During this period, and for some time thereafter, the market was choked with vituperative tracts, vitriolic pamphlets, animadversions, lampoons, and scarcely lyrical scurrilities that had considerable influence upon Restoration poetry. During the Restoration, the more refined, cavalier mode of the courtiers and their near relations (Dorset, Rochester, Sedley, Dryden, Etherege) prevailed; their tone was most often witty, classical, relaxed – although they were certainly capable of vicious and scatological invectives and *jeux d'esprit*.

John Oldham, on the other hand, was far removed from court and courtly writing. A schoolteacher and tutor most of his life in Gloucestershire, his actual writing career spans only about six years (1677–83). Unlike Samuel Butler (similarly removed from Court), however, he aspired to more austere and classical forms of satire. Oldham's most renowned and sustained work are his four *Satyrs upon the Jesuits*. Born into a nonconformist family and himself a staunch Whig, Oldham responded to the Popish Plot by harshly attacking the Catholics as conspirators seeking to infiltrate and to overthrow the Anglican monarchy; he was especially intemperate about Loyola's Society of Jesus, which he considered to be made up of a pack of ruthless torturers and spies: "Racks, gibbets, halters, were their Arguments." In such a climate, Oldham felt himself vengefully "driven" to write:

> 'Tis pointed *Satyr*, and the *sharps* of Wit
> For such a *prize* are th' only Weapons fit:
> Nor needs there *Art*, or *Genius* here to use,
> Where *Indignation* can create a muse....
> All this urge on my rank envenom'd spleen,
> And with keen Satyr edg my stabbing Pen....

This particular satire met with considerable success in London, and is clearly his one major triumph. It is harsh, dense, and unrelenting, though often wanting in polish or finesse. In an era when the indirection, lightness, and sophistication of Horace were more and more coming into vogue, Oldham patently prefers the caustic muse of Juvenal (and, indeed, in tone and versification, he often sounds like the Elizabethan satirist John Marston). John Oldham did in fact freely translate two of Juvenal's satires (III, XIII) into English, and has sometimes been designated "the English Juvenal."

His *A Satyr Against Vertue* attempts ironically to celebrate vice, but Oldham is unequal to such subtlety, and many readers misunderstood (as they did Defoe's similar irony). Some of his Pindaric odes are at least workmanlike and competent in that genre, and several of his little-known imitations and translations of Horace represent some of his best work. In all, Oldham's *métier* seems to have been the heroic couplet. He wrote a number of satires and even some lighter lyrics (his drinking-song, "The Careless Good Fellow," is still anthologized). Unfortunately, his life was cut short, and he died of smallpox at the age of thirty.

His uneven, abrupt, and too often scattergun verse struck Alexander Pope as "indelicate," and Dryden tended to agree. Yet it was John Dryden, in one of the most moving elegies in the language, "To the Memory of Mr. Oldham," who perhaps does an intense and would-be satirist some justice:

> O early ripe! to thy abundant store
> What could advancing Age have added more?
> It might (what Nature never gives the young)
> Have taught the numbers of thy native Tongue.
> But Satyr needs not those, and Wit will shine
> Through the harsh cadence of a rugged line.
> A noble Error, and but seldom made,
> When Poets are by too much force betray'd.

Oldham did indeed suffer from harsh ruggedness and excessive force, but there *was* some nobility in his poetry.

—John R. Clark

PARNELL, Thomas. English. Born in Dublin, Ireland, in 1679. Educated at Dr. Jones's school, Dublin; Trinity College, Dublin, 1693–1700, B.A. 1697, M.A. 1700; B.D. and D.D. of Dublin University, 1712. Married Anne Minchin in 1706 (died, 1711); two sons and one daughter. Ordained deacon, 1700, priest, 1703; Minor Canon of St. Patrick's, Dublin, 1704; Archdeacon of Clogher, 1706–16; Prebend of Dunlavin, 1713; frequently visited London after 1706: on intimate terms with Swift and other members of the Tory Party by 1711; contributed to the *Spectator*, 1712–13; Member of the Scriblerus Club, 1713; appointed Vicar of Finglas, 1716. *Died* (buried) *24 October 1718.*

PUBLICATIONS

Collections

> *Works, in Verse and Prose.* 1755.
> *Poems*, edited by L. Robinson. 1927.
> *Minor Poets of the Eighteenth Century*, edited by Hugh I'A. Fausset. 1930.

Verse

> *An Essay on the Different Styles of Poetry.* 1713.
> *Homer's Battle of the Frogs and Mice.* 1717.
> *Poems on Several Occasions*, edited by Alexander Pope. 1722.
> *Posthumous Works.* 1758.

Reading List: *Parnell* by Alfred H. Cruickshank, 1921.

*   *   *

Thomas Parnell is a witty and graceful minor poet, who was a friend and close literary associate of Swift and especially of Pope. He was a protégé of Swift in his literary and his clerical career, and an original member of the Scriblerus Club. He helped Pope with his translation of the *Iliad*, and wrote the "Essay on the Life, Writings, and Learning of Homer" prefixed to the translation. He also translated the pseudo-Homeric *Battle of the Frogs and Mice*, published in 1717 together with some satirical apparatus designed to support Pope in the controversy surrounding his Homeric enterprise. The main collection of Parnell's work is *Poems on Several Occasions*, edited by Pope. Pope altered Parnell's text, although we do not know exactly how, since the papers he used did not survive. Some autograph versions of these poems have, however, recently been discovered, along with many new poems. Two later collections, the *Works, in Verse and Prose* and the *Posthumous Works*, can also largely be authenticated by manuscripts. Most of the manuscripts are in my custody at the University of Warwick, and a complete edition is in preparation.

The poems, published and unpublished, include a large group of religious meditations; a verse *Essay on the Different Styles of Poetry*; some rather feeble satires; political poems on the Peace of Utrecht and related matters; poems in praise of Swift, Pope, and other Scriblerians, and contributions to Scriblerian warfare, chiefly against Pope's literary enemies; translations from Greek and Latin (*The Battle of the Frogs and Mice*, "The Vigil of Venus"); some attractive lyrics ("When thy beauty appears," "My days have been so wondrous free"); and a variety of hymns, "imitations," epigrams, and other works. But perhaps his two best-known poems are "The Hermit" (a retelling of a pious fable) and "A Night-Piece on Death" (an early example of eighteenth-century "graveyard" poetry). Oliver Goldsmith wrote a life of Parnell in 1770, and Johnson included him in the *Lives of the Poets*.

—C. J. Rawson

PHILIPS, Ambrose. English. Born in Shrewsbury, Shropshire, c. 1675. Educated at St. John's College, Cambridge, B.A. 1696, M.A. 1700. Fellow of St. John's College, 1699–1707; member of Addison's circle, London, in the early 1700's; Justice of the Peace for Westminster; Commissioner for the Lottery, 1717; Founder-Editor, *The Freethinker*, 1718–19; held various posts in Ireland from 1724: Secretary to the Bishop of Armagh, 1724, and to the Lord Chancellor, 1726; Member of the Irish Parliament for Armagh, 1727; Judge of the Prerogative Court, 1733; returned to London, 1748. *Died 18 June 1749*.

PUBLICATIONS

Collections

Poems, edited by Mary G. Segar. 1937.

Verse

Pastorals. 1710; edited by R. H. Griffith, as *A Variorum Text of Four [of the Six] Pastorals*, in *Texas University Studies*, 1932.
An Epistle to Charles Lord Halifax. 1714.
An Epistle to James Craggs. 1717.
An Ode in the Manner of Pindar on the Death of William, Earl Cowper. 1723.
To the Honourable Miss Carteret. 1725.
To Miss Georgiana. 1725.
To the Lord Carteret. 1726.
Supplication for Miss Carteret in the Smallpox. 1726.
To Miss Margaret Pulteney. 1727.
Farmer Pope and His son, with *Codrus* by Edmund Curll and Elizabeth Thomas. 1728.
Pastorals, Epistles, Odes, and Other Original Poems, with Translations from Pindar, Anacreon, and Sappho. 1748.

Plays

The Distressed Mother, from a play by Racine (produced 1712). 1712.
The Briton (produced 1722). 1722.
Humfrey, Duke of Gloucester (produced 1723). 1723.

Other

The Freethinker.   3 vols., 1722.

Editor, *Life of John Williams,* by J. Hacket.   1700.
Editor, *Letters to Several Ministers of State,* by Hugh Boulter.   2 vols., 1769–70.

Translator, *Persian Tales,* by Petis de la Croix.   1709.

*   *   *

Ambrose Philips is perhaps chiefly remembered for his pastorals, and this largely because of the quarrel with Pope their publication engendered. Addison had written a series of articles in *The Guardian* in which he acclaimed Philips as the true successor of Theocritus, Virgil, and Spenser. This enraged Pope, who had recently published his own youthful pastorals, and he sent to Steele, the *Guardian's* editor, a further anonymous article in which he quoted passages from his own work beside parallel passages from Philips, ironically praising the latter. He later satirised Philips in the character sketch entitled "Umbra." Gay's pastorals *The Shepherd's Week* owe their genesis to the same quarrel. Philips had argued that simple rusticity was the main quality to be aimed at in the pastoral and, following Spenser, had given English names, such as Hobbinol and Rosalind, to his shepherds. Gay parodied this by using names like Grubbinol and Blowselind, and giving to these characters some of the real manners and much of the folk lore of genuine English peasants. Philips's goal of simplicity too often landed him in mere insipidity – and indeed "insipid" seems to be the epithet which inevitably comes up in any discussion of Philips's work. His pastorals do however contain passages of some charm.

Philips's tragedy *The Distressed Mother* was an adaptation of Racine's *Andromaque.* With some assistance from promotion by Addison in the *Spectator,* and Addison's claque in the theatre, it achieved success and held the stage for some time. Of his other two plays, *The Briton* and *Humfrey, Duke of Gloucester,* Johnson remarks, in the *Lives of the Poets* that they "are not below mediocrity, nor above it." Johnson further remarked of Philips's translations of Pindar that "he found the art of reaching all the obscurity of the Theban bard, however he may fall below his sublimity; he will be allowed, if he has less fire, to have more smoke." His translations of Sappho appeared in a *Spectator* paper for the first time introducing the Greek lyric poetess to English readers. Philips made a thoroughly rococo job of the "Ode to Aphrodite," but his version of the "Ode to Anactoria" has some of the directness, if not the intensity, of the original.

Later in his career Philips abandoned some of the stricter canons of Augustan taste. His poems to persons of quality (some of them addressed to children) are written in short trochaic couplets. These verses earned him from Henry Carey (author of *Sally in Our Alley*) the nickname of "Namby-Pamby." The *faux naif* quality of these verses seems to have earned them the esteem of such Victorian anthologists and critics as Palgrave and Edmund Gosse, but the contemporary reader may be disposed to echo Carey's view of them. To us it may seem that Philips's "Epistle to the Earl of Dorset" (from Copenhagen) is perhaps his best poem. Here he exhibits originality and descriptive force in rendering a northern winter scene.

—John Heath-Stubbs

PHILIPS, John.   English.   Born in Bampton, Oxfordshire, 30 December 1676. Educated at Winchester College (scholar), 1691–97; Christ Church, Oxford, matriculated 1697. Employed by Harley and St. John as a propagandist. Consumptive. *Died 15 February 1709.*

PUBLICATIONS

Collections

  Poems, edited by M. G. Lloyd Thomas.   1927.

Verse

  The Sylvan Dream; or, The Mourning Muses.   1701.
  The Splendid Shilling: An Imitation of Milton.   1701.
  Blenheim.   1705.
  Cerealia: An Imitation of Milton.   1706; revised edition, 1706.
  Honoratissimo Viro Henrico Saint John, Armigero: Ode.   1707.
  Ode Gratulatoria Willielmo Cowper.   1707.
  Cider.   1708.
  Poems.   1712.

Bibliography: in *Poems*, 1927.

Reading List: *The English Georgic* by John Chalker, 1969.

*   *   *

In his own time John Philips owed a large part of his fame to a couple of earlier works. Neither *The Splendid Shilling* nor *Blenheim* compels an equivalent degree of admiration today, when their adaptation of Miltonic style is liable to seem coy and archaic. To contemporaries, *The Splendid Shilling* appeared daring in its strategy of turning Milton's verbal gestures to a low subject-matter – the work provides a picture of the distressed poet, skulking in penury as the bailiffs make their rounds. Classical epic had been much burlesqued, but this was the first extended mock-Miltonic, that is to say a poem travestying specifically *English* modes of poeticism. Humour and a whiff of first-person authenticity help to carry off the effect. *Blenheim* attempts to enlist the grand style for propagandist ends, and falls at times into awkward postures, such as a parenthesis within parentheses at lines 16–20.

Philips's most successful poetry, both for local felicities and for overall coherence, is found in *Cyder*. To all intents and purposes a formal Georgic in two books, this mixes the comic burlesque of *The Splendid Shilling* with the patriotic aims of *Blenheim*. If it had achieved nothing else, the poem would have had the merit of showing subsequent English poets how to make use of the Virgilian combination (husbandry plus politics) for their own needs: Pope's *Windsor-Forest* is directly indebted to *Cyder* at several points. Philips is particularly successful in counterpointing an innocent rural vocation against the threats of a more active life in less temperate climes. He inserts, for example, an elevated passage describing an earthquake in a lost Roman city (usually identified with Hereford, and thus prolonging a regional theme in the poem). As John Chalker, Philips's best modern critic, observes, "By temporarily going beyond his bucolic subject matter to the wider world of a lost heroic age, and by setting his 'humble' subject against that extensive background, Philips deliberately encourages the reader to consider the value of the activities which are the subject of the poem." As well as the technical accounts of arboriculture and cider-making which provide opportunities for joking inflation of humdrum reality, Philips affords us an easy modulation into scrutiny of the natural order, the connection of beauty and use in the landscape, the values of an agrarian society. The blank verse of *Cyder*, grandiloquent as it often is, has ceased to be merely a parodic instrument; it opens the way for the garrulous, loose-jointed, and histrionic idiom of Thomson and Cowper, poets who were the freer because Philips had gone over the top. He writes of

> *Sylvan* Shades, and silent Groves,
> (Haunt of the *Druids*) whence the Hearth is fed
> With copious Fuel; whence the sturdy Oak,
> A Prince's Refuge once, th'aeternal Guard
> Of *England*'s Throne, by sweating Peasants fell'd,
> Stems the vast Main, and bears tremendous War
> To distant Nations, or with Sov'ran Sway
> Aws the divided World to Peace and Love.

At such moments the false heroics of burlesque turn into something very like mythopoeic invention, and it was on this that John Philips's successors were able to build.

—Pat Rogers

PHILIPS, Katherine (née Fowler). Pseudonym: Orinda.   English.   Born in London, 1 January 1631. Educated at Mrs. Salmon's School, Hackney, London. Married James Philips in 1647; one son and one daughter. After marriage divided her time between her husband's estate in Cardigan and London: centre of a literary circle that included Henry Vaughan, Jeremy Taylor, and Abraham Cowley; adopted the name Orinda to which contemporaries prefixed the epithet "matchless." *Died 22 June 1664.*

PUBLICATIONS

Collections

Selected Poems, edited by Louise Imogen Guiney.   2 vols., 1904–05.

Verse

Poems. 1664.
Poems, to Which Is Added Corneille's Pompey and Horace, edited by Sir Charles Cotterell.   1667.

Plays

Pompey, from the play by Corneille (produced 1663).   1663.

Horace, completed by John Denham, from the play by Corneille (produced
   1668).   1678.

Other

Familiar Letters (by Rochester, Thomas Otway, and Philips), edited by Tom Brown and
   Charles Gildon.   2 vols., 1697.
Letters from Orinda to Poliarchus.   1705.

Reading List: *The Matchless Orinda* by P. W. Souers, 1931.

*   *   *

If "the matchless Orinda" no longer inspires, as Langbaine predicted in 1691, an immortal
memory "honour'd of all Men that are Favourers of Poetry," she still merits study as more
than historically the first significant English poetess. As one of the few active poets during the
decade before the Restoration, Katherine Philips shows in her work the tension between
metaphysical elevation of ingenuity and an evolving neo-classical admiration for pellucid
thought in "easy" versification. She is also interesting as the purest English expression of the
vogue of Platonic *Précieuse* – an ideal of love and honor and literacy adapted from
seventeenth-century French romances in reaction to what she perceived to be the "dull and
sullen" excesses of the Interregnum. Platonic friendship is her most characteristic theme, and
her many poems to Lucasia and Rosania escape artificiality because of the same authentic
intensity which inspired admiration in friends like Henry Vaughan, Jeremy Taylor, and
Abraham Cowley.

Adopting the cavalier vein of William Cartwright, Orinda's lyrics move in a realm of
empyrean abstraction far above the compromises and contradictions of contemporary affairs.
Yet somehow she is best when she is abstract, for the concrete seems to have stimulated the
artificial in her and only in hymning an ideal passion does she seem unpretentious. Her best
songs continue the Caroline genius for song – lyric yet resonant with the spoken word,
wittily ingenious without self-indulgent audacity. If there is too much of the affectation of the
Précieuse in "To Mrs. M. A. at Parting," which Keats admired, her "To My Excellent
Lucasia, on Our Friendship" is nearly perfect:

> I did not live until this time
>   Crown'd my felicity,
> When I could say without a crime,
>   I am not thine, but Thee.

Although her songs are her enduring claim to distinction, Orinda's didactic poems or
couplet essays are worth study as innovations in a form that was to flower in Dryden and
Pope. Nor are her couplets contemptible. They draw strength from their approximation to
human speech in the second line – an idiomatic effect often achieved by forcing the syntax of
the initial line: "Silence with things transcendent nearest suits,/The greatest Emperors are
serv'd by mutes." At their best, as in "The World," her couplets are concise without
sacrificing suggestiveness: "We live by chance and slip into events;/Have all of beasts except
their innocence." In the couplets of *Pompey* Katherine Philips produced what her
contemporaries considered one of the literary triumphs of the age and what may still be the
best verse translation of Corneille in English. If some of the sublimity of the French is
inevitably lost, *Pompey* is nonetheless meticulously faithful to the spirit and phrase of the
original and is uniquely successful in translating Corneille's rhetorical devices.

However, it is not her writings in verse that the present age is apt to find most engaging but her letters to the courtier Sir Charles Cotterell. These, published as *Letters from Orinda to Poliarchus*, give an almost Richardsonian reality to Katherine's personal and literary life and deserve a place in the development of the epistolary novel. As a writer of letters Katherine Philips is inferior to no seventeenth-century woman with the possible exception of her friend Dorothy Temple. The attractive portrait that emerges from the *Letters* gives a unique vividness to the personality which Dryden and his age regarded as the paragon of female poets.

—Harry M. Solomon

POMFRET, John. English. Born in Luton, Bedfordshire, in 1667. Educated at Bedford Grammar School; Queens' College, Cambridge, B.A. 1684, M.A. 1688. Married Elizabeth Wingate in 1692; one son. Took holy orders: Rector of Maulden, Bedfordshire, 1695–1702, and of Millbrook, Bedfordshire, 1702. *Died* (buried) *1 December 1702.*

PUBLICATIONS

Verse

An Epistle to Charles, Earl of Dorset. 1690.
The Sceptical Muse. 1699.
Poems. 1699; revised edition, 1702, 1710, 1790.
A Prospect of Death. 1700.
Reason. 1700.
The Choice or Wish. 1700.
Two Love Poems. 1701.
Quae Rara, Chara: A Poem on Panthea's Confinement. 1707.

Reading List: "Pomfret's *Choice*" in *Reconsiderations* by E. E. Kellett, 1928.

*   *   *

Students of the eighteenth century have often sought out John Pomfret's *Choice* simply because Samuel Johnson thought it possibly the most often "perused" poem of his lifetime. The search is rewarding because the poem, published at the very beginning of the century, so well sets forth the calm moderation, the distrust of extremes, which strongly appealed to the age. The political and religious controversies and violence of the seventeenth century seemed ended when William and Mary came to the throne. Pomfret remembered Monmouth's Insurrection of 1685 and wrote of it in one early poem, "Cruelty and Lust." But by the end of the century he was writing *The Choice* in an altogether different mood. The way now seemed open for man to examine his various options and to make deliberate choice of the way he wished to live. The idea was to recur throughout the century; Goldsmith's *Traveller* is a case in point, and Johnson's first title for *Rasselas* was *The Choice of Life.*
Pomfret's formulation of the good life evidently appealed strongly to cultivated readers, at

least in theory. Avoiding the extremes of rustic and urban, he would live *near* some "fair town" in a house neither too little nor too large; he would wish a modest fortune for genteel, not great, life. His table would be spread with frugal plenty, healthy but not luxurious. He would have a small wine cellar but no "high drinking." He would wish three friends, two male and one female. The latter would be a modest and obliging neighbor ("for I'd have no wife") whom he would visit occasionally: "But so divine, so noble a repast/I'd seldom, and with moderation, taste." One cannot but sympathize with the bishop who is reputed to have hesitated giving Pomfret a living because of these lines, but, as Johnson says, "It had happened to Pomfret as to almost all other men who plan schemes of life; he had departed from his purpose, and was then married."

The Choice describes a quiet life devoted to studies and friends, all worries evidently excluded. The well-turned couplets illustrate the moderation which they preach, never irregular, never disappointing ear or mind, never rising to heights of imagination, wit, or intensity. Its charm today lies in its portrayal of a world remote from modern life.

Although *The Choice* is Pomfret's best poem, several of the others have a similar antiquarian interest, chiefly those concerned with love: "Love Triumphant over Reason," "The Fortunate Complaint," "Strephon's Love for Delia Justified," and especially "An Epistle to Delia." These poems, totally unromantic of course, were all written when the poet was a young man (he died in his mid-thirties) yet reveal a strangely controlled and rational view of the matter, part of the business of life and a choice to be exercised with discretion. Most detached and prudential of all is his advice "To a Friend Inclined to Marry," setting forth his requirements for a wife as to her birth, fortune, and personal qualities. Pomfret's other poems (only nineteen are published in all) run to religious themes and Pindaric affectations. There is little reason to disturb them.

—Harlan W. Hamilton

POPE, Alexander. English. Born in London, 21 May 1688; lame at birth. Attended several schools but because of ill health did not remain long at any of them; lived at his father's house at Binfield, Windsor Forest, after 1700, and completed his education by reading; also studied Italian and French, in London, 1703. Inherited a small income from his father; excluded, as a Roman Catholic, from attending university or holding public office, he lived solely and successfully as a man of letters. Associated with the Whig writers, Congreve, William Walsh, Addison and Steele, 1706–11; with the Tory wits, Swift, Dr. Arbuthnot, John Gay, Thomas Parnell, and the politicians Oxford and Bolingbroke, from 1712: with the others formed the Scriblerus Club, 1713; supported himself by working on translations of Homer and by editing Shakespeare, 1713–26; lived at Twickenham, Middlesex, after 1718. *Died 30 May 1744.*

PUBLICATIONS

Collections

Works, edited by W. Elwin and W. J. Courthope. 10 vols., 1871–89.
Correspondence, edited by George Sherburn. 5 vols., 1956.
Poems, edited by John Butt and others. 10 vols., 1939–67; revised edition of vols. 1–6, 1 vol., 1963.
Poetical Works, edited by Herbert Davis. 1966.

Verse

An Essay on Criticism. 1711; edited by R. M. Schmitz, 1962.
Windsor-Forest. 1713; edited by R. M. Schmitz, 1952.
Ode for Music. 1713.
The Rape of the Lock. 1714; edited by J. S. Cunningham, 1966.
The Temple of Fame: A Vision. 1715.
To the Ingenious Mr. Moore, Author of the Celebrated Worm-Powder. 1716.
A Roman Catholic Version of the First Psalm. 1716.
The Court Ballad. 1717.
Works. 2 vols., 1717–35.
Duke upon Duke. 1720; as *An Excellent Old Ballad, Called Pride Will Have a Fall,* 1720.
The Discovery. 1727; as *The 'Squire Turned Ferret,* 1727.
Miscellanies in Prose and Verse, with others. 4 vols., 1727–32; *Peri Bathos; or, The Art of Sinking in Poetry,* edited by E. L. Steeves, 1952.
The Dunciad: An Heroic Poem in Three Books. 1728; revised edition, 1728 (twice); *The Dunciad Variorum,* 1729; *The New Dunciad,* 1742; *The Dunciad in Four Books,* 1743.
An Epistle to Richard, Earl of Burlington. 1731; as *Of Taste,* 1732; as *Of False Taste,* 1732.
Of the Use of Riches: An Epistle to Bathurst. 1732; edited by E. R. Wasserman, 1960.
An Essay on Man. 4 vols., 1733–34.
The Impertinent. 1733.
The First Satire of the Second Book of Horace, Imitated. 1733; with the second satire, 1734.
An Epistle to Richard Lord Viscount Cobham. 1733.
Sober Advice from Horace. 1734.
An Epistle to Dr. Arbuthnot. 1734; edited by John Butt, 1954.
Of the Characters of Women. 1735.
Bounce to Fop. 1736.
Horace His Ode to Venus, lib. iv, Ode i, Imitated. 1737.
The Second Book of the Epistles of Horace Imitated (two poems). 1737.
The Sixth Epistle of the First Book of Horace Imitated. 1738.
An Imitation of the Sixth Satire of the Second Book of Horace (by Swift, completed by Pope). 1738.
The First Epistle of the First Book of Horace Imitated. 1738.
One Thousand Seven Hundred and Thirty Eight [*Epilogue to the Satires, Dialogue i*]. 1738; *Dialogue ii,* 1738.
The Universal Prayer. 1738.
Poems and Imitations of Horace. 1738 (published as *Works,* vol. 2, part 2).
Epistles of Horace Imitated. 1738.
A Blast upon Bays; or, A New Lick at the Laureate. 1742.

Plays

Three Hours after Marriage, with Arbuthnot and Gay (produced 1717). 1717; revised version in *Supplement to the Works of Pope,* 1757; 1717 edition edited by Richard Marton and William Peterson, 1961.
Esther: An Oratorio, with Arbuthnot and Samuel Humphreys, music by Handel (produced 1732). 1732.

Other

The Critical Specimen. 1711.
The Narrative of Dr. Robert Norris. 1713.
A Key to the Lock. 1715; revised edition, 1715.
The Dignity, Use, and Abuse of Glass-Bottles. 1715.
A Full and True Account of a Horrid and Barbarous Revenge by Poison on the Body of Mr. Edmund Curll, Bookseller. 1716; *A Further Account,* 1716.
God's Revenge Against Punning. 1716.
The Plot Discovered; or, A Clue to the Comedy of the Non-Juror. 1718.
A Receipt to Make a Soup. 1727.
Letters of Mr. Pope and Several Eminent Persons. 1735; revised edition, 5 vols., 1735–37.
Works. 7 vols., 1736–41.
Works in Prose. 2 vols., 1737–41.
Works, with His Last Corrections, Additions, and Improvements, edited by William Warburton. 9 vols., 1751.
A Supplement to the Works. 1757.
Additions to the Works. 2 vols., 1776.

Editor, *Miscellaneous Poems and Translations by Several Hands.* 1714.
Editor, *Poems on Several Occasions.* 1717; as *Pope's Own Miscellany,* edited by N. Ault, 1735.
Editor, *Poems on Several Occasions,* by Thomas Parnell. 1722.
Editor, *The Works of John Sheffield, Duke of Buckingham.* 2 vols., 1723.
Editor, *The Works of Shakespeare.* 6 vols., 1725.

Translator, *The Iliad of Homer.* 6 vols., 1715–20.
Translator, *The Odyssey of Homer.* 5 vols., 1725–26.

Bibliography: *Pope: A Bibliography* by R. H. Griffith, 2 vols., 1922–27; *Pope: A List of Critical Studies 1895–1944* by T. E. Tobin, 1945.

Reading List: *On the Poetry of Pope* by Geoffrey Tillotson, 1938, revised edition, 1950; *Pope's Dunciad: A Study of Its Meaning* by Aubrey Williams, 1955; *The Major Satires of Pope* by Robert W. Rogers, 1955; *Pope: The Poetry of Allusion* by R. A. Brower, 1959; *Essential Articles for the Study of Pope* edited by Maynard Mack, 1964, revised edition, 1968; *The World of Pope's Satires* by Peter Dixon, 1968; *The Garden and the City* by Maynard Mack, 1969; *Pope* by Elizabeth Gurr, 1971; *Writers and Their Background: Pope* edited by Peter Dixon, 1972; *Pope: The Critical Heritage* edited by John Barnard, 1973; *The Social Milieu of Pope* by Howard Erskine-Hill, 1975; *An Introduction to Pope* by Pat Rogers, 1976.

*   *   *

Alexander Pope found his voice so early, and began to acquire friends and influence so young, that he has seemed to hostile readers a safe establishment poet. In fact, he was a member of a beleaguered minority – the papists – and further handicapped by his wretched health, a topic well handled by Marjorie Hope Nicolson and G. S. Rousseau in their book *This Long Disease, My Life* (1968). Much of Pope's later work can be viewed as the struggle to forge a rhetoric of dissent, that is a poetic idiom expressing Opposition ideology and – in a strict sense – reactionary values, as the England of George II and Robert Walpole struck off on a new course. But from the start he had shown the capacity to deliver the unexpected, at the level of phrasing or of larger poetic strategies. A tame, house-trained writer would never have needed to evolve such a resourceful, dense, or energetic style.

By the time he was thirty Pope was exceedingly famous, with a collection of impressive works all decked out to advantage in his *Works* (1717), a sort of retrospective exhibition and also a catalogue raisonné of his preoccupations up to that date. His themes had ranged from politics to pastoralism, from history to mythology, and from the low jinks of high society to the profession of an erotic faith by a religious devotee. Generally a lyrical element is present, and while this is not undercut as it was to be in *The Dunciad* Pope often finds ways of misapplying the lyricism or of bending it to unusual purposes. Only the "Pastorals" (1709) make their claim exclusively in this vein, with their mellifluous diction, their rather passive relation to tradition, and their elaborate phonetic patterning – devices that are principally used, in fact, to image the "turn" of the year and recurrent items in the natural cycle.

Elsewhere, the lyrical element has to earn its place alongside motifs that may be harsh or humdrum. In his *Essay on Criticism*, Pope is lecturing the age upon its pedantry, ill-breeding, and narrowmindedness: but, unlike many lecturers, he avoids these qualities in his own discourse. Still more remarkable, he shows himself able to set out aesthetic theory in an aesthetically pleasing manner. The separate lines and couplets are so memorable that dozens are known out of context ("A little Learning is a dang'rous Thing"; "snatch a Grace beyond the Reach of Art"; "First follow Nature"; "True Wit is Nature to Advantage drest,/What oft was Thought, but ne'er so well Exprest"; "True Ease in Writing comes from Art, not Chance"; "To Err is Humane; to Forgive, Divine"; "For Fools rush in where Angels fear to tread"; and many more). Solemn Popians tell us we ought not to squeeze these phrases out of the poem, but really they survive their conversion to proverbial uses amazingly well. Pope's task was to instruct us through wit, and the most eloquent passages have a vivid life of their own beyond the immediate needs of the argument.

Windsor-Forest exaggerates Pope's usual habit of doing three things at once. It takes on perhaps too much: using Pope's boyhood home near Windsor as a focus of pastoral retreat and also as a fount of patriotism, the work attempts to celebrate a topical event (the signing of a peace treaty by the Tory ministry) while dealing with wider currents of history and mythology. Like many of the early poems, it raises large questions about artistic vocation. Even though we no longer misread *Windsor-Forest* as a failed nineteenth-century nature poem, its studied organisation and overpacked symbolism still ensure that it has not become a general favourite, even among those attuned to Pope's style. Neither for that matter has *The Temple of Fame*, despite Wilson Knight's impassioned advocacy and its starkly eloquent contemplation of the nature of heroism. Even "Eloisa to Abelard," direct and dramatic, as far from the marmoreal face of stoical classicism as one could get, draws readers for what it says rather than the way it is said. Although Pope is registering the feelings of a distracted woman, his rhetoric goes on defining the emotions with total accuracy. There is no linguistic breakdown, no fraying of the poetic medium, no loss of expressive control to match the speaker's nervous crisis.

Unquestionably it is *The Rape of the Lock* which comes home most strongly to the present age, as it has to most generations of readers. It is concerned with events ridiculous in their triviality and their temporality, yet it creates something that can fairly be called sublime in the fulfilment of its imaginative design. A strange vein of wonder runs through the poem, which serves (more than the chance plot-similarities) to establish a deep kinship with *A Midsummer Night's Dream*. Pope's particular genius shows itself in the way he builds around the everyday happenings in a not-very-intelligent court circle the power of a supernatural fable. From a silly book that had less to do with the Rosicrucian enlightenment than with the popular taste for blending sex with the occult, he picked up the idea of the elementals who stand in for the divine "machinery" of serious epic. Everything is proportionately downgraded, just as Swift scaled physical details down in Lilliput. A distant, heroic, masculine, martial, historic world is replaced by a drearily contemporary, petty, feminine (or effeminate), card-playing, resolutely *ephemeral* setting. Only the language remains: enough of the noble diction of epic, at least, to allow Pope reminders of the world we have lost. A kind of familiarising intimacy, appropriate to the cosy boudoir atmosphere of Belinda's life, suffuses the texture of the poetry. *The Rape of the Lock* is a living classic, which along with social and psychological observation acts out a myth of sexuality: biology and upbringing are at war, while the sylphs and the gnomes contend for the heroine's soul.

After a decade spent translating Homer and editing Shakespeare, Pope returned to original composition with the first version of *The Dunciad* in 1728. This is often treated as his swan-song, and it ought to be remembered that only the fourth book (and not even the famous conclusion to *that*) is really a late work. In some respects it might be better to think of *The Dunciad* as a "middle-period" work, still fanciful in execution and somewhat veiled in its methods. Scores of individuals do come in for attack in the poem, but only very obliquely are the King and his prime minister indicted, although the essential logic of the fable requires that they occupy a central role. (It is possible that the original intention was to produce a mock-coronation ceremony for the new king.) As it is, *The Dunciad* is an uproarious and splendidly comic version of recent political and literary history. In either version it makes powerful inroads into the court defences, especially through the medium of the poet laureate, Colley Cibber, when he is elevated to the throne of Dulness. But by the standards of Pope's true "later" style – that is, the urgent mode of topicalised Horace he perfected in the 1730's – *The Dunciad* might be regarded as just a little dispersed and wayward. Its highest merit lies in masterful use of the arts of language rather than in a completely sustained portrayal of civilisation in decay.

What I have called the "later" style was evolving around 1730, when Pope began to publish fragments of what he planned as a great moral work on a monumental scale. The outlying parts that remain are *An Essay on Man* (1733–34) and the four *Moral Essays* (1731–35). The *Essay* has today a reputation for windy eloquence and optimistic Panglossian metaphysics: neither expectation is wholly borne out by the text, but there is enough to explain the common belief on these points. As to the *Moral Essays*, they represent Pope at just about his very best – or at least three of the four do. The *Epistle to Burlington* and the *Epistle to Bathurst* both illustrate Pope's capacity to draw large poetic meanings out of tiny social circumstances. As Howard Erskine-Hill's recent book shows, he makes the small change of political and economic history into fictions expressing "the deeper loyalties and antipathies of his life." Again, in the "Epistle to a Lady," we are led with consummate skill in poetic construction from trivial aspects of the feminine round to the very inmost existential state of woman.

It is perhaps the *Imitations of Horace* (1733–38) which best exemplify Pope's mature accomplishment. They are mostly couched in a conversational idiom, now jaunty, now abrupt; vigorous, off the cuff, racily contemporaneous. Pope sets out not to translate Horace literally, but to find equivalents in his own surroundings. More anxious and more subjective than the Roman satirist, Pope confronts his own destiny as a writer while identifying the ills of society at large. The famous *Epistle to Dr. Arbuthnot*, later designated as the prologue to these imitations, exemplifies the blend of public and private themes, although it has no precise Horatian antecedent. By now Pope has become more frontal in his attack on the Walpolian system of government; poet and minister had become, as Maynard Mack puts it, "mighty opposites," spokesmen for contending orders of value. It is in these later poems that Pope became, paradoxically, both a more overtly political writer and a more nakedly confessional poet. But he had not wrung the neck of his early rhetoric: he simply pared down his style, loosened it slightly (e.g., by admitting more elisions) and let out the constraints on syntax by a notch or two. His formal skills allowed him to do even more when his themes darkened, so that his later manner has no need to repudiate its origins.

—Pat Rogers

PRIOR, Matthew. English. Born near Wimborne Minster, Dorset, 21 July 1664. Educated at Westminster School, London, under the patronage of Lord Dorset (King's Scholar, 1681); St. John's College, Cambridge, B.A. 1686, M.A. 1700. Appointed Fellow of St. John's College, 1688; tutor to one of Lord Exeter's sons, 1688; Secretary to Lord Dursley, Ambassador to the Hague, 1689–97; secretary in the negotiations for the Treaty of Ryswick, 1697; secretary to the embassy in Paris, 1698; Under-Secretary of State, England, 1699; Member of Parliament for East Grinstead, 1701; Commissioner of Trade and Plantations, 1701–07; joined the Tory party, 1702; appointed commissioner of Customs, 1711; sent to Paris by Oxford's Tory government to negotiate for the end of the War of the Spanish Succession, 1711: helped draft the Treaty of Utrecht, popularly known as "Matt's peace," 1713; recalled from Paris on the fall of the Tory government and imprisoned in the Tower of London in the belief that he would incriminate Oxford as a traitor, 1715, released, 1717; through a gift of Lord Harley bought Down Hall, Essex, 1719, and retired there. *Died 18 September 1721.*

PUBLICATIONS

Collections

    Literary Works, edited by H. B. Wright and M. K. Spears.   2 vols., 1959.

Verse

    On the Coronation.   1685.
    The Hind and the Panther Transversed to the Story of the Country Mouse and the City Mouse, with Charles Montagu.   1687.
    An Ode in Imitation of the Second Ode of the Third Book of Horace.   1692.
    For the New Year: To the Sun.   1694.
    To the King: An Ode on His Majesty's Arrival in Holland.   1695.
    An English Ballad in Answer to Mr. Despreaux's Pindarique Ode on the Taking of Namure.   1695.
    Verses Humbly Presented to the King at His Arrival in Holland.   1696.
    Carmen Saeculare for the Year 1700 (with Latin translation by Thomas Dibben).   1700.
    To a Young Gentleman in Love.   1703.
    A Letter to Monsieur Boileau Depreaux Occasioned by the Victory at Blenheim.   1704.
    An English Padlock.   1705.
    Pallas and Venus: An Epigram.   1706.
    An Epistle from the Elector Bavaria to the French King.   1706.
    An Ode Humbly Inscribed to the Queen.   1706.
    Poems on Several Occasions.   1707; revised edition, 1709, 1718.
    Horace lib. I epist ix Imitated.   1711.
    To the Right Honorable Mr. Harley, Wounded by Guiscard.   1711.
    Archibaldi Pitcarnii Scoti Carmen Imitated.   1712.
    Walter Danniston ad Amicos Imitated.   1712(?).
    Earl Robert's Mice.   1712.
    Two Imitations of Chaucer.   1712.
    A Fable of the Widow and Her Cat.   1712.
    A Memorial Against the Mortifying of the Ports of Dunkirk and Mardike.   1715.
    The Dove.   1717.

The Conversation.   1720.
Colin's Mistakes.   1721.
A Supplement to Mr. Prior's Poems.   1722.
The Turtle and the Sparrow.   1723.
Down-Hall.   1723.

Other

A New Answer to an Argument Against a Standing Army.   1697.
The History of His Own Time (miscellany), edited by J. Bancks.   1740.
Original Letters from Prior (and others), edited by R. Warner.   1817.

Reading List: *Prior: Poet and Diplomatist* by C. K. Eves, 1939; *Prior* by R. W. Ketton-Cremer, 1957.

*   *   *

Matthew Prior is best remembered for his curt, colloquial poetic tales ("Hans Carvel," "The Ladle," "Paulo Purganti and His Wife," "Protagenes and Apelles"), for his dialogues ("Henry and Emma, A Poem, Upon the Model of The Nut-brown Maid," "The Turtle and the Sparrow"), for his amorous and cynical love lyrics to Chloes, Phyllisses, and Lisettas, for caustic epigrams, and for witty verse epistles. Yet he was also a man of action, verse-man but also politician. For over twenty years he had served with signal success (until the death of Queen Anne) as a distinguished diplomat. In a sense, Prior realized the ideals of the Restoration and Neo-Classical Age: despite his lowly birth, he was a man of wit and banter and yet a sophisticated and Horatian man of the world.

In his *The Conversation: A Tale*, he can step back and ironically take a cool look at himself. In the poem, one Damon in a tavern engages a stranger in conversation; Damon boasts of knowing Matt. Prior well. Needless to say, the "stranger" in the case is Prior himself. But listen to Damon hold forth:

> But (pass His Politics and Prose)
> I never herded with his Foes;
> Nay, in his Verses, as a Friend,
> I still found Something to commend:
> Sir, I excus'd his NUT-BROWN MAID;
> Whate'er severer Critics said:
> Too far, I own, the Girl was try'd:
> The Women All were on my Side.
> For ALMA I return'd Him Thanks:
> I lik'd Her with her little Pranks:
> Indeed poor SOLOMON in Rhime
> Was much too grave to be Sublime.

Prior displays clear perception. He had hoped that the retelling of the old "Nut-Brown Maid," called "Henry and Emma," would achieve tragic strength by his heroic couplets; and had similarly assumed that "Alma: or, The Progress of the Mind" (1718) would, though told amusingly and skeptically, portray nonetheless a serious philosophy; and he aspired in his long "Solomon on The Vanity of the World" (1708) to give grandeur to the themes and tones of Ecclesiastes.

But Matt. Prior is *not* recollected for these longer pieces. Nor is he remembered for a host of panegyrical verses, pindarics, birthday odes, and poems of praise and political celebrations of contemporary figures and events (the longest of these last being the *Carmen Seculare* to William III). There is a note of something strained when Prior seeks to be elevated or grandly auspicious. He did, after all, admire Spenser all his life (and was indeed buried at his feet), but the severe and archaic epic tone was none of his equipment.

His admiration, however, for Anacreon, for Horace, for the Chaucer of the *fabliaux*, for Montaigne is more felicitous. His lightsome verse epistles, his epigrams, love songs, and burlesque moral fables more frequently succeed. He has learned much from Jonson's casual poems, from the Cavalier poets, from Charles Sackville, Earl of Dorset (Dorset was his patron); and he has learned much indeed from Samuel Butler. His most effective moments in verse stem from his lighter, octosyllabic verse in the iambic or the anapestic vein, and he is doubtless one of the most successful writers of correct yet relaxed four-foot lines. Often too, Prior could be what Dr. Johnson disapprovingly would term "amorous" or "sensual". Nevertheless, the humor and whimsicality are always tempered by a slight and wistful melancholy; he frequently speaks of Life's "Fantastick Mazes," wherein we find but "imagin'd Pleasures" "To combat against real Cares." And there is a recurrent note that we often discover in Horace's later Odes, as in "*Quid sit futurum Cras fuge quaerere*":

> For what To-morrow shall disclose,
> May spoil what You To-night propose:
> ENGLAND may change; or Cloe stray:
> Love and Life are for To-day.

But for all of that, Matthew Prior found his proper niche: although much abroad in 1712 and 1713, he served on the outer fringe of the renowned Scriblerus Club, composed of Swift, Pope, Gay, Arbuthnot, and Parnell; Prior improved with such company and became one of England's masters of the *sermo pedestris*, or low style. He was a correct, polished, and facile maker of pleasant verses; if he was something of the epicurean and the skeptic, he always retained a knowing cheerfulness together with a spritely, almost acid wit. He had managed to become, after all, two things that the century admired – a self-made poet and a self-made man.

In despite of some of Dr. Johnson's strictures, then, Matthew Prior has been able to prevail. What William Cowper said more than fifty years after his death (in a letter of 17 January 1782) about his poetry's "charming ease" most aptly sums the poet up:

> Every man conversant with verse-writing knows, and knows by painful experience, that the familiar style is of all styles the most difficult to succeed in. To make verse speak the language of prose, without being prosaic, – to marshal the words of it in such an order as they might naturally take in falling from the lips of an extemporary speaker, yet without meanness, harmoniously, elegantly, and without seeming to displace a syllable for the sake of the rhyme, is one of the most arduous tasks a poet can undertake. He that could accomplish this task was Prior....

—John R. Clark

RAMSAY, Allan. Scottish. Born in Leadhills, Crawford, Lanarkshire, 15 October 1686. Educated at Crawford village school until 1700; apprenticed to a wigmaker in Edinburgh, 1701. Married Miss Christian Ross in 1712 (died, 1743); eight children including the painter Allan Ramsay. Started his own business, and became prosperous, as a wigmaker in Edinburgh; member of the Jacobite Easy Club, 1712–15: Club Laureate, 1715; changed his business to that of bookseller, 1718, and founded the first circulating library in Scotland, 1728; ceased to write after 1730; built and managed the first theatre in Edinburgh, 1736–37; retired from bookselling, 1755. *Died 7 January 1758.*

PUBLICATIONS

Collections

Works, edited by Burns Martin and others.   6 vols., 1951–74.
Poems of Ramsay and Robert Fergusson, edited by Alexander M. Kinghorn and Alexander Law.   1974.

Verse

The Battle; or, Morning Interview: A Heroi-Comical Poem.   1716.
Christ's Kirk on the Green.   1718; revised edition, 1718.
Edinburgh's Address to the Country.   1718(?).
Scots Songs.   1718; augmented edition, 1719, 1720.
Elegies on Maggy Johnston, John Cowper, and Lucky Wood.   1718.
The Scribblers Lashed.   1718.
Tartana; or, The Plaid.   1718.
Content.   1719.
Familiar Epistles Between W— H— and A— R—.   1719.
Richy and Sandy: A Pastoral on the Death of Addison.   1719(?).
An Epistle to W[illiam] H[amilton].   1720(?).
Edinburgh's Salutation to the Marquess of Carnarvon.   1720.
To Mr. Law.   1720.
An Ode with a Pastoral Recitative on the Marriage of James Earl of Wemyss and Mrs. Janet Charteris.   1720.
Patie and Roger: A Pastoral.   1720.
A Poem on the South Sea.   1720; as *Wealth; or, The Woody,* 1720.
The Prospect of Plenty: A Poem on the North-Sea Fishery.   1720; as *To the Royal Burrows of Scotland,* 1720.
The Rise and Fall of Stocks 1720, The Satire's Comic Project.   1720.
Poems.   1721; revised edition, 2 vols.,1728
Robert, Richy, and Sandy: A Pastoral on the Death of Prior.   1721.
Fables and Tales.   1722; as *Collection of Thirty Fables,* 1730.
A Tale of Three Bonnets.   1722.
The Fair Assembly.   1723.
Jenny and Meggy: A Pastoral, Being a Sequel to Patie and Roger.   1723.
Health.   1724; revised edition, 1724 (twice), 1730.
The Monk and the Miller's Wife; or, All the Parties Pleased.   1724.
Mouldy-Mowdiwart; or, The Last Speech of a Wretched Miser.   1724.
The Poetic Sermon.   1724.
On Pride: An Epistle.   1724.
On the Royal Company of Archers Marching under the Command of His Grace Duke of Hamilton.   1724.
On Seeing the Archers Diverting Themselves.   1724.
A Scots Ode to the British Antiquarians.   1726.
To the Right Honourable Duncan Forbes of Culloden.   1737.

The Vision. 1748.
Curiosities of a Scots Charta Chest 1600–1800 (includes letters), edited by Mrs. Atholl
  Forbes. 1897.

Plays

*The Nuptials: A Masque on the Marriage of James Duke of Hamilton and Lady Anne
  Cochran.* 1723.
The Gentle Shepherd: A Scots Pastoral Comedy (produced 1729). 1725.

Other

Some Few Hints in Defence of Dramatic Entertainments. 1727(?).
An Address of Thanks from the Society of Rakes. 1735.

Editor, *The Tea-Table Miscellany.* 3 vols., 1723–27; vols. 1–2 issued as *A New
  Miscellany of Scots Song,* 1727; 4 vols., 1740.
Editor, *The Ever Green, Being a Collection of Scots Poems Before Sixteen Hundred.* 2
  vols., 1724.
Editor, *A Collection of Scots Proverbs.* 1737.

Bibliography: *Bibliography of the Writings of Ramsay* by Burns Martin, 1931.

Reading List: *Ramsay* by W. H. O. Smeaton, 1896; *New Light on Ramsay* by Andrew
Gibson, 1927; *Ramsay* by Burns Martin, 1931.

*   *   *

Noticing in his preface to *The Ever Green* that "Readers of the best and most exquisite
Discernment frequently complain of our *Modern Writings*, as filled with affected Delicacies
and studied Refinements, which they would gladly exchange for that natural Strength of
Thought and Simplicity of Stile our Forefathers practised," Allan Ramsay achieved a great
deal in his lifetime to gratify this preference.

  He practised his literary art at a crucial point in Scotland's cultural history, when political
union seemed complete, if uneasy, and when the pressures of commerce, cultural attitude,
and political pressure seemed likely to iron out local customs, speech-values, and writing in
favour of the metropolitan, which in this case meant literary London. Ramsay, a practical
man of business in an enlightened city which felt fiercely proud of its Scottishness, if
uncertain how best to express it, researched, published, popularised Scottish writing, both the
original verse of his immensely popular *Gentle Shepherd*, and the rescued oral literature of
the *Tea-Table Miscellany*, and the late mediaeval Scots verse published in the pages of *The
Ever Green*. His style was uneven, and in preparing older work for the press, he often made
interpolations which pleased his contemporaries, yet jar modern scholarship. Yet he proved
himself a witty and versatile practitioner of verse in Scots and English, in long and short
poems, in pastoral and epigram as well as lyric and descriptive verse.

  He proclaimed in the same preface his scorn of "one's expressing his *Ignorance* of his
native Language": as a man who rescued the poetry of Scotland from threatened oblivion
and helped popularise it at a time of growing national consciousness, he plainly played an
important part in the coming "golden age" of Scottish culture. Like many men of this period,
he was a keen participant in societies of literary interest, in amateur and professional
theatricals, and an amateur of the arts in general. His works have recently been given the

thorough and scholarly editing they deserve, by the Scottish Texts Society, and in the process
been revealed in their extensiveness and variety. The explosion of talent in the two following
generations plainly owes a good deal to this pioneer. In him, too, we see some of the
ambiguities of the golden age, the uncertainty over language; the attitude to the past as
something to be maintained, yet modified to the standards of the present; a curious double
standard which exults in the Scottish for Scottish readers yet maintains a curiously defensive
tone for non-Scots. A man of talent born at the threshold of an exciting period, Ramsay was
an accomplished writer who deserves to be remembered for more than just his one successful
pastoral.

—Ian Campbell

ROCHESTER, 2nd Earl of; John Wilmot.   English.   Born in Ditchley, near Woodstock,
Oxfordshire, 10 April 1647; succeeded his father as earl in 1658. Educated at Burford School,
Oxfordshire; Wadham College, Oxford, M.A. 1661. Associated with Elizabeth Barry, servant
to Lady Shelton of Norfolk, and had a daughter by her; kidnapped Elizabeth Malet, and was
imprisoned for his actions, 1665; married her, 1667; one son and three daughters. Travelled
in France and Italy, 1663–64, then attended the court of Charles II: joined Sir Thomas
Teddeman on board the *Royal Katherine*, and took part in an unsuccessful attack on Dutch
ships at Bergen, 1665, and served in the Channel under Sir Edward Spragge, 1666; an
associate of the most dissolute set at court – Villiers, Sedley, and Savile; known for his
drunken exploits and his amorous and obscene lyrics; companion to Charles in the king's
amorous adventures: frequently dismissed from court in disgrace, then reinstated; appointed
gentleman of the king's bedchamber, 1666; summoned to the House of Lords, 1667;
appointed Keeper of Woodstock Park, 1674; retired from court when his health failed, 1679;
under the influence of Bishop Burnet said to have repented of the excesses of his life on his
death-bed. *Died 26 July 1680.*

PUBLICATIONS

Collections

> *Complete Poems,* edited by D. M. Vieth.   1968.
> *Satires Against Man: The Poems,* edited by Dustin H. Griffin.   1973.
> *The Debt to Pleasure: An Anthology,* edited by John Adlard.   1976.

Verse

> *Poems on Several Occasions.*   1680; edited by James Thorpe, 1950.
> *Corydon and Cloris: or, The Wanton Shepherdess.*   1676(?).
> *A Satire Against Reason and Mankind.*   1679.
> *A Letter from Artemisia in the Town to Chloe in the Country.*   1679.
> *Upon Nothing.*   1679.
> *A Very Heroical Epistle from My Lord All-Pride to Dol-Common.*   1679.

The Famous Pathologist: or, The Noble Mountebank, with Thomas Alcock, edited by V. de S. Pinto. 1961.

Plays

Valentinian, from the play by Fletcher (produced 1684). 1685.
Sodom: or, The Quintessence of Debauchery, edited by L. S. A. M. von Römer. 1904; edited by Patrick J. Kearney, 1969 (probably not by Rochester).

Other

A Letter to Dr. Burnet. 1680.
Familiar Letters (by Rochester, Thomas Otway, and Katherine Philips), edited by Tom Brown and Charles Gildon. 2 vols., 1697.
Miscellaneous Works, with the Earl of Roscommon. 1707.
The Rochester-Savile Letters 1671–1680, edited by J. H. Wilson. 1941.

Reading List: Rochester by C. Williams, 1935; Rochester by V. de S. Pinto, 1935, revised edition, as Enthusiast in Wit, 1962; Attribution in Restoration Poetry: A Study of Rochester's Poems of 1680 by D. M. Vieth, 1963; Rochester: The Critical Heritage edited by David Farley-Hills, 1972; Lord Rochester's Monkey, Being the Life of Rochester by Graham Greene, 1974.

*   *   *

John Wilmot, Earl of Rochester, is one of that number of English poets who seem in the popular mind more important for what they did than for what they wrote. Certainly Rochester's wild, licentious, and short life – he died at the age of 33 – gave him a posthumous reputation for wickedness that even Byron might envy. But, unlike Byron, Rochester did not live to complete a single masterpiece. Instead, even his best poems are marred by poor lines, shoddy rhymes, flat phrases. All of which suggest that he took poetry no more seriously than Congreve took play-writing (Voltaire was shocked by Congreve's refusal to discuss dramatic matters and by his insistence on talking only of "gentlemanly" ones). Certainly, Rochester is no professional writer, in the sense that the term can be applied to his great contemporary Dryden. Yet it would be absurd to dismiss Rochester as a mere dilettante. For all the technicolour quality of the life, his art represents a solid achievement.

Some lapidary phrases of Dr. Johnson get to the heart of the matter. "The glare of his general character diffused itself upon his writings.... In all his works there is sprightliness and vigour, and everywhere may be found tokens of a mind, which study might have carried to excellence." Johnson perhaps slightly overstates his case, but in the main what he says carries the unmistakable ring of truth. The exception I find to be in Rochester's Songs, where I can detect very little of either sprightliness or vigour, though there is a good deal of, largely spurious, elegance. This is not to deny that the songs have a cavalier-like polish to them, reminiscent of Carew, Lovelace, or Suckling. But the point is rather that they typically exhibit a no doubt fashionable cynicism in their statements about love and the relationship between men and women which from our vantage point looks distressingly trivial and modish. If this is particularly true of the famous and much-anthologised "Love a Woman," it seems to me equally the case with the majority of the rest, not excepting the equally famous "Song of a Young Lady to her Ancient Lover," which compares poorly with Burns's "John Anderson, My Jo."

Mention of Burns has its point. Like Rochester, the great Scottish poet was renowned for his licentious life. Yet the differences are more important than the similarities. For in Burns's love poetry one finds a much more certain regard for women than one does in Rochester, who is nearer to Byron in thinking of all women as "the sex."

All women? What then of his wife, with whom we are told he was deeply in love, and to whom he would regularly return from the dissipations of court life. She is probably the woman addressed in the song "Absent from thee I languish still."

> When wearied with a world of Woe
>   To thy safe Bosom I retire,
> Where Love, and Peace, and Truth does flow,
>   May I contented there expire.

The usual view of Rochester's marriage is that his wife represented a safe harbour from the wreck of his London life, and that he was truly appreciative of the fact. It may be so, but I do not see why her point of view should not be considered. Never mind the time he spent with her – what of the time he was away? Rochester's placing his wife in retirement so that he could visit her when exhausted by the drunken lechery of his town life is surely indicative of a thoroughly selfish and sentimental view of "the best of women." And that explains, I think, not only the slightness of the songs, but the rancid disgust of his famous pornographic satires "The Imperfect Enjoyment" and "A Ramble in St. James's Park." In the last analysis Rochester, I think, hated women, turned them into things of use, and then was ferociously appalled at their willingness to be so used. We are asked to see in this a fearless readiness to take Hobbesian philosophy at face value and discover the truth of man as natural force. (A century later the Marquis de Sade was supposed to be making similar fearless discoveries.) I can see in this argument no more than a piece of not very sophisticated special pleading. I do not think Rochester set out to prove how futile life was, but that he assuredly came to recognise that *his* life was futile. And it is for this reason that he matters as a poet.

"Huddled in dirt the reasoning engine lies/That was so proud, so witty, and so wise": Tennyson reportedly could never read this couplet, from Rochester's most substantial poem, *A Satire Against Mankind*, without the tears starting to his eyes. My guess is that Tennyson is misreading the lines, and converting into "Tennysonian melancholy" and pathos what is in truth hard-edged, contemptuous, and snarlingly witty. It is the word "engine" which does the trick. It suggests that man can be seen as a mechanical object, a kind of well-oiled war weapon, a tool of aggression lacking all compassion, love, fellow-feeling. And Rochester's best work, which lies in his satires, is directed towards his sure sense of the ultimate sterility and meaninglessness of the kind of life towards which he was drawn. That is why I think that his famous deathbed conversion, for all the sugary sentimentalities with which it is coated in Bishop Burnet's famous *Some Passages of the Life and Death of the Right Honourable John Earl of Rochester*, cannot be dismissed as the vagary of an ill man. For what comes over most strongly in any encounter with Rochester's poetry is the reek of disgust at a certain kind of life. The satirist in him is likely to inflate that kind of life to life in general (and the less cautious critics assume the inflation to be no more than sober truth), but of course in the end he is writing about the life he knew best: the male dominated, trivial, sexually rapacious, mean-spirited world of Charles's court. Rochester is the best, because severest, critic of that life.

—John Lucas

SACKVILLE, Charles. See **DORSET, Earl of.**

SAVAGE, Richard.   English.   Born in England c. 1697; claimed to be the illegitimate son of the fourth Earl Rivers and Lady Macclesfield. Very little is known for certain about his early life: probably of humble parentage, and probably had little education; chose literature for a livelihood c. 1715; acted at Drury Lane, 1718, 1723; killed a gentleman in a tavern brawl, and sentenced to die, 1727, obtained royal pardon, 1728; published his accounts of his birth: given a pension by his alleged mother's nephew, Lord Tyrconnel, on condition he abstain from further attacks on her, 1728–34; applied unsuccessfully for post of Poet Laureate, 1730; given a pension by Queen Caroline, 1732–37; subsequently lived in great poverty; died in debtor's prison in Bristol. *Died 1 August 1743.*

PUBLICATIONS

Collections

> *Works.*   2 vols., 1775.
> *Poetical Works*, edited by Clarence Tracy.   1962.

Verse

> *The Convocation; or, A Battle of Pamphlets.*   1717.
> *A Poem Sacred to the Glorious Memory of Our Late King George.*   1727.
> *The Bastard.*   1728.
> *Nature in Perfections; or, The Mother Unveiled.*   1728.
> *The Wanderer: A Vision.*   1729.
> *Verses Occasioned by the Viscountess Tyrconnel's Recovery at Bath.*   1730.
> *An Epistle to Sir Robert Walpole.*   1732.
> *A Collection of Pieces in Verse and Prose, on the Occasion of The Dunciad.*   1732.
> *The Volunteer Laureat: A Poem to Her Majesty on Her Birthday.*   1732 (similar verses
>   annually until 1738).
> *On the Departure of the Prince and Princess of Orange.*   1734.
> *The Progress of a Divine: A Satire.*   1735.
> *A Poem on the Birthday of the Prince of Wales.*   1735; as *Of Public Spirit in Regard to
>   Public Works: An Epistle,* 1737.
> *A Poem Sacred to the Memory of Her Majesty.*   1738.
> *London and Bristol Compared: A Satire.*   1744.
> *Various Poems: The Wanderer, The Triumph of Mirth and Health, The Bastard.*   1761.

Plays

> *Love in a Veil,* from a play by Calderón (produced 1718).   1719.
> *The Tragedy of Sir Thomas Overbury* (produced 1723).   1724.

Other

> *An Author to Be Let.*   1729.

> Editor, *Miscellaneous Poems and Translations by Several Hands.*   1726.

Bibliography: "Some Uncollected Authors: Savage" by Clarence Tracy, in *Book Collector*, 1963.

Reading List: *The Artificial Bastard: A Biography of Savage* by Clarence Tracy, 1953.

*   *   *

Richard Savage's earliest poems, written about 1715 but never published in his lifetime, express Jacobite sympathies; but a depressingly large proportion of his later poems consists of panegyrics upon the illustrious house of Hanover. Such works as the 1727 elegy on George I, or the series of annual "Volunteer-Laureat" addresses on Queen Caroline's birthday, or the 1732 epistle addressed to Walpole, or the *Poem on the Birth-day of the Prince of Wales* (later republished as *Of Public Spirit in Regard to Public Works*) all express in bombastic terms unimpeachably Whig principles. These, and others in similar vein, constitute Savage's appeal for patronage either from the Government or from the Prince's opposition court; and, though Savage never obtained that patronage which he thought he deserved, he was favoured with the royal pardon in 1728 when under sentence of death for murder.

The trial and pardon added to the notoriety that Savage had already gained by repeatedly pressing his claims to be the son of the Countess of Macclesfield by her adultery with the Earl Rivers – a claim which the Countess vehemently denied – and ensured the immediate popularity of *The Bastard*. This short piece, invigorated by Savage's anger, self-pity, and extravagant egotism, remains his best poem because it is the only one in which his feelings seem to be fully engaged. His longest and most ambitious work is *The Wanderer: A Vision* in five cantos where, influenced by his friend Thomson's early poems on the Seasons, but, unlike Thomson, writing in heroic couplets, he makes a great excursion through the grandest works of Nature and offers moral reflections upon them. The most interesting feature of this would-be sublime poem is Savage's romantic conception of the poet as prophetic bard. Also in 1729, but in a very different vein is the prose pamphlet *An Author to Be Lett* "by Iscariot Hackney." Savage had provided Pope with many facts and scurrilous inventions for the notes to *The Dunciad Variorum*, and this little squib is so lively a supplement to Pope's attacks on the dunces that one wishes Savage had written more prose satire.

Though Savage never found a patron – or a mother – he had the friendship of Pope and Thomson, and especially of Johnson who had walked about London with him hungry, penniless, and homeless, and whose great *Life of Savage* (1744) rather too indulgently represents its subject as a self-destructive genius.

—A. J. Sambrook

SCOTT, John. English. Born in Bermondsey, London, 9 January 1730; moved with his family to Amwell, Hertfordshire, 1740, and lived there for the reest of his life. Privately educated. Married 1) Sarah Frogley in 1767 (died, 1768); 2) Mary de Horne in 1770, one daughter. Wrote verse for *The Gentleman's Magazine*, London, 1753–58; visited London occasionally from 1760: attended Mrs. Montagu's parties; met Samuel Johnson, 1766, and entertained him at Amwell. *Died 12 December 1783.*

PUBLICATIONS

Collections

The Works of the English Poets 17, edited by Alexander Chalmers.   1810.

Verse

Four Elegies, Descriptive and Moral.   1760.
Elegy Written at Amwell.   1769.
Amwell: A Descriptive Poem.   1776.
Moral Eclogues.   1778.
Poetical Works.   1782.

Other

*The Constitution Defended and the Pensioner Exposed, in Remarks on the False
    Alarm.*   1770.
A Digest of the Present Act for Amendment of the Highways.   1773.
Observations on the Present State of the Parochial and Vagrant Poor.   1773.
Remarks on the Patriot.   1775.
Digests of the General Highway and Turnpike Laws.   1778.
A Letter to the Critical Reviewers.   1782.
Critical Essays on Some of the Poems of Several English Poets.   1785.

Bibliography: "Some Uncollected Authors: Scott" by N. Russell, in *Book Collector,* 1965.

Reading List: *Scott of Amwell* by Lawrence D. Stewart, 1956.

*   *   *

John Scott's greatest impact on his time was made with his essays on social problems, politics, and literature, and with his poetry on a variety of subjects, especially nature. In his essay on the poor, Scott spoke out for the laboring classes, directing attention to the brutal harshness of the vagrancy laws and the vicious practice of farming out work houses. He blamed the misery of the village poor upon grasping landowners who had enclosed the commons. But he provided no solutions to the problems that he discussed.

Despite his friendship with Johnson and despite Quaker objections to participation in secular politics, Scott was moved to answer Johnson's *False Alarm* (1770), a defence of the government's harsh views of John Wilkes, in *The Constitution Defended* (1770). Characteristically, Scott objected to Johnson's Toryism, the doctrines of divine hereditary right and passive obedience to the will of kings. Looking back to the Revolution like a genuine Whig, Scott insisted upon limiting the prerogatives of monarchy, protecting and extending individual rights in a system of representative government with the people as the supreme authority, and regarding Wilkes as a popular champion of libertarian principles.

These liberal and Whiggish ideas he had expressed a few years before in a "Sonnet, on Arbitrary Government" and verses addressed to the egalitarian Catherine Macaulay. Scott also wrote against Johnson in *Remarks on the Patriot* (1775).

In his poems, Scott often wrote about personal matters, although maintaining an outer conventional form that rendered an impression of classical simplicity. For example, his intensely personal distaste for war is seen in the oft-reprinted "Ode XIII (I hate that drum's discordant sound)" directed against the recruitment of soldiers. Scott also wrote about exotic places – Mexico, China, Arabia, India, enriching the substance of his poems with details drawn from travel books. However, his greatest achievement is the result of close and continued observation of nature, especially in his "Amoebaean Eclogues," in which he introduced rural imagery not usually noticed in a series of loosely structured, hence "amoebaean" verse essays. His loco-descriptive *Amwell* he regarded as his *magnum opus*. In this poem Scott celebrated in 451 blank verse lines the picturesque rural scene around Ware, "the semblance fair of Nature's forms," and explained why through personal, literary, and historical associations the rustic scenery "Gave rapture to [his] soul." Scott's poetry, like the scenery in the poem, is not characterized by the awful sublime. His poetry is in what he himself thought (in Ode XIX) was the unfashionable classic mode and style, and his models were Horace, Virgil, Akenside, and Shenstone.

In his criticism, Scott applied his "criterion of merit," that is, "classical simplicity" (letter to Beattie, 6 June 1783), to nine important seventeenth and eighteenth century poems from Denham's *Cooper's Hill* to Gray's *Elegy*. What he meant by this measure, it becomes clear, is lucidity, conciseness, neatness and elegance, and rational consistency, a consistency determined by testing figure and diction against the sentiment intended. For example, in his essay on Pope's *Windsor Forest*, which is typical of his method, he engaged in an analysis of the diction and thought, and noted evidences of mental confusion in the imagery. Though Scott sometimes brings a rash insensitivity to the organic integrity of the creative imagination, his criticism has the virtue of forcing us to read the poems afresh and to reach an understanding and perhaps an appreciation of their subtleties of image, diction, and sense. Independent in his criticism, as in his views of politics and society, Scott courageously judges for himself and often takes issue with Samuel Johnson and prevailing taste.

—Martin Kallich

SEDLEY, Sir Charles, Baronet.   English.   Born in Aylesford, Kent, c. 1639; succeeded to the baronetcy, 1656. Educated at Wadham College, Oxford, but left without taking a degree. Married Catherine Savage, daughter of Earl Rivers, 1657; one daughter. Entered the court of Charles II, and became notorious as a fashionable profligate; withdrew from court after the death of Charles. Member of Parliament for New Romney, 1668–81, 1690–95, and 1696–1701. *Died 20 August 1701.*

PUBLICATIONS

Collections

Poetical and Dramatic Works, edited by V. de S. Pinto.   2 vols., 1928.

Verse

The Happy Pair; or, A Poem on Matrimony.   1702; revised edition, 1705.
The Poetical Works, and His Speeches in Parliament, edited by W. Ayloffe.   1707
   (contains some spurious material).

Plays

Pompey the Great, with others, from a play by Corneille (produced 1664).   1664.
The Mulberry Garden (produced 1668).   1668; edited by A. Norman Jeffares, in
   Restoration Comedy, 1974.
Antony and Cleopatra, from the play by Shakespeare (produced 1677).   1677; revised
   version, as *Beauty the Conqueror,* in *Miscellaneous Works,* 1702.
Bellamira; or, The Mistress, from the play *The Fatal Contract* by William Hemmings
   (produced 1687).   1687.
The Grumbler, from a play by D. A. de Brueys and Jean Palaprat.   1719.
The Tyrant King of Crete, from the play *Pallantus and Eudora* by Henry Killigrew, in
   Works.   1722.

Other

Reflections upon Our Late and Present Proceedings in England.   1689.
The Speech of Sedley in the House of Commons.   1691.
The Miscellaneous Works, edited by W. Ayloffe.   1702.

Bibliography: in *Poetical and Dramatic Works,* 1928.

Reading List: *Sedley* by V. de S. Pinto, 1927; *Court Wits of the Restoration* by John H.
Wilson, 1948.

*   *   *

With Rochester and Dorset, Sir Charles Sedley was one of the chief court poets of Charles
II's reign. He is best known today, as he was in the Restoration, for his love poems and songs,
which modern critics group into two categories: the gentler strain of poems which tend to
plead with the beloved, often seeking to ingratiate the lover to the beloved, and the wittily
satiric poems which are filled with such wordly wisdom as, "Tis early to begin to fear/The
devil at fifteen." His poetry betrays the cynicism of Charles's Restoration court, and, as a
result, it has always been overshadowed by that of the more prolific Rochester and Dorset.
His satirical poems and plays all treat, sardonically, middle- and upper-class manners of the
period. Sedley is undoubtedly a minor poet, but one with a perceptive eye and a cutting pen.
His dramatic efforts are imitative of Etherege, Shadwell, and Dryden, and his poetry often
resembles Rochester's, but his wit is always sharp.

—John J. Perry

SEWARD, Anna. Known as the "Swan of Lichfield." English. Born in Eyam, Derbyshire, 12 December 1742; moved with her family to Lichfield, Staffordshire, 1754, and remained there for the rest of her life. Educated privately; encouraged to write by Dr. Erasmus Darwin. Lived at home, caring for her father; acquainted with Dr. Johnson and his circle at Lichfield; met Boswell c. 1776 and supplied him with anecdotes about Johnson; inherited the family estate, 1790; met Scott, 1807, who became her literary executor and editor. *Died 25 March 1809.*

PUBLICATIONS

Collections

> *Poetical Works,* edited by Walter Scott.   3 vols., 1810.
> *Letters 1784–1807,* edited by A. Constable.   6 vols., 1811.

Verse

> *Elegy on Captain Cook, to Which Is Added an Ode to the Sun.*   1780; revised edition, 1784.
> *Monody on Major André.*   1781.
> *Poem to the Memory of Lady Miller.*   1782.
> *Louisa: A Poetical Novel in Four Epistles.*   1784.
> *Ode on General Elliott's Return from Gibraltar.*   1787.
> *Llangollen Vale with Other Poems.*   1796.
> *Original Sonnets on Various Subjects, and Odes Paraphrased from Horace.*   1799.
> *Blindness.*   1806.

Other

> *Variety: A Collection of Essays.*   1788.
> *Memoirs of the Life of Dr. Darwin.*   1804.
> *Memoirs of Abelard and Eloisa.*   1805.
> *Monumental Inscriptions in Ashbourn Church, Derbyshire,* with B. Boothby.   1806.
> *Miss Seward's Enigma.*   1855.

Reading List: *The Singing Swan: An Account of Seward* by Margaret Ashmun, 1931; *Seward: An Eighteenth-Century Handelian* by R. M. Myers, 1947.

*   *   *

Anna Seward was known as the Swan of Lichfield, and, as the term suggests, she did produce a considerable body of forgettable poems. Her *Poetical Works,* published after her death, came to three volumes, and her *Letters* came to six. A contemporary critic refers to all this literary work as "written almost throughout with a disgusting affectation of verbal ornament, and everywhere tinctured with personal, political, and poetical prejudices." Nevertheless, she was a brilliant woman who never achieved a major literary accomplishment; and a reason may have been that she was part of a provincial literary circle that despised the London literary world of Samuel Johnson. Further, she received too much flattery within that limited circle of her friends in the Midlands, William Hayley, Cowper, Erasmus Darwin, without ever having to confront the major literary world of London. She was a minor writer by choice, and as such she presaged the tendency in our society for minor writers deliberately to break off into regional groupings.

One major contribution that she did make to English literature, however, came through her friendship and sometime infatuation with Erasmus Darwin, who had helped teach her to make poems when she was a girl growing up in Lichfield and who also chose deliberately to be a regional and minor writer with all the self-consciousness and sense of limits that go with that choice. Her *Memoirs of the Life of Dr. Darwin* is written in a less affected and more direct manner. She makes incisive and critical statements in that book about him and about the whole literary world of the Midlands. The book, in fact, may be her most valuable contribution to our literary heritage. During her lifetime she received the most fame for her two elegiac poems *Elegy on Captain Cook* and *Monody on Major André*. She probably received help on the Captain Cook elegy from Dr. Darwin just as she helped him with the opening lines of his poem *The Botanic Garden*. The avowedly minor writers at this time often worked together establishing the sense of small community that provided some compensation for the realization that epic works were not being produced. In this sense, Anna Seward, the assertive woman and minor writer, seems very modern.

—Donald M. Hassler

SHENSTONE, William.   English.   Born at Leasowes, Halesowen, Worcestershire, 13 November 1714. Educated at Halesowen Grammar School; Solihull Grammar School, Warwickshire; Pembroke College, Oxford, 1732–42, left without taking a degree. Inherited the Leasowes estate, 1735, settled there, 1745, and devoted himself thereafter to laying out the grounds. *Died 11 February 1763.*

PUBLICATIONS

Collections

> *Works.*   3 vols., 1773.
> *Poetical Works,* edited by George Gilfillan.   1854.

Verse

> *Poems upon Various Occasions.*   1737.
> *The Judgment of Hercules.*   1741.
> *The School-Mistress.*   1742; revised edition, in *A Collection of Poems by Several Hands I,* edited by Robert Dodsley, 1748.

Other

Letters, edited by Marjorie Williams.   1939.
Letters, edited by Duncan Mallam.   1939.
The Correspondence of Thomas Percy and Shenstone, edited by Cleanth Brooks.   1977.

Editor, *Miscellaneous Poems, Revised and Corrected*, by Joseph Giles.   1771.
Editor, *Shenstone's Miscellany*, edited by Ian A. Gordon.   1952.

Bibliography: in *Seven 18th-Century Bibliographies* by Iolo A. Williams, 1924.

Reading List: *A Study of Shenstone and His Critics* by Alice I. Hazeltine, 1918; *Shenstone* by

Arthur R. Humphreys, 1937.

*   *   *

William Shenstone is one of the minor writers of the eighteenth century, but his influence on the direction of English poetry was out of all proportion to the intrinsic merits of his verse. He began writing poetry when Pope was at his zenith, and his *Poems upon Various Occasions* appeared in the same year (1737) as several of Pope's epistles. Shenstone firmly rejected Pope's heroic couplet and the Augustan ideal of correctness and public poetry. His first volume was made up of ballads, songs, and the earliest version of *The School-Mistress*, written in unfashionable Spenserian stanzas. Thereafter Shenstone went his own way, retreating to live in the country, to become an arbiter of the altering taste of the mid-eighteenth century.

When Robert and James Dodsley launched their influential anthology *A Collection of Poems* (1748), Shenstone's poetry appeared in company with such forward-looking poetry as odes by Gray and by Collins, Warton's *Enthusiast*, and Dyer's *Grongar Hill*. He became the adviser to the Dodsleys for the later volumes, and was responsible for the inclusion of Gray's *Elegy in a Country Churchyard*, Akenside's "Hymn to the Naiads," and many of his own best lyrics (e.g., "Pastoral Ballad," "Rural Elegance,""Slender's Ghost," "Written at an Inn"). Shenstone became a close associate of Bishop Percy and had a considerable hand in the selection and editing of the old ballads (published after his death) in Percy's *Reliques of Ancient English Poetry* (1765). His own anthology of old ballads, Elizabethan lyrics, and verse by his contemporaries remained in manuscript until it was discovered and published in our own day.

Shenstone's reputation was for a long time diminished by the slighting references in Dr. Johnson's *Lives of the Poets*. Johnson's Augustan judgment of his lyrics – "all of the light and airy kind, such as trip lightly and nimbly along, without the load of any weighty meaning" – misses Shenstone's achievement. He was an innovator both in theme and in his metrical freedom. Gray in his own day thought highly of *The School-Mistress*; and, in the next generation of poets, Shenstone found favour with Robert Burns, who quoted in the preface to his Kilmarnock volume (1768) the "divine elegies" of "that celebrated poet."

—Ian A. Gordon

SMART, Christopher. English. Born in Shipbourne, near Tunbridge, Kent, 11 April 1722. Educated at Durham Grammar School, 1733–39; Pembroke College, Cambridge, matriculated 1739, B.A. 1742, M.A. 1747. Married Anna Maria Carnan in 1753; two daughters. Fellow of Pembroke College, 1745–53, and Praelector in Philosophy and Keeper of the Common Chest, Cambridge University, 1746–47 (awarded Seatonian Prize, at Cambridge, 5 times, 1750–53, 1755); confined for a short period in Bedlam, 1751; left Cambridge to become a writer in London, 1755: worked for the bookseller John Newbery for whom he edited, as Mary Midnight, *The Midwife*, 1751–53, and various other periodicals; Co-Editor, *Universal Visitor*, 1756–59; confined to Bedlam, 1763; impoverished during his later years; died in a debtor's prison. *Died 21 May 1771.*

PUBLICATIONS

Collections

> *Collected Poems*, edited by Norman Callan. 2 vols., 1949.
> *Poems* (selection), edited by Robert Brittain. 1950.
> *Religious Poetry*, edited by Marcus Walsh. 1972.

Verse

> *The Horatian Canons of Friendship, Being the Third Satire of the First Book of Horace Imitated.* 1750.
> *On the Eternity of the Supreme Being.* 1750.
> *A Solemn Dirge, Sacred to the Memory of Frederic, Prince of Wales.* 1751.
> *The Nut-Cracker.* 1751.
> *On the Immensity of the Supreme Being.* 1751.
> *Poems on Several Occasions.* 1752.
> *On the Omniscience of the Supreme Being.* 1752.
> *The Hilliad: An Epic Poem*, book 1. 1753.
> *On the Power of the Supreme Being.* 1754.
> *On the Goodness of the Supreme Being.* 1756.
> *Hymn to the Supreme Being on Recovery from a Dangerous Fit of Illness.* 1756.
> *Mrs. Midnight's Orations and Other Select Pieces.* 1763.
> *A Song to David.* 1763; edited by J. B. Broadbent, 1960.
> *Poems.* 1763.
> *Poems on Several Occasions.* 1763.
> *Ode to the Earl of Northumberland, with Some Other Pieces.* 1764.
> *The Psalms of David* (with *Hymns and Spiritual Songs for the Fasts and Festivals of the Church of England*). 1765.
> *The Parables of Our Lord and Saviour Jesus Christ, Done into Familiar Verse for the Use of Younger Minds.* 1768.
> *Hymns for the Amusement of Children.* 1771(?); edited by Edmund Blunden, 1947.
> *Rejoice in the Lamb [Jubilate Agno]: A Song from Bedlam*, edited by W. F. Stead. 1939; edited by W. H. Bond, 1954.

Plays

> *The Grateful Fair; or A Trip to Cambridge* (produced 1747?).
> *The Judgment of Midas*, in *Poems.* 1752.

Hannah: An Oratorio, music by John Worgan (produced 1764).   1764.
Abimelech: An Oratorio, music by S. Arnold (produced 1768).   1768.
Providence: An Oratorio.   1777.

Other

Mother Midnight's Comical Pocket-Book.   1753.

Editor, *An Index to Mankind; or, Maxims Selected from the Wits of all Nations.*   1751.
Editor, with others, *The Student; or, Oxford and Cambridge Monthly Miscellany.*   2 vols., 1750–51.
Editor, *The Muses' Banquet; or, A Present from Parnassus.*   2 vols., 1752.
Editor, *Be Merry and Be Wise; or, The Dream of the Jests, and the Marrow of Maxims, for the Conduct of Life.*   1753.
Editor, with Richard Rolt, *The Universal Visitor and Memorialist for the Year 1756.*   1756.
Editor, *A Collection of Poems for the Amusement of Children Six Foot High* and *Three Feet High.*   2 vols., 1756.
Editor, *The Nonpareil; or, The Quintessence of Wit and Humour* (selections from *Midwife; or, Old Woman's Magazine*).   1757.

Translator, *Carmen Cl. Alexandri Pope in S. Caeciliam, Latine Redditum.*   1743.
Translator, *The Works of Horace Translated Literally into English Prose.*   2 vols., 1756.
Translator, *The Fables of Phaedrus* (in verse).   1765.
Translator, *The Works of Horace Translated into Verse with a Prose Interpretation.*   4 vols., 1767.

Bibliography: *A Bibliography of the Writings of Smart* by G. J. Gray, 1903.

Reading List: *Smart: A Biographical and Critical Study* by E. G. Ainsworth and C. E. Noyes, 1943; *Poor Kit Smart* by Christopher Devlin, 1961; *Smart* by Geoffrey Grigson, 1961; *Smart as a Poet of His Times: A Reappraisal* by Sophia Blaydes, 1966; *Smart: Scholar of the University* by Arthur Sherbo, 1967; *Poetry of Vision: Five Eighteenth-Century Poets* by P. M. Spacks, 1967; *The Poetry of Smart* by Moira Dearnley, 1968; *Smart* by Frances E. Anderson, 1974.

*   *   *

After a notable though brief academic career at Cambridge, Christopher Smart became a professional writer in London, where he achieved a modest reputation composing verse in mostly minor and conventional modes. His collection of *Poems on Several Occasions* contains odes, lyrics, ballads, a masque, Latin versions of Pope and Milton, and a blank-verse georgic poem, "The Hop-Garden." The most significant works of these early London years are the poems on the attributes of the Supreme Being with which Smart five times won the Seatonian Prize of Cambridge University (1750–55). These are Miltonic blank verse exercises in conventional religious sublimity, in which Smart had yet to find his own form and voice, but they surpass the usual level of prize poetry, and already introduce Smart's favourite theme of the grateful chorus of nature in praise of its Creator.

Confinement in the madhouse allowed Smart to escape some of the restrictions of demand and tradition, and create the distinctive religious verse which is his main achievement. Much recent attention has focussed on the *Jubilate Agno,* written on a daily basis from 1759 to 1763, though not published until 1939. The *Jubilate* is an antiphonal poem, formed on the model of Hebrew poetry, and particularly of the Psalms. "Let" verses calling man and the creatures to praise are echoed by more imaginative and personal "For" verses: "Let Chesed rejoice with Strepsiceros, whose weapons are the ornaments of his peace. For I preach the very GOSPEL of CHRIST without comment & with this weapon shall I slay envy" (B1.9). It may be (the incompleteness of the surviving manuscript demands caution) that the *Jubilate* has an overall prophetic scheme, the replacement of Israel by the English as the chosen race; but the responsive structure breaks down early in the poem and the later parts, though not incoherent, have partly the character of a journal, an imaginative exercise in mnemonics by a learned man striving to preserve the stock of his knowledge.

Less ambiguous is Smart's accomplishment in the religious verse written in the madhouse and published in the early 1760's. In these poems Smart developed for himself a distinctive high lyric style, using varied but relatively simple stanzaic forms as defining framework for a poetic language characteristically compressed, metaphoric and allusive. Smart's masterpiece is *A Song to David*, a poem of energetic and committed devotion in which he writes in praise of, and identifies himself with, David the psalmist, "the great Author of The Book of Gratitude," the model of the inspired poet-priest. After describing the virtues of David and the subjects of his divine verse, the *Song* moves into "an exercise upon the decalogue" which uses many parts of the Bible including the New Testament, presents David as the leader of the natural chorus of Adoration in an extended passage which is Smart's finest expression of the theme, and concludes with a rhetorical climax which brings together David, Christ and Smart:

> Glorious – more glorious is the crown
> Of Him that brought salvation down
>   By meekness, call'd thy Son;
> Thou at stupendous truth believ'd,
> And now the matchless deed's atchiev'd,
>   DETERMINED, DARED, and DONE.

The *Song* is constructed with what Smart himself called "exact Regularity and Method," its subjects organised in numerically balanced stanza groups. The *Hymns and Spiritual Songs for the Fasts and Festivals of the Church of England* are a collection of liturgical poems which resemble the *Song* in their careful structure and condensed and figurative style. The best hymns of the cycle ("New Year," "St. Mark," and "The Nativity of Our Lord and Saviour Jesus Christ," for example) are religious lyrics of high quality. The more sophisticated poetic character and orthodox Anglican theology of Smart's *Hymns* differentiate them from the popular hymns of Smart's century. With the *Hymns* were published his monumental, and inevitably more mechanical, *Translation of the Psalms of David*, in which the Psalter is versified, and thoroughly christianized. Though it is not certain whether Smart's *Hymns* were intended to be sung, the *Psalms* were "adapted to the Divine Service," and music was written specially for them by William Boyce and others.

The production of Smart's last years is more various. Biblical stories are the basis of the two oratorios *Hannah* and *Abimelech*; *Hannah* dramatises the adoration theme with some success. The *Poetical Translation of the Fables of Phaedrus* and the versification of the parables were written for the new reading public of children. The verse translation of the works of Horace is an ambitious attempt to write English poetry in the style of Horace's "unrivalled peculiarity of expression." The *Hymns for the Amusement of Children* distil into a language of expressive simplicity the themes of praise and gratitude.

Smart is a difficult case for critical judgment, a considerable poet who commanded no following. The spiritual, formal, and stylistic distinctness of his major religious lyrics seems to have discouraged a contemporary readership, and in his own time, and later, his madness has been too much taken into account. Reliable evaluation will depend on fuller consideration of the published religious verse, and the inaccessible verse Horace.

—Marcus Walsh

SOMERVILLE, William.   English.   Born in Colwich, Staffordshire, 2 September 1675. Educated at Winchester College, 1690–94; New College, Oxford, 1694–96; Middle Temple, London, 1696. Married Mary Bethel in 1708 (died, 1731). Fellow, New College, until 1705; thereafter spent his life as a country squire at the family seat of Edstone, Warwickshire. *Died 17 July 1742.*

PUBLICATIONS

Collections

   Poetical Works.   2 vols., 1766.

Verse

   The Two Springs: A Fable.   1725.
   Occasional Poems, Translations, Fables, Tales.   1727.
   The Chace.   1735; revised edition, 1749.
   Hobbinol; or, The Rural Games: A Burlesque Poem in Blank Verse.   1740.
   Field Sports.   1742.
   A Collection of Miscellaneous Poems, edited by F. G. Waldron.   1802.

Bibliography: "Somerville's The Chace, 1735" by J. D. Fleeman, in *Publications of the Bibliographical Society of America 58,* 1964.

*   *   *

   The verse of that Warwickshire squire and one-time Oxford fellow, William Somerville, reflects the literary and sporting interests of a well-educated country gentleman. Johnson went so far as to say "he writes very well for a gentleman." Some occasional poems addressed to Addison or referring to Marlborough must have been written about 1712, but the rest of Somerville's early verse, collected into *Occasional Poems* is not easy to date. It consists of unremarkable odes, addresses, epistles, fables, imitations of Horace, and salacious tales in octosyllabic couplets on such subjects as "The Night-Walker Reclaim'd" or "The Inquisitive Bridegroom." His gift for burlesque is admirably shown in a spirited and facetious piece of minor Augustan mock-epic in heroic couplets, "The Bowling-Green"; but more interesting, in view of his later development, is the imitation of John Philips's burlesque Miltonic blank verse in Somerville's poem written as early as 1709, "The Wicker-Chair," which was eventually revised and published with a dedication to Hogarth, under the title of *Hobbinol; or, The Rural Games; A Burlesque Poem.* Here Somerville has certainly followed the advice he gave to Thomson to "read Philips much," for *Hobbinol* very deliberately combines the country-subject of *Cyder* with the comedy of *The Splendid Shilling* in a mock-heroic description, at perhaps too great a length, of village sports. Somerville exposes the boorishness of the country fellow at play, but not without a touch of the John Bullish, roast-beef patriotism of his age and some genuine admiration for "the British freeholders, who, when dressed in their holiday clothes ... eat and drink as plentifully, and fight as heartily, as the greatest hero in the Iliad" (Preface to *Hobbinol*).
   Somerville's best poem is his blank-verse didactic piece *The Chace.* This relates the history of the chase and describes in plain, vivid terms the techniques of hunting the fox, stag, hare, otter, and other creatures; it provides detailed instructions upon such matters as the construction of kennels and the breeding of hounds; it reflects upon the psychology of bitches

and the mystery of the scent; and intersperses all this with moral and patriotic digressions, and with romantic, exotic excursions describing such pursuits as "the Asiatic way of hunting" and "the ancient way of hunting the tiger with a mirror." Somerville brought into currency the definition of hunting as "the sport of kings; image of war without its guilt"; and by his references to heroic poetry and tactful echoes of Virgil's *Georgics* he contrives to dignify hunting by associating it with patriotism, sociability, health, and even virtue. Though *The Chace* can have few readers today, it was very popular for a century after first publication, and was the favourite reading of Surtees' Mr. Jorrocks. Somerville's last poem, *Field Sports*, is a languid supplement to *The Chace*, describing hawking and angling – "the more polite entertainments of the field."

—A. J. Sambrook

STEELE, Sir Richard. Irish.   Born in Dublin, baptized 12 March 1672.   Educated at Charterhouse, London, where he met Joseph Addison, 1684–89; matriculated at Christ Church, Oxford, 1690; postmaster at Merton College, Oxford, 1691–94, but left without taking a degree. Enlisted as a cadet in the Duke of Ormonde's guards, 1694; Ensign in Lord Cutts's Regiment, 1695, and served as Cutts's confidential secretary, 1696–97; Captain, stationed at the Tower of London, by 1700; transferred as Captain to Lord Lucas's Regiment in 1702. Married 1) Margaret Ford Stretch in 1705 (died, 1706); 2) Mary Scurlock in 1707 (died, 1718), two sons and two daughters. Wrote extensively for the theatre, 1701–05; Gentleman-Writer to Prince George of Denmark, 1706–08; Gazetteer (i.e., Manager of the *Gazette*, the official government publication), 1707–10; Commissioner of Stamps, 1710–13; Editor, *The Tatler*, to which Addison was the major contributor, 1709–11; Editor, with Addison, *The Spectator*, 1711–12; Editor, *The Guardian*, 1713; elected Member of Parliament for Stockbridge, Hampshire, 1713, but expelled for anti-government views; Editor, *The Englishman*, 1713–14, *The Lover*, 1714, and *The Reader*, 1714; on accession of George I, 1714, appointed Justice of the Peace, Deputy Lieutenant for the County of Middlesex, Surveyor of the Royal Stables at Hampton Court, and Supervisor of the Drury Lane Theatre, London: granted life patent of Drury Lane, 1715; Member of Parliament for Boroughbridge, Yorkshire, 1715; Editor, *Town Talk*, 1715–16, *The Tea-Table*, and *Chit-Chat*, 1716; appointed Commissioner for Forfeited Estates in Scotland, 1716; quarrelled with Addison, 1719; Editor, *The Plebeian*, 1719, and *The Theatre*, 1720; Member of Parliament for Wendover, Buckinghamshire, 1722; retired to Wales, 1724. Knighted, 1715. *Died 1 September 1729.*

PUBLICATIONS

Collections

   Correspondence, edited by R. Blanchard.   1941; revised edition, 1968.
   Plays, edited by Shirley S. Kenny.   1971.

Essays and Prose Writings

The Christian Hero, An Argument Proving That No Principles But Those of Religion Are Sufficient to Make a Great Man. 1701; edited by R. Blanchard, 1932.
The Tatler, with Addison. 4 vols., 1710–11; edited by G. A. Aitken, 4 vols., 1898–99; selections edited by L. Gibbs, 1953.
The Spectator, with Addison. 8 vols., 1712–15; edited by D. F. Bond, 5 vols., 1965; selections edited by R. J. Allen, 1957.
An Englishman's Thanks to the Duke of Marlborough. 1712.
A Letter to Sir M. W[arton] Concerning Occasional Peers. 1713.
The Importance of Dunkirk. 1713.
The Guardian, with others. 2 vols., 1714; edited by Alexander Chalmers, 1802.
The Englishman (2 series, and an epistle). 3 vols., 1714–16; edited by R. Blanchard, 1955.
The Crisis, with Some Seasonable Remarks on the Danger of a Popish Successor. 1714.
The French Faith Represented in the Present State of Dunkirk. 1714.
A Letter Concerning the Bill for Preventing the Growth of Schism. 1714.
Mr. Steele's Apology for Himself and His Writings. 1714.
A Letter from the Earl of Mar to the King. 1715.
A Letter Concerning the Condemned Lords. 1716.
Account of Mr. Desagulier's New-Invented Chimneys. 1716.
An Account of the Fish Pool, with Joseph Gillmore. 1718.
The Joint and Humble Address to the Tories and Whigs Concerning the Intended Bill of Peerage. 1719.
A Letter to the Earl of O – d Concerning the Bill of Peerage. 1719.
The Plebeian. 1719; edited by R. Hurd, in Addison's *Works,* 1856.
The Spinster, in Defence of the Woollen Manufactures. 1719.
The Crisis of Property. 1720.
A Nation a Family; or, A Plan for the Improvement of the South-Sea Proposal. 1720.
The State of the Case Between the Lord Chamberlain and the Governor of the Royal Company of Comedians. 1720.
The Theatre. 1720; edited by John Loftis, 1962.
Tracts and Pamphlets, edited by R. Blanchard. 1944.
Steele's Periodical Journalism 1714–16 : The Lover, The Reader, Town Talk, Chit-Chat, edited by R. Blanchard. 1959.

Plays

The Funeral; or, Grief a-la-Mode (produced 1701). 1702.
The Lying Lover; or, The Ladies' Friendship (produced 1703). 1704.
The Tender Husband; or, The Accomplished Fools (produced 1703). 1705.
The Conscious Lovers (produced 1722). 1723.

Verse

The Procession : A Poem on Her Majesty's Funeral. 1695.
Occasional Verse, edited by R. Blanchard. 1952.

Other

Editor, *The Ladies Library.* 3 vols., 1714.
Editor, *Poetical Miscellanies.* 1714.

Reading List: *Steele* by Willard Connely, 1934; *Steele at Drury Lane* by John Loftis, 1952; *Steele, Addison, and Their Periodical Essays* by Arthur R. Humphreys, 1959; *Steele: The Early Career*, 1964, and *The Later Career*, 1970, both by Calhoun Winton.

*   *   *

Though best remembered as a periodical essayist, Sir Richard Steele's literary career began in the theatre – if, that is, one forgets and forgives his moralizing tract *The Christian Hero*, an unsuccessful attempt at self-admonition. His plays were frank attempts to make piety more palatable, while avoiding the sexual excesses for which Collier had condemned the stage, and which increasingly middle-class audiences were also finding offensive.

The first, *The Funeral*, has several touches of originality, notably in its satire of the undertaking business, its sprightly yet sympathetic treatment of its female characters, and its liveliness of plotting. Indeed, two of the participants in Gildon's *A Comparison Between the Two Stages* allege that in this latter respect the play resembles a farce more than it does a comedy, and it may be regretted that Steele never successfully evaded formal considerations of this kind – though two fragments, *The School of Action* and *The Gentleman*, do begin to assert the kind of freedom from the rules that Gay and Fielding more happily achieved.

The Lying Lover was unalleviated by realism, displayed less comic spirit, and was, as Steele ruefully admitted, "damn'd for its piety." Loosely derived from Corneille's *Le Menteur*, it features a pathetic repentance scene, in which its hero, Young Bookwit, awakens in prison to find that he has killed a rival in a drunken duel. For this he is duly contrite in blank verse, to the extent of putting forgiveness before honour. There is some wit in the quixotic Bookwit's romancing in the earlier scenes, and his respectful welcome to Newgate by his fellow inmates hints at the inverted morality of *The Beggar's Opera*: yet, just a few scenes later, Steele perpetrates a double shift in the plot lacking any sense of its own fatal absurdity.

The Tender Husband, Steele's third play, also proved to be his last to reach the stage for nearly eighteen years. It has a female Quixote, or prototype Lydia Languish, as its heroine – and, indeed, the original of Tony Lumpkin in that heroine's cousin, Humphry Gubbin. Unfortunately, the sub-plot featuring the eponymous husband, who devises an unlikely test of his wife's faithfulness by disguising his own mistress as a suitor, disrupts the comic flow, and complicates the conclusion with a sentimental reconciliation.

In the following years, Steele was increasingly active as a Whig politician, his major literary achievement being, of course, the succession of periodicals he created, some written in collaboration with Joseph Addison. Of these, the best remembered are *The Spectator*, and *The Guardian*, with the irrelevantly titled *The Theatre* probably the most important of the later series. Whether or not Steele succeeded in his aim "to make the pulpit, the bar, and the stage all act in concert in the cause of piety, justice, and virtue" is arguable: but he certainly perfected a distinctive new form of clubable *belles lettres*, incidentally exploring techniques of characterization for his recurrent *personae* which were to be of significance to the early novelists, and publishing some first-rate dramatic criticism.

Although *The Conscious Lovers*, which did not reach the stage till 1722, was influential in the development of the *comédie larmoyante* in France, to the modern mind it merely demonstrates that, at its most sentimental, eighteenth-century comedy was no laughing matter. With the exception of its scenes below stairs – their purpose all too evidently to sugar a didactic pill – it is a distinctly unfunny play: yet, according to Steele, an audience's pleasure might be "too exquisite for laughter," and thus better expressed in the tears evoked by the inexpressibly virtuous behaviour of his hero, Young Bevil, and by the convenient reshufflings of the characters in the closing scene.

The mercantile morality of the play is at once over-explicit and interruptive, and its characters are neither in the humours nor the manners tradition, but mere ethical absolutes. No wonder that Fielding's Parson Adams considered it the first play fit for a Christian to read since the pagan tragedies – but then good Parson Adams lacked both irony and a sense of incongruity, as does *The Conscious Lovers*. Steele is better remembered by the feeling for both irony *and* incongruity in his earlier plays, and, of course, by his largeness of heart as a periodical essayist.

—Simon Trussler

SWIFT, Jonathan.   English.   Born in Dublin, Ireland, 30 November 1667, of English parents. Educated at Kilkenny Grammar School, 1674–82; Trinity College, Dublin, 1682–88. Married Esther (Stella) Johnson in 1716 (died, 1728). Companion and Secretary to Sir William Temple at Moor Park, Farnham, Surrey, 1689–91, 1691–94, 1695–99; ordained in the Anglican Church, in Dublin, 1695, and held first living at Kilroot, Northern Ireland, until 1698; Chaplain to the Earl of Berkeley, Lord Lieutenant of Ireland, 1700; vicar of Laracor; Prebend, St. Patrick's Cathedral, Dublin, 1701; editor of several volumes of Temple's works during the 1700's; aligned with the Tory ministry of Oxford and Bolingbroke, 1710: lived in London, wrote political pamphlets, and contributed to *The Examiner*, 1710–14; Dean of St. Patrick's Cathedral, Dublin, from 1713; a leader of the Irish resistance movement from 1724; visited London, 1726, 1727, but otherwise resided in Dublin until his death. D.D.: University of Dublin,1701. *Died 19 October 1745.*

PUBLICATIONS

Collections

> *Poems,* edited by Harold Williams.   3 vols., 1937.
> *Prose Works,* edited by Herbert Davis.   14 vols., 1939–68.
> *Gulliver's Travels and Other Writings,* edited by Louis A. Landa.   1960.
> *The Correspondence,* edited by Harold Williams.   5 vols., 1963–65.
> *A Tale of a Tub and Other Satires,* edited by Kathleen Williams.   1975.
> *Selected Poems,* edited by C. H. Sisson.   1977.

Verse

> *Baucis and Philemon, Imitated from Ovid.*   1709.
> *Part of the Seventh Epistle of the First Book of Horace Imitated.*   1713.
> *The First Ode of the Second Book of Horace Paraphrased.*   1713.
> *The Bubble.*   1721.
> *Cadenus and Vanessa.*   1726.
> *Miscellanies in Prose and Verse,* with others.   4 vols., 1727–32.
> *Horace, Book I, Ode XIV, Paraphrased.*   1730.
> *The Lady's Dressing Room, to Which Is Added A Poem on Cutting Down the Old Thorn at*
>   *Market Hill.*   1732.
> *An Elegy on Dicky and Dolly.*   1732.

The Life and Genuine Character of Doctor Swift, Written by Himself.   1733.
On Poetry: A Rhapsody.   1733.
An Epistle to a Lady.   1734.
A Beautiful Young Nymph Going to Bed, Written for the Honour of the Fair Sex.   1734.
An Imitation of the Sixth Satire of the Second Book of Horace, completed by Pope.
   1738.
Verses on the Death of Dr. Swift.   1739.

Fiction

*A Tale of a Tub, Written for the Universal Improvement of Mankind, to Which Is Added
   an Account of a Battle Between the Ancient and Modern Books in St. James's
   Library.*   1704; revised edition, 1710; edited by G. C. Guthkelch and D. N. Smith,
   1958.
Travels into Several Remote Nations of the World, by Captain Lemuel Gulliver.   1726;
   revised edition, 1735; edited by Angus Ross, 1972.

Other

*A Discourse of the Contests and Dissensions Between the Nobles and the Commons in
   Athens and Rome.*   1701; edited by F. H. Ellis, 1967.
Predictions for the Year 1708.   1708.
A Project for the Advancement of Religion and the Reformation of Manners.   1709.
A New Journey to Paris.   1711.
The Conduct of the Allies.   1711.
Some Remarks on the Barrier Treaty.   1712.
A Proposal for Correcting, Improving, and Ascertaining the English Tongue.   1712.
Mr. Collin's Discourse of Free-Thinking.   1713.
The Public Spirit of the Whigs.   1714.
A Proposal for the Universal Use of Irish Manufacture.   1720.
*Fraud Detected: or, The Hibernian Patriot, Containing All the Drapier's Letters to the
   People of Ireland.*   1725; as *The Hibernian Patriot,* 1730.
A Short View of the Present State of Ireland.   1728.
*A Modest Proposal for Preventing the Children of Poor People from Being Burthen to
   Their Parents or the Country.*   1729.
*An Examination of Certain Abuses, Corruptions, and Enormities in the City of
   Dublin.*   1732.
The Works.   1735.
A Complete Collection of Genteel and Ingenious Conversation.   1738; edited by E.
   Partridge, 1963.
Some Free Thoughts upon the Present State of Affairs Written in the Year 1714.   1741.
Three Sermons.   1744.
Directions to Servants.   1745.
The Last Will and Testament of Swift.   1746.
Brotherly Love: A Sermon.   1754.
The History of the Four Last Years of the Queen.   1758.

Editor, *Letters Written by Sir William Temple and Other Ministers of State.*   3 vols.,
   1700–03.
Editor, *Miscellanea: The Third Part,* by William Temple.   1701.
Editor, *Memoirs: Part III,* by William Temple.   1709.

Bibliography: *A Bibliography of the Writings of Swift* by H. Teerink, 1937, revised edition, edited by Arthur H. Scouten, 1963; *A Bibliography of Swift Studies 1945–1965* by J. J. Stathis, 1967.

Reading List: *The Mind and Art of Swift* by Ricardo Quintana, 1936; *The Sin of Wit* by Maurice Johnson, 1950; *Swift: The Man, His Works, and the Age* by Irvin Ehrenpreis, 2 vols. (of 3), 1962–67; *Swift and the Satirist's Art* by E. W. Rosenheim, Jr., 1963; *Swift and the Age of Compromise* by Kathleen Williams, 1968, and *Swift: The Critical Heritage* edited by Williams, 1970; *Swift: A Critical Introduction* by Denis Donoghue, 1969; *Swift* edited by C. J. Rawson, 1971, and *Gulliver and the Gentle Reader* by Rawson, 1973.

*   *   *

Swift began as a poet, and wrote many poems throughout his life. His poetic achievement has been overshadowed by his major prose satires, but deserves to be recognised. After a brief early period of Cowleyan odes, Swift abandoned "serious" or "lofty" styles (both terms are his own), and became one of the masters in a great English tradition of "light" verse, informal but far from trivial, which includes the works of Skelton, Samuel Butler, Prior, Byron, and Auden. Byron admired him especially, and said he "beats us all hollow." Swift seldom wrote what he called "serious Couplets," avoiding a form which his friend Pope was bringing to a high refinement of precision and masterfulness. He preferred looser and more popular metres, and most often the loose octosyllabic couplet chiefly associated with Butler's *Hudibras*, a poem Swift greatly admired. These looser forms reflected the disorders of life, rather than seeming to subdue or iron out these disorders within the reassuring contours of a style which overtly proclaimed the author's triumphant and clarifying mastery. Even the few poems which, exceptionally, Swift wrote in the heroic couplet, the "Description of the Morning" and the "Description of a City Shower," tend to flatten that eloquently patterned metre into an idiom of bare realistic notation, registering the chaotic and unstructured energies of common city scenes rather than any sense of the satirist's control.

These two poems also parody some conventions of grand poetic description, and Swift's impulse to undercut the loftier orderings of "serious" poets runs through virtually all his work as a poet. The celebrated "excremental" poems ("The Lady's Dressing Room," "A Beautiful Young Nymph Going to Bed," "Strephon and Chloe," "Cassinus and Peter") are among other things parodies of the false idealisations of love-poetry. The famous plaintive cry that "Celia, Celia, Celia shits," which occurs in two of the poems and has shocked healthy-minded readers like D. H. Lawrence and Aldous Huxley, has this dimension of parody, although more than mere parody is at work. The words are too playful to support any simple view that Swift hated the human body or was a misogynist. Through his foolish Strephons, Swift mocks those who cannot accept the physical facts and seek refuge in idealising poeticisms. But he also tells us that the body is ugly and perishable, and that in matters of love and of friendship the moral and intellectual virtues are a sounder guide. These themes also run through many non-scatological poems which he wrote to women friends, notably the moving and tender poems to Stella and the archly self-justifying "Cadenus and Vanessa."

The latter, a defence of his role in a one-sided love-affair, is one of several autobiographical poems which Swift, at various periods, wrote as apologies for some aspect of his private or public life. Of these, the most interesting are "The Author upon Himself" and *Verses on the Death of Dr. Swift*. The latter is perhaps his best-known poem, a comprehensive and in many places light-hearted and low-key defense of his literary and political career, rising towards the end to a pitch of self-praise which some readers have found distasteful. *An Epistle to a Lady* is a revealing poem about Swift's unwillingness to write in a "lofty Stile"; and *On Poetry: A Rapsody* whose title implies a similar point, is in the main an angry and witty account of the world of bad poets and hireling politicians.

In the 1730's Swift also wrote a series of angry poems on Irish affairs, of which "The Legion Club" is the best known. These attacks on prominent public men in Ireland sometimes have the force to ritual curses, and are perhaps the only places where Swift attempts what is often (and almost always wrongly) attributed to him, a Juvenalian grandeur of denunciation.

Swift's earliest major work is the prose *Tale of a Tub* (published 1704, but begun about 1696 and largely written by 1700), a brilliantly inventive and disturbing display of his satiric powers. It is the last and greatest English contribution to the long Renaissance debate on the relative merits of the Ancients and the Moderns. Through a deliberately diffuse and all-embracing parody, the *Tale* mimics the laxity, muddle, and arrogance of Modern thought, both in religion and in the various branches of literature and learning. This parody is sometimes very specific, as when Dryden's garrulous self-importance, or the mystical nonsense of some "*dark* Author" like Thomas Vaughan, is mocked. But it extends beyond specific examples to the whole contemporaneous republic of bad authors and to all deviant religions, which for Swift meant mainly the dissenting sects and Roman Catholicism. The cumulative force of its many-sided and probing irony reaches even further, however, transcending parody altogether and turning into a comprehensive anatomy of modern culture and indeed of human folly in general. Many readers, from Swift's time to our own, have felt that its effect was so destructive as to undermine even those things to which Swift claimed to be expressing loyalty, including the Church of England and indeed religion itself. Swift defended himself against such charges, but they stuck, and were to damage his career as a churchman. Whether or not Swift's defense is wholly accepted, the work shows Swift's deep and characteristic tendency to put his most powerful energies into the destructive or critical side of his vision, leaving the positive values to emerge by implication from the wreckage. The *Tale* was published with two accompanying pieces, *The Battle of the Books* and the *Discourse Concerning the Mechanical Operation of the Spirit*. The first extends the *Tale*'s satire on learning, the second on religious abuses.

In the years after 1704, Swift wrote a number of tracts on matters of religion and ecclesiastical politics. Of these, the "Argument Against Abolishing Christianity," has exceptional distinction as an ironic *tour de force*, subtle, inventive, slippery and playful, yet charged with an urgency of purpose and a sense of cherished values under threat.

During the period of Swift's early fame, 1710–14, Swift became a protégé of Harley and wrote many political tracts in support of his Tory ministry and of the controversial Peace of Utrecht. Harley put him in charge of the *Examiner*, for which he wrote some of his best brief polemical pieces, notably against the Duke of Marlborough, hero of the war against France. Of his other political writings in this period perhaps the most important is *The Conduct of the Allies*. Swift was one of the members of the Scriblerus club, a group of satirical wits associated with Harley (now Earl of Oxford), whose other regular members were Pope, Gay, Arbuthnot, and Thomas Parnell. The Club mostly met in 1714, and was effectively dispersed after Queen Anne's death in that year and the consequent collapse of the Tory administration. But the Club's activities not only resulted in the collectively composed *Memoirs of Martinus Scriblerus* (which Pope published much later, in 1741), but also influenced other writings by individual Scriblerians, including *Gulliver's Travels* (1726), and Pope's *Dunciad* (1728). In 1713, Swift became Dean of St. Patrick's Cathedral in Dublin, the highest preferment he could achieve in the Church. He regarded it as a blow to his hopes, and thought of his native Ireland as a place of exile.

After the Queen's death in 1714, he remained in Ireland for almost the whole of his life, and became actively involved in Irish political affairs. His Irish writings of the 1720's and (to a lesser degree) the 1730's earn him his honoured place as a defender of Ireland's rights. He was one of a series of great Anglo-Irishmen who fought to relieve Ireland's wrongs at the hands of the English oppressor: the list includes Charles Stewart Parnell and W. B. Yeats. The most important literary text among Swift's Irish writings is *A Modest Proposal*, an ironic pamphlet advocating the selling of Irish infants for food as a means of helping the economy. This *Proposal* is the climax of a whole series of tracts, which includes *A Proposal for Universal Use of Irish Manufacture*, the *Drapier's Letters*, and *A Short View of the State of Ireland*, in which the economic and political weaknesses of Ireland are bitterly exposed, and remedies suggested. The common view that these works are mainly or entirely anti-English is only partially true. It is becoming increasingly recognised that Swift was also concerned to expose the Irish for their failure to help themselves: their slavish temperament, economic fecklessness, commercial disreputability, the draining of the country's resources by absentee landlords. These criticisms underlie *A Modest Proposal*, which is more accurately read as a cry of exasperation against Irishmen of all classes and parties than as an attack on the English oppressor (although it is that too). Swift disliked the Irish while feeling called upon to defend their political rights. He thought of himself as English, accidentally "dropped" in Ireland by birth and kept there by an unhappy turn in his career. But he fought powerfully for Irish interests, achieved some practical successes (especially with the *Drapier's Letters*), and became and has remained a national hero.

Gulliver's Travels was published in 1726. It bears strong traces of Swift's involvement in Irish affairs. But its reach is, of course, much wider. Like *A Tale of a Tub*, it has a framework of parody (in this case mainly of travel-books), but its principal satiric concerns, unlike those of the *Tale*, are not in themselves enshrined in the parody. Neither work deals merely with bad books, and both are concerned with a fundamental exploration of the nature of man. But in the *Tale*, the follies of unregulated intellect and impulse are directly expressed in the kind of book and the features of style which Swift mimics, whereas in *Gulliver's Travels* the travel-book format is mainly a convenient framework for a consideration of human nature which is only marginally concerned with the character of travel-writers.

In the first two books, an allegory of human pride begins to establish itself. The tiny Lilliputians of Book I are a minuscule and self-important replica of the society of England; the giants of Book II demonstrate that in the eyes of larger creatures we ourselves seem as ludicrous as the Lilliputians seem to us. The two Books have a complementary relationship which is forceful and clear: a neat balancing of narrative structures which supports and illustrates the basic satiric irony, and is able to accommodate a wide range of detailed satiric observation about English and European mores and institutions.

This exceptionally tidy structural arrangement gives way in the rest of the work to something more complex and less predictable. Book III takes us to a miscellany of strange lands, all of them inhabited by humans of normal size, and between them illustrating particular social and political institutions (repressive government, insane and inhumane scientific research projects, wild follies of intellect). If the schematic relationship between Books I and II is not continued, much of Book III adds to or develops the exposure of particular human characteristics and institutions which had begun in the earlier books. But towards the end of Book III a new note is struck. Gulliver visits the land of the Struldbruggs, who have the gift of immortality but without perpetual youth. The horror which these hideous creatures arouse as they decay into increasing senility is no longer primarily concerned with moral culpability. It is a portrayal of certain grim features of the human situation which are independent of good and evil.

In Book IV satire becomes absolute, transcending all mere particularities of vice and folly of the kind encountered so far. The savage Yahoos have most of the vices and follies satirised earlier, but they embody a sense of the radical ugliness of the human animal, in his moral and his physical nature, which amounts (or so it seems to many readers) to a more fundamental disenchantment. The Houyhnhnms, the horse-shaped rulers of the humanoid Yahoos, are by contrast absolutely reasonable and virtuous, as the Yahoos are absolutely irrational and vicious. Swift said that he wished to disprove the traditional definition of man as a "rational animal," and he did so partly by enshrining an ideal rationality in a beast commonly named in philosophical discourse as an example of the non-rational animal: the horse. Swift's analysis has usually been considered a bleak and disturbing one, although some recent critics have held that Swift really believed that man both was and ought to be a creature who came somewhere between Yahoo and Houyhnhnm, a liberal and humane though fallible creature of the sort exemplified by the good Portuguese captain, who appears briefly near the end. This latter view seems to me misguided.

—C. J. Rawson

THOMSON, James.   Scottish.   Born in Ednam, Roxburghshire, baptized 15 September 1700. Educated at Jedburgh Grammar School; University of Edinburgh, matriculated 1715; studied for the ministry. Abandoned his studies and went to London, 1725: Tutor to Thomas Hamilton, afterwards Earl of Haddington; Companion and Tutor to Charles Talbot, the future Lord Chancellor's son, 1730–33; Secretary of Briefs, 1733–37; appointed Surveyor-General of the Leeward Islands, 1744. Received a pension from the Prince of Wales, 1738–48. *Died 27 August 1748.*

PUBLICATIONS

Collections

Works, edited by George Lyttelton.   4 vols., 1750.
Complete Poetical Works, edited by J. L. Robertson.   1908.
Letters and Documents, edited by Alan D. McKillop.   1958.

Verse

Winter.   1726, revised edition, 1726, 1730; *Summer,* 1727, revised edition, 1730; *Spring,* 1728, revised edition, 1731; complete version, as *The Seasons,* 1730, revised edition, 1730, 1744, 1746; edited by A. J. Sambrook, with *The Castle of Indolence,* 1972.
A Poem Sacred to the Memory of Sir Isaac Newton.   1727.
Britannia.   1729; revised edition, 1730.
A Poem to the Memory of Mr. Congreve.   1729.
The Four Seasons and Other Poems.   4 vols., 1735.
Ancient and Modern Italy Compared, Being the First Part of Liberty.   1735; *Greece,* 1735; *Rome,* 1735; *Britain,* 1736; *The Prospect,* 1736; complete version, as *Liberty,* 1738.
A Poem to the Memory of Lord Talbot, Late Chancellor of Great Britain.   1737.
The Castle of Indolence.   1748; edited by J. A. Sambrook, with *The Seasons,* 1972.
Poems on Several Occasions.   1750.

Plays

The Tragedy of Sophonisba (produced 1730).   1730.
Agamemnon (produced 1738).   1738.
Edward and Eleonora.   1739.
Alfred: A Masque, with David Mallet, music by Thomas Arne (produced 1740).   1740; revised version (produced 1751), 1751; as *Alfred the Great,* 1753.
Tancred and Sigismunda (produced 1745).   1745.
Coriolanus (produced 1749).   1749.

Other

Works.   1736; revised edition, 2 vols., 1744.

Reading List: *The Background of Thomson's Seasons* by Alan D. McKillop, 1942; *Thomson: Poet of the Seasons* by Douglas Grant, 1951; *The Varied God: A Critical Study of Thomson's Seasons*, 1959, and *The Poetry of Vision*, 1967, both by Patricia M. Spacks; *The Unfolding of the Seasons* by Ralph Cohen, 1970.

*   *   *

Winter is a religious-sublime poem in which James Thomson's descriptions of the terrible beauties of that season prompt the poet to reflect upon the power of God. Thomson added poems on the other seasons, written like *Winter* in blank verse and Miltonic diction, and revised and expanded them all repeatedly, until the final version of *The Seasons* (1746) was over fourteen times as long as the first version of *Winter*. In this process of growth *The Seasons* assumed a somewhat more secular character. Since Thomson regarded Nature as the work of God and Newton as the great interpreter of this work, he inevitably brings a great deal of imaginatively exciting new science into his poem, but this tends to concentrate the reader's attention upon second causes, rather than upon the First Cause. *The Seasons* under revision also grows more and more to resemble the *Georgics*, as Thomson draws upon Virgil's practical advice on husbandry, his myths, his exotic excursions, his anthropomorphic mock-heroic accounts of beasts, and, above all, his great patriotic rhapsodies. Like all English readers of the *Georgics*, Thomson is moved by Virgil's appealing myth of the innocence, felicity, vigour, patriotism, and piety of the husbandman's life. In the later stages of revision Thomson brings in ever-longer geographical excursions to describe the wonders of Nature in the Arctic and the tropics; he brings in longer reflections upon society and history; and he interpolates sentimental stories to add a human interest which he may have thought was lacking at first. However, there is a more significant human interest. Thomson's poem describes external nature, but it is, as Wordsworth said, "written nobly from himself." The subject is not so much religion, science, philosophy, history, and nature as a mind responding to these things. The unity of this apparently shapeless poem is in the movement of Thomson's own mind, and the poet is his own subject; standing alone, he finds in the shapes and sounds of unconscious external nature the self-conscious life of his own thought and feeling. Down to the middle of the nineteenth century *The Seasons* was probably the best-known of all English poems after *Paradise Lost*. Until the effect of Wordsworth's poetry came to be widely felt, it was the dominant influence upon English nature poetry, and did much to shape what is sometimes called the "romantic" view of external nature.

Thomson's occasional lyrical poems are unremarkable, except for his "Hymn on Solitude" (written 1725) which is one of the earliest and finest of eighteenth-century imitations of Milton's "L'Allegro" and "Il Penseroso." The blank-verse *Poem Sacred to the Memory of Sir Isaac Newton* blends panegyric, patriotism, religion, and science; its best lines are a dramatic, subtly personified, account of the spectrum. *Britannia*, also in blank verse, is a piece of anti-Walpole invective which rises to imaginative vision only in the lines on the wreck of the Spanish Armada "where loud the Northern Main/Howls thro' the fractur'd *Caledonian* Isles." The social, political, patriotic, and party interests of *Britannia* reappear in the series of five much longer blank-verse poems (1735-6) collected under the title of *Liberty*, in which Thomson dutifully, but not very animatedly, traces the progress of civilization through Europe from ancient times to modern. Here, as always in Thomson, there is imaginative vitality when landscape description is used to evoke states of mind and feeling; but for the most part the poet seems to be only half engaged with his subject. *Liberty* was a fruit of that same mistaken ambition which led Thomson to devote most of his energies to the writing of high-minded and languid heroic tragedies: *Sophonisba*, *Agamemnon*, *Edward and Eleonora*, *Tancred and Sigismunda*, and *Coriolanus*. He also wrote, in collaboration with David Mallet, the masque *Alfred* in which first appeared Thomson's best known lyric – "Rule Britannia."

The Castle of Indolence, in two cantos, is one of the happiest eighteenth-century imitations of Spenser. In the opening of the first canto Thomson richly evokes a dreamy, honeyed, languorous drowsiness where the Castle becomes the symbol of one kind of poetic imagination and Indolence becomes the poet's dream; but in the remainder of the poem Thomson elaborates an allegory in which the Castle is destroyed by the Knight of Arts and Industry. Indolence is condemned, and progress is praised in its various moral, intellectual, social, and material forms. It looks as if Thomson − consciously or not − is dramatizing a conflict between the moralizing, didactic public poet who was responsible for most of his writings, and the inward-looking visionary who wrote the most imaginative descriptions in *The Seasons*.

—A.J. Sambrook

TICKELL, Thomas. English. Born in Bridekirk, Cumberland, in 1686. Educated at Queen's College, Oxford, matriculated 1701, B.A. 1705, M.A. 1709. Married Clotilda Eustace in 1726; two sons and two daughters. Fellow, Queen's College, 1710–26; Professor of Poetry, Oxford University, 1711; moved to London and associated with Addison, through whose influence he entered diplomatic service: employed by Addison when Secretary to the Lord Lieutenant of Ireland, 1714, and made Under-Secretary by Addison when Secretary of State, 1717; Secretary to the Lord Justices in Ireland, 1724–40. *Died 23 April 1740.*

PUBLICATIONS

Collections

Poetical Works, edited by Thomas Park. 1807.

Verse

Oxford. 1707.
A Poem to the Lord Privy-Seal on the Prospect of Peace. 1713.
An Imitation of the Prophecy of Nereus, from Horace, Book 1, Ode XV. 1715.
The First Book of Homer's Iliad. 1715.
An Epistle from a Lady in England to a Gentleman at Avignon. 1717.
An Ode Occasioned by the Earl Stanhope's Voyage to France. 1718.
An Ode to the Earl of Sunderland at Windsor. 1720.
Kensington Garden. 1722.
To Sir Godfrey Kneller, at His Country Seat. 1722.
Lucy and Colin: A Song Written in Imitation of William and Margaret. 1725.
A Poem in Praise of the Horn-Book. 1728.
On Her Majesty's Re-Building the Lodgings of the Black Prince and Henry V and Queen's College, Oxford. 1733.

Other

Editor, The Works of Addison. 4 vols., 1721.

Reading List: *Tickell and the Eighteenth-Century Poets* by R. E. Tickell, 1931.

*   *   *

Thomas Tickell began his poetical career with *Oxford* of which Bonamy Dobrée in *English Literature in the Early Eighteenth Century* says that its decasyllabic couplets "conduct one gravely round a tour of the sights of Oxford, with the expected references to the great men, especially the poets, who had lived there." Other works include occasional pieces, and political poems like *Epistle from a Lady in England to a Gentleman at Avignon* (which favoured the Hanoverian Succession) and "The Prospect of Peace." But it is chiefly as the loyal friend of Addison that he is remembered. His translation of the first book of Homer's *Iliad* earned him the emnity of Pope. Pope suspected, apparently with some reason, that Addison was encouraging Tickell to enter into competition with his own projected translation of Homer. After Addison's death Tickell edited his works, and produced his "Elegy on the Death of Mr. Addison." Johnson, in the *Lives of the Poets*, says "neither he nor Addison ever produced nobler lines than are contained in the third and fourth paragraphs; nor is a more sublime or more elegant funeral-poem to be found in the whole compass of English literature." Edmund Gosse, in Ward's *English Poets*, was probably nearer the mark when he said, "In it a sublime and public sorrow for once moved a thoroughly mediocre poet into utterance that was sincere and original." It is certainly true that Tickell's personal feeling breaks through the formality of this poem, and redeems it from the triviality of much eighteenth-century funerary writing:

> What mourner ever felt poetic fires?
> Slow comes the verse, that real woe inspires:
> Grief unaffected suits but ill with art,
> Or flowing numbers with a bleeding heart.

Kensington Garden is fanciful mock-heroic poem of some charm, though Johnson criticised Tickell for mixing Greek gods with Gothic fairies. To some extent this poem belongs to the same world as Pope's *Rape of the Lock*, though falling a long way below that masterpiece. *Lucy and Colin* is of interest as one of the earliest examples of the eighteenth-century fashion for sentimental exploitation of the traditional ballad form – a fashion which was to have important consequences for the Romantic movement.

—John Heath-Stubbs

———————

WALSH, William.   English.   Born in Abberley, Worcestershire, in 1663, and lived on the family estate there for all of his life. Educated at Wadham College, Oxford, matriculated 1678, but did not take a degree. Whig Member of Parliament for Worcestershire, 1698, 1701, 1702, and for Richmond, Yorkshire, 1705–08; Gentleman of the Horse in Queen Anne's household; a friend and literary adviser of Alexander Pope. *Died 18 March 1708.*

PUBLICATIONS

Collections

Works in Prose and Verse. 1736.

Verse

Letters and Poems Amorous and Gallant. 1692.
A Funeral Elegy upon the Death of the Queen. 1695.
Ode for the Thanksgiving Day. 1706.

Play

Squire Trelooby, with Congreve and Vanbrugh, from a play by Molière (produced 1704). Revised version by James Ralph published as *The Cornish Squire,* 1734.

Other

A Dialogue Concerning Women, Being a Defence of the Sex. 1691.

Reading List: articles by Phyllis Freeman, in *Bodleian Quarterly Review,* 1934, and *Review of English Studies,* 1948, 1957.

*   *   *

William Walsh was a late member of that seventeenth-century "mob of gentlemen who wrote with ease." He had the reputation among his contemporaries of an amiable beau; and the bulk of his verse consists of light, pretty, but languid amatory verses, written in a variety of lyrical forms, including – a relatively uncommon one in his day– the sonnet. A collection of these verses together with some elaborately gallant love-letters published in 1692 (*Letters and Poems, Amorous and Gallant*) carried a preface in which Walsh condemns Petrarchan conceits and Donne-like wit, praises controlled and precise workmanship, and argues for propriety, good sense, and elegance. This preface treats of pastoral, too, where Walsh accepts the neo-classical view that pastoral must represent a golden age of truth, sincerity and innocence. His own four pastoral eclogues and his pastoral elegy "Delia," to the memory of Mrs. Tempest, are wholly conventional.

Walsh's political verse shows more vigour. As a zealous Whig he was provoked by some violently Jacobite Messianic poems hailing Queen Anne's accession to write, in his "The Golden Age Restor'd" (1703), a neat, ironic, insolently urbane satire upon the Tories, in which, like some of the poets he attacks, he takes Virgil's fourth eclogue as his model. His imitation of Horace Book III, Ode iii (1705) adapts Horace's vision of Roman greatness to praise the memory of William III.

Walsh, Congreve, and Vanbrugh each wrote one act of a farce adapted from Molière's *Monsieur de Pourceaugnac* under the title *Squire Trelooby,* acted in 1704, of which the text is now lost (but see *Philological Quarterly,* 1968, pp. 145–56). A poem "In Defence of Painting" where Walsh claims that art and reason must compensate for the defects of nature was sent to Dryden in 1686 but not published until 1951 (see *Modern Language Notes,* pp. 518–23). Dryden befriended Walsh, contributed a preface to his prose *Dialogue Concerning Women,*

Being a Defence of the Sex and, in his own postscript to the translation of Virgil (1697), declared that Walsh was "without Flattery ... the best critic of our Nation"; but there is hardly enough in the surviving letters and other writings (whether or not one includes the Preface to the Pastorals in Dryden's Virgil which has sometimes been attributed to Walsh) to justify such a high estimate. However, Pope submitted his own juvenile pastorals to Walsh for correction, adopted some of Walsh's notions in his "Discourse on Pastoral Poetry," probably conceived the *Essay on Criticism* under Walsh's influence, and certainly ends that poem with high praise of Walsh as "the Muse's Judge and Friend." It was Walsh who asked Pope to make "correctness" his study and aim. Johnson's judgement remains true, that Walsh "is known more by his familiarity with greater men, than by anything done or written by himself."

—A. J. Sambrook

WARD, Ned (Edward Ward). English. Born in Oxfordshire in 1667. Married; one daughter. In early life visited the West Indies; afterwards a publican in Moorfields, London; moved to Fulwood's Rents, where he kept a punch shop and tavern, possibly the King's Head, next door to Gray's Inn, 1699–1731; also a journalist: edited *The Weekly Comedy*, 1699; *The Infallible Astrologer*, with Tom Brown, 1700–01; and *The London Terraefilius*, 1707–08. Pilloried for attacks on the government, 1705. *Died 20 June 1731*.

PUBLICATIONS

Verse

> *The Poet's Ramble after Riches; or, A Night's Transactions upon the Road Burlesqued.* 1691.
> *The Miracles Performed by Money.* 1692.
> *Sot's Paradise; or, The Humours of a Derby Ale-House, with a Satire upon the Ale.* 1698.
> *Ecclesia et Factio: A Dialogue Between Bow-Steeple Dragon and the Exchange Grasshopper.* 1698.
> *O Raree-Show, O Pretty-Show; or, The City Feast.* 1698.
> *The Insinuating Bawd and the Repenting Harlot.* 1699.
> *The Cockpit Combat; or, The Baiting of the Tiger.* 1699.
> *A Walk to Islington, with a Description of the New Tunbridge Wells and Sadler's Music House.* 1699.
> *The Wealthy Shop-Keeper; or, The Charitable Citizen.* 1700; revised edition, as *The Character of a Covetous Citizen,* 1702.
> *A Journey to Hell; or, A Visit Paid to the Devil.* 3 vols., 1700–05; as *The Infernal Vision,* n.d.
> *Bribery and Simony; or, A Satire upon the Corrupt Use of Money.* 1703.
> *All Men Mad; or, England a Great Bedlam.* 1704.
> *The Dissenting Hypocrite or Occasional Conformist.* 1704.
> *Helter Skelter; or, The Devil upon Two Sticks.* 1704.

The Libertine's Choice; or, The Mistaken Happiness of the Fool in Fashion.   1704.
Honesty in Distress, But Relieved by No Party.   1705.
A Satire Against Wine, with a Poem in Praise of Small Beer.   1705.
A Trip to Germany; or, The Poet Turned Carbineer.   1705.
The Rambling Fuddle-Caps; or, A Tavern Struggle for a Kiss.   1706.
Hudibras Redivivus; or, A Burlesque Poem on the Times.   2 vols., 1707.
Marriage Dialogues; or, A Poetical Peep into the State of Matrimony.   1708; as
    Matrimony Unmasked, 1710; revised edition, as *Nuptial Dialogues and Debates*, 1723.
The Modern World Disrobed; or, Both Sexes Stript of Their Pretended Virtue (prose and
    verse).   1708; as *Adam and Eve Stripped of Their Furbelows*, 1710.
*The Forgiving Husband and Adultress Wife; or, A Seasonable Present to the Unhappy
    Pair in Fenchurch-Street.*   1709.
Vulgus Britannicus; or, The British Hudibras.   1710.
Don Quixote Translated into Hudibrastic Verse.   2 vols., 1711–12.
The Poetical Entertainer; or, Tales, Satires, Dialogues, etc., Serious and Comical.   5
    vols., 1712.
The Quack Vintners; or, A Satire upon Bad Wine.   1712.
The History of the Grand Rebellion.   3 vols., 1713–15.
The Field Spy; or, The Walking Observator.   1714.
The Mourning Prophet; or, Faction Revived by the Death of Queen Anne.   1714.
The Hudibrastic Brewer; or, A Preposterous Union Between Malt and Meter.   1714.
The Republican Procession; or, The Tumultuous Cavalcade: A Merry Poem.   1714;
    revised edition, 1714, 1727.
*The Lord Whiglove's Elegy, with a Pious Epitaph upon the Late Bishop of
    Addlebury.*   1715.
St. Paul's Church; or, The Protestant Ambulators.   1716.
British Wonders.   1717.
The Vanity of Upstarts.   1717.
The Delights of the Bottle; or, The Complete Vintner.   1720.
The Northern Cuckold; or, The Garden House Intrigue.   1721.
*The Merry Travellers; or, A Trip upon Ten-Toes from Moorfields up to Bromley, Intended
    as The Wandering Spy.*   1721.
The Parish Guttlers; or, The Humours of a Select Vestry.   1722.
The Wandering Spy; or, The Merry Travellers, part 2.   1722.
The Wandering Spy; or, The Merry Observator.   6 vols., 1724.
News from Madrid: The Spanish Beauty; or, The Tragi-Comical Revenge.   1726.
*Apollo's Maggot in His Cups; or, The Whimsical Creation of a Little Satirical Poet: A
    Lyric Ode.*   1729.
Durgen; or, A Plain Satire upon a Pompous Satirist.   1729; as *The Cudgel; or, A Crab-
    Tree Lecture*, 1742.
To the Right Honourable Humphrey Parsons.   1730.

Fiction and Satirical Prose

The School of Politics; or, The Humours of a Coffee-House.   1690; revised edition,
    1691.
Female Policy Detected; or, The Arts of a Designing Woman Laid Open.   1695.
The London Spy.   2 vols., 1698–99; revised edition, 1703, 1704, 1706, 1753; edited by
    K. Fenwick, 1955.
A Trip to Jamaica; with a True Character of the People of the Island.   1698.
A Hue and Cry after a Man-Midwife.   1699.
*A Frolic to the Horn-Fair with a Walk from Cuckold's Point Through Deptford and
    Greenwich.*   1699.

Modern Religion and Ancient Loyalty: A Dialogue. 1699.
A Trip to New-England, with a Character of the Country and the People, both English and Indians. 1699.
The World Bewitched: A Dialogue Between Two Astrologers and the Author. 1699.
The Dancing School with the Adventures of the Easter Holidays. 1700.
The English Nun; or, A Comical Description of a Nunnery. 1700.
The Reformer: Exposing the Vices of the Age in Several Characters. 1700.
The Grand Mistake; or, All Men Happy If They Please. 1700(?).
Labour in Vain; or, What Signifies Little or Nothing. 1700.
Laugh and Be Fat; or, An Antidote Against Melancholy. 1700.
The Metamorphosed Beau; or, The Intrigues of Ludgate. 1700.
The Pleasures of Single Life or the Miseries of Matrimony. 1700(?).
The Rambling Rakes; or, London Libertines. 1700.
A Step to the Bath, with a Character of the Place. 1700.
A Step to Stir-Bitch-Fair, with Remarks upon the University of Cambridge. 1700.
Aesop at Paris, His Life and Letters. 1701.
Battle Without Bloodshed; or, Martial Discipline Buffooned by the City Train-Bands. 1701.
The Revels of the Gods; or, A Ramble Through the Heavens. 1701.
Three Nights Adventures or Accidental Intrigues. 1701.
The Rise and Fall of Madam Coming Sir. 1703.
The Secret History of the Calves-Head Club; or, The Republican Unmasked. 1703; revised edition, 1706; as *The Whig's Unmasked,* 1713.
Female Dialogues; or, Ladies' Conversations. 1704.
Fair Shell but a Rotten Kernel; or, A Bitter Nut for a Facetious Monkey. 1705.
A Comical View of London and Westminster; or, The Merry Quack, with A Legacy for the Ladies; or, Characters of the Women of the Age, by Tom Brown. 1705.
The Barbeque-Feast; or, The Three Pigs of Peckham, Broiled under an Apple-Tree. 1706.
The Wooden World Dissected in the Character of a Ship of War. 1706.
Mars Stript of His Armour; or, The Army Displayed in All Its True Colours. 1708.
The Wars of the Elements; or, A Description of a Sea Storm. 1708.
The History of the London Clubs; or, The Citizen's Pastime. 2 vols., 1709; as *The Secret History of the Clubs,* 1709; revised edition, as *A Complete and Humorous Account of All the Remarkable Clubs and Societies,* 1756.
The Tory Quaker; or, Aminadab's New Vision of the Fields. 1717.
The Dancing Devils; or, The Roaring Dragon: A Dumb Farce. 1724.
The Amorous Bugbears; or, The Humours of a Masquerade. 1725.
The Bachelor's Estimate; or, The Expenses of a Married Life. 1725.
A Fiddler's Fling at Roguery. 1730.

Other

A Collection of the Writings. 1700.
The Writings. 4 vols., 1703–09.
Five Travel Scripts Commonly Attributed to Ward, edited by H. W. Troyer. 1933.

Translator, *A Seasonable Sketch of an Oxford Reformation,* by J. Allibond. 1717.

Reading List: *Ned Ward of Grubstreet: A Study of Subliterary London in the Eighteenth Century* by H. W. Troyer, 1946 (includes bibliography).

*   *   *

Ned Ward is one of the best examples of the late Restoration journalist, attempting rather successfully to enliven literary English by incorporating colloquial idiom and vulgar imagery. He was satirical poet, prose humorist, low-life reporter, Tory propagandist. In his verse he was greatly influenced by Samuel Butler, whose manner he vulgarized in *Hudibras Redivivus*, so scurrilous in its attacks on the Whigs that it earned Ward two stands in the pillory. The quality of his verse, direct and aggressive, and the cynicism with which he wrote are both illustrated in these lines from *Hudibras Redivivus*:

> For he that writes in such an Age,
> When Parties do for Pow'r engage,
> Ought to chuse one Side for the Right,
> And then, with all his Wit and Spite,
> Blacken and Vex the Opposite.
> Scurrility's a useful Trick,
> Approv'd by the most Politic;
> Fling Dirt enough, and some will stick.

Though Ward's verse-writing led him into competition with Pope and to being satirized in *The Dunciad*, to which he replied in his own way in *Durgen* and *Apollo's Maggot in His Cups*, he is best known and most influential for his prose journalism, which at times was inventive enough to approach fiction. His best work was undoubtedly contained in the *London Spy*, a series of eighteen monthly numbers which consist mainly of reportage of London low life, pungently written, with a great deal of slang interspersed, and decorated with metaphors of startling vulgarity and vigour. Ward's personal experience was broad. He travelled widely for a man of his day, making a visit to the Caribbean, described in *Trip to Jamaica*, and another to the American colonies that gave him the material for *Trip to New England*, but he was most at home in London, where he kept a tavern for several years, watching his customers and listening to their ways of speaking. Taverns, prisons, brothels, London parks at ambiguous nightfall, all feature prominently in his descriptive reports.

There seems little doubt that – just as his later series of periodical essays, *The Humours of a Coffee-House*, not only predated but also influenced *The Tatler* – the vivid descriptions of low life in the *London Spy* helped create a style of reportage and a taste among readers for verisimilitude in describing the seamier aspects of social life, both of which Defoe later used for his own purposes in such novels as *Moll Flanders* and *Captain Singleton*. The *London Spy* is still good reading for anyone interested in low-life reportage and in the relationship between literary and colloquial writing, but Ward's importance is mainly historical – that of a vigorous pioneer in the craft of journalism and, less directly, in the development of a viable tradition of realism in fiction.

—George Woodcock

WARTON, Joseph. English. Born in Dunsfold, Surrey, baptized 22 April 1722; elder brother of Thomas Warton, *q.v.* Educated at Basingstoke Grammar School, Hampshire; Winchester College, 1735–40; Oriel College, Oxford, matriculated 1740, B.A. 1744, M.A. 1759, B.D. and D.D. 1768. Married 1) Mary Daman in 1748 (died, 1772), three sons and three daughters; 2) Charlotte Nicholas in 1773, one daughter. Took holy orders, 1744, and served as Curate to his father at Basingstoke, 1744–45; subsequently served as Curate at Chelsea, London; appointed Rector of Winslade, 1748; Travelling Chaplain with the Duke of

Bolton, 1751; contributed to *The Adventurer*, 1753–56; Rector of Tunworth, 1754–55; Second Master, 1755–66, and Headmaster, 1766–93, Winchester College; Rector of Wickham, Hampshire, 1783–1800, and Upham, Hampshire, 1790–1800; retired to Wickham on leaving Winchester. Member, Literary Club, 1773. *Died 23 February 1800.*

PUBLICATIONS

Collections

Poems, in *British Poets 68*, edited by Thomas Park. 1822.
The Three Wartons: A Choice of Their Verse, edited by Eric Partridge. 1927.

Verse

The Enthusiast; or, The Lover of Nature. 1744.
Odes on Various Subjects. 1746.
An Ode Occasioned by Reading West's Translation of Pindar. 1749.
An Ode to Evening. 1749.

Other

Ranelagh House: A Satire in Prose. 1747.
An Essay on the Writings and Genius of Pope. 2 vols., 1756–82.

Editor, *Poems on Several Occasions*, by Thomas Warton, the Elder. 1748.
Editor and Translator, *The Works of Virgil in Latin and English.* 4 vols., 1753.
Editor, *Sidney's Defence of Poetry.* 1787.
Editor, with others, *The Works of Pope.* 9 vols., 1797.

Reading List: *Biographical Memoirs of Warton* (includes letters) by John Wooll, 1806; *The Ascendancy of Taste: The Achievement of Joseph and Thomas Warton* by Joan Pittock, 1973.

*   *   *

Joseph Warton's poem *The Enthusiast*, published when he was only 22, celebrates in Miltonic blank verse the new preference for the irregularities of nature over rigid classical forms. While still at school Warton had been friendly with William Collins, with whom he planned to publish a volume of odes. In the event Warton's *Odes on Various Subjects* were preferred by Dodsley to those of Collins, presumably because they were more congenial to the taste of the time. The odes were frequently reprinted throughout the century. In the Preface to the *Odes* Warton complained that "the fashion of moralizing in verse has been carried too far," insisting that invention and imagination alone characterise true poetry. From 1753, Warton was responsible for the papers on literary criticism in *The Adventurer*; and in the same year appeared the work on which Warton placed his hopes of preferment, an edition of the works of Virgil. This included his own translations of the *Eclogues* and *Georgics*. In his *Essay on the Writings and Genius of Pope*, Warton pursued his campaign against the didactic and satiric verse modes popularised by Pope (a second volume was not published until 1782), and he edited Pope's works in nine volumes. Most of the material incorporated in the notes came from the *Essay*. At the time of his death Warton was engaged in preparing an edition of Dryden.

As a member of the Literary Club Warton was acquainted with Johnson, Burke, Garrick, Reynolds in the leading literary coterie of the mid-century. In later life he corresponded with Wilkes on friendly terms. His correspondence, part of which was published in Wooll's *Biographical Memoirs*, and in manuscript in the Bodleian and in the British Library, reveals an enthusiastic, ambitious, and kindly personality, an indefatigable seeker in the field of literary enterprises.

—Joan Pittock

WARTON, Thomas. English. Born in Basingstoke, Hampshire, 9 January 1728; younger brother of Joseph Warton, *q.v.* Educated at Basingstoke Grammar School; Trinity College, Oxford, matriculated 1744, B.A. 1747, M.A. 1750, B.D. 1767. Took holy orders, 1748; Fellow of Trinity College, 1751 until his death: Professor of Poetry, 1757–67, and Camden Professor of History, 1785–90, Oxford University; Rector of Kidlington, 1771. Member, Literary Club, 1782. Fellow, Society of Antiquaries, 1771. Poet Laureate, 1785 until his death. *Died 21 May 1790.*

PUBLICATIONS

Collections

Poetical Works, edited by R. Mant.   2 vols., 1802.
Poetical Works of Goldsmith, Collins, and Warton, edited by George Gilfillan.   1854.
The Three Wartons: A Choice of Their Verse, edited by Eric Partridge.   1927.

Verse

The Pleasures of Melancholy.   1747.
The Triumph of Isis.   1749.
Newmarket: A Satire.   1751.
Ode for Music as Performed at Oxford 1751.   1751.
Mons Catharinae prope Wintoniani.   1774.
Poems.   1777; as *Poems on Various Subjects,* 1791.
Verses on Reynolds's Painted Window at New College Oxford.   1782.
Verses Left under a Stone.   1790(?).
The Hamlet: An Ode.   1859.

Other

A Description of Winchester.   1750.
Observations on the Faerie Queene of Spenser.   1754.
A Companion to the Guide, and a Guide to the Companion: A Supplement to All Accounts of Oxford.   1760(?).
The Life of Sir Tho. Pope.   1772.
The History of English Poetry.   3 vols., 1774–81; edited by W. C. Hazlitt, 4 vols., 1871; *An Unpublished Continuation,* edited by R. M. Baine, 1953.
Specimen of the History of Oxfordshire.   1781; as *A History of Kidlington,* 1783.
An Enquiry into the Authenticity of the Poems Attributed to Rowley.   1782.
Essays on Gothic Architecture, with others.   1800.
Correspondence of Thomas Percy and Warton, edited by M. G. Robinson and Leah Dennis, constitutes *Percy Letters,* vol. 3.   1951.

Editor, *The Union; or, Select Scots and English Poems.*   1753.
Editor, *Inscriptionum Romanorum Metricarum Delectus.*   1758.
Editor, *The Life and Literary Remains of Ralph Bathurst.*   2 vols., 1761.
Editor, *The Oxford Sausage; or, Select Poetical Pieces.*   1764.
Editor, *Anthologiae Graecae.*   1766.
Editor, *Theocrite Syracusii quae Supersunt.*   2 vols., 1770.
Editor, *Poems upon Several Occasions by Milton.*   1785; revised edition, 1790.

Reading List: *Warton: A Biographical and Critical Study* by Clarissa Rinaker, 1916 (includes bibliography); *The Ascendancy of Taste: The Achievement of Joseph and Thomas Warton* by Joan Pittock, 1973.

*   *   *

Thomas Warton was one of the most celebrated figures of eighteenth-century Oxford. His versatility and resourcefulness as a minor poet are evident in his popular *Pleasures of Melancholy* and his defence of Oxford in *The Triumph of Isis,* as well as in the facetious verses he composed for *The Oxford Sausage.* His *Verses on Reynolds's Painted Window* uniquely illustrate the mental agonies and doubts which the violent shifting of aesthetic values imposed on men like Warton. In 1785 he was appointed Poet Laureate, but his lack of success in versifying on royal topics excited the mockery of Peter Pindar and the compilers of *The New Rolliad.*

Warton was a principal agent in obtaining the degree of M.A. for Johnson, and was a prominent member of the Literary Club. His enthusiasm for early poetry, in particular that of Spenser and Milton, imparts a freshness and originality to his work which makes it of greater intrinsic interest than that of his brother Joseph. His *Observations on the Faerie Queene of Spenser* displays a high level of critical and scholarly imagination, and his substantial correspondence with Thomas Percy reveals his passionate interest in early literature and his wealth of antiquarian information.

Warton's *History of English Poetry,* despite its faults, established for the first time a British literary tradition in which the focal achievement is the work of the Elizabethans. His edition of Milton's minor poems is itself a kind of conclusion to his observations in the *History,* for it is preoccupied with the ways in which the imagination of a great poet employs fiction and allegory from various sources to create works of classic importance. Warton's love of poetry and his critical acumen are expressed with imagination and authority in his contribution to the Chatterton controversy, *An Enquiry into the Authenticity of the Poems Attributed to Rowley.* Characteristically, his lectures as Poetry Professor dealt with the delight of Greek literature, a novel topic at that time.

—Joan Pittock

WATTS, Isaac. English. Born in Southampton, Hampshire, 17 July 1675. Educated at Southampton Grammar School, until 1690, and at a nonconformist academy in Stoke Newington, London, 1690–94. Wrote first hymn c. 1695, and thereafter wrote more than 600 hymns throughout his life; tutor in the family of Sir John Hartopp, Stoke Newington, 1696–1702; non-conformist minister: Assistant Pastor, 1699–1702, and Pastor, 1702–48, Mark Lane, London; because of ill-health turned over part of his pastoral duties to an assistant in 1713, and lived the remainder of his life with his friends Sir Thomas and Lady Abney at their homes at Theobalds and Stoke Newington. D.D.: University of Edinburgh, 1728. *Died 25 November 1748.*

PUBLICATIONS

Collections

Works, edited by D. Jennings and F. Doddridge.   6 vols., 1753; revised edition, edited by G. Burder, 6 vols., 1810–11.

Verse

Horae Lyricae: Poems Chiefly of the Lyric Kind.   1706; revised edition, 1709; edited by Robert Southey, 1834.
Hymns and Spiritual Songs.   1707; revised edition, 1709; edited by S. L. Bishop, 1962.
Divine Songs Attempted in Easy Language for the Use of Children.   1715; revised edition, 1740; as *Divine and Moral Songs for Children,* 1787.
The Psalms of David Imitated.   1719.

Other

An Essay Against Uncharitableness.   1707.
A Guide to Prayer.   1715; edited by Harry Escott, 1948.
The Art of Reading and Writing English.   1721.
Sermons on Various Subjects.   3 vols., 1721–27.
The Christian Doctrine of the Trinity.   1722.
Death and Heaven; or, The Last Enemy Conquered and Separate Spirits Made Perfect.   1722.
Three Dissertations Relating to the Christian Doctrine of the Trinity.   1724.
Logic.   1725.
The Knowledge of the Heavens and the Earth Made Easy; or, The First Principles of Astronomy and Geography.   1726.
A Defense Against the Temptation of Self-Murder.   1726.
An Essay Towards the Encouragement of Charity Schools.   1728.
A Caveat Against Infidelity.   1729.
Catechisms; or, Instructions in the Principles of the Christian Religion.   1730.
An Humble Attempt Towards the Revival of Practical Religion among Christians and Particularly Protestant Dissenters.   1731.
Philosophical Essays on Various Subjects.   1733.
Reliquiae Juveniles: Miscellaneous Thoughts in Prose and Verse.   1734.
The Redeemer and the Sanctifier.   1736.
Humility Represented in the Character of St. Paul.   1737.

A New Essay on Civil Power in Things Sacred.   1739.
The Doctrine of the Passions Explained and Improved.   1739.
The Improvement of the Mind; or, A Supplement to the Art of Logic.   1741.
The World to Come; or, Discourses on the Joys and Sorrows of Departed Souls.   2 vols.,
   1745.
Useful and Important Questions Concerning Jesus.   1746.
The Glory of Christ as God-Man Displayed in Three Discourses.   1746.
Evangelical Discourses on Several Subjects.   1747.
*The Rational Foundation of a Christian Church and the Terms of Christian
   Communion.*   1747.
Discourses on the Love of God and Its Influence on All Passions.   1760 (4th edition).
A Treatise on the Education of Children and Youth.   1769 (2nd edition).
Nine Sermons Preached in 1718–19, Now First Published.   1812.

Reading List: *The Hymns of Wesley and Watts: Five Informal Papers* by B. L. Manning,
1942; *Watts: His Life and Works* by A. P. Davis, 1943 (includes bibliography); *Watts* by Erik
Routley, 1961; *Watts, Hymnographer: A Study of the Beginnings, Development, and
Philosophy of the English Hymns* by Harry Escott, 1962.

*   *   *

Though Isaac Watts wrote a large number of spiritual works in prose, and a *Logic* which
remained in use for a hundred years after his death, his most notable literary achievement is
as a writer of hymns, and as a major originator of the English hymn tradition. At the
beginning of the eighteenth century, the Church of England and most of the Protestant sects
(Watts himself was an Independent) used metrical versions of the Psalms rather than hymns
in worship. Watts was not the first but was certainly the most influential advocate for the
replacement of the Psalms, arguing in his "Short Essay Toward the Improvement of
Psalmody" suffixed to his *Hymns and Spiritual Songs* that "when we sing, especially unto
God, our chief design is, or should be, to speak our own hearts and our words to God," and
that we must therefore sing composures suitable to our own case. Watts claimed that the
Psalms, based on Hebrew culture and an Old Testament morality, could not satisfy the needs
of contemporary Christian devotion. Watts therefore planned a system of evangelical
hymnody, containing both christianised psalms and original hymns.

Watts's *Hymns and Spiritual Songs* are divided into three sections, the first based on
particular scriptural texts, the second of "mere human composure," and the third "Prepared
for the Holy Ordinance of the Lord's Supper." In this collection appear some of the finest and
best-known English hymns, including "There is a land of pure delight," "Come, let us join
our cheerful songs," and "When I survey the wondrous cross." Intended for the social
worship of all classes, stating important points of doctrine clearly, and keeping the major
topics of belief in the mind of the congregation, the *Hymns* are consciously unpoetic in style.
Watts speaks in his Preface of suiting the metaphors "to the level of vulgar capacities," of
aiming at plainness of sense and regularity of rhythm, of rejecting the "beauties" of poetry.
Watts normally uses a familiar imagery of Protestant belief, metaphors articulating meaning
explicitly. Occasionally some of the more sophisticated stylistic and formal features of the
seventeenth-century devotional lyric appear in Watts's writing; "When I survey the
wondrous cross," for example, is a meditation, stanza four of which is omitted in most hymn
books because of the vivid, punning metaphor of Christ on the cross: "His dying crimson,
like a robe,/Spreads o'er his body on the tree." Generally, however, those of his hymns
which contained "expressions ... not suited to the plainest capacity," and therefore not fitted
to congregational use, were set apart by Watts, and published rather in his *Horae Lyricae*.
Horae Lyricae contains three books, one of poems "sacred to devotion and piety," a second
including pieces in such distinctly literary forms as odes, epistles, and epigrams, and a third of

elegies and epitaphs, "sacred to the memory of the dead." The more literary nature of this work is confirmed both by the important critical Preface, in which Watts argues for the turning of poetry to divine subjects, and by the fact that Samuel Johnson chose to represent Watts only by this collection in the *Works of the English Poets*.

A decade later, Watts undertook an evangelical version of the Psalms of David, "imitated in the language of the New Testament, and applied to the Christian state and worship." The intention was to make the Psalms once more an appropriate vehicle for Christian devotion, christianised, simplified in style, purged of the distinctively judaic, adapted to an eighteenth-century English context. Some of Watts's finest and most familiar "hymns" are in fact to be found in his version of the Psalms, notably "Our God, our help in ages past" and "Jesus shall reign where'er the sun."

The *Divine Songs Attempted in Easy Language for the Use of Children* is a collection of pedagogical and catechismal, rather than devotional, poetry, and lies outside Watts's system of hymnody. The Christian message is presented here more generally, avoiding, for the most part, the theological particularity which may be found in the *Hymns* and *Psalms*. Style is simplified further, "to the level of a child's understanding," and indeed to the point of being liable to parody: Lewis Carroll's "'Tis the voice of the lobster" and "How doth the little crocodile" are both based on poems by Watts in this collection. Yet here too Watts offered an influential model, reflected not only in eighteenth-century children's poetry, but also, formally at least, in William Blake's *Songs of Innocence*, though Blake would not have found acceptable the authoritarian and conventional morality of Watts's *Songs*.

Few poets have had a greater effect on the culture of the English-speaking world than Watts, yet the nature of his religious poetry poses difficulties for the critic, for whom it was not designed. Watts has more often been admired for his exemplary life (as by Samuel Johnson in his *Life* of Watts), or for his unquestionable historical importance, than for his specifically artistic merits. Yet the simplicity and restraint of Watts's writing are themselves the result of an artistic process of selection and exclusion, and are in themselves a poetic virtue. The exact economy of Watts's style makes his best hymns classic and authoritative statements of an important aspect of popular religious belief and experience.

—Marcus Walsh

WESLEY, Charles. English. Born in Epworth, Lincolnshire, 18 December 1707; younger brother of the founder of Methodism, John Wesley. Educated at Westminster School, London, 1716–26 (King's Scholar, 1721; Captain of the School, 1725); Christ Church, Oxford, matriculated 1726, B.A. 1730, M.A. 1733; joined with other students in strict method of religious observance and study: nicknamed "methodists." Married Sarah Gwynne in 1749; eight children. Involved in the Methodist movement, under his brother's lead, from 1730: ordained deacon and priest, 1735; accompanied his brother to Georgia as Secretary to the governor, James Oglethorpe, 1735–36; involved in study, Oxford, 1736–38; believed himself "converted" 1738; involved in evangelical work in London, 1738–39; settled at Bristol, and preached through the West of England and Wales, 1730–56; because of ill-health retired to Bath and gave up active ministry, 1761; diverged from his brother on various points of doctrine from 1762; settled in London, 1771, and occasionally preached in London until the end of his life. Composed nearly 9,000 hymns, of which 500 are still in use. *Died 29 March 1788.*

PUBLICATIONS

Collections

Poetical Works of John and Charles Wesley.   13 vols., 1868–72.
Representative Verse, edited by Frank Baker.   1962.

Verse

Hymns and Sacred Poems.   2 vols., 1749.

Other

Sermons, edited by S. Wesley.   1816.
Journal, edited by T. Jackson.   2 vols., 1849.
The Early Journal, 1736–39, edited by John Telford.   1909.

Bibliography: *A Bibliography of the Works of John and Charles Wesley* by R. Green, 1896.

Reading List: *The Evangelical Doctrines of Wesley's Hymns* by J. E. Rattenbury, 1941; *Wesley as Revealed in His Letters,* 1948, and *Wesley's Verse,* 1964, both by Frank Baker; *The Hymns of Wesley: A Study of Their Structure* by R. N. Flew, 1953; *Wesleys Hymnen* by E. Mayer, 1957; *Singer of a Thousand Songs: A Life of Wesley* by E. Myers, 1965.

*   *   *

The 8989 extant hymns of Charles Wesley echo the essence of the Evangelical Revival of eighteenth-century England. Certainly, not every poem evidences the same degree of quality, but together the hymns convey the intensity of the poet's deep personal feelings. Few subjects or occasions escaped his notice: his own conversion and marriage; domestic upheavals from panics, earthquakes, religious riots, rumored invasions; festivals of the Church and doctrines of the faith; scenes from the paraphrases of Scripture; deaths of friends; the education of children; the effects of local surroundings. As with his elder brother John, Charles Wesley spent little time contemplating and transmitting abstract themes; instead, he emphasized the personal and the concrete. His lines thus reflected the experiences of thousands of believers and an equal number of those struggling to believe.

Although Wesley's hymns demonstrate the influence of a variety of British poets upon the hymnodist – from Shakespeare to Edward Young – the content and language of Scripture remained his principal source. Thus, in "Waiting for the Promise," we see:

> Fainting soul, be bold, be strong;
> Wait the leisure of thy Lord:
> Though it seem to tarry long,
> True and faithful is His word.

Wesley's contemporaries would have recognized the words of Psalm 27:16, from Coverdale's prose version in the *Book of Common Prayer*: "O tarry thou the Lord's leisure," indicating that Methodism's bard continued to hold to his Anglican upbringing and education. No doubt, that is true; yet, Wesley must not be relegated to a mere paraphraser of Scriptures, a versifier who combined experience with emotionalism and pumped both into the liturgy of the Methodist service. Instead, he must be remembered as a legitimate, devotional poet who established the idea that a hymn is indeed a poem. John Wesley, in the preface to *A Collection of Hymns for the Use of the People Called Methodists* (1780), set forth what still stands as the most accurate assessment of his brother's poetry: "In these hymns there is no doggerel, no botches, nothing put in to patch the rhyme, no feeble explatives. ... Here are... both the purity, the strength and the elegance of the ENGLISH language: and at the same time the utmost simplicity and plainness, suited to every capacity." The Methodist patriarch challenged critics to judge "whether there is not in some of the following verses, the true Spirit of Poetry: such as cannot be acquired by art and labour; but must be the gift of nature." He concluded that through labor "a man may become a tolerable imitator.... But unless he is born a Poet, he will never attain the genuine SPIRIT OF POETRY."

Despite his brother's exuberance, Charles Wesley met with only limited success and acceptance outside of Methodism. Today, there is little doubt of the overall popularity and the wide poetic and hymnodic acceptability of such pieces as "All praise to Him who dwells in bliss"; "Christ the Lord is risen to-day"; "Christ, whose glory fills the sky"; "Come, let us join our friends above"; "Come, Thou long-expected Jesus"; "Hail the day that sees Him rise"; "Hark! how all the welkin sings"; "Hark, the herald-angels sing"; "Lo! He comes, with clouds descending"; "Love Divine, all loves excelling"; "Jesu, Lover of my soul." However, by mid-eighteenth century, English congregational song had been nurtured by the common metres and generalized experiences from the voices of Protestant Dissent: Watts, Doddridge, Gibbons, and Hart. Wesley's specific experiences, his departure from the simple metres of the old Psalmody, his enthusiastic and controversial spirit – all appeared foreign to the tastes of Britons unfamiliar with the influences and teachings of Wesleyan Methodism.

Not until the late nineteenth century, when Methodism finally emerged from the abuse and contempt initiated by contemporary rivals of the Wesleys, did Charles Wesley's devotional poetry achieve the recognition it deserves. Essentially, the major pieces were seen to reflect the poet's sincere faith arising from his far-ranging loyalties and desires to interpret Christian experience. The hymns transmit that faith because he relied upon what people knew and felt, upon the essence of their own values. Culturally superior to the majority of persons whom he addressed, Wesley intentionally held back his own knowledge and, instead, wove his reactions and concerns through Scriptures, attempting to educate his readers with essential theological lessons. In the end, there remains little doubt as to the purpose and direction of a new voice who spoke with and for certain eighteenth-century Britons seeking God in times of trouble:

> Weary of all this wordy strife,
>   These notions, forms, and modes, and names,
> To Thee, the Way, the Truth, the Life,
>   Whose love my simple heart inflames,
> Divinely taught, at last, I fly,
> With Thee, and Thine to live, and die.

—Samuel J. Rogal

WHITEHEAD, William. English. Born in Cambridge, baptized 12 February 1715. Educated at Winchester College, 1729–35; Clare Hall, Cambridge (sizar), matriculated 1735, B.A. 1739, M.A. 1743. Fellow of Clare Hall from 1742; tutor to the future Earl of Jersey and Lord Villiers, 1745; gave up his fellowship, and settled in London, to devote himself to writing: quickly became known as poet and playwright; accompanied Villiers and Lord Nuneham on a tour of Germany and Italy, 1754–56; appointed Secretary and Registrar of the Order of Bath, 1756, and Poet Laureate, 1757; Reader of Plays for David Garrick, at Drury Lane, London, from 1762. *Died 14 April 1785.*

PUBLICATIONS

Collections

Plays and Poems.   2 vols., 1774; revised edition, 3 vols., 1788.

Plays

The Roman Father, from a play by Corneille (produced 1750).   1750.
Fatal Constancy, in *Poems on Several Occasions.*   1754.
Creusa, Queen of Athens (produced 1754).   1754.
The School for Lovers, from a play by Fontenelle (produced 1762).   1762.
A Trip to Scotland (produced 1770).   1770.

Verse

The Danger of Writing Verse.   1741.
Anne Boleyn to Henry the Eighth: An Epistle.   1743.
An Essay on Ridicule.   1743.
Atys and Adrastus: A Tale, in the Manner of Dryden's Fables.   1744.
On Nobility: An Epistle.   1744.
An Hymn to the Nymph of Bristol Spring.   1751.
Poems on Several Occasions.   1754.
Elegies, with an Ode to the Tiber.   1757.
Verses to the People of England.   1758.
A Charge to the Poets.   1762.
Variety: A Tale for Married People.   1776.
The Goat's Beard: A Fable.   1777.

Reading List: *Whitehead, Poeta Laureatus* (in German) by August Bitter, 1933.

*   *   *

William Whitehead began to write poetry during Pope's later years, but lived and wrote through the era variously known as the age of Pre-Romanticism, Reason, or Johnson. Most of the qualities implied by those associations can be found somewhere in his work. "The Enthusiast," for example, whose deism and nature description have been considered pre-romantic, is deeply indebted to the *Essay on Man*; the enthusiast for nature is finally taught that "man was made for man," and drawn from solitude to society. Many of his early poems pay their respects to Pope – verbally, ideologically, or both – and supply us with bad examples of late Augustan "definite-article verse" ("the vacant mind," "the social bosom," "the mutual morning task they ply"). Generally they are light, occasional, often epistolary, and gently satirical, when not congratulating the Royal Family on a marriage or birth. His commonest mood is mild, free-floating mockery, directed both at self and at a rather amusing environment. Whitehead publishes twelve quarto pages of heroic couplets under the title "The Danger of Writing Verse"; playfully emulates Spenser and the early Milton in the freely enjambed blank verse of *An Hymn to the Nymph of Bristol Spring*; and begins "The Sweepers" like a Johnson and Boswell joke: "I sing of Sweepers, frequent in thy streets,/ Augusta." Passion is seldom indulged and never intense, and Reason is often praised. The recurrent Tory patriotism was duly rewarded: as Laureate from 1757 to 1785, Whitehead had to compose birthday odes to George III throughout the American Revolution, a task he performed unflinchingly amid the customary howls of poets and critics.

Whitehead's interest in theatre began while he was a schoolboy at Winchester, where he played Marcia in a production of *Cato*, but reached new heights when the leading actor of the day took over Drury Lane in 1747. In "To Mr. Garrick" he warned the new manager – a nervous man anyway – that "A nation's taste depends on you/– Perhaps a nation's virtue too." The poem inaugurated a long association: Whitehead served as both playwright and play-reader for Drury Lane, and Garrick took leading roles in three of the poet's plays, all fairly successful. *The Roman Father*, a blank-verse tragedy based on Corneille's *Horace*, is distinctly reminiscent of *Cato*; the title-character Horatius (Garrick) is honoured to donate his sons' lives to Rome, and the closing paean to patriotism as the "first, best passion" was a sure clap-trap. Certain scenes, indeed, could be played as *parodies* of Addison, an idea which seems less far-fetched in view of *Fatal Constancy*, a fragmentary "sketch of a tragedy ... in the heroic taste." Though Whitehead gives only the hero's speeches and the scene directions, they are enough to suggest why he wrote no more tragedies after 1754. "My starting eyeballs hang/Upon her parting steps" cries the protagonist as his lover departs, after which they "Exeunt severally, languishing at each other." (Significantly, the play's forte is ingenious exits.) Unlike his plays designed for the stage, *Fatal Constancy* has the lightness of most of his verse, and a keen eye for theatrical absurdities. *Creusa, Queen of Athens*, with Garrick as Alestes, was produced to "great applause" and the approbation of Horace Walpole the same year.

Whitehead's only full-length comedy, *The School for Lovers*, caught and perpetuated the vogue of genteel or "sentimental" drama, though it also included stock bits of comic business that turn up in Goldsmith and Sheridan. The rhetoric of the prologue ("with strokes refin'd .../Formed on the classic scale his structures rise") conveys Whitehead's pure and reformist intentions as a playwright. *The Dramatic Censor* (1770) complained that "a dreadful soporific languor drowses over the whole, throwing both auditors and readers into a poppean lethargy," but the play, with Garrick as Dorilant, had a good first run and several revivals. Likewise *A Trip to Scotland*, Whitehead's only farce, pleased audiences for several seasons despite an unimpressive text. None of his plays reads well today, yet none failed, and *The Roman Father* and *The School for Lovers* were still being revived at the end of the eighteenth century.

—R. W. Bevis

WILMOT, John.   See ROCHESTER, 2nd Earl of.

WINCHILSEA, Countess of; Anne Finch, née Kingsmill.   English.   Born in Sidmonton, Hampshire, c. 1661. Educated privately. Married Heneage Finch in 1684 (4th Earl of Winchilsea, 1712). Maid of Honour to Mary of Modena, the consort of James II: after downfall of the Stuarts retired to the country with her husband. *Died 5 August 1720.*

PUBLICATIONS

Collections

Poems, edited by Myra Reynolds.   1903.
Poems (selection), edited by J. Middleton Murry.   1928.

Verse

The Spleen : A Pindaric Ode, with *A Prospect of Death,* by John Pomfret.   1709.
Free-Thinkers : A Poem in Dialogue.   1711.
Miscellany Poems on Several Occasions.   1713.

*   *   *

The Countess of Winchilsea is a minor poet who for generations has endeared herself to her readers, partly by the freshness, delicacy, and originality of her talent, partly by the personal touches that abound in her verses.

Wordsworth was so struck by her "Nocturnal Reverie" that he wished a selection of her poems might be published. Gosse secured the inclusion of a few specimens in Ward's *English Poets,* and there Matthew Arnold discovered her and was impressed. Most anthologies of 18th-century poetry print a few of her pieces. The scholarly edition by Myra Reynolds, draws on manuscript as well as printed sources, and reveals the range of her literary activities. Pindaric odes, fables in the manner of La Fontaine, satires, even a tragedy, besides verse epistles, songs, and meditative lyrics, flowed from her pen. Many are commonplace; but when the best are assembled, they add up to something unusual and attractive.

Anne Kingsmill, as she was before her marriage to Heneage Finch, later Earl of Winchilsea, was a Maid of Honour to Mary of Modena, James II's consort. The downfall of the Stuarts meant a life of retirement in the country for Anne and her husband, but this was no disaster. Not only were they devoted to one another, as her poems show, but neither of them depended on urban pleasures. Lady Winchilsea asked nothing better than "an Absolute Retreat," in which she could enjoy "contemplations of the mind" and the joys of friendship. For someone of her epoch, her delight in landscape, her feeling for birds and beasts, trees and flowers, was unusually deep and sensitive. This no doubt commended her to Wordsworth. Her diction, too, is pure, and her best poems have a spontaneous air about them.

Unlike the later 18th-century Bluestockings, the Countess of Winchilsea was not a lady of formidable learning, but she resembled them in being a defender of a woman's right to cultivate her mind and express herself in print. In several poems she protests against the conventions that condemned women to "the dull manage of a servile house." She insists on developing her own gifts, "Nor will in fading silks compose/Faintly the inimitable Rose." *The Spleen,* from which these lines are taken, is at least as interesting an account of depression as Matthew Green's more famous, and later, treatment of the same subject.

—Margaret Bottrall

YOUNG, Edward. English. Born in Upham, Hampshire, baptized 3 July 1683. Educated at Winchester School; New College, and Corpus Christi College, Oxford, Bachelor of Civil Laws, 1714, Doctor 1719. Married Lady Elizabeth Lee in 1731 (died, 1741); one stepdaughter and one son. Law Fellow, All Souls College, Oxford, 1708; moved to London: member of Addison's circle; Tutor/Companion to the Marquis of Wharton in Ireland, 1716, and later Tutor to the Marquis of Exeter; took holy orders, 1724, and appointed Royal Chaplain, 1727; Rector of Welwyn, Hertfordshire, 1730 until his death; Clerk to the Closet of the Princess Dowager of Wales, 1761. *Died 5 April 1765.*

PUBLICATIONS

Collections

> *Complete Works,* edited by J. Nichols. 2 vols., 1854.
> *Correspondence,* edited by Henry Pettit. 1971.
> *(Selected Poems),* edited by Brian Hepworth. 1975.

Verse

> *An Epistle to Lord Lansdown.* 1713.
> *A Poem on the Last Day.* 1713.
> *An Epistle to the Lord Viscount Bolingbroke, Sent with A Poem on the Last Day.* 1714.
> *The Force of Religion; or, Vanquished Love: A Poem.* 1714.
> *On the Late Queen's Death, and His Majesty's Accession to the Throne.* 1714.
> *A Paraphrase on Part of the Book of Job.* 1719.
> *A Letter to Mr. Tickell Occasioned by the Death of Joseph Addison.* 1719.
> *The Universal Passion.* 7 vols., 1725–28; revised edition, as *Love of Fame: The Universal Passion, in Seven Characteristical Satires,* 1728.
> *Poetic Works.* 1726.
> *Cynthio.* 1727.
> *Ocean: An Ode Occasioned by His Majesty's Late Royal Encouragement of the Sea-Service, to Which Is Prefixed An Ode to the King, and A Discourse on Ode.* 1728.
> *Imperium Pelagi: A Naval Lyric Written in Imitation of Pindar's Spirit, Occasioned by His Majesty's Return September 1729 and the Succeeding Peace.* 1730; as *The Merchant,* 1730.
> *Two Epistles to Mr. Pope Concerning the Authors of the Age.* 1730.
> *The Foreign Address: or, The Best Argument for Peace, Occasioned by the British Fleet, and the Posture of Affairs when the Parliament Met 1734.* 1735.
> *Poetical Works,* edited by E. Curll. 2 vols., 1741.
> *The Complaint; or, Night-Thoughts on Life, Death, and Immortality: Night the First* to *Night the Eighth.* 8 vols., 1742–45; *The Consolation* [Night the Ninth] *and Some Thoughts Occasioned by the Present Juncture,* 1746; complete version (nine nights), 1750.
> *A Sea Piece Containing the British Sailor's Exultation and His Prayer Before Engagement, Occasioned by the Rumour of War.* 1755.
> *The Poetical Works.* 4 vols., 1757.
> *Resignation.* 1761; revised edition, 1762.

Plays

> *Busiris, King of Egypt* (produced 1719).   1719.
> *The Revenge* (produced 1721).   1721.
> *The Brothers*, from a play by Thomas Corneille (produced 1753).   1753.

Other

> *A Vindication of Providence: or, A True Estimate of Human Life, in Which the Passions Are Considered in a New Light* (sermon).   1728.
> *An Apology for Princes; or, The Reverence Due to Government* (sermon).   1729.
> *The Centaur Not Fabulous, in Five Letters to a Friend on the Life in Vogue.*   1755; augmented edition, 1755.
> *An Argument Drawn from the Circumstances of Christ's Death for the Truth of His Religion* (sermon).   1758.
> *Conjectures on Original Composition in a Letter to the Author of Sir Charles Grandison.*   1759; edited by E. J. Morley, 1918.

Bibliography: *Young: A Handlist of Critical Notices and Studies* by Francesco Cordasco, 1950.

Reading List: *Le Poète Young* by Walter Thomas, 1901 (includes bibliography); *The Life and Letters of Young* by H. C. Shelley, 1914; *Das Pseudoklassizistische und Romantische in Youngs Night Thoughts* by K. Laux, 1938; *Young and the Fear of Death* by C. V. Wicker, 1952; *Young: Versuch einer Gedanklichen Interpretation auf Grund der Frühwerke* by Erich König, 1954; *Young* by I. St. J. Bliss, 1969.

*   *   *

Edward Young, the contemporary of Addison, is also the precursor of the Romantics. He is yet another of those mid-eighteenth-century figures who mark the progress to what is yet to be.

His early work such as, for example, *The Force of Religion: or, Vanquish'd Love*, is cast in heroic couplets. This is a narrative poem on the last days of Lady Jane Grey, but its dramatic qualities make it not surprising that Young tried his hand at work for the stage. *Busiris*, though it proved a success on the stage, is as turgid and flat as most tragedies of its day, and it cannot be said that *The Revenge* is any better. Well-constructed though both of them are, there are too much rhetoric and inflated feeling and too little real passion and sense of relentless overwhelming circumstances for them to be convincing.

Young practised that fashionable mode of the time, the satire in heroic couplets. *Love of Fame: The Universal Passion* appeared in seven parts. It covers a variety of topics – human vanity, the state of contemporary learning, women, the praise of war, and the corruption of courts, but, despite its title, it lacks both an organising principle and a coherent plan. Young's satires are fluent and stand precursor to much of Pope's best work, especially in their character-sketches, though Young is more genial and more general than Pope.

The sadness of personal bereavement may have led Young to his greatest and longest work, *The Complaint; or, Night-Thoughts*, in which he turned to blank verse. It is by this poem that he is now chiefly remembered though not always to his credit. The poem grew, one *Night* following upon another, and, as it grew, each *Night* grew longer. Young had already treated apocalyptic themes in *The Last Day*. Now at the climax of a long development in the poetry of melancholy which issued also in Gray's *Elegy*, Young employs an occasion of deepest personal trouble as a point of departure to consider "the nature, proof and importance of personal immortality" (Heading of *Nights* VI and VII).

He uses the moral argument; he appeals to cosmological evidence; he is still in the Augustan fashion reasoning his way to faith; but, more and more, feeling keeps breaking in. Indeed, *Night-Thoughts*, far from being a gloomy poem, is a poem of triumph, of death as "the crown of life," giving, if life has been lived aright, the entry to immortal bliss. Even cosmology teaches the same lesson; night is not darkness but a plenitude of burning wonders of God's creation. Young, the Christian, moves on, however, to emphasise the God of history and especially the Christ of the Incarnation and the Passion. On the Cross "There hangs all human hope: that nail supports/The falling universe: that gone, we drop." He sees life as a time of probation and hence he considers the infidelity of his interlocutor, Lorenzo, to be senseless. Immortality is all, and in the seventh *Night* he seeks by a series of psychological arguments – man's misery here, his enlightened self-love, his fundamental sense of aspiration – to suggest the likelihood of everlasting life. The intuitive and assertive element in this is important. It shows Young's relationship with the Evangelicals and reminds us of the pre-Romantic position which he will assume again in *Conjectures on Original Composition*.

This work was preceded by the prose treatise *The Centaur Not Fabulous*, in which Young attacked the infidelity and, even more, the immoralities of the day. Like others of its author's output, it shows a sincerity which, unfortunately, loses something of its impact as a result of prolixity. The *Conjectures* departs from that tradition of authority and "imitation" that marks neo-classicism, lauds originality, the literary equivalent of "enthusiasm" in religion, and emphasises "natural genius." In adumbrating his theories Young also suggests the two levels of the creative mind, the conscious and ordinary and the unconscious and inscrutable.

—Arthur Pollard

NOTES ON CONTRIBUTORS

BAREHAM, T. Senior Lecturer in English, New University of Ulster, Coleraine. Author of *George Crabbe: A Critical Study,* 1977, *A Bibliography of Crabbe* (with S. Gattrell), 1978, and articles on Shakespeare and Malcolm Lowry. **Essays:** Sir Richard Blackmore; William Lisle Bowles; George Crabbe; Stephen Duck; Sir Samuel Garth.

BEVIS, R. W. Member of the Department of English, University of British Columbia, Vancouver. Editor, *Eighteenth Century Drama: Afterpieces,* 1970. **Essay:** William Whitehead.

BOTTRALL, Margaret. Biographer and Critic. University Lecturer, Department of Education, and Senior Tutor, Hughes Hall, Cambridge University, until 1972. Author of *George Herbert,* 1954, and *Every Man a Phoenix: Studies in Seventeenth-Century Autobiography,* 1958. Editor of *Personal Records,* 1961, and *Songs of Innocence and Experience,* by Blake, 1970. **Essay:** Anne Finch, Countess of Winchilsea.

CAMPBELL, Ian. Lecturer in English Literature, University of Edinburgh. Author of *Thomas Carlyle,* 1974, and of articles on Scottish literature since 1750. Associate Editor of the Duke-Edinburgh edition of *Carlyle Letters,* and editor of Carlyle's *Reminiscences* and *Selected Essays.* **Essay:** Allan Ramsay.

CLARK, John R. Professor and Chairman, Department of English, University of South Florida, Tampa. Author of *Form and Frenzy in Swift's "Tale of a Tub,"* 1970, and of many essays, reviews, and translations in periodicals. Editor of *Satire – That Blasted Art* (anthology), 1971, and of the satire issue of *Seventeenth-Century News,* 1975. **Essays:** Tom Brown; Earl of Dorset; John Oldham; Matthew Prior.

CRADDOCK, Patricia. Associate Professor of English, Boston University. Author of "Gibbon: The Man in His Letters," in *The Familiar Letter in the Eighteenth Century,* edited by H. Anderson and others, 1966; "Gibbon's Revisions of *The Decline and Fall,*" in *Studies in Bibliography 21,* 1968; "An Approach to the Distinction of Similar Styles: Two English Historians," in *Style 2,* Spring 1968. Editor of *The English Essays of Gibbon,* 1972, and editor and translator, with N. Murstein, of *Gibbon's Essai sur l'étude de la littérature* (forthcoming). **Essay:** Edward Gibbon.

GORDON, Ian A. Professor of English, University of Wellington, 1936–74; also taught at the University of Leeds and the University of Edinburgh. Author of *John Skelton,* 1943; *The Teaching of English,* 1947; *Katherine Mansfield,* 1954; *The Movement of English Prose,* 1966; *John Galt,* 1972. Editor of *English Prose Technique,* 1948, and of works by William Shenstone, John Galt, and Katherine Mansfield. **Essay:** William Shenstone.

HAMILTON, Harlan W. Professor Emeritus of English, Case Western Reserve University, Cleveland. Author of *Doctor Syntax: A Silhouette of William Combe,* 1969, and articles on Johnson and Combe in *English Studies Today, Western Humanities Review,* and *PMLA.* **Essays:** William Combe; John Pomfret.

HASSLER, Donald M. Associate Professor of English, Kent State University, Kent, Ohio. Author of *Erasmus Darwin,* 1972. **Essays:** Erasmus Darwin; Anna Seward.

HEATH-STUBBS, John. Writer and Lecturer. Author of several books of verse, the most recent being *The Watchman's Flute,* 1978, a book of plays, and of *The Darkling Plain: A*

Study of the Later Fortunes of Romanticism, 1950, *Charles Williams,* 1955, and studies of the verse satire, the ode, and the pastoral. Editor of anthologies and works by Shelley, Tennyson, Swift, and Pope; translator of works by Giacomo Leopardi, Alfred de Vigny, and others. **Essays:** Mark Akenside; Charles Churchill; William Mickle; Ambrose Philips; Thomas Tickell.

JEFFARES, A. Norman. Professor of English Studies, University of Stirling, Scotland; Editor of *Ariel: A Review of International English Literature,* and General Editor of the Writers and Critics series and the New Oxford English series; Past Editor of *A Review of English Studies.* Author of *Yeats: Man and Poet,* 1949; *Seven Centuries of Poetry,* 1956; *A Commentary on the Collected Poems* (1958) and *Collected Plays* (1975) *of Yeats.* Editor of *Restoration Comedy,* 1974, and *Yeats: The Critical Heritage,* 1977. **Essay:** William Cowper.

JOSEPH, M. K. Professor of English, University of Auckland. Author of several books of verse, most recently *Inscription on a Paper Dart,* 1974; three novels, most recently *A Soldier's Tale,* 1976; and of *Byron the Poet,* 1964. Editor of *Frankenstein* by Mary Shelley, 1969. **Essay:** William Falconer.

KALLICH, Martin. Professor of English, Northern Illinois University, De Kalb. Author of *The Psychological Milieu of Lytton Strachey,* 1961; *The American Revolution Through British Eyes* (with others), 1962; *Heav'n's First Law: Rhetoric and Order in Pope's Essay on Man,* 1967; *Oedipus: Myth and Drama* (with others), 1968; *The Other End of the Egg: Religious Satire in Gulliver's Travels,* 1970; *The Association of Ideas and Critical Theory in 18th-Century England,* 1970; *Horace Walpole,* 1971; *The Book of the Sonnet* (with others), 1972. **Essays:** Edmund Burke; John Scott.

KELSALL, Malcolm. Professor of English, University College, Cardiff; Advisory Editor of *Byron Journal.* Editor of *The Adventures of David Simple* by Sarah Fielding, 1969, *Venice Preserved* by Thomas Otway, 1969, and *Love for Love* by William Congreve, 1970. **Essay:** Joseph Addison.

LEWIS, Peter. Lecturer in English, University of Durham. Author of *The Beggar's Opera* (critical study), 1976, and articles on Restoration and Augustan drama and modern poetry. Editor of *The Beggar's Opera* by John Gay, 1973, and *Poems '74* (anthology of Anglo-Welsh poetry), 1974. **Essay:** John Gay.

LINDSAY, Maurice. Director of the Scottish Civic Trust, Glasgow, and Managing Editor of *The Scottish Review.* Author of several books of verse, the most recent being *Walking Without an Overcoat,* 1977; plays; travel and historical works; and critical studies, including *Robert Burns: The Man, His Work, The Legend,* 1954 (revised, 1968), *The Burns Encyclopedia,* 1959 (revised, 1970), and *A History of Scottish Literature,* 1977. Editor of the Saltire Modern Poets series, several anthologies of Scottish writing, and works by Sir Alexander Gray, Sir David Lyndsay, Marion Angus, and John Davidson. **Essays:** John Armstrong; James Beattie; Robert Burns.

LUCAS, John. Professor of English and Drama, Loughborough University, Leicestershire; Advisory Editor of *Victorian Studies, Literature and History,* and *Journal of European Studies.* Author of *Tradition and Tolerance in 19th-Century Fiction,* 1966; *The Melancholy Man: A Study of Dickens,* 1970; *Arnold Bennett,* 1975; *Egilssaga: The Poems,* 1975; *The Literature of Change,* 1977; *The 1930's Challenge to Orthodoxy,* 1978. Editor of *Literature and Politics in the 19th Century,* 1971, and of works by George Crabbe and Jane Austen. **Essays:** Matthew Green; William Mason; John Wilmot, Earl of Rochester.

MacLAINE, Allan H.   Professor of English, University of Rhode Island, Kingston. Author of *The Student's Comprehensive Guide to the Canterbury Tales*, 1964, *Robert Fergusson*, 1965, and of articles on Burns. **Essays:** Robert Fergusson; Thomas Gray.

MINER, Earl.   Townsend Martin Professor of English and Comparative Literature, Princeton University, New Jersey. Author of *Dryden's Poetry*, 1967; *An Introduction to Japanese Court Poetry*, 1968; *The Metaphysical Mode from Donne to Cowley*, 1969; *The Cavalier Mode from Jonson to Cotton*, 1971; *Seventeenth-Century Imagery*, 1971; *The Restoration Mode from Milton to Dryden*, 1974; *Japanese Linked Poetry*, 1978. **Essays:** Samuel Butler; Charles Cotton; John Dryden.

MOORE, Catherine E.   Associate Professor of English, North Carolina State University, Raleigh. **Essay:** Anna Barbauld.

MUIR, Kenneth.   Professor Emeritus of English Literature, University of Liverpool; Editor of *Shakespeare Survey*, and Chairman, International Shakespeare Association. Author of many books, including *The Nettle and the Flower*, 1933; *King Lear*, 1952; *Elizabethan Lyrics*, 1953; *John Milton*, 1955; *Shakespeare's Sources*, 1957; *Shakespeare and the Tragic Pattern*, 1959; *Shakespeare the Collaborator*, 1960; *Introduction to Elizabethan Literature*, 1967; *The Comedy of Manners*, 1970; *The Singularity of Shakespeare*, 1977; *Shakespeare's Comic Sequence*, 1978. Editor of several plays by Shakespeare, and of works by Wyatt and Middleton; translator of five plays by Racine. **Essay:** William Blake.

OLIVER-MORDEN, B. C.   Teacher at the Open University and the University of Keele. Editor of the 18th-Century section of *The Year's Work in English 1973*. **Essays:** William Collins; Oliver Goldsmith; George Lyttelton, James Macpherson.

PERRY, John J.   Member of the Department of English, State University of New York, Brockport. **Essay:** Sir Charles Sedley.

PITTOCK, Joan.   Member of the Department of English, University of Aberdeen, Scotland. Author of *The Ascendancy of Taste: The Achievement of Joseph and Thomas Warton*, 1973. **Essays:** Joseph Warton; Thomas Warton.

POLLARD, Arthur.   Professor of English, University of Hull, Yorkshire. Author of *Mrs. Gaskell, Novelist and Biographer*, 1965, and *Anthony Trollope*, 1978. Editor of *The Letters of Mrs. Gaskell* (with J. A. V. Chapple), 1966; *The Victorians* (Sphere History of Literature in English), 1970; *Crabbe: The Critical Heritage*, 1972; *Thackeray: Vanity Fair* (casebook), 1978. **Essays:** John Byrom; John Langhorne; Edward Young.

RAWSON, C. J.   Professor of English, University of Warwick, Coventry; Joint Editor of *Modern Language Review* and *Yearbook of English Studies*, and General Editor of the Unwin Critical Library. Author of *Henry Fielding*, 1968; *Fielding and the Augustan Ideal under Stress*, 1972; *Gulliver and the Gentle Reader*, 1973; *Focus: Swift*, 1978. Editor of *Fielding: A Critical Anthology*, 1973, and *Yeats and the Anglo-Irish Literature: Critical Essays* by Peter Ure, 1973. **Essays:** Thomas Parnell; Jonathan Swift.

ROGAL, Samuel J.   Associate Professor of English, Mary Holmes College, West Point, Mississippi. Author of articles on hymns and sacred music, John Wesley, George Eliot, Pope, and Milton, in *The Serif, Eighteenth-Century Life, Nineteenth-Century Fiction, Milton Quarterly*, and other periodicals. **Essay:** Charles Wesley.

ROGERS, Pat.   Professor of English, University of Bristol. Author of *Grub Street: Studies in a Subculture*, 1972, and *The Augustan Vision*, 1974. Editor of *A Tour Through Great*

Britain by Daniel Defoe, 1971, *Defoe: The Critical Heritage*, 1972, and *The Eighteenth Century*, 1978. **Essays:** William Diaper; John Philips; Alexander Pope.

ROTHSTEIN, Eric.   Professor of English, University of Wisconsin, Madison. Author of *George Farquhar*, 1967, and *Restoration Tragedy: Form and the Process of Change*, 1967. Co-Editor of *The Augustan Milieu: Essays Presented to Louis A. Landa*, 1970. **Essay:** Christopher Anstey.

RUOFF, James E.   Associate Professor of English, City College of New York. Author of *Elizabethan Poetry and Prose*, 1972, *Crowell Handbook of Elizabethan and Stuart Literature*, 1973, and *Major Shakespearean Tragedies* (with Edward G. Quinn), 1973. **Essay:** John Bunyan.

SAMBROOK, A. J.   Reader in English, University of Southampton, Hampshire. Author of *A Poet Hidden: The Life of Richard Watson Dixon*, 1962, and *William Cobbett: An Author Guide*, 1973. Editor of *The Scribleriad*, 1967, *The Seasons and The Castle of Indolence* by James Thomson, 1972, and *Pre-Raphaelitism: Patterns of Literary Criticism*, 1974. **Essays:** Robert Blair; John Cunningham; James Grainger; David Mallet; Lady Mary Wortley Montagu; Richard Savage; William Somerville; James Thomson; William Walsh.

SOLOMON, Harry M.   Associate Professor of English, Auburn University, Alabama. Author of *Sir Richard Blackmore* (forthcoming), and of articles on Shaftesbury, Swift, and others for *Southern Humanities Review, Keats-Shelley Journal, Studies in English Literature*, and other periodicals. **Essays:** William King; Katherine Philips.

TAYLOR, Donald S.   Member of the English Department, University of Oregon, Eugene. Editor of *The Complete Works of Thomas Chatterton*, 2 vols., 1971. **Essay:** Thomas Chatterton.

TRUSSLER, Simon.   Editor of *Theatre Quarterly.* Theatre Critic, *Tribune*, 1969–76. Author of several books on theatre and drama, including studies of John Osborne, Arnold Wesker, John Whiting, Harold Pinter, and Edward Bond, and of articles on theatre bibliography and classification. Editor of two collections of eighteenth-century plays and of *The Oxford Companion to the Theatre*, 1969. **Essay:** Sir Richard Steele.

WALSH, Marcus.   Lecturer in English, University of Birmingham. Editor of *The Religious Poetry of Christopher Smart*, 1972. **Essays:** James Boswell; John Dyer; Samuel Johnson; Christopher Smart; Isaac Watts.

WOODCOCK, George.   Free-lance Writer, Lecturer, and Editor. Author of verse (*Selected Poems*, 1967), plays, travel books, biographies, and works on history and politics; critical works include *William Godwin*, 1946; *The Incomparable Aphra*, 1948; *The Paradox of Oscar Wilde*, 1949; *The Crystal Spirit* (on Orwell), 1966; *Hugh MacLennan*, 1969; *Odysseus Ever Returning: Canadian Writers and Writing*, 1970; *Mordecai Richler*, 1970; *Dawn and the Darkest Hour* (on Aldous Huxley), 1972; *Herbert Read*, 1972; *Thomas Merton*, 1978. Editor of anthologies, and of works by Charles Lamb, Malcolm Lowry, Wyndham Lewis, and others. **Essay:** Ned Ward.

DRAMA

INTRODUCTION

From 1660 to 1800 there appeared a body of dramatic literature, frequently scorned in the 19th and early 20th centuries, that has found increasing appreciation in modern times. It was once the dull duty of the literary historian (often a specialist in Elizabethan drama) to comment on the immorality and licentiousness of the Restoration comedies as he proceeded to chronicle the decay and downfall of English drama, but a look at recent bibliographies or publishers' advertisements will show the remarkable increase of editions of these plays and the general respect being accorded by modern critics. The dramatic works by the authors during this one hundred and forty year period are so diverse in nature that they prove recalcitrant to easy categorization. To avoid broad generalisations which would scarcely be valid for so many writers over such a long period of time, I will break my account into three sections: the reign of Charles II, 1660–1685; 1685 until the Stage Licensing Act of 1737; and 1737 until 1800, or thereabouts.

As Robert Hume points out in his important study, *The Development of English Drama in the Late Seventeenth Century,* literary historians have not yet been able to establish a terminal date for Restoration drama. Most of them set the period from 1660 to 1700, using the premiere of *The Way of the World* as the culmination of the type of play called the comedy of manners. Others want to include Farquhar and hence extend the date to 1707, the year of *The Beaux Stratagem,* and some push the terminus three more years, to include the retirement of Thomas Betterton, the great actor-manager who had performed in many of the major successes of the age. Finally, John Loftis, the editor of the Nebraska Regents series of reprints, stretched the period to 1737. This extension led of course to ludicrous difficulties. In one case, a critic, who shall be nameless here, called Susannah Centlivre's *The Busy Body* (1709) a lively Restoration comedy, but classified Nicholas Rowe's farce *The Biter* (1704) as "a tedious eighteenth century play." Hence I will be a strict constructionist and apply the term "Restoration" to those plays, lively or tedious, which were acted after the restoration of good King Charles to the English throne.

The year 1737 provides a valid dividing point for the second section, as the Stage Licensing Act ended the theatrical career of Henry Fielding and the experimental dramatists whose innovative plays he had been staging. Furthermore, a number of years passed after 1737 before new, full-length plays were produced; thus there is a real, though brief, break in continuity.

1. The Drama from 1660 to 1685

The major rupture of continuity, of course, was the eighteen-year cessation of acting during the interregnum. The result of this hiatus was that most of the new Restoration plays differed so considerably from those of the Elizabethan period that historians have not been able to agree on the relative importance of the different causes of the change. Some account, then, should be given of the influence of contemporary French drama, the burden of Italian and French Neoclassic theories, trends in Caroline drama, the vogue of the Spanish Romance, and the historical and social background of the literary scene in the 1660's.

Years ago, when Restoration comedy was in disrepute, its emergence was attributed to the influence of French drama, thereby removing a stain from the purity of English literature. From the record of new plays in London during the first decade of the restoration of the monarchy, we can see that this ascription is fallacious, in so far as comedy is concerned. Much has been made of English borrowings from Molière, but the essential form of the new satiric wit-comedy characteristic of Restoration drama had already been established by the time of *The Misanthrope* and *Tartuffe* in 1666 and 1667.

Royalist exiles waiting in Paris for Oliver Cromwell to die did have the opportunity to see tragedies by Corneille and admire the emphasis placed on *gloire* and on loyalty to the monarch. They also became accustomed to the musical and psychological effects of the rhymed alexandrine couplet. Furthermore, all persons interested in literature, whether expatriates or quietly living in England, were becoming conversant with the propositions concerning dramatic literature propounded by French Neoclassic critics. The goal of perfecting tragedy by moving it in the direction of the epic (the queen of literary forms) was most attractive, and even before 1660 we find English writers such as Hobbes and Davenant speculating on this topic. Besides, Englishmen visiting Paris or the northern Italian cities were impressed by the spectacle incorporated into the staging of tragedies and operas. Hence we can see that a potential audience was already being prepared for the heroic play when English dramatists came to compose them. English devotees of the theatre evinced great interest in the introduction of rhymed verse for the language of tragedy. The campaign being carried out in Paris to refine, correct, polish, and preserve the French language could not fail to impress English observers, who soon realised that this mode provided a route whereby they could surpass the literary giants of the Elizabethan age, "the race before the flood." All these points are discussed at length by John Dryden in his *Essay of Dramatic Poesy,* the best introduction to Restoration Drama that has ever been written.

The attractiveness of the heroic play was further enhanced by the active support of Charles II himself. He too had seen the French serious dramas in Paris, certainly not overlooking their support of the values of a hierarchical society, and he suggested to Roger Boyle, Earl of Orrery, the composition of such a play. Later, when productions of the heroic drama were under way, he and his brother, the Duke of York, not only brought the court to attend performances but also lent royal robes to the actors for costumes. When we add to these influential forces at work the fact that "love-and-honour" plays had previously been acted for Queen Henrietta Marie and her court in the time of Charles I and thus had already become part of the native tradition in serious drama, we should be prepared for an early advent of the heroic play on the London stage.

The first one, *The General,* was composed in 1661 by Lord Orrery, and first performed in Dublin in 1662. However, the first heroic play witnessed by a London audience was *The Indian Queen,* a collaboration of Sir Robert Howard and John Dryden, in January 1664. It was followed immediately by Orrery's *The History of Henry the Fifth* in August of that year, and others by Dryden, Orrery, Elkanah Settle, John Caryl, and Samuel Pordage appeared in the next few years. The wild rant and extravagant action in these plays make them objectionable, worse yet, even ludicrous to the modern reader. Accordingly, to understand the admiration which the original audiences had for these plays, we must remember Erich Auerbach's explanation in *Mimesis* of the fascination which the courtiers had for works which presented the crisis of leaders, torn by contrary demands from their private life and their duties as rulers.

The other major influence on the new dramatists came from Spain. The borrowed elements are relatively novel and can be easily traced as they appear. One feature was a highly complicated plot, giving rise, in English hands, to a sub-genre which Allardyce Nicoll termed "intrigue plays." Of the borrowed character types, the Spanish fathers turn out to be unusually choleric and bombastic, the young male leads are haughty though idealistic, but it is the high-spirited heroines who set the tone of the work. These young ladies are both virtuous and loquacious. They object wittily and vociferously to marriages which their fathers have arranged, but they are women of high moral fibre and while they talk audaciously, they never say anything indecent. Their high moral standards do not lead them to a submissive attitude in the presence of their suitors; instead, the young ladies engage in a free, open, and even equal basis, and are ready to out-talk any man who starts an argument. The initial English use of this material appeared in the first major box-office success of the Restoration period, *The Adventures of Five Hours* (1663), by Sir Samuel Tuke. Pepys and other commentators quickly noticed both the liveliness of the play and the complete lack of anything bawdy. The playwrights soon employed the Spanish romance to their advantage. In *The Carnival*, Thomas Porter presents the young male lead and the heroine as the two main characters, rather than designating the man as the protagonist, and achieves what John Harrington Smith was later to call "the gay couple." This achievement of an almost complete equality of the sexes engaged in a duel of wits came to be the distinguishing sign of Restoration comedy. Dryden saw that all he needed to add was some racy language to the women's parts, and he would have perfect material for the theatre – especially when the actress was Nell Gwyn. The best example of the dramatic possibilities is found in the famous encounter between Dorimant and Harriet in Etherege's *The Man of Mode* (1676).

This presentation of foreign elements does not mean that there was no connection between the new drama and the old. The break with Elizabethan tragedy was complete, but various aspects of the older comedy continued on in the Restoration plays. Fletcher's comedies were at the peak of their reputation in the 1660's; they were offered frequently in the theatre and were imitated by young playwrights. In contrast to the exphasis on action and complicated plot-turns in the Spanish plays, Fletcher's comedies put the major emphasis on dialogue. The last Caroline plays before the outbreak of war blossomed again in the Restoration, especially festive comedies like Brome's *The Jovial Crew*, whose cheerful and optimistic tone is perpetuated in the newly-discovered *The Country Gentleman*, by Sir Robert Howard and George Villiers, 2nd Duke of Buckingham. But the most influential of all the Elizabethan writers was Ben Jonson. We mistake the true nature of his influence if we seek only for some Restoration comedies containing "humors" characters. Jonson's use of humors characters was only a device; the medical metaphor was outmoded in the late seventeenth century anyhow; and the members of the *dramatis personae* labelled with a "humor" in some Restoration plays are actually "social" types (fop, rake, cast-off mistress) rather than humor characters. Nor is the adulation lavished on the name of Ben Jonson a reliable sign. Almost everyone, it appears, praised him, but they went to see Shakespeare's plays in the theatres. The recorded number of performances of Jonson's comedies in the years 1660–1700 is very low, and not at all in line with the number of allusions to him in essays, prologues, poems, and the like.

The true relation between Ben Jonson's comedies and most Restoration comedies is that both share the same pessimistic view of the nature of man and his hostility toward his fellow man; both demonstrate an unceasing animosity between the different social classes; and both sets of comedies modulate toward being open-ended. To illustrate the difference from Elizabethan or eighteenth-century comedy, we can invoke Shakespeare. At the beginning of his comedy *The Tempest*, practically everybody is hostile to some other person or group; plots and counter-plots abound. But by the end of the play, everyone but Caliban realises that there is a universal harmony; everyone becomes reconciled and Prospero can break his staff. Again, what could exceed the hostility shown in *The Merchant of Venice*? Yet all is resolved in universal harmony at Belmont. But when we turn to Ben Jonson's *The Alchemist*, the play just stops. The cleverest rascal gets off, scotfree, and there is little doubt he will ply his trade again. So too in Sir Robert Howard's charming comedy *The Committee* (1662). Here, the demure heroine Ruth blackmails the greedy, social climbing Puritan Mrs. Day into a stalemate, without any resolution. The Puritans (in the play) still control England; they hate the Royalists and seek to humiliate them as well as take their estates; the frustrated Cavaliers return the hatred. *The Country-Wife* (1675) ends when Margery Pinchwife is corrupted; the dance stops with the music, and will resume when the musicians start playing again, but the hostility between Horner and Pinchwife has not the least abated. *The Man of Mode* stops when Dorimant agrees to visit Harriet's country home, but the play presents no resolution. This open-ended nature of the structure of much Restoration comedy certainly proclaims the debt to the master satirist Ben Jonson.

As can be seen from the presentation of the Puritans in Howard's *The Committee*, the historical and social background had much to do in shaping the nature of early Restoration drama. To the young people of the 1660's, the recent Civil War was a monstrous stroke of folly. The events in it and the conduct of the leaders showed that older people were incapable of running the country properly, and that no one should pay the least attention to the elderly anyhow. The recently-found comedy *The Country Gentleman* does treat an older man in a favorable light, but otherwise the situation in Restoration comedies of the 1660's was the same as in Paris in May 1968 − no one over thirty was fit to be trusted.

The "noble experiment" of Puritan rule was regarded with cynicism. After they had won the civil war, the Puritan leaders, proud of their high ethics, determined not to confiscate captured property as conquerors throughout history had done; instead, they set up sequestration courts and committees. However, if a Royalist nobleman returned to claim his property, he might find himself executed or jailed. Most of the Cavaliers lacked cash to pay their taxes, and saw their estates pass into the greedy hands of the sequestration committees, so that either way the loyal supporters of the Stuarts lost their lands. Nor was the Restoration settlement acceptable all around. To regain one's property, a man needed money and lawyers for the long rounds in the law courts. Many Londoners bitterly resented the return of Charles II, and there were several abortive revolts. This situation made the Stuart supporters nervous, ill-tempered, and reckless, so that hedonism became the vogue.

It is not surprising then to see the new young playwrights hit back at the Puritans. No later than Charles's return, and possibly slightly before, John Tatham brought out his vindictive satire, *The Rump,* presenting the frenzied scrambles first for power and then for safety on the part of the deceased Cromwell's lieutenants. This piece was followed in 1661 by the poet Cowley's satire on the Puritans, *Cutter of Coleman Street.* In 1662 came Howard's *The Committee,* the best of the group, followed in the next year by John Wilson's *The Cheats* and John Lacy's *The Old Troop.* These were the first new plays of the Restoration, not the celebrated wit comedies or sex comedies.

Another factor affecting the playwrights and the development of the drama was the audience. In 1600, when London was a city of from 150,000 to possibly 200,000 people, the drama was at the height of its popularity, and despite the opposition to the theatre by the Puritans, the city was able to support six or seven established theatrical troupes. In 1660, the King issued two licenses (to Davenant and Killigrew) to create a monopoly, and itinerant troupes were crushed or absorbed. Thus until nearly the end of Charles's reign, the city of London, now with a population of about 400,000, was only barely maintaining two theatrical companies. In spite of royal patronage, the two companies did not prosper uniformly, and by 1682 the King's Company had lost so much money that it was ended, with the players being absorbed by the Duke's company. Thus in the last three years of Charles's reign, and on into 1695, only one company was staging plays.

Not only had the drama lost its popular base, as the chief form of entertainment for Londoners, but the bulk of the remaining theatregoers constituted a coterie audience. It is true that in recent years closer study of the evidence has shown that some business men, clerks, and servants occasionally attended the theatre, but the great majority of the regular audience were members of the court, or lesser figures in government administration, or other members of the upper middle class, or the law students. The result was that the dramatists were no longer writing for a large, heterogeneous audience, and the new plays were designed for this smaller coterie audience. Accordingly, many of the plays were highly topical and included specific, personal satire.

This brief survey of the main influences on the new playwrights has already dealt with several of the emerging types of drama: the heroic play, intrigue comedy, the beginnings of wit comedy, and the political plays. What remains now is to focus on the main lines of development in comedy and tragedy. Though the new comedies each season exhibited considerable variety, a type was developing which has been called wit comedy or the comedy of manners. Dryden took the lead, as he had with the heroic drama, and presented a gay couple in *The Wild Gallant* (1663) and an even more vivacious pair in *Secret Love* (1667). James Sutherland points out that the playwright James Howard contributed two plays, *The English Monsieur* and *All Mistaken,* in the pattern which evolved into the comedy of manners. The first two plays of George Etherege are more instructive in showing us what happened. Into the first, *The Comical Revenge* (1664), Etherege crammed four plots, with the *dramatis personae* for each drawn from a different class of London society. The first complication concerns noblemen who had participated in the Civil War, and is in the context of the love-and-honour heroic drama. The main plot presents a rake and a widow, both from the upper middle class. The third group comprises of gamblers, sharpers, and their victim, and the last episode deals with servants. A just treatment of these several lines would require a novel, possibly in more than one volume. Whether Etherege saw this problem or not, he turned his focus of interest to one group in his next play – *She Wou'd If She Cou'd* (1668) – the members of middle-class London society. The protagonist is a rake who is looking out for sexual experiences while pursuing his main goal – marriage to a rich heiress. Looking backwards through the drama, we can see that Etherege fixed the group to be dealt with in this art form, and the group he presented is in the same category as those ever since, in the comedy of manners, down through Oscar Wilde and Somerset Maugham. Etherege was an objective observer, and William Wycherley, now looked on as the best comic dramatist among this early group, introduced more satiric drive in his plays. Because of the virulent satire in *The Country-Wife* (1675) and *The Plain-Dealer* (1676), this type of Restoration play is often called satiric comedy. The first wave of the comedy of manners reached its peak in 1676, with the production in that year of *The Plain-Dealer*, Etherege's polished masterpiece, *The Man of Mode*, and Shadwell's satire on the dabblers in science, *The Virtuoso*. No one knew it at the time but the artistic achievement of these plays marked the close of the first wave of the comedy of manners. Wycherley and Etherege had written their last play, and the next group of comic dramatists took comedy in a different direction. Tom D'Urfey and Aphra Behn began a series of racy plays which we may call sex-comedy, marked by the bawdy language so offensive to our Victorian ancestors. Dryden, who should have known better, composed a play of this type, *Mr. Limberham* (1678), which proved quite a shocker, in spite of Dryden's protest that he was writing satire. At any rate, the comedies of the next few years certainly degenerated in dramatic quality, regardless of whether the reader is amused or offended by the indecency of language and situation. Comedy, which had gotten off to such a promising start in the 1660's, was in a decline by the end of Charles's reign.

Meanwhile, the progress of tragedy was following a different route. From the beginning, the artificiality of the heroic drama had led to objections and eventually to a diminution of audience interest. Also, other poets could not equal the nervous rhymed couplets of Dryden's plays. Dryden himself wearied of the heroic play and turned away from it. A period of experimentation went on, with mediocre authors like Settle reviving the old revenge play. Then two able playwrights appeared in the persons of Thomas Otway and Nathaniel Lee. Both turned to the high road of English tragedy – tragedy of character. Neither was entirely successful, but Otway achieved the best tragedy of the entire period under consideration in this volume, *Venice Preserved* (1682), and Lee's *The Rival Queens* (1677) held the stage for over a century and a half. Dryden himself showed renewed vitality in the tragic form with *All for Love* (1677) and *Don Sebastian* (though the latter play was held back and not acted until 1689). An initial conclusion then would indicate that after the delay occasioned by the false start with the heroic play, English tragedy was on the way to new heights. Unfortunately, Otway died in 1684, poor Nathaniel Lee lost his senses and was committed to Bedlam in 1684, and the renewal of tragic form proved to be temporary and illusory. Worse yet, a minor playwright, John Banks, was to alter the nature of contemporary tragedy by abandoning the tragic hero. The process of enervating the male lead had been begun by Dryden in his depiction of Antony's degeneration in *All for Love*, and Castalio in Otway's *The Orphan* (1680) and Jaffeir in *Venice Preserved* are both weaklings. But John Banks completely subordinated the hero in *The Unhappy Favourite*, in 1681, and arranged for the women to take over. In the next year, he wrote *Anna Bullen*, where a weak, vacillating woman is the main character. Contemporary critics sneered and termed the plays "she-tragedies," but the damage was done. With the beautiful and tender Anne Bracegirdle available for the role, dramatists now composed tragedies featuring a tender woman in distress. The consequence was that the quality of tragedy plummeted rapidly.

With the prevailing cynicism of the age, it is not surprising to find the emergence of burlesque and farce. The sceptics had rejected the heroic play from the beginning, and the Duke of Buckingham, aided by several friends, put all the objections to bad drama together to create *The Rehearsal* (1671). More lively burlesque came from the pen of Thomas Duffett, as he pounced on Settle with *The Empress of Morocco* (1673) and on the attempts to create dramatic opera in his *The Mock-Tempest* (1674) and *Psyche Debauched* (1675).

Farcical episodes were prevalent in Elizabethan drama, but in the Restoration period authors began systematically to compose full-length five-act farces. The popularity of the *commedia dell'arte* led John Lacy, Nahum Tate, and Edward Ravenscroft, among others, to plunder these improvised comedies of the strolling Italian companies for use on the London stage. The most popular of all of the Restoration farces was Ravenscroft's *Mamamouchi* (1672), adapted and completely Englished from Molière. The most notorious full-length farce was Ravenscroft's *The London Cuckolds* (1681), where the hostility of the dramatists towards the London business men is made explicit. Much of the contents are pure slapstick comedy, and the play eschews the double-entendre and smutty talk of such comedies as *Mr. Limberham*. Ravenscroft drew upon both European folklore and scenes from Elizabethan comedy as sources for his amusing *lazzi* in this play. There was a good deal of contemporary commentary about the new mode of full-length farce, and Dryden and Shadwell got into a controversy over farce. Nahum Tate even wrote a serious justification of farce, as a preface to his successful assay, *A Duke and No Duke* (1684). The Lord Chamberlain's records show Charles II in frequent attendance at farces, and we can draw upon the irony implicit in this datum of fact to close this introduction to the development of drama in the time of this monarch.

2. The Drama from 1685 to 1737

English dramatists would never again enjoy as strong a royal patron as the Merry Monarch had been. It is true that his successor, James II, sponsored the drama, but he was out of office in three years, and William and Mary were not devotees of the theatre. Queen Anne would protect the players because of traditional Stuart support of the stage, but she took little interest in it. The Brunswick Georges preferred opera. For whom then would the dramatists write? It was the conjecture of John Harrington Smith that they tried to please "the Ladies," and that this change led to the introduction of sentimental elements (though Smith preferred the term "exemplary comedy" as a more accurate label for such plays). Unfortunately, we cannot be sure about the constituency of this new audience because of the numerous signs that the composition of the audience was changing. The first of these signals was lack of success for new plays for which great expectations had been entertained: Southerne's important comedy, *The Wives Excuse* (1691), failed on the night of its premiere. This mishap was followed by what might be called a general audience revolt at the turn of the century. Beginning in the autumn of 1697, almost all the new plays at both theatres were failures. Some fifteen new plays failed in this season of 1697–98, a disaster previously unheard of in theatre history. This rejection of new plays lasted for about six seasons, reaching a total of about seventy failures. What complicates the matter still more is the great variety in the kinds of dramas which were not being accepted. Congreve's artistic masterpiece, *The Way of the World*, achieved only a few performances, probably a total of six, when people in the theatre world expected a smash hit. In the same month, March 1700, William Burnaby's cynical and satiric comedy of manners, *The Reformed Wife*, also failed and had to be withdrawn. The contemporary play which we might consider at the furthest extreme of difference from these two comedies was Sir Richard Steele's whining, sentimental opus *The Lying Lover* (1703); yet it too was rejected and had to be dropped. A further sign of uncertainty in the audience was the failure of plays which later enjoyed great success. In 1703, Rowe's new tragedy, *The Fair Penitent*, failed, though it was in the new style of having a distressed heroine as the chief character in the play. It was revived in 1715, and went on to become one of the six or eight most popular tragedies of the century. The same pattern held for Colley Cibber's comedy *She Would and She Would*

Not. This play just barely reached a sixth night in November 1702, with such a small audience on the last night that the play was withdrawn. It was attempted again in 1707, when it again failed. Revived in 1714, it went on to become one of the most frequently acted plays on record, both in longevity and in total performances. Cibber's *Richard III* also failed in 1699 when it was first presented, and all students of the drama are generally aware of the tremendous and prolonged success that this adaptation from Shakespeare later enjoyed.

Proof that the composition of the audience was changing and that this pattern of theatrical failures did not arise from the antipathy of theatre-goers against a particular dramatist or type of play can be found in the surprising phenomenon of changing hours for the commencement of theatrical performances. For the convenience of the leisure class, plays throughout the Restoration had begun at four o'clock in the afternoon. The theatre is a relatively conservative institution, and starting times, once established, are rarely changed. However, from 1700 to 1705, the two playhouses began to push the opening time back, albeit irregularly, to four-thirty, then five, and sometimes to as late as six-thirty. From apologies in the newspapers and new advertisements announcing a four-thirty or five o'clock opening, we can infer that veteran theatre-goers had been protesting against the new hours, but subsequent playbills then announce the later hour of five-thirty or six. Such reversals certainly indicate an unstable situation and a changing audience.

I have presented this dreary and melancholy account (which can be studied fully in *The London Stage*) not to give a history of the period but to show the effect upon the dramatists. Let us see what happened. Thomas Southerne stopped writing comedies and wrote tragedies instead. Farquhar joined the army and was absent from the stage for three or four years. Vanbrugh turned his attention to architecture and stopped writing plays. But the most important withdrawal was that of William Congreve. It was Congreve who had revived the drama and whose sparkling comedies, *The Old Batchelor* (1693) and *Love for Love* (1695), had drawn large crowds to the theatre and had gotten the new company at Lincoln's Inn Fields off to a flying start. When *The Way of the World* did not answer expectations, Congreve stopped his playwriting. It would be difficult to exaggerate the severe consequences on English comedy caused by these withdrawals. When Wycherley and Etherege stopped composing plays, other, less able writers kept supplying the theatres with new plays, even if the quality was lowered. The withdrawal of a major dramatist – Congreve – and two excellent practitioners, Southerne and Vanbrugh, left only Farquhar. After his early death in 1707, there were not enough remaining playwrights of real ability, and comedy withered and declined.

After this general account of conditions in the theatre world at the beginning of the eighteenth century, it is time to trace the main directions of tragedy and comedy. The serious drama was now moving definitely in the direction of pathetic tragedy, with Southerne's *The Fatal Marriage* (1694) and Nicholas Rowe's *Jane Shore* (1714) becoming the most successful examples of the numerous attempts in this mode. Close study of the new tragedies, season by season, reveals authorial anxiety over the language of tragedy. Some writers even tried to revive the high-flown diction and rhymed couplets of the heroic play. D'Urfey went so far as to write his ten-act, two part *The Famous History of the Rise and Fall of Massaniello* (1699) in prose, a major break with convention. The full impact of the influence of neoclassic dramatic theory and of Racine came in the 1690's and the early eighteenth century. The results were meagre, as no plays of genuine dramatic tension appeared. The one real stage success was Addison's *Cato,* but its favorable reception came from an ideological basis, not an aesthetic one. The later neoclassic plays became increasingly derivative, with the last prominent example, Aaron Hill's *Zara* (1735), being adapted from Voltaire.

However, just as tragedy seemed at its nadir, a brief revival came in an attempt to restore domestic tragedy. Yet even the six or seven new plays in this style were clumsily written. In spite of this handicap, one of these, George Lillo's *The London Merchant* (1731), suggested the potentiality of this type of play and was indeed influential on German dramatic theory and practice. However, no systematic attempt was made in England to develop what Lillo had begun, and tragedy very nearly became extinct.

In contrast, a strong revival of comedy can be seen in the period now under consideration. A second wave of the comedy of manners was begun by Southerne in 1691 with his brilliant psychological study, *The Wives Excuse.* Two years later, the Irish dramatist William Congreve presented his first success, *The Old Batchelor,* and a new though brief rejuvenation of comic form was under way. Within a few years, Vanbrugh, Burnaby, and Farquhar added their contributions. Historically, the most striking aspect of their work was their originality. Traditional comedy, before and after this group, presented the formula of boy-meets-girl, boy-wins-girl. The comedies of this short period, say 1691 to 1707, deal with marital incompatibility, and in most of the plays either the hero or the heroine or both are already married as the play begins. If the main characters are not married, as with Mirabell and Millamant, we encounter a long proviso scene dealing with the causes of marital discord. A variant approach, found in Lord Lansdowne's comedy *The She Gallants* (1695), is the inclusion of a symposium on the problem of marital disharmony. (The play is so self-conscious that one at first suspects it was funded by the Arts Council.) There is no doubt that the playwrights were fully aware of the novelty of their structure and their break with convention. In the last comedy of this group, *The Beaux Stratagem,* Farquhar several times quotes or paraphrases from Milton's second divorce tract. Oblique evidence of authorial awareness can be found in the comparison of Vanbrugh's plots. In *The Relapse* (1696), the heroine, Amanda, is a sweet, innocent, virtuous woman, beyond the reach of the most passionate appeals of a would-be seducer. Her husband, Careless, is a confirmed woman-chaser. The point of the play is that he is incapable of reform. In *The Provok'd Wife* (1697), the husband, Sir John Brute, is a vulgar scoundrel, a vicious drunkard; his wife despises him and would like to cheat, save that she lacks the intestinal fortitude to commit adultery – virtue or morality are not her concern. In Vanbrugh's incompleted work *A Journey to London* (revised and finished later by Colley Cibber as *The Provoked Husband*), the male lead, Sir Francis Headpiece, is thoroughly honest and decent; his young wife is a huzzy who wants to go to London in the hope of getting sexual experiences. Vanbrugh's plan for ending the play was to have Sir Francis turn this rotten woman out of the house. The plays of this "Marriage Group" certainly deserve more attention.

Farce and burlesque again burgeoned. The most famous burlesque was the completely original ballad opera, *The Beggar's Opera* (1728). In it, John Gay achieves the irony peculiar to the Augustan age, in fact, so much so that some critics have erroneously called Swift the author. Originality also marks the lively experiments of Henry Fielding during his tenure as manager of the little theatre in the Haymarket. In *The Author's Farce* (1730), he attempted non-representational drama. His satire *Pasquin* (1736) enjoyed a sensational run. Fielding introduced footlights, offered two new plays on the same night, abandoned older drama, encouraged experimental work by young authors, employed the greatest care and pains to produce Lillo's tragedy of fate, *Fatal Curiosity* (1736), used actors in the audience, and invented an entirely original kind of dramatic burlesque in *The Tragedy of Tragedies* (1731). This experimental and innovative activity was completely ended by Sir Robert Walpole's interference in the Stage Licensing Act of 1737.

3. The Drama from 1737 to 1800

The drama experienced considerable change in the last half of the eighteenth century, though the differences may be more apparent to us than to audiences of the time. The age was dominated by comedy and comic opera, in spite of a large number of new tragedies. The plays become more thematic than before, and plot becomes increasingly important, leading to complex and involved structures by the end of the century in melodrama. Again, the audiences saw superior acting. Nevertheless, while some roles in new plays were designed for specific actors or actresses, this practice diminished in contrast to that of earlier periods, yielding to skilled ensemble acting. And in spite of some striking individual triumphs, the dramatists lost their previous pre-eminence of creating new dramatic forms, and were affected by foreign influences, notably the Italian comic opera, the French *comédie larmoyante,* and the lurid German melodramas of Kotzebue.

First, however, one should consider the altered conditions in the theatres for which the dramatists wrote. As a consequence of the restriction of legitimate drama in London to two theatres stipulated by the Stage Licensing Act of 1737, a considerable number of veteran players were available to the managers of the two remaining theatrical companies, Drury Lane and Covent Garden. Given a monopoly and a surplus of experienced actors, the managers preferred to drill, rehearse, and perfect their forthcoming productions of older works, especially after David Garrick became manager at Drury Lane, than to give up the proceeds of the third nights of the opening run to authors of new plays. A glance at the daily calendar in *The London Stage* will show how few new five-act plays appeared in the 1740's and 1750's. Meanwhile, partly from the sponsorship and financial backing of the "Ladies Shakespeare Club," a highly popular revival of Shakespeare's plays got under way. David Garrick soon learned that polished presentations of *Richard III, Hamlet, Romeo and Juliet,* and Jonson's *Every Man in His Humour,* alternated with later favorites, such as *The Beaux Stratagem* and *The Provok'd Wife,* would yield enormous financial rewards and avoid not only payments to authors but also disastrous failures at premieres. In this situation, it is not surprising that the best creative writers turned to writing novels, and English drama lost the high status it had maintained since the 1580's.

The players to sustain the roles were certainly available. At first there were Garrick, Spranger Barry, Kitty Clive, Peg Woffington, and Susannah Arne Cibber; later came J. P. Kemble, John Palmer, and Sarah Siddons. Numerous commentators called the cast for the premiere of *The School for Scandal* (1777) the best that had ever been assembled.

In time, new playwrights emerged. Their offerings in tragedy had little merit, but a number of popular comedies appeared, reflecting and refracting the mores of upper-middle-class Georgian society. Some of these comedies retained aspects of satiric analysis associated with Restoration drama, though a capacity for feeling becomes a test of individual value by the end of the play. Nevertheless, in portraying the idiosyncrasies of the individual in society, most of the dramatists – from the talented to the mediocre – were what Stuart Tave has called "amiable humorists." Yet we must not forget that these playwrights were concerned with the problems of the current social world.

In older histories of English literature, these plays are written off as sentimental, with the implication that the audiences must have been naive to accept such simple stuff. This traditional estimate overlooks two important aspects of late eighteenth-century England: the cultural polish of the age and the concern with problem-solving. The reader needs to remember that the new elite which was coming into ascendancy early in the century (and which was the butt of the Tory satirists) was now in its second and third generation. For this new class, the brothers Adam designed and decorated the interiors of the houses, Thomas Chippendale and Thomas Sheraton made their chairs, Josiah Wedgwood their dinner ware, John Baskerville and William Caslin created the type for the books they read, and Joshua Reynolds, George Romney, Henry Raeburn, and Thomas Gainsborough painted their portraits. If these artifacts indicate a measure of elegance, why should the recipients lose their sophistication when they attended the theatre? Were not the plays an integral part of Georgian culture?

To illustrate the study of society in the drama of the period, I want to examine one play, Charles Macklin's highly popular comedy *The Man of the World* (1764). The author presents a nouveau riche Scot, Sir Pertinax Macsycophant, a recently created knight, firmly on the road to success. His grand plan is to marry his son, Egerton, into a noble family and obtain an estate. (Macsycophant had legally changed his son's name to get a small inheritance and to conceal his Scottish origin.) An heiress, Lady Rodolpha, is found, the daughter of land-poor Lord Lumbercourt, whose control over rotten boroughs provides him with two representatives in Parliament. Macsycophant supplies the money and enriches the noble lord, but Lumbercourt's lawyer delays the transaction, When the Scot discovers that this attorney wants to become an M.P., he quickly promises him the seat, with the result that the lawyers on both sides are working for the Scot. Meanwhile, Macsycophant sends his son out to attend levees of influential noblemen and expand his connections by flattering his way into their good graces. Egerton, just arrived from his course of studies at Oxford, refuses, whereupon the father denounces the Oxford tutor, Sidney, as "subversive." The irony here is delicious: Macsycophant had arranged for the best education for his son that money could buy, and Sidney had been dutifully transmitting to Egerton the newest ideas of the time – the revolutionary principles of the French Enlightenment, including the doctrine of the equality of mankind – and consequently really was subversive. In plotting this situation, Macklin was hardly less satiric than John Wilkes in his essays in the *North-Briton* on the Scottish invasion in the time of Lord Bute. George III was drawing upon the full powers of government to imprison and punish Wilkes, while the Lord Chamberlain refused for seventeen years to license *The Man of the World* for a stage performance.

Also, as I have indicated, there was a shift in the focus of interest in the ideas of the time, so that people were concerned with solving problems rather than raising them. In the seventeenth century, speaking broadly, one can say that the prime interest was in raising difficult questions. The authors of the heroic play showed the prince in agonized distress over the conflict between his private and personal interests and his duties as the ruler of a kingdom. The comic dramatists showed an irreconcilable clash between man's natural desires and the artificial conventions of the society in which he lived. In *The Country-Wife,* Lady Fidget wants to go to bed with any available man, but as the wife of a prominent London businessman, she has social constraints upon her behaviour. The consequences of truth-telling make up the contents of *The Plain-Dealer,* and the possible disadvantages arising from a liberal education afford matter for Shadwell's *The Squire of Alsatia* (1688). Southerne shows the impasse when a virtuous woman is married to a cowardly and inveterate woman-chaser, in *The Wives Excuse.* From these and other Restoration plays, we can observe that the playwrights were fond of dealing with discordant aspects of society. In the eighteenth century, however, the major thrust of the Enlightenment was towards the reform and solution of social ills, and the intellectuals wanted to see problems solved. In Richard Cumberland's *The West Indian* (1771), often called the prototype or model for late eighteenth-century comedy, the protagonist, Belcour, opens the play as a rake and a confirmed girl-chaser. After a number of adventures, Belcour is shown that he can become a useful member of society. In the penultimate speech of the play, Stockwell gives his verdict: "Yes, Belcour, I have watched you with a patient, but enquiring eye, and I have discovered through the veil of some irregularities, a heart beaming with benevolence, an animated nature, fallible indeed, but not incorrigible; and your election of this excellent young lady makes me glory in acknowledging you to be my son." There is no denial of the presence of evil: *Each One Has His Fault* (1792) Mrs. Inchbald announces as the title of her play; but intelligent and reasonable people can learn through experience.

Looking at the entire period, we can distinguish five relatively distinct varieties or types of drama: genteel comedy, humanitarian drama, musical comedy, farce, and tragedy. The works in the first category are those which deal with upper-middle-class society, from which they derive the nomenclature of "genteel." This was the term by which they were known at the time and it is a more accurate and hence more useful designation than the label of "sentimental comedy." The comic dramatists of this era were not trying to imitate *The Man of Mode,* nor should each of their works be measured against *The Way of the World* in order to assign a school grade, but should rather be studied in the context of literature and society of the Georgian period. Some, like Cumberland's *The West Indian,* place more stress on "feeling" and susceptibility to emotion than, say, Macklin's *The Man of the World.* The best known are the sparkling comedies of Sheridan (*The Rivals,* 1775, and *The School for Scandal*) and Goldsmith (*She Stoops to Conquer,* 1773), delightful plays which have held the stage since their premiere. A number of authors contributed at least one successful comedy of this sort. The earliest was Benjamin Hoadley's *The Suspicious Husband,* which opened at Drury Lane in 1747 and which was described at that time as the first good, full-length comedy in many years. The elder Colman's popular work, *The Clandestine Marriage* (1766), in which he was assisted by Garrick is an excellent example of genteel comedy, with its satire on social climbers and ridicule of fads in landscape gardening. Equally popular was *The Way to Keep Him* (1760), one of several comic treatments of marital incompatibility with which Arthur Murphy regaled theatre-goers. In addition to its long record of stage performances, this play was drawn upon for private theatricals possible more than any other drama of the time. Hugh Kelly's *False Delicacy* (1768), containing the criticism indicated by its title, was another lively, problem-solving comedy which enjoyed great popularity. A final example is Frederick Reynolds's *The Dramatist* (1789), in which the playwright Vapid upsets the villain's machinations by leaping up from concealment in a closet to spout the needed hemistich to a line in an epilogue on which he had been straining his wits all day. All of these plays have been revived in modern times, and all contain considerable merit.

One entirely new species emerged toward the end of the century. It is known as "humanitarian drama," and the reasons for its failure as dramatic art are instructive. The chief practitioners were Thomas Holcroft, Richard Cumberland, and Elizabeth Inchbald. They were devoted to those basic principles of the European Enlightenment which Sir Pertinax Macsychophant had denounced as subversive. These playwrights were particularly interested in propagating the doctrines of the equality of mankind and the brotherhood of man. In the prologue to his chief stage success, *The Road to Ruin* (1792), Holcroft states that he is "Telling us that Frenchman, and Polishman, and every man is our brothers:/And that all men, ay, even poor Negro men, have a right to be free, one as well as another!" Cumberland even composed a play called *The Jew* (1794) for the explicit purpose of illustrating the concept of the brotherhood of man. In *Such Things Are* (1787), Mrs. Inchbald presented the prison reformer John Howard as a character in the play. In *Love's Frailties* (1794), Holcroft has one character say, "I WAS BRED TO THE MOST USELESS, AND OFTEN THE MOST WORTHLESS, OF ALL PROFESSIONS: THAT OF A GENTLEMAN." (Allardyce Nicoll points out that Holcroft had these words printed in capital letters.) Strong language indeed, yet there is not a play among this group of "humanitarian" dramas which has literary or dramatic merit. A look at some of these plays will show what went wrong. In *The Road to Ruin*, whose prologue insisted that every man is our brother, the villain, Silky, is a Jew. In *Duplicity* (1781), to the second edition of which Holcroft inserted a preface saying that he "would rather have the merit of driving one man from the gambling table, than of making a whole theatre merry," a person named Osborne manipulates Harry's finances to prevent him from being ruined by the Jews, and people from Somersetshire are presented as boobies. In *The Deserted Daughter* (1795), Holcroft offers a stereotyped comic butt in the Scot Donald. The melodramatic structure of Cumberland's *The Fashionable Lover* (1772) requires a villain, and the author provides a Scot for this purpose, along with a comic Jew, Naphtali. Mrs. Inchbald's plays are, as Allardyce Nicoll says, crammed with impossibilities, amazing discoveries, and heavy use of the "obscure birth" device as a plot solution. She also leans heavily upon stock characters. It is not a matter of lack of talent, for her plays include a number of valid and realistic touches. The trouble is that these playwrights were trying to put new wine into old bottles, unable to escape from the dominant theatrical conventions of the stock character – the stereotype. As a consequence, these plays do not generate dramatic conflict, and the use of stereotyped characters makes the message ludicrous.

It was the thesis of Bonamy Dobrée that high, satiric comedy emerged when a country had a highly cultured and stable society maintained over a considerable period of time, such as France in the age of Louis XIV. To a certain extent, conditions in late eighteenth-century London fit this formula, and hence the question may be asked why comedy did not develop beyond *The School for Scandal* and *The Clandestine Marriage*. The answer may seem facetious but it can be supported by stage history: high comedy lost out in competition with musical comedy. In the 1740's and 1750's, ballad opera had flourished, but these musical pieces were usually presented as the afterpiece to some longer work in the double-feature structure of London theatre programmes. Also, a few Italian comic operas had appeared from time to time. But this general situation was to change with the advent of Bickerstaff and

Dibdin. Peter Tasch shows, in his book on Isaac Bickerstaff, some amazing statistics abstracted from *The London Stage* to demonstrate the change. In 1755, the Covent Garden theatre was open on 184 nights. Tragedies and Shakespeare's history plays occupied 84 of these, comedy 85, and a musical production, either opera or oratorio, took up the remaining 15 performances. Ten years later, Covent Garden opened its doors for 189 performances, of which 81 were of musical comedies. The leader of this innovation was Isaac Bickerstaff, who found not only that English lyrics could be wed to music after the Italian manner but also the person who could perform the operation, the composer Charles Dibdin. Bickerstaff's first full-length musical comedy, *Love in a Village* (1762), was done with Thomas Arne, but Dibdin went on to compose or arrange the music for eight pieces by Bickerstaff, and to compose many more alone after Bickerstaff left the country. It will be noted that most of Dibdin's comic operas were based on French plays. General John Burgoyne supplied two more musical comedies, and showed full awareness that he was developing a new sub-genre by writing a defence of comic opera as a preface to his popular opus *The Lord of the Manor* (1780). The most popular of all of the many musical comedies was Sheridan's *The Duenna* (1775), a lively piece which achieved a run of seventy-five performances, the longest yet known on the London stage. Its success led to a nearly complete domination of musical comedy. The chief practitioner in the closing years of the century was John O'Keeffe, who composed about twenty comic operas, apart from his genuine comedy *Wild Oats.*

The particular satiric sting which we associate with Restoration comedy had gradually disappeared from the majority of five-act plays, as we have seen, but sharp ridicule reappeared in an odd metamorphosis in the last half of the eighteenth century in the farces used as afterpieces in the double- and even triple-feature offerings of the London playhouses. Satire, invective, and mimicry all appear in the irregular pieces composed by Samuel Foote in his thirty-year residency at the Little Theatre in the Haymarket. Most of these plays or playlets were closely topical and directed at specific individuals, such as the attack on the Methodist evangelist George Whitefield in *The Minor* (1760). However, Foote achieved one artistic success in the mode of the great Augustan satirists – parodic satire – when he produced his farce *Piety in Pattens* (also known as *The Primitive Puppet-Shew*) in 1773. In it, as Samuel Bogorad writes in his recent edition of this farce, "Foote reduced to absurdity the sentimental vogue by portraying in Polly a housemaid who attempts to display the palpitatingly tender emotions of her betters." Richardson's *Pamela,* sentimental comedies, the new musical comedies, and the language of contemporary drama are all devastated in the opening lines of the piece: "In what a perilous State is a poor Maiden like me, beset every where, & no Friend to advise with. The Squire on one side, & the Butler on the other, no sooner as Mrs. Candy our Housekeeper says, have I escap'd the Silly of the Master, but I fall plump into the Cribbige of the Man." Successful as *Piety in Pattens* was on the stage, together with a tremendous amount of newspaper publicity, Foote never published his masterpiece. Two manuscripts, however, have been found in modern times, at the Folger and the Huntington libraries, and the farce has now been printed. Those who read it will realize that some textbook generalisations about the period will have to be altered.

In the 1760's, satiric farces flourished, led by Arthur Murphy, who exploited the comic possibilities of *l'idée fixe* in *The Apprentice* (1756) and *The Upholsterer* (1758) and skillfully built a harsh verbal duel from a dispute over a card game by a newly married couple in *Three Weeks after Marriage* (1764). The elder Colman contributed one lively piece in *Polly Honeycombe* (1760), and the actor Charles Macklin another in *Love A-la-Mode* (1759), with various other authors supplying satiric afterpieces until the end of the century. The last farce of the period to be a smash hit at the box office was Prince Hoare's *No Song, No Supper,* the music by Storace. The material in this musical farce came entirely from folklore, a sign of changing times.

The weakest drama of the period is found in the tragedies. The Augustan age did not lack a concept of tragedy, but an author who wished to present it would, for example, write it in prose in several volumes and call it *The Decline and Fall of the Roman Empire.* Not only were the playwrights unable to formulate a genuine tragedy but audiences preferred softened versions of Shakespeare's tragedies, such as Nahum Tate's emasculation of *King Lear*. Furthermore, the new serious plays which appeared were so completely under the domination of either French Classical tragedy or the new romantic stuff of Kotzebue and Schiller's *Die Rauber* that they merit only brief discussion. The most discussed new tragedy was John Home's *Douglas* (1756), looked on today as a most tedious play. Edward Moore made a feeble attempt to continue domestic tragedy in *The Gamester* (1753). The newer romantic mode is shown in Robert Jephson's *Braganza*. Actually, there was little room on the stage for tragedy, as the various forms or genres of drama at the end of the century tended to coalesce or merge, combining catastrophe, song, dance, comic stereotypes, and spectacle into the amorphous conglomeration called melodrama.

READING LIST

1. Bibliographies, handbooks, etc.
Summers, Montague, *A Bibliography of the Restoration Drama*, 1934.
Harbage, Alfred B., *Annals of English Drama 975–1700*, 1940; revised edition, edited by Samuel Schoenbaum, 1964.
Woodward, Gertrude L., and James G. McManaway, *A Check-list of English Plays 1641–1700*, 1945.
Scouten, Arthur H., and others, editors, *The London Stage 1660–1800 · A Calendar of Plays, Entertainments, and Afterpieces*, 11 vols., 1960–68.
Stratman, Carl J., *Bibliography of English Printed Tragedy 1565–1900*, 1966.
Arnott, J. F., and J. W. Robinson, *English Theatrical Literature 1559–1900*, 1970.
Stratman, Carl J., D. G. Spencer, and M. E. Devine, editors, *Restoration and Eighteenth-Century Theatre Research · A Bibliographical Guide 1900–1968*, 1971.

2. General histories
Genest, John, *Some Account of the English Stage, from the Restoration to 1830*, 10 vols., 1832.
Ward, A. W., *A History of English Dramatic Literature to the Death of Queen Anne*, 3 vols., 1899.
Nettleton, G. H., *English Drama of the Restoration and Eighteenth Century*, 1914.
Nicoll, Allardyce, *A History of the Restoration Drama 1660–1700*, 1923; *A History of Early Eighteenth-Century Drama 1700–1750*, 1923; *A History of Late Eighteenth-Century Drama 1750–1800*, 1927; revised edition, 3 vols., 1952.
Dobrée, Bonamy, *Restoration Comedy*, 1924; *Restoration Tragedy*, 1929.
Bateson, F. W., *English Comic Drama 1700–1750*, 1929.
Craik, T. W., general editor, *The Revels History of Drama in English: Volume V: 1660–1750*, by John Loftis, Richard Southern, Marion Jones, and Arthur H. Scouten, 1976; *Volume VI: 1750–1880*, by M. R. Booth, Richard Southern, F. and L. Marker, and Robertson Davies, 1975.
Hume, Robert, D., *The Development of English Drama in the Late Seventeenth Century*, 1976.

3. Topics, themes, short periods, etc.

Palmer, J., *The Comedy of Manners*, 1913.

Bernbaum, E., *The Drama of Sensibility 1696–1780*, 1915.

Krutch, Joseph Wood, *Comedy and Conscience after the Restoration*, 1924; revised edition, 1949.

Lynch, Kathleen, *The Social Mode of Restoration Comedy*, 1926.

Hotson, Leslie, *The Commonwealth and Restoration Stage*, 1928.

Green, C. C., *The Neo-Classic Theory of Tragedy in England During the Eighteenth Century*, 1934.

Nolte, Fred O., *The Early Middle-Class Drama 1696–1774*, 1935.

Green, F. C., *Minuet*, 1935.

Summers, Montague, *The Playhouse of Pepys*, 1935.

Prior, M. E., *The Language of Tragedy*, 1947.

Wilson, J. H., *The Restoration Court Wits*, 1948.

Smith, J. H., *The Gay Couple in Restoration Comedy*, 1948.

Fujimura, T. H., *The Restoration Comedy of Wit*, 1952.

Kronenberger, Louis, *The Thread of Laughter*, 1952.

Hughes, Leo, *A Century of English Farce*, 1956.

Sherbo, Arthur, *English Sentimental Drama*, 1957.

Holland, Norman N., *The First Modern Comedies · The Significance of Etherege, Wycherley, and Congreve*, 1959.

Loftis, John, *Comedy and Society from Congreve to Fielding*, 1959.

Waith, Eugene M., *The Herculean Hero*, 1962.

Knight, G. Wilson, *The Golden Labyrinth · A Study of English Drama*, 1962.

Singh, S., *The Theory of Drama in the Restoration Period*, 1963.

Brown, John Russell, and B. Harris, editors, *Restoration Theatre*, 1965.

Loftis, John, editor, *Restoration Drama: Modern Essays in Criticism*, 1966.

Miner, Earl, editor, *Restoration Dramatists: A Collection of Critical Essays*, 1966.

Rothstein, E., *Restoration Tragedy: Form and Process and Change*, 1967.

Muir, Kenneth, *The Comedy of Manners*, 1970.

Birdsall, V. O., *Wild Civility: The English Comic Spirit on the Restoration Stage*, 1970.

Loftis, John, *The Spanish Plays of Neoclassical England*, 1973.

4. Anthologies of primary works

Bell's British Theatre, 21 vols., 1776–81; supplement, 4 vols., 1785.

Inchbald, Mrs., editor, *British Theatre*, 25 vols., 1808; supplement, 7 vols., 1809.

Spingarn, J. E., editor, *Critical Essays of the Seventeenth Century*, 3 vols., 1908–09.

Summers, Montague, editor, *Restoration Comedies*, 1922.

Stevens, D. H., editor, *Types of English Drama*, 1923.

MacMillan, Dougald, and Howard Mumford Jones, editors, *Plays of the Restoration and 18th Century*, 1931.

Elson, J. J., editor, *The Wits* (interregnum drolls), 1932.

Nettleton, G. H., and Arthur E. Case, editors, *British Dramatists from Dryden to Sheridan*, 1939; revised edition, edited by G. W. Stone, 1975.

Hughes, Leo, and Arthur H. Scouten, editors, *Ten English Farces*, 1948.

Wilson, J. H., editor, *Six Restoration Plays*, 1959.

Spencer, Christopher, editor, *Five Restoration Adaptations of Shakespeare*, 1965.

Trussler, Simon, editor, *Burlesque Plays of the Eighteenth Century*, 1969.

Bevis, R. W., editor, *Eighteenth-Century Drama · Afterpieces*, 1970.

Rubsamen, W. H., editor, *The Ballad Opera*, 28 vols., 1974.

Sutherland, James, editor, *Restoration Tragedies*, 1977.

BANKS, John.   English.   Very little is known about his life: flourished 1677–96. Studied law; a member of the society of the New Inn.

PUBLICATIONS

Plays

> *The Rival Kings; or, The Loves of Oroondates and Statira* (produced 1677).   1677.
> *The Destruction of Troy* (produced 1678).   1679.
> *The Unhappy Favourite; or, The Earl of Essex* (produced 1681).   1682; edited by James
>   Sutherland, in *Restoration Tragedies*, 1976.
> *Virtue Betrayed; or, Anna Bullen* (produced 1682).   1682.
> *The Island Queens; or, The Death of Mary, Queen of Scotland.*   1684; revised version,
>   as *The Albion Queens* (produced 1704), 1704.
> *The Innocent Usurper; or, The Death of the Lady Jane Gray.*   1694.
> *Cyrus the Great; or, The Tragedy of Love* (produced 1695).   1696.

Reading List: Introduction by Thomas M. H. Blair to *The Unhappy Favourite*, 1939; *Banks: Eine Studie* by Hans Hochuli, 1952.

*   *   *

John Banks is certainly one of the weakest playwrights in the long history of English drama and he was not even considered a poet by his later contemporaries. Yet he was responsible for a major change in tragedy and he was an innovator in turning to recent English history as subject matter for his most popular plays. In making a woman the central character, he brought about a sweeping change in the nature of English tragedy. The prevailing pattern of earlier drama showed the fall of a strong hero – Faustus, Richard III, Bussy d'Ambois, Lear, Coriolanus; the current mode of the heroic play had its Almanzors and Montezumas; Banks offered, instead, a heroine in distress. In fact, in two of his most popular plays both the heroine and the villain are women. Critics sneered and termed his plays "she-tragedies," but the dramatists fell in line – Otway, Southerne, Congreve, and especially Nicholas Rowe – to follow this major shift in tragic structure.

A basic characteristic of the contemporary heroic drama was its distant setting, and the action was often set at a remote time. Banks showed considerable initiative in choosing his material for historical events in the lifetime of Queen Elizabeth I. Deficient as he was in attempting verse, he had no difficulty in recognizing tragic episodes from history: the plight of Anne Boleyn, the ordeal of decision by Queen Elizabeth on the Earl of Essex and Mary, Queen of Scots. Some of these events were scarcely a century old, it will be recalled. This fact, together with the native setting, probably created a strong sense of realism for Restoration audiences, and provided a striking contrast to the purposeful artificiality of the heroic drama. The subject matter of "real" versus "usurping" rulers and the deposition and execution of queens led of course to many of the plays being banned from the stage.

—Arthur H. Scouten

BEHN, Aphra (Johnson). English. Born, probably in Harbledown, Kent, baptized 14 December 1640. Probably married a Mr. Behn c. 1664 (died before 1666). Lived in Surinam, Dutch Guiana, c. 1663–64; employed by the English as a spy in Antwerp in 1666; imprisoned for debt in late 1660's; professional writer. *Died 16 April 1689.*

PUBLICATIONS

Collections

> *Works,* edited by Montague Summers. 6 vols., 1915.
> *Selected Writings,* edited by Robert Phelps. 1950.

Plays

> *The Forced Marriage; or, The Jealous Bridegroom* (produced 1670). 1671.
> *The Amorous Prince; or, The Curious Husband* (produced 1671). 1671.
> *The Dutch Lover* (produced 1673). 1673.
> *Abdelazar; or, The Moor's Revenge,* from the play *Lust's Dominion* (produced 1676). 1677.
> *The Town Fop; or, Sir Timothy Tawdrey* (produced 1676). 1677.
> *The Debauchee; or, The Credulous Cuckold,* from the play *A Mad Couple Well Matched* by Richard Brome (produced 1677). 1677.
> *The Rover; or, The Banished Cavaliers* (produced 1677). 1677; edited by Frederick M. Link, 1967.
> *Sir Patient Fancy* (produced 1678). 1678.
> *The Feigned Courtesans; or, A Night's Intrigue* (produced 1679). 1679.
> *The Young King; or, The Mistake* (produced 1679). 1683.
> *The Revenge; or, A Match in Newgate,* from the play *The Dutch Courtesan* by Marston (produced 1680). 1680.
> *The Second Part of The Rover* (produced 1681). 1681.
> *The Roundheads; or, The Good Old Cause,* from the play *The Rump* by John Tatham (produced 1681). 1682.
> *The False Count; or, A New Way to Play an Old Game* (produced 1681). 1682.
> *The City Heiress; or, Sir Timothy Treat-All,* from the play *A Mad World, My Masters* by Middleton (produced 1682). 1682.
> *The Lucky Chance; or, An Alderman's Bargain* (produced 1686). 1687; edited by A. Norman Jeffares, in *Restoration Comedy,* 1974.
> *The Emperor of the Moon* (produced 1687). 1687; edited by Leo Hughes and Arthur H. Scouten, in *Ten English Farces,* 1948.
> *The Widow Ranter; or, The History of Bacon in Virginia* (produced 1689). 1690.
> *The Younger Brother; or, The Amorous Jilt* (produced 1696). 1696.

Fiction

> *Love Letters Between A Nobleman and His Sister.* 3 vols., 1683–87.
> *The Fair Jilt; or, The History of Prince Tarquin and Miranda.* 1688.
> *Oroonoko; or, The Royal Slave.* 1688.
> *The History of the Nun; or, The Fair Vow-Breaker.* 1689.
> *The Lucky Mistake.* 1689.

Histories and Novels.   1696; revised edition, 1697, 1700.

Verse

Poems upon Several Occasions, with a Voyage to the Island of Love.   1684.
A Pindaric on the Death of Our Late Sovereign.   1685.
A Pindaric Poem on the Happy Coronation of His Sacred Majesty James II and His Illustrious Consort Queen Mary.   1685.
A Poem to Catherine, Queen Dowager.   1685.
To Christopher, Duke of Albemarle, on His Voyage to Jamaica: A Pindaric.   1687.
To the Memory of George, Duke of Buckingham.   1687.
A Poem to Sir Roger L'Estrange.   1688.
A Congratulatory Poem to Her Majesty.   1688.
A Congratulatory Poem to the King's Most Sacred Majesty.   1688.
To Poet Bavius.   1688.
Lycidus; or, The Lover in Fashion, Together with a Miscellany of New Poems by Several Hands, with others.   1688.
A Congratulatory Poem to Her Sacred Majesty Queen Mary, upon Her Arrival in England.   1689.
A Pindaric Poem to the Rev. Dr. [Thomas] Burnet.   1689.

Other

Editor, *Convent Garden Drollery.*   1672; edited by G. Thorn-Drury, 1928.
Editor, *Miscellany, Being a Collection of Poems by Several Hands* (includes Behn's translation of La Rochefoucauld).   1685.

Translator, *La Montre; or, The Lover's Watch,* by Balthasar de Bonnecorse.   1686.
Translator, *The Fatal Beauty of Agnes de Castro,* by J. B. de Brillac.   1688.
Translator, *A Discovery of New Worlds,* by Fontennelle.   1688; as *The Theory of New Worlds,* 1700.
Translator, *The History of Oracles, and the Cheats of the Pagan Priests,* by Fontennelle.   1688.
Translator, with others, *Cowley's Six Books of Plants.*   1689.

Reading List: *Behn* by V. Sackville-West, 1927; *The Incomparable Aphra* by George Woodcock, 1948; *New Light on Behn* by W. J. Cameron, 1961; *Behn* by Frederick M. Link, 1968 (includes bibliography); *The Passionate Shepherdess: Behn* by Maureen Duffy, 1977.

*   *   *

Aphra Behn began her literary career as a dramatist. Her early plays are undistinguished imitations of the romantic tragi-comedy deriving from Beaumont and Fletcher; *Abdelazar*, for instance, is a successful but conventional tragedy of blood and lust. Her first good play is *The Town Fop*, a racy London comedy combining complex intrigue, farce, and expert dialogue. This formula, often augmented by a pair of witty lovers, she repeats in later plays like *The Rover, Sir Patient Fancy, The Feigned Courtesans, The Second Part of The Rover,* and *The Lucky Chance. The False Count* is a romantic farce in the traditional manner; *The Emperor of the Moon* a fine farce in the new *commedia dell' arte* style. *The Roundheads* is clumsy Tory propaganda, but Behn's other political play, *The City Heiress*, is coherent and witty enough to rank with her best work. Two plays were produced posthumously; three others are usually attributed to her, *The Revenge* with near certainty.

Behn's comedies are action-focused. At their best, they show sure craft, an accurate ear for speech rhythms, considerable wit, and mastery of stagecraft. Most of them borrow from earlier European or English sources; a play wholly original, like *The Feigned Courtesans*, is unusual. Some works, like *The Lucky Chance*, make minor use of sources. Others, like *Sir Patient Fancy*, *The City Heiress*, and *The Emperor of the Moon*, borrow both plot suggestions and the outline of characters. *The Town Fop* and *The Rover* are among Behn's adaptations of earlier plays which are in every case better than the originals. What she borrows she makes her own; plot ideas may come from Killigrew or Molière, but dialogue, pace, organization, most detail, and stagecraft are nearly always original. Her themes sometimes go beyond the conventional, especially in her emphasis on mature relationships between the sexes and on the evils of marriages made for money instead of love, and many of her characters (Hellena in *The Rover*, for example) have a vitality that transcends the stereotypes of the period.

Behn's poetry is occasional. The elegies and panegyrics are inconsequential and often clumsy; the prologues, epilogues, and songs for the plays are generally successful and often excellent. Several forgettable translations of French and Latin works belong to her later years when she was desperate for money; even so, her version of La Rochefoucauld is better than one might expect. Her short fiction has been overrated. *The Fair Jilt*, a study of the *femme fatale*, and *The Wandering Beauty*, a pastoral fairy tale, are worth reading, but *Oroonoko*, which contrasts the nobility of a savage with the baseness of supposedly civilized Englishmen in Surinam, is the only piece comparable to her best comedies. The majority of these were stage successes; indeed, *The Rover* and *The Emperor of the Moon* survived nearly a century. Taken together, they rank Aphra Behn with Dryden, Etherege, Wycherley, and Shadwell among the comic dramatists of her day – no mean achievement for the first Englishwoman to make her living by her pen.

—Frederick M. Link

BICKERSTAFF, Isaac.   Irish.   Born in Dublin, 26 September 1733. Soldier: Page to Lord Chesterfield, Lord Lieutenant of Ireland, 1745; commissioned Ensign in the Fifth Regiment of Foot, 1745, and 2nd Lieutenant, 1746 until he resigned, 1755; 2nd Lieutenant, 91st Company, Plymouth Marine Corps, 1758–63. Wrote for the stage, 1756–71; fled England to avoid arrest as a homosexual, 1772, and spent the remainder of his life in exile abroad. *Died c. 1808*.

PUBLICATIONS

Plays

>   *Thomas and Sally; or, The Sailor's Return*, music by Thomas Arne (produced 1760).   1761; revised edition, 1780.
>   *Judith* (oratorio), music by Thomas Arne (produced 1761).   1761.
>   *Love in a Village*, music by Thomas Arne and others (produced 1762).   1763.
>   *The Maid of the Mill*, music by Samuel Arnold and others (produced 1765).   1765.

Daphne and Amintor, from a work by Saint-Foix (produced 1765).   1765.
The Plain Dealer, from the play by Wycherley (produced 1765).   1766.
Love in the City, music by Charles Dibdin and others (produced 1767).   1767;
    shortened version, as *The Romp* (produced 1774), 1786.
Lionel and Clarissa, music by Charles Dibdin (produced 1768).   1768; revised version,
    as *The School for Fathers* (produced 1770), 1770.
The Absent Man (produced 1768).   1768.
The Padlock, music by Charles Dibdin (produced 1768).   1768.
The Royal Garland, music by Samuel Arnold (produced 1768).   1768.
Queen Mab (cantata), music by Charles Dibdin (produced 1768).   1768.
The Hypocrite, from the play *The Non-Juror* by Cibber (produced 1768).   1769.
Doctor Last in His Chariot, from a play by Molière (produced 1769).   1769.
The Captive, music by Charles Dibdin, from the play *Don Sebastian* by Dryden
    (produced 1769).   1769.
The Ephesian Matron; or, The Widow's Tears, music by Charles Dibdin (produced
    1769).   1769.
Tis Well It's No Worse, from a play by Calderón (produced 1770).   1770.
The Recruiting Serjeant, music by Charles Dibdin (produced 1770).   1770.
He Would If He Could; or, An Old Fool Worse Than Any, music by Charles Dibdin, from
    a play by G. A. Federico (as *The Maid the Mistress*, produced 1770; as *He Would If He
    Could*, produced 1771).   1771.
The Sultan; or, A Peep into the Seraglio, from a play by C. S. Favart, music by Charles
    Dibdin and others (produced 1775).   1780.

Fiction

The Life and Adventures of Ambrose Gwinnet.   1768.

Verse

Leucothoë: A Dramatic Poem.   1756.

Reading List: *The Dramatic Cobbler: The Life and Works of Bickerstaff* by Peter A. Tasch,
1971; *English Theatre Music in the Eighteenth Century* by Roger Fiske, 1973.

*   *   *

Between 1760 and 1772, Isaac Bickerstaff was the dramatist primarily responsible for
originating English comic opera and making it fashionably popular. His plots were not new –
he adapted and borrowed from English and French plays more than he ever acknowledged –
but he paired music, much of it by continental composers, and only some of it commissioned
for his operas, with often witty and always singable lyrics.
    Love in a Village is by critical assent the first English comic opera and the most popular in
the eighteenth century. Thomas Arne composed the music specifically for five of the forty-
two songs and used thirteen of his earlier melodies. Bickerstaff borrowed from Wycherley's
The Gentleman's Dancing Master and plundered Charles Johnson's *The Village Opera*.
Despite harsh criticism of his plagiarism, the comic opera was an overwhelming success (37
performances at Covent Garden during its first season). Bickerstaff repeated his success with
The Maid of the Mill in which Charles Dibdin, who became his composer two years later,
played the comic role of Ralph.
    As successful as Bickerstaff and Dibdin were to be, their first superb effort, *Love in the City*,

failed because its satire was too apposite for the London audience. Profiting from their mistake, they returned to pastoral plots for their next comic opera, *Lionel and Clarissa*. In the four comic operas which Bickerstaff wrote during the 1760's for Covent Garden, he developed the form of musical comedy which lasted until the time of Gilbert and Sullivan a hundred years later.

Unable to compete with Covent Garden, Garrick hired Bickerstaff and Dibdin, but their only full-length opera for Drury Lane was their revised *Lionel and Clarissa, School for Fathers*. However, Bickerstaff did write the musical farce, *The Padlock*, with Dibdin's music; and Dibdin played the comic servant Mungo in blackface – the first such occurrence on the London stage. Bickerstaff also adapted comedies like Wycherley's *The Plain Dealer* for Garrick. Although his most popular comedy, *The Hypocrite*, was based on Cibber's *Non-Juror*, Bickerstaff's character Maw-worm was original and kept the play alive well into the nineteenth century.

Bickerstaff's and Dibdin's most interesting musical works were two serenatas for Ranelagh House: *The Ephesian Matron* and *The Recruiting Serjeant*. These short Italianate light operas (similar in style to *La Serva Padrona*) might have led the two men to new musical dramatic forms, but in 1772 Bickerstaff's career ended when he fled to France to avoid arrest as a homosexual. Despite his short career, Bickerstaff is important to English drama because to it he contributed comic opera.

—Peter A. Tasch

BOYLE, Roger; Baron Broghill; 1st Earl of Orrery.   Irish.   Born in Lismore, 25 April 1621. Educated at Trinity College, Dublin; may have studied at Oxford University. Married Lady Margaret Howard in 1641; two sons and five daughters. Travelled in France and Italy for several years after leaving university, then went to England, and commanded the Earl of Northumberland's troops in the Scottish expedition; returned home to Ireland at the time of the rebellion, 1641: under the Earl of Cork took part in the defence of Lismore, and held a command at the battle of Liscarrol, 1642; served under the parliamentarians, 1647–48, but continued to support the Royalist, and later the Restoration, cause, until offered a general's command by Cromwell in the war against the Irish, 1650; after the defeat of the Irish appointed Governor of Munster, and given control of various estates in Ireland, including Blarney Castle; served the Commonwealth government as Member of Parliament for Cork, 1654, and for Edinburgh, 1656, as Lord President of the Council, 1656, as a Member of the House of Lords, 1657, and as one of Cromwell's special council; after death of Cromwell concluded that Richard Cromwell's attempts to consolidate the government were hopeless: obtained command of Munster, and with Sir Charles Coote, secured Ireland for Charles II; served as Lord President of Munster until 1668; appointed a Lord Justice of Ireland, 1660; Member of Parliament for Arundel, 1661; impeached by the House of Commons for taxing without the king's authority, 1668, which proceedings were stopped by the King's proroguing Parliament. Created Baron Broghill, 1627; Earl of Orrery, 1660. *Died 16 October 1679.*

PUBLICATIONS

Collections

Dramatic Works, edited by William S. Clark, II.   2 vols., 1937.

Plays

> The General (as Altamire, produced 1662; as The General, produced 1664). Edited by
>   J. O. Halliwell, 1853.
> Henry the Fifth (produced 1664). With Mustapha, 1668.
> Mustapha, Son of Solyman the Magnificent (produced 1665). With Henry the Fifth,
>   1668; edited by Bonamy Dobrée, in Five Heroic Plays, 1960.
> The Black Prince (produced 1667). In Two New Tragedies, 1669.
> Tryphon (produced 1668). In Two New Tragedies, 1669.
> Guzman (produced 1669). 1693.
> Mr. Anthony (produced 1669). 1690.
> Herod the Great, in Six Plays. 1694.
> King Saul. 1703.
> Zoroastres, in Dramatic Works. 1937.

Fiction

> Parthenissa. 6 vols., 1654–69.
> English Adventures. 1676.
> The Martyrdom of Theodora and Didymus. 1687.

Verse

> Poems on Most of the Festivals of the Church. 1681.

Other

> A Treatise of the Art of War. 1677.
> A Collection of the State Letters. 1742.

Reading List: "An Unheroic Dramatist" by Graham Greene, in The Lost Childhood and
Other Essays, 1951; Boyle by Kathleen M. Lynch, 1965.

*   *   *

Despite the opinion of Graham Greene – "Roger Boyle ... is one of the great bores of
literature" – the First Earl of Orrery remains a fascinating representative of Cavalier culture.
Nobleman, statesman, servant of the Stuart kings and of Cromwell, he also found time to
pursue a career as a man of letters. His plays, which include the first important attempts to
introduce rhymed heroic tragedy on the English stage, were admired by Dryden and
Davenant, and retained some popularity after the Restoration.

His contemporaries also knew him as the author of a work which has proved less
accessible to posterity – Parthenissa, one of the earliest and best English experiments with
long heroic romance in the manner of such French salon-writers as La Calprenède and the de
Scudérys. Orrery points out in his Preface that the book is a deliberate amalgam of history
and fiction, real and imaginary people, because "Historyes are for the most Part but mixt
Romances, and yet the Pure Romance Part, may be as Instructive as, if not more than, the
Historicall." Like its French models, Parthenissa interlaces pseudo-philosophical dialogues on
Platonic love and honour with descriptions of action – the pageantry of tournaments, and
battles on land and sea. It is structured around the intersecting stories of four pairs of high-

born lovers, of whom Parthenissa and Artabanes are the most important. The couples assemble at the Temple of Hierophanus in Syria to consult the oracle, and there exchange tales of trials in love and friendship, and hazards in war, in a prose which, though sometimes florid, often has a pleasing dignity and serenity. Orrery's aim was to bring all of his lovers to felicity, but the romance remained unfinished, and only one of the stories is resolved.

—J. C. Hilson

BROOKE, Henry. Irish.   Born in Rantavan, County Cavan, c. 1703. Educated at Trinity College, Dublin, 1720; The Temple, London. Married his cousin Catherine Meares; 22 children. From c. 1725 divided his time between London and Dublin; became involved in English politics: because of difficulties caused by his championing the Prince of Wales against George II returned to Dublin and settled there, 1740: appointed Barrack-Master, Dublin, c. 1745; in later years suffered from mental debility. *Died 10 October 1783.*

PUBLICATIONS

Collections

> *Poetical Works*, edited by Charlotte Brooke.   4 vols., 1792.

Plays

> *Gustavus Vasa, The Deliverer of His Country* (as *The Patriot*, produced 1744; as *Gustavus Vasa*, produced 1805).   1739.
> *The Female Officer* (produced 1740).   In *A Collection of Plays and Poems*, 1778.
> *The Earl of Westmorland* (as *The Betrayer of His Country*, produced 1742; as *Injured Honour*, produced 1754).   In *A Collection of Plays and Poems*, 1778.
> *The Triumph of Hibernia*, music by Niccolo Pasquali (produced 1748).
> *Little John and the Giants* (as *Jack the Giant Queller*, produced 1749).   In *A Collection of Plays and Poems*, 1778.
> *The Earl of Essex* (produced 1750).   1761.
> *The Victims of Love and Honour* (produced 1762).   In *A Collection of Plays and Poems*, 1778.

Fiction

> *The Fool of Quality; or, The History of Henry, Earl of Moreland.*   5 vols., 1764–70; edited by E. A. Baker, 1902.
> *Juliet Grenville; or, The History of the Human Heart.*   1774.

Verse

Universal Beauty. 1735.
Constantia; or, The Man of Law's Tale, in *The Canterbury Tales Modernised,* edited by
    George Ogle. 1741.
Fables for the Female Sex, with Edward Moore. 1744.
New Fables. 1749.
A Description of the College Green Club: A Satire. 1753.
Redemption. 1772.

Other

The Farmer's Six Letters to the Protestants of Ireland. 1745; as *Essays Against Popery,*
    1750.
The Secret History and Memoirs of the Barracks of Ireland. 1745.
A New Collection of Fairy Tales. 1750.
The Spirit of Party. 2 vols., 1753–54.
The Interests of Ireland Considered. 1759.
The Case of the Roman Catholics of Ireland. 1760.
Trial of the Cause of the Roman Catholics. 1761.
A Proposal for the Restoration of Public Wealth and Credit. 1762(?).
A Collection of Plays and Poems (includes, besides the plays listed above, *The Vestal
    Virgin, The Marriage Contract, Montezuma, The Imposter, The Contending Brother,
    The Charitable Association, Cymbeline, Antony and Cleopatra*). 4 vols., 1778.

Translator, *Tasso's Jerusalem Delivered* (books 1–2). 1738.
Translator, *A New System of Fairy; or, A Collection of Fairy Tales,* by Comte de
    Caylus. 2 vols., 1750.

Reading List: *Brookiana: Anecdotes of Brooke* by C. H. Wilson, 2 vols., 1804; *Memoirs of
Brooke* by Isaac D'Olier, 1816; *Brooke* by H. Wright, 1927.

*   *   *

The eighteenth century so abounds in truly great novelists that excellent or eccentric
second-raters are ignored. John Wesley hailed *The Fool of Quality* as "one of the most
beautiful pictures that ever was drawn in the world; the strokes are so fine, the touches so
easy, natural, and affecting, that I know not who can survey it with tearless eyes, urless he
has a heart of stone." Now it may win only a notice in some learned discussion of William
Law's *A Serious Call to the Devout and Holy Life* or of Shaftesbury's sentimental philosophy.
In fact, Brooke's sentimental and discursive picaresque novel, with its variety, vivacity, and
breeziness, ought to be linked with the "free fantasia" school of fiction in Sterne's wake, and
with an eye to the influence of Rousseau.

Brooke's tragedy *Gustavus Vasa* (banned in London as revolutionary but produced in
Dublin as *The Patriot*), is better know than *The Fool of Quality*. It deals with the Job-like
tribulations of the Nordic giant who in the years following 1521 strove to unify and
strengthen the kingdom of Sweden. Strindberg's play of the same name centers on the man
himself; Brooke centers on the manipulations of the plot, and ends with fustian bombast.
Brooke's *Earl of Essex* escaped the "bow-wow" attack of Dr. Johnson on *Gustavus Vasa*, but
is inferior to it.

Brooke's verse is of interest for two reasons. "Conrade," purporting to be a fragment of old
Celtic saga, fits into the poetic revival of Irish poetry exemplified by the Ossian controversy.

Pope is said to have assisted Brooke in *Universal Beauty*, and the poem was highly praised in its day. Bonamy Dobrée (in *English Literature in the Early Eighteenth Century*) says that Brooke "most nearly made a real poem out of science"; like Erasmus Darwin's *Temple of Love*, it repays investigation. Brooke was also a sincere and articulate political writer, especially on the Jacobite tendencies of the Irish Catholics and the notorious penal laws.

—Leonard R. N. Ashley

BUCKINGHAM, 2nd Duke of; George Villiers.   English.   Born in Westminster, London, 30 January 1628; succeeded to the dukedom, 1628; raised by King Charles I with his own children. Educated at Trinity College, Cambridge M.A. 1642. At the beginning of the Civil War joined the King at Oxford and served under Prince Rupert at the storming of Lichfield Close, 1643; later committed to the care of the Earl of Northumberland; sent on a Continental tour, lived in Florence and Rome; served under the Earl of Holland, in Surrey, during the second civil war, 1648; after defeat of the Royalists, escaped to France; appointed by Charles II a Member of the Order of the Garter, 1649, and Privy Councillor, 1650; appointed General of the Eastern Association of Forces, 1650, also commissioned to raise forces for the King on the Continent; Commander-in-Chief of the English royalists in Scotland, 1651; lands sequestered, 1651; accompanied Charles II on his expedition to England, quarrelled with the King, and returned to exile in Holland, 1651; returned to England, 1657; imprisoned in the Tower of London, 1658–59; served with the forces of Lord Fairfax, 1660. Married Mary Fairfax in 1657; later associated with the Countess of Shrewsbury, by whom he had a son. Recovered his estates at the Restoration; became gentleman of the king's bedchamber, 1660, and Privy Councillor, 1662; Lord Lieutenant of the West Riding of Yorkshire, 1661–67; briefly imprisoned and stripped of office for opposition to government policies, 1667; served as the King's principal minister in the "Cabal" administration, 1667–69; appointed master of the horse, 1668; replaced by Arlington in the King's confidence and kept ignorant of private negotiations with the French King, 1669, 1670; negotiated treaties with France for attack upon Holland, 1670, 1672; appointed Lieutenant General, 1673; quarrelled openly with Arlington, whom the King supported, 1673, and censured by Parliament for the French treaties, and deprived of his offices by the King, 1674; joined the Country Party, and thereafter acted as a leader of the opposition in the House of Lords, working for the establishment of a Whig parliament; admitted Freeman of the City of London, 1681; after the accession of James II abandoned public career and retired to Yorkshire. *Died 16 April 1687.*

PUBLICATIONS

Collections

    Works, edited by Tom Brown.   1704; revised edition, 2 vols., 1715.
    Works, edited by T. Percy.   1806(?).

Plays

    The Chances, from the play by Fletcher (produced 1667).   1682.

The Rehearsal (produced 1671).   1672; revised version, 1675; edited by D. E. L. Crane, 1976.
The Militant Couple, The Belgic Hero Unmasked, and *The Battle,* in *Works.*   1704.
The Country Gentleman, with Robert Howard, edited by Arthur H. Scouten and Robert D. Hume.   1976.

Other

A Letter to Sir Thomas Osborn upon the Reading of a Book Called The Present Interest of England.   1672.
A Short Discourse upon the Reasonableness of Men's Having a Religion.   1685.

Reading List: *Plays about the Theatre* by Dane F. Smith, 1936; *Great Villiers* by Hester W. Chapman, 1949; *The Burlesque Tradition in the English Theatre after 1660* by V. C. Clinton-Baddeley, 1952; *A Rake and His Times* by John H. Wilson, 1954; "*The Rehearsal:* A Study of Its Satirical Methods" by Peter Lewis, in *Durham University Journal,* March 1970.

*   *   *

Just as *Don Quixote* and *The Dunciad* have outlived the hack writing they parodied, so Buckingham's *The Rehearsal* survives as an eminently stageworthy play, while the heroic tragedies it burlesqued are studied more often for the theories justifying their form than for their intrinsic interest. *The Rehearsal* was Buckingham's single major contribution to the drama (though his adaptation of Fletcher's *The Chances* is still occasionally preferred to its original), for he was, as Dryden claimed in *Absalom and Achitophel,* "everything by starts, and nothing long," a man of curious vice, and considerable virtuosity.

Though first drafted in the mid-1660's, *The Rehearsal* did not reach the stage till 1671, by which time the heroic dramas of Davenant, Boyle, Dryden, Stapylton, and the Howards had successfully caught and held the public taste. In the following year, Dryden, recently created laureate, could still claim that heroic verse was "in possession of the stage," and that "very few tragedies, in this age, shall be received without it." That he himself shortly afterwards abandoned the form for good was in no small part due to the success of *The Rehearsal,* in which he is caricatured as the mock-dramatist Bayes.

The play anticipates many of the techniques perfected in the great age of burlesque, the early eighteenth century, in its rehearsal framework, and in its employment of "bathos," as re-defined by Pope. Its "plot" – the attempted usurpation of the two-seater throne of the Kingdom of Brentford – is bedecked with ludicrous imagery, absurd discoveries (a banquet appears out of a coffin), and contrived twists and turns in the action. Moreover, the framework permits Bayes to make a fool of himself in his own annotations to his play. Heroic drama could withstand charges of unreality (it was, after all, concerned with elevated behaviour): but Buckingham made it appear downright absurd, and so hastened its end.

—Simon Trussler

BURGOYNE, John.   English.   Born at Sutton Park, Bedfordshire, in 1722. Educated at Westminster School, London. Married Lady Charlotte Stanley in 1743 (died, 1776); had four children by Susan Caulfield. Soldier: cornet, 1740, lieutenant, 1741, and captain, 1744, in the 13th Light Dragoons; sold his commission and lived in France to escape his creditors,

1749–55; returned to England, obtained captaincy in the 11th Dragoons, 1756, and exchanged that commission for captaincy and lieutenant-colonelcy in the Coldstream Guards, 1758; served in expeditions to Cherbourg and St. Malo, 1758, 1759; devised schemes for creation of the King's Light Dragoons and Queen's Light Dragoons, 1759; sent to Portugal as Brigadier-General to assist the Portuguese against Spain: captured Valencia de Alcantara, 1762; Tory Member of Parliament for Midhurst, 1762–68, and for Preston, 1768–74; appointed Governor of Fort William, Scotland, 1769; Major-General, 1772; sent to the American colonies to reinforce General Gage's forces, 1774; during the Revolutionary War, Commander of the British attack of the United States from Canada: captured Ticonderoga and Fort Ward, and promoted to Lieutenant-General, then defeated by, and surrendered to, General Gates at Saratoga, 1777; on his return to England condemned for his actions by the House of Commons and the press, and deprived by the king of his commands and the governorship of Fort William; supported by the opposition and on return of Whigs to power appointed Commander-in-Chief in Ireland, 1782–83; thereafter devoted himself to writing. *Died 4 June 1792.*

PUBLICATIONS

Collections

Dramatic and Poetical Works.   2 vols., 1808.

Plays

The Maid of the Oaks, music by F. H. Barthelemon (produced 1774; revised version, produced 1774).   1774.
The Lord of the Manor, music by William Jackson, from a play by Jean-François Marmontel (produced 1780).   1781.
The Heiress (produced 1786).   1786.
Richard Coeur de Lion, music by Thomas Linley, from an opera by Michel Jean Sedaine, music by Grétry (produced 1786).   1786.

Other

A Letter to His Constituents upon His Late Resignation.   1779.
A State of the Expedition from Canada.   1780; supplement, 1780.
Political and Military Episodes Derived from the Life and Correspondence, by E. B. de Fonblanque.   1786.
The Orderly Book from His Entry in the State of New York until His Surrender at Saratoga, edited by E. B. O'Callaghan.   1860.

Reading List: *Gentleman Johnny Burgoyne* by Francis J. Hudleston, 1927; *The Man Who Lost America* by Paul Lewis, 1973.

*   *   *

At Saratoga in 1777 General John Burgoyne lost an army. The fault was not his and the American commander who forced the surrender owed less to his own skill than to the complacency of the British Government and to the indolence of Burgoyne's superiors in North America. But Saratoga, the first battle-honour of the United States Army, spelt for Burgoyne the end of a long, gallant, and thoughtful career as a soldier. The fifteen years that were left to him Burgoyne used energetically and not often wisely. In Parliament as M.P. for Preston he was always ready to intervene on behalf of the Army and particularly of its private soldiers and non-commissioned officers, but his speeches were muddled and prolix and he was, not unnaturally, testy about his own military reputation. He wenched, he gambled, he roistered. But he also wrote, and the honours that had been denied him in his prime profession came his way eventually by way of the theatre.

His first dramatic piece, *The Maid of the Oaks* had been staged at Drury Lane before the American Revolution. It was damned by Horace Walpole (who damned almost everything that Burgoyne attempted whether in the Army, in Parliament, or for the stage), but David Garrick, better-qualified then Walpole to judge an entertainment, proclaimed it "a great success," and the play survived in the repertory for several months and, in book form, enjoyed a considerable vogue for many years. But it is in truth a heavy-handed and stylised piece, remarkable only for its mawkishness and portentous morality so utterly out of keeping with the author's personal inclinations and activities.

In *The Lord of the Manor* Burgoyne abandoned the ludicrously inappropriate pastoral idyll and took to the world he knew. Sergeant Sash, Corporal Dill, and Corporal Snip are caricatures only in the sense that they are exaggerations of reality, and Burgoyne understood the reality that is the British soldier. An eighteenth-century audience was never averse to a resounding platitude and Burgoyne gave them many to applaud, most of them from the lips of his *alter ego* hero, Trumore. *The Lord of the Manor* was written as a libretto, for the music of William Jackson of Exeter. Most of its faults are the faults of the operatic genre but they are as nothing when compared to the faults of Burgoyne's second attempt at opera, his adaptation of a serious French libretto, *Richard Coeur de Lion*.

The Heiress is a different matter. The plot is thin and moved forward in a flurry of coincidences. The characterisation is simplistic and is moulded almost entirely by the names of the participants (Lord Gayville; Mr. Rightly, the honest lawyer, and Mr. Alscrip, his devious colleague; Chignon, the prissy French hairdresser; the social climbers, Mr. and Mrs. Blandish) but the play has pace, the wit is sharp, and the social comment incisive.

With *The Heiress* Burgoyne made only £200 but he won the affection of the theatre-going public, of the critics, not only in England but also in France and Germany, and even of Horace Walpole: "Burgoyne's battles and speeches will be forgotten, but his delightful comedy *The Heiress* will continue the delight of the stage and one of the most pleasing domestic compositions."

—J. E. Morpurgo

CAREY, Henry. English. Born, probably in Yorkshire, c. 1687; believed by some scholars to have been the natural son of Henry Savile, Marquis of Halifax. Studied music with Olaus Linnert, Roseingrave, and Geminiani. Married in 1708; four children. Taught music in various boarding schools; settled in London, 1710; a member of Addison's circle; produced the magazine *The Records of Love*, 1710; wrote farces and songs for the London stage, 1715–39. *Died* (by suicide) *4 October 1743.*

PUBLICATIONS

Collections

Poems, edited by Frederick T. Wood.   1930.

Plays

The Contrivances; or, More Ways Than One (produced 1715).   1715; revised version, music by the author (produced 1729), 1729.
Hanging and Marriage; or, The Dead-Man's Wedding (produced 1722).   1722; revised version, as *Betty; or, The Country Bumpkins*, music by the author (produced 1732), songs published 1732.
Amelia, music by J. F. Lampe (produced 1732).   1732.
Teraminta, music by J. C. Smith (produced 1732).   1732.
The Happy Nuptials, music by the author (produced 1733).   Extracts in *Gentleman's Magazine*, November 1733; revised version, as *Britannia; or, The Royal Lovers* (produced 1734).
The Tragedy of Chrononhotonthologos, music by the author (produced 1734).   1734.
The Honest Yorkshireman, music by the author (produced 1735).   1736; pirated version, as *A Wonder*, 1735.
The Dragon of Wantley, music by J. F. Lampe (produced 1737).   1737.
Margery; or, A Worse Plague Than the Dragon, music by J. F. Lampe (produced 1738).   1738.
Nancy; or, The Parting Lovers, music by the author (produced 1739).   1739.
Dramatic Works.   1743.

Verse

Poems on Several Occasions.   1713; revised edition, 1720, 1729.
Works (songs and cantatas, with music by Carey).   1724; revised edition, 1726.
Of Stage Tyrants: An Epistle.   1735.
The Musical Century (songs).   2 vols., 1737; revised edition, 1740, 1743.
An Ode to Mankind, Addressed to the Prince of Wales.   1741.

Other

A Learned Dissertation on Dumpling.   1726.
Pudding and Dumpling Burnt to Pot; or, A Complete Key to the Dissertation on Dumpling.   1727.
Cupid and Hymen: A Voyage to the Islands of Love and Matrimony, with others.   1748.

Reading List: *English Comic Drama 1700–1750* by F. W. Bateson, 1929; *The Burlesque Tradition in the English Theatre after 1660* by V. C. Clinton-Baddeley, 1952; "Carey's *Chrononhotonthologos*: A Plea" by Samuel L. Macey, in *Lock Haven Review*, 1969; "Carey's *Chrononhotonthologos*" by Peter Lewis, in *Yearbook of English Studies*, 1974.

*   *   *

Henry Carey thought himself a musician who wrote poetry for diversion. Posterity remembers him, if at all, for "Sally in Our Alley" and – debatably – for "God Save the King." Contemporaries knew him as a writer of popular songs, ballad operas, and burlesques. His poetic gift was meager; the classical imitations, moralistic and satiric pieces, and the heavier amatory verses are pedestrian at best. His only good poems are parodies like "Namby-Pamby," popular ballads like "Sally" and "The Town Spark and the Country Lass," and the lighter songs in his plays – "Oh, London Is a Dainty Place," from *The Honest Yorkshireman*, for example. Nor was Carey a well-trained musician. What he had was a knack for light rhymes and catchy tunes, and these together account for much of his success.

His first play, *The Contrivances*, was a smash hit after he turned if from farce to ballad opera; it was played nearly 200 times during the century. Carey also wrote both words and music for *Nancy; or, The Parting Lovers*, a short musical piece popular under several titles for decades. He supplied the music for a hit pantomime (*Harlequin Doctor Faustus*, 1723) and for a popular masque (*Cephalus and Procris*); much of the music for his ballad opera *The Honest Yorkshireman* is also original. *Amelia* and *Teraminta* show his interest in promoting English opera, but his librettos are flat and conventional; it was certainly J. F. Lampe's music which made *Amelia* a success.

Carey's real achievements, aside from *The Contrivances*, came late in his career. *Chrononhotonthologos* burlesques contemporary (and earlier) tragedy. No reader will easily forget the King of Queerumania and his court, or the opening lines of the play. Although not as directly parodic as *The Rehearsal*, it is delightful to read and stands comparison with *Tom Thumb*, its immediate predecessor. *The Dragon of Wantley*, a burlesque with music by Lampe, is even better, and was as popular for the rest of the century as *The Contrivances*. The plot, based on a laundered version of the ballad, is deliberately thin, and the burlesque of the Italian opera – evident in the music as well as the text – pointed and hilarious. So successful was the piece, indeed, that it nearly drove Italian opera off the English stage for a year or two. *Margery*, like most sequels, was less successful.

Carey is said to have heard his tunes everywhere he went. The modern reader is not so fortunate. No available edition of *The Dragon of Wantley*, for example, includes the music, yet it is as difficult to appreciate Carey's achievement without it as to judge *West Side Story* on its libretto. Like Isaac Bickerstaff and several other successful authors of the century, Carey remains largely inaccessible.

—Frederick M. Link

CENTLIVRE, Susanna. English. Born in or near Holbeach, Lincolnshire, 1669. Possibly married a nephew of Sir Stephen Fox, c. 1684, and an officer named Carroll, c. 1685; married Joseph Centlivre, principal cook to Queen Anne and George I, 1707. Actress in the provinces, often appearing in her own works, written under the name S. Carroll; devoted herself to writing from 1700; lived in London from 1712. *Died 1 December 1723.*

PUBLICATIONS

Collections

Works.   3 vols., 1760–61; as *Dramatic Works*, 1872.

Plays

The Perjured Husband; or, The Adventures of Venice (produced 1700). 1700.
The Beau's Duel; or, A Soldier for the Ladies (produced 1702). 1702.
The Stolen Heiress; or, The Salamanca Doctor Outplotted (as The Heiress, produced 1702). 1703.
Love's Contrivance; or, Le Medecin Malgré Lui (produced 1703). 1703.
The Gamester, from a play by J. F. Regnard (produced 1705). 1705.
The Basset-Table (produced 1705). 1706.
Love at a Venture (produced 1706?). 1706.
The Platonic Lady (produced 1706). 1707.
The Busy Body (produced 1709). 1709.
The Man's Bewitched; or, The Devil to Do about Her (produced 1709). 1710.
A Bickerstaff's Burying; or, Work for the Upholders (produced 1710). 1710; as The Custom of the Country (produced 1715).
Mar-Plot; or, The Second Part of the Busy Body (produced 1710). 1711.
The Perplexed Lovers (produced 1712). 1712.
The Wonder! A Woman Keeps a Secret (produced 1714). 1714.
The Gotham Election. 1715; as The Humours of Election, 1737.
A Wife Well Managed (produced 1724). 1715.
The Cruel Gift; or, The Royal Resentment (produced 1716). 1717.
A Bold Stroke for a Wife (produced 1718). In A Collection of Plays 3, 1719; edited by Thalia Stathas, 1967.
The Artifice (produced 1722). 1723.

Verse

A Trip to the Masquerade; or, A Journey to Somerset House. 1713.
A Poem to His Majesty upon His Accession to the Throne. 1715.
An Epistle to Mrs. Wallup, Now in the Train of the Princess of Wales. 1715.
A Woman's Case, in an Epistle to Charles Joye. 1720.

Bibliography: "Some Uncollected Authors 14" by Jane E. Norton, in Book Collector, 1957.

Reading List: The Celebrated Mrs. Centlivre by John W. Bowyer, 1952.

*   *   *

Mrs. Centlivre wrote seventeen comedies, including three short farces, and strayed once or twice into tragedy. (Her poems are unimportant, orthodox complimentary or epistolary effusions for the most part.) Few of the plays were outright flops, and at least four enjoyed considerable success. The least merited popularity, perhaps, was that attached to The Gamester, a sentimental comedy rebuking the age for its addiction to gambling. A sequel, The Basset-Table, met with a less favourable reception, but it displays more vivacity in places, as in the scenes involving the uxorious City drugster Sago and his extravagantly flighty wife.

Throughout the eighteenth and nineteenth centuries, the dramatist's name was kept alive by two comedies which held the boards for decade after decade and which each totted up many hundreds of performances across the English-speaking world. Probably the better play is the earlier, entitled The Busie Body, constructed around the "sly, cowardly, inquisitive fellow" Marplot, who frustrates all the schemes he attempts to abet. This was a true acting part, and Theophilus Cibber, Henry Woodward, and Garrick all enjoyed great success in the role. Equally well-known was The Wonder! A Woman Keeps a Secret, which introduced some of Mrs. Centlivre's favourite Latin lovers – in this case melodramatic Portuguese grandees. Both the male and female leads provide fine opportunities for an accomplished player, and Garrick, Kemble, Mrs. Yates, and Susanna Cibber at various times all made a striking impact in the play.

Mrs. Centlivre's outstanding comedy is probably *A Bold Stroke for a Wife*, which traces the attempts of Colonel Fainwell to obtain the hand of Mrs. Lovely, a spirited heiress. The hero has to overcome the objections of four guardians, and he adopts a succession of disguises to deceive each of these well-marked "humour" characters – an antiquated beau, a foolish virtuoso, a grasping stock-jobber, and a sanctimonious Quaker. The play clearly exhibits the author's talent for lively dialogue, energetic stage business, and vivid portrayal of eccentric traits. It is worth adding that the unacted farce called *A Gotham Election* was an unlucky victim of political censorship. It is short but exceedingly amusing. The principal characters are conventional in outline, but nicely realised: for example, the amorous Squire Tickup, a Tory and seemingly a Jacobite into the bargain, who is opposed by the pompous Whig Sir Roger Trusty, a ready orator with a mouthful of high-minded party rhetoric always at his disposal. Around the gentry there are placed a wide range of rustic wiseacres, apparently foolish peasants with a vein of peasant shrewdness. As some of the names indicate – Shallow, Sly, Gabble – there is an echo of the Shakespearian clown in their speech, which is compounded of strange Mummerzet dialect and brutally direct colloquialisms. It is a pity that Susanna Centlivre did not get the opportunity to develop this vein of comedy; the play shows her capable of a realistic dramatic idiom rarely encountered on the eighteenth-century stage.

—Pat Rogers

CIBBER, Colley.   English.   Born in London, 6 November 1671. Educated at the Free School, Grantham, Lincolnshire, 1682–87. Joined the Earl of Devonshire's Volunteers, 1688, and remained in the service of the Earl of Devonshire, 1688–90. Married Katherine Shore in 1693; ten children. Actor in the Drury Lane Company, London, 1691–1706, and Adviser to the Manager after 1700, and Actor at the Haymarket, London, 1706 until the two theatres consolidated, 1708; Co-Owner/Manager of the Drury Lane Company, 1708–32; retired officially as an actor in 1733, but occasionally appeared on the stage until 1745. Poet Laureate, 1730 until his death. *Died 11 December 1757.*

PUBLICATIONS

Collections

Dramatic Works.   4 vols., 1760; 5 vols., 1777.
Three Sentimental Comedies (includes *Love's Last Shift, The Careless Husband, The Lady's Last Stake*), edited by Maureen Sullivan.   1973.

Plays

Love's Last Shift; or, The Fool in Fashion (produced 1696).   1696; in *Three Sentimental Comedies,* 1973.

Woman's Wit; or, The Lady in Fashion (produced 1697).   1697.

Xerxes (produced 1699).   1699.

King Richard III, from the play by Shakespeare (produced 1700).   1700; edited by Christopher Spencer, in *Five Restoration Adaptations of Shakespeare*, 1965.

Love Makes a Man; or, The Fop's Fortune (produced 1700).   1701.

She Would and She Would Not; or, The Kind Imposter (produced 1702).   1703.

The Schoolboy; or, The Comical Rival, from his own play *Woman's Wit* (produced 1703).   1707.

The Careless Husband (produced 1704).   1705; in *Three Sentimental Comedies*, 1973.

Perolla and Izadora (produced 1705).   1706.

The Comical Lovers (produced 1707).   1707; as *Marriage a la Mode* (produced 1707; as *Court Gallantry*, produced 1715).

The Double Gallant; or, The Sick Lady's Cure (produced 1707).   1707.

The Lady's Last Stake; or, The Wife's Resentment (produced 1707).   1708; in *Three Sentimental Comedies*, 1973.

The Rival Fools (produced 1709).   1709.

The Rival Queens (produced 1710).   1729; edited by William M. Peterson, 1965.

Hob; or, The Country Wake, from the play *The Country Wake* by Thomas Dogget (produced 1710).   1715.

Ximena; or, The Heroic Daughter, from a play by Corneille (produced 1712).   1719.

Bulls and Bears (produced 1715).

Myrtillo, music by J. C. Pepusch (produced 1715).   1715.

Venus and Adonis, music by J. C. Pepusch (produced 1715).   1715.

The Non-Juror, from a play by Molière (produced 1717).   1718.

Plays.   2 vols., 1721.

The Refusal; or, The Ladies' Philosophy, from a play by Molière (produced 1721).   1721.

Caesar in Egypt (produced 1724).   1724.

The Provoked Husband; or, A Journey to London, from a play by Vanbrugh (produced 1728).   1728; edited by Peter Dixon, 1975.

Love in a Riddle (produced 1729).   1729; shortened version, as *Damon and Phillida* (produced 1729), 1729; revised version, 1730.

Polypheme, from an opera by Paul Rolli, music by Nicholas Porpora (produced 1734).

Dramatic Works.   5 vols., 1736.

Papal Tyranny in the Reign of King John, from the play *King John* by Shakespeare (produced 1745).   1745.

Verse

A Poem on the Death of Queen Mary.   1695.

The Sacred History of Arlus and Odolphus.   1714.

An Ode to His Majesty for the New Year.   1731.

An Ode for His Majesty's Birthday.   1731.

A Rhapsody upon the Marvellous Arising from the First Odes of Horace and Pindar.   1751.

Verses to the Memory of Mr. Pelham.   1754.

Other

An Apology for the Life of Mr. Colley Cibber, Comedian.   1740; revised edition, 1750, 1756; edited by B. R. S. Fone, 1968.

A Letter to Mr. Pope.   1742; *Second Letter*, 1743; *Another Letter*, 1744.

The Egoist; or, Colley upon Cibber.   1743.
The Character and Conduct of Cicero Considered.   1747.
The Lady's Lecture: A Theatrical Dialogue Between Sir Charles Easy and His Marriageable Daughter.   1748.

Bibliography: by Leonard R. N. Ashley, in *Restoration and 18th-Century Theatre Research* 6, 1967.

Reading List: *Mr. Cibber of Drury Lane* by R. H. Barker, 1939; *Cibber* by Leonard R. N. Ashley, 1965; "Cibber's *Love's Last Shift* and Sentimental Comedy" by B. R. S. Fone, in *Restoration and Eighteenth Century Theatre Research 7*, May 1968.

*   *   *

Colley Cibber was a superb actor. In a career which lasted from 1691 (when he acted in a bit part in *Sir Anthony Love* by Thomas Southerne) till 1745 (when he starred in ten performances of his own *Papal Tyranny in the Reign of King John*) he created an army of coxcombs ("first in all foppery") and sneering villains (including his adaptation of *Richard III*). In all he played about 130 different parts. He was also one of the most important actor-managers in the history of the English stage. With others, he ran, for decades, the Theatre Royal in Drury Lane, and though he was sometimes criticized for his treatment of authors and inevitably made mistakes, he had a long and generally favorable influence on the stage.

He told the story of his public life in a brilliant autobiography, *An Apology for the Life of Mr. Colley Cibber, Comedian*. The real Cibber much resembles the striking, colored bust by Roubillac in London's National Portrait Gallery: a cheerful, shrewd, frank, ruddy face, the humorous expression of the rather thin lips suggesting that they might speak, probably with some self-satisfied vanity and with more than a little determination, some wisdom and more wit. The *Apology* covers 40 years of the London stage from the pen of a man who had a chief part in shaping its goals and achievements. The writer's style is conversational, his prejudices betrayed (or clearly stated), his friends defended, his enemies attacked, but this is a discussion of his professional, not his private, life. There is little here of Cibber the family man, the gambler, the *beau garçon*. His versatility and vitality dazzle us, his talent and tenacity win our admiration, and his very flaws and frailties endear him to us, for he is a true original (as Edward Young would say) even when he comes to us like an eastern potentate bedecked in light feathers.

Cibber aroused even more opposition than the *Apology* stimulated by gaining the appointment as Poet Laureate, though Gay was at pains to point out that a better man would not have accepted the job and a worse one could not have held it. Bad as he was, Cibber was, after all, the best Poet Laureate since Dryden, and it must be admitted that the odes which Joseph Knight recklessly called "the most contemptible things of literature" do not look so bad alongside those which Masefield (and more recent) laureates have perpetrated. Pope was biased but right to say Cibber's poetry was "prose on stilts," but Dr. Johnson was right too: "Colley Cibber, Sir, was by no means a blockhead."

Cibber's true worth was in his plays. His first play, *Love's Last Shift*, he wrote out of his "own raw uncultivated Head" and it was so good his enemies later swore it must have been stolen. It was a landmark in the history of English drama and launched the long vogue of sentimental comedy. For that (and the follow-up in this genre, *The Careless Husband*) Cibber's name must be featured in every history of the drama. Even his enemy John Dennis described it as having "a just Design, distinguished Characters, and a proper Dialogue." It's a good comedy. And *The Careless Husband* is a better one.

Cibber's tragedies are, on the whole, inferior to his comedies, though he has a deft hand with melodrama, and it must be noted that his version of *Richard III* replaced Shakespeare on the stage for about 125 years. The most famous of Cibber's *rifacimenti*, however, was

Molière's *Tartuffe* adapted as *The Non-Juror*; and the best-loved of Cibber's plays in his own time (second only to Shakespeare in popularity) was the comedy *The Provok'd Husband*. All of these are still worth attention.

Thus let us put Cibber down as Laureate and regret his odes, read his *Apology* and declare it too smug, praise his brilliant portrayals of the fop onstage and regret some of his private life offstage, criticize some of his comedic carpentry but recognize his occasional excellences and his undoubted place in the history of the drama, and accept Pope's diatribe in the *Dunciad* (which, after all, immortalized Cibber) while balancing it against Warburton's judicious estimate: "Cibber, with a great stock of levity, vanity, and affectation, had sense, and wit, and humor."

Leonard R. N. Ashley

COLMAN, George, the Elder.   English.   Born in Florence, Italy, where his father was envoy at court, in April 1732; returned to London, 1733. Educated at Westminster School, London, 1746–51; Christ Church, Oxford, matriculated 1751, B.A. 1755, M.A. 1758; Lincoln's Inn, London, 1755–57; called to the Bar, 1757. Married the actress Miss Ford (died, 1771); children include George Colman the Younger, *q.v.* Founding Editor, with Bonnell Thornton, *Connoisseur*, 1754–56; practised law on the Oxford circuit, 1759–64; left an income by his patron, the Earl of Bath, which allowed him to abandon the law, 1764; purchased one-quarter of the Covent Garden Theatre, 1767; Manager, 1767–74; retired to Bath; contributed to the *London Packet*, 1775; bought the Little Theatre, Haymarket, and managed it, 1777–89; paralysed by a stroke, 1785, and thereafter became increasingly feeble-minded; succeeded at the Haymarket by his son, 1789. *Died 14 August 1794.*

PUBLICATIONS

Plays

> *Polly Honeycombe: A Dramatic Novel* (produced 1760).   1760; edited by Richard Bevis, in *Eighteenth Century Drama: Afterpieces*, 1970.
> *The Jealous Wife*, from the novel *Tom Jones* by Fielding (produced 1761).   1761; edited by Allardyce Nicoll, 1925.
> *The Musical Lady* (produced 1762).   1762.
> *Philaster*, from the play by Beaumont and Fletcher (produced 1763).   1763.
> *The Deuce Is in Him* (produced 1763).   1763.
> *A Fairy Tale*, from the play *A Midsummer Night's Dream* by Shakespeare (produced 1763).   1763.
> *The Clandestine Marriage*, with David Garrick (produced 1766).   1766.
> *The English Merchant*, from a play by Voltaire (produced 1767).   1767.
> *The Oxonion in Town* (produced 1767).   1769.
> *King Lear*, from the play by Shakespeare (produced 1768).   1768.
> *Man and Wife; or, The Shakespeare Jubilee* (produced 1769).   1770.
> *The Portrait*, music by Samuel Arnold, from a play by Louis Anseaume, music by Grétry (produced 1770).   1770.

Mother Skipton, music by Samuel Arnold (produced 1770).   Songs published 1771.

The Fairy Prince, music by Thomas Arne, from the masque *Oberon* by Jonson (produced 1771).   1771.

Comus, music by Thomas Arne, from the masque by Milton (produced 1773).   1772.

An Occasional Prelude (produced 1772).   1776.

Achilles in Petticoats, music by Thomas Arne, from a work by John Gay (produced 1773).   1774.

The Man of Business (produced 1774).   1774.

The Spleen; or, Islington Spa (produced 1776).   1776.

Epicoene; or, The Silent Woman, from the play by Jonson (produced 1776).   1776.

New Brooms! An Occasional Prelude, with David Garrick (produced 1776).   1776.

Polly, from the play by John Gay (produced 1777).   1777.

The Sheep Shearing, music by Thomas Arne and others, from the play *A Winter's Tale* by Shakespeare (produced 1777).   1777.

The Spanish Barber; or, The Fruitless Precaution, music by Samuel Arnold, from a play by Beaumarchais (produced 1777).

The Distressed Wife (produced 1777).

Dramatic Works.   4 vols., 1777.

The Female Chevalier, from the play *The Artful Wife* by William Taverner (produced 1778).

The Suicide (produced 1778).

Bonduca, music by Samuel Arnold, from the play by Fletcher (produced 1778).   1778.

The Separate Maintenance (produced 1779).

The Manager in Distress (produced 1780).   1790.

The Genius of Nonsense, music by Samuel Arnold (produced 1780).   Songs published 1781.

Preludio to The Beggar's Opera (produced 1781).

Harlequin Teague; or, The Giant's Causeway, with John O'Keeffe (produced 1782).   Songs published 1782.

Fatal Curiosity, from the play by Lillo (produced 1782).   1783.

The Election of the Managers (produced 1784).

Tit for Tat; or, The Mutual Deception, from a work by Marivaux (produced 1786).   1788.

Ut Pictura Poesis! or, The Enraged Musicians: A Musical Entertainment Founded on Hogarth, music by Samuel Arnold (produced 1789).   1789.

Verse

Two Odes, with Robert Lloyd.   1760.

Poems on Several Occasions.   3 vols., 1787.

Other

The Connoisseur, with Bonnell Thornton.   4 vols., 1757.

A Letter of Abuse to D—d G—k.   1757.

A True State of the Differences (on Covent Garden Theatre).   1768.

An Epistle to Dr. Kenrick.   1768.

T. Harris Dissected.   1768.

Prose on Several Occasions.   3 vols., 1787.

Some Particulars of the Life of George Colman, Written by Himself.   1795.

Editor, with Bonnell Thornton, *Poems by Eminent Ladies*.   2 vols., 1755.

Editor, *The Works of Beaumont and Fletcher.* 10 vols., 1778.

Translator, *The Comedies of Terence.* 1765; revised edition, 1766.
Translator, *The Merchant,* in *Comedies of Plautus.* 1769.
Translator, *Epistola de Arte Poetica,* by Horace. 1783.

Reading List: *Memoirs of the Colman Family, Including Their Correspondence* by Richard B. Peake, 2 vols., 1841; *Colman the Elder* by Eugene R. Page, 1935; "Bickerstaff, Colman, and the Bourgeois Audience" by Peter A. Tasch, in *Restoration and 18th Century Theatre Research 9,* May 1970.

*   *   *

The work of the many-faceted George Colman the Elder – lawyer, essayist, editor, translator, playwright, and theatre manager – is divisible into two phases: before and after 1764. In that year his uncle and patron, William Pulteney, Earl of Bath, died without fulfilling his nephew's great expectations, and this rude jolt sent a number of aftershocks through Colman's life and consciousness, as may be seen in his plays. Prior to 1764 he thought he was merely amusing himself at the bar and in the theatre until he could be made "easy," and his early dramatic efforts are commensurately light-hearted. *Polly Honeycombe,* "A Dramatick Novel of One Act," was an auspicious beginning; with strong acting by such comedians as Yates, King, and Miss Pope, who played the titular heroine on whom Sheridan modelled Lydia Languish, it pleased the town and gained a place in the repertory, giving Colman a quick reputation as a bright young man and a promising new comic voice. He followed this up the next season – with some editorial help from Garrick, according to tradition – by adapting *Tom Jones* for the stage as *The Jealous Wife,* his first full-length comedy and another success. *The Musical Lady* and *The Deuce Is in Him* kept his name before the public in the next two years without adding to his lustre or altering his "image"; both are two-act afterpieces.

What is notable about these first four plays – especially in view of his later work – is their general antipathy to sentiment, supposedly the prevailing taste at the time. *Polly* is a spirited attack on the sentimental novel (first cousin to the sentimental comedy), *The Deuce Is in Him* on one species of sentimentalist (the Tortuous Tester of Motives; compare Sheridan's Faulkland). *The Musical Lady,* supposedly culled from the overlong first draft of *Jealous Wife* but reminiscent of *Polly* in plot, is a thin wisp of manners satire. *The Jealous Wife* is mellower – as audiences expected a *main*piece to be – and has one rather sentimental reform scene, but is basically what Goldsmith later called a "laughing comedy." In these early plays Colman clearly feels that he is witty and amusing, and that he is free to choose his satiric targets without considering which of the drama's patrons might be in the line of fire.

The discovery that he was not to be a gentleman of leisure altered Colman's whole intellectual and emotional orientation from the free-wheeling to the careful; if he must "live to please," he "must please to live." After 1764 his tone changed rather suddenly from that of Foote to that of Garrick, and his mind kept reverting – understandably – to the simple but enormous difference between bourgeois and aristocrat. *The Clandestine Marriage,* co-authored with Garrick, tells the story of a poor young clerk who secretly marries his rich boss's daughter and then has to watch her being wooed by noblemen until the truth is revealed in act five. It is a very class-conscious play – at times almost an essay in sociology – that strikes a rough balance between laughter and sentiment, ridicule and sympathy, which made it quite popular with audiences of the time and gave Colman his greatest success. The 1975 London production survived by making Lord Ogleby, a comically senile rake probably created by Garrick, the centre of the play, leaving the distressed lovers to take care of themselves.

In 1767 Colman became manager of Covent Garden Theatre. His biggest coup in that position was producing *She Stoops to Conquer* in 1773 after Garrick had rejected it; otherwise his stewardship of Covent Garden (and later the Haymarket) was undistinguished. Presumably it was the demands of his managerial duties that made his subsequent efforts at dramatic authorship diffuse and relatively disappointing. He essayed most of the genres then current, but with a marked preference for the shorter, lighter and easier forms: farces, burlettas, spectacles, alterations. *The English Merchant*, adapted from Voltaire, is notable as Colman's most sentimental comedy, perhaps his only real one; both it and *The Man of Business* reveal his continuing preoccupation with the problems of the bourgeois, but their heaviness mars their gestures at social significance in a comic framework. Of his afterpieces in these years, *The Oxonian in Town* and *Man and Wife*, a gibe at Garrick's Shakespeare Jubilee in Stratford, have some entertainment value, while *New Brooms!* makes some interesting comments on theatrical taste and managerial dilemmas at the end of the Garrick era, when Sheridan took over Drury Lane.

Colman worked at a time when traditional tragedy and comedy were breaking down into new genres; perhaps he is best remembered as one of the first English writers of the *drame* or problem play. *The Man of Business* might be called a "comedy of fiscal responsibility," yet is also kin to the domestic tragedy of Lillo. It is filled with improving epigrams ("Regularity and punctuality are the life of business") and home questions ("What has a man of business to do with men of pleasure? Why is a young banker to live with young noblemen?") that the middle-class audience found piquant and relevant, and to which Colman himself could not have been oblivious. *The Suicide* returns to the theme of a young bourgeois toying with aristocratic vices, but in a bolder, darker, and more interesting way; it deserves more attention than it has ever received. Some of Colman's best writing is in the opening scene, of revellers returning at dawn to a London household just beginning to stir, and in the black comedy of the pseudo-suicide itself. His late play *The Separate Maintenance*, while less original, again shows Colman immersed in a contemporary social problem of genuine concern to his audience. Although he never decided exactly *what* point he wanted to make about the relationship between the bourgeoisie and the aristocracy, Colman's persistence in bringing living issues onto the London stage, at a time when most comedy was escapist, is significant on the eve of the French Revolution.

—R. W. Bevis

COLMAN, George, the Younger.   English.   Born in London, 21 October 1762; son of George Colman the Elder, *q.v.* Educated at a school in Marylebone, London, until 1771; Westminster School, London, 1772–79; Christ Church, Oxford, 1779–81; King's College, Aberdeen, 1781–82; Lincoln's Inn, London. Married 1) Clara Morris in 1784 (died); 2) the actress Mrs. Gibbs. Took over management of his father's Haymarket Theatre, 1789–1813 (purchased the Haymarket patent, 1794; disposed of all of his shares to his partner by 1820); appointed Lieutenant of the Yeoman of the Guard by George IV, 1820; Examiner of Plays, 1824 until his death. *Died 17 October 1836.*

PUBLICATIONS

Collections

Poetical Works. 1840.
Broad Grins, My Night-Gown and Slippers, and Other Humorous Works, edited by G. B. Buckstone. 1872.

Plays

The Female Dramatist, from the novel Roderick Random by Smollett (produced 1782).
Two to One, music by Samuel Arnold (produced 1785).   1784.
Turk and No Turk, music by Samuel Arnold (produced 1785).   Songs published 1785.
Inkle and Yarico, music by Samuel Arnold (produced 1787).   1787.
Ways and Means; or, A Trip to Dover (produced 1788).   1788.
The Battle of Hexham, music by Samuel Arnold (produced 1789).   1790.
The Surrender of Calais, music by Samuel Arnold (produced 1791).   1792.
Poor Old Haymarket; or, Two Sides of the Gutter (produced 1792).   1792.
The Mountaineers, music by Samuel Arnold (produced 1793).   1794.
New Hay at the Old Market (produced 1795).   1795; revised version, as Sylvester
    Daggerwood (produced 1796), 1808.
The Iron Chest, music by Stephen Storace, from the novel Caleb Williams by William
    Godwin (produced 1796).   1796; edited by Michael R. Booth, in Eighteenth Century
    Tragedy, 1965.
The Heir at Law (produced 1797).   1800.
Blue Beard; or, Female Curiosity! A Dramatic Romance, music by Michael Kelly, from
    a play by Michel Jean Sedaine (produced 1798).   1798.
Blue Devils, from a play by Patrat (produced 1798).   1808.
The Castle of Sorrento, with Henry Heartwell, music by Thomas Attwood, from a
    French play (produced 1799).   1799.
Feudal Times; or, The Banquet-Gallery, music by Michael Kelly (produced
    1799).   1799.
The Review; or, The Wags of Windsor, music by Samuel Arnold (produced
    1800).   1801.
The Poor Gentleman (produced 1801).   1802.
John Bull; or, An Englishman's Fireside (produced 1803).   1803.
Love Laughs at Locksmiths, music by Michael Kelly, from a play by J. N. Bouilly
    (produced 1803).   1803.
The Gay Deceivers; or, More Laugh Than Love, music by Michael Kelly, from a play by
    Theodore Hell (produced 1804).   1808.
The Children in the Wood (produced 1805?).   1805.
Who Wants a Guinea? (produced 1805).   1805.
We Fly by Night; or, Long Stories (produced 1806).   1808.
The Forty Thieves, with Sheridan, music by Michael Kelly (produced 1806).   1808; as
    Ali Baba, 1814.
The Africans; or, War, Love, and Duty, music by Michael Kelly (produced
    1808).   1808.
X.Y.Z. (produced 1810).   1820.
The Quadrupeds of Quedlinburgh; or, The Rovers of Weimar (produced 1811).
Doctor Hocus Pocus; or, Harlequin Washed White (produced 1814).
The Actor of All Work; or, First and Second Floor (produced 1817).
The Law of Java, music by Henry Bishop (produced 1822).   1822.
Stella and Leatherlungs; or, A Star and a Stroller (produced 1823).
Dramatic Works.   4 vols., 1827.

Verse

My Nightgown and Slippers; or, Tales in Verse.   1797; revised edition, as Broad Grins,
    1802.
Poetical Vagaries.   1812.
Vagaries Vindicated; or, Hypocrite Hypercritics.   1813.

Eccentricities for Edinburgh.   1816.

Other

Random Records (autobiography).   2 vols., 1830.

Editor, *Posthumous Letters Addressed to Francis Colman and George Colman the Elder.*   1820.

Reading List: *Colman the Younger* by Jeremy F. Bagster-Collins, 1946; "The Early Career of Colman" by Peter Thomson, in *Essays on Nineteenth-Century British Theatre* edited by Kenneth Richards and Thomson, 1971.

*   *   *

The younger George Colman was a shrewd judge of the theatrical public's taste. As such, he earned for himself a reputation as a superior writer without ever achieving anything more than popularity. His dramatic work was of four main kinds. Firstly, he was the originator of a new kind of play (his contemporary, James Boaden, writes of "a sort of Colman drama of three acts"), in which Elizabethan blank verse and a serious theme are lightened by frequent songs and imported comic characters. *The Battle of Hexham*, *The Surrender of Calais*, *The Mountaineers*, and *The Iron Chest* are all in this style, and Colman was still ready to exploit it in 1822, when he wrote *The Law of Java*. They are plays that eased the important passage of traditional tragedy into nineteenth-century melodrama. Secondly, he wrote comedies that were generally saved by his sense of humour from conceding too much to the contemporary vogue for sentimentality. *Inkle and Yarico*, his first striking success and still an interesting piece to stage, is a comedy with songs, *Ways and Means* an imitative comedy of manners, and *The Heir at Law* shows some ingenuity in the creation of Pangloss and an ability to handle the full five-act form. *The Poor Gentleman* is too much in the mawkish shadow of Cumberland's *The West Indian*, but Colman's finest comedy, *John Bull*, merits more attention than it has received. It is robust and not at all mealy-mouthed. Thirdly, there are the ephemeral theatre-pieces, *Doctor Hocus Pocus*, a pantomime, *Blue Beard*, a spectacular, *Love Laughs at Locksmiths*, a farce, and many others. Finally, there are pieces that grew out of his work as a theatre-manager. *Poor Old Haymarket* was a prelude to the new season at the small summer theatre which he had inherited from his ailing father. It reveals a fondness for the Haymarket, and a felt sense of the difference between it and the vast patent houses. *New Hay at the Old Market* exhibits Colman's familiarity with the contemporary theatre, and furnishes us with a lot of information about it.

His autobiographical *Random Records* is honest to its title. It tells regrettably little about his final years as Examiner of Plays. He was much abused for his strictness, not least because his own light verse has prurient edges; but abuse is an inevitable concomitant of the office. Colman's Examinership was unimpressive but not malicious. The submerged tradition that he was the author of *Don Leon*, a witty and obscene poem in heroic couplets proposing an explanation of the collapse of Lord Byron's marriage, may owe its currency to a contemporary delight in taxing with immorality the official guardian of theatrical morals.

—Peter Thomson

CONGREVE, William. English. Born in Bardsey, Yorkshire, baptized 10 February 1670; moved with his family to Ireland, 1674. Educated at school in Kilkenny, 1681–85; Trinity College, Dublin; Middle Temple, London, 1691. Involved with Henrietta, Duchess of Marlborough, who bore him a daughter. Manager, Lincoln's Inn Theatre, London, 1697–1705; wrote little for the stage after failure of *The Way of the World*, 1700; associated with Vanbrugh in managing the Queen's Theatre, London, 1705; retired from the theatre, 1706, and thereafter, at the intercession of friends, held various minor government posts, including Commissioner of Wine Licenses, Undersearcher of Customs, and Secretary for Jamaica. *Died 19 January 1729.*

PUBLICATIONS

Collections

Complete Works, edited by Montague Summers.   4 vols., 1923.
Works, edited by F. W. Bateson.   1930.
Letters and Documents, edited by John C. Hodges.   1964.
Complete Plays, edited by Herbert J. Davis.   2 vols., 1967.
The Comedies, edited by Anthony G. Henderson.   1977.

Plays

The Old Bachelor (produced 1693).   1693.
The Double-Dealer (produced 1693).   1694.
Love for Love (produced 1695).   1695.
The Mourning Bride (produced 1697).   1697.
The Way of the World (produced 1700).   1700.
The Judgement of Paris (produced 1701).   1701.
Semele, in *Works*.   1710.
Squire Trelooby, with Vanbrugh and William Walsh, from a play by Molière (produced 1704).   Revised version by James Ralph published as *The Cornish Squire*, 1734.

Fiction

Incognita; or, Love and Duty Reconciled.   1692; edited by A. Norman Jeffares, with *The Way of the World*, 1966.
An Impossible Thing: A Tale.   1720.

Other

Amendments of Mr. Collier's False and Imperfect Citations.   1698.
Works.   3 vols., 1710.
A Letter to the Viscount Cobham.   1729.
Last Will and Testament.   1729.

Editor, *The Dramatic Works of Dryden.*   6 vols., 1717.

Reading List: *Congreve* by D. Crane Taylor, 1931; *Congreve the Man: A Biography* by John

C. Hodges, 1941; *A Congreve Gallery* by Kathleen M. Lynch, 1951; *Congreve* by Bonamy Dobrée, 1963; *The Cultivated Stance: The Designs of Congreve's Plays* by W. Van Voris, 1966; *Congreve* by Maximillian E. Novak, 1971 (includes bibliography); *Congreve: A Collection of Critical Studies,* edited by Brian Morris, 1972.

*   *   *

William Congreve is now largely read for his plays; his poems, some of which had made his name in London by 1692, are polished and epigrammatic; he wrote translations, short lyrics, and occasional poems as well as ballads, his neat songs being perhaps his best contribution. But his first literary work of note is *Incognita*, a novel largely influenced by stage techniques. Congreve wrote it, he tells us in his *Preface*, in a fortnight; he decided to imitate dramatic writing in the plot. This is a double one with two pairs of lovers. Mistaken identities, the lovers unaware their elders have already arranged the marriages as they themselves would wish them, family feuds ultimately settled by the marriages – all of it echoes polite society and permits romantic feeling. It is finely controlled, and the comic situations bring out the sophistication with which Congreve wrote this elegant, flowing story. He told the story with obvious enjoyment and embellished it with somewhat cynical comments.

His first play was *The Old Batchelor*, a light comedy full of witty conversation, yet with undertones of reality in the character of Heartwell, the surly old bachelor who prides himself on speaking truth. He is different from the stock characters of Restoration comedy, the rakes and fops; and, of course, he is entrapped and then exposed. The situation is comic, the flippancy of Bellmour and Vainlove matched by the mockery of Belinda. And the whole play moves quickly, with a liveliness that probably owed much to Congreve's careful study of Plautus, Terence and Juvenal, as well as of Ben Jonson and the Restoration playwrights.

The Double-Dealer followed, a sombre play indeed, which verges upon the tragic, although it has its lively songs, its coxcombs and coquettes and its wit. Maskwell is Iago-like in his machinations and Lady Touchwood's fate, after her infamy is exposed, is hardly the stuff of comedy, however much Congreve thought comedy should expose the follies of vicious people. By making them ashamed of these faults, he remarked, it should instruct them, while delighting good people "who are at once both warn'd and diverted at the expense of the Vicious." The comedy was too black for its time, however much the reader can admire the classical skill Congreve showed in its construction, its unity of time – a few hours in one evening – and place – for the action takes place in the long gallery of Lord Touchwood's house (except for two episodes in a room opening off it). The absurdity of Mr. Brisk and Lord Froth, pert and solemn coxcombs respectively, Lady Froth, the coquette who pretends to poetry, wit, and learning, and Sir Paul Plyant, an uxorious old fool, all relieve the play's starkness, and indeed we realise Cynthia and Mellefont are convincingly in love, however she may doubt the merits of marriage. The comedy centres upon Maskwell's continuous capacity for intrigue, and the passion displayed not only by the Touchwoods but by Mellefont suggests that Congreve's concept of comedy was dominated in writing this play by satiric ambitions.

His next play, *Love for Love*, rightly brought him back to public favour. This is his best acting play; it has a clear plot, abundant absurdity, humorous characterisation, and satire in plenty. Here are the stock ingredients of the comedy of manners: youth and age in conflict, contrasts between city and country ways, questions of debts and inheritances, conversations between master and servant, intrigues and marriages, deceits and witty conversations. Foresight, with his passion for astrology, his hypochondria, and his credulity, is Jonsonian; Sir Sampson Legend, authoritarian father and self-deluding lover, matches him in comic characterisation, and is akin to one of Molière's creations.

Miss Prue, the wilful ingenue, is matched by the bluff young sailor Ben, another Jonsonian character whose "humour" is marked out by his nautical language. Scandal's affair with Mrs. Foresight follows the conventional pattern of comedy which recognises the relationship of rakes and cynical married women who enjoy intrigue; Mrs. Frail, wanting to marry Valentine for his money, is tricked into marriage with Tattle whom she despises, and Valentine marries Angelica. But he has to live down his past; she is enigmatic in her response to him until he renounces his inheritance and so proves he is not primarily interested in her wealth. The "humour, plot and satire" claimed in the Prologue are all there, but this relationship between Valentine and Angelica moves a little from Restoration conventions; a touch of idealism suddenly penetrates the cynicism of Restoration comic conventions. Wit and gallantry, Angelica argues at the end of the play, are not enough. And the idealism is, perhaps, founded upon disillusion, and upon a certain fastidiousness.

In *The Mourning Bride* Congreve tried his hand at the heroic play, that strange genre which flourished in Charles the Second's age and is somewhat baffling to us. Here we have the classical use of rhetoric and music, exalted verse, and a lively plot. Congreve exhibits his dramatic sense in welding together two themes – the love of Alphonso and Almeira, and the passion of Zara, her murder of Selim, and her suicide – against a broad background of a popular resistance movement against a tyrant. For the play is violently dramatic and arresting, its language exalted yet affective.

Congreve, who had written "An Essay Concerning Humour in Comedy" in 1695 which, as well as distinguishing between wit and humour, offers us an excellent defence of English eccentricity, was now forced into a situation where he had, in effect, to defend humour on the stage. Jeremy Collier's attack on the immorality and profanity of the English stage prompted Congreve's *Amendments of Mr. Collier's False and Imperfect Citations*. It is an example of how not to reply in anger; but it shows us something more of Congreve's attitudes to comedy: that the satirical portrayal of well bred people was justifiable if their manners were ridiculous, that the author's own ideas must not be thought the same as those of the foolish people he exposed on the stage, that passages from those plays should not be taken out of context.

There followed Congreve's most brilliant comedy, *The Way of the World*, virtually his last work for the stage. (He subsequently wrote a masque, *The Judgement of Paris*, and an "Ode for St. Cecilia's Day.") This is a complex play, revolving around marriage and money, in which information is slowly revealed, and things turn out not to be what they seem. Lady Wishfort, gullible and gulled, is finally forced to allow Mirabell and Millamant to marry, Fainall is exposed, Mrs. Marwood and Mrs. Fainall suffer. The minor characters, Sir Wilfull Witwoud the buffoon, Petulant and Witwoud the fops, the servants Foible, Mincing, and Waitwell, are all brilliantly drawn, differentiated, from their first appearance on stage, by their language and attitudes. And Mirabell and Millamant mark a new refinement; they foreshadow a new sensibility, a humane quality. And they are witty, polished, epigrammatic in speech. The whole play is sparkling and lively, it brings order out of chaos, and shows Congreve was fundamentally serious, moral, idealistic. This is an impression confirmed by the few letters of his which survive. In these his warmth of heart balances his astuteness, his taste and delicacy show why his contemporaries looked upon him with – in Steele's words – "the greatest affection and veneration."

—A. Norman Jeffares

COWLEY, Hannah (née Parkhouse). English. Born in Tiverton, Devon, in 1743. Privately educated. Married Captain Thomas Cowley c. 1768 (died, 1797); one son and one daughter. Wrote for the stage, 1776–95; as Anna Matilda engaged in poetical correspondence with Robert Merry ("Della Crusca") in *World*, 1787. *Died 11 March 1809.*

PUBLICATIONS

Collections

Works: Dramas and Poems.   3 vols., 1813.

Plays

The Runaway (produced 1776).   1776.
Who's the Dupe? (produced 1779).   1779.
Albina, Countess Raimond (produced 1779).   1779.
The Belle's Stratagem (produced 1780).   1781; edited by T. H. Lacy, 1867.
The School of Eloquence (produced 1780).
The World as It Goes; or, A Party at Montpellier (produced 1781); as *Second Thoughts Are Best* (produced 1781).
Which Is the Man? (produced 1783).   1782.
A Bold Stroke for a Husband (produced 1783).   1784.
More Ways Than One (produced 1783).   1784; as *New Ways to Catch Hearts* (produced 1783).
A School for Greybeards; or, The Mourning Bride, from the play *The Lucky Chance* by Behn (produced 1786).   1786.
The Fate of Sparta; or, The Rival Kings (produced 1788).   1788.
A Day in Turkey; or, The Russian Slaves (produced 1791).   1792.
The Town Before You (produced 1794).   1795.

Verse

The Maid of Aragon: A Tale.   1780.
The Scottish Village; or, Pitcairne Greene.   1786.
The Poetry of Anna Matilda.   1788.
The Siege of Acre: An Epic Poem.   1801; revised edition, 1810.

Bibliography: "Some Uncollected Authors 16: Cowley" by J. E. Norton, and "Cowley" by William B. Todd, in *Book Collector 7*, 1958.

*   *   *

Hannah Cowley's first play, *The Runaway*, was a country-house comedy dedicated to Garrick, who "nourished" and "embellished" it. According to *The Gentleman's Magazine* for 1809, the play was written in a fortnight; if so, Cowley wrote fluently, for it is an unusually good first effort and lasted ten seasons on the stage. Her second work, *Who's the Dupe?*, a two-act farce, became one of the most popular afterpieces of the period. Later plays, including the comic opera *A Day in Turkey*, are five-act mainpieces. The two tragedies were fairly successful – *Albina, Countess Raimond* ran for seven nights and *The Fate of Sparta* for nine – but their plots are hackneyed and their language and characters dull.

The comedies, however, are among the best of their day. *The Belle's Stratagem* was the fourth most popular mainpiece written between 1776 and 1800 and was revived as late as 1913. It mixes fast-paced comic intrigue with witty dialogue and sets off a sparkling heroine and her lover in the main plot against a more sentimental pair in the sub-plot. This pattern is often repeated in later successes like *Which Is the Man?* and *More Ways Than One*. In the latter, for example, Miss Archer recalls Letitia Hardy of *The Belle's Stratagem* and Arabella parallels Lady Touchwood; in each case, the witty heroine better reflects the tone of the play than the sober one. Occasionally the blocking action opposes a father to a daughter or ward; more often, the obstacle is the attitude of one of the principals, in which cases Cowley has the other use some "stratagem" to assure the comic resolution. These comedies and *The Town Before You*, Cowley's last play, often suggest the gaiety of earlier comedy, particularly in their dialogue and heroines. Intrigue is nevertheless prominent and sometimes central, as in *A School for Greybeards*, based on Aphra Behn's *The Lucky Chance*; it sometimes sinks into farce and sometimes produces developed characters like Lord Sparkle in *Which Is the Man?*

Cowley is a mediocre poetess. *The Maid of Aragon*, *The Scottish Village*, "Edwina," and *The Siege of Acre* are included in her collected works but will not bear rereading. The last-named is interesting as an epic by a woman, but Cowley's patriotism cannot excuse her couplets. As a comic dramatist she deserves to be better known. Most of her mainpieces are fresh enough in language to play successfully today. Though she draws her characters and comic situations from the large pool used by all the dramatists of the century, she chooses and combines these elements well and is usually able to vivify the stereotype. Her best characters, especially, are memorable creations.

—Frederick M. Link

CROWNE, John. English. Born, probably in Shropshire, c. 1640; emigrated with his family to Nova Scotia, where they were granted territory by Cromwell, 1656; returned to England after the Restoration when the French seized the land, 1660. Early in the reign of Charles II worked as a gentleman-usher to a lady in London; began writing in 1665; wrote for the theatre from 1671. *Died in April 1712.*

PUBLICATIONS

Collections

   Dramatic Works, edited by James Maidment and W. H. Logan.   4 vols., 1872–74.

Plays

   Juliana; or, The Princess of Poland (produced 1671).   1671.
   The History of Charles the Eighth of France; or, The Invasion of Naples by the French (produced 1671).   1672.
   Andromache, from a play by Racine (produced 1674).   1675.
   The Prologue to Calisto, with Choruses Between the Acts.   1675
   Calisto; or, The Chaste Nymph, music by Nicholas Staggins (produced 1675).   1675.
   The Country Wit (produced 1676).   1675.
   The Destruction of Jerusalem by Titus Vespasian, 2 parts (produced 1677).   1677; part 1 edited by Bonamy Dobrée, in *Five Heroic Plays,* 1960.
   The Ambitious Statesman; or, The Loyal Favourite (produced 1679).   1679.

The Misery of Civil War, from a play by Shakespeare (produced 1680).   1680; as *Henry the Sixth,* part 2, 1681.
Thyestes (produced 1680).   1681.
Henry the Sixth, part 1, from the play by Shakespeare (produced 1681).   1681.
City Politics (produced 1683).   1683; edited by John H. Wilson, 1967.
Sir Courtly Nice; or, It Cannot Be (produced 1685).   1685; edited by A. Norman Jeffares, in *Restoration Comedy,* 1974.
Darius, King of Persia (produced 1688).   1688.
The English Friar; or, The Town Sparks (produced 1690).   1690.
Regulus (produced 1692).   1694.
The Married Beau; or, The Curious Impertinent (produced 1694).   1694.
Caligula (produced 1698).   1698.

Fiction

Pandion and Amphigenia; or, The History of the Coy Lady of Thessalis.   1665.

Verse

A Poem on the Death of King Charles the II.   1685.
Daeneids; or, The Noble Labours of the Great Dean of Notre-Dame in Paris: An Heroic Poem, from a poem by Boileau.   1692.
The History of the Love Between a Parisian Lady and a Young Singing Man: An Heroic Poem.   1692.

Other

Notes and Observations on The Empress of Morocco by Settle, with Dryden and Shadwell.   1674.

Bibliography: *The First Harvard Playwright: A Bibliography of Crowne* by George P. Winship, 1922.

Reading List: *Crowne: His Life and Dramatic Works* by Arthur F. White, 1922; *The Restoration Court Stage, with a Particular Account of the Production of Calisto* by Eleanore Boswell, 1932; Introduction by Charlotte B. Hughes to *Sir Courtly Nice,* 1966.

*   *   *

John Crowne's strengths are his sharp characterizations and a sense of the stage as medium. A competent and successful dramatist, Crowne combined an understanding of contemporary taste with consistent ethical principles. His tragedies reflect the shifting forms and politics of his age, and his comedies the growing demand for sentimental reform. His contempt for political and religious faction, for fanaticism, and for tyranny of all sorts underlies much of his work.

Although Sir Courtly Nice is Crowne's best known character, his Sir Mannerly Shallow, Ramble, and the Molierian servant girl Isabella in *The Country Wit* and Young Ranter and Father Finical in *The English Friar* are well drawn satiric figures. Each represents a familiar London type and benefits from the tradition of humours characters while bearing wider implications. Ranter, for example, is a rake and a bully, a farcical rowdy, yet his father and society's tolerance contribute to his immorality. The characterizations benefit from lively dialogue often sprinkled with witty conceits, idiomatic phrases, and graceful sentences. Crowne writes far better than most of his peers and individualizes almost every character. Bartoline lisps, Artall delights in his wit, and Florio pretends piety in *City Politiques*. A number of characters refer to Adam, Eve, Eden, and the serpent in *The Married Beau*, and their words ("we are sons of Adam/And he ne'er got much honour by his sons") suit their morals. Although Crowne's tragedies have more conventional characters, some of them are notable. The Constable of France in *The Ambitious Statesman*, Caligula, and Atreus are merciless tyrants: Phraartes, the rational opponent of religion in *The Destruction of Jerusalem*, and Memnon, the son of the Amazon in *Darius*, are original heroes. Crowne is particularly good at pairing characters. The courageous, honorable Valerius contrasts to the posturing, mad Caligula: *The History of Charles the Eighth of France* has three heroes; Airy and Laura represent two types of irresponsibility in *The English Friar*.

Crowne's comic plots are rich in intrigue, discoveries, stage business, and satire. Laura chases Young Ranter with a sword: Surly smudges and belches upon the fastidious Sir Courtly Nice, and Florio and Artall anticipate Wycherley's Horner in feigning illness in order to gain access to other men's wives. Crowne's tragedies abound with virtuous maidens, wronged queens, noble warriors, tyrants, conspirators, and ghosts in plots familiar to any student of the heroic play. Within the conventions, however, Crowne produces some well-plotted, effective plays. He arranges Antigone's visit to her imprisoned mother immediately before the scene in which her lover finds his exiled father in a cave (*Thyestes*); he portrays Phraartes's frenzied reaction to Cleonora's death just before Titus Vespasian renounces Berenice in the interest of Titus's duty to Rome. Crowne, however, is capable of extravagant language and excessive violence. The Constable of France racks his own son on stage; Atreus serves Thyestes his son's blood and then the butchered body is displayed; Darius's ghost appears and gloats over the mangled bodies of his murderers.

In addition to his tragedies and comedies, Crowne wrote a court masque, *Calisto*, an adaptation of Racine's *Andromache*, two adaptations of Shakespearian plays, and a tragicomedy, *Juliana*.

—Paula R. Backscheider

CUMBERLAND, Richard.   English.   Born in Cambridge, 19 February 1732. Educated at a school in Bury St. Edmunds, Suffolk; Westminster School, London, 1744–47; Trinity College, Cambridge, 1747–51, B.A. 1751. Married Elizabeth Ridge in 1759; 4 sons and 3 daughters. Fellow of Trinity College, 1752; Private Secretary to Lord Halifax in the 1750's, and Ulster Secretary under Halifax, 1761–62; Clerk of Reports, 1762–75, and Secretary, 1775–80, Board of Trade; retired to Tunbridge Wells, Kent. D.C.L.: University of Dublin, 1771. *Died 7 May 1811*.

PUBLICATIONS

Plays

The Banishment of Cicero.   1761.

The Summer's Tale, music by Thomas Arne (produced 1765). 1765; revised version, as *Amelia* (produced 1768), 1768; revised version, music by Charles Dibdin (produced 1771), 1771.

The Brothers (produced 1769). 1770.

The West Indian (produced 1771). 1771.

Timon of Athens, from the play by Shakespeare (produced 1771). 1771.

The Fashionable Lover (produced 1772). 1772.

The Squire's Return (produced 1772).

The Note of Hand; or, The Trip to Newmarket (produced 1774). 1774.

The Choleric Man (produced 1774). 1775.

The Princess of Parma (produced 1778).

The Election (produced 1778).

Calypson: A Masque, in *Miscellaneous Poems.* 1778; revised version, music by Thomas Butler (produced 1779), 1779.

The Bondman, from the play by Massinger (produced 1779).

The Duke of Milan, from the play by Massinger (produced 1779).

The Widow of Delphi; or, The Descent of the Deities, music by Thomas Butler (produced 1780). Songs published 1780.

The Walloons (produced 1782). In *Posthumous Dramatic Works,* 1813.

The Mysterious Husband (produced 1783). 1783.

The Carmelite (produced 1784). 1784.

The Natural Son (produced 1784). 1785; revised version (produced 1794).

Alcanor (as *The Arab,* produced 1786). In *Posthumous Dramatic Works,* 1813.

The Country Attorney (produced 1787; as *The School for Widows,* produced 1789).

The Imposters (produced 1789). 1789.

An Occasional Prelude (produced 1792).

The Clouds, from the play by Aristophanes. 1792.

The Armourer (produced 1793). Songs published 1793.

The Box-Lobby Challenge (produced 1794). 1794.

The Jew (produced 1794). 1794.

The Wheel of Fortune (produced 1795). 1795.

First Love (produced 1795). 1795.

The Defendant (produced 1795).

The Days of Yore (produced 1796). 1796.

Don Pedro (produced 1796). In *Posthumous Dramatic Works,* 1813.

The Last of the Family (produced 1797). In *Posthumous Dramatic Works,* 1813.

The Village Fete (produced 1797).

False Impressions (produced 1797). 1797.

The Eccentric Lover (produced 1798). In *Posthumous Dramatic Works,* 1813.

The Passive Husband (as *A Word for Nature,* produced 1798). In *Posthumous Dramatic Works,* 1813.

Joanna of Montfaucon, music by Thomas Busby, from a work by Kotzebue (produced 1800). 1800.

Lover's Resolutions (produced 1802). In *Posthumous Dramatic Works,* 1813.

The Sailor's Daughter (produced 1804). 1804.

The Death and Victory of Lord Nelson (produced 1805). 1805.

A Hint to Husbands (produced 1806). 1806.

The Jew of Mogadore, music by Michael Kelly (produced 1808). 1808.

The Robber (produced 1809).

The Widow's Only Son (produced 1810).

Posthumous Dramatic Works (includes the unproduced plays *The Confession, Torrendal, Tiberius in Capreae, The False Demetrius*). 2 vols., 1813.

The Sybil; or, The Elder Brutus (produced 1818). In *Posthumous Dramatic Works,* 1813.

Fiction

> *Arundel.* 1789.
> *Henry.* 1795.
> *John de Lancaster.* 1809.

Verse

> *An Elegy Written on Saint Mark's Eve.* 1754.
> *Odes.* 1776.
> *Miscellaneous Poems.* 1778.
> *Calvary; or, The Death of Christ.* 1792.
> *A Poetical Version of Certain Psalms of David.* 1801.
> *The Exodiad,* with J. B. Burges. 1801.
> *Retrospective: A Poem in Familiar Verse.* 1811.

Other

> *A Letter to the Bishop of O—d.* 1767.
> *Anecdotes of Eminent Painters in Spain During the 16th and 17th Centuries.* 2 vols., 1782.
> *A Letter to Richard, Lord Bishop of Llandaff.* 1783.
> *Character of the Late Viscount Sackville.* 1785.
> *An Accurate Catalogue of the Paintings in the King of Spain's Palace at Madrid.* 1787.
> *The Observer.* 5 vols., 1788; edited by A. Chalmers, in *British Essayists,* 1817.
> *A Few Plain Reasons Why We Should Believe in Christ.* 1801; as *The Anti Carlile,* 1826.
> *Memoirs.* 2 vols., 1806–07; edited by Henry Flanders, 1856.

> Editor, *Pharsalia,* by Lucan. 1760.
> Editor, *The London Review.* 2 vols., 1809.
> Editor, *The British Drama.* 14 vols., 1817.

Reading List: *Cumberland: His Life and Dramatic Works* by Stanley T. Williams, 1917 (includes bibliography); *Dramatic Character in the English Romantic Age* by Joseph Donohue, 1970; *Cumberland* by Richard J. Dircks, 1976.

*   *   *

Richard Cumberland is better remembered as the original of Sir Fretful Plagiary in Sheridan's *The Critic* than for his own prolific output, although *The West Indian* gets a mention in most theatrical histories as an archetype of sentimental comedy. Yet Cumberland was the author of around fifty plays in most contemporary forms, including a new version of *Timon of Athens* and, in *The Jew,* an enlightened plea for its time on behalf of a persecuted people. Sensitive to criticism though Cumberland was (and as his own *Memoirs* affirms), Sheridan's satire did nothing to discourage a dramatic career which began with *The Banishment of Cicero* in 1761 and ended with *The Widow's Only Son* just a year before his death, fifty years later.

Goldsmith, in his posthumous *Retaliation,* describes him as: "A flattering painter who made it his care/To draw men as they ought to be, not as they are." And it is true that his comedies too often tended to be the "bastard tragedies" Goldsmith elsewhere dubbed them.

Yet Cumberland's first play was a true tragedy, and he also tried his hand at comic opera before attempting his first comedy, *The Brothers*, in 1769. Presumably it was the relatively favourable reception accorded this play that encouraged him to continue in this vein with *The West Indian*, whose titular hero, Belcour, blunders his good-natured but untutored way through London society, a sort of diluted, colonial version of Tom Jones.

The plot of the play is convoluted even by the standards of its time, and few of the characters do more than exemplify their required vice or virtue: but Belcour himself is strong enough to sustain a certain interest through the twists and turns of the plotting, and the Irish Major O'Flaherty, an honest soldier of fortune, serves occasionally to deflate the more sententious exchanges. If Cumberland lacked much originality, his work remains nevertheless an interesting link between sentimental comedy and melodrama, and the moral code enshrined in the one is often expressed in the exclamatory style of the other in his later work.

—Simon Trussler

DENNIS, John. English. Born in London in 1657. Educated at Harrow School, 1670–75; Caius College, Cambridge, 1675–79, B.A. 1679; awarded M.A. at Trinity Hall, Cambridge, 1683. Fellow of Trinity Hall, 1679–80, then settled in London: noted early in his career as a political pamphleteer, subsequently as a playwright, and later, most notably, as a literary critic; enjoyed patronage of the Duke of Marlborough; "royal waiter" in the Port of London, 1705–20; involved in a literary feud with Alexander Pope from 1711; lived in great poverty at the end of his life. *Died 6 January 1734.*

PUBLICATIONS

Plays

A Plot and No Plot (produced 1697).   1697.
Rinaldo and Armida (produced 1698).   1699.
Iphigenia (produced 1699).   1700.
The Comical Gallant; or, The Amours of Sir John Falstaff, from the play *The Merry Wives of Windsor* by Shakespeare (produced 1702).   1702.
Liberty Asserted (produced 1704).   1704.
Gibraltar; or, The Spanish Adventure (produced 1705).   1705.
Orpheus and Eurydice.   1707.
Appius and Virginia (produced 1709).   1709.
The Invader of His Country; or, The Fatal Resentment, from the play *Coriolanus* by Shakespeare (produced 1719).   1720.

Verse

Poems in Burlesque.   1692.

Poems and Letters upon Several Occasions. 1692.
The Passion of Byblis, from Ovid. 1692.
Miscellanies in Verse and Prose. 1693; as *Miscellany Poems,* 1697.
The Court of Death: A Pindaric Poem to the Memory of Queen Mary. 1695.
The Nuptials of Britain's Genius and Fame: A Pindaric Poem on the Peace. 1697.
The Monument: A Poem to the Memory of William the Third. 1702.
Britannia Triumphans. 1704.
The Battle of Ramillia. 1706.
A Poem upon the Death of Queen Anne and the Accession of King George. 1714.

Other

The Impartial Critic; or, Some Observations upon "A Short View of Tragedy" by Rymer. 1693.
Remarks on a Book Entitled King Arthur. 1696.
Letters upon Several Occasions. 1696.
The Usefulness of the Stage. 1698.
The Seamen's Case. 1700(?).
The Advancement and Reformation of Modern Poetry: A Critical Discourse. 1701.
The Danger of Priestcraft to Religion and Government. 1702.
An Essay on the Navy. 1702.
A Proposal for Putting a Speedy End to the War. 1703.
The Person of Quality's Answer to Mr. Collier's Letter. 1704.
The Grounds of Criticism in Poetry. 1704.
An Essay on the Operas after the Italian Manner. 1706.
An Essay upon Public Spirit, Being a Satire in Prose upon the Manners and Luxury of the Times. 1711.
Reflections Critical and Satirical upon a Late Rhapsody Called "An Essay upon Criticism." 1711.
An Essay upon the Genius and Writings of Shakespeare. 1712.
Priestcraft Distinguished from Christianity. 1715.
A True Character of Mr. Pope and His Writings. 1716.
Reflections upon Mr. Pope's Translation of Homer, with Two Letters Concerning "Windsor Forest" and "The Temple of Fame." 1717.
Select Works. 2 vols., 1718; revised edition, 1718–21.
The Characters and Conduct of Sir John Edgar and His Three Deputy Governors. 1720; *Third and Fourth Letter,* 1720.
Original Letters, Familiar, Moral, and Critical. 2 vols., 1721.
A Defense of Sir Fopling Flutter. 1722.
Julius Caesar Acquitted and His Murderers Condemned. 1722.
Remarks upon a Play Called "The Conscious Lovers." 1723.
Vice and Luxury Public Mischiefs; or, Remarks on a Book Entitled "The Fable of the Bees." 1724.
The Stage Defended from Scripture, Reason, Experience, and the Common Sense of Mankind. 1726.
Miscellaneous Tracts, vol. 1. 1727.
Remarks upon Mr. Pope's "Rape of the Lock," in Several Letters to a Friend. 1728.
Remarks upon Several Passages in the Preliminaries to "The Dunciad," and in Pope's Preface to His Translation of Homer's Iliad. 1729.
Critical Works, edited by Edward N. Hooker. 2 vols., 1939–43.

Translator, with others, *The Annals and History of Tacitus,* vol. 3. 1698.
Translator, *The Faith and Duties of Christians,* by Thomas Burnet. 1728.

Translator, *A Treatise Concerning the State of Departed Souls,* by Thomas Burnet. 1730.

Reading List: *Dennis: His Life and Criticism* by Harry G. Paul, 1911; *The Word "Sublime" and Its Context 1650–1760* by Theodore E. B. Wood, 1972.

*   *   *

John Dennis attained greater stature as a critic than as a playwright, and it is on his criticism, chiefly, that his reputation as an arch-classicist rests. According to Pope (*Essay on Criticism*), Don Quixote (in the Georgian continuation)

> Discours'd in Terms as just, with Looks as Sage,
> As e'er cou'd *Dennis,* of the *Grecian* Stage;
> Concluding all were desp'rate Sots and Fools,
> Who durst depart from *Aristotle*'s Rules.

If the second couplet is aimed at Dennis it misses the mark. Throughout his career, Dennis (like Pope) did regard Aristotle, Horace, and other ancients as the clear, unchanging universal light of "methodiz'd" Nature in which contemporary literature should be examined; his classicism is particularly evident in the cogent attacks on *The Conscious Lovers* as a misunderstanding of traditional comedy. But – as Edward N. Hooker writes in the indispensable introduction to the *Critical Works* – Dennis was an "intelligent classicist," a man alive to the power of passion in life and art, not the dry expounder of dead rules that Pope satirized. He knew and approved Longinus on the sublime; he felt, and admitted that he felt, the sublimity of the Alps and of Shakespeare. The latter, indeed, gave him difficulties, but also brought out his critical honesty: he testified to Shakespeare's greatness as well as to his disregard of the "Rules of dramatick Composition" which Dennis espoused, and then followed his logic beyond the point where angels and prudence bad him stop. Shakespeare would have written even better had he possessed "Learning and the Poetical Art," and his plays could now be improved by remedying these defects. Dennis proceeded to "regularize" *The Merry Wives of Windsor* as *The Comical Gallant,* and *Coriolanus* ("Where Master-strokes in wild Confusion lye") as *The Invader of His Country.* Both failed.

Whenever he turned from theory to practice, in fact, Dennis struggled as if in an alien medium. He could not contrive to embody his ideas in dramatic form so as to move spectators or readers, though he tried everything, even abandoning his own critical precepts; Dennis's plays were much more hospitable to "romantic" influences such as the heroic drama than his relevant critical prose would lead one to expect. The Preface to *Rinaldo and Armida* announces a *telos* of Sophoclean terror, but the text itself is a rather entertaining hodge-podge of masque, opera, and tragi-comedy with debts to Tasso, Spenser, Dryden, and Milton ("perhaps the greatest genius" in 1700 years). It contains a song with the deathless couplet – "All around venereal Turtles/Cooing, billing, on the Myrtles" – which gives some idea of the distance between Dennis and a neoclassicist such as Addison. *Iphigenia* indulged in spectacular costumes and a mighty tempest that later occasioned Dennis's only contribution to English idiom: "They've stolen my thunder!" *Liberty Asserted,* set in Canada, features a half-breed noble savage and exhibits a fondness for rant: "These are Events surpassing all Examples;/These are th'amazing Miracles of Fate!" His few comic pieces are quite unclassical.

It is easy to see why critics and audiences did not like Dennis's plays: bombast, uncertain plotting, awkward exposition, a certain laborious lifelessness. Unfortunately the repeated failures brought out a captious streak in Dennis that allowed Pope to liken him to Appius, the irascible tyrant of one of his own tragedies.

In one overlong preface after another Dennis blamed his woes on audiences, managers, theatres, the acting, the weather, or a combination thereof, and his strictures on successful playwrights such as Steele became suspect. Dennis could not accept the verdict of theatrical audiences – whom he considered ignorant, mercantile, and debased – as final, appealing instead to the reading public, to posterity; but posterity has so far seen no reason to overturn the original decision against his plays, though it has sometimes endorsed his criticism.

—R. W. Bevis

DIBDIN, Charles. English. Born in Southampton, Hampshire, baptized 4 March 1745. Chorister, Winchester Cathedral, Hampshire, 1756–60. Married c. 1764, but later left his wife; associated with the actress Harriet Pitt, 1767–74: had three children by her, including the playwrights Charles Isaac Mungo Dibdin and Thomas Dibdin; later married Anne Wylde, four children. Settled in London, 1760; singer and actor from 1762, and appeared in theatres in London and the provinces; playwright and composer: wrote some 1400 songs; contract composer at Drury Lane, London, 1769–76; lived in France, 1776–78; returned to Drury Lane, 1778–81; Joint Manager of the Royal Circus, later called the Surrey, 1782–85; proprietor of the periodicals *The Devil*, 1786–87, and *The Bystander: or, Universal Weekly Expositor*, 1789–90; solo performer of "entertainments" from 1787, and had his own theatre, the Sans Souci, 1796–1805. Granted Civil List pension, 1803. *Died 25 July 1814.*

PUBLICATIONS

Plays

The Shepherd's Artifice, music by the author (produced 1764).   1765.
The Mischance, music by the author (produced 1773).
The Ladle, music by the author, from the poem by Prior (produced 1773).   1773.
The Wedding Ring, music by the author, from a play by Goldoni (produced 1773).   Songs published 1773.
La Zingara; or, The Gipsy, music by F. H. Barthélémon, from a play by Mme. Favart (produced 1773).
The Deserter, music by the author, from a play by Michel Jean Sedaine, music by P. A. Monsigny and F. A. Philidor (produced 1773).   1773.
The Waterman; or, The First of August, music by the author (produced 1774).   1774.
The Cobbler; or, A Wife of Ten Thousand, music by the author, from a play by Michel Jean Sedaine (produced 1774).   1774.
The Quaker, music by the author (produced 1775).   1777.
The Comic Mirror, music by the author (produced 1775).
The Metamorphoses, music by the author, from plays by Molière (produced 1775).   1776.
The Seraglio, with E. Thompson, music by the author (produced 1776).   1776.

Poor Vulcan, music by the author, from a play by P. A. Motteux (produced 1778).   1778.

She Is Mad for a Husband, music by the author (produced 1778).

The Gipsies, music by Samuel Arnold, from a play by Mme. Favart (produced 1778).   1778.

Rose and Colin, music by the author, from a play by Michel Jean Sedaine (produced 1778).   1778.

The Wives Revenged, music by the author, from a play by Michel Jean Sedaine (produced 1778).   1778.

Annette and Lubin, music by the author, from a play by Santerre and Mme. Favart (produced 1778).   1778.

The Chelsea Pensioner, music by the author (produced 1779).   1779.

The Touchstone; or, Harlequin Traveller, music by the author (produced 1779).   Songs published 1779.

The Mirror; or, Harlequin Everywhere, music by the author (produced 1779).   1779.

The Shepherdess of the Alps, music by the author, from an opera by J. F. Marmontel, music by Joseph Kohaut (produced 1780).   1780.

The Islanders, music by the author, from plays by Saint-Foix and Framéry (produced 1780).   Songs published 1780; revised version, as *The Marriage Act* (produced 1781), 1781.

Harlequin Freemason, with J. Messink, music by the author (produced 1780).

Jupiter and Alcmena, music by the author, from the play *Amphitryon* by Dryden (produced 1781).

None So Blind as Those Who Won't See, music by Samuel Arnold, from a play by Dorvigny (produced 1782).

The Graces, music by the author (produced 1782).   1782.

The Passions, music by the author (produced 1783).

The Regions of Accomplishment, music by the author (produced 1783).

The Cestus, music by the author (produced 1783).   1783.

Harlequin Phantom of a Day, music by the author (produced 1783).   1783.

The Lancashire Witches; or, The Distress of Harlequin, music by the author (produced 1783).

The Talisman of Orosmanes, music by the author (produced 1783).   1783(?).

The Long Odds, music by the author (produced 1783).   1783.

The Milkmaid, music by the author (produced 1783).

The Saloon, music by the author (produced 1784).

The Statue; or, The Bower of Confidence, music by the author (produced 1785).

Life, Death, and Renovation of Tom Thumb, music by the author (produced 1785).   1785(?).

Clump and Cudden; or, The Review, music by the author (produced 1785).   1785.

Liberty Hall; or, A Test of Good Fellowship, music by the author (produced 1785).   1785.

Harvest Home, music by the author (produced 1787).   1787.

The Fortune Hunters; or, You May Say That, music by the author (produced 1789).

A Cure for a Coxcomb; or, The Beau Bedevilled, music by the author and John Collins (produced 1792).

A Loyal Effusion, music by the author (produced 1794).

A Pennyworth of Wit; or, The Wife and the Mistress, music by John Davy (produced 1796).

First Come, First Served, music by the author (produced 1797).

Hannah Hewit; or, The Female Crusoe, music by the author, from his own novel (produced 1798).   Songs published in *Chorus of Melody*, n.d.

The Broken Gold, music by the author (produced 1806).

The Round Robin (produced 1811).

Other plays and entertainments: *The False Dervise, The Land of Simplicity, Pandora, The Refusal of Harlequin, The Razor-Grinder, England Against Italy, The Imposter, The Old Woman of Eighty;* performer in *The Whim of the Moment* and *The Oddities,* 1789, and *The Wags,* 1790 – performances continued until 1809.

Fiction

Hannah Hewit; or, The Female Crusoe.   1792.
The Younger Brother.   1793.
Henry Hooka.   1807.

Verse

The Harmonic Preceptor.   1804.
The Lion and the Water-Wagtail.   1809.
The Songs, edited by George Hogarth.   2 vols., 1842.

Other

The Musical Tour (autobiography).   1778.
Royal Circus Epitomized.   1784.
A Letter on Music Education.   1791.
A Complete History of the English Stage.   5 vols., 1800.
Observations on a Tour Through England and Scotland.   2 vols., 1801–02.
The Professional Life of Dibdin, Written by Himself, with the Words of 600 Songs.   4 vols., 1803; revised edition, 6 vols., 1809.
Music Epitomized.   1808.
The English Pythagoras; or, Every Man His Own Music Master.   1808.

Bibliography: *A Dibdin Bibliography* by Edward R. Dibdin, 1937.

Reading List: *A Brief Memoir of Dibdin* by William Kitchiner, 1884; *English Theatre Music in the 18th Century* by Roger Fiske, 1973.

*   *   *

Despite his prodigious outpouring of songs, operas, entertainments, stage histories, didactic poetry, satires, novels, and autobiography, for most of his career Charles Dibdin was a Sullivan without an appropriate Gilbert. His first and best partner and librettist was Isaac Bickerstaff with whom, from 1765 to 1772, Dibdin collaborated on about eight musical pieces for the London theatres and for Garrick's Shakespeare Jubilees (1769). He wrote all the music for the popular afterpiece, *The Padlock* (1768), and in it played the servant Mungo in blackface – the first foretaste of the nineteenth-century minstrel shows. Two of Bickerstaff's and Dibdin's musical entertainments or serenatas for Ranelagh House, *The Ephesian Matron* (1769) and *The Recruiting Serjeant* (1770), are witty, short pieces modelled after the form of *La Serva Padrona* and are still occasionally performed.

After Bickerstaff exiled himself, although Dibdin continued to write for Garrick (whom he detested) until 1776, he turned out thirty pantomimes and musical dialogues between 1772 and 1782 for Thomas King at Sadler's Wells. Dibdin's often-produced ballad opera, *The Waterman; or, The First of August,* was first played at the Little Theatre in the Haymarket. A comic opera, *The Quaker*, had one performance sloppily produced at Drury Lane in 1775, but it was not until 1777, when Dibdin was in France avoiding creditors, that the opera was successfully staged. Perpetually in debt, always quarreling with theatre managers and collaborators, constantly flirting with, but not exploring, new forms of popular entertainment, Dibdin shifted from one theatre to another. He even became a partner in a new theatre, the Royal Circus, later named the Surrey, in 1782, for which he wrote upwards of sixty works, but ended up in debtor's prison for his efforts. In 1785 he wrote the comic opera *Liberty Hall* which is remembered (if at all) for three songs: "The Highmettled Racer," "Jock Ratlin," and "The Bells of Aberdovey." Two years later he toured the country with his own one-man show to raise money for an aborted voyage to India. Typical of Dibdin's energy was his *The Whim of the Moment* (1789), one of about thirty "table entertainments" for which he was manager, author, composer, narrator, singer, and accompanist. Renamed *The Oddities* and produced at the Lyceum, it includes Dibdin's most famous song, "Tom Bowling."

At his own theatre, the Sans Souci, Dibdin introduced many of his popular, uplifting, patriotic sea songs. In all he wrote about 1,400 songs and a huge number of stage productions from puppet shows and brief musical dialogues to comic operas. Although he was awarded a £200 pension in 1803 for celebrating the bravery and loyalty of the British sailor, Dibdin's creative energies were most fully realized when he collaborated early in his career with Bickerstaff.

—Peter A. Tasch

DODSLEY, Robert. English. Born near Mansfield, Nottinghamshire, 13 February 1703. Apprenticed to a stocking weaver in Mansfield, from whom he ran away. Married; his wife died in 1754. Became a footman to the Hon. Mrs. Lowther in London, who encouraged him in his writing and secured him other patrons, including Alexander Pope; set up as a bookseller, at "Tully's Head" in Pall Mall, 1735, and subsequently published works by Johnson, Pope, and others; suggested to Johnson the scheme of an English dictionary, 1746, and was one of the publishers of the first edition, 1755; started various journals, *The Publick Register*, 1741, *The Museum*, 1746–47, *The Preceptor*, 1748, and *The World*, 1753–56; founded *the Annual Register*, initially edited by Edmund Burke, 1758; retired from bookselling and publishing, 1759. *Died 23 December 1764.*

PUBLICATIONS

Collections

Works of the English Poets 15, edited by A. Chalmers.   1810.

Plays

An Entertainment for Her Majesty's Birthday.   1732.
An Entertainment for the Wedding of Governor Lowther.   1732.

The Toy-Shop (produced 1735). 1735; with *Epistles and Poems on Several Occasions*, 1737.
The King and the Miller of Mansfield (produced 1737). 1737.
Sir John Cockle at Court, Being the Sequel to The King and the Miller (produced 1738). 1738.
The Blind Beggar of Bethnal Green, from the play by John Day and Henry Chettle (produced 1741). 1741.
Rex and Pontifex, in *Trifles*. 1745.
The Triumph of Peace, music by Thomas Arne (produced 1749). 1749.
Cleone (produced 1758). 1758.

Verse

Servitude. 1729; as *The Footman's Friendly Advice*, 1731.
An Epistle from a Footman to Stephen Duck. 1731.
A Sketch of the Miseries of Poverty. 1731.
A Muse in Livery; or, The Footman's Miscellany. 1732.
The Modern Reasoners: An Epistle to a Friend. 1734.
An Epistle to Mr. Pope, Occasioned by His Essay on Man. 1734.
Beauty; or, The Art of Charming. 1735.
The Art of Preaching, in Imitation of Horace's Art of Poetry. 1738.
Colin's Kisses, Being Twelve New Songs. 1742.
Pain and Patience. 1742.
Public Virtue, book 1: Agriculture. 1753.
Melpomene; or, The Regions of Terror and Pity. 1757.

Other

The Chronicle of the Kings of England, Written in the Manner of the Ancient Jewish Historians. 2 vols., 1740–41.
Trifles. 2 vols., 1745–77.
The Oeconomy of Human Life, Translated from an Indian Manuscript. 1751.

Editor, *A Select Collection of Old Plays.* 12 vols., 1744; edited by W. C. Hazlitt, 15 vols., 1874–76.
Editor, *A Collection of Poems by Several Hands.* 3 vols., 1748; revised edition, 6 vols., 1748–58; edited by I. Reed, 6 vols., 1782.
Editor, *Select Fables of Aesop and Other Fabulists.* 1761.
Editor, *Fugitive Pieces on Various Subjects.* 2 vols., 1761.
Editor, *The Works of William Shenstone.* 2 vols., 1764.

Reading List: *Dodsley, Poet, Publisher, and Playwright* by Ralph Straus, 1910 (includes bibliography).

*　　*　　*

Footman, poet, and playwright, Robert Dodsley was the most important publisher of the eighteenth century both in terms of the men whose works he issued – Pope, Young, Akenside, Gray, Johnson, Burke, Shenstone, Sterne, among others – and in terms of the works he edited or initiated. His *Collection of Poems by Several Hands* rescued from pamphlet obscurity many of the best and most representative poems of the mid-century. *A Select*

Collection of Old Plays did the same for the lesser Elizabethan dramatists. His enormously successful society periodical *The World* is second in quality only to *The Spectator*; and *The Annual Register*, which he astutely contracted Burke to edit, established a tradition of excellence in assembling the best of each year's poetry and prose. A labor of love, his popular *Select Fables* included the first comprehensive, orginal study of that genre of English.

Although he is not an important poet, many of Dodsley's verses are better than his amusingly ill-considered lines "To the Honourable Lady Howe, Upon the Death of Her Husband": "But let this thought alleviate/The sorrows of your mind:/He's gone – but he is gone so late/You can't be long behind." If, in its celebration "of various Manures" and its delineation of sheep diseases, there is a turgid frivolity to the blank verse of his ambitious georgic *Agriculture*, the couplets of *The Art of Preaching*, a satire on abuses of the clergy, show facility and cleverness. The more ephemeral the subject, the surer Dodsley's touch. A few of his epigrams are excellent. "An Epistle to Stephen Duck" ingratiatingly compares Dodsley, the aspiring footman, to the thresher poet, newly called to eminence by the Queen. "Colin's Kisses," variations on a pastoral theme, are always melodious and often charming. Dodsley's one success in a more august mode – *Melpomene; or, the Regions of Terrour and Pity* – was applauded as sublime by his contemporaries, and even today the stanza and imagery of this homostrophic ode effectively present the various tragic tableaux.

Three of Dodsley's plays deserve particular mention. The plotless but good-humored *Toy-Shop* offers a satiric merchant who philosophizes over every sale. *The King and the Miller of Mansfield*, the democratically biased tale of a monarch lost in Sherwood Forest who is entertained incognito by an honest tradesman, was a theatrical triumph, establishing Dodsley as the most important sentimentalist of the 1730's. A disappointing sequel, *Sir John Cockle at Court*, reverses the premise of the original play by taking the blunt miller to London. Dodsley's greatest success and the play in which he comes closest to "the sentiment sublime, the language of the heart" which he recommends in *Melpomene* is *Cleone*, a domestic drama of traduction, murder, and madness which avoids the stilted heroics usual in mid-century tragedies. Although psychologically unconvincing, the play does achieve by flashes an authentic tragic tone worthy of Otway, to whose work Johnson compared it. Eighteenth-century audiences found the pathetic madness and death of Cleone so emotionally disturbing that Sarah Siddons had to discontinue the role.

—Harry M. Solomon

DRYDEN, John.   English.   Born in Aldwinckle All Saints, Northamptonshire, 19 August 1631. Educated at Westminster School, London (King's Scholar), 1646–50; Trinity College, Cambridge (pensioner), 1650–54, B.A. 1654. Married Lady Elizabeth Howard in 1663. Remained in Cambridge, 1654–57; settled in London, 1657, and possibly held a minor post in Cromwell's government; thereafter supported himself mainly by writing plays. Appointed Poet Laureate, 1668, and Historiographer Royal, 1669: converted to Roman Catholicism, c. 1685, and lost his royal offices at the accession of William and Mary, 1689. Member, Royal Society, 1660. *Died 1 May 1700.*

PUBLICATIONS

Collections

The Works, edited by Sir Walter Scott. 18 vols., 1808; revised edition edited by George Saintsbury, 1882–92.
Dramatic Works, edited by Montague Summers. 6 vols., 1931–32.
Letters, edited by Charles E. Ward. 1942.
Works, edited by Edward N. Hooker and H. T. Swedenberg, Jr. 1956 –
Poems, edited by James Kinsley. 4 vols., 1958.
Four Comedies, Four Tragedies (includes *Secret Love, Sir Martin Mar-All, An Evening's Love, Marriage A-la-Mode, The Indian Emperor, Aureng-Zebe, All for Love, Don Sebastian*), edited by L. A. Beaurline and Fredson Bowers. 2 vols., 1967.
A Selection, edited by John Conaghan. 1978.

Plays

The Wild Gallant (produced 1663). 1669; in *Works 8*, 1962.
The Indian Queen, with Sir Robert Howard (produced 1664). In *Four New Plays*, by Howard, 1665.
The Rival Ladies (produced 1664). 1664; in *Works 8*, 1962.
The Indian Emperor; or, The Conquest of Mexico by the Spaniards, Being the Sequel of The Indian Queen (produced 1665). 1667; in *Works 9*, 1966.
Secret Love; or, The Maiden Queen (produced 1667). 1668; in *Works 9*, 1966.
Sir Martin Mar-All; or, The Feigned Innocence, from a translation by William Cavendish of a play by Molière (produced 1667). 1668; in *Works 9*, 1966.
The Tempest; or, The Enchanted Island, with William Davenant, from the play by Shakespeare (produced 1667). 1670; edited by Vivian Summers, 1974.
An Evening's Love; or, The Mock Astrologer (produced 1668). 1671; in *Works 10*, 1970.
Tyrannic Love; or, The Royal Martyr (produced 1669). 1670; in *Works 10*, 1970.
The Conquest of Granada by the Spaniards, 2 parts (produced 1670, 1671). 1672; in *Works 2*, 1978.
Marriage A-la-Mode (produced 1672). 1673; in *Works 2*, 1978.
The Assignation; or, Love in a Nunnery (produced 1672). 1673; in *Works 2*, 1978.
Amboyna (produced 1673). 1673.
Aureng-Zebe (produced 1675). 1676; edited by Frederick M. Link, 1971.
The State of Innocence and Fall of Man. 1677.
All for Love; or, The World Well Lost, from the play *Antony and Cleopatra* by Shakespeare (produced 1677). 1678; edited by David M. Vieth, 1974.
The Kind Keeper; or, Mr. Limberham (produced 1678). 1680; edited by A. Norman Jeffares, in *Restoration Comedy*, 1974.
Oedipus, with Nathaniel Lee (produced 1678). 1679.
Troilus and Cressida; or, Truth Found Too Late, from the play by Shakespeare (produced 1679). 1679.
The Spanish Friar; or, The Double Discovery (produced 1680). 1681.
The Duke of Guise, with Nathaniel Lee (produced 1682). 1683.
Albion and Albanius, music by Lewis Grabu (produced 1685). 1685.
Don Sebastian, King of Portugal (produced 1689). 1690; in *Four Tragedies*, 1967.
Amphitryon; or, The Two Socias (produced 1690). 1690.
King Arthur; or, The British Worthy, music by Henry Purcell (produced 1691). 1691.
Cleomenes, The Spartan Hero (produced 1692). 1692.

Love Triumphant; or, Nature Will Prevail (produced 1694).   1694.
The Secular Masque, in *The Pilgrim*, by Vanbrugh (produced 1700).   1700.
Comedies, Tragedies, and Operas.   2 vols., 1701.

Verse

Heroic Stanzas to the Memory of Oliver, Late Lord Protector, in *Three Poems upon the Death of His Late Highness Oliver, Lord Protector*, with Waller and Sprat.   1659.
Astraea Redux: A Poem on the Happy Restoration and Return of His Sacred Majesty Charles the Second.   1660.
To His Sacred Majesty: A Panegyric on His Coronation.   1661.
To My Lord Chancellor, Presented on New Year's Day.   1662.
Annus Mirabilis, The Year of Wonders 1666: An Historical Poem.   1667.
Ovid's Epistles, with others.   1680.
Absalom and Achitophel.   1681; *Second Part*, with Nahum Tate, 1682; edited by James and Helen Kinsley, 1961.
The Medal: A Satire Against Sedition.   1682.
Mac Flecknoe; or, A Satire upon the True-Blue-Protestant Poet T[homas] S[hadwell].   1682.
Religio Laici; or, A Layman's Faith.   1682.
Miscellany Poems.   1684; *Sylvae; or, The Second Part*, 1685; *Examen Poeticum, Being the Third Part*, 1693; *The Annual Miscellany, Being the Fourth Part*, 1694; *Fifth Part*, 1704; *Sixth Part*, 1709.
Threnodia Augustalis: A Funeral-Pindaric Poem Sacred to the Happy Memory of King Charles II.   1685.
The Hind and the Panther.   1687.
A Song for St. Cecilia's Day 1687.   1687.
Britannia Rediviva: A Poem on the Birth of the Prince.   1688.
Eleonora: A Panegyrical Poem Dedicated to the Memory of the Late Countess of Abingdon.   1692.
The Satires of Juvenal, with others, *Together with the Satires of Persius.*   1693.
An Ode on the Death of Henry Purcell.   1696.
The Works of Virgil, Containing His Pastorals, Georgics, and Aeneis.   1697; edited by James Kinsley, 1961.
Alexander's Feast; or, The Power of Music: An Ode in Honour of St. Cecilia's Day.   1697.
Fables Ancient and Modern.   1700.
Ovid's Art of Love, Book 1, translated.   1709.
Hymns Attributed to Dryden, edited by George Rapall and George Reuben Potter.   1937.
Prologues and Epilogues, edited by William B. Gardner.   1951.

Other

Of Dramatic Poesy: An Essay.   1668; revised edition 1684; edited by George Watson, in *Of Dramatic Poesy and Other Critical Essays*, 1962.
Notes and Observations on The Empress of Morocco, with John Crowne and Thomas Shadwell.   1674.
His Majesty's Declaration Defended.   1681.
The Vindication.   1683.
A Defence of An Essay of Dramatic Poesy.   1688.
Works.   4 vols., 1695.

Critical and Miscellaneous Prose Works, edited by Edmond Malone.   4 vols., 1800.
Essays, edited by W. P. Ker.   2 vols., 1900.
Literary Criticism, edited by A. C. Kirsch.   1966.

Editor, *The Art of Poetry*, by Nicolas Boileau, translated by William Soames, revised edition.   1683.

Translator, *The History of the League*, by Louis Maimbourg.   1684.
Translator, *The Life of St. Francis Xavier*, by Dominique Bouhours.   1688.
Translator, with Knightly Chetwood, *Miscellaneous Essays*, by Saint-Evremond.   1692.
Translator, with others, *The Annals and History of Tacitus*.   3 vols., 1698.

Bibliography: *Dryden: A Bibliography of Early Editions and of Drydeniana* by Hugh Macdonald, 1939; *Dryden: A Survey and Bibliography of Critical Studies 1895–1974* by David J. Latt and Samuel J. Monk, 1976.

Reading List: *The Poetry of Dryden* by Mark Van Doren, 1920, revised edition, 1931; *Dryden: Some Biographical Facts and Problems* by J. M. Osborn, 1940, revised edition, 1965; *Dryden and the Conservative Myth* by B. N. Schilling, 1961; *Life of Dryden* by Charles E. Ward, 1961; *Dryden's Imagery* by Arthur W. Hoffman, 1962; *Essential Articles for the Study of Dryden* edited by H. T. Swedenberg, Jr., 1966; *Dryden's Major Plays* by Bruce King, 1966; *Dryden's Poetry* by Earl Miner, 1967; *Contexts of Dryden's Thought* by Philip Harth, 1968; *Dryden: The Critical Heritage* edited by James and Helen Kinsley, 1971; *Dryden* by William Myers, 1973; *Dryden and the Development of Panegyric* by James Dale Garrison, 1975; *Dryden, The Public Writer 1660–1685* by George McFadden, 1978.

*   *   *

John Dryden's life is largely obscure until he commences as author. He was born on 19 August 1631 at Aldwinckle All Saints in Northamptonshire, and about 1646 he entered, as a King's Scholar, Westminster School under the famous master Richard Busby. Much later he recalled that about 1648 he had translated Persius's third satire as a Thursday night exercise for the school. His first published poem, "Upon the Lord Hastings," appeared in 1649; on 18 May of the following year he was admitted as pensioner to Trinity College, Cambridge, proceeding B.A. in 1654. The next years are yet more obsucre. Some color is given to the tradition he served the Protectorate by the publication in 1659 of the *Heroique Stanza's* on Cromwell's death.

His career may be said to begin, however, with the Restoration, and its first period to run from 1660–1680. Early in these years he published poems on the new order, bringing together historical, political, religious, and heroic elements. Although such a poem as *Astraea Redux* is inferior to the poem on Cromwell, it is more ambitious. Somewhat of the new effort succeeds in *Annus Mirabilis*, whose year of wonders (1666) included the second naval war with Holland and the Great Fire of London. Dryden seeks too hard to connect these diverse events, and his execution is uneven. But it has bounding energy and is his sole fully narrative poem till far later. His talents were being recognized – in 1668 he succeeded Davenant as poet laureate, and in 1669 Howell as historiographer royal. By the end of this period he had completed but not published his first poetic masterpiece, *Mac Flecknoe*. If Elkanah Settle was its first dunce hero, Thomas Shadwell finally gained the honor. The poem assesses good and bad art, using a mock coronation skit. Father Flecknoe abdicates for his son (Shadwell). Art, politics, and religious matters combine with paternal love to assess both the dunces and true drama. Flecknoe is "King by Office" and "Priest by Trade." He passes to his son *Love's Kingdom*, his own dull play, as "Sceptre." From "this righteous Lore" comes Shadwell's soul, his opera *Psyche*. Humor and allusion combine to establish the true canons of drama and to fix Shadwell immemorially.

Mac Flecknoe shows that Dryden's chief interest in these decades is the stage. After a first comedy, he turned to the rhymed heroic play, rising to the high astounding terms of the two-part *Conquest of Granada*. He approached earth thereafter. *Marriage A-la-mode* consists of a mingling of serious and comic plots especially congenial to him, and a favorite still. In the Prologue to his heroic play *Aureng-Zebe*, he professes himself "weary" of rhyme, and in *All for Love* he wrote a blank verse tragedy on Antony and Cleopatra, thought by many his finest play. His collaboration with Nathaniel Lee for *Oedipus* altered his smooth earlier blank verse style to a harsher, more various medium that appears again in his adaptation of *Troilus and Cressida*. After his enormously popular *Spanish Fryar* (1680), he wrote no plays single-handedly till 1689.

The next period, 1680–1685, is dominated by engagement with the tumultuous times. In the state of near revolution over the Popish Plot and efforts to seize power from Charles II, Dryden published *Absalom and Achitophel*, his poem most admired today. Using the biblical parallel of the plot against David (Charles), Dryden creates an epic-historic-satiric blend for the machinations of Achitophel (Earl of Shaftesbury) and his dupe Absalom (Duke of Monmouth). The Chaucer-like portraits of individuals and the personal statement on government (ll. 751–810) show Dryden in full command of a public poetry.

1682 brought Dryden further attention. *Mac Flecknoe* now first appeared in print, pirated. When Shaftesbury was released from prison by a Whig jury in November 1681, a triumphant medal was struck. Next March Dryden's one bitter poem, *The Medall*, appeared. Perhaps his anger was feigned. His usual composure is evident in *Religio Laici*, his first religious poem, which curiously begins with rich imagery and progresses to a direct, non-metaphorical style unique in his poetry. In 1684 he published one of his poems most popular today, "To the Memory of Mr. Oldham," on a young poet recently dead. In that year and the next he joined the bookseller Jacob Tonson in putting out the first two of a series of "Dryden miscellanies," collections of poetry by various hands. Charles II died, and James acceded, in 1685. Dryden celebrated these events in *Threnodia Augustalis*, his first pindaric ode after one of his finest poems, the translation of Horace, *Odes*, III, xxix.

The next period, 1685–1688, coincides with the brief rule by James II. Probably about the summer of 1685 Dryden became a Roman Catholic, and in 1687 published his second religious poem, *The Hind and the Panther*, whose 2592 lines make it his longest poem apart from translations. Its style is as complex as that of *Religio Laici* had been simple. Using sacred zoögraphy (the Hind represents Catholicism, the Panther Anglicanism, etc.), fables, myth, allusion, allegory, and the slightest of plots, Dryden sets forth a timeless version of the times, including the recent and distant past (Part I), present contentions (II), and the ecclesiastical as well as national future (III). Each part has a moving personal passage and those who have most opposed Dryden's doctrine or his fable have often called the style of this poem his finest. The poetic and personal confidence thereby implied finds expression in the ode, so praised by Dr. Johnson, on Anne Killigrew, whose small poetic abilities nonetheless may represent the artist's high vocation. Music is an equally confidently used metaphor in *A Song for Cecilia's Day*, which enacts history from Creation to Judgment.

When James fled late in 1688, and when William and Mary were invited as sovereigns by Parliament, Dryden entered into the most difficult period of his career, 1688–1694. Stripped of offices and denied full engagement with his times, he turned again to "the ungrateful stage." Two plays that now seem his greatest resulted: *Don Sebastian*, concerned with tragic fate, and *Amphitryon*, a very bleak comedy. Both deal with human identity in a hostile world. In 1691 he enjoyed a fortunate collaboration with Henry Purcell on *King Authur*, an opera. In 1694, his last play, *Love Truimphant*, featured a happy ending engineered by an unconvincing change of heart. Such doubts and sputters in these years had fullest exercise in the *Satires* of 1693 (translating Juvenal and Persius) and the Preface to *Examen Poeticum*, the third miscellany.

In the last period, 1694–1700, Dryden worked through his problems. If he could not address all his contemporaries, he could focus on individuals. In 1694 two of his finest poetic addresses appear: "To my Dear Friend Mr. Congreve" and "To Sir Godfrey Kneller." Gloom remains in both, but the gloomier "Kneller" shows chastened faith even in "these Inferiour Times," The "Congreve" bears uncanny resemblance in motif to *Mac Flecknoe*. Drama is again the topic, with comparisons again settling values. Now Dryden must abdicate and Congreve have legitimate succession, even if a usurper should sneak in for a time. The "son" merits, however, and the "father" loves.

Addresses lacked the capaciousness to adjust new strains to old hopes. Such scale was achieved in the 1697 *Virgil*. Although it and his comedies most require re-assessment, it does seem that he darkens the second half of his *Aeneis* (as if the military and the public worlds do not quite merge), and that he renders the *Georgics* even more heroically and sympathetically than Virgil to show the terms on which hope remained. His real epic was to come in cento, *Fables Ancient and Modern* (1700). It combines seventeen poems made over from Ovid, Boccaccio, Chaucer, and Homer with four solely Dryden's: those two handsome ones to the Duchess of Ormonde and to John Dryden of Chesterton toward the beginning, as also *Alexander's Feast* and "The Monument of a Fair Maiden Lady" toward the end. In redoing the *Metamorphoses* as Milton had redone the *Aeneid* in *Paradise Lost*, Dryden relates his poems by links, themes, motifs, and central subject – the human search for the good life. A serene wisdom shows that such a life can finally be gained only on Christian terms. Yet the vain and sinful race continues to endear itself to the old poet. *Fables* is once again becoming a favorite of readers as it had been for the Romantics and Dryden's own contemporaries. He died on May Day 1700 of degenerative diseases, yet calm of mind to the end.

The limitations of such periodizing are represented by its failure to allow for his constant writing in "the other harmony of prose" (Preface to *Fables*). He was by no means the modern stylist some claim. He writes in numerous styles and sometimes shows no more knowledge than Milton of modern paragraph and sentence writing. In his styles, however, he established English criticism, struggling like others before him to create the critical essay. As early as *The Rival Ladies* (1664) he found his way in use of the preface, employing a method inquisitive, devoted to current issues, and yet enough assured to deal with general principles. *Of Dramatick Poesy. An Essay* is really a dialogue, his most elaborate criticism, a semi-fiction, offering heroic debate on the proper character of drama. In the "Parallel Betwixt Poetry and Painting" (a preface to *De Arte Graphica* in 1695) we see most clearly his attempt to unite neo-Aristotelian mimesis with neo-Horatian affectivism. Once more he asserted the poet's right to heighten – to take a better or worse "likeness" and remain true, or to deal with the best "nature," unlike the scientist. In a way prescient for his career, the "Account" prefixed to *Annus Mirabilis* (1667) had placed historical poetry and panegyric (by implication satire also) under the aegis of epic. These prefaces, the *Dramatick Poesy*, and his poems as well dealt with the concept of hope for human progress, which was relatively new in England, and also introduced critical and historical principles. The element most neglected by historians of criticism was his historical understanding, which permitted him to compare and differentiate and evolve a historical relativism that would later undermine mimetic presumptions. To him we owe the concept of a historical age or period possessing its own temper or Zeitgeist, with all that such assumptions have meant to subsequent thought about literature.

Such diversity – there are over thirty plays, operas, and cantatas alone – yields to no easy summary. We can observe what joins him to, or differentiates him from, his great contemporaries – or the next century. Like Marvell, Dryden was a gifted lyric poet, although in odes rather than ruminative lyrics. Like Butler, he was a learned satirist, but where Butler degrades Dryden exalts. Like Milton, he excelled in varieties of narrative and drama, just as both also overcame crises toward the end of their lives. Dryden had what Milton lacked – wit, humor, and generosity. But his extraordinary intellectual power to liken and assimilate was incapable of Milton's higher fusion of all into a single intense reality. And where Milton, like Spenser, created an artistic language spoken by no one, Dryden like Donne and Jonson created a more natural language founded on actual speech. Born early enough to remember the outbreak of civil war (1642) and to live through four different national constitutions,

Dryden wrote of subjects that poets no longer treat directly – the most momentous events of their times. For all that, his powers took on greatness only in the second half of his life, developing to the end. He practiced every literary kind except the novel, never repeating himself except in songs for plays. He is a rare example of a writer whose finest work comes at the end of a lifetime, of a century, and of a distinct period of literature. The next equivalent of *Fables* is not heroic poetry but the novel.

—Earl Miner

D'URFEY, Thomas.   English.   Born in Exeter, Devon, in 1653. Settled in London; an intimate of Charles II and of James II; wrote for the stage from 1676; also composed numerous songs; Editor, *Momus Ridens; or, Comical Remarks on the Public Reports,* weekly, 1690–91. *Died 26 February 1723.*

PUBLICATIONS

Plays

   The Siege of Memphis; or, The Ambitious Queen (produced 1676).   1676.
   Madame Fickle; or, The Witty False One, from the play *A Match at Midnight* by William
      Rowley (produced 1676).   1677; edited by A. Norman Jeffares, in *Restoration
      Comedy,* 1974.
   The Fool Turned Critic (produced 1676).   1678.
   A Fond Husband; or, The Plotting Sisters (produced 1677).   1677.
   Trick for Trick; or, The Debauched Hypocrite, from the play *Monsieur Thomas* by
      Fletcher (produced 1678).   1678.
   Squire Oldsapp; or, The Night-Adventurers (produced 1678).   1679.
   The Virtuous Wife; or, Good Luck at Last (produced 1679).   1680.
   Sir Barnaby Whigg; or, No Wit Like a Woman's (produced 1681).   1681.
   The Royalist (produced 1682).   1682.
   The Injured Princess; or, The Fatal Wager, from the play *Cymbeline* by Shakespeare
      (produced 1682).   1682.
   A Commonwealth of Women, from the play *The Sea Voyage* by Fletcher and Massinger
      (produced 1685).   1686.
   The Banditti; or, A Lady's Distress (produced 1686).   1686.
   A Fool's Preferment; or, The Three Dukes of Dunstable, from the play *The Noble
      Gentleman* by Beaumont and Fletcher (produced 1688).   1688.
   Love for Money; or, The Boarding School (produced 1691).   1691.
   Bussy D'Ambois; or, The Husband's Revenge, from the play by Chapman (produced
      1691).   1691.
   The Marriage-Hater Matched (produced 1692).   1692.
   The Richmond Heiress; or, A Woman Once in the Right (produced 1693).   1693.
   The Comical History of Don Quixote, 3 parts (produced 1694–95).   3 vols., 1694–96.

Cinthia and Endimion; or, The Loves of the Deities (produced 1696).   1697.
The Intrigues at Versailles; or, A Jilt in All Humours (produced 1697).   1697.
The Campaigners; or, The Pleasant Adventures at Brussels (produced 1698).   1698.
The Rise and Fall of Massaniello, 2 parts (produced 1699).   1699–1700.
The Bath; or, The Western Lass (produced 1701).   1701.
The Old Mode and the New; or, Country Miss with Her Furbeloe (produced 1703).   1703.
Wonders in the Sun; or, The Kingdom of the Birds (produced 1706).   1706.
The Modern Prophet; or, New Wit for a Husband (produced 1709).   1709.
New Operas, with Comical Stories and Poems (includes *The Two Queens of Brentford, or, Bayes No Poetaster; The Grecian Heroine, or, The Fate of Tyranny; Ariadne, or, The Triumph of Bacchus*).   1721.

Fiction

Tales Tragical and Comical.   1704.
Stories Moral and Comical.   1707.

Verse

Archery Revived; or, The Bow-Man's Excellence: An Heroic Poem, with Robert Shotterel.   1676.
The Progress of Honesty; or, A View of Court and City: A Pindaric Poem.   1681.
Butler's Ghost; or, Hudibras, The Fourth Part.   1682.
Scandalum Magnatum; or, Potapski's Case: A Satire Against Polish Oppression.   1682.
A New Collection of Songs and Poems.   1683.
Choice New Songs.   1684.
Several New Songs.   1684.
A Third Collection of New Songs.   1685.
An Elegy upon the Late Blessed King Charles II, and Two Panegyrics upon Their Present Sacred Majesties King James and Queen Mary.   1685.
A Complete Collection of Songs and Odes, and *A New Collection of Songs and Poems.*   2 vols., 1687.
A Poem Congratulatory on the Birth of the Young Prince.   1688.
New Poems, Consisting of Satires, Elegies, and Odes.   1690.
Collin's Walk Through London and Westminster: A Poem in Burlesque.   1690.
A Pindaric Ode on New Year's Day.   1691.
A Pindaric Poem on the Royal Navy.   1691.
The Moralist; or, A Satire upon the Sects.   1691.
The Triennial Mayor; or, The New Raparees.   1691.
The Weasels: A Satirical Fable.   1691.
The Weasel Trapped.   1691.
A Pindaric Ode upon the Fleet.   1692.
Gloriana: A Funeral Pindaric Poem Sacred to the Memory of Queen Mary.   1695.
Albion's Blessings: A Poem Panegyrical on His Sacred Majesty King William the III.   1698.
A Choice Collection of New Songs and Ballads.   1699.
An Ode for the Anniversary Feast Made in Honour of St. Cecilia.   1700.
The Trophies; or, Augusta's Glory: A Triumphant Ode.   1707.
Honor and Opes; or, The British Merchant's Glory.   1708.
Musa et Musica; or, Honour and Music.   1710.
Songs, edited by Cyrus L. Day.   1933.

Other

The Canonical Statesman's Grand Argument Discussed. 1693.

Editor, *Songs Complete, Pleasant, and Divertive.* 5 vols., 1719; revised edition, as *Wit and Mirth; or, Pills to Purge Melancholy,* 6 vols., 1719–20.

Reading List: *A Study of the Plays of D'Urfey* by Robert S. Forsythe, 2 vols., 1916–17; *Dates and Performances of D'Urfey's Plays* by Cyrus L. Day, 1950.

*   *   *

Thomas D'Urfey is probably best-known today for his delightful and influential collection of ballads and songs, *Pills to Purge Melancholy.* However, he was a dramatist of some consequence in his day, contributing about 30 comedies, tragedies, and operas between 1676 and 1709. He is a useful author for the literary historian, as he participated in the successive trends of contemporary drama; nevertheless, his real merit lies in the distinct individuality he achieved within his otherwise imitative productions.

With *A Fond Husband,* D'Urfey followed the influential vogue of sex-intrigue comedy established by Wycherley and Etherege, yet he peoples his landscape with grotesque "humours" characters designed for the low comedians James Nokes and Anthony Leigh. D'Urfey experienced the undoubted satisfaction of seeing Charles II in attendance at three of the first five performances of this comedy.

When Ravenscroft led the way toward farce, D'Urfey quickly turned in this direction with several plays, but in one of them, *The Virtuous Wife,* he inserted a serious presentation of female virtue, introduced by a hilarious "induction" scene in which the profligate and immoral actress Elizabeth Barry announced her refusal to play the role of a virtuous woman. Again, James Nokes scored a triumph as the elderly Lady Beardly in a farcical part.

To the phase of political satires, D'Urfey offered *Sir Barnaby Whigg* and *The Royalist.* When this vogue ended, Shadwell began experimenting with exemplary drama, to which D'Urfey contributed the two works which entitle him to a place in the history of English drama: *Love for Money* and *The Richmond Heiress.* In the former, he introduced a vulgar and realistic account of a girls' boarding school for the functional purpose of securing atmosphere by means of "local colour." The main plot-line shows a distressed heroine, who speaks in the high pathetic style, and a hero who is a "man of sense" rather than the customary town rake we associate with Restoration comedy. This hero tests the heroine and seeks dominance over her, not for sentimental reasons but for future financial security. I doubt that Stendhal would have disclaimed this play, so carefully has D'Urfey built his various ironic patterns. In *The Richmond Heiress,* D'Urfey presented several innovations. The action deals with fortune hunters, all of whom are severely ridiculed, and the play ends without a marriage of the principal characters. Also, the serious treatment of the morality of the characters and the emphasis on "The Papers" (showing legal control of the estate) suggest plays of a century later.

With the three-part *Comical History of Don Quixote,* D'Urfey followed the vogue of the bawdy which led to the famous attack by Jeremy Collier. Indecent language and incident are presented with verve and vitality. The best invention is Sancho's low-life daughter, Mary the Buxom, whose rough, coarse speeches carry vividly.

Originality appears in the two-part drama *Massaniello,* in which D'Urfey chooses prose as the language of tragedy. The harsh, realistic portrayal of a bestial mob raised to power well illustrates D'Urfey's creative skill. His plays became longer and longer, containing multiple plots, and hence can be viewed as a precursor of the coming genre of the novel.

—Arthur H. Scouten

ETHEREGE, Sir George. English. Born, probably at Maidenhead, Berkshire, c 1635. Little is known of his early life: may have studied at Cambridge University, and at the Inns of Court, London, and may have spent many years abroad: unknown when his first play was produced in 1664. Had one daughter by the actress Mrs. Barry; married Mary Arnold c. 1680. Prominent figure in Restoration London, in the circle of Sedley and the Earl of Rochester; also served the court as a diplomat: Secretary to the Ambassador to Constantinople, Sir Daniel Harvey, 1668–71; on diplomatic assignment in The Hague, 1671; Ambassador to the Imperial Court at Ratisbon (Regensburg), Bavaria, 1685–89; possibly served in Paris, 1691. Knighted c. 1685. *Died in 1691.*

PUBLICATIONS

Collections

> *Works,* edited by H. F. B. Brett-Smith.   2 vols. (of 3), 1927.
> *Poems,* edited by James Thorpe.   1963.
> *Letters,* edited by Frederick Bracher.   1974.

Plays

> *The Comical Revenge; or, Love in a Tub* (produced 1664).   1664.
> *She Would If She Could* (produced 1668).   1668; edited by Charlene M. Taylor, 1971.
> *The Man of Mode; or, Sir Fopling Flutter* (produced 1676).   1676; edited by John Conaghan, 1973.

Other

> *The Letterbook,* edited by Sybil M. Rosenfeld.   1928.

Reading List: *Etherege: Sein Leben, Seine Zeit, und Seine Dramen* by V. Meindl, 1901; *Etherege: A Study in Restoration Comedy* by Frances S. McCamic, 1931; *Etherege and the 17th-Century Comedy of Manners* by Dale Underwood, 1957.

*   *   *

Although Sir George Etherege wrote only three plays, he exerted enormous influence on his successors and is usually regarded as the originator of the Restoration comedy of manners. All of his plays contain the wit and satire that characterize this kind of comedy, but it was his last and best play, *The Man of Mode,* that provided the characters, values, and language that became models for later dramatists.

Etherege's plays depict the sophisticated, fashionable world of courtier-rakes and coquettes, and satirize the affectations and foibles of a society Etherege knew intimately. The appeal of Etheregean comedy, which is chiefly based on brilliant wit and polished dialogue, is usually intellectual, although occasional farcical elements are present, while plot complications derive from sexual and romantic intrigue.

Each of Etherege's plays affirms a unique and complex set of values which carefully defines a hierarchy of characters and modes of behavior, and by which each character and event is measured. The action in each play centers around a battle of wits between hero and heroine. The hero, who has not seriously considered marriage, is captured by a heroine who is the only character who fully understands the hero. The hero and heroine are contrasted with minor characters whose activities help delineate the characters of the hero and heroine. Each hero is superior to the other men in his play in that he exhibits greater knowledge of self and environment, is able to determine the proper balance between convention and nature, can manipulate his fellow-creatures to his advantage, and follows the most "reasonable" course of action circumstances allow. Each heroine is able to meet and outmaneuver the hero on his own ground, recognizes her unique limitations, comprehends the difficulty and implications of the problem she faces, and makes the hero feel that marriage is the most desirable course of action. Etherege's heroes and heroines are always evenly matched, and because they seldom face problems imposed by the external world, happiness is achieved when they overcome obstacles resulting from their own characters.

Despite these broad similarities, Etherege's plays differ significantly in structure and quality. Etherege steadily refined his art until he produced, in *The Man of Mode*, one of the most brilliant comedies in the English language.

The Comical Revenge contains four largely separate plots, each of which provides implicit commentary on the others. The main plot is a battle between evenly matched and resourceful lovers, Sir Frederick Frollick and Widow Rich. Comedy derives from their verbal and tactical adeptness in trying to force each other into confessions of love. The "heroic" plot is written in couplets, contains long speeches on courtly love and honor, and depicts the adventures of four lovers and a faithful friend. The two remaining "low" plots deal with the nearly successful duping of a country booby, Sir Nicholas Cully, and the imprisonment of Sir Frederick's servant, Dufoy, in a tub.

Sir Frederick and Widow Rich constitute a mean between the heroic and low plots. Love is depicted as an honorable passion, free from lust and based on purity, in the heroic plot, a conception burlesqued by Sir Frederick's continual understatement, and as a "disease" whose end-product is literally venereal disease in the Dufoy plot. Sir Frederick's concept of love is both "natural," in that it is not opposed to physical appetite and freedom, and "reasonable," in that it takes practical considerations into account. Like later Etherege heroes, Sir Frederick is able to manipulate others and to dissemble, and is generally in control of events, except those involving Widow Rich, whose self-sufficiency and resourcefulness he underestimates.

Many of the minor characters in *The Comical Revenge* are not differentiated from one another, nor is the Sir Frederick–Widow Rich plot developed as fully as the main plots in Etherege's later plays. Moreover, much of the play's humor depends on farce and burlesque, and it is not always easy to see the relationship of individual parts to one another or to the whole.

There is no heroic plot in *She Would If She Could*, but there are two sets of heroes and heroines. Characters who are able to recognize the proper relationship between social decorum and honesty are contrasted with characters entirely ruled by custom. The older, unsympathetic characters return to the country, always an undesirable place in Etheregean comedy, with the same mistaken notions they brought to town. Although minor distinctions among the four sympathetic lovers are made, the hierarchy of values is not nearly as complex as in *The Man of Mode*.

Like *She Would If She Could*, *The Man of Mode* contrasts characters who do not recognize the necessity for occasional plain-dealing with those who do, but it also contrasts those who do not understand the importance of social conventions with those who do. Characters of all shades inhabit the ground between the extremes in *The Man of Mode*. Instead of two sets of lovers, Harriet and Dorimant dominate the action of the play and regulate our response to the other characters. Dorimant is contrasted with each of the other male characters, from the completely affected Sir Fopling Flutter to such near-misses as Young Bellair, who, despite good breeding, lacks Dorimant's wit. Dorimant is acquainted with and able to profit from all fashionable modes of behavior, but is still able to maintain his identity. His only match in the play is Harriet, who is contrasted with all other women in the play, from Loveit, who sacrifices all necessary conventional restraints to emotion, to Bellinda, who, though attractive and witty, is unable to control Dorimant. Harriet's intellect, beauty, wealth, familiarity with the world, understanding of self and others, and powers of manipulation enable her to make Dorimant desire marriage. Their union represents an Etheregean ideal in which both retain individuality, freedom, and the excitement of the chase, and in which no fundamental character changes occur.

The Etheregean hero and heroine become progressively more refined in each play. Sir Frederick's drunken rowdiness is replaced by Dorimant's polished wit and naturally easy sense of propriety, much as Widow Rich's occasional coarseness gives way to Harriet's restraint and quiet aggressiveness. Sir Frederick is closer than Dorimant to the good-natured hero of sentimental comedy; in *The Man of Mode*, "good nature" can be feigned, but is not a necessary virtue.

Language is a more important source of pleasure in each successive play. In *The Comical Revenge*, language is important primarily because the sections written in couplets contrast with the prose parts; in *The Man of Mode*, Harriet and Dorimant demonstrate their superiority partially through mastery of language, and much intellectual pleasure derives from extended metaphors. In general, wit changes from frankly physical allusions to complex sexual puns and sophisticated dialogue.

The differences between *The Comical Revenge* and *The Man of Mode* illustrate Etherege's growth as a playwright. In the former, the reader is sometimes puzzled by scenes that have little relationship to preceding and following scenes, interest is divided among four plots, and our feelings about the hero and heroine are sometimes ambivalent when Etherege clearly wishes them to be positive. In the latter, plot elements are unified, our sympathies are wholly engaged by the Harriet–Dorimant relationship, and interest is fully maintained throughout by Etherege's varied and complex portrait of Restoration society.

—James S. Malek

FARQUHAR, George.   Irish.   Born in Londonderry, Northern Ireland, c. 1677. Educated at a school in Londonderry; Trinity College, Dublin (sizar), 1694–95. Married Margaret Pemell in 1703; two daughters. Corrector for the press of a Dublin bookseller, 1696; actor at the Smock Alley Theatre, Dublin, 1696–97, but gave up acting after accidentally wounding a fellow-actor; settled in London, 1697, and began writing for the stage; also an army officer: commissioned Lieutenant in the Militia, and served in Holland, 1700; Lieutenant in the Grenadiers, 1704, engaged in recruiting in Lichfield and Shrewsbury, 1705–06. *Died 29 April 1707.*

PUBLICATIONS

Collections

Complete Works, edited by Charles Stonehill.   2 vols., 1930.

Plays

Love and a Bottle (produced 1698).   1699.

The Constant Couple; or, A Trip to the Jubilee (produced 1699).   1700; edited by A.
   Norman Jeffares, in *Restoration Comedy*, 1974.
Sir Harry Wildair, Being the Sequel of The Trip to the Jubilee (produced 1701).   1701.
The Inconstant; or, The Way to Win Him, from the play *The Wild Goose Chase* by
   Fletcher (produced 1702).   1702.
The Twin-Rivals (produced 1702).   1703.
The Stage Coach, from a play by Jean de la Chapelle (produced 1704).   1704.
The Recruiting Officer (produced 1706).   1706; edited by John Ross, 1978.
The Beaux' Strategem (produced 1707).   1707; edited by Charles N. Fifer, 1977.

Verse

*Love and Business in a Collection of Occasionary Verse and Epistolary Prose, A Discourse
   Likewise upon Comedy in Reference to the English Stage.*   1702.
Barcelona; or, The Spanish Expedition.   1710.

Fiction

The Adventures of Covent Garden.   1698.

Reading List: *Young George Farquhar: The Restoration Drama at Twilight* by W. Connely,
1949; *Farquhar* by Albert J. Farmer, 1966; *Farquhar* by Eric Rothstein, 1967; *The
Development of Farquhar as a Comic Dramatist* by Eugene N. James, 1972.

*   *   *

Of the many comic writers who have emerged from Ireland, George Farquhar is among
the very best, keeping company with such fellow-dramatists as Goldsmith and Wilde. During
his short life (he died at about age thirty), he wrote eight plays (all comedies), an interesting
critical essay entitled "A Discourse upon Comedy in reference to the English Stage," and
some much less important miscellaneous poetry and prose. Farquhar is usually regarded as
the last major dramatist writing "Restoration" comedy, but it is important to distinguish him
from both his predecessors, notably Etherege and Wycherley, and his contemporaries, such
as Vanbrugh and Congreve.
   Farquhar's theatrical career spans the years from 1698 to 1707, which belong to a period
of transition in comic drama, partly in response to increasing demands during the 1690's and
early eighteenth century for more decorum and positive moral standards on the stage. The
preoccupation with sexual licence, bawdry, and satire of the early Restoration playwrights,
especially in the 1670's, gradually gave way to a more genteel and morally exemplary
conception of comedy, culminating in eighteenth-century "sentimental" comedy. Although
Farquhar's plays look back to the first masters of "wit" or "manners" comedy and are
certainly not lacking in bawdy, they do exhibit features characteristic of this new tendency
towards greater propriety. Most of Farquhar's heroes, for example, prove to be much less
rakish in their conduct than their witty speech suggests, and they seem benevolent, good-
hearted, and almost chaste in comparison to such calculating cynics and sexual athletes as
Wycherley's Horner in *The Country Wife* and Etherege's Dorimant in *The Man of Mode*.
Consequently critics have argued that Farquhar is more wholesome, humane, and morally
nutrient as well as being emotionally softer than most Restoration dramatists. Yet this does
not mean that he sacrifices comic liveliness to sentiment and sententiousness. On the
contrary, there is more low comedy in Farquhar, especially in his two masterpieces, *The
Recruiting Officer* and *The Beaux' Stratagem*, than in the stylistically refined though sexually

squalid world of much contemporary "manners" comedy. *The Recruiting Officer* is built around an army recruiting campaign in Shrewsbury, and *The Beaux' Stratagem*, set in Lichfield, features a gang of highwaymen, prefiguring another great play of the century, Gay's *The Beggar's Opera*. Farquhar's great innovation in these, his last two plays, was to breathe new life into the conventions of Restoration comedy, which were becoming stale and outworn by the time he was writing, and he achieved this mainly by setting the actions in the provinces, not in London like most of his previous plays, and by drawing heavily on his personal experience of provincial life. The Restoration comedy of manners is virtually synonymous with London and with a small section of London Society at that, the beau monde. Characters from the provinces are almost invariably laughing-stocks because of their boorish country habits, crude speech, and ignorance of the ways of the fashionable world, and are contrasted unfavourably with modish city wits. By breaking out of the claustrophobic confines of London high society to include a much wider social spectrum, and by departing from Restoration stereotypes, Farquhar let more than a draught of fresh air into comic drama. By placing his characters in the world of small-town justices, innkeepers, tradesmen, soldiers, military recruits, highwaymen, and country wenches, Farquhar necessarily put the emphasis on humour rather than on wit, and opened up new possibilities for comedy; sadly these were not much exploited by subsequent dramatists in England, although one of the three or four great plays of the eighteenth century not by Farquhar, Goldsmith's *She Stoops to Conquer*, is certainly indebted to his example. Farquhar's real successor in this respect is the Fielding of *Joseph Andrews* and *Tom Jones*. Farquhar did, however, exert a strong influence on the development of German drama in the eighteenth century, mainly as a result of Lessing's enthusiasm for him, and even in the twentieth century he has had some impact on the German theatre; he, like his younger contemporary John Gay, was one of the British dramatists who influenced Brecht.

Farquhar's first play, *Love and a Bottle*, is an entertaining but overloaded ragbag of traditional comic devices and conventions, including mistaken identities, multiple disguises, and a complex intrigue plot. His next play, *The Constant Couple; or, A Trip to the Jubilee*, is a considerable advance, and is cleverly plotted, inventive, and full of well-drawn comic characters, yet tinged with sentimentalism. It was a great theatrical success in its first season and remained a favourite with audiences throughout the eighteenth century. Much of its popularity was due to the appealing central character, Sir Harry Wildair, who superficially resembles the rakes and libertines of Restoration comedy but differs from them in that beneath his affectation of fast-living and profligacy he is really good-natured and well-intentioned. He is unconventional, impulsive, and imprudent rather than corrupt or debauched. Encouraged by the public response to *The Constant Couple*, Farquhar wrote a sequel featuring the same principal characters, *Sir Harry Wildair*, which is even more inferior to its predecessor than most sequels. Two of his next three plays are adaptations of other plays. *The Inconstant*, based on Fletcher's *The Wild-Goose Chase* but with substantial changes, is full of broad humour and lively action. The other adaptation is the much slighter *The Stage-Coach*, a popular farcical afterpiece taken from a contemporary French play. Between these two adaptations came an original, serious, and morally explicit play upholding strict poetic justice, *The Twin-Rivals*, which differs from his previous work in its pervasive sentimentalism. In form it is a comedy, but, with its virtuous heroes and heroines, its licentious rake who is finally redeemed at a stroke, and its deformed villain, as well as its exposé of vice and evil in society, it approximates to a *drame* and falls uneasily between comedy and social-problem play.

It was after completing *The Stage-Coach* that Farquhar, now in the Army, spent some time in the provinces as a recruiting officer, visiting both Shrewsbury and Lichfield. His experiences on this mission were crucial to his artistic development, and in *The Recruiting Officer* and *The Beaux' Stratagem* he transmuted these experiences into excellent drama, at the same time revitalising the conventions of comedy. *The Recruiting Officer* contains plenty of boisterous humour, especially in the scenes satirizing corrupt recruiting methods and involving the ingenious and roguish Sergeant Kite, but at its centre is the perennial theme of comedy, love and its problems. The recruiting officer himself and the romantic hero, Captain Plume, is a descendant of Sir Harry Wildair and proves to be a man of sensibility for all his dashing military qualities, while the resourceful and practical heroine, Silvia, recalls Rosalind in *As You Like It* and Viola in *Twelfth Night*, and like them spends part of the play disguised as a young man. The triumph of romantic love over all obstacles is also a major theme of *The Beaux' Stratagem*, in which two fashionable young men-about-town, short of money and attempting to recoup their losses in the provinces, meet two country ladies and eventually fall in love with them after initially trying to trick them. Partly because the two men are mistaken for both highwaymen and Jesuits, the plot is full of comic misunderstandings and complications that give the play much of its theatrical dynamism. Both of these plays, which celebrate human vitality and variety in an almost Shakespearean way, were immediately recognised to be outstanding contributions to the genre of comedy, and time has certainly not withered their vitality and variety.

—Peter Lewis

FIELDING, Henry.   English.   Born in Sharpham Park, Glastonbury, Somerset, 22 April 1707; brother of Sarah Fielding. Educated at Eton College; studied literature at the University of Leyden, 1728–29; entered the Middle Temple, London, 1737; called to the Bar, 1740. Married 1) Charlotte Craddock in 1734 (died, 1742); 2) Mary Daniel in 1747. Settled in London, 1727; successful playwright, in London, 1728–37; Author/Manager, Little Theatre, Haymarket, 1737 (theatre closed as a result of Licensing Act); Editor, with James Rolph, *The Champion*, 1739–41; lawyer and novelist from 1740, also writer/editor for *The True Patriot*, 1745–46, *The Jacobite's Journal*, 1747–48, and the *Convent Garden Journal*, 1752; Principal Justice of the Peace for Middlesex and Westminster, 1748; Chairman, Westminster Quarter Sessions, 1749–53. *Died 8 October 1754.*

PUBLICATIONS

Collections

   Complete Works, edited by W. E. Henley.   16 vols., 1903.
   Works (Wesleyan Edition), edited by W. B. Coley.   1967–.

Plays

   Love in Several Masques (produced 1728).   1728.
   The Temple Beau (produced 1730).   1730.
   The Author's Farce, and The Pleasures of the Town (produced 1730).   1730; revised version (produced 1734), 1750; 1730 version edited by Charles B. Woods, 1966.
   Tom Thumb (produced 1730).   1730; revised version, as *The Tragedy of Tragedies; or, The Life and Death of Tom Thumb the Great* (produced 1731), 1731; edited by LeRoy J. Morrissey, 1973.
   Rape upon Rape; or, The Justice Caught in His Own Trap (produced 1730).   1730; revised version, as *The Coffee-House Politician* (produced 1730), 1730.
   The Letter-Writers; or, A New Way to Keep a Wife at Home (produced 1731).   1731.

The Welsh Opera; or, The Grey Mare the Better Horse (produced 1731).   1731; as *The Genuine Grub Street Opera,* 1731; edited by LeRoy J. Morrissey, 1973.
The Lottery (produced 1732).   1732.
The Modern Husband (produced 1732).   1732.
The Covent Garden Tragedy (produced 1732).   1732.
The Old Debauchees (produced 1732).   1732; as *The Debauchees; or, The Jesuit Caught,* 1745.
The Mock Doctor; or, The Dumb Lady Cured, from a play by Molière (produced 1732).   1732; edited by J. Hampden, 1931.
The Miser, from a play by Molière (produced 1733).   1733.
Deborah; or, A Wife for You All (produced 1733).
The Intriguing Chambermaid, from a play by J. F. Regnard (produced 1734).   1734.
Don Quixote in England (produced 1734).   1734.
An Old Man Taught Wisdom; or, The Virgin Unmasked (produced 1735).   1735.
The Universal Gallant; or, The Different Husbands (produced 1735).   1735.
Pasquin: A Dramatic Satire on the Times, Being the Rehearsal of Two Plays, Viz a Comedy Called The Election and a Tragedy Called The Life and Death of Common Sense (produced 1736).   1736; edited by O. M. Brack, Jr., and others, 1973.
Tumble-Down Dick; or, Phaeton in the Suds (produced 1736).   1736.
Eurydice (produced 1737).   In *Miscellanies,* 1743.
The Historical Register for the Year 1736 (produced 1737).   With *Eurydice Hissed,* 1737; revised version, 1737; edited by William W. Appleton, 1967.
Eurydice Hissed; or, A Word to the Wise (produced 1737).   With *The Historical Register,* 1737; revised version, 1737; edited by William W. Appleton, 1967.
Plautus, The God of Riches, with W. Young, from a play by Aristophanes.   1742.
Miss Lucy in Town: A Sequel to The Virgin Unmasqued, music by Thomas Arne (produced 1742).   1742.
The Wedding Day (produced 1743).   In *Miscellanies,* 1743.
Dramatic Works.   2 vols., 1745.
The Fathers; or, The Good-Natured Man (produced 1778).   1778.

Fiction

An Apology for the Life of Mrs. Shamela Andrews.   1741; edited by A. R. Humphreys, with *Joseph Andrews,* 1973.
The History of the Adventures of Joseph Andrews and of His Friend Mr. Abraham Adams.   1742; revised edition, 1742; edited by Martin C. Battestin, in *Works,* 1967.
The Life of Mr. Jonathan Wild the Great, in *Miscellanies.*   1743.
The History of Tom Jones, A Foundling.   1749; revised edition, 1749, 1750; edited by Fredson Bowers and Martin C. Battestin, in *Works,* 2 vols., 1975.
Amelia.   1752; revised edition, in *Works,* 1762.

Verse

The Masquerade.   1728; edited by C. E. Jones, in *The Female Husband and Other Writings,* 1960.
The Vernon-iad.   1741.

Other

Of True Greatness: An Epistle to George Dodington, Esq.   1741.

The Champion; or, The British Mercury.   2 vols., 1741; excerpt edited by S. J. Sackett, as *The Voyages of Mr. Job Vinegar,* 1958.
The Opposition: A Vision.   1742.
A Full Vindication of the Duchess Dowager of Marlborough.   1742.
Some Papers Proper to Be Read Before the Royal Society.   1743.
Miscellanies.   3 vols., 1743; vol. 1 edited by Henry Knight Miller, in *Works,* 1972.
An Attempt Toward a Natural History of the Hanover Rat.   1744.
The Charge to the Jury.   1745.
The History of the Present Rebellion in Scotland.   1745.
A Serious Address to the People of Great Britain, in Which the Certain Consequences of the Present Rebellion Are Fully Demonstrated.   1745.
A Dialogue Between the Devil, The Pope, and the Pretender.   1745.
The Female Husband; or, The Surprising History of Mrs. Mary, Alias Mr. George Hamilton, Taken from Her Own Mouth since Her Confinement.   1746; edited by C. E. Jones, in *The Female Husband and Other Writings,* 1960.
A Dialogue Between a Gentleman of London, Agent for Two Court Candidates, and an Honest Alderman of the Country Party.   1747.
Ovid's Art of Love, Adapted to the Present Times.   1747; as *The Lover's Assistant,* 1759.
A Proper Answer to a Late Scurrilous Libel, Entitled An Apology for the Conduct of a Late Celebrated Second-Rate Minister.   1747.
A Charge Delivered to the Grand Jury.   1749.
A True State of the Case of Bosavern Penlez, Who Suffered on Account of the Late Riot in the Strand.   1749.
An Enquiry into the Causes of the Late Increase of Robbers.   1751.
A Plan of the Universal Register Office, with John Fielding.   1752.
Examples of the Interposition of Providence in the Detection and Punishment of Murder.   1752.
A Proposal for Making an Effectual Provision for the Poor.   1753.
A Clear State of the Case of Elizabeth Canning.   1753.
The Journal of a Voyage to Lisbon.   1755; edited by H. E. Pagliaro, 1963.
The Covent Garden Journal, edited by G. E. Jensen.   1915.
The True Patriot, and the History of Our Own Times, edited by M. A. Locke.   1964.
Criticism, edited by Ioan Williams.   1970.
The Jacobite's Journal, edited by W. B. Coley, in *Works.*   1974.

Translator, *The Military History of Charles XII, King of Sweden,* by M. Gustavus Alderfeld.   3 vols., 1840.

Bibliography: by Martin C. Battestin, in *The English Novel* edited by A. E. Dyson, 1973.

Reading List: *The History of Fielding* by Wilbur L. Cross, 3 vols., 1918; *Fielding the Novelist: A Study in Historical Criticism* by Frederic T. Blanchard, 1926; *Fielding: His Life, Works, and Times* by F. Homes Dudden, 2 vols., 1952; *Fielding* by John Butt, 1954, revised edition, 1959; *The Moral Basis of Fielding's Art* by Martin C. Battestin, 1959; *Essays on Fielding's "Miscellanies"* by Henry Knight Miller, 1961; *Fielding's Social Pamphlets* by Marvin R. Zinker, Jr., 1966; *Fielding and the Language of Irony* by Glenn W. Hatfield, 1968; *Fielding and the Nature of the Novel* by Robert Alter, 1968; *Fielding and the Augustan Ideal under Stress* by Claude J. Rawson, 1972; *Fielding: A Critical Anthology* edited by Claude J. Rawson, 1973; *Fielding's "Tom Jones": The Novelist as Moral Philosopher* by Bernard Harrison, 1975; *Occasional Form: Fielding and the Chains of Circumstance* by J. Paul Hunter, 1975.

*   *   *

Though Henry Fielding is remembered chiefly as a novelist – as, indeed, along with Defoe and Richardson, one of the founders of the modern novel and as the author of one of the dozen or so greatest novels in English, *Tom Jones* – he began his literary career as a poet and a dramatist. A young man of twenty, without much money but with strong family connections to the Whig establishment, he came to London from the West Country in 1727 determined to make his mark as a wit and to solicit the patronage of the Court at a time when, because of the uncertain political climate following the death of George I, a talented writer might expect that his services would be appreciated by the prime minister, Sir Robert Walpole. Contrary to the usual view of Fielding as a staunch and unswerving opponent of Walpole and the Court, his earliest poems and plays reveal that when he was not actively seeking the king's and Walpole's favors he prudently adopted a neutral attitude in politics: to judge from the title of his first published work, *The Coronation: A Poem, and An Ode on the Birthday* (issued in November 1727 but now lost), he began, even in a Cibberian vein, by openly declaring his loyalty to George II; and beside several other poems soliciting Walpole's patronage in 1729–31, he dedicated to the prime minister his most ambitious, if unsuccessful, comedy, *The Modern Husband*. Indeed, as B. L. Goldgar persuasively argues in *Walpole and the Wits* (1976), of the fifteen comedies and farces which Fielding produced between 1728 – when his first play, *Love in Several Masques*, was acted at Drury Lane – and 1734 all but one were calculated shrewdly to amuse the widest possible audience without offending the Court; only in *The Welsh Opera* (1731) – a transparent political allegory satirizing not only Walpole and the leader of the Opposition, but the royal family itself – did he abandon this cautious policy, the result being, predictably, that the play was first withdrawn for revision and then suppressed.

These were the years in which Fielding established himself as London's most popular living playwright. With the exception of *The Modern Husband*, which treats rather too earnestly the disturbing theme of adultery and marital prostitution in high life, his more conventional comedies are entertaining and skillful, but by inviting comparison with the greater works of Congreve and Molière they have suffered the condescension of historians of the drama. No other critic, certainly, has endorsed Shaw's declaration that Fielding was "the greatest practising dramatist, with the single exception of Shakespeare, produced by England between the Middle Ages and the nineteenth century...." Where Fielding did shine was in the lesser modes of farce, burlesque, and satire – in *The Tragedy of Tragedies*, for example, an hilarious travesty of heroic drama, or in *The Author's Farce*, a delightful adaption of the "rehearsal play" concluding with a satiric "puppet show" performed by live actors, a work which in fact anticipates the expressionism of modern experimental drama.

Despite his reputation as the theatrical gadfly of the Court, it was only in the final three years (1734–37) of his dramatic career that Fielding moved, rather hesitantly, into the camp of the Opposition. Though he dedicated *Don Quixote in England* to Chesterfield, who had recently joined their ranks, the political satire in this play – as indeed even in *Pasquin*, which is usually said to be vehemently antiministerial – is in fact directed at the venality and incompetence of both parties. Only with *The Historical Register* and its after-piece *Eurydice Hiss'd* did he at last drop the mask of impartiality and, by ridiculing Walpole all too effectively, help to precipitate the Theatrical Licensing Act of 1737, which terminated his career as a playwright.

Forced by an Act of Parliament to abandon the stage, Fielding began preparing for the bar and, to supplement the meager income he would earn as a barrister, enlisted as a hackney author in the Opposition's campaign against Walpole. In this latter capacity, during his editorship of *The Champion* (1739–41), he almost certainly drafted his first work of fiction, *The Life of Jonathan Wild the Great*, a mock biography of an infamous real-life criminal whom he ironically praises for the very qualities of unscrupulous self-aggrandisement by which the prime minister himself had achieved "greatness." This work, however, which Walpole appears to have paid Fielding to suppress, was withheld from publication until 1743, a year after the Great Man's fall from power, when it was issued as part of the *Miscellanies*; by this time Fielding presumably had revised the novel substantially, generalizing the political satire and perhaps expanding the narrative to accommodate the more positive, contrasting element of Wild's relationship with the good-natured Heartfrees. Also included in the *Miscellanies* was *A Journey from This World to the Next*, a satirical fiction done in brisk imitation of Lucian.

It was not politics, however, but a quite remarkable literary event that provoked Fielding into finding his true voice as a novelist. Amused and not a little exasperated by the extraordinary success of Richardson's *Pamela* (1740), Fielding responded first by parodying the novel, hilariously, in *Shamela* (1741) and then by offering in *Joseph Andrews* (1742) his own alternative conception of the art of fiction. Though Fielding's improbably virtuous hero is meant to continue the ridicule of Richardson's indomitable virgin, *Joseph Andrews* is much more than merely another travesty of *Pamela*. Modelled in some respects on Cervantes' masterpiece, it yet enacts Fielding's own original theory of the "comic epic-poem in prose," whose subject is "the true ridiculous" in human nature, exposed in all its variety as Joseph and the amiable quixote Parson Abraham Adams journey homeward through the heart of England. In contrast to the brooding, claustrophobic world evoked in the letters of Richardson's beleaguered maidens, Fielding's is cheerful and expansive, presided over by a genial, omniscient narrator who seems a proper surrogate of that beneficent Providence celebrated by Pope in *An Essay on Man* (1733–34).

In *Joseph Andrews* Fielding founded, as he put it, a "new province of writing." *Tom Jones*, his masterpiece, fulfilled the promise of that ambitious, splendid beginning. Generations of readers have delighted in the comic adventures and nearly disastrous indiscretions of the lusty foundling boy who grows to maturity, discovers the identity of his parents, and marries the beautiful girl he has always loved – a story simple enough in outline, but crowded with entertaining characters, enlivened by the wit and humanity of the narrator, and complicated by the intricacies of an ingenious plot which Coleridge called one of the most perfect in all literature. Like most great books, moreover, *Tom Jones* offers us more than superficial pleasures: it is the realization of its author's profoundest philosophy of life, an artfully constructed model of a world abundant, orderly, and ultimately benign, as the Christian humanist tradition conceived it to be. Thus Fielding declares his subject to be "human nature" and his book to be nothing less than "a great creation of our own." His foundling hero stands for all of us: like the protagonists of romance, he is a kind of wayfaring Everyman who, having been expelled from "Paradise Hall," must through hard experience gain that knowledge of himself which will enable him to be united with the girl, Sophia, whose name signifies Wisdom. *Tom Jones* is, as few books have managed to be, the consummate expression of a particular form and conception of literary art.

With the publication of *Tom Jones* Fielding's life and work entered a new phase. As a reward for his services as publicist for the Pelham administration, he was appointed to the magistracy, an office which he exercised with an energy and diligence which shortened his life. His new role as a public figure, working actively to preserve the peace and to improve the wretched condition of the poor, affected his art in interesting, but most critics would say regrettable, ways. *Amelia*, his last novel, is a very different book from *Tom Jones*: Fielding's tone has become darker, more monitory, in keeping with his subject – no longer the follies of men, but their errors and cupidities and the doubtful efficacy of those institutions, the law and the church, meant to preserve the social order; his narrator less frequently appears upon the stage, and his voice, wavering between anger and a maudlin sentimentality, no longer inspires confidence. Though his ostensible focus is the domestic tribulations of the feckless Captain Booth and his long-suffering wife, Fielding's true intentions are all too patently didactic: scene after scene is calculated to expose the imperfections of the penal laws, the destructiveness of infidelity, the injustices of the patronage system, and the immoralities of an effete and pleasure-loving society. To be sure, *Amelia* is less fun to read than any of Fielding's other novels, but in the starkness and candor of its social commentary it is compelling none the less. It is in fact the first true novel of social protest and reform in England, sounding themes that would not be resumed until the next century.

—Martin C. Battestin

FOOTE. Samuel. English. Born in Truro, Cornwall, baptized 27 January 1720. Educated at Truro Grammar School; Worcester College, Oxford, 1737–40, left without taking a degree; entered the Temple, London, 1740. Married Mary Hickes in 1741; two sons. Jailed for debt, Fleet Prison, London, 1742–43; actor in London and Dublin from 1744; began writing for the stage in the 1740's; operated an unlicensed "lecture" theatre, London, 1762–66; lost a leg in a riding accident, 1766; granted a patent to erect a theatre; built and ran the Haymarket Theatre, London, 1766–77. *Died 21 October 1777.*

PUBLICATIONS

Collections

>   *Dramatic Works,* edited by John Badcock.   3 vols., 1830.

Plays

>   *The Auction of Pictures* (produced 1748).
>   *The Knights* (produced 1749; revised version, produced 1754).   1754.
>   *Taste* (produced 1752).   1752; revised version, as *The Diversions of the Morning* (produced 1758, and regularly thereafter), in *Dramatic Works,* 1830.
>   *The Englishman in Paris* (produced 1753).   1753.
>   *The Englishman Returned from Paris* (produced 1756).   1756.
>   *The Author* (produced 1757).   1757.
>   *The Minor* (produced 1760; revised version, produced 1760).   1760.
>   *Tragedy a la Mode,* from the play *Fatal Constancy* by William Whitehead (as *Modern Tragedy,* produced 1761).   In *The Wandering Patentee* by Tate Wilkinson, 1795; as *Lindamira,* in *Thespian Gleanings* by Thomas Matthews, 1805.
>   *The Liar,* from a play by Molière (produced 1762).   1764.
>   *The Orators* (produced 1762).   1762.
>   *The Young Hypocrite,* from a French play, in *The Comic Theatre.*   1762.
>   *The Mayor of Garret* (produced 1763).   1764.
>   *The Trial of Samuel Foote for a Libel on Peter Paragraph* (produced 1763).   In *The Wandering Patentee* by Tate Wilkinson, 1795.
>   *The Patron* (produced 1764).   1764.
>   *The Commissary* (produced 1765).   1765; edited by R. W. Bevis, in *Eighteenth Century Drama: Afterpieces,* 1970.
>   *The Tailors: A Tragedy for Warm Weather,* revised by Colman the Elder (produced 1767).   1778.
>   *An Occasional Prelude* (produced 1767).   In *Memoirs of Foote* by William Cooke, 1805.
>   *The Devil upon Two Sticks* (produced 1768).   1778.
>   *The Lame Lover* (produced 1770).   1770.
>   *The Maid of Bath* (produced 1771).   1771; revised version, 1778.
>   *The Nabob* (produced 1772).   1778.
>   *Piety in Pattens* (produced 1773).   Edited by Samuel N. Bogorad and Robert G. Noyes, in *Theatre Survey,* Fall 1973.
>   *The Bankrupt* (produced 1773).   1776.
>   *The Cozeners* (produced 1774).   1778.
>   *A Trip to Calais* (as *The Capuchin,* produced 1776).   1778.

Other entertainments: *A Writ of Inquiry; Comic Lectures; Morning Lectures.*

Other

A Treatise on the Passions, So Far as They Regard the Stage. 1747.
The Roman and English Comedy Considered and Compared, with Remarks on The Suspicious Husband. 1747.
A Letter to the Author of The Remarks Critical and Christian on The Minor. 1760.
Apology for The Minor, in a Letter to Mr. Baine. 1771.

Editor, *The Comic Theatre* (French plays). 5 vols., 1762.

Reading List: *Foote: A Biography* by Percy H. Fitzgerald, 1910; *The Dramatic Work of Foote* by Mary M. Belden, 1929 (includes bibliography); *The Life and Works of Foote* by John W. Wilkinson, 1936; *Foote, Comedian* by Simon Trefman, 1971.

*　　*　　*

If Samuel Foote possessed the "wit of escape," as Dr. Johnson said, "in an eminent degree," he often had to employ it to escape from situations created by his wit in the first place. For most of his thirty years on the London stage Foote was something of a dramatic outlaw, "wanted" by the Lord Chamberlain's office either for evasion of the Licensing Act or slander and libel. When he emerged as a mimic in the 1740's the issue was his right to perform at all. Having no patent, Foote would invite his friends to "Tea" or "Chocolate," or (as the Examiner of Plays caught up with each name) "Diversions" or an "Auction," for which admission was charged, and then provide "free entertainment": such topical skits as a night-club comedian might devise today. Eventually this satirical pot-pourri became *Taste*. Foote was a man of many dodges, and in the end the law came over to him, so to speak: in 1766, after he had lost a leg in a riding accident, his friends procured him a summer patent at the Haymarket as a kind of disability pension. For the next few years he wrote plays around crippled heroes (*The Lame Lover, The Devil upon Two Sticks*). Long before that, however, the issue had become the angry protests of the victims of his take-offs. Virtually every one of Foote's twenty-odd plays mimicked a living individual (including George Whitefield, Thomas Sheridan, and Thomas Arne) or satirized an influential group (Methodists, nabobs, war profiteers). Usually Foote's wit extricated him from the scrape – the nabobs who came to chastise him were so charmed they stayed to dinner – or else he converted the outcry into profitable publicity; but his portrait of the Duchess of Kingston as Lady Kitty Crocodile in *A Trip to Calais* was a fatal mistake. She had the play banned, and her deputy harried Foote out of the theatre on a sodomy charge. Though acquitted, he died the following year.

Foote's extreme topicality also brought critical disapproval: only general satire of human types should be admissible and would survive, he was warned, whereas the individual eccentricities he so cruelly mimicked were by their nature ephemeral and would deservedly perish. The playwright's unfailing response was to wave the banner of Old Comedy (his favourite of many nicknames was "the English Aristophanes"). If Socrates could be spoofed on the classical Athenian stage, asked Foote, why should a modern nuisance not be pilloried likewise? He liked to think of himself as a dramatic magistrate or watchman, and of his plays as quasi-legal instruments "for the correction of individuals." Foote insisted, moreover, on calling his plays "comedies," though his contemporaries (and later critics) slighted them as "farces" and "sketches." If they are thought of as Aristophanic or *old* comedy the perfunctory and truncated plots seem less damaging, since they were merely vehicles for the main cargo of satire.

For the theatre historian Foote was an important (though not quite respectable) influence on the drama of his time. Taking up the satirical afterpiece where Fielding left off, he developed it considerably in range and style over the next three decades. Several of his long-forgotten playlets contributed stock plots and characters to Georgian comedy; Sheridan, for example, was indebted to *The Minor* and *The Author*. And perhaps the most obscure of them all was once the most influential: *Piety in Pattens*, a shrewd and amusing send-up of sentimentalism, was credited by several writers with bringing the Muse of the Woeful Countenance into disrepute just days before the première of *She Stoops to Conquer*.

To the general reader unmoved by such *arcana*, Foote can still appeal by virtue of his delight in language: not the periods of Johnson, or the wit of Sheridan, but the spoken language of the kingdom in his day. The "genius for mimicry" to which his contemporaries testified comes across now as a good ear for colloquial speech, of which Foote was a student. Although he did not hold the mirror up to nature or man, he did create a remarkably sensitive, albeit primitive, recording device, on which the voices of the men and women of Georgian England can yet be heard. The dialogue of *The Patron* and *The Commissary* remains vivid after two centuries: its tones as brash, its distortion as poignant, as an old vaudeville record.

—R. W. Bevis

GARRICK, David.   English.   Born in Hereford, 19 February 1717. Educated at Lichfield Grammar School, Staffordshire; Samuel Johnson's Academy at Edial, Staffordshire, 1736–37. Married Eva Marie Violetti in 1749. Moved to London with Samuel Johnson, 1737; wine merchant, with his brother, in London, 1738–42; appeared on the stage from 1741, and came to be regarded as the greatest actor of his age, noted for his portrayal of tragic heroes; Joint Manager, with Sheridan, Theatre Royal, Dublin, 1745–46; Joint Owner/ Manager, with James Lacy, 1747–73, and Sole Owner/Manager, 1773 until he retired, 1776, Drury Lane Theatre, London. *Died 20 January 1779.*

PUBLICATIONS

Collections

>   *Poetical Works.*   2 vols., 1785.
>   *Dramatic Works.*   3 vols., 1798.
>   *Three Farces* (includes *The Lying Valet, A Peep Behind the Curtain, Bon Ton*), edited by Louise B. Osborn.   1925.
>   *Three Plays* (includes *The Meeting of the Company, Harlequin's Invasion, Shakespeare's Garland*), edited by E. P. Stein.   1926.
>   *Letters*, edited by David M. Little and George R. Kahrl.   3 vols., 1963.

Plays

>   *Lethe; or, Aesop in the Shades*, from the play *An Hospital for Fools* by James Miller (produced 1740).   1745; revised version, 1757.
>   *The Lying Valet*, from the play *All Without Money* by Peter Motteux (produced 1741).   1741; in *Three Farces*, 1925.
>   *Miss in Her Teens; or, The Medley of Lovers*, from a play by F. C. Dancourt (produced 1747).   1747; edited by Richard Bevis, in *Eighteenth Century Drama: Afterpieces*, 1970.

Albumazar, from the play by Thomas Tonkis (produced 1747; revised version, produced 1773).   1773.

Romeo and Juliet, from the play by Shakespeare (produced 1748).   1750.

Every Man in His Humour, from the play by Jonson (produced 1751).   1752.

The Chances, from the play by Fletcher (produced 1754).   1773.

The Fairies, from the play *A Midsummer Night's Dream* by Shakespeare (produced 1755).   1755.

Catharine and Petruchio, from the play *The Taming of the Shrew* by Shakespeare (produced 1756).   1756.

King Lear, from the play by Shakespeare (produced 1756).   In *Bell's Shakespeare*, 1786.

Florizel and Perdita; or, The Winter's Tale, from the play by Shakespeare (produced 1756).   1758.

Lilliput (produced 1756).   1757.

The Tempest, music by J. C. Smith, from the play by Shakespeare (produced 1756).   1756.

The Male Coquette; or, Seventeen Hundred Fifty Seven (as *The Modern Fine Gentleman*, produced 1757).   1757.

Isabella; or, The Fatal Marriage, from the play by Thomas Southerne (produced 1757).   1757.

The Gamesters, from the play *The Gamester* by Shirley (produced 1757).   1758.

Antony and Cleopatra, with Edward Capell, from the play by Shakespeare (produced 1759).   1758.

The Guardian, from a play by B. C. Fagan (produced 1759).   1759.

Harlequin's Invasion: A Christmas Gambol (produced 1759).   In *Three Plays*, 1926.

The Enchanter; or, Love and Magic, music by J. C. Smith (produced 1760).   1760.

Cymbeline, from the play by Shakespeare (produced 1761).   1762.

The Farmer's Return from London (produced 1762).   1762.

A Midsummer Night's Dream, from the play by Sheakespeare (produced 1763).   1763.

The Clandestine Marriage, with Colman the Elder (produced 1766).   1766.

Neck or Nothing, from a play by Le Sage (produced 1766).   1766.

The Country Girl, from the play *The Country Wife* by Wycherley (produced 1766).   1766.

Cymon: A Dramatic Romance, music by Michael Arne (produced 1767).   1767.

Linco's Travels, music by Michael Arne (produced 1767).

A Peep Behind the Curtain; or, The New Rehearsal (produced 1767).   1767; in *Three Farces*, 1925.

The Elopement (produced 1767).

Dramatic Works.   3 vols., 1768.

The Jubilee, music by Charles Dibdin (produced 1769).   1769; revised version, as *Shakespeare's Garland; or, The Warwickshire Jubilee*, music by Dibdin and others (produced 1769), 1769; in *Three Plays*, 1926.

King Arthur; or, The British Worthy, music by Thomas Arne, from the play by Dryden, music by Purcell (produced 1770).   1770; as *Arthur and Emmeline*, 1784.

The Institution of the Garter; or, Arthur's Round Table Restored, music by Charles Dibdin, from the poem by Gilbert West (produced 1771).   1771.

The Irish Widow (produced 1772).   1772.

Hamlet, from the play by Shakespeare (produced 1772).

A Christmas Tale, music by Charles Dibdin, from a play by C. S. Favart(?) (produced 1773).   1774; revised version, 1776.

The Alchemist, from the play by Jonson (produced 1774?).   1777.

The Meeting of the Company; or, Bayes's Art of Acting (produced 1774).   In *Three Plays*, 1926.

Bon Ton; or, High Life above Stairs (produced 1775).   1775; in *Three Farces*, 1925.

The Theatrical Candidates, music by William Bates (produced 1775).   With *May Day*, 1775.
May Day; or, The Little Gipsy, music by Thomas Arne (produced 1775).   1775.

Verse

An Ode on the Death of Mr. Pelham.   1754.
The Fribbleriad.   1761.
An Ode upon Dedicating a Building and Erecting a Statue to Shakespeare at Stratford upon Avon.   1769.

Other

Mr. Garrick's Answer to Mr. Macklin's Case.   1743.
An Essay on Acting.   1744.
Reasons Why David Garrick Should Not Appear on the Stage.   1759.
The Diary of Garrick, Being a Record of His Memorable Trip to Paris in 1751, edited by R. C. Alexander.   1928.
The Journal of Garrick Describing His Visit to France and Italy in 1763, edited by G. W. Stone.   1939.
Letters of Garrick and Georgiana Countess Spencer 1759–1779, edited by Earl Spencer and Christopher Dobson.   1960.

Bibliography: *A Checklist of Verse by Garrick* by Mary E. Knapp, 1955; "Garrick: An Annotated Bibliography" by Gerald M. Berkowitz, in *Restoration and Eighteenth-Century Theatre Research 11*, 1972.

Reading List: *Memoirs of the Life of Garrick* by Thomas Davies, 1780; *The Life of Garrick* by Arthur Murphy, 2 vols., 1801; *Garrick, Dramatist* by E. P. Stein, 1938; *Garrick* by Carola Oman, 1958; *Garrick, Director* by Kalman A. Burnim, 1961; *Garrick and Stratford*, 1962, and *Garrick's Jubilee*, 1964, both by Martha England; *Theatre in the Age of Garrick* by Cecil Price, 1973; *A Splendid Occasion: The Stratford Jubilee of 1769* by Levi Fox, 1973.

*   *   *

Although David Garrick was the author of poems, prologues, epilogues, and plays, he is remembered for his complete mastery of the British stage. His style of acting – comparatively natural contrasted to the earlier bombast of Quin and other tragedians – broke with the old way and began a tradition which with inevitable changes still continues. "If this young fellow be right," Quin exclaimed, "then we have been all wrong." His success at Drury Lane proved him right and forced his competitors at Covent Garden and the theatres in Dublin and the provinces to follow his example of acting style and dramatic repertory. Only comic opera, successful at Covent Garden in the early 1760's, escaped Garrick's management for a few years until he augmented his company by inviting Covent Garden's major composer and author to work for him. Under Garrick's and James Lacy's management, Drury Lane prospered; when Garrick died his estate was estimated at up to £100,000.

As a patentee of Drury Lane, and director, manager, author, and actor, Garrick tilted the balance to a theatre dominated by the performer rather than by the author. The names associated with the "Age of Garrick" are most likely to be those of his fellow actresses and actors: Clive, Abington, Shuter, Woffington, Moody, King. But despite contemporary satires which portrayed Garrick discouraging talented dramatists (as in Smollett's *Roderick*

Random), Garrick helped authors to rewrite their plays for a demanding but frivolous audience. As George Winchester Stone, Jr. points out (in *The London Stage*, Part 4), Garrick produced 63 new mainpieces and 107 new afterpieces during his 29-year reign. If his worst missteps were to reject John Home's *Douglas* (which succeeded at Covent Garden) and support Hugh Kelly's *False Delicacy* over Goldsmith's *Good Natur'd Man*, they are covered by the great strides Drury Lane took in stagecraft and prestige under his management.

Of the 212 different mainpieces produced by Garrick from 1747 to 1776, Stone shows that the first three of the ten most frequently performed tragedies were by Shakespeare. Of the 15 most popular comedies, three were Shakespeare's and two were by Jonson. Almost 20% of the total performances were plays by Shakespeare. Following custom, Garrick altered plays by Jonson and Shakespeare, among others, to make them vehicles for his own acting and for his repertory company, and entertaining for eighteenth-century audiences. Thus, though he did not treat *The Alchemist* or *Hamlet*, for instance, as literature, he recognized that drama must be performed if it is to be preserved. His most ambitious venture was the Shakespeare Jubilee at Stratford-on-Avon in 1769, an elaborate self-congratulatory celebration which attracted most of London's fashionable artists and their admirers. Though itself a failure, the Jubilee – at which nothing by Shakespeare was performed – can be considered one of the beginnings of Shakespearean idolatry.

Garrick's adaptations of comedies and his original farces like *The Lying Valet* and *Bon Ton; or, High Life above Stairs* amused; but *The Clandestine Marriage*, most of which was by George Colman the Elder, is an accomplished comedy unfairly overshadowed by Goldsmith's plays. Its Epilogue, a miniature comic opera by Garrick, satirizes fashionable playgoers and their infatuation with comic opera; it epitomizes Garrick's skill at light verse and bantering dialogue.

Of the over ninety roles which Garrick performed, among his most famous were Ranger (*Suspicious Husband*, Hoadly), Abel Drugger (*Alchemist*, Jonson), Hamlet and Lear, Benedick (*Much Ado*, Shakespeare), Archer and Scrub (*Beaux' Stratagem*, Farquhar), Don Felix (*The Wonder*, Centlivre), and Bayes (*The Rehearsal*, Villiers). On stage, departing from tradition, Garrick remained in character even when other performers spoke. Whatever the role, Frederick Grimm wrote in 1765, Garrick "abandons his own personality, and puts himself in the situation of him he has to represent ... he ceases to be Garrick." Of "middle stature, small rather than big," Garrick's "vivacity is extreme." Unlike many other actors, Garrick could switch from tragedy to comedy; but whether he was Richard III or Sir John Brute in Vanbrugh's *Provok'd Wife*, Garrick's "negative capability" enabled him to convince his audience that he had become that person.

Now, when actors have been knighted and performers are often associated with American politics, it might be easy to minimize Garrick's importance. But like Samuel Johnson, Garrick was an arbiter of taste. Sterne turned to him for early approval of *Tristram Shandy*, as well he should have since Garrick held shares in two London newspapers, *St. James Chronicle* (which he helped found with the elder Colman and others) and the *Public Advertiser*; his enemies accused him of being a censor-general of London's press. Artists like Reynolds and Hogarth caught his naturalness on canvas, and Goldsmith, Burke, and others of the Literary Club counted him a member. "In his time," concluded one of his early biographers, Arthur Murphy, "the theatre engrossed the minds of men to such a degree that it may now be said there existed in England a *fourth estate*, King, Lords, and Commons, and *Drury-Lane playhouse*." His funeral was magnificent; appropriately, Garrick was buried in the Poets' Corner at the foot of Shakespeare's monument. Summarizing Garrick's career, Burke wrote, "He raised the character of his profession to the rank of a liberal art."

—Peter A. Tasch

GAY, John. English.   Born in Barnstaple, Devon, baptized 16 September 1685. Educated at the free grammar school in Barnstaple; apprenticed to a silk mercer in London. Secretary to the household of the Duchess of Monmouth, 1712–14; Secretary to the Earl of Clarendon on his diplomatic mission to Hanover, 1714; accompanied William Pulteney, later Earl of Bath, to Aix, 1717; lived at Lord Harcourt's estate in Oxfordshire, 1718; earned considerable income from publication of his collected poems, 1720, and made and lost a fortune in South Sea funds speculation; Commissioner for the Public Lottery, 1722–31; recovered much of his fortune from the success of the *Beggar's Opera*, 1728; lived with his patrons the Duke and Duchess of Queensberry, 1728–32. *Died 4 December 1732.*

PUBLICATIONS

Collections

> *Poetical, Dramatic, and Miscellaneous Works.*   6 vols., 1795.
> *Plays.*   2 vols., 1923.
> *Poetical Works,* edited by G. C. Faber.   1926.
> *Letters,* edited by Chester F. Burgess.   1966.
> *Poetry and Prose,* edited by Vinton A. Dearing and Charles Beckwith.   2 vols., 1974.
> *Selected Works,* edited by Samuel Joseloff.   1976.

Plays

> *The Mohocks.*   1712.
> *The Wife of Bath* (produced 1713).   1713; revised version (produced 1730), 1730.
> *The What D'ye Call It* (produced 1715).   1715.
> *Three Hours after Marriage,* with Pope and Arbuthnot (produced 1717).   1717; revised
> version, in *Supplement to the Works of Pope,* 1757; 1717 edition edited by Richard
> Morton and William Peterson, 1961.
> *Acis and Galatea,* music by Handel (produced 1719).   1732.
> *Dione,* in *Poems on Several Occasions.*   1720.
> *The Captives* (produced 1724).   1724.
> *The Beggar's Opera* (produced 1728).   1728; edited by Peter Lewis, 1973.
> *Polly, Being the 2nd Part of The Beggar's Opera* (version revised by Colman the Elder
> produced 1777).   1729; in *Poetical Works,* 1926.
> *Achilles* (produced 1733).   1733.
> *The Distressed Wife* (produced 1734).   1743; as *The Modern Wife* (produced 1771).
> *The Rehearsal at Goatham.*   1754.

Verse

> *Wine.*   1708.
> *Rural Sports.*   1713; revised edition, 1720; edited by O. Culbertson, 1930.
> *The Fan.*   1714.
> *The Shepherd's Week.*   1714.
> *A Letter to a Lady.*   1714.
> *Two Epistles, One to the Earl of Burlington, The Other to a Lady.*   1715(?).
> *Trivia; or, The Art of Walking the Streets of London.*   1716.
> *Horace, epode iv, Imitated.*   1717(?).

The Poor Shepherd.   1720(?).
Poems on Several Occasions.   2 vols., 1720.
A Panegyrical Epistle to Mr. Thomas Snow.   1721.
An Epistle to Her Grace Henrietta Duchess of Marlborough.   1722.
A Poem Addressed to the Quidnunc's.   1724.
Blueskin's Ballad.   1725.
To a Lady on Her Passion for Old China.   1725.
Daphnis and Cloe.   1725(?).
Molly Mog.   1726.
Fables.   2 vols., 1727–38; edited by Vinton A. Dearing, 1967.
Some Unpublished Translations from Ariosto, edited by J. D. Bruce.   1910.

Other

The Present State of Wit.   1711.
An Argument Proving That the Present Mohocks and Hawkubites Are the Gog and Magog Mentioned in the Revelations.   1712.

Bibliography: in *Poetical Works,* 1926; *Gay: An Annotated Checklist of Criticism* by Julie T. Klein, 1973.

Reading List: *Gay, Favorite of the Wits* by William H. Irving, 1940; *Gay, Social Critic* by Sven M. Armens, 1954; *Gay* by Oliver Warner, 1964; *Gay* by Patricia M. Spacks, 1965.

*   *   *

Although John Gay was one of the most talented English writers in the first third of the eighteenth century, he is overshadowed by his two close friends and fellow-members of the Scriblerus Club, Swift and Pope. Comparisons with the two literary giants of the period are therefore inevitable and usually to Gay's detriment, which is unfortunate since his gifts are significantly different from theirs. It is unfair to think of Gay as a lesser Swift or a lesser Pope. Gay certainly lacks the emotional intensity, intellectual power, and penetrating insight of Swift's great satires, and rarely equals Pope in refined verbal wit, imaginative inventiveness, and incisive irony. The all-embracing cultural survey of *Gulliver's Travels* or even the moral breadth of Pope's *Moral Essays* and *Imitations of Horace* were beyond Gay, as were the gloomy visionary quality and sustained mock-heroic elaboration of *The Dunciad*. Gay's mature work does not seem to stem from a firm ideological foundation of inter-connected philosophical ideas, political convictions and moral values in the way that Swift's and Pope's do. Nevertheless Swift and Pope are not the measure of all Augustan writers as they are sometimes thought to be, and Gay, although influenced by his two friends, usually followed his own creative impulses and did not attempt to do what they were doing. As a result he acquired a distinctive literary voice, less relentless and angry than Swift's, less acerbic and barbed than Pope's, more genial, warm-hearted and gentle than both. His satirical and burlesque works, for example, are less single-minded than theirs, so that his ridicule is often tempered with sentiment, producing a bitter-sweet amalgam that is very much Gay's own and that is particularly evident in his masterpiece, *The Beggar's Opera.* Furthermore Gay, with his less fixed intellectual commitment, was much more chameleon-like than his friends, which helps to explain the extraordinary diversity of his output.

In addition to being a versatile poet, he was a fairly prolific playwright in both verse and prose, and the only member of the Scriblerus Club to devote himself to drama. Indeed it is as the author of *The Beggar's Opera* that he is best remembered today. As a dramatist he did not restrict himself to the "regular" and neoclassically respectable genres of tragedy and comedy but attempted most of the theatrical forms of the period; and with *The Beggar's Opera* he actually invented the ballad opera, which became very popular in the eighteenth century and is the precursor of English comic opera and of the modern musical, as well as being an important influence on Brecht. Gay began his dramatic career with a short farce, *The Mohocks*, and followed this with an undistinguished comedy based on Chaucer, *The Wife of Bath*, before turning his hand to two very different satirical plays. The popular *The What D'Ye Call It* is a fine burlesque of contemporary tragedy, especially "pathetic" plays, that succeeds in transcending burlesque, while the controversial *Three Hours after Marriage*, written as a Scriblerian enterprise with Pope and Arbuthnot, is a lively and frequently farcical dramatic satire attacking a number of well-known contemporary intellectuals and artists. Not long after this he provided Handel with a libretto for his pastoral opera *Acis and Galatea* and then made two not particularly successful attempts at tragedy, *Dione*, written in couplets and in a pastoral and sentimental vein, and *The Captives*, a blank-verse tragedy in a more heroic manner that ends happily with virtue rewarded and poetic justice established. Next came by far his greatest theatrical success, *The Beggar's Opera*, a truly original work of genius and one of the very few eighteenth-century plays to hold the stage until the present day. By using a mixture of speech and song and by providing his own words for well-known tunes, Gay created a new kind of music theatre, the ballad opera, while simultaneously burlesquing Italian opera, which was enjoying a vogue in England. In addition *The Beggar's Opera*, set in the London underworld, is a most unusual love story, both romantic and anti-romantic, as well as a pungently ironic social and political satire. Amazingly enough, Gay was able to weld these diverse elements together into a unified work of art that manages to be both highly topical and universal. After the unprecedented commercial success of *The Beggar's Opera*, Gay wrote an inferior sequel, *Polly*, which was banned from the stage by the Government, offended by the scathing political ridicule of its predecessor. None of his three posthumous plays, *Achilles*, a farcical treatment of a classical legend in ballad-opera form, and the two satirical comedies, *The Distress'd Wife* and *The Rehearsal at Goatham*, adds much to his dramatic achievement.

The range and variety of his dramatic work is matched by that of his poetry, although the quality is again decidedly uneven. He wrote mock-heroic poetry, notably *The Fan*, which is indebted to *The Rape of the Lock*; an extended georgic in the manner of Virgil, *Rural Sports*; a group of pastoral poems, *The Shepherd's Week*, which burlesque Ambrose Philips's *Pastorals* yet are much more than burlesque; a long mock-georgic about London life, laced with acute social observations, guide-book advice and moral precepts, *Trivia; or, The Art of Walking the Streets of London*; a number of urbane verse *Epistles* to friends on various topics; a set of ironic Eclogues, mainly Town Eclogues about fashionable women and love; two series of *Fables* in the manner of Aesop and La Fontaine; various narrative poems, including bawdy tales inspired by Chaucer's *fabliaux*; a few meditative poems such as "A Contemplation on Night" (1714); some lyrics and ballads including the well-known "Sweet William's Farewell to Black-ey'd Susan" (1720); and translations of Ovid and Ariosto. Although much of his poetry is written in decasyllabic couplets, the standard form of the time, Gay is again more varied than many of his contemporaries since he uses the lighter and racier octosyllabic couplets for the *Fables* and some of the tales, blank verse for his early mock-heroic *Wine*, ottava rima for one of his Epistles, "Mr. Pope's Welcome from Greece," and a variety of stanza forms for his songs and ballads. His finest poetic achievement is the first series of *Fables*, ostensibly written to entertain a young member of the Royal Family but, as in the case of earlier fable literature, having a much wider moral, social, and political significance than the apparently innocuous subject-matter suggests. Gay's *Fables* are not of the supreme quality of La Fontaine's, but they remain the best examples of their kind in English since Henryson's admirable adaptations of Aesop into Middle Scots. *Trivia*, which has been claimed to be the finest poem about London in the language, is also a genuinely individual work revealing some of his best qualities: his observant eye for detail, his great sympathy for ordinary humanity, his down-to-earth good sense, his sturdy versification, and plain, unfussy diction. *The Shepherd's Week* is probably the most important Augustan contribution to the genre of pastoral. Much of Gay's work is now of interest only to the specialist, but in a few cases, notably the *Fables* and above all *The Beggar's Opera*, he transcends his own time and must therefore rank as a major Augustan writer.

—Peter Lewis

GOLDSMITH, Oliver.   Irish.   Born in Pallas, near Ballymahon, Longford, 10 November 1728. Educated at the village school in Lissoy, West Meath, 1734–37; Elphin School, 1738; a school in Athlone, 1739–41, and in Edgeworthstown, Longford, 1741–44; Trinity College, Dublin (sizar), 1745–49 (Smyth exhibitioner, 1747), B.A. 1749; studied medicine at the University of Edinburgh, 1752–53; travelled on the Continent, in Switzerland, Italy, and France, 1753–56, and may have obtained a medical degree. Settled in London, 1756; tried unsuccessfully to support himself as a physician in Southwark; worked as an usher in Dr. Milner's classical academy in Peckham, 1756, and as a writer for Ralph Griffiths, proprietor of the *Monthly Review*, 1757–58; Editor, *The Bee*, 1759; contributed to the *British Magazine*, 1760; Editor, *The Lady's Magazine*, 1761; also worked for the publisher Edward Newbery; worked as a proof-reader and preface writer, contributed to the *Public Ledger*, 1760, and prepared a *Compendium of Biography*, 7 volumes, 1762; after 1763 earned increasingly substantial sums from his own writing; one of the founder members of Samuel Johnson's Literary Club, 1764. *Died 4 April 1774.*

PUBLICATIONS

Collections

> *Collected Letters*, edited by Katharine C. Balderston.   1928.
> *Collected Works*, edited by Arthur Friedman.   5 vols., 1966.
> *Poems and Plays*, edited by Tom Davis.   1975.

Plays

> *The Good Natured Man* (produced 1768).   1768.
> *The Grumbler*, from a translation by Charles Sedley of a work of Brueys (produced 1773).   Edited by Alice I. P. Wood, 1931.
> *She Stoops to Conquer; or, The Mistakes of a Night* (produced 1773).   1773; edited by Arthur Friedman, 1968.
> *Threnodia Augustalis, Sacred to the Memory of the Princess Dowager of Wales*, music by Mattia Vento (produced 1772).   1772.
> *The Captivity* (oratorio), in *Miscellaneous Works*.   1820.

Fiction

> *The Vicar of Wakefield*.   1766; edited by Arthur Friedman, 1974.

Verse

The Traveller; or, A Prospect of Society.   1764.
Poems for Young Ladies in Three Parts, Devotional, Moral, and Entertaining.   1767.
The Deserted Village.   1770.
Retaliation.   1774.
The Haunch of Venison: A Poetical Epistle to Lord Clare.   1776.

Other

An Enquiry into the Present State of Polite Learning in Europe.   1759.
The Bee.   1759.
The Mystery Revealed.   1762.
The Citizen of the World; or, Letters from a Chinese Philosopher Residing in London to
    His Friends in the East.   2 vols., 1762.
The Life of Richard Nash of Bath.   1762.
An History of England in a Series of Letters from a Nobleman to His Son.   2 vols., 1764.
An History of the Martyrs and Primitive Fathers of the Church.   1764.
Essays.   1765; revised edition, 1766.
The Present State of the British Empire in Europe, America, Africa, and Asia.   1768.
The Roman History, from the Foundation of the City of Rome to the Destruction of the
    Western Empire.   2 vols., 1769; abridged edition, 1772.
The Life of Thomas Parnell.   1770.
The Life of Henry St. John, Lord Viscount Bolingbroke.   1770.
The History of England, from the Earliest Times to the Death of George II.   4 vols.,
    1771; abridged edition, 1774.
The Grecian History, from the Earliest State to the Death of Alexander the Great.   2
    vols., 1774.
An History of the Earth and Animated Nature.   8 vols., 1774.
A Survey of Experimental Philosophy, Considered in Its Present State of
    Improvement.   2 vols., 1776.

Editor, The Beauties of English Poesy.   2 vols., 1767.

Translator, The Memoirs of a Protestant, by J. Marteilhe.   2 vols., 1758; edited by A.
    Dobson, 1895.
Translator, Plutarch's Lives.   4 vols., 1762.
Translator, A Concise History of Philosophy and Philosophers, by M. Formey.   1766.
Translator, The Comic Romance of Scarron.   2 vols., 1775.

Bibliography: Goldsmith Bibliographically and Biographically Considered by Temple Scott,
1928.

Reading List: Goldsmith by Ralph Wardle, 1957; Goldsmith by Clara M. Kirk, 1967;
Goldsmith: A Georgian Study by Ricardo Quintana, 1967; Life of Goldsmith by Henry A.
Dobson, 1972; Goldsmith by A. Lytton Sells, 1974; Goldsmith: The Critical Heritage, edited
by George S. Rousseau, 1974; The Notable Man: The Life and Times of Goldsmith by John
Ginger, 1977.

*   *   *

Oliver Goldsmith's reputation is made up of paradox. His blundering, improvident nature nevertheless won him the loyalty and friendship of figures like Dr. Johnson, Sir Joshua Reynolds, and Edmund Burke. While in society he was a buffoon, his writing testifies to personal charm and an ironic awareness of his own and others' absurdity. Critical opinion of his work similarly varies from acceptance of Goldsmith as the sensitive apologist for past values to appraisal of him as an accomplished social and literary satirist. Indeed, his work can operate on both levels, a fact perhaps recognised by the young Jane Austen in her *Juvenilia* when she took Goldsmith's abridgements of history for young persons as a model for her own exercise in irony.

Drifting into authorship after a mis-spent youth (as Macaulay notes in his disapproving *Life*), Goldsmith turned to hack writing, contributing articles to the *Monthly* and *Critical Reviews* from 1757. His more ambitious *Inquiry into the Present State of Polite Learning* of 1759 won him the reputation of a man of learning and elegant expression. In this last essay he reveals his fundamental dislike of the contemporary cult of sensibility which was to generate not only his own "laughing" form of comedy in the drama but also *The Vicar of Wakefield*. Meeting Smollett, then editor of the *British Magazine*, Goldsmith was encouraged to expand his contributions to literary journalism. He produced the weekly periodical *The Bee*; many papers collected and published in 1765 and 1766 as *Essays*; and, most important, the "Chinese Letters" of 1760–61 collected as *The Citizen of the World*.

The "citizen" is, of course, an Oriental traveller, observing the fashions and foibles of the *bon ton* in London with wide-eyed innocence that carries within it implicit comment and criticism not unmixed with humour. The device was borrowed from the French, notably Montesquieu's *Lettres Persanes* (1721). In each essay the absurdities of behaviour are marked, the whole inter-woven by continuing narratives around the Man in Black, Beau Tibbs, the story of Hingo and Zelis, for instance. In many ways the ironies, improbabilities, and apparent innocence of the Chinese letters prefigure the extended prose romance of *The Vicar of Wakefield*.

This could be seen as Goldsmith's answer to Sterne's *Tristram Shandy* (1759). He had attacked Sterne's sentimental fiction as "obscene and pert" in *The Citizen*; in many ways *The Vicar* parodies Sterne's novel but with such a light hand that it has been taken on face value for many generations as the tale indeed of a family "generous, credulous, simple, and inoffensive." However, Goldsmith early establishes for the observant the manifest danger of complacency in such apparent virtues. His Yorkshire parson displays the moral duplicity of a feeling heart, for Goldsmith's approach to life and art is the opposite of Sterne's relativism and dilettante values.

Goldsmith's moral seriousness (while softened by genial good humour) dominates that other work now considered "classic," *The Deserted Village*. His earlier sortie in the genre of topographical/philosophical verse, *The Traveller*, did much to establish his reputation. It is an accomplished use of convention, where the poet climbs an eminence only to have his mind expanded into contemplation of universal questions. In *The Deserted Village*, however, the poet comes to terms with a particular social problem in a particular landscape as opposed to former abstract musings above imaginary solitudes. "Sweet Auburn" can be identified closely with the village of Nuneham Courtenay, where the local land-owner had recently moved the whole community out in order to extend and improve his landscape park. The fact becomes a catalyst for Goldsmith in a consideration of where aesthetic values and irresponsible wealth lead: a symbol taken from life and not from poetic convention.

Goldsmith's rhymed couplets have grace and ease, particularly when his verse is unlaboured, as in the prologues and epilogues to his own and others' plays. The charm and humour of these can be observed in his later poem *Retaliation*, which has a pointed raciness born out of the settling of personal scores. Always the butt of jokes in the group known as The Club, here he gets his own back with a series of comic epitaphs for the other members. Notable is that for Garrick – "On the stage he was natural, simple, affecting;/Twas only that when he was off he was acting" – but he labels himself the "gooseberry fool."

As a dramatist, Goldsmith exploited both verbal dexterity and the comedy of situation, looking back to Shakespeare in the rejection of the so-called genteel comedy of Hugh Kelly or Richard Cumberland. Affected and strained in tone and action, the drama of sentiment offered to Goldsmith nothing of the "nature and humour" that he saw as the first principle of theatre. However he might despise the sentimental school, he cannot avoid using some of its conventions, the good-natured hero, of course, and the device of paired lovers, but the way these are treated is particular to himself. Together with Sheridan, Goldsmith exploits the theatrical unreality of comedy, using the stage as a separate world of experience with its own laws and therefore demanding the suspension of disbelief in order that farcical unreality might unmask farcical reality. His character Honeydew in *The Good Natured Man* has something in common with Charles Surface in *School for Scandal*, but the tone of Goldsmith's comedy is less brittle than that of Sheridan. This mellow tone, a fundamental wholesomeness, is magnificently encapsulated in *She Stoops to Conquer*.

Goldsmith's first play met with a poor response, as being too "low" in its matter (especially the bailiffs scene), and, though *She Stoops to Conquer* was open to similar criticism, its riotous humour overcame prejudice. In short, it was good theatre and this is testified by its continuing popularity in production. Characters like Tony Lumpkin, Mrs. Hardcastle, and the old Squire have become literary personalities, while the pivot of the plot, Marlow's loss of diffidence in apparently more relaxed circumstances, holds true to human nature. The character of Kate is a liberated heroine in the Shakespearean style, contrasted as in the older comedy with a foil. One is able to relate Goldsmith's "laughing" comedy to that of Shakespeare in many ways, for the Lord of Misrule dominates both.

The range of Goldsmith's work is touched by this same humour and sensitivity, the good heart that is so easily squandered as he himself acknowledged in *The Good Natured Man*, but is just as easily extended with purpose to the reader. As Walter Scott observed, no man contrived "so well to reconcile us to human nature."

—B. C. Oliver-Morden

HILL, Aaron. English. Born in London, 10 February 1685. Educated at Barnstaple Grammar School, Devon; Westminster School, London. Married Miss Morris in 1710 (died, 1731); nine children. Visited his relative, Lord Paget, then Ambassador in Constantinople, and sent by Paget on a tour of the east, 1700–03; subsequently travelled as a tutor to Sir William Wentworth; settled in London: Manager of the Drury Lane Theatre, 1709–10, and the opera in the Haymarket, 1710–13; managed the Little Theatre, Haymarket, c. 1720–33; Editor, with William Bond, *The Plain-Dealer*, 1724–25; Editor, *The Prompter*, 1734–36; also involved in various unsuccessful business ventures, including extracting oil from beechmast, 1713, colonizing in Georgia, 1718, etc.; retired to Essex, 1738. *Died 8 February 1750.*

PUBLICATIONS

Collections

Works. 4 vols., 1753.
Dramatic Works. 2 vols., 1760.

Plays

Elfrid; or, The Fair Inconstant (produced 1710).   1710; revised version, as Athelwold
(produced 1731), 1732.
The Walking Statue; or, The Devil in the Wine Cellar (produced 1710).   With Elfrid,
1710.
Rinaldo, music by Handel, from a play by Giacomo Rossi (produced 1711).   1711.
Il Pastor Fido, The Faithful Shepherd, music by Handel, from a play by Giacomo Rossi
(produced 1712).   1712.
The Fatal Vision; or, The Fall of Siam (produced 1716).   1716.
The Fatal Extravagance, with Joseph Mitchell (produced 1721).   1720; revised version
(produced 1730), 1726.
King Henry the Fifth; or, The Conquest of France by the English, from the play by
Shakespeare (produced 1723).   1723.
The Tragedy of Zara, from a work by Voltaire (produced 1735).   1736.
Alzira, from a work by Voltaire (produced 1736).   1736.
Merope, from a work by Voltaire (produced 1749).   1749.
The Roman Revenge, from a work by Voltaire (produced 1753?).   1753.
The Insolvent; or, Filial Piety, from the play The Guiltless Adultress by Davenant based
on The Fatal Dowry by Massinger (produced 1758).   1758.
The Muses in Mourning, Merlin in Love, The Snake in the Grass, Saul, and Daraxes, in
Dramatic Works.   1760.

Verse

Camillus.   1707.
The Invasion: A Poem to the Queen.   1708.
The Dedication of the Beech Tree.   1714.
The Northern Star.   1718; revised edition, 1739.
The Creation: A Pindaric.   1720.
The Judgment-Day.   1721.
The Progress of Wit: A Caveat.   1730.
Advice to the Poets.   1731.
The Tears of the Muses.   1737.
The Fanciad: An Heroic Poem.   1743.
The Impartial: An Address Without Flattery.   1744.
The Art of Acting.   1744.
Free Thoughts on Faith; or, The Religion of Reason.   1746.
Gideon; or, The Patriot: An Epic Poem.   1749.

Other

A Full Account of the Present State of the Ottoman Empire.   1709.
An Enquiry into the Merit of Assassination.   1738.
A Collection of Letters Between Hill, Pope, and Others.   1751.
Selections from The Prompter, edited by W. A. Appleton and K. A. Burnim.   1966.

Editor, The Plain-Dealer (periodical).   2 vols., 1730.

Translator, with Nahum Tate, The Celebrated Speeches of Ajax and Ulysses, by
Ovid.   1708.

Reading List: *The Life and Works of Hill* by H. Ludwig, 1911; *Hill, Poet, Dramatist, Projector* by Dorothy Brewster, 1913.

*   *   *

Aaron Hill was a man of great ambition but very frequently a loser. As a teenager he visited Constantinople (where a relative, Lord Paget, was British ambassador) but his book on the Ottoman Empire was written too early in life and later he deprecated it. He addressed a poem to Lord Peterborough but failed to take the preferment it occasioned. He wrote another in honor of Peter the Great and was awarded a gold medal – which he never collected. He proposed the colonization of Georgia but then dropped the idea. He invented some gadgets and processes – he patented one for extracting oil from beechmast – but nothing came of it. He wrote the libretto for Handel's *Rinaldo* (1711) but did not benefit either from the subsequent popularity for opera or from the spate of parodies, ballad operas, and other reactions which followed the Italian fad. He was appointed by William Collier to manage the Theatre Royal in Drury Lane but the actors beat him up and rioted: for this Powell was dismissed and Booth, Bickerstaff, Keen and Leigh disciplined, but in the end Hill suffered most. He defended Shakespeare against the attacks of Voltaire when the French genius was temporarily touted over the native one and said some nasty things about Pope in *The Progress of Wit*, which gained him the notoriety of a mention in *The Dunciad*. He adapted several of Voltaire's plays for the English stage but Arthur Murphy rather upstaged him with *The Orphan of China* (1759). His version of Voltaire's *Merope* was commanded as a benefit performance by Frederick, Prince of Wales – but Hill died the night before the performance.

As a playwright, Hill was not notable, though his early farce *The Walking Statue* showed more promise than such poems as *Camillus* and *The Northern Star*. *Elfrid; or, The Fair Inconstant* betrayed some of the jejune quality in *A Full Account of the Ottoman Empire*, and, while rhodomontade might pass on the stage, when *Aethelwold* (the revised version of *Elfrid*) appeared in print it was greeted with well-deserved ridicule. I must confess that Voltaire's pseudo-classical plays leave me cold and that Hill's English *réchauffages* are no help. Even the poetry of Stephen Duck (1705–1756) is probably better than Hill's if one must have a Wiltshire bard of the time, though Hill retired to family farms in Wiltshire after London rejected him, while Duck committed suicide after his brief vogue. Hill's verse is more pompous than that of John Home's *Douglas* (1757) but far less impressive, and Hill's greatest contribution to poetry was (when he was self-importantly setting himself up as *censor elegantiarum* in competition with Pope) in recognizing true talent in James Thomson's *Winter* (1726, brought to Hill's attention by Thomson's friend David Mallet) and generously publicizing it. One might add that Hill regarded Thomson's *Liberty* as "mighty work" and "the last stretched blaze of our expiring genius" – probably because Thomson was then the heir-apparent to Pope. In his controversy with Pope, Hill was lively but did not really emerge as well as Colley Cibber. In the end he made up with Pope and numbered him and Richardson and many other celebrities among his friends. He befriended Richard Savage and wrote about him in his newspaper.

It was his journalism and his letters that saved Hill from being "a bit of a bore." *The Plain-Dealer* (23 March 1724 to 7 May 1725), conducted with William Bond, "maintained a good philosophic literary level" (Bonamy Dobrée, *English Literature in the Early Eighteenth Century*, 1959), and *The Prompter* (12 November 1734 to 2 July 1736) is of interest to all students of the theatre, its 173 numbers full of good criticism. Moreover Hill's letters are "always in the centre of the literary scene" (Dobrée) and concern Pope and *The Dunciad*; projects involving real estate and potash; coffee, sugar, and the tax on Madeira; Drury Lane and actors like Barton Booth and Robert Wilks; an ill-fated attempt to run the opera at the Haymarket; advice to Thomson on the use of capitals and to actors about tone and delivery; a letter to Sir Robert Walpole on "the encouragement of able *writers*" and one to Lady Walpole on rock-gardens; praise of Richardson's *Pamela* and criticism of Mallet's *Euridice*;

communications to celebrities as different as Peterborough and Voltaire. Perhaps Hill was, as Pope waspishly said, a "bad author" but he was a fascinating individual, and the letters do much to prove the truth of another judgment of the Wasp of Twickenham: that Aaron Hill was "not quite a swan, not wholly a goose." If only as the author of *The Prompter*, Hill deserves a more modern study than those of Brewster or Ludwig.

—Leonard R.N. Ashley

HOLCROFT, Thomas.   English.   Born in London, 10 December 1745. Self-educated. Married four times, lastly to Louisa Mercier; one son and two daughters. Worked as a stableboy in Newmarket, Suffolk, 1757–60, and in his father's cobbler's stall, London, 1761–64; taught school in Liverpool, 1764; resumed his trade of shoemaker, London, 1764–69, and contributed to the *Whitehall Evening Post*; tutor in the family of Granville Sharp, 1769; prompter at a Dublin theatre, 1770–71; strolling player in the provinces in England, 1771–78; returned to London, 1778, and thereafter a prolific writer: contributed to the *Westminster Magazine*, *Wit's Magazine*, *Town and Country*, and early numbers of the *English Review*; actor and playwright at Drury Lane Theatre, 1778–84; Correspondent in Paris for the *Morning Herald*, 1783; joined the Society for Constitutional Information, 1792: indicted for treason, imprisoned, then discharged, 1794; moved to Hamburg, 1799, and tried, unsuccessfully, to establish the *European Repository*; lived in Paris, 1801–03, then returned to London: set up a printing business with his brother-in-law, 1803, which subsequently failed. *Died 23 March 1809.*

PUBLICATIONS

Plays

>   *The Crisis; or, Love and Fear* (produced 1778).
>   *Duplicity* (produced 1781).   1781; as *The Masked Friend* (produced 1796).
>   *The Noble Peasant*, music by William Shield (produced 1784).   1784.
>   *The Follies of a Day; or, The Marriage of Figaro*, from a play by Beaumarchais (produced 1784).   1785; revised version, 1881; revised version, from the opera by da Ponte, music by Mozart (produced 1819), 1819.
>   *The Choleric Fathers*, music by William Shield (produced 1785).   1785.
>   *Sacred Dramas Written in French by la Comtesse de Genlis.*   1785.
>   *Seduction* (produced 1787).   1787.
>   *The School for Arrogance*, from a play by Destouches (produced 1791).   1791.
>   *The Road to Ruin* (produced 1792).   1792; edited by Ruth I. Aldrich, 1968.
>   *Love's Frailties* (produced 1794).   1794.
>   *Heigh-Ho! for a Husband.*   1794.
>   *The Rival Queens; or, Drury Lane and Covent Garden* (produced 1794).
>   *The Deserted Daughter*, from a work by Diderot (produced 1795).   1795.
>   *The Man of Ten Thousand* (produced 1796).   1796.
>   *The Force of Ridicule* (produced 1796).
>   *Knave or Not?*, from plays by Goldoni (produced 1798).   1798.
>   *He's Much to Blame* (produced 1798).   1798.

The Inquisitor (produced 1798).   1798.

The Old Clothesman, music by Thomas Attwood (produced 1799).   Songs published 1799(?).

Deaf and Dumb; or, The Orphan Protected, from a play by de Bouilly (produced 1801).   1801.

The Escapes; or, The Water-Carrier, music by Thomas Attwood, songs by T. J. Dïbdin, from an opera by J. N. Nouilly, music by Cherubini (produced 1801).

A Tale of Mystery, from a play by Pixérécourt (produced 1802).   1802.

Hear Both Sides (produced 1803).   1803.

The Lady of the Rock (produced 1805).   1805.

The Vindictive Man (produced 1806).   1806.

Fiction

Alwyn; or, The Gentleman Comedian, with William Nicholson.   1780.

The Family Picture; or, Domestic Dialogues on Amiable Subjects.   1783.

An Amorous Tale of the Chaste Loves of Peter the Long and His Most Honoured Friend Dame Blanche Bazu.   1786.

Anna St. Ives.   1792; edited by Peter Faulkner, 1970.

The Adventures of Hugh Trevor.   1794; edited by Seamus Deane, 1973.

Memoirs of Bryan Perdue.   1805.

Verse

Elegies.   1777.

Human Happiness; or, The Sceptic.   1783.

Tales in Verse, Critical, Satirical, Humorous.   1806.

Other

A Plain and Succinct Narrative of the Late [Gordon] Riots.   1780; edited by Garland Garvey Smith, 1944.

The Trial of the Hon. George Gordon.   1781.

Memoirs of Baron de Tott, Containing the State of the Turkish Empire and the Crimea.   2 vols., 1785.

The Secret History of the Court of Berlin.   2 vols., 1789.

A Narrative of Facts Relating to a Prosecution for High Treason.   2 vols., 1795.

A Letter to William Windham on the Intemperance and Danger of His Public Conduct.   1795.

Travels from Hamburg Through Westphalia, Holland, and the Netherlands.   2 vols., 1804.

Memoirs, completed by William Hazlitt.   3 vols., 1816; edited by Elbridge Colby, as *The Life of Holcroft*, 2 vols., 1925.

Editor, *Letter on Egypt*, by Mr. Savary.   2 vols., 1786.

Editor, and Translator, *Posthumous Works of Frederick, King of Prussia.*   13 vols., 1789.

Editor, *The Theatrical Recorder*   2 vols., 1805–06.

Translator, *Philosophical Essays with Observations on the Laws and Customs of Several Eastern Nations*, by Foucher d'Osbornville.   1784.

Translator, *Tales of the Castle*, by la Comtesse de Genlis.   5 vols., 1785.
Translator, *Caroline of Lichtfield*, by Baroness de Montolieu.   2 vols., 1786.
Translator, *Historical and Critical Memoirs of the Life and Writings of Voltaire*, by Chaudon.   1786.
Translator, *The Present State of the Empire of Morocco*, by Chenier.   2 vols., 1788.
Translator, *The Life of Baron Frederick Trenck.*   3 vols., 1788.
Translator, *Essays on Physiognomy*, by J. C. Lavater.   3 vols., 1789.
Translator, *Travels Through Germany, Switzerland, and Italy*, by Frederick Leopold, Count Stolberg.   2 vols., 1796–97.
Translator, *Herman and Dorothea*, by Goethe.   1801.

Bibliography: *A Bibliography of Holcroft* by Elbridge Colby, 1922.

Reading List: *Holcroft and the Revolutionary Novel* by Rodney M. Baine, 1965; *The English Jacobin Novel* by Gary Kelly, 1976.

*   *   *

Thomas Holcroft was a self-taught man of letters, and one of the leading radical writers of the period of the French Revolution. His early writing was mostly for the theatre, and both *The School for Arrogance* and *The Road to Ruin* were successful in combining sentimental melodrama with the new philosophy. But with changing theatrical taste, Holcroft's plays passed into an oblivion from which they are yet to be restored. He chose to use the novel form for the fuller exposition of his political outlook, an outlook clearly influenced by his friendship with William Godwin, the most famous radical intellectual of the day, and his acquaintance with other radicals like Tom Paine and Mary Wollstonecraft.

Holcroft's two major novels are *Anna St. Ives* and *The Adventures of Hugh Trevor*. *Anna St. Ives* may be regarded as the equivalent in fiction of Godwin's *Political Justice*. It expresses its criticism of society through the contrasting contenders for the hand of the heroine, Anna: the rationalist Frank Henley, the virtuous son of the steward of Anna's father, and the aristocratic rake Coke Clifton. Clifton is a character in the line of Richardson's Lovelace in *Clarissa*, confident, witty, and unprincipled. He is allowed to express himself with a theatrical exuberance which gives the novel some vitality: "Should I be obliged to come like Jove to Semele, in flames, and should we both be reduced to ashes in the conflict, I will enjoy her!" However, the novel has a clear doctrinaire intention, which results in the defeat of Clifton and the marriage of Frank and Anna. The extravagance of Holcroft's idealism comes out in the final conversion of Clifton himself to the high-minded radicalism of his two unfailing friends.

Hugh Trevor is less diagrammatic in its rendering of life, but no less didactic in intention. The story of Trevor's life is basically picaresque, with a variety of adventures and events, but the moral of his experiences is clear: society is corrupt, and reason must guide the individual if he is to avoid its coercions. But there is also some psychological development, which would seem to have an autobiographical origin, in Trevor's gradual development of control over his original impulsiveness. When this is allied with a vigorous satirical attack on various aspects of society, including the Church, the law and reactionary politicians, the overall effect is a novel of considerable interest. Together with *Anna*, it justifies Holcroft's claim to be considered as a significant participant in an important tradition of rationalist social idealism.

—Peter Faulkner

HOME, John. Scottish. Born in Leith, near Edinburgh, 21 September 1722. Educated at the grammar school in Leith; University of Edinburgh, graduated 1742. Fought on the Hanoverian side in the Edinburgh volunteers, subsequently as a Lieutenant in the Glasgow volunteers, 1745–46: taken prisoner at Falkirk, 1746. Married Mary Home in 1770. Licensed to preach by the presbytery of Edinburgh, 1745; Minister of Athelstaneford, East Lothian, 1747 until he resigned before he could be tried on charges of profanity in his play *Douglas*, 1757; Private Secretary to the Earl of Bute, and subsequently tutor to the Prince of Wales, from 1757: granted pension by George III on his accession, 1760; Conservator of Scots privileges at Campvere, Holland, from 1763; built a mansion in Kilduff, East Lothian, and lived there, 1770–79; settled in Edinburgh, 1779. *Died 5 September 1808.*

PUBLICATIONS

Collections

Works. 3 vols., 1822.

Plays

Douglas (produced 1756). 1757; edited by Gerald D. Parker, 1972.
Agis, music by William Boyce (produced 1758). 1758.
The Siege of Aquileia (produced 1760). 1760.
Dramatic Works. 1760; revised edition, 2 vols., 1798.
The Fatal Discovery (produced 1769). 1769.
Alonzo (produced 1773). 1773.
Alfred (produced 1778). 1778.

Other

The History of the Rebellion in the Year 1745. 1802.

Reading List: *The Works of Home* by Henry Mackenzie, 1822; *Home: A Study of His Life and Works* by Alice E. Gipson, 1917.

* * *

Although John Home wrote six tragedies, his reputation is based almost entirely on *Douglas,* the second of his plays in order of composition but the first to be performed. After Garrick declined the play at Drury Lane, *Douglas* was performed with great success in Edinburgh, which led to a remarkably heated controversy concerned chiefly with the impropriety of a minister contributing to "wicked" theatrical activity. *Douglas* was also an immediate success when performed at Covent Garden in London, quickly became standard repertory fare, and remained popular for over a century.

One of the eighteenth century's best blank-verse tragedies, *Douglas* deals with the untimely death of the valiant Douglas and the ensuing suicide of his mother, Lady Randolph, with whom he has been reunited after having been separated since infancy. The contrast between

Lady Randolph's past suffering and current, though temporary, joy is central to the play, which seeks to evoke "celestial melancholy" by focusing on tragic irony and pity for Lady Randolph's frustrated maternal love. The play's popularity can also be attributed to its fervid language, highly romantic setting, and appeal to Scottish national pride.

Of Home's five other plays, *Agis*, *The Siege of Aquileia*, *The Fatal Discovery*, and *Alonzo* were moderately well-received on the eighteenth-century stage, while his last effort, *Alfred*, ran for only three nights. With the exception of *The Siege of Aquileia*, these plays also employ tragic irony, melancholy atmospheres, or romantic settings to evoke pathos, but are generally inferior to *Douglas*.

Agis, written before *Douglas*, deals with the assassination of a political hero who fails to recognize the treachery of his enemies. In *The Fatal Discovery*, based on one of James Macpherson's Ossianic fragments, the heroine, Rivine, commits suicide after placing love above personal honor. Rivine is made to appear an innocent victim of deception; hence emphasis is placed on the growing pathos of her situation as the play progresses. *Alonzo* is nearly identical to *Douglas* in plot conception and in stressing frustrated maternal affection; however, Lady Randolph's suicide is well-motivated and moving, whereas Ormisinda, in *Alonzo*, kills herself for no apparent reason at the moment when various misunderstandings could be corrected and disaster averted. *Alfred* is a melodrama that deserves to remain the most obscure of Home's plays. It consists of a series of schemes devised by Alfred to save his betrothed from Hinguar, the Danish king.

The best of these five plays is *The Siege of Aquileia*, in which Aemilius, a Roman consul and governor, must either sacrifice his sons or betray his country and personal honor. Home handles Aemilius's dilemma effectively, making the choice progressively more difficult. This is the only one of Home's plays in which the protagonist must choose between equally worthy, conflicting sets of values; hence it allows for more complex tragic effects than the pathos that remains uppermost in all of Home's other plays.

—James S. Malek

HOWARD, Sir Robert. English. Born in England in 1626; son of the Earl of Berkshire; brother-in-law of John Dryden, *q.v.* Probably educated at Magdalen College, Oxford. Married 1) Ann Kingsmill in 1645, one daughter; 2) Lady Honora O'Brien in 1665, one son; 3) Annabella Dives in 1692. Royalist: knighted for bravery at the second battle of Newbury, 1644; imprisoned during the Commonwealth at Windsor Castle; after the Restoration became Member of Parliament for Stockbridge, Hampshire, was made a Knight of the Bath, and became Secretary to the Commissioners of the Treasury; Auditor of the Exchequer, 1677 until his death; Member of Parliament for Castle Rising, Norfolk, 1678–98; Privy Councillor, 1688; commissioner to enquire into the state of the fleet, 1690; commander of the militia horse, 1690. *Died 3 September 1698.*

PUBLICATIONS

Plays

The Blind Lady, in *Poems*. 1660.
The Surprisal (produced 1662). In *Four New Plays*, 1665.

The Committee; or, The Faithful Irishman (produced 1662).   In *Four New Plays*, 1665; edited by Carryl N. Thurber, 1921.

The Indian Queen (produced 1664).   In *Four New Plays*, 1665; revised version, music by Purcell (produced 1695); in *Works 8* by Dryden, 1962.

The Vestal Virgin; or, The Roman Ladies (produced 1665).   In *Four New Plays*, 1665.

Four New Plays.   1665; expanded edition, as *Five New Plays*, 1692; as *Dramatic Works*, 1722.

The Great Favourite; or, The Duke of Lerma (produced 1668).   1668; edited by D. D. Arundell, in *Dryden and Howard*, 1929.

The Country Gentleman, with George Villiers, edited by Arthur H. Scouten and Robert D. Hume.   1976.

Verse

Poems.   1660.
The Duel of the Stags.   1668.

Other

An Account of the State of His Majesty's Revenue.   1680.
The Life and Reign of King Richard the Second.   1680.
Historical Observations upon the Reigns of Edward I, II, III, and Richard II.   1689.
A Letter to Mr. Samuel Johnson.   1692.
The History of Religion.   1694; as *An Account of the Growth of Deism*, 1709.

Reading List: *Howard: A Critical Biography* by Harold J. Oliver, 1963 (includes bibliography).

*   *   *

Sir Robert Howard was active in various aspects of the revival of drama upon the re-opening of the theatres in 1660, as he not only wrote comedies and one of the earliest heroic plays but also engaged in dramatic theory. A new kind of tragedy was emerging, and Harold J. Oliver calls Howard's first play, *The Blind Lady*, "half-way between Jacobean tragedy and Heroic drama." Howard then went all the way towards creating a new form in *The Indian Queen*. Here we find an epic hero, a conflict between the claims of Love and Honour, serious debates, and spectacular stage effects. The reception of this new type of drama led Howard into unprofitable literary controversies over the place of rhymed verse in tragedy and the validity of tragi-comedy.

Of his four comedies, *The Committee* was his great success, holding the stage into the nineteenth century. This vivacious work presents an implacable conflict between the puritans and the royalists toward the end of the Commonwealth period and contains an intrinsically comic figure in the Irish servant Teague. More important, however, in a critical analysis of Howard as a playwright is his achieving what strikes the reader as a genuine rather than an artificial portrayal of women in his imaginative creation of the heroine Ruth and the villain Mrs. Day, a former dairy maid who has risen to become the wife of the chairman of the sequestration committee. These two women are more than a match for the men throughout the play.

Similar psychological insight and emphasis on the role of women appear in *The Country Gentleman*, the long-lost political comedy by Howard and George Villiers, which was discovered in 1973. In the play, Howard experiments with the love game between the romantic couples, a technique which was to become standard practice in later sex-comedies of the Restoration. Yet Howard proceeds with sturdy independence to present an exemplary father (unheard of in this early period), to champion the country against the city, and to engage in satire which includes positive as well as negative examples. His neoclassical taste is revealed in the structure of this comedy, all of which is set in two rooms of one house, with the time of the action only slightly exceeding the actual time of the representation.

After a promising beginning as a playwright, Howard abandoned literature and turned to a full career in politics.

—Arthur H. Scouten

HUGHES, John.   English.   Born in Marlborough, Wiltshire, 29 January 1677; brother of the translator Jabez Hughes. Educated at a dissenting academy, probably in Little Britain, London. Worked in the Ordnance Office, London, and served as Secretary to various commissions for the purchase of lands for the royal dockyards; Secretary to the commissions of peace in the court of chancery, from 1717. *Died 17 February 1720.*

PUBLICATIONS

Collections

   Poems on Several Occasions, with Some Select Essays, edited by W. Duncombe.   2
      vols., 1735.

Plays

   Six Cantatas, music by J. C. Pepusch (produced 1710).   1710.
   Calypso and Telemachus, music by J. E. Galliard (produced 1712).   1712.
   Apollo and Daphne: A Masque, music by J. C. Pepusch (produced 1716).   1716.
   Orestes.   1717.
   The Siege of Damascus (produced 1720).   1720.

Verse

   The Triumph of Peace.   1698.
   The Court of Neptune.   1699.
   The House of Nassau: A Pindaric Ode.   1702.
   An Ode in Praise of Music.   1703.
   An Ode to the Creator of the World, Occasioned by the Fragments of Orpheus.   1713.
   An Ode for the Birthday of the Princess of Wales.   1716.
   The Ecstasy: An Ode.   1720.

Other

A Review of the Case of Ephraim and Judah. 1705.
The Lay-Monastery, Consisting of Essays, Discourses, etc., with Richard
    Blackmore. 1714.
A Layman's Thoughts on the Late Treatment of the Bishop of Bangor. 1717.
Charon; or, The Ferry-Boat: A Vision. 1719.
The Complicated Guilt of the Late Rebellion. 1745.
Letters of Several Eminent Persons Deceased, with others, edited by J.
    Duncombe. 1772; as The Correspondence of Hughes and Several of His Friends, 2
    vols., 1773.

Editor, A Complete History of England, vols. 1–2, by W. Kennett. 1706.
Editor, Advice from Parnassus, by Traiano Boccalini. 1706.
Editor, The Works of Spenser. 6 vols., 1715; commentary edited by Scott Elledge, in
    Eighteenth-Century Critical Essays, vol. 1, 1961.

Translator, Fontenelle's Dialogues of the Dead, with Two Original Dialogues. 1708.
Translator, The History of the Revolutions in Portugal, by the Abbot de Vertot. 1712.
Translator, Letters of Abelard and Heloise, Extracted Chiefly from Bayle. 1718 (3rd
    edition).

Reading List: "Some Sources for The Siege of Damascus" by John R. Moore, in Huntington
Library Quarterly 21, 1958.

*   *   *

Critics have been reluctant to pass favourable judgment on John Hughes. Eminent
contemporaries were less than generous towards his achievement, and Johnson's Life is non-
committal. Gibbon, on the other hand, praised The Siege of Damascus for its "rare merit of
blending nature and history...." As a playwright Hughes had some success in the sphere of
high tragedy; but his more ambitious poems such as The House of Nassau and the Ode to the
Creator of the World lack coherence, while his shorter verses are overburdened with
Augustan conventionalities. What redeems Hughes's considerable talent is his excellent
understanding of other authors' intentions (as in the "Essay on Allegorical Poetry" prefixed
to his 1715 edition of Spenser) and his discerning views on the potentialities of sung poetry.
    At a time when Italian vocal music was all the rage, Hughes aimed "to improve a sort of
(English) verse, in regular measures, purposely fitted for music ... which, of all the modern
kinds, seems to be the only one that can now properly be called lyrics." Rejecting Edmund
Waller's notion that "soft words with nothing in them make a song" and paying due respect
to the composer's demand for a congenial text, Hughes produced Six Cantatas (set by J. C.
Pepusch) and other brief works in which the airs and recitatives employ suitably contrasting
accentuations. On a more ambitious scale are several odes, also intended for music. The
inventiveness they display is again evident in stage masques written as an alternative genre to
Italianate music drama. A more resourceful composer than Pepusch might have created a
minor masterpiece out of Apollo and Daphne; for his opera Calypso and Telemachus Hughes
had collaborated with J. E. Galliard, for whose music Handel had a high regard. This work
constituted an attempt to refute "a late Opinion among some, that English words are not

proper for Musick" and bears out Hughes's contention that the alleged shortcomings of the English language need not deter an inventive librettist.

Hughes's prose writings include translations and periodical essays. His work as a whole reveals a wide knowledge of general literature; although overshadowed by Steele, Addison, and Pope his critical abilities place him well above the level of incorrigible mediocrity.

—E. D. Mackerness

INCHBALD, Elizabeth (née Simpson). English.   Born in Stanningfield, near Bury St. Edmunds, Suffolk, 15 October 1753. Married the actor and painter Joseph Inchbald in 1772 (died, 1779). Settled in London, 1772; debut as an actress, playing opposite her husband, Bristol, 1772; subsequently appeared in various Scottish towns, 1772–76, various English towns, 1776–78, and under Tate Wilkinson in Yorkshire, 1778–80; appeared on the London stage, 1780 until her retirement, 1789. *Died 1 August 1821.*

PUBLICATIONS

Plays

A Mogul Tale: or, The Descent of the Balloon (produced 1784).   1788.
I'll Tell You What (produced 1785).   1786.
Appearance Is Against Them (produced 1785).   1785.
The Widow's Vow, from a play by Patrat (produced 1786).   1786.
Such Things Are (produced 1787).   1788.
The Midnight Hour: or, War of Wits, from a play by Dumaniant (produced 1787).   1787.
All on a Summer's Day (produced 1787).
Animal Magnetism (produced 1788).   1788(?).
The Child of Nature, from a play by Mme. de Genlis (produced 1788).   1788.
The Married Man, from a play by Philippe Néricault-Destouches (produced 1789).   1789.
The Hue and Cry, from a play by Dumaniant (produced 1791).
Next Door Neighbours, from plays by L. S. Mercier and Philippe Néricault-Destouches (produced 1791).   1791.
Young Men and Old Women, from a play by Gresset (produced 1792).
Every One Has His Fault (produced 1793).   1792; edited by Allardyce Nicoll in *Lesser English Comedies of the Eighteenth Century*, 1931.
The Wedding Day (produced 1794).   1794.
Wives as They Were and Maids as They Are (produced 1797).   1797.
Lovers' Vows, from a play by Kotzebue (produced 1798).   1798.
The Wise Men of the East, from a play by Kotzebue (produced 1799).   1799.
To Marry, or Not to Marry (produced 1805).   1805.
The Massacre and *A Case of Conscience*, in *Memoirs of Mrs. Inchbald* by James Boaden.   2 vols., 1833.

Fiction

> *A Simple Story*. 1791; edited by J. M. S. Tompkins, 1967.
> *Nature and Art*. 1796; edited by W. B. Scott, 1886.

Other

> Editor, *The British Theatre; or, A Collection of Plays with Biographical and Critical Remarks*. 25 vols., 1808.
> Editor, *A Collection of Farces and Other Afterpieces*. 7 vols., 1809.
> Editor, *The Modern Theatre*. 10 vols., 1809.

Bibliography: "An Inchbald Bibliography" by George L. Joughlin, in *Studies in English*, 1934.

Reading List: *Memoirs of Mrs. Inchbald* by James Boaden, 2 vols., 1833; *Inchbald and Her Circle* by Samuel R. Littlewood, 1921; *Inchbald, Novelist* by William MacKee, 1935; *Inchbald et la Comédie "Sentimentale" Anglaise au XVIII Siècle* by Françoise Moreux, 1971.

*   *   *

"Now Mrs. Inchbald was all heart," said James Boaden, her biographer, and the statement is as true of her writings as of her life. It is not the whole truth, of course; Boaden's memoir bears ample evidence of her independent spirit, her chasteness of mind and morals, her political liberalism, her candour, and her ardent and life-long pursuit of intellectual self-improvement. These too went to shape her plays and novels. Her plays reveal a fairly constant moral interest, combined with concern for domestic virtues set against the temptations of fashionable society, and working on the conventions of sentimental comedy and the social, scientific, religious, political, and literary topics of the day. She kept well abreast of changing theatrical tastes in the last two decades of the century, but constantly strove to give her slender subjects, complicated plots, and conventional characters some serious moral content. So, as the writer of an epilogue to one of her adaptations from French put it, her version had "the merit/Of giving Gallic Froth – true BRITISH SPIRIT." Her dramas, even those taken from French or German originals (such as Kotzebue's *Lovers' Vows*), were made her own not so much by their themes or techniques as by her thorough subordination of her borrowed materials to her personal version of the moral and aesthetic values of the time. As J. Taylor put it in his prologue to her last play, *To Marry or Not to Marry*, "In all, her anxious hope was still to find,/Some useful moral for the feeling mind."

Her novels were her real achievement, however, and to them she devoted the painstaking care of the conscious artist. These fictions carry many of the same themes and techniques as her plays, and her skill at stagecraft is everywhere apparent in dialogue and the management of scenes, but what she adds in her novels to the technical proficiency of the experienced playwright is an acutely observed sentimental realism. For in both her novels, but especially in the first, *A Simple Story*, can be felt the pressure of autobiography, of the many hours the young woman, wife, and widow had devoted not just to study, but to reflection, and to the practice of that candour which was self-knowledge. From her knowledge of herself, combined with her varied social experience, and informed by her reading in moral writers of all kinds, came that authenticity of psychological observation which made her novels so admired by the likes of William Godwin and Maria Edgeworth. For her, as for so many of the women writers of her day, moral education, the chastening of sensibility by experience, reflection, reason, and reading, was the basic form to be sought in life. In her first novel this form is given all the symmetry, deployed through parallels and contrasts in plot, character, and incident, that could be expected from a kind, even a fictitious kind, of moral discourse. In her second novel, moral education is made more of a public issue, diffused into a satire on the institutions of society, but still shaped by the kind of antithesis represented by the novel's title, *Nature and Art*. Autobiography and moral and social issues are not separate in her novels, then, but fused successfully in fictional form. It was this achievement that won her novels admiration in her own day, and makes them still worth reading now.

—Gary Kelly

KELLY, Hugh. Irish. Born in Killarney in 1739. Received very little formal education; apprenticed to a staymaker. Married in 1761; had five children. Moved to London, 1760, and worked as a staymaker and attorney's copying-clerk, and as writer for one of the daily papers; subsequently Editor of the *Court Magazine* and of the *Lady's Museum* from 1761; also wrote political pamphlets for the bookseller Pottinger, contributed series of essays "The Babler" to Owen's *Weekly Chronicle*, edited the *Public Ledger*, and gained a reputation as a theatrical critic; began to write for the theatre, 1768; employed as a writer by the government from c. 1770, and subsequently received a pension from Lord North; studied law, called to the Bar, Middle Temple, London, 1774, and gave up writing to practise law at the Old Bailey and Middlesex sessions. *Died 3 February 1777.*

PUBLICATIONS

Plays

    L'Amour A-la-Mode; or, Love-a-la-Mode. 1760.
    False Delicacy (produced 1768). 1768.
    A Word to the Wise (produced 1770). 1770.
    Clementina (produced 1771). 1771.
    The School for Wives, with William Addington, from a play by Molière (produced 1773). 1774.
    The Romance of an Hour, from a story by J. F. Marmontel (produced 1774). 1774.
    The Man of Reason (produced 1776).

Fiction

    Memoirs of a Magdalen; or, The History of Louisa Mildmay. 1767.

Verse

    An Elegy to the Memory of the Earl of Bath. 1765 (2nd edition).
    Thespis; or, A Critical Examination into the Merits of All the Principal Performers Belonging to Drury Lane Theatre. 1766; revised edition, 1766; part 2, 1767.

Other

The Babler.   2 vols., 1767.
Works.   1778.

Reading List: "Kelly: His Place in the Sentimental School" by Mark Schorer, in *Philological Quarterly*, 1933; "Some Remarks on 18th Century Delicacy, with a Note on Kelly's *False Delicacy*" by C. J. Rawson, in *Journal of English and Germanic Philology 61*, 1962.

*   *   *

Hugh Kelly typifies the mid-eighteenth-century Grub-Street hack: he edited two magazines, the *Lady's Museum* and the *Court Magazine*, and contributed essays and poetic ephemerae to others. His sentimental novel, *Memoirs of a Magdalen: or, The History of Louisa Mildmay*, appeared first in Owen's *Weekly Chronicle*, as did his series of essays *The Babler* (1763–1766). He wrote pro-government pieces for, and edited, *The Public Ledger* for which the administration rewarded him with a £200 pension – but he died poor. Imitating Charles Churchill's poetic satire on the theatres, *The Rosciad*, Kelly wrote *Thespis*, the two parts of which delineated the actors and writers of Drury Lane and of Covent Garden. Having criticized the contemporary theatre, Kelly then wrote *False Delicacy* for Drury Lane, a comedy that Johnson characterized as "totally void of character," but which outplayed Covent Garden's offering, Goldsmith's *Good Natur'd Man*. Critics have increasingly suggested that the work is less a sentimantal comedy than a mildly witty reproof of delicacy. At each of the two performances of Kelly's second produced comedy, *A Word to the Wise*, Kelly's friends and supporters of Wilkes, who were paying Kelly back for being a ministry writer, caused near riots. (In 1777, to benefit Kelly's widow and six children, Johnson wrote a prologue to this comedy for a performance at Covent Garden.)

Kelly's next play, the verse tragedy *Clementina*, was brought out anonymously, and though it lasted nine performances it has no merit: a contemporary reported, "A man can't hiss and yawn at the same time." *The School for Wives*, however, at first ascribed for protection to Captain William Addington, received good printed reviews, as did Kelly's afterpiece, *The Romance of an Hour*, adapted from Marmontel's tale *L' Amitié à l'épreuve*. *The Man of Reason*, Kelly's final comedy, lasted one performance.

Essays in *The Babler*, and the comedies *False Delicacy*, *A Word to the Wise*, and *A School for Wives*, offer the Horatian precept that art must morally instruct (and possibly therefore ennoble) as it entertains. *Thespis* is important as a gossip's recounting of Drury Lane and Covent Garden performers. Neither of Kelly's best plays, *False Delicacy* and *A School for Wives*, seems likely to be revived, but they provided good acting roles which sport with the conventions of sentimentality and are graceful theatrical properties.

—Peter A. Tasch

LEE, Nathaniel.   English.   Born in Hatfield, Hertfordshire, probably in 1653. Educated at Westminster School, London; Trinity College, Cambridge, 1665–68, B.A. 1668. Settled in London, and at first attempted to become an actor; abandoned acting for writing for the stage c. 1672; a friend of Rochester and his circle: led a dissolute life, and undermined his health and reason by drinking: confined in Bethlehem Hospital (Bedlam), 1684–89. *Died* (buried) *6 May 1692.*

PUBLICATIONS

Collections

Works, edited by Thomas B. Stroup and Arthur L. Cooke.   2 vols., 1954–55.

Plays

Nero, Emperor of Rome (produced 1674).   1675.
Sophonisba; or, Hannibal's Overthrow (produced 1675).   1675; edited by Bonamy
    Dobrée, in Five Heroic Plays, 1960.
Gloriana; or, The Court of Augustus Caesar (produced 1676).   1676.
The Rival Queens; or, The Death of Alexander the Great (produced 1677).   1677; edited
    by Paul F. Vernon, 1970.
Oedipus, with Dryden (produced 1678).   1679.
Mithridates, King of Pontus (produced 1678).   1678.
Caesar Borgia, The Son of Pope Alexander the Sixth (produced 1679).   1679.
Lucius Junius Brutus, Father of His Country (produced 1680).   1681; edited by John
    Loftis, 1967.
Theodosius; or, The Force of Love (produced 1680).   1680.
The Princess of Cleve, from a novel by Mme. de la Fayette (produced 1681).   1689.
The Duke of Guise, with Dryden (produced 1682).   1683.
Constantine the Great (produced 1683).   1684.
The Massacre of Paris (produced 1689).   1689.

Verse

To the Prince and Princess of Orange upon Their Marriage.   1677.
To the Duke on His Return.   1682.
On the Death of Mrs. Behn.   1689.
On Their Majesties' Coronation.   1689.

Bibliography: by A. L. McLeod, in Restoration and 18th-Century Theatre Research 1, 1962.

Reading List: Otway and Lee by Roswell G. Ham, 1931; "The Satiric Design of Lee's The
Princess of Cleve" by Robert D. Hume, in Journal of English and Germanic Philology, 1976.

*   *   *

Nathaniel Lee was the most "poetic" of the tragic dramatists in the Restoration period. His twelve tragedies (on characters drawn chiefly from classical and Renaissance history) exude figurative language. Tropes flowed from his pen, reaching a torrent of passionate utterance, with the result that his prolific imagery became both his strength and his weakness. The following passage from Act 3 of his Lucius Junius Brutus will illustrate his fondness for clusters of imagery:

As in that glass of nature thou shalt view
Thy swoln drown'd eyes with the inverted banks,
The tops of Willows and their blossoms turn'd,
With all the Under Sky ten fathom down,
Wish that the shaddow of the swimming Globe
Were so indeed, that thou migh'st leap at Fate.

All his works are characterized by overcharged emotion and verbal extravagance; furthermore, the hysterical emphasis on passion was rarely balanced by any change of pace or variation of manner. He was fond of spectacle, on-stage tortures, and melodramatic turns. His early plays betray a heavy indebtedness to Elizabethan revenge tragedy and to the bombastic "love and honor" drama of his own time. However, he broke away from these influences to develop his own style, and in *The Rival Queens* he used blank verse and thus abandoned the heroic rhymed couplet before Dryden did.

His own genius showed itself in the depiction of his heroines – Sophonisba, Rosalinda, Statira, Roxana – and in his return to the high road of English tragedy in emphasising the complex character of the protagonist and presenting interior conflict. In *Caesar Borgia*, produced during the anti-Catholic frenzy of 1679, when one would expect only rant and a stereotyped villain, Lee portrays in Borgia (as Allardyce Nicoll says) a struggle "of manliness and vicious influence, of conscience warring against the pernicious atmosphere." Even more dramatic is Alexander in Lee's masterpiece, *The Rival Queens*, a strong protagonist who is torn by internal conflicts and by flaws in his character. The resultant catastrophe is not predetermined but brought on by his own actions. In *Lucius Junius Brutus*, Lee achieved new heights with a drama of ideas, presenting, as James Sutherland says, "a historical tragedy that had a disquieting relevance to contemporary England." Artistically, Brutus seems as fully realised as Addison's Cato but in 1680 no government official stood ready to give the actor £50, as Bolingbroke rewarded Booth; instead, the government banned the play. We ought no longer accept that political verdict as a critical evaluation of the play and should instead recognize the merits of Lee as a tragic dramatist.

In addition, Lee wrote a remarkable "sex" comedy, *The Princess of Cleve*, in the satiric tradition of Wycherley's *The Plain Dealer*, Dryden's *Mr. Limberham*, and Otway's *Friendship in Fashion*. Montague Summers, many years ago, and Robert Hume, in his recent *Development of English Drama*, both show that in the character of Nemours (a comedy of manners "gallant") Lee offers a hostile, even savage depiction of Lord Rochester. Those critics who deny the existence of satire in Restoration drama should read this play.

—Arthur H. Scouten

LILLO, George. English. Born in Moorfields, London, 4 February 1693. Very little is known about his life: Partner in his father's jewelry business in the City of London; began writing for the theatre c. 1730. *Died 3 September 1739.*

PUBLICATIONS

Collections

Works.   2 vols., 1775.

Plays

Silvia; or, The Country Burial (produced 1730).   1730.
The London Merchant; or, The History of George Barnwell (produced 1731).   1731;
    edited by William H. McBurney, 1965.
The Christian Hero (produced 1735).   1735.
Fatal Curiosity (produced 1736; as Guilt Its Own Punishment, produced 1736).   1737;
    edited by William H. McBurney, 1966.
Marina, from the play Pericles by Shakespeare (produced 1738).   1738.
Elmerick; or, Justice Triumphant (produced 1740).   1740.
Britannia and Batavia.   1740.
Arden of Faversham, completed by John Hoadly, from the anonymous play (produced
    1759).   1762.

Reading List: Introduction by Adolphus W. Ward to The London Merchant and Fatal
Curiosity, 1906; Lillo und Siene Bedeutung für die Geschichte des Englischen Dramas by G.
Loccack, 1939; "Notes for a Biography of Lillo" by D. B. Pallette, and "Further Notes" by C.
F. Burgess, in Philological Quarterly, 1940, 1967.

*   *   *

George Lillo is a dramatist who was once immensely popular and influential, but who has
not held the stage for a long time and is now virtually unactable because of the melodramatic
and sentimental qualities of his work. Today his plays are almost unknown except to students
of the eighteenth century, yet in his time he was an artistic innovator, although not the
revolutionary figure in the history of drama he was once thought to be. The view that Lillo
pioneered "bourgeois" tragedy almost single-handed is no longer tenable, but it remains true
that in the play with which his name is always linked, The London Merchant; or, The History
of George Barnwell, he developed a form of domestic tragedy in prose about middle-class life
that is the precursor of the social drama of Ibsen and his successors. Lillo inherited a tradition
of domestic tragedy descending from the Elizabethan theatre and proceeded to modify it in
such a way as to make it conform to the increasingly widespread philosophical and ethical
tenets of sentimentalism and benevolism, while at the same time making it reflect the
concerns of the merchant class. Judging by the almost ecstatic way it was received at the time
of its first production, it is obvious that The London Merchant, like Steele's slightly earlier and
equally popular and influential "sentimental" comedy The Conscious Lovers (1722),
responded to an unspoken demand for a new kind of serious drama, radically different from
the dominant types of comedy and tragedy, still heavily influenced by late seventeenth-
century modes. Subsequently The London Merchant was championed by Continental
intellectuals, being highly praised by Rousseau and Diderot in France and imitated by Lessing
in Germany. Lessing's enthusiasm for Lillo was shared by such prominent members of the
next generation of German writers as Goethe and Schiller, and, particularly through his other
original domestic tragedy, Fatal Curiosity, Lillo exerted a decisive influence on the growth of
German Schicksalstragödie (tragedy of fate) at the end of the eighteenth century. To modern
critics, Lillo's influence seems out of proportion to the instrinsic value of his plays but there is
no denying that he is a dramatist of considerable historical significance.

As has been noted, domestic tragedy was by no means new in the 1730's. There are a
number of Elizabethan and Jacobean examples, including such fine plays as Heywood's A
Woman Killed with Kindness and the anonymous A Yorkshire Tragedy and Arden of
Feversham, and certain late seventeenth- and early eighteenth-century dramatists, notably
Otway, Banks, Southerne, and Rowe, wrote tragedies much more domestic and pathetic than
heroic and classical in conception. Yet these Restoration and Augustan plays do not deal with
everyday English life and could not be called "bourgeois." Whereas prose comedy usually

dealt with contemporary life and ordinary people, poetic tragedy almost invariably adhered to the neoclassical principle that only characters of high birth and social or political eminence, preferably historically or geographically remote ones, could be tragic protagonists. Following the example of Aaron Hill in *The Fatal Extravagance* (1721), ten years before *The London Merchant*, Lillo shattered this doctrine, but whereas Hill's play is a reworking of *A Yorkshire Tragedy*, Lillo's play, which is based on an old ballad and has no dramatic source, is a more conscious attempt to break new ground. The idea of a London apprentice being a tragic hero would have seemed incongruous or even ludicrous to many people at the time, and it is said that some people went to the theatre to sneer, but Lillo won even the sceptics over and his success established that even humble members of society and their private lives were deserving of tragic treatment. Also indicative of his artistic daring is his choice of the medium of comedy, prose; and even though his prose is heightened and sometimes indistinguishable from blank verse it is a decisive step towards greater naturalism in tragic drama and so towards Büchner and Ibsen.

As a tragedy *The London Merchant* is as didactic as a Morality play, contains propaganda on behalf of the merchant class, is incorrigibly sentimental in its treatment of Barnwell's guilt and remorse, and blurs his responsibility for his actions by making him a victim of a power outside himself, the ruthless woman who has led him astray, Millwood. Consequently he is as much a wronged innocent as a culpable human being, even though he is involved in theft and murders his uncle. Many critics have found Lillo's other important play, *Fatal Curiosity*, superior to *The London Merchant* as a domestic tragedy, even though he reverts to blank verse. The provincial setting of *Fatal Curiosity*, the Cornish port of Penryn, makes it more unconventional for a tragedy of its time than the earlier play. As the title suggests, the role of fate is very pronounced, much more so than in *The London Merchant*, and the characters seem to be the helpless playthings and unfortunate victims of fortune. There are certainly no villains. It is out of desperation and necessity and as an alternative to suicide rather than for any evil motive that a destitute, old couple murder an apparent stranger for his wealth, only to discover that he is their long-lost son, a virtuous man of sensibility who has returned in order to help his parents. From the tragic irony of this situation, Lillo extracts a great deal of sentiment. This kind of tragedy of fate was beginning to become popular in the eighteenth century before Lillo, but with this play he did more than any other single dramatist to consolidate it. Discussion of Lillo's interest in domestic tragedy would be incomplete without mentioning his *Arden of Feversham*, staged posthumously in 1759 and obviously based on the Elizabethan play of the same name. The substantial changes Lillo makes in tone and characterization are symptomatic of the impact of sentimentalism on contemporary tragedy, the result being a softening of the tragic intensity of the original. In particular Arden's wife is transformed, so that instead of being the determined and callous prime mover of her husband's murder she is an essentially compassionate woman dominated by her ruthless lover.

Lillo's five other extant dramatic works are of lesser importance (the manuscript of his unpublished comedy, *The Regulators*, was lost in the eighteenth century). His first play, *Silvia*, is a ballad opera in form, but differs from the general run of such works in its moral seriousness and sentimentalism, being about the victory of virtue over vice and the reformation of a libertine. *The Christian Hero* and *Elmerick ; or, Justice Triumphant*, both of which have foreign settings, are more conventional tragedies than *The London Merchant* and *Fatal Curiosity*. The first is true to its title in being heroic in conception and idiom, while the second is more deeply tinged with sentiment and pathos. *Marina* is an adaptation of Shakespeare's *Pericles*, while the short masque, *Britannia and Batavia*, is a political allegory. None of these works attracted much attention at the time, and they add almost nothing to his achievement in developing domestic tragedy.

—Peter Lewis

MACKLIN, Charles. Irish.   Born in Culdaff, Inishowen, in 1699. Educated in a school at Island Bridge, near Dublin. Married 1) Ann Grace in 1739 (died, 1758), one son and one daughter; 2) Elizabeth Jones in 1759 (died, 1781). Lived in London, working in a public house in the Borough district; Badgeman, or Scout, at Trinity College, Dublin, 1713; subsequently joined a strolling company of actors in Bristol; debut as an actor, London, 1725; played with the Drury Lane Company, 1733, the Haymarket Company, 1734, and again with Drury Lane, 1734–48; accidentally killed a fellow actor, tried for murder and acquitted, 1735; taught acting from 1743; appeared in Dublin for Sheridan, 1748–50, and at Covent Garden, London, 1750 until his retirement from the stage, 1753; proprietor of a tavern and coffee house in Covent Garden, 1754–58; returned to the stage, 1759, and continued to act in London, and occasionally in Dublin, until he again retired, 1789. *Died 11 July 1797.*

PUBLICATIONS

Collections

  Four Comedies (includes *Love A-la-Mode, The True-Born Irishman, The School for Husbands, The Man of the World*), edited by J. O. Bartley.   1968.

Plays

  King Henry VII; or, The Popish Imposter (produced 1746).   1746.
  A Will and No Will; or, A Bone for the Lawyers, from a play by J. F. Regnard (produced 1746).   Edited by Jean B. Kern, with *The New Play Criticized,* 1967.
  The New Play Criticized; or, The Plague of Envy (produced 1747).   Edited by Jean B. Kern, with *A Will and No Will,* 1967.
  The Club of Fortune-Hunters; or, The Widow Bewitched (produced 1748).
  The Lover's Melancholy, from the play by Ford (produced 1748).
  Covent Garden Theatre; or, Pasquin Turned Drawcansir, Censor of Great Britain (produced 1752).   Edited by Jean B. Kern, 1965.
  Love A-la-Mode (produced 1759).   1784; in *Four Comedies,* 1968.
  The School for Husbands; or, The Married Libertine (produced 1761).   In *Four Comedies,* 1968.
  The True-Born Irishman; or, The Irish Fine Lady (produced 1762; revised version, as *The Irish Fine Lady,* produced 1767).   In *Plays,* 1793; in *Four Comedies,* 1968.
  The Man of the World (as *The True Born Scotsman,* produced 1764; revised version, as *The Man of the World,* produced 1781).   1785; in *Four Comedies,* 1968.
  The Whim; or, A Christmas Gambol (produced 1764).
  Plays.   1793.

Other

  The Case of Charles Macklin, Comedian.   1743.
  Mr. Macklin's Reply to Mr. Garrick's Answer.   1743.
  Epistle from Tully in the Shades to Orator M—n in Covent Garden.   1755.
  An Apology for the Conduct of Mr. Charles Macklin, Comedian.   1773.
  The Genuine Arguments for a Conspiracy to Deprive Charles Macklin of His Livelihood.   1774.

Riot and Conspiracy: The Trial of Thomas Leigh and Others for Conspiring to Ruin in His Profession Charles Macklin. 1775.

Reading List: *Macklin: An Actor's Life* by William W. Appleton, 1960; "The Comic Plays of Macklin: Dark Satire at Mid-18th Century" by R. R. Findlay, in *Educational Theatre Journal,* 1968.

*   *   *

Charles Macklin was more important to the eighteenth-century English stage as an actor than as a playwright, and his plays frequently adopt the actor's perspective on the world. All ten of them (nine comedies and the ill-starred *Henry VII*) were composed during a busy theatrical career, either as a vehicle for himself or for someone else in the profession, and all are directed towards audiences, not readers. They keep reverting to the nature of the dramatic illusion – whether the stage presents an imitation of our reality, some other reality, or simply unreality – which was also debated by the critics of the time. *A Will and No Will* begins with a "Prologue by the Pit" in which some "members of the audience" onstage discuss the play to come, concluding that they will now see "a Prologue by the Pit." Similarly, at the end of *The New Play Criticized* Heartly asks Lady Critic to write a farce based on the events of the last hour and called *The New Play Criticized*; it will close with his marriage to her daughter. She agrees, and thus Heartly wins his Harriet. Another Harriet, the heroine of *The School for Husbands*, informs Lord Belville that he has been the victim of an elaborate charade by telling him, "We have all been acting a sort of comedy at your expence." More than half of Macklin's comedies play at confusing, at least momentarily, the boundaries commonly supposed to divide life from dramatic art.

This preoccupation is understandable in a man whose consciousness must have been almost wholly histrionic, whose life was the fixed backdrop of Georgian theatre. His acting career spanned sixty-five years, from the days of Cibber and Quin and *The Beggar's Opera*, fifteen years before Garrick's début, to the dawn of melodrama a dozen years after the latter's death. He worked with Fielding at the Haymarket before the Licensing Act, evolved the naturalistic Shylock that made Pope exclaim, "This is the Jew/That Shakespeare drew," tutored Sam Foote in acting, watched Goldsmith and Sheridan come and go, gave some of the earliest lessons in ensemble playing, and opened as the star of his own last comedy when over eighty. On the whole his influence on eighteenth-century theatre rivals Garrick's.

Macklin's forte as a dramatist was a particular kind of verisimilitude: on occasion he commanded the energy to "bounce" an audience into belief in his illusion, as Forster said a novelist should do. He could take a conventional scene (e.g., social climbing in *The True-Born Irishman*, raking and exposure in *The School for Husbands*) and bring it alive through his mastery of colloquial speech and his eye for realistic detail. Had he been able to do this more often we should have heard and thought more of him.

Macklin's best-known full-scale comedy was and is *The Man of the World*, an interesting if flawed prototype of the Victorian problem play; Sir Pertinax Macsycophant, played by Macklin, remains a powerful character. More successful are his short satiric afterpieces, particularly *Love A-la-Mode*, his most popular and lucrative work. The classic testing of Charlotte's four humorous suitors – the fop, the horsey squire, the Scot, and the Teague – gave Macklin an opportunity for writing some of his best dialogue and provided him with a symmetrical structure. The farce as a whole gives an accurate idea of what Macklin could and could not do. It concludes with Sir Callaghan O'Brallaghan remarking that "the whole business is something like the catastrophe of a stage play": another involuted reminder of Macklin's profession.

—R. W. Bevis

MOORE, Edward. English. Born in Abingdon, Berkshire, 22 March 1712. Educated by his uncle, a schoolmaster in Bridgwater, Somerset, and at a school in East Orchard, Dorset. Married Jenny Hamilton in 1749; one son. Apprenticed to a linendraper in London, then worked as a factor in Ireland, then returned to London to set up as a linendraper on his own: turned to literature when the business failed; enjoyed the patronage of Lord Lyttelton: through Lyttelton's influence appointed Editor of *The World* magazine, 1753–56. *Died 1 March 1757.*

PUBLICATIONS

Collections

Poetical Works, edited by Thomas Park.   1806.

Plays

Solomon: A Serenata, music by William Boyce (produced 1743).   1750.
The Foundling (produced 1748).   1748.
Gil Blas, from the novel by Le Sage (produced 1751).   1751.
The Gamester (produced 1753).   1753.

Verse

Fables for the Female Sex.   1744.
The Trial of Selim the Persian for Divers High Crimes and Misdemeanors.   1748.
An Ode to David Garrick.   1749.

Other

The World, with others.   6 vols., 1755–57.
Poems, Fables, and Plays.   1756.

Reading List: *The Life and Works of Moore* by John H. Caskey, 1927; Introduction by Charles H. Peake to *The Gamester*, 1948.

*   *   *

It is not hard to see how George Lillo's *George Barnwell; or, The London Merchant* (1731) was one of the greatest hits of the eighteenth-century London stage. The most significant of later eighteenth-century dramatists in the line of Lillo was Edward Moore, best-known as the author of the bourgeois prose tragedy *The Gamester*. The *Poems, Fables, and Plays* show he had wider scope, but it is as a dramatist of domestic dolors that he stands out in John H. Caskey's study and in literary history. He is an important link between Lillo and what came after.

True, he has a secure place in the history of the journalistic essay. After Johnson's *Rambler* and Hawksworth's *Adventurer* came over 200 numbers of *The World* (1753–56) which

Moore edited. He wrote a lot of it himself and attracted contributors such as Chesterfield, Horace Walpole, Soame Jenyns, Richard Owen Cambridge, and Hanbury Williams.

But it was when he went bankrupt as a London linen-draper that Moore came into the theatre and into his own. *Gil Blas* is a lively comedy of disguise based on an episode of Le Sage in which a young lady dresses up as a student in order to capture a man who has caught her eye. Moore adequately handles the quick changes of the young lady back and forth but lacks the verbal lightness for really effective quick exchanges of dialogue. The borrowed plot remains the redeeming feature.

The Foundling was more in Moore's style, a sentimental and moral excursion along the lines that Cibber had more or less invented and Steele had made more or less popular, an earnest endeavor such as Moore's friend Fielding has his Parson Adams damn with feinting praise like this: "there are some things almost solemn enough for a sermon." The remark may underline for us how far comedy had strayed at that period from corrective laughter. If comedy was full of fine feeling and nearly devoid of fun, just imagine the domestic tragedy between, say, *The London Merchant* and Kelly's *False Delicacy*. *The Foundling* was nominally a comedy but is hardly a laugh riot. I find the work with which Moore started to make money as a writer, *Fables for the Female Sex*, funnier. The play is well constructed, however.

Then when Garrick (who played in it) gave Moore a hand with *The Gamester*, Moore had a first-rate piece of its kind. If you have tears, prepare to shed them now as we note the sad story of Beverley, a victim (like Barnwell) of evil in the vile form of Stukeley (who owes something to Lillo's Millwood, something to Shakespeare's Iago, and something to Fielding's Jonathan Wild). Beverley is sunk in a mire of gambling debts. Under the mercantile ethic (presented in numerous middle-class plays as well as in novels from Defoe and others throughout the century) squandering money was the foulest of crimes. In a comedy, by some stratagem finances as well as love affairs all come right in the end. In this tragedy, Beverley poisons himself in despair just before it transpires that he was to inherit the estate of his rich uncle! The distraught Mrs. Beverley wrings every drop of sentiment out of her husband's fate, though the play is not a "she-tragedy" of the Otway or Rowe variety. It is rather in the Elizabethan tradition of domestic melodrama and a milestone in the "road to ruin" genre which began to concentrate more and more not on the gambler himself but, as in temperance dramas, on the dire effects upon guiltless wives and suffering children.

The weakness in the genre is that the gambler is generally either a villain (in which case he attracts no sympathy) or a sap (like Barnwell or Beverley). It is hard to bring naturalism to the hysteria and histrionics. Moore's dialogue is more "natural" than Lillo's, but what Goldsmith would have called "natural" (as when he spoke of Garrick's "simple, natural, affecting" acting) may look pretty stilted and posturing to us.

Diderot adapted *The Gamester* as a *drame bourgeois* and Thomas Holcroft echoed some aspects of Moore in *The Road to Ruin* (1792). Moore's play has relevance to all the sentimental plays of the latter part of the eighteenth century and all the melodramatic ones of the first half of the nineteenth century; in its confusion of tragic hero and hapless victim, of sentiment and seriousness, of tragedy and melodrama, it is related to such works as Arthur Miller's *Death of a Salesman*. *The Gamester* is a masterpiece of the second-rate and as such of first-rate importance in the history of the theatre.

—Leonard R. N. Ashley

MORTON, Thomas. English. Born in Durham c. 1764. Educated at Soho Square School, London; entered Lincoln's Inn, 1784, but was not subsequently admitted to the bar. Married; one daughter and two sons, including the playwright John Maddison Morton. Full-time playwright from 1792. Senior Member of Lord's, London; Honorary Member, Garrick Club, 1837. *Died 28 March 1838.*

PUBLICATIONS

Plays

Columbus; or, A World Discovered (produced 1792). 1792.
The Children in the Wood, music by Samuel Arnold (produced 1793). 1794.
Zorinski, music by Samuel Arnold (produced 1795). 1795.
The Way to Get Married (produced 1796). 1796.
A Cure for the Heart-Ache (produced 1797). 1797.
Secrets Worth Knowing (produced 1798). 1798.
Speed the Plough (produced 1800). 1800; edited by Allardyce Nicoll in *Lesser English Comedies of the Eighteenth Century,* 1931.
The Blind Girl; or, A Receipt for Beauty, music by Joseph Massinghi and William Reeve (produced 1801). Songs published 1801.
Beggar My Neighbour; or, A Rogue's a Fool, from a play by A. W. Iffland (produced 1802; as *How to Tease and How to Please,* produced 1810).
The School of Reform; or, How to Rule a Husband (produced 1805). 1805.
Town and Country (produced 1807). 1807.
The Knight of Snowdoun, music by Henry Bishop, from the poem "The Lady of the Lake" by Scott (produced 1811). 1811.
Education (produced 1813). 1813.
The Slave, music by Henry Bishop (produced 1816). 1816.
Methinks I See My Father; or, Who's My Father? (produced 1818). 1850(?).
A Roland for an Oliver, from a play by Scribe (produced 1819). 1819.
Henri Quatre; or, Paris in the Olden Time, music by Henry Bishop (produced 1820). 1820.
A School for Grown Children (produced 1827). 1827.
The Invincibles, music by A. Lee (produced 1828). 1829.
The Sublime and Beautiful (produced 1828).
Peter the Great; or, The Battle of Pultawa, with James Kenney, music by Tom Cooke and William Carnaby, from a play by Frédéric du Petit-Mère (produced 1829).
Separation and Reparation (produced 1830).
The King's Fireside (produced 1830).
The Writing on the Wall!, with J. M. Morton (produced 1852). N.d.

*   *   *

Thomas Morton's first five-act comedy, *The Way to Get Married*, gave good acting parts to Lewis, Quick, Munden, and Fawcett. It also established his method, which is to embed a pathetic tale of poverty and remorse amid comic episodes and eccentric characters. Scenes of convulsive anguish alternate with amusing encounters and adventures whose general intention is to commend generosity and expose the mercenary motives of a heartless society. Morton was, in effect, writing melodrama before the word had reached the English theatre. He had, generally, the tact to give his comedians more stage time than his "heavies," and to allow one of his comic men to make the crucial discovery that makes all well. *Secrets Worth Knowing* is an exact example of the style. The comedy survives well, but the suffering resists contemporary staging. The same is true of Morton's best play, *Speed the Plough*, in which the real life belongs to the characters least involved in the main plot. Sir Philip Blandford's remorse over a dead wife, lost child, and murdered brother is tediously related in embarrassingly pompous prose. The child (not lost), the brother (not murdered), and the daughter also speak in grandiose archaisms. By extraordinary contrast, the uxorious Sir Abel Handy, his well-intentioned son, his wife, Farmer and Mrs. Ashfield, and their daughter are all finely observed and provided with sprightly dialogue. It is Mrs. Ashfield's obsessive concern with what Mrs. Grundy (who never appears) may say that has provided Morton's best known monument. *The School of Reform* is an attempt to repeat the success of *Speed the Plough*, but the influence of the German dramatists, particularly of Kotzebue's guilt-laden stories of sexual sin, swamps most of Morton's own talent. The character of Robert Tyke, and the final sensation scene in a Gothic chapel, underline the close relations between contemporary comedy and melodrama. *A Cure for the Heart-Ache* is the only one of Morton's comedies to suit the description, though even that play is not without pathetic attitudinising.

—Peter Thomson

MURPHY, Arthur. Irish. Born in Clomquin, Roscommon, 27 December 1727; lived with his family in Dublin, 1729–35, and in London from 1735. Studied at the English College in St. Omer, France, 1738–44. Clerk to a merchant in Cork, 1747–49; worked in the City banking house of Ironside and Belchier, London, 1749–51; publisher of, and leading contributor to, *Gray's Inn Journal*, 1752–54; appeared as an actor at Covent Garden and Drury Lane, 1754–55, and began writing for the stage, 1756; admitted to Lincoln's Inn, London, 1757, was subsequently called to the bar, and practised in London; also edited the weekly papers, *The Test* and *The Auditor*; retired from the law and the theatre, 1788; appointed a commissioner of bankrupts and granted a pension by George III, 1803. *Died 18 June 1805.*

PUBLICATIONS

Collections

The Way to Keep Him and Five Other Plays (includes The Apprentice, The Upholsterer, The Old Maid, Three Weeks after Marriage, Know Your Own Mind), edited by John P. Emery. 1956.

Plays

The Apprentice (produced 1756). 1756; in The Way to Keep Him and Five Other Plays, 1956.
The Englishman from Paris (produced 1756).
The Upholsterer; or, What News? (produced 1758). 1758; edited by R. W. Bevis, in Eighteenth Century Drama: Afterpieces, 1970.
The Orphan of China, from a play by Voltaire (produced 1759). 1759.
The Tears and Triumphs of Parnassus, with Robert Lloyd, music by John Stanley (produced 1760).
The Way to Keep Him, from a play by Moissy (produced 1760). 1760; revised version (produced 1761), 1761; in The Way to Keep Him and Five Other Plays, 1956; 1760 version edited by R. W. Bevis, in Eighteenth Century Drama: Afterpieces, 1970.

The Desert Island, from a play by Metastasio (produced 1760).   1760.
All in the Wrong (produced 1761).   1761.
The Old Maid, from a play by Fagan (produced 1761).   1761.
The Citizen, from a play by Destouches (produced 1761).   1763.
No One's Enemy But His Own, from a play by Voltaire (produced 1764).   1764.
What We Must All Come To (produced 1764).   1764; as *Three Weeks after Marriage*
    (produced 1776), 1776; in *The Way to Keep Him and Five Other Plays*, 1956.
The Choice (produced 1765).   In *Works*, 1786.
The School for Guardians, from a play by Molière (produced 1767).   1767.
Zenobia (produced 1768).   1768.
The Grecian Daughter (produced 1772).   1772.
Alzuma (produced 1773).   1773.
News from Parnassus (produced 1776).   In *Works*, 1786.
Know Your Own Mind, from a play by Destouches (produced 1777).   1778; in *The Way
    to Keep Him and Five Other Plays*, 1956.
The Rival Sisters (produced 1793).   In *Works*, 1786.
Arminius.   1798.
Hamlet, with Alterations, from the play by Shakespeare, in *Life of Murphy* by J. Foot.
    1811; edited by Martin Lehnert, in *Shakespeare Jahrbuch 102*, 1966.

Verse

A Poetical Epistle to Samuel Johnson.   1760.
An Ode to the Naiads of Fleet Ditch.   1761.
The Examiner: A Satire.   1761.
*Seventeen Hundred and Ninety-One: A Poem in Imitation of the Thirteenth Satire of
    Juvenal.*   1791.
The Bees: A Poem from the Fourteenth Book of Vaniere's Praedium Rusticum.   1799.
The Game of Chess, from a poem by Vida.   1876.

Other

The Gray's Inn Journal.   2 vols., 1756.
A Letter to Voltaire on The Desert Island.   1760.
Works.   7 vols., 1786.
An Essay on the Life and Genius of Samuel Johnson.   1792.
The Life of David Garrick.   2 vols., 1801.
New Essays, edited by Arthur Sherbo.   1963.

Editor, *Works*, by Fielding.   4 vols., 1762.

Translator, *The Works of Tacitus.*   4 vols., 1793.
Translator, *The Works of Šallust.*   1807.

Reading List: *Murphy: An Eminent English Dramatist of the Eighteenth Century* by John P.
Emery, 1946; *The Dramatic Career of Murphy* by Howard Hunter Dunbar, 1946;
Introduction by Simon Trefman to *The Englishman from Paris*, 1969.

*   *   *

A man of broad interests and a prolific writer, Arthur Murphy was a journalist, biographer, editor, actor, translator of the classics, lawyer, political writer, and one of the most successful playwrights of the third quarter of the eighteenth century. Of particular interest among Murphy's various non-dramatic writings are his *Gray's Inn Journal* and biographies of Garrick, Fielding, and Johnson. These works contain much perceptive practical criticism, Murphy's generally traditional literary theories, and a great deal of information about the theater and literary life of his age.

About twenty of Murphy's plays were performed during the eighteenth century. These range from short farces and satires used as afterpieces to full-length tragedies and comedies. Although at least minimally successful in all the dramatic genres he attempted, Murphy's greatest skill is evident in his comedies and farces. One of the best of these is *The Way to Keep Him*, which was first performed as a three-act afterpiece and was a miniature comedy, not a farce. After Murphy rewrote it in five acts, the resulting full-fledged comedy of manners remained popular for a century. The play, which deals with various modes of marital behavior, contains some sentimental elements, but generally shares the same spirit as the comedies of Congreve and Sheridan. *All in the Wrong, The School for Guardians*, and *Know Your Own Mind* also display Murphy's talent for writing comedies of manners.

Murphy's farces are among the best in an age that is noted for good farces. Whether focusing on satire or outlandish situations, his farces are usually fast-paced and his characters, often "humours" types, well-drawn. *The Apprentice* and *The Upholsterer* satirize stage-struck apprentices and tradesmen who are excessively interested in politics, respectively. The latter contains a character, Mrs. Termagant, who may have been a source for Sheridan's Mrs. Malaprop. Other farces worthy of mention are *The Old Maid, No One's Enemy But His Own*, and *Three Weeks after Marriage*. The ingenious situational humor and riotous quarrel scenes make the latter an especially lively theatrical piece.

—James S. Malek

O'KEEFFE, John. Irish. Born in Dublin, 24 June 1747. Educated at a Jesuit school in Saul's Court, Dublin; afterwards studied art in the Dublin School of Design. Married; one daughter and two sons. Originally an actor: member of Henry Mossop's stock company, Dublin, 1762–74; wrote for the stage from 1767; settled in London, c. 1780, and thereafter wrote comic pieces for the Haymarket and Covent Garden theatres; blind from the mid-1780's; received an annuity from Covent Garden, 1803, and a royal pension, 1820. *Died 4 February 1833.*

PUBLICATIONS

Plays

> *The She Gallant; or, Square-Toes Outwitted* (produced 1767).   1767; revised version, as *The Positive Man*, music by Samuel Arnold and Michael Arne (produced 1782), in *Dramatic Works*, 1798.
> *Colin's Welcome* (produced 1770).
> *Tony Lumpkin in Town* (produced 1774).   1780.

The Poor Soldier (as *The Shamrock, or, St. Patrick's Day*, produced 1777; revised version, as *The Poor Soldier*, music by William Shield, produced 1783). 1785.

The Son-in-Law, music by Samuel Arnold (produced 1779). 1783.

The Dead Alive, music by Samuel Arnold (produced 1781). 1783.

The Agreeable Surprise, music by Samuel Arnold (produced 1781). 1784.

The Banditti; or, Love's Labyrinth, music by Samuel Arnold (produced 1781). Songs published 1781; revised version, as *The Castle of Andalusia* (produced 1782), 1783; revised version (produced 1788).

Harlequin Teague; or, The Giant's Causeway, music by Samuel Arnold (produced 1782). Songs published 1782.

Lord Mayor's Day; or, A Flight from Lapland, music by William Shield (produced 1782). Songs published 1782.

The Maid the Mistress, from a play by G. A. Federico (produced 1783). Songs published 1783.

The Young Quaker (produced 1783). 1784.

The Birthday; or, The Prince of Arragon, music by Samuel Arnold, from a play by Saint-Foix (produced 1783). 1783.

Gretna Green (lyrics only), play by Charles Stuart, music by Samuel Arnold (produced 1783). 1791.

Friar Bacon; or, Harlequin's Adventures in Lilliput, Brobdignag etc. (lyrics only), play by Charles Bonner, music by William Shield (produced 1783; as *Harlequin Rambler*, produced 1784). Songs published 1784.

Peeping Tom of Coventry, music by Samuel Arnold (produced 1784). 1786.

Fontainbleau; or, Our Way in France, music by William Shield (produced 1784). 1785.

The Blacksmith of Antwerp (produced 1785). In *Dramatic Works*, 1798.

A Beggar on Horseback, music by Samuel Arnold (produced 1785). In *Dramatic Works*, 1798.

Omai; or, A Trip round the World, music by William Shield (produced 1785). Songs published 1785.

Love in a Camp; or, Patrick in Prussia, music by William Shield (produced 1786). 1786.

The Siege of Curzola, music by Samuel Arnold (produced 1786). Songs published 1786.

The Man Milliner (produced 1787). In *Dramatic Works*, 1798.

Love and War, from the play *The Campaign* by Robert Jephson (produced 1787).

The Farmer, music by William Shield (produced 1787). 1788.

Tantara-Rara, Rogues All, from a play by Dumaniant (produced 1788). In *Dramatic Works*, 1798.

The Prisoner at Large (produced 1788). 1788.

The Highland Reel, music by William Shield (produced 1788). 1789.

Aladdin; or, The Wonderful Lamp, music by William Shield (produced 1788). Songs published 1788.

The Lie of the Day (as *The Toy*, produced 1789; revised version, as *The Lie of the Day*, produced 1796). In *Dramatic Works*, 1798.

The Faro Table, from the play *The Gamester* by Mrs. Centlivre (produced 1789).

The Little Hunch-Back; or, A Frolic in Bagdad (produced 1789). 1789.

The Czar Peter, music by William Shield (as *The Czar*, produced 1790; as *The Fugitive*, produced 1790). In *Dramatic Works*, 1798.

The Basket-Maker, music by Samuel Arnold (produced 1790). In *Dramatic Works*, 1798.

Modern Antiques; or, The Merry Mourners (produced 1791). 1792.

Wild Oats; or, The Strolling Gentleman (produced 1791). 1791; edited by Clifford Williams, 1977.

Tony Lumpkin's Ramble to Town (produced 1792).
Sprigs of Laurel, music by William Shield (produced 1793).   1793; revised version, as
   The Rival Soldiers (produced 1797).
The London Hermit; or, Rambles in Dorsetshire (produced 1793).   1793.
The World in a Village (produced 1793).   1793.
Life's Vagaries (produced 1795).   1795.
The Irish Mimic; or, Blunders at Brighton, music by William Shield (produced
   1795).   1795.
Merry Sherwood; or, Harlequin Forester (lyrics only), play by Mark Lonsdale and
   William Pearce, music by William Reeve (produced 1795).   Songs published 1795.
The Wicklow Gold Mines; or, The Lad of the Hills, music by William Shield (produced
   1796).   1814; revised version, as *The Wicklow Mountains* (produced 1796), 1797.
The Doldrum; or, 1803 (produced 1796).   In *Dramatic Works,* 1798.
Alfred; or, The Magic Banner (produced 1796).   1796.
Olympus in an Uproar; or, The Descent of the Deities, from the play *The Golden Pippin*
   by Kane O'Hara (produced 1796).
Britain's Brave Tars; or, All for St. Paul's, music by Thomas Attwood (produced 1797).
She's Eloped (produced 1798).
The Eleventh of June; or, The Daggerwoods at Dunstable (produced 1798).
A Nosegay of Weeds; or, Old Servants in New Places (produced 1798).
Dramatic Works.   4 vols., 1798.

Verse

Oatlands; or, The Transfer of the Laurel.   1795.
A Father's Legacy to His Daughter, Being the Poetical Works, edited by Adelaide
   O'Keeffe.   1834.

Other

Recollections of the Life of O'Keeffe, Written by Himself.   2 vols., 1826.

* * *

John O'Keeffe wrote for a living, and was the slave of a public about which he must
sometimes have grumbled but which he hated to upset. Between 1778, when the elder
Colman bought for the Haymarket his opportunistic afterpiece *Tony Lumpkin in Town,* and
1800, when Thomas Harris awarded him a benefit at Covent Garden, O'Keeffe was a
provider of theatrical pieces for those two theatres. Most of these pieces depend as much on
song as on dialogue. Of the some 60 he admits to in his *Recollections,* over 20 are called
"operas," a way of assuring contemporary audiences that the dialogue would be frequently
interrupted by songs. In the three acts of *The Castle of Andalusia* there are over 20 such
interruptions. The music for this popular piece was arranged by Dr. Arnold, but borrowed
from Italy, Ireland, and the London streets. The plot calls for a noble bandit, a resourceful
rogue, two pairs of lovers, an ageing and covetous widow, and the audience's ready
acceptance of the convention of gullibility without which plays of mistaken identity will
crumble about their ears. In *Fontainbleau* there are fewer songs and a greater dependence on
bright dialogue and quirky characters like Colonel Epaulette, the anglophile Frenchman who
makes his first entrance singing "Rule Britannia, Britannia rule de vay." The Jonsonian
"humour" is close to journey's end in mere risible eccentricity, although there is comic
resource and energy in O'Keeffe's handling of a slender story. He was bound by convention
to attempt the more exacting five-act comedy form. *The Young Quaker* was moderately

successful at the small Haymarket, and *The Toy*, later reduced to three acts as *The Lie of the Day*, was an effective vehicle for William Lewis, Quick, and Aickin.

But it was *Wild Oats* that made and has preserved O'Keeffe's reputation as a writer of comedy. The play depends on an alias, a carefully contrived mistaken identity, a sequence of coincidences, and a lost baby miraculously rediscovered in the person of the leading character, a strolling player conditionally named Rover. Plot and characters are not original, but if not of invention, there is a sufficient freshness of deployment to explain the success of the 1976 revival by the Royal Shakespeare Company. Rover, who has a dramatic quotation for every emergency, was created by Lewis and has proved the play's main attraction in the theatre. In a reading, the hostility towards Quaker puritanism and a veiled egalitarianism are quite as striking. O'Keeffe was proud to boast of Sheridan's calling him "the first that turned the public taste from the dullness of sentiment ... towards the sprightly channel of comic humour." He was *not* the first, but *Wild Oats* is a substantial alternative to the sentimental plays that surrounded it. Of the three other five-act comedies performed in his lifetime, *She's Eloped* survived only one night while *The World in a Village* and *Life's Vagaries* were moderately successful.

—Peter Thomson

ORRERY, Earl of.   See BOYLE, Roger.

OTWAY, Thomas.   English.   Born in Trotten, Sussex, 3 March 1652. Educated at Winchester College, Hampshire, 1668; Christ Church, Oxford, 1669–71, left without taking a degree. Served in the Duke of Monmouth's Regiment in the Netherlands, 1678–79. Settled in London, 1671, and worked temporarily as an actor; wrote for the Duke's Company at the Dorset Garden Theatre, London, from 1675. *Died 14 April 1685.*

PUBLICATIONS

Collections

   The Works, edited by J. C. Ghosh.   2 vols., 1932.

Plays

   Alcibiades (produced 1675).   1675.
   Don Carlos, Prince of Spain (produced 1676).   1676.

Titus and Berenice, from a play by Racine (produced 1676).   1677.
The Cheats of Scapin, from a play by Molière (produced 1676).   In Titus and Berenice,
    1677.
Friendship in Fashion (produced 1678).   1678.
The History and Fall of Caius Marius (produced 1679).   1680.
The Orphan; or, The Unhappy Marriage (produced 1680).   1680; edited by Aline M.
    Taylor, 1976.
The Soldier's Fortune (produced 1680).   1681.
Venice Preserved; or, A Plot Discovered (produced 1682).   1682; edited by Malcolm
    Kelsall, 1969.
The Atheist; or, The Second Part of the Soldier's Fortune (produced 1683).   1684.

Verse

The Poet's Complaint of His Muse; or, A Satire Against Libels.   1680.
Windsor Castle in a Monument to Our Late Sovereign Charles II.   1685.

Other

Familiar Letters (by Rochester, Otway, and Katherine Philips), edited by Tom Brown
    and Charles Gildon.   2 vols., 1697.

Translator, The History of the Triumvirates, by Samuel de Broe.   1686.

Reading List: Otway and Lee by Roswell G. Ham, 1931; Next to Shakespeare by Aline M.
Taylor, 1950; Gestalt und Funktion der Bilder im Otway und Lee by Gisela Fried, 1965; Die
Künstlerische Entwicklung in der Tragödien Otways by Helmut Klinger, 1971.

*   *   *

In the eight years between 1675 and 1683 Thomas Otway wrote and had produced at
Dorset Garden Theatre ten plays. Two of his six tragedies are of lasting quality; the other four
are of varying merit. The four comedies are generally regarded as having little to recommend
them, though a farce entitled The Cheats of Scapin held the stage for many years. The first
two plays, Alcibiades and Don Carlos, belong to the prevailing genre of Heroic Tragedy, being
written in heroic couplets of elevated rhetoric to be spoken by supremely noble characters,
and emphasizing the themes of love, honour, and valour. Yet even in these Otway broke out
of the stereotype, especially in the latter play, to create scenes of unaffected sincerity,
tenderness, and simplicity. The later tragedies are derived, as was becoming the fashion by
1677, more directly in form and substance from Elizabethan and Jacobean antecedents. His
comedies likewise follow, though with less success, Elizabethan and Jacobean structure and
variety – brought up to date with fashionable cynicism, vulgarity, and attempts at Restoration
wit.
    For his direct source Otway went to Plutarch (Alcibiades), Racine (Titus and Berenice),
Molière (The Cheats of Scapin), Roger Boyle (The Orphan), Shakespeare (Don Carlos and
Caius Marius) and Saint Réal (Don Carlos). Just as importantly, he drew in his bitter comedies
upon the cynical tone and wit of Wycherley, and upon Shakespeare for the same qualities in
all his plays, as well as for dramatic situation, structure, and poetry. Out of his own poverty,
disappointment in patronage, unhappy army experience, and hopeless love for Mrs. Barry
came also much of his fatalism, cynicism, and despair, tones which fit well the popular
Hobbesism of the time. His striking this popular mood of the theatre-goers – the nobles,

courtiers, and wits – doubtless accounted for his considerable success in his own day. Furthermore, the slightly veiled parallels and references in his plays (in the comedies and in *Caius Marius* and *Venice Preserved*) to current political intrigues, especially the popish plot and attacks upon the Whigs and the Earl of Shaftesbury, brought patrons to Dorset Garden. But his temperament and his attraction to Shakespeare's special brand of satire perhaps account best for Otway's more lasting qualities.

And his success upon the tragic stage has been considerable. For his two powerful tragedies he has been called "Next to Shakespeare," the title of Aline Taylor's full account of the remarkable stage success of *Venice Preserved* and *The Orphan*. Contributing greatly to this success have been the superb actors who have played the chief roles. But other lasting qualities have contributed to their survival and retained a place for them and the rest of Otway's plays in the history of dramatic literature. Otway became an excellent dramatic craftsman, and he also had something important, though quite unflattering, to say about the human condition.

Otway's exposition usually follows an immediate plunge into the midst of the action, such as the opening quarrel of *Venice Preserved*, which creates effective suspense. The suspense is intensified through the complication, and the direct, swift action brings on the powerful climax. The result is a shattering recognition for the principals, especially in the tragedies, which is followed by an unrelieved dénouement of defeat and despair in the tragedies and only cynicism in the comedies. The movement in the tragedies is often, like that of Greek tragedy, direct and inevitable. In *The Orphan* onlooker and reader alike are held horrified in their anxiety: surely Castalio will tell Polydore that he is married to Monimia; surely someone will light a taper! But the light comes too late; the recognition is too great for the principals to bear, as is also true in *Venice Preserved*, *Don Carlos*, and *Caius Marius*. Such inability reflects the basic fault in Otway's main characters. His dramas rise from the weaknesses of his characters: they are strong in emotion, but weak in judgment, more given to blaming fate than recognizing their own crucial errors – which lead to self-destruction.

This same quality of irresponsibility gave rise to a sort of perverse wit, bitter and sardonic, in both his comedies and tragedies. Inherited from Shakespeare and Marston in large part, it is perhaps best exemplified in *Venice Preserved*. Pierre makes his nervous midnight entrance upon the Rialto for his assignation with Jaffeir. Like Bernardo in *Hamlet*, he improperly challenges the one who is already on the scene: "Speak, who goes there?" He gets the reply: "A dog, that comes to howl/At yonder moon: What's he that asks the Question?" Pierre answers "A Friend to Dogs, for they are honest creatures." (In *Julius Caesar* Brutus reproves Cassius with "I'd rather be a dog and bay the moon/Than such a Roman.") The following speeches revile priesthood and condemn prayer and religion.

This same sort of cynicism in Otway's plays gives rise to numerous oaths, curses, and orations, all of which make for intense dramatic effect. Pierre's notable speech before the Senate asks in four ironic rhetorical questions whether the chains that bind him are "the wreaths of triumph ye bestow," for his service to the state. Jaffeir's solemn oath to remain faithful to the conspiracy becomes ironic as he, for love of Belvidera, fails to keep the oath and then denounces his own failure before the Senate. He curses Old Priuli, as might a primitive Irish satirist: "Kind Heav'n! let heavy Curses/Gall his old Age; Cramps, Aches rack his Bones...." Belvidera calls upon heaven to pour down curses with vengeance, despair, danger, etc. upon her; and Jaffeir in a final curse, such as Polydore's in *The Orphan*, asks that a "Final destruction seize the world...." And this is just what happens to his world as he and Belvidera commit suicide. All is left in ruins. Though one may argue that underlying *Venice Preserved* is the affirmation of the integrity of the family (as one may argue for the same in *Coriolanus*), such integrity does not prevail at the end of the play – only the corrupt Senate prevails. The very title is ironic: Venice preserved indeed!

Just such lack of affirmation, just such lack of hope characterize Otway's plays. Fortune, Chance, Fate control – not men or benevolent gods. Even the earlier *Alcibiades*, *Don Carlos*, and *Caius Marius* lack a just settling of accounts; the comedies, *The Soldier's Fortune* and *The Atheist*, are dissertations upon Fortune and Chance.

The ritualistic use of formal curses, prayers, oaths, and set speeches make Otway's plays dramatically effective. But the sardonic and cynical quality be gives them belong rather to satire than pure comedy or tragedy. As a part of rhetoric, style, and invention this quality reverses the normal processes of expression and appeals both to emotion and intellect. It is inherently dramatic, and Otway uses it with great effect. Yet it cannot rise to affirmation. The conclusions of his plots bring no sense of order or justice having been reasserted. Rather, chaos prevails, and an effective catharsis does not take place. The audience are left to face a meaningless, unintelligible world, anticipating the school of the absurd of the mid-twentieth century.

Otway's dozen poems outside the plays and his half-dozen love letters are useful chiefly in explaining the partisanship, political and historical allusions, and tone of the plays. The love letters reveal in effective, if sometimes maudlin, prose the poet's hopeless passion for Mrs. Barry; hence the character of his tragic heroines. Of the poems, *The Poet's Complaint of His Muse* and *Windsor Castle* seem most significant. The former is autobiographical, consisting of twenty-one strophes shot through with allusions to contemporary events and political affairs. It ends with a tribute to James, Duke of York, as he takes precautionary leave of England because of the Popish Plot. The latter is an extensive panegyric upon the ascension of James II, who "By mighty deeds has earnrown he wears." Both indicate directly the poet's scornful opposition to the Whigs and his sympathy and admiration for the Royalists – attitudes revealed implicitly in his plays.

—Thomas B. Stroup

RAVENSCROFT, Edward. English. Born in England c. 1650. Very little is known about his life: descended from an ancient Flintshire family; member of the Middle Temple, London, 1671; career as a playwright extended over a quarter century, but he is thought to have died comparatively young: nothing is recorded about him after 1697.

PUBLICATIONS

Plays

The Citizen Turned Gentleman, from a play by Molière (produced 1672).   1672; as
    Mamamouchi, 1675.
The Careless Lovers (produced 1673).   1673.
The Wrangling Lovers; or, The Invisible Mistress (produced 1676).   1677.
Scaramouche a Philosopher, Harlequin a School-Boy, Bravo, Merchant and Magician
    (produced 1677).   1677.
The English Lawyer, from a Latin play by George Ruggle (produced 1677).   1678.
King Edgar and Alfreda (produced 1677).   1677.
The London Cuckolds (produced 1681).   1682; edited by A. Norman Jeffares, in
    Restoration Comedy, 1974.
Dame Dobson; or, The Cunning Woman, from a play by Thomas Corneille (produced
    1683).   1684.

Titus Andronicus; or, The Rape of Lavinia, from the play by Shakespeare (produced 1686). 1687.
The Canterbury Guests; or, A Bargain Broken (produced 1694).   1695.
The Anatomist; or, The Sham Doctor (produced 1696).   1697; edited by Leo Hughes and Arthur H. Scouten, in *Ten English Farces*, 1948.
The Italian Husband (produced 1697).   1698.

*   *   *

In the prologue to his *Assignation* Dryden jeered at his rival Edward Ravenscroft for pleasing the crowd but being condemned by the critics for his very first play, *The Citizen Turn'd Gentleman*. The Laureate's judgment proved prophetic. In an age which insisted on interpreting Horace as requiring *edification*, Ravenscroft found his success in *entertainment*.

His early comedies, all following a common Restoration pattern of combining scenes from as many as three plays by Molière, were generally successful. His serious attempts, a play borrowed from early English history, *King Edgar and Alfreda*, an adaptation of Shakespeare's *Titus Andronicus*, and an equally macabre borrowing from the Italian called *The Italian Husband*, won no lasting acclaim. *Scaramouche*, borrowed from both Molière and his *commedia dell'arte* neighbors, anticipates in many ways the vastly popular pantomimes of the next century and provides something of a pattern for his two most successful pieces: *The London Cuckolds*, which lasted 102 years but eventually proved too bawdy for an increasingly squeamish age, and *The Anatomist*, an even livelier but less risqué piece which proved more fortunate in its long theatrical history. *The London Cuckolds* borrows only its theme, the absurdity of attempting by contrivance to avoid even the risk of cuckoldry, from *The School for Wives*, but Ravenscroft multiplies Molière's Arnolphe by three, adds several farce turns wholly unconnected with the French play, and succeeds in being shocking and amusing at one and the same time. Borrowed from Hauteroche but much improved by some additional farce turns of his own, *The Anatomist* was turned into a one-act afterpiece at Goodman's Fields just a few months before David Garrick began his illustrious career at that theatre. *The Anatomist* was a favorite of Garrick's. He repeatedly attached it to his own pieces or to his own performances throughout his career. Beyond Garrick's time it waned somewhat in popularity but lasted until the mid-nineteenth century, well beyond the term of a hundred years which, according to Dr. Johnson's dictum, is "commonly fixed as the test of literary merit." In Ravenscroft's case perhaps *theatrical* merit would be the more appropriate term.

—Leo Hughes

ROWE, Nicholas.   English.   Born in Little Barford, Bedfordshire, baptized 30 June 1674. Educated at Westminster School, London (King's Scholar); entered the Middle Temple, London, 1691. Married Antonia Parons in 1698. Inherited the family estate, 1692, and gave up the law for playwriting; also held various official appointments: Under-Secretary to the Duke of Queensbury, Secretary of State for Scotland, 1709–11. First modern editor of Shakespeare, 1709. Poet Laureate, 1715 until his death. *Died 6 December 1718.*

PUBLICATIONS

Collections

Plays edited by Anne D. Devenish.   2 vols., 1747.
Works.   2 vols., 1764.
Three Plays (includes *Tamerlane, The Fair Penitent, Jane Shore*), edited by James R.
Sutherland.   1929.

Plays

The Ambitious Step-Mother (produced 1700).   1701.
Tamerlane (produced 1701).   1701; edited by Landon C. Burns, 1966.
The Fair Penitent, from the play *The Fatal Dowry* by Massinger and Nathan Field
(produced 1703).   1703; edited by Malcolm Goldstein, 1969.
The Biter (produced 1704).   1705.
Ulysses (produced 1705).   1706.
The Royal Convert (produced 1707).   1708; as *Ethelinda* (produced 1776).
The Tragedy of Jane Shore (produced 1714).   1714; edited by Harry William Pedicord,
1974.
Tragedies.   2 vols., 1714.
Lady Jane Gray (produced 1715).   1715.

Verse

A Poem upon the Late Glorious Successes of Her Majesty's Arms.   1707.
Poems on Several Occasions.   1714.
Poetical Works.   1715.
Ode for the New Year 1716.   1716.
Ode for the Year 1717.   1717.
Ode to the Thames for the Year 1719.   1719.

Other

Editor, with J. Tonson, *Poetical Miscellanies 5–6*, by Dryden.   2 vols., 1704–09.
Editor, *Works of Shakespeare.*   6 vols., 1709.

Translator, *The Life of Pythagoras* (verse only).   1707.
Translator, with others, *Callipaedia*, by Claudius Quillet.   1712.
Translator, with others, *Ovid's Metamorphoses.*   1717.
Translator, *Lucan's Pharsalia.*   1718.

Reading List: *Pity and Tears: The Tragedies of Rowe* by Landon C. Burns, 1974; *Rowe and
Christian Tragedy* by J. Douglas Canfield, 1977.

*   *   *

Nicholas Rowe, a lawyer-turned-playwright, wrote some of the best and most frequently acted tragedies between 1700 and 1740: *Tamerlane, Jane Shore*, and *The Fair Penitent*. He knew Addison and Pope, and honored the theory of tragedy Pope described in his Prologue to Addison's *Cato*.

Rowe, as Shakespeare's first modern editor (1709), compared copies of the texts available to him instead of merely reprinting the First Folio, improving many obscure passages, discovering a missing scene in *Hamlet*, and adding for the first time consistent act and scene divisions, exits and entrances, and other stage directions. He demonstrated, as Alan S. Downer explains (*The British Drama: A Handbook and Brief Chronicle*), how inaccurately the Elizabethan tradition was understood 100 years later. His Preface preserves facts and traditions about Shakespeare plus observations on the way he handled various types of plays, many typical of his time, though others transcend it.

Rowe was sentimental and melodramatic in his own plays, achieving his greatest effects in pathos, though with power, in *The Fair Penitent, Jane Shore*, and *Lady Jane Gray*. These looked back chiefly to Thomas Otway's tender love scenes in *Venice Preserved* and *The Orphan*, and provided powerful emotional roles for actresses such as Mrs. Siddons.

Dr. Johnson, in his life of Rowe, commended Rowe's plays for interesting fables, delightful language, easily imagined domestic stories of common life, and exquisitely harmonious and appropriate diction. He declared that Lothario in *The Fair Penitent*, however, retained too much of the spectator's kindness. Rowe, borrowing *The Fair Penitent*'s plot from Massinger's *The Fatal Dowry*, has Calista seduced and abandoned by the gay Lothario (whom she really loved), married to the noble Altamount to save her honor, and reduced to utter despair when Altamount bursts in upon a love tryst and kills Lothario. Crushed by grief, she kills herself beside Lothario's coffin with her father's dagger, at his suggestion, but is tearfully received again as his daughter before she expires, thus lacing the play with Otway's pathos from a middle-class viewpoint and in the manner soon to dominate the sentimental novel.

Tamerlane, which demonstrated political tragedy's potential but failed to express, according to John Loftis (*The Politics of Drama in Augustan England*), the "lively conflicts embodying rival political philosophies," praised the amiable William III (Tamerlane) and attacked Louis XIV (Bajazet), and was produced annually on November 4 (William's birthday) and November 5 (the anniversary of his landing in England in 1688). Gone, however, was Marlowe's amoral Herculean superman with his boundless aspiration, love, cruelty, and wrath.

Jane Shore, "written in imitation of Shakespeare's style" plus much pathos, was typical of that phase of English drama (stimulated by Dryden's *All for Love*, with its love versus duty theme) when dramatists selected Shakespearean stories but developed different themes. Purportedly a Restoration heroic tragedy, the play shows political scheming as applicable to Queen Anne's time as to Elizabeth's, especially concerning Gloster, the civil war, and the uncertain succession. Richard of Gloster throws Jane, mistress to Edward IV, out into the street to starve, forbidding anyone to feed or shelter her under penalty of death. Her disguised husband saves her from rape by Lord Hastings, but the insanely jealous Alicia, Hastings's lover and Jane's close friend, pretending to appeal for Jane's banishment, substitutes a letter damning both Jane and Hastings as the crown's enemies. This prompts Gloster to execute Hastings, but drives the love-mad Alicia wild when she cannot embrace him one last time. Ironically, only Jane's still loving husband helps her, and he is taken to prison after she dies. Alicia's concluding madness recalls Otway's ending to *Venice Preserved* when Pierre and Jaffeir die on the scaffold and their ghosts appear to Belvidera, who then goes mad and dies. Rowe's handling of the Jane Shore story, the best since Shakespeare's day, advocated and applauded domestic virtue in the context of Richard of Gloster's ruthless tyranny, presenting Jane caught by as fierce a royal decree as that which tormented Sophocles' Antigone.

Rowe's last play, *Lady Jane Gray*, again focuses on a lady in distress. Though superior to the other "she-tragedies" in dramatic technique (interest is concentrated on Jane rather than being dispersed), it was never as popular. Jane, a defiant Protestant martyr, forfeits her pardon from Mary and prays from the scaffold for a monarch "To save the altars from the rage of Rome."

Nicholas Rowe helped to define a new sort of tragedy, where sympathy for love in distress and admiration for the hero's struggles against impossible odds replaced Aristotelian catharsis with its pity and terror. Characters were wept out of their evil ways; pity for the poor fallen sinners, and the implicit grim warning to others to avoid their errors, purposefully create a chasm between the tragic hero and the audience. In his best work, Rowe avoided the excesses of crass sentimentality which mars the tragedies of dramatists such as George Lillo, thus establishing his modest claim to success in tragedy.

—Louis Charles Stagg

SETTLE, Elkanah. English. Born in Dunstable, Bedfordshire, 1 February 1648. Educated at Westminster School, London; Trinity College, Oxford, matriculated 1666, but left without taking a degree. Married Mary Warner in 1673. Settled in London, 1666, and was immediately successful as a playwright; enjoyed the patronage of Rochester; involved in a literary feud with Dryden; appointed Official Poet to the City of London, 1691, and wrote the Lord Mayor's Pageants until 1708; wrote drolls for Bartholomew Fair in his old age; poor brother of the Charterhouse from 1718. *Died 12 February 1724.*

PUBLICATIONS

Plays

    Cambyses, King of Persia (produced 1667?).   1671; revised version, 1675.
    The Empress of Morocco (produced 1671?).   1673; edited by Bonamy Dobrée, in *Five Heroic Plays*, 1960.
    Love and Revenge, from the play *The Fatal Contract* by William Hemmings (produced 1674).   1675.
    The Conquest of China by the Tartars (produced 1675).   1676.
    Ibrahim the Illustrious Bassa, from the novel by Mme. de Scudéry (produced 1676).   1677.
    Pastor Fido; or, The Faithful Shepherd, from a play by Guarini (produced 1676).   1677.
    The Female Prelate, Pope Joan (produced 1680).   1680.
    Fatal Love: or, The Forced Inconstancy (produced 1680).   1680.
    The Heir of Morocco (produced 1682).   1682.
    Distressed Innocence; or, The Princess of Persia (produced 1690).   1691.
    The Triumphs of London (produced 1691).   1691 (later pageants performed and published in 1692–95, 1698–1702, 1708).
    The Fairy Queen, music by Henry Purcell, from the play *A Midsummer Night's Dream* by Shakespeare (produced 1692).   1692.
    The New Athenian Comedy.   1693.
    The Ambitious Slave; or, A Generous Revenge (produced 1694).   1694.
    Philaster; or, Love Lies A-Bleeding, from the play by Beaumont and Fletcher (produced 1695).   1695.

The World in the Moon, music by Daniel Purcell and Jeremiah Clarke (produced 1697).   1697.

The Virgin Prophetess; or, The Fate of Troy, music by Gottfried Finger (produced 1701).   1701; as *Cassandra,* 1702.

The Siege of Troy (Bartholomew and Southwark fairs droll).   1707.

The City-Ramble; or, A Play-House Wedding (produced 1711).   1711.

The Lady's Triumph, with Lewis Theobald (produced 1718).   1718.

Fiction

Diego Redivivus.   1692; edited by Spiro Peterson, in *The Counterfeit Lady Unveiled,* 1961.

The Notorious Impostor.   2 vols., 1692; revised edition, as *The Complete Memoirs of That Notorious Impostor Will Morrell,* 1694; edited by Spiro Peterson, in *The Counterfeit Lady Unveiled,* 1961.

Verse

Mare Clausam; or, A Ransack for the Dutch.   1666.

Absalom Senior; or, Achitophel Transprosed: A Poem.   1682; edited by Harold W. Jones, in *Anti-Achitophel,* 1961.

Some 80 complimentary poems are cited in the bibliography by Frank C. Brown, below.

Other

Notes and Observations on The Empress of Morocco Revised.   1674.

The Character of a Popish Successor.   1681.

A Defence of Dramatic Poetry.   1698.

Editor, *Herod and Mariamne,* by Samuel Pordage.   1673.

Reading List: *Settle: His Life and Works* by Frank C. Brown, 1910 (includes bibliography).

*   *   *

Faustus solicited Helen of Troy to make him immortal with a kiss. Dryden made Elkanah Settle immortal with a gibe. This very minor writer is embedded in the amber of *Absalom and Achitophel* as a fly which once buzzed around the laureate.

The facts of Settle's life are quickly told and help to explain Dryden's antagonism. Settle attended Westminster School and Trinity College, Oxford, but took no degree, setting off to seek fame and fortune in London and within a year having his first, rodomontade tragedy produced. It was pompous "in King Cambyses' vein" and indeed was called *Cambyses, King of Persia.* Its "bombastic grandiloquence" echoed Thomas Preston's tragedy of the same name (1569) and was calculated to appeal to the self-important young lawyers of Lincoln's Inn, then much impressed with the fad of heroic drama. Full of sound and fury, Settle's tyro effort threatened to eclipse Dryden and Sir Robert Howard's *Indian Emperor.*

Dryden was in the ascendant. Soon he was to become Poet Laureate and Historiographer Royal. He was to score in the theatre with *Tyrannic Love; or, The Royal Martyr* (1669) and *The Conquest of Granada* (1670). But he was doing it on his own. Settle was set up as his rival by John Wilmot, Earl of Rochester. Settle's *Empress of Morocco* was played at Whitehall by lords and ladies and was a resounding success. The Duke of Buckingham and some of his smart friends pilloried Dryden as Bayes in *The Rehearsal*, a satiric swipe at the "heroic" plays of Davenant and Dryden which must have hurt Dryden. Settle's public success was used as another club with which to beat Dryden.

After 1675 Settle lost some of his backers but little of his public. Recruited to the Whig faction by the Earl of Shaftesbury, Settle entered the pamphlet wars and attacked Dryden's interests from many angles; when Dryden turned Catholic, Settle was hired by Shaftesbury to write a "pope-burning" pageant. Settle's career stretched from 1673 into the next century and ended with his writing and performing drolls for Bartholomew Fair. Meanwhile, Dryden ticked him off as Og, while Thomas Shadwell was Doeg and held up to ridicule in *Absalom and Achitophel* and *Mac Flecknoe*.

Honestly speaking, the whole "heroic drama" was a bore and Settle's pieces are not much less bombastic than Dryden's or anyone else's. Only in *The Female Prelate*, dealing with Pope Joan, does he step really far beyond the bounds of taste in this rather tasteless period. He may have ended up in the Charterhouse while Dryden ended up in the literary Pantheon, but it was not "heroic drama" that basically explained these two extreme fates. Thomas Duffett's burlesque of *The Empress of Morocco*, clever as it is, cannot really make it sound worse than the inflated junk so cruelly pricked in *The Rehearsal*. Settle never got really much better than *The Empress of Morocco* in that unpromising genre and his operatic *Fairy Queen* (based on *A Midsummer Night's Dream*) is still remembered, albeit chiefly for the music by Henry Purcell. Settle had none of the collaborators of Dryden, nor does Settle enjoy or deserve Dryden's fame. His work was done at a time when too many plays were actually what Davenant called his 1656 entertainments at Rutland House, *Declamations and Musick*. The whole "heroic drama" was a mistake – and Settle was not even the best of that lot.

—Leonard R. N. Ashley

SHADWELL, Thomas.   English.   Born in Broomhill, Norfolk, c. 1642. Educated at home for five years, then at King Edward VI Grammar School, Bury St. Edmunds, Suffolk, 1654–56; admitted as a pensioner to Caius College, Cambridge, 1656, but left without taking a degree; entered the Middle Temple, London, 1658, and studied there for some time. Married the actress Anne Gibbs c. 1665; three sons and one daughter. Travelled abroad, then returned to London and began writing for the theatre and the opera c. 1668; involved in a feud with Dryden from 1682; succeeded Dryden as Poet Laureate and Historiographer Royal, 1689. *Died 19 November 1692.*

PUBLICATIONS

Collections

   Complete Works, edited by Montague Summers.   5 vols., 1927.

Plays

   The Sullen Lovers; or, The Impertinents (produced 1668).   1668.
   The Royal Shepherdess, from the play *The Rewards of Virtue* by John Fountain (produced 1669).   1669.

The Humorists (produced 1670).   1671.

Epsom Wells (produced 1672).   1673; edited by Dorothy M. Walmsley, with *The Volunteers*, 1930.

The Miser (produced 1672).   1672.

The Tempest; or, The Enchanted Island, from the play by Shakespeare (produced 1674).   1674; edited by Christopher Spencer, in *Five Restoration Adaptations of Shakespeare*, 1965.

The Triumphant Widow; or, The Medley of Humours, with William Cavendish (produced 1674).   1677.

Psyche, music by Matthew Locke (produced 1675).   1675.

The Libertine (produced 1675).   1676; edited by Oscar Mandel, in *The Theatre of Don Juan*, 1963.

The Virtuoso (produced 1676).   1676; edited by Marjorie Hope Nicolson and David Stuart Rodes, 1966.

A True Widow (produced 1678).   1679.

Timon of Athens, The Man-Hater, from the play by Shakespeare (produced 1678).   1678.

The Woman Captain (produced 1679).   1680.

The Lancashire Witches and Tegue o Divelly the Irish Priest (produced 1681).   1682.

The Squire of Alsatia (produced 1688).   1688; edited by A. Norman Jeffares, in *Restoration Comedy*, 1974.

Bury Fair (produced 1689).   1689.

The Amorous Bigot, with the Second Part of Tegue o Divelly (produced 1690).   1690.

The Scourers (produced 1690).   1691.

The Volunteers; or, The Stock Jobbers (produced 1692).   1693; edited by Dorothy M. Walmsley, with *Epsom Wells*, 1930.

Verse

The Medal of John Bayes: A Satire Against Folly and Knavery.   1682.

A Lenten Prologue.   1683.

The Tenth Satire of Juvenal.   1687.

A Congratulatory Poem on His Highness the Prince of Orange His Coming into England.   1689.

A Congratulatory Poem to the Most Illustrious Queen Mary upon Her Arrival in England.   1689.

Ode on the Anniversary of the King's Birth.   1690.

Ode to the King, on His Return from Ireland.   1690(?).

Votum Perenne: A Poem to the King on New Year's Day.   1692.

Ode on the King's Birthday.   1692.

Other

Notes and Observations on The Empress of Morocco by Settle, with Dryden and John Crowne.   1674.

Some Reflections upon the Pretended Parallel in the Play The Duke of Guise.   1683.

Reading List: *Shadwell: His Life and Comedies* by Albert S. Borgman, 1928; *Shadwell* by Michael W. Alssid, 1967; *The Drama of Shadwell* by Don Kunz, 1972.

*   *   *

Thomas Shadwell is best known today as the target of John Dryden's satiric poem *Mac Flecknoe* (1678). Reading this cunning, exquisitely amusing lampoon, one is utterly convinced that Shadwell was no more than a clumsy, dull, nonsensical dramatist who repeated the same formula in play after play like one of his own comic humours. But reading Shadwell's drama beside Dryden's, one make a fairer assessment: while Shadwell was not nearly as accomplished a poet as his rival Dryden, he was a skillful and successful playwright. Actually, Dryden was able to enjoy a dramatic triumph over Shadwell only in the extravagantly imaginative fiction of his own poetic satire. The facts are that Shadwell was a very prolific, shrewdly professional, and highly popular Restoration dramatist.

Shadwell wrote during a literary epoch familiar to most of us either through Dryden's poetry or through some dozen outstanding plays written by a handful of gentlemen amateurs and companions to Charles II – men like the Second Duke of Buckingham, Sir Charles Sedley, Sir George Etherege, and William Wycherley. Like Dryden, Shadwell consorted with this group of witty courtiers, but he was a middle-class writer whose living depended increasingly more on box-office receipts than on their patronage. As a professional writer Shadwell was compelled to engage in nearly constant experimentation with a variety of dramatic kinds in order to appeal to an audience hungry for novelty. For example, his first play, *The Sullen Lovers*, was clearly a comedy of humours written in imitation of Ben Jonson, who along with Shakespeare had undergone a successful revival in the newly reopened theatres after Charles II's restoration to the throne. However, by the time he wrote *Epsom Wells*, Shadwell had already mastered the more modern, sophisticated comedy of wit made popular by Sedley and Etherege. Similarly, as spectacular operatic performances came into vogue, Shadwell adapted *The Tempest* and the story of Psyche; when his audience clamored for bombastic heroic tragedy, for which Dryden had created a following, Shadwell produced *The Libertine* and *Timon of Athens*. Later when political turmoil made it impossible to stage anything but farce and propaganda, Shadwell obliged with *The Woman Captain* and *The Lancashire Witches*. And when the taste was for sentimental comedy, he offered *The Squire of Alsatia* and *Bury Fair*.

Altogether between 1668 and 1692 Shadwell wrote at least eighteen plays. According to his editor, Montague Summers, some of these, like *Epsom Wells*, merited command performances at court; others, like *The Tempest*, set records for box-office receipts; fifteen of his plays continued to be performed after 1700 and six of them compiled distinguished stage histories, remaining in repertory for forty to eighty years. It was a living.

The remarkable variety in the canon of a professional playwright like Shadwell does much to dispel the common notion that Restoration drama consists essentially of heroic plays and comedies of wit. Similarly, reading Shadwell results in further correction of the gradually waning Victorian hypothesis that Restoration drama is noteworthy principally for its licentiousness and trivial frivolity. Despite their sometimes irreverent tone and frothy surface Shadwell's plays have a consistently orthodox Christian moral core; and, although they may go to extravagant lengths to entertain, invariably some socially utilitarian message is worked out in the dramatic action. His artistic credo is stated succinctly in his prologue to *The Lancashire Witches*: "Instruction is an honest Poet's aim,/And not a large or wide, but a good Fame." Among his contemporaries Shadwell enjoyed both. And sometimes envy as well.

Most of Shadwell's poetry was written in connection with his drama. He composed satiric prologues and epilogues notable for their wit and verve, their rapidly shifting tone and perspective, and their ingenious metaphors defining the playwright's relationship to his audience and plays – conceits which ranged anywhere from depicting the author as a warrior on a battlefield to a procurer in a bawdy-house. His songs typically treat of love or drinking, hunting or war; ensconced in the plays, they work to develop character or amplify theme in addition to providing a seemingly impromptu entertainment. His best poetry displays his natural ability as a dramatist: amusing characterizations, a swiftly developing argument, and clever turns of phrase.

The remainder of Shadwell's poetry consists of vituperative, Juvenalian invective like *The*

Medal of John Bayes or lavish panegyrics on public figures. His most conventional and unimaginative poetry was written in fulfillment of his duty as Poet Laureate – a post in which he succeeded Dryden in 1689 and served until his death in 1692. These official birthday odes, celebrations of monarchical arrivals, and congratulations for battlefield victories are frankly dull enough to have been written by Mac Flecknoe. But once again in poetry as well as drama Shadwell is notable for his range from the crude and scurrilous to the elegant and highly stylized.

Unquestionably Shadwell's real talent was for dramatic satire and comedy – pieces like *Epsom Wells*, *The Virtuoso*, and *The Squire of Alsatia*. These seem to have been inspired by a volatile combination of mischief, social purpose, and exuberant delight at the folly surrounding him. Quite likely the rest was composed because a patron or playhouse wanted it or because a reputation needed living up to or because he needed the money. This is to say that such hack work was a practical necessity, making possible that drama which is the principal justification of Shadwell's career.

—Don Kunz

SHERIDAN, Richard Brinsley (Butler).   Irish.   Born in Dublin, 30 October 1751; moved with his family to Bath, 1770. Educated at Harrow School, Middlesex, 1762–68; Waltham Abbey School, 1772–73; Middle Temple, London, 1773. Married 1) Elizabeth Ann Linley in 1773 (died, 1792), one son; 2) Esther Jane Ogle in 1795, one son. Part-owner and Director of the Drury Lane Theatre, London, 1776; served in Parliament, first as Member for Stafford, then Westminster, then Ilchester, 1780–1812: Under-Secretary of State for Foreign Affairs in the Rockingham Administration, 1782, and Secretary of the Treasury in the coalition ministry, 1783; manager of the Warren Hastings trial by Parliament, 1788–94; Treasurer of the Navy, 1806; Member of the Privy Council. *Died 7 July 1816.*

PUBLICATIONS

Collections

> *Works*, edited by F. Stainworth.   1874.
> *Plays and Poems*, edited by R. Crompton Rhodes.   3 vols., 1928.
> *Letters*, edited by Cecil Price.   3 vols., 1966.
> *Dramatic Works*, edited by Cecil Price.   2 vols., 1973.

Plays

> *The Rivals* (produced 1775).   1775; edited by R. L. Purdy, 1935.
> *St. Patrick's Day; or, The Scheming Lieutenant* (produced 1775).   1788.
> *The Duenna*, music by Thomas Linley and others (produced 1775).   1775.
> *A Trip to Scarborough*, from the play *The Relapse* by Vanbrugh (produced 1777).   1781.

The School for Scandal (produced 1777).   1780.
The Camp, music by Thomas Linley (produced 1778).   1795.
The Critic; or, A Tragedy Rehearsed (produced 1779).   1781.
The Storming of Fort Omoa (interlude in *Harlequin Fortunatus* by Henry Woodward; produced 1780).
Robinson Crusoe; or, Harlequin Friday, music by Thomas Linley (produced 1781).   Songs published 1781.
The Glorious First of June, with James Cobb (benefit entertainment, produced 1794).   Songs published 1794; revised version, as *Cape St. Vincent* (produced 1797), songs published 1797.
The Stranger, from a translation by Benjamin Thompson of a play by Kotzebue (produced 1798).
Pizarro, from a play by Kotzebue (produced 1799).   1799.
The Forty Thieves, with Charles Ward and Colman the Younger, music by Michael Kelly (produced 1806).   1808; as *Ali Baba*, 1814.

Verse

The Ridotto of Bath: A Panegyric.   1771.
The Love Epistle of Aristaenetus, with Nathaniel Halhed.   1771.
The Rival Beauties, with Miles Peter Andrews(?).   1772.
Verses to the Memory of Garrick.   1779; as *The Tears of Genius*, 1780.

Other

A Familiar Epistle to the Author of the Epistle to William Chambers.   1774.
Speeches.   5 vols., 1816.

Bibliography: in *Plays and Poems*, 1928.

Reading List: *Sheridan* (biography) by Walter S. Sichel, 2 vols., 1909; *Harlequin Sheridan: The Man and the Legends* by R. Crompton Rhodes, 1933; *Sheridan of Drury Lane* by Alice Glasgow, 1940; *Sheridan* by Lewis Gibbs, 1947; *Sheridan and Kotzebue: A Comparative Essay* by G. Sinko, 1949; *Sheridan: The Track of a Comet* by Madeleine Bingham, 1972; *Sheridan's Comedies: Their Contexts and Achievements* by Mark S. Auburn, 1977; *Sheridan and the Drama of Georgian England* by John Loftis, 1977.

*   *   *

Sheridan's first comedy, *The Rivals*, was produced in 1775, as were *St. Patrick's Day; or, The Scheming Lieutenant*, a farce, and *The Duenna*, a comic opera. *The Duenna* made his name. Then he adapted Vanbrugh's *The Relapse* (1696) to suit the greater refinement of his own age and called it *A Trip to Scarborough*; it was staged in February 1777, and followed in the same year by *The School for Scandal*; two years later came *The Critic*. With the exception of *Pizarro*, which he adapted from the German of Kotzebue in 1799, and some minor work, his dramatic career was compressed into four years.

The Rivals is characterized by liveliness and vitality. The plot is skilfully devised, the dialogue is fresh, and the characters, though types, are well differentiated and probably created with particular actors and actresses in mind, for Sheridan knew about the theatre from an early age: his father was an actor and the author of a successful farce as well as a teacher of elocution, and his mother had written successful comedies. Sheridan set the action of *The Rivals* in Bath, where his father had set up his school of elocution in 1770, and where his own youth had been socially successful. He danced and flirted and observed the fashionable life of this elegant spa, with its concerts, plays, and balls, its circulating libraries, cards, and scandal occupying the time of the people of distinction who frequented it. He captured its ethos well in *The Rivals*. One heroine, Lydia Languish, headlong and romantic, derives much of her silliness from her diet of light reading, and the other, Julia Melville, is sentimental in the eighteenth-century manner. Jack Absolute refuses his father's plans for him until he finds that the girl chosen is Lydia whom he loves – but there is the complication that he has pretended to be Ensign Beverley, to cater to Lydia's romantic nature. Jack's relationship with his autocratic father adds to the play's liveliness, but the other hero, Faulkland, who suffers from jealousy, can seem sickly to a modern audience in his fashionably sentimental speeches to Julia. But Sir Lucius O'Trigger, the fire-eating Irishman, and Mrs. Malaprop, vulgar, ambitious, a magnificent mishandler of language, give the play its own particular comic – and farcical – flavour. Vitality and speed of action have kept this play successful on the stage.

The *School for Scandal* is more serious, for Sheridan was satirising the excesses of contemporary journalism and scandal-mongering. But what he created in his mockery of the polite world of his own day was lasting comedy. He used proven ingredients, lovers kept apart and finally rewarded, mistaken identity, the country girl out of her depth in the life of the town, the reassessment of an apparent rake, and, above all, the exposure – and, significantly, the explanation – of hypocrisy. It is all done very effectively, with sparkling conversation, a clever, indeed complex, plot of intrigue, a comedy of manners which exposes the soulful sentimentality of contemporary drama, the slandering, the malice, selfishness, and hypocrisy of contemporary society. Sheridan's ironies are clear: he distinguished between appearance and reality brilliantly, without the coarseness or indeed the immorality of Restoration comedy; he supplied suspense, the ludicrous situation, the unexpected reversal; he knew what kept – and still keeps – an audience amused. And so the contrast between the Surface brothers, the effect of the screen's falling upon the main characters, the reconciliation of Sir Peter and Lady Teazle, the marriage of Charles and Maria are all timeless in achievement.

Sheridan's views of comedy emerge not only in the second prologue to *The Rivals* but in *The Critic*, which was inspired by Buckingham's *The Rehearsal*. In it he mocked his contemporary Cumberland in the character of Sir Fretful Plagiary, and contemporary critics in the characters Puff and Sneer. This play is an amusing parody of contemporary dramatic techniques, which were often fairly crude – and so there are often references which are obscure to modern audiences or readers. *The Critic* is in effect a series of sketches, designed as an after-play to *Hamlet* – hence when Tilburina burlesques Ophelia's speech the audiences would have had the original in mind. Sheridan is exposing dull dialogue, artificial devices and asides, the melodrama inherent in plots which were unsophisticatedly resolved, the insistence upon fashion in dress, stereotyped delivery of lines, and crude acting in badly illuminated auditoriums. In fact, he is giving us a somewhat exasperated manager's view of the unsatisfactory elements of the stage in his own day: but he does it, as usual, with the light touch and sense of absurdity which illuminate all his own drama.

—A. Norman Jeffares

SOUTHERNE, Thomas. Irish. Born in Oxmantown, near Dublin, in Autumn 1660. Educated at Trinity College, Dublin (pensioner), 1676–78, M.A. 1696; entered the Middle Temple, London, 1678. Served as an Ensign in Princess Anne's Regiment, and rose to the command of a company, 1685–88. Thereafter devoted himself entirely to writing for the stage, at first as a protégé and disciple of Dryden; retired in 1726. *Died 22 May 1746.*

PUBLICATIONS

Collections

Plays, edited by T. Evans.   3 vols., 1774.

Plays

The Loyal Brother; or The Persian Prince (produced 1682).   1682; edited by P.
Hamelius, 1911.
The Disappointment; or, The Mother in Fashion (produced 1684).   1684.
Sir Anthony Love; or, The Rambling Lady (produced 1690).   1691.
The Wives' Excuse; or, Cuckolds Make Themselves (produced 1691).   1692; edited by
Ralph R. Thornton, 1973.
The Maid's Last Prayer; or, Any, Rather Than Fail (produced 1693).   1693; edited by
Ralph R. Thornton, 1978.
The Fatal Marriage; or, The Innocent Adultery, from the story "The Nun" by Aphra
Behn (produced 1694).   1694.
Oroonoko, from the story by Aphra Behn (produced 1695).   1696; edited by
Maximillian E. Novak and David Stuart Rodes, 1976.
The Fate of Capua (produced 1700).   1700.
The Spartan Dame (produced 1719).   1719.
Money the Mistress (produced 1726).   1726.

Reading List: *Southerne, Dramatist* by John W. Dobbs, 1933; *The Comedy of Manners* by
Kenneth Muir, 1970.

*   *   *

Thomas Southerne's career as a dramatist was, like his life's span, a lengthy one. His first
play, *The Loyal Brother,* a panegyric to the Duke of York, appeared in the troubled year
1682; his last, *Money the Mistress,* a failed comedy, in 1726. His major works came apace
between 1690 and 1696: three comedies in the manners genre and two extraordinarily
popular tragedies in the pathetic vein.
Of the comedies, *Sir Anthony Love* was best received; its success gave rise to a new
practice, the author's sixth-night benefit. The action is conventionally vigorous, the intrigues
multiplex; Southerne's twist lies in representing his rake-hero, Sir Anthony, by "the female
Montford bare above the knee." The next comedy, *The Wives' Excuse,* a flat failure,
paradoxically excites critical interest today as the link between the older plays of Etherege and
Wycherley and the revival of the manners genre by Congreve and Vanbrugh. The foibles of
fashionable Londoners are exhaustively chronicled, but the play devolves into a "problem
play" with its distressed heroine consciously choosing not to take the usual revenge on an
impertinent coxcomb of a husband. Stung by the failure, Southerne reverted to the sure-fire
formula of gallantry and intrigue in *The Maid's Last Prayer,* adding genuinely comic (nigh
farcical) scenes of amateur "musick-meetings," Lady Susan's dogged pursuit of men, any
man, rather than fail, and, curiously, one of the darkest scenes of sexual revenge in dramatic
literature.
The success of *The Fatal Marriage* and *Oroonoko* confirmed Southerne's popular

reputation in his own generation. Adapting both plots from the works of Aphra Behn, Southerne commingled new action and characters, as well as counterpoint comic sub-plots, to accentuate the pathos and distressed nobility of his sentimentalized tragic protagonists. Each play remained an actor's vehicle well into the nineteenth century, Garrick having altered *The Fatal Marriage* in 1757 to *Isabella*.

Of the remaining plays, *The Disappointment* is an olio of dramatic elements; it points, however, to an interest in the distressed-heroine problem play. *The Fate of Capua*, a neo-classical tragedy set in the Second Punic War, was unsuccessful, despite moving individual scenes. *The Spartan Dame* was Southerne's true valedictory to the theatre, though it was really an old play, having been largely completed in 1687 but denied production because of its fable (from Plutarch) – usurpation by a daughter.

In a partisan age, Southerne managed to maintain widespread and abiding friendships: Dryden, Wycherley, Congreve, Dennis, Gildon, the Earls of Orrery; later Pope and his circle regarded him with affection; his literary mid-wifery to unproduced dramatists was legendary; and his dedications to Whigs or Tories were made with an eye to profit, not politics. In the theatre, Southerne's astute eye caught the changes in the audiences' taste and composition; he learned early to supply these new arbiters of the box and pit with drama of pathos – she-tragedies – not the out-of-style realistic, satiric comedy. Therein his popularity lay.

—Ralph R. Thornton

STEELE, Sir Richard. Irish. Born in Dublin, baptized 12 March 1672. Educated at Charterhouse, London, where he met Joseph Addison, 1684–89; matriculated at Christ Church, Oxford, 1690; postmaster at Merton College, Oxford, 1691–94, but left without taking a degree. Enlisted as a cadet in the Duke of Ormonde's guards, 1694; Ensign in Lord Cutts's Regiment, 1695, and served as Cutts's confidential secretary, 1696–97; Captain, stationed at the Tower of London, by 1700; transferred as Captain to Lord Lucas's Regiment in 1702. Married 1) Margaret Ford Stretch in 1705 (died, 1706); 2) Mary Scurlock in 1707 (died, 1718), two sons and two daughters. Wrote extensively for the theatre, 1701–05; Gentleman-Writer to Prince George of Denmark, 1706–08; Gazetteer (i.e., Manager of the *Gazette*, the official government publication), 1707–10; Commissioner of Stamps, 1710–13; Founding Editor, *The Tatler*, to which Addison was the major contributor, 1709–11; Founder, and Editor with Addison, *The Spectator*, 1711–12; Founding Editor, *The Guardian*, 1713; elected Member of Parliament for Stockbridge, Hampshire, 1713, but expelled for anti-government views; Founding Editor, *The Englishman*, 1713–14, *The Lover*, 1714, and *The Reader*, 1714; on accession of George I, 1714, appointed Justice of the Peace, Deputy Lieutenant for the County of Middlesex, Surveyor of the Royal Stables at Hampton Court, and Supervisor of the Drury Lane Theatre, London: granted life patent of Drury Lane, 1715; Member of Parliament for Boroughbridge, Yorkshire, 1715; Founding Editor, *Town Talk*, 1715–16, *The Tea-Table*, and *Chit-Chat*, 1716; appointed Commissioner for Forfeited Estates in Scotland, 1716; quarrelled with Addison, 1719; Founding Editor, *The Plebeian*, 1719, and *The Theatre*, 1720; Member of Parliament for Wendover, Buckinghamshire, 1722; retired to Wales, 1724. Knighted, 1715. *Died 1 September 1729.*

PUBLICATIONS

Collections

Correspondence, edited by R. Blanchard.   1941; revised edition, 1968.
Plays, edited by Shirley S. Kenny.   1971.

Plays

The Funeral; or, Grief a-la-Mode (produced 1701).   1702.
The Lying Lover; or, The Ladies' Friendship (produced 1703).   1704.
The Tender Husband; or, The Accomplished Fools (produced 1703).   1705.
The Conscious Lovers (produced 1722).   1723.

Verse

The Procession: A Poem on Her Majesty's Funeral.   1695.
Occasional Verse, edited by R. Blanchard.   1952.

Other

The Christian Hero, An Argument Proving That No Principles But Those of Religion Are Sufficient to Make a Great Man.   1701; edited by R. Blanchard, 1932.
The Tatler, with Addison.   4 vols., 1710–11; edited by G. A. Aitken, 4 vols., 1898–99; selections edited by L. Gibbs, 1953.
The Spectator, with Addison.   8 vols., 1712–15; edited by D. F. Bond, 5 vols., 1965; selections edited by R. J. Allen, 1957.
An Englishman's Thanks to the Duke of Marlborough.   1712.
A Letter to Sir M. W[arton] Concerning Occasional Peers.   1713.
The Importance of Dunkirk.   1713.
The Guardian, with others.   2 vols., 1714; edited by Alexander Chalmers, 1802.
The Englishman (2 series, and an epistle).   3 vols., 1714–16; edited by R. Blanchard, 1955.
The Crisis, with Some Seasonable Remarks on the Danger of a Popish Successor.   1714.
The French Faith Represented in the Present State of Dunkirk.   1714.
A Letter Concerning the Bill for Preventing the Growth of Schism.   1714.
Mr. Steele's Apology for Himself and His Writings.   1714.
A Letter from the Earl of Mar to the King.   1715.
A Letter Concerning the Condemned Lords.   1716.
Account of Mr. Desagulier's New-Invented Chimneys.   1716.
An Account of the Fish Pool, with Joseph Gillmore.   1718.
The Joint and Humble Address to the Tories and Whigs Concerning the Intended Bill of Peerage.   1719.
A Letter to the Earl of O—d Concerning the Bill of Peerage.   1719.
The Plebeian.   1719; edited by R. Hurd, in Addison's *Works,* 1856.
The Spinster, in Defence of the Woollen Manufactures.   1719.
The Crisis of Property.   1720.
A Nation a Family; or, A Plan for the Improvement of the South-Sea Proposal.   1720.
The State of the Case Between the Lord Chamberlain and the Governor of the Royal Company of Comedians.   1720.

The Theatre.   1720; edited by John Loftis, 1962.
Tracts and Pamphlets, edited by R. Blanchard.   1944.
Steele's Periodical Journalism 1714–16: The Lover, The Reader, Town Talk, Chit-Chat,
    edited by R. Blanchard.   1959.

Editor, *The Ladies Library.*   3 vols., 1714.
Editor, *Poetical Miscellanies.*   1714.

Reading List: *Steele* by Willard Connely, 1934; *Steele at Drury Lane* by John Loftis, 1952;
Steele, Addison, and Their Periodical Essays by Arthur R. Humphreys, 1959; *Steele: The
Early Career,* 1964, and *The Later Career,* 1970, both by Calhoun Winton.

*   *   *

Though best remembered as a periodical essayist, Sir Richard Steele began his literary
career in the theatre – if, that is, one forgets and forgives his moralizing tract *The Christian
Hero,* an unsuccessful attempt at self-admonition. His plays were frank attempts to make
piety more palatable, while avoiding the sexual excesses for which Collier had condemned
the stage, and which increasingly middle-class audiences were also finding offensive.

The first, *The Funeral,* has several touches of originality, notably in its satire on the
undertaking business, its sprightly yet sympathetic treatment of its female characters, and its
liveliness of plotting. Indeed, two of the participants in Gildon's *A Comparison Between the
Two Stages* allege that in this latter respect the play resembles a farce more than it does a
comedy, and it may be regretted that Steele never successfully evaded formal considerations
of this kind – though two fragments, *The School of Action* and *The Gentleman,* do begin to
assert the kind of freedom from the rules that Gay and Fielding more happily achieved.

The Lying Lover was unalleviated by realism, displayed less comic spirit, and was, as Steele
ruefully admitted, "damn'd for its piety." Loosely derived from Corneille's *Le Menteur,* it
features a pathetic repentance scene, in which its hero, Young Bookwit, awakens in prison to
find that he has killed a rival in a drunken duel. For this he is duly contrite in blank verse, to
the extent of putting forgiveness before honour. There is some wit in the quixotic Bookwit's
romancing in the earlier scenes, and his respectful welcome to Newgate by his fellow inmates
hints at the inverted morality of *The Beggar's Opera*: yet, just a few scenes later, Steele
perpetrates a double shift in the plot, lacking any sense of its own fatal absurdity.

The Tender Husband, Steele's third play, also proved to be his last to reach the stage for
nearly eighteen years. It has a female Quixote, or prototype Lydia Languish, as its heroine –
and, indeed, the original of Tony Lumpkin in that heroine's cousin, Humphry Gubbin.
Unfortunately, the sub-plot featuring the titular husband, who devises an unlikely test of his
wife's faithfulness by disguising his own mistress as a suitor, disrupts the comic flow, and
complicates the conclusion with a sentimental reconciliation.

In the following years, Steele was increasingly active as a Whig politician, his major
literary achievement being, of course, the succession of periodicals he created, some written
in collaboration with Joseph Addison. Of these, the best remembered are *The Tatler, The
Spectator,* and *The Guardian,* with the irrelevantly titled *The Theatre* probably the most
important of the later series. Whether or not Steele succeeded in his aim "to make the pulpit,
the bar, and the stage all act in concert in the cause of piety, justice, and virtue" is arguable:
but he certainly perfected a distinctive new form of clubable *belles lettres,* incidentally
exploring techniques of characterization for his recurrent *personae* which were to be of
significance to the early novelists, and publishing some first-rate dramatic criticism.

Although *The Conscious Lovers,* which did not reach the stage until 1722, was influential
in the development of the *comédie larmoyante* in France, to the modern mind it merely
demonstrates that, at its most sentimental, eighteenth-century comedy was no laughing
matter. With the exception of its scenes below stairs – their purpose all too evidently to sugar

a didactic pill – it is a distinctly unfunny play: yet, according to Steele, an audience's pleasure might be "too exquisite for laughter," and thus better expressed in the tears evoked by the inexpressibly virtuous behaviour of his hero, Young Bevil, and by the convenient reshufflings of the characters in the closing scene.

The mercantile morality of the play is at once over-explicit and interruptive, and its characters are in neither the humours nor the manners tradition, but mere ethical absolutes. No wonder that Fielding's Parson Adams considered it the first play fit for a Christian to read since the pagan tragedies – but then good Parson Adams lacked both irony and a sense of incongruity, as does *The Conscious Lovers*. Steele is better remembered by the feeling for both irony *and* incongruity in his earlier plays, and, of course, by his largeness of heart as a periodical essayist.

—Simon Trussler

TATE, Nahum. Irish. Born Nahum Teate in Dublin in 1652. Educated at Trinity College, Dublin, 1668–72, B.A. 1672. Settled in London, 1672; began writing for the theatre, 1678; also subsequently involved in extensive work as editor and translator of various authors; Editor, with M. Smith, *The Monitor*, 1713; appointed Poet Laureate, 1692, and Historiographer Royal, 1702. *Died 30 July 1715.*

PUBLICATIONS

Plays

> *Brutus of Alba; or, The Enchanted Lovers* (produced 1678).   1678.
> *The Loyal General* (produced 1679).   1680.
> *King Richard the Second*, from the play by Shakespeare.   1681; as *The Sicilian Usurper* (produced 1680), 1691; as *The Tyrant of Sicily* (produced 1681).
> *King Lear*, from the play by Shakespeare (produced 1681).   1681; edited by James Black, 1975.
> *The Ingratitude of a Commonwealth; or, The Fall of Caius Martius Coriolanus*, from the play by Shakespeare (produced 1681).   1682.
> *A Duke and No Duke*, from the play *Trappolin Supposed a Prince* by Aston Cokayne (produced 1684).   1685; edited by Leo A. Hughes and Arthur H. Scouten, in *Ten English Farces*, 1948.
> *Cuckold's Haven; or, An Alderman No Conjuror*, from the play *Eastward Ho* by Jonson, Chapman, and Marston (produced 1685).   1685.
> *The Island Princess*, from the play by Fletcher (produced 1687).   1687.
> *Dido and Aeneas*, music by Henry Purcell (produced 1689).   1690; edited by G. A. Macfarren, 1841.
> *Injured Love; or, The Cruel Husband.*   1707.

Verse

Poems. 1677; revised edition, 1684.
The Second Part of Absalom and Achitophel, with Dryden.   1682.
On the Sacred Memory of Our Late Sovereign. 1685.
A Pastoral in Memory of the Duke of Ormonde. 1688.
A Poem Occasioned by His Majesty's Voyage to Holland. 1691.
A Poem Occasioned by the Late Discontents. 1691.
Characters of Virtue and Vice, Attempted in Verse from a Treatise by Joseph Hall. 1691.
An Ode upon Her Majesty's Birthday. 1693.
A Present for the Ladies. 1693.
A Poem upon the Late Promotion of Several Eminent Persons. 1694.
In Memory of Joseph Washington: An Elegy. 1694.
An Ode upon the University of Dublin's Foundation. 1694.
Mausolaeum: A Funeral Poem on Our Late Queen. 1695.
An Elegy on the Late Archbishop of Canterbury. 1695.
The Anniversary Ode for His Majesty's Birthday. 1698.
A Consolatory Poem to Lord Cutts. 1698.
Elegies. 1699.
An Essay of a Character of Sir George Treby. 1700.
Funeral Poems. 1700.
Panacea: A Poem upon Tea. 1700; as *A Poem upon Tea,* 1702.
An Elegy in Memory of Ralph Marshall. 1700.
A Congratulatory Poem on the New Parliament. 1701.
The Kentish Worthies. 1701.
A Monumental Poem in Memory of Sir George Treby. 1702.
Portrait-Royal: A Poem upon Her Majesty's Picture. 1703.
The Song for New Year's Day. 1703.
The Triumph: A Poem on the Glorious Successes of the Last Year.   1705.
Britannia's Prayer for the Queen. 1706.
The Triumph of Union. 1707.
A Congratulatory Poem to Prince George of Denmark. 1708.
The Muse's Memorial to the Earl of Oxford. 1712.
The Muses Bower. 1713.
The Triumph of Peace. 1713.
A Poem Sacred to the Memory of Queen Anne. 1714.

Other

An Essay for Promoting of Psalmody. 1710.

Editor, *Poems by Several Hands.* 1685.
Editor, *A Memorial for the Learned,* by J. D. 1686.
Editor, *The Life of Alexander the Great,* by Quintus Curtius Rufius. 1690.
Editor, *The Political Anatomy of Ireland,* by Sir William Petty. 1691.
Editor, *Guzman,* by Roger Boyle. 1693.
Editor, *The Four Epistles of A. G. Bushbequius.* 1694.
Editor, *Miscellanea Sacra; or, Poems on Divine and Moral Subjects.* 1696; revised edition, 1698.
Editor, *An Essay on Poetry,* by John Sheffield, Duke of Buckingham. 1697.
Editor, *The Original of the Soul* (Nosce Teipsum), by Sir John Davies. 1697.
Editor, *The Innocent Epicure; or, The Art of Angling,* by J. S. 1697.

Translator, with others, *Ovid's Epistles.* 1680.
Translator, *Syphilus: A Poetical History of the French Disease,* by Fracastoro. 1686.
Translator, with "a person of quality," *The Aethiopian History,* by Heliodorus. 1686;
as *The Triumphs of Love and Constancy,* 1687.
Translator, with others, *Cowley's Six Books of Plants.* 1689.
Translator, *The Life of the Prince of Condé.* 2 vols., 1693.
Translator, with others, *The Satires of Juvenal,* with *The Satires of Persius* translated by
Dryden. 1693.
Translator, with Nicholas Brady, *An Essay of a New Version of the Psalms of
David.* 1695; revised edition, 1695, 1696; *Supplement,* 1700.
Translator, *Majesta Imperii Britannici, The Glories of Great Britain,* by Mr.
Maidwell. 1706.
Translator, with Aaron Hill, *The Celebrated Speeches of Ajax and Ulysses,* by
Ovid. 1708.
Translator, with others, *The Works of Lucian.* 4 vols., 1710–11.
Translator, with others, *Ovid's Art of Love and His Remedy of Love.* 1712.

Reading List: *Tate* by Christopher Spencer, 1972.

*   *   *

Nahum Tate is best known for his scaled-down version of *King Lear* with its love story
between Cordelia and Edgar and its happy ending in which Lear retires and leaves his
kingdom to the lovers. After Tate's version was finally replaced in the theatre by
Shakespeare's in 1838, the word "Tatefication" was coined to refer to the debasement of
great literary works; however, the term ignores the ingenuity with which the adaptation was
fitted to the Restoration theatre and its long success. The farce *A Duke and No Duke* (based on
Aston Cokayne's *Trappolin Supposed a Prince,* 1633) also continued to please audiences until
well into the 19th century; for the second edition (1693) Tate wrote an extended defence of
farce. Tate's libretto for Henry Purcell's operatic masterpiece *Dido and Aeneas* contains verse
that, though undistinguished as poetry, is well designed for setting to music.

Tate was not a vigorous or original writer, and his best work was done in adaptation,
translation, or collaboration. He joined successfully with Dryden in Ovid's *Epistles* and
Juvenal's *Satires,* as well as *The Second Part of Absalom and Achitophel* (1682). With a
clerical family background and experience in translation and in writing for music, Tate was
well-qualified to collaborate with Nicholas Brady in versifying the Psalms. Their *New Version
of the Psalms of David* was more polished and elegant than the old Sternhold and Hopkins
version of 1562, and was generally used in Anglican churches for more than a century. Some
of the Tate-Brady renderings are included as hymns in modern hymnals, e.g., "Thro' All the
Changing Scenes of Life" (Psalm 34) and "As Pants the Hart for Cooling Streams" (Psalm
62). The carol "While Shepherds Watched Their Flocks by Night" first appeared in the
Supplement to the New Version.

Of the 102 poems in Tate's two collections (1677, 1684), many are on melancholy themes
but some suggest Cavalier or Metaphysical models or echo Shakespeare or Milton. The odes,
elegies, and other occasional poems that Tate felt were a laureate's duty generally do an
adequate job of expressing (sometimes to musical accompaniment by Purcell or John Blow)
the grand thoughts that are appropriate for the public occasion. A more relaxed poem
(perhaps his best original work) is the amusing, mock-heroic *Panacea: A Poem upon Tea.*

—Christopher Spencer

VANBRUGH, Sir John. English. Born in London, baptized 24 January 1664. Educated at the King's School, Chester, to age 19; also studied in France, 1683–85. Commissioned ensign in the 13th foot regiment of Lord Huntingdon, 1686; arrested in Calais for espionage, and imprisoned in France, 1688–92; Captain in Lord Berkeley's Marine Regiment, 1696; Captain in Lord Huntingdon's Regiment, 1702. Married Henrietta Maria Yarborough in 1719; one son. Architect: designed Castle Howard, 1701, Haymarket Theatre, 1703, Blenheim Palace, 1705, Fleurs (Floors Castle), 1716, Seaton Delavel, 1720, etc.; Comptroller to the Public Works, 1702–13, 1715; Manager, with Congreve, Haymarket Theatre, London, 1705–06; appointed Carlisle Herald, 1703, and Clarenceux King-at-Arms, 1704–26, in the College of Heralds; Surveyor of Greenwich Hospital, 1715. Knighted, 1723. *Died 26 March 1726.*

PUBLICATIONS

Collections

Complete Works, edited by Bonamy Dobrée and Geoffrey Webb. 4 vols., 1927–28.

Play

The Relapse; or, Virtue in Danger (produced 1696). 1697; edited by Bernard Harris, 1971.
Aesop, 2 parts, from a play by Boursault (produced 1696–97). 2 vols., 1697.
The Provoked Wife (produced 1697). 1697; edited by Peter Dixon, 1975.
The Country House, from a play by Dancourt (produced 1698). 1715.
The Pilgrim, from the play by Fletcher (produced 1700). 1700.
The False Friend, from a play by Le Sage (produced 1702). 1702.
Squire Trelooby, with Congreve and William Walsh, from a play by Molière (produced 1704). Revised version by James Ralph published as *The Cornish Squire,* 1734.
The Confederacy, from a play by Dancourt (produced 1705; also produced as *The City Wives' Confederacy).* 1705.
The Mistake, from a play by Molière (produced 1705). 1706.
The Cuckold in Conceit (produced 1707).
Plays. 2 vols., 1719.
A Journey to London, completed by Cibber (as *The Provoked Husband,* produced 1728). 1728.

Other

A Short Vindication of The Relapse and The Provoked Wife from Immorality and Profaneness. 1698.
Vanbrugh's Justification of What He Deposed in the Duchess of Marlborough's Late Trial. 1718.

Reading List: *Vanbrugh, Architect and Dramatist,* 1938, and *The Imagination of Vanbrugh and His Fellow Artists,* 1954, both by Laurence Whistler; *Vanbrugh* by Bernard Harris, 1967; "Vanbrugh and the Conventions of Restoration Comedy" by Gerald M. Berkowitz, in *Genre*

6, 1973; *Masks and Façades: Vanbrugh: The Man in His Setting* by Madeleine Bingham, 1974; *Vanbrugh* by Kerry Downes, 1977.

*   *   *

Vanbrugh's reputation as a major comic dramatist rests on two plays produced within six months of each other at the end of the seventeenth century, *The Relapse* and *The Provok'd Wife*. Like Etherege and Wycherley, the two finest comic playwrights of the previous generation, Vanbrugh was not a professional writer and devoted only a fairly short period of his life to the theatre, so that his output, like theirs, is relatively small. Indeed he is at least as renowned for his architecture, especially Castle Howard and Blenheim Palace, as for his plays. Belonging to the generation of dramatists that includes Congreve, Farquhar, Steele, and Colley Cibber, Vanbrugh was writing after the Glorious Revolution of 1688 when the theatre was again coming under moralistic attacks because of its alleged licentiousness and obscenity. Vanbrugh himself was criticized in the most influential of these, Jeremy Collier's comprehensive *A Short View of the Immorality and Profaneness of the English Stage* (1698), and published a reply in the same year, *A Short Vindication*, in which he defends *The Relapse* and *The Provok'd Wife* against Collier's strictures. At a time when comic drama was beginning to undergo the transformation that led to the homiletic "exemplary" or "sentimental" comedy of the eighteenth century, which concentrated on providing models of virtue and examples of moral reformation to be emulated rather than on comedy's traditional function of ridiculing vice, folly, and affectation, Vanbrugh was intent on keeping alive the satirical mainstream of seventeenth-century comedy descending from Ben Jonson. Like Congreve, he was greatly indebted to the dramatists of Charles II's reign who developed the so-called "wit" or "manners" comedy of the Restoration, but because of his originality in handling its conventions he made a distinctive contribution to this kind of comedy. This is partly because of his essentially serious preoccupation with the subject of marriage, especially the tensions between husband and wife in ill-matched and unhappy relationships, and partly because of the robust energy of his plays that manifests itself in his rich characterization and his inventiveness in creating comic situations. Vanbrugh does in fact cross Shadwell's comedy of "humours" with Etherege's and Congreve's comedy of "wit." Although less caustically satirical than Wycherley, less stylistically refined than Congreve, and less genial than Farquhar, he is undoubtedly one of the wittiest of Restoration writers and for sheer vitality he has few equals among his contemporaries and eighteenth-century successors.

Vanbrugh wrote *The Relapse*, his first play to be staged, in response to Cibber's *Love's Last Shift* (1696), in which Amanda employs subterfuge and deception, including seduction, to win back her rakish husband Loveless who has deserted her. Cibber presents Amanda's reprehensible conduct as admirable, and Loveless, overwhelmed by her display of wifely love, is instantly reconciled to her and morally reformed. Vanbrugh clearly found this sentimental and sententious dénouement facile, dishonest, and unconvincing, and in *The Relapse* wrote a sequel that is also a reply to *Love's Last Shift*. *The Relapse* does, however, stand as a completely independent work that can be appreciated without reference to Cibber's considerably inferior play. Vanbrugh's main plot continues the story of Amanda and Loveless after the penitent's apparent rehabilitation and shows how temporary such reformations usually are. Loveless soon reverts to his promiscuous ways when temptation arrives in the form of Amanda's widowed cousin Berinthia, whereas the virtuous Amanda resists Worthy's offer of adulterous love. At the end of the play Vanbrugh presents no solution to the problem of Amanda and Loveless's marriage, which is left unresolved. Interesting and unusual as this part of the play is, it almost takes second place to the sub-plot concerning Lord Foppington. Vanbrugh again draws on *Love's Last Shift*, since Lord Foppington is Cibber's Sir Novelty Fashion elevated to the peerage, but Vanbrugh also transforms Cibber's amusing portrait of a fop into not only the most rounded presentation of a fashionable beau in contemporary drama but one of the great comic characters of the English stage. Almost as unforgettable is Sir Tunbelly Clumsey, Vanbrugh's version of another stereotype of Restoration comedy, the boorish country knight. Structurally *The Relapse* may be faulty, and Vanbrugh, a fundamentally moral writer, is unable to eschew completely the sentimentality that mars Cibber's play so badly, but its sustained comic brilliance more than compensates for its defects.

The Provok'd Wife, a better organised play than its predecessor, also contains one of the best comic characters of the period, Sir John Brute, the most memorable of the numerous husbands in Restoration comedy who are heartily sick of marriage and their wives and who try, not very successfully, to devote themselves to a life of debauchery. The surly, rude, and stubborn Sir John has ruined his marriage, and Vanbrugh explores sympathetically the predicament of Lady Brute who is maltreated by her husband but who is too virtuous to give herself to her admirer Constant. Vanbrugh deals with the issue of marital incompatibility, at a time when divorce was virtually impossible, in a sensitive and humane way, not in the flippant and jokey manner typical of contemporary comedy, and is too realistic to offer an easy theatrical solution producing a happy ending for Lady Brute. As in *The Relapse*, there is no tidy resolution of the main plot.

Apart from the unfinished *A Journey to London*, which reached the stage in 1728 in a version revised, completed, and sentimentalized by Colley Cibber entitled *The Provok'd Husband*, Vanbrugh's other dramatic works are either adaptations or translations of earlier plays. His one attempt to revamp an English play, a prose version of Fletcher's *The Pilgrim*, impoverishes rather than enriches the original, but the opposite occurs in the case of some of his translations. As a translator of recent French plays, including some of Molière's, Vanbrugh was far from slavish and felt free to alter and add to his sources, the result being that he imbued them with some of his typical vigour and broad humour. The outstanding example is *The Confederacy*, a superb adaptation of Dancourt's *Les Bourgeoises à la Mode*, itself a lively and witty comedy that Vanbrugh, by transferring the action from Paris to London, nevertheless succeeds in enhancing from beginning to end. Also worthy of note is *Aesop*, based on Boursault's *Les Fables d'Ésope*, in which Vanbrugh characteristically tones down the sentiment of the original in favour of comic action. Vanbrugh's two masterpieces still hold the stage and *The Confederacy* has been revived in recent years, but they are not produced as frequently as they deserve.

—Peter Lewis

VILLIERS, George.   See BUCKINGHAM, 2nd Duke of.

WHITEHEAD, William. English. Born in Cambridge, baptized 12 February 1715. Educated at Winchester College, 1729–35; Clare Hall, Cambridge (sizar), matriculated 1735, B.A. 1739, M.A. 1743. Fellow of Clare Hall from 1742; tutor to the future Earl of Jersey and Lord Villiers, 1745; gave up his fellowship, and settled in London, to devote himself to writing: quickly became known as poet and playwright; accompanied Villiers and Lord Nuneham on a tour of Germany and Italy, 1754–56; appointed Secretary and Registrar of the Order of Bath, 1756, and Poet Laureate, 1757; Reader of Plays for David Garrick, at Drury Lane, London, from 1762. *Died 14 April 1785.*

PUBLICATIONS

Collections

Plays and Poems.   2 vols., 1774; revised edition, 3 vols., 1788.

Plays

The Roman Father, from a play by Corneille (produced 1750).   1750.
Fatal Constancy, in *Poems on Several Occasions.*   1754.
Creusa, Queen of Athens (produced 1754).   1754.
The School for Lovers, from a play by Fontenelle (produced 1762).   1762.
A Trip to Scotland (produced 1770).   1770.

Verse

The Danger of Writing Verse.   1741.
Anne Boleyn to Henry the Eighth: An Epistle.   1743.
An Essay on Ridicule.   1743.
Atys and Adrastus: A Tale, in the Manner of Dryden's Fables.   1744.
On Nobility: An Epistle.   1744.
An Hymn to the Nymph of Bristol Spring.   1751.
Poems on Several Occasions.   1754.
Elegies, with an Ode to the Tiber.   1757.
Verses to the People of England.   1758.
A Charge to the Poets.   1762.
Variety: A Tale for Married People.   1776.
The Goat's Beard: A Fable.   1777.

Reading List: *Whitehead, Poeta Laureatus* (in German) by August Bitter, 1933.

*   *   *

William Whitehead began to write poetry during Pope's later years, but lived and wrote through the era variously known as the age of Pre-Romanticism, Reason, or Johnson. Most of the qualities implied by those associations can be found somewhere in his work. "The Enthusiast," for example, whose deism and nature description have been considered pre-romantic, is deeply indebted to the *Essay on Man*; the enthusiast for nature is finally taught that "man was made for man," and drawn from solitude to society. Many of his early poems pay their respects to Pope – verbally, ideologically, or both – and supply us with bad examples of late Augustan "definite-article verse" ("the vacant mind," "the social bosom," "the mutual morning task they ply"). Generally they are light, occasional, often epistolary, and gently satirical, when not congratulating the Royal Family on a marriage or birth. His commonest mood is mild, free-floating mockery, directed both at self and at a rather amusing environment. Whitehead publishes twelve quarto pages of heroic couplets under the title "The Danger of Writing Verse"; playfully emulates Spenser and the early Milton in the freely enjambed blank verse of *An Hymn to the Nymph of Bristol Spring*; and begins "The Sweepers" like a Johnson and Boswell joke: "I sing of Sweepers, frequent in thy streets,/ Augusta." Passion is seldom indulged and never intense, and Reason is often praised. The recurrent Tory patriotism was duly rewarded: as Laureate from 1757 to 1785, Whitehead had to compose birthday odes to George III throughout the American Revolution, a task he performed unflinchingly amid the customary howls of poets and critics.

Whitehead's interest in theatre began while he was a schoolboy at Winchester, where he played Marcia in a production of *Cato*, but reached new heights when the leading actor of the day took over Drury Lane in 1747. In "To Mr. Garrick" he warned the new manager – a nervous man anyway – that "A nation's taste depends on you/– Perhaps a nation's virtue too." The poem inaugurated a long association: Whitehead served as both playwright and play-reader for Drury Lane, and Garrick took leading roles in three of the poet's plays, all fairly successful. *The Roman Father*, a blank-verse tragedy based on Corneille's *Horace*, is distinctly reminiscent of *Cato*; the title-character Horatius (Garrick) is honoured to donate his sons' lives to Rome, and the closing paean to patriotism as the "first, best passion" was a sure clap-trap. Certain scenes, indeed, could be played as *parodies* of Addison, an idea which seems less far-fetched in view of *Fatal Constancy*, a fragmentary "sketch of a tragedy ... in the heroic taste." Though Whitehead gives only the hero's speeches and the scene directions, they are enough to suggest why he wrote no more tragedies after 1754. "My starting eyeballs hang/Upon her parting steps" cries the protagonist as his lover departs, after which they "Exeunt severally, languishing at each other." (Significantly, the play's forte is ingenious exits.) Unlike his plays designed for the stage, *Fatal Constancy* has the lightness of most of his verse, and a keen eye for theatrical absurdities. *Creusa, Queen of Athens*, with Garrick as Alestes, was produced to "great applause" and the approbation of Horace Walpole the same year.

Whitehead's only full-length comedy, *The School for Lovers*, caught and perpetuated the vogue of genteel or "sentimental" drama, though it also included stock bits of comic business that turn up in Goldsmith and Sheridan. The rhetoric of the prologue ("with strokes refin'd .../Formed on the classic scale his structures rise") conveys Whitehead's pure and reformist intentions as a playwright. *The Dramatic Censor* (1770) complained that "a dreadful soporific languor drowses over the whole, throwing both auditors and readers into a poppean lethargy," but the play, with Garrick as Dorilant, had a good first run and several revivals. Likewise *A Trip to Scotland*, Whitehead's only farce, pleased audiences for several seasons despite an unimpressive text. None of his plays reads well today, yet none failed, and *The Roman Father* and *The School for Lovers* were still being revived at the end of the eighteenth century.

—R. W. Bevis

WILSON, John. English. Born in London, baptized 27 December 1626; lived with his family in Plymouth, 1634–44. Educated at Exeter College, Oxford, matriculated 1644, but left without taking a degree; entered Lincoln's Inn, London, 1646: called to the Bar, 1652. Courtier and royalist: chairman of a board of sequestration after the Restoration; may have accompanied the Duke of Ormonde to Ireland, 1677; Recorder of Londonderry, 1681–89; possibly served as Secretary to the Viceroy of Ireland, 1687; lived in Dublin, 1689–90; returned to London, 1690. *Died c. 1695.*

PUBLICATIONS

Collections

Dramatic Works, edited by James Maidment and W. H. Logan. 1874.

Plays

> The Cheats (produced 1663). 1664; edited by Milton C. Nahm, 1935.
> Andronicus Comnenius. 1664.
> The Protectors. 1665.
> Belphegor; or, The Marriage of the Devil (produced 1675). 1691.

Verse

> To His Grace James, Duke of Ormonde. 1677.
> To His Excellence Richard, Earl of Arran. 1682.
> A Pindaric to Their Sacred Majesties James II and Queen Mary on Their Joint Coronation. 1685.

Other

> A Discourse of Monarchy. 1684.
> Jus Regium Coronae. 1688.

> Translator, Moriae Encomium; or, The Praise of Folly, by Erasmus. 1668.

Reading List: Wilsons Dramen by K. Faber, 1904; "John Wilson and 'Some Few Plays' " by Milton C. Nahm, in Review of English Studies, 1938.

* * *

Like many of the more important Restoration dramatists, John Wilson devoted only a small part of his life to writing. In his case the crucial years were those immediately following the Restoration of the monarchy in 1660, when he wrote two prose comedies, The Cheats and The Projectors, a blank-verse tragedy, Andronicus Comnenius, and made his well-known translation of Erasmus's Moriae Encomium (The Praise of Folly). After the 1660's he wrote only one play, the tragi-comic Belphegor (performed in Dublin in 1675 and in London in 1690), and a few poems and tracts.

His reputation as a dramatist rests mainly on his first play, The Cheats, which was revived and reprinted from time to time during the rest of the seventeenth century and the first quarter of the eighteenth century. Wilson, a lawyer and a man of considerable learning, knew the work of Ben Jonson and his pre-Commonwealth followers intimately, and his two comedies belong to the Jonsonian comic tradition, especially to the "low" city comedy that Middleton specialized in; they therefore illustrate the element of continuity in seventeenth-century drama despite the closure of the theatres between 1642 and 1660. As comedies of "humours," both The Cheats and The Projectors contain numerous satirical portraits of the type found in the plays of Jonson and his "sons," as the names of the characters indicate; the cast of The Projectors, for example, includes Suckdry (a relative of Jonson's Volpone), Sir Gudgeon Credulous (very similar to Fitzdottrel in Jonson's The Devil Is an Ass), Jocose, Squeeze, and Leanchops. The world of Wilson's comedies is the familiar Jonsonian one of knaves and gulls, deceivers and deceived, cheats and cheated, and many of Wilson's targets, such as hypocrites, casuists, usurers, and misers, are identical to Jonson's. Derivative and backward-looking as Wilson's comedies are, they are lively and varied, and contain some memorable "humour" figures. Although Belphegor is a tragi-comedy set in Italy, it too shows Jonson's influence, being partly modelled on The Devil Is an Ass; Wilson's main source, however, is Machiavelli's version of a legend about a devil taking human form in order to discover the truth about women and marriage. In his one attempt at tragedy, *Andronicus Comnenius*, a study of a revengeful tyrant who indulges in wholesale slaughter to become Emperor of Constantinople, Wilson observes many of the neo-classical proprieties and rules, but is influenced by Shakespeare as well as Jonson, one scene being closely based on Richard's wooing of Anne in *Richard III*. Despite the abundance of off-stage action and murder, *Andronicus Comnenius* is a static play lacking in subtlety, and is much less interesting than Shakespeare's relatively immature history play about a similar character. Wilson's talent was for satirical comedy.

—Peter Lewis

WYCHERLEY, William. English. Born in Clive, near Shrewsbury, Shropshire, in 1640. Lived in Paris, 1655–60; spent a short time at Queen's College, Oxford (gentleman commoner), 1660; entered the Inner Temple, London, 1660, but never practised law. Married 1) the Countess of Drogheda in 1679 (died, 1681); 2) Elizabeth Jackson in 1715. Served in the Army, and may have been both an actor and theatre manager before he began to write for the theatre in 1671; enjoyed the patronage of Charles II until 1680 when the king banished him from court because of his marriage; gaoled for debt on his wife's estate, 1682: released and given a pension by James II, 1686; retired to Clive and devoted himself to writing poetry. *Died 31 December 1715.*

PUBLICATIONS

Collections

    Complete Works, edited by Montague Summers.   4 vols., 1924.
    Complete Plays, edited by Gerald Weales.   1967.

Plays

    Love in a Wood; or, St. James's Park (produced 1671).   1672.
    The Gentleman Dancing-Master (produced 1672).   1673.
    The Country-Wife (produced 1675).   1675; edited by David Cook and John Swannell, 1975.
    The Plain-Dealer (produced 1676).   1677.

Verse

    Hero and Leander in Burlesque.   1669.
    Epistles to the King and Duke.   1683.
    Miscellany Poems.   1704.
    The Idleness of Business: A Satire.   1705.
    On His Grace the Duke of Marlborough.   1707.

Other

Posthumous Works, edited by Lewis Theobald and Alexander Pope.   2 vols., 1729.

Reading List: *Wycherley: Sa Vie, Son Oeuvre* by Charles Perromat, 1921 (includes bibliography); *Brawny Wycherley* by Willard Connely, 1930; *Wycherley's Drama: A Link in the Development of English Satire* by Rose A. Zimbardo, 1965; *Wycherley* by P. F. Vernon, 1965; *Wycherley* by Katharine M. Rogers, 1972.

*   *   *

Like so many literary gentlemen of the Restoration, William Wycherley fancied himself a poet, but it was not until he was in his sixties and the Restoration had begun to turn into the eighteenth century, spiritually as well as chronologically, that his *Miscellany Poems* appeared. The collection, in which long, tedious philosophic poems share space with love-and-seduction verses, is, as Macaulay said, "beneath criticism." Its publication did attract Alexander Pope, then a bright teen-ager on the literary make, who became a friend of the aging Wycherley. Pope's promise to polish the old man's verse was not kept during Wycherley's life, but it did lead to a volume, *Posthumous Works*, in which it is impossible to separate standard Wycherley from bad Pope. Wycherley occasionally dipped to prurience in his poems, as in "The Answer," a verse reply to "A Letter from Mr. Shadwell to Mr. Wycherley," but he seldom rose to the kind of wit that can be found on almost any page of *The Country-Wife*.

From the little we know about Wycherley, he was ambitious for social position and greedy for money but finally inept in his attempts to get what he wanted; he was also an urban snob as only a transplanted country boy can be. How so conventional a Restoration figure and so dull a poet could have written the comedies that mark him as one of the major English playwrights is still one of the mysteries of English literary history. We do not even know why he wrote them. He may have needed money; he may have wanted to impress the Restoration Wits – Rochester, Dorset, Sedley, Etherege – with whom he had become friends; he may have been overcome by a temporary artistic afflatus. For whatever reason, between 1671 and 1676, he wrote three good plays and one fine one, comedies that provide the theater's best and harshest view of Restoration society, and then, after the publication of *The Plain-Dealer* in 1677, he turned his back on the theater. He did return once, in 1696, to write a pedestrian prologue which was probably never performed for Catharine Trotter's preposterous *Agnes de Castro*. Strange company for the creator of Horner and Mrs. Pinchwife!

Wycherley's plays, like most of the Restoration comedies, are about the endless quest for sex and money, in and out of marriage, and the central theme is enriched by the playwright's marvelous sense for social pretension and polite hypocrisy. Whether he sends Alderman Gripe (*Love in a Wood*) into an old bawd's house, a pious prayer on his lips, or allows Lady Fidget (*The Country-Wife*) to reach from behind her prim exterior for the ever available Horner, he raises laughter at surface behavior which is the child of mendacious society by deep-seated lubricity. Except when a voice of pure delight, like that of the titular country wife, is needed to set off the shady machinations of most of the characters, there is no place for healthy sexuality in Wycherley's plays. Even Mrs. Pinchwife has to learn to deceive, but to her credit and to the play's advantage she remains a child trickster, the happy side of corruption. For the most part sex is a game (and often a brutal one) or a commodity (and often a shoddy one). From bawds and pimps to courting couples, Wycherley's characters know that sex is money, that whatever other entry marriage supplies, it opens purses. When Manly in *The Plain-Dealer* loses his jewels to the scheming Olivia, he is not simply robbed, he is unmanned.

Because Wycherley has always seemed so much a part of the world he depicts, some critics have taken Horner as an author surrogate and read the plays as a celebration of a society in which the true wits are successful manipulators, properly winning sex or money from the imperfect pretenders who deserve being used. Because that depicted world is essentially an ugly one, some critics have taken Manly as Wycherley (the playwright's later pseudonymous use of The Plain-Dealer in letters and in the preface to *Miscellany Poems* helped feed the notion) and taken Manly's abusive attacks on society as the playwright's true voice. There are obvious satiric elements in Wycherley's plays – conventional portraits of literary poseurs, bumbling cuckolds, overeager importers of foreign dress and manners – and they help prove the case for the concerned critic whether he sees Wycherley as Horner or Manly. On a deeper level, however, neither approach really works. On closer look, the clever Horner becomes a sex machine, servicing his clientele with all the efficiency and false gaiety of a fast-food shop, and Manly, who so hates hypocrisy, can be seen as a man for whom plain-dealing is a mask, a self-righteous, self-absorbed individual who uses the falseness of society as an excuse to act dishonestly. The strength of Wycherley's plays is that they are not ordinary period satires. He is the most modern of the Restoration writers because he refuses to provide a place for the audience to stand. His good characters, like Christina in *Love in a Wood*, turn fool through overstatement; his clever characters become butts; his fools refuse to remain skewered. John Dennis, praising Wycherley, once said " 'tis the Business of a Comick Poet to paint the Age in which he lives," and that Wycherley has done superbly, but without providing an ideational frame to fence in his presentation.

In emphasizing the ugliness of the world in which Wycherley's characters play their dead-serious games, I am in danger of falsifying the quality of the playwright's work, as have a number of recent revivals in which plain-dealing directors have displayed a chic fondness for sordid detail. Although the plays are harshly realistic in their approach to life, they are artificial in a theatrical sense. The characters are stereotypical and the exchanges between them are as set as vaudeville comic routines. Take, as an instance, the scene in *Love in a Wood* in which Dapperwit is about to introduce Ranger to his mistress, for whom he is pimping. The realistic content of the scene – the need to get the money in hand – need not interfere with the theatrical effect of a comic turn in which Dapperwit's loquacity, established in an earlier scene, becomes a hesitation device, enticing Ranger and then putting verbal obstacles in his path. Like so much that goes on in Wycherley's plays, this is overtly funny aside from any satirical implications; yet, unlike so much popular comedy, the theatrical fun of the scene does not disguise or weaken the essential nastiness of the situation. As though to emphasize the theatricality of his plays, Wycherley introduces in-jokes – references to his own work (*The Plain-Dealer*), to his actors (*The Gentleman Dancing-Master*), to the fact that the audience is in a theater. "She's come, as if she came expresly to sing the new Song she sung last night," says Hippolita in *The Gentleman Dancing-Master*, and a character who has no other function in the play walks on stage to perform a number. This kind of playfulness not only underscores the conscious artifice in Wycherley's work, it reminds the audience that there is a distance between the action and its referent, that these very funny plays are about a world in which the comic stereotypes have painful counterparts. Only occasionally, as when the brutality of Manly threatens the comic surface of *The Plain-Dealer*, does the real world come dragging its unpleasantness onto the stage. For the most part, Wycherley invokes laughter haunted by a suspicion which, a beat or two beyond the laugh, asks what was so funny. At his best, which means at almost any point in *The Country-Wife*, the laughter and the questioning come at the same time, the play's artistry and its documentary integrity go hand-in-hand.

—Gerald Weales

NOTES ON CONTRIBUTORS

ASHLEY, Leonard R. N. Professor of English, Brooklyn College, City University of New York. Author of *Colley Cibber*, 1965; *19th-Century British Drama*, 1967; *Authorship and Evidence · A Study of Attribution and the Renaissance Drama*, 1968; *History of the Short Story*, 1968; *George Peele · The Man and His Work*, 1970. Editor of the *Enriched Classics* series, several anthologies of fiction and drama, and a number of facsimile editions. **Essays:** Henry Brooke; Colley Cibber; Aaron Hill; Edward Moore; Elkanah Settle.

BACKSCHEIDER, Paula R. Associate Professor of English, University of Rochester, New York. Author of "Defoe's Women: Snares and Prey" in *Studies in Eighteenth Century Culture*, 1977, and "Home's *Douglas* and the Theme of the Unfulfilled Life" in *Studies in Scottish Literature*, 1978. Editor of the Garland series *Eighteenth-Century Drama* (60 vols.) and of *Probability, Time, and Space in Eighteenth Century Literature*, 1978. **Essay:** John Crowne.

BATTESTIN, Martin C. William R. Kenan, Jr., Professor of English, University of Virginia, Charlottesville. Author of *The Moral Basis of Fielding's Art*, 1959, *The Providence of Wit · Aspects of Form in Augustan Literature and the Arts*, 1974, and a forthcoming biography of Fielding. Editor of the Wesleyan Edition of Fielding's works, and of *Joseph Andrews, Tom Jones,* and *Amelia*. **Essay:** Henry Fielding.

BEVIS, R. W. Member of the Department of English, University of British Columbia, Vancouver. Editor, *Eighteenth Century Drama · Afterpieces*, 1970. **Essays:** George Colman, the Elder; John Dennis; Samuel Foote; Charles Macklin; William Whitehead.

FAULKNER, Peter. Member of the Department of English, University of Exeter, Devon. Author of *William Morris and W. B. Yeats*, 1962; *Yeats and the Irish Eighteenth Century*, 1965; *Humanism in the English Novel*, 1976; *Modernism*, 1977. Editor of *William Morris · The Critical Heritage*, 1973, and of works by Morris. **Essay:** Thomas Holcroft.

HILSON, J. C. Lecturer in English, University of Leicester. Editor of *Augustan Worlds* (with M. M. B. Jones and J. R. Watson), 1978, and *An Essay on Historical Composition*, by James Moor, 1978. Author of articles on Hume, Richardson, Smollett, and Conrad. **Essay:** Roger Boyle, Earl of Orrery.

HUGHES, Leo. Professor of English, University of Texas, Austin. Author of *A Century of English Farce*, 1956, and *The Drama's Patrons*, 1971. Editor of *Ten English Farces* (with Arthur H. Scouten), 1948, and *The Plain Dealer* by William Wycherley, 1967. **Essay:** Edward Ravenscroft.

JEFFARES, A. Norman. Professor of English Studies, University of Stirling, Scotland; Editor of *Ariel · A Review of International English Literature*, and General Editor of the Writers and Critics series and the New Oxford English series; Past Editor of *A Review of English Studies*. Author of *Yeats · Man and Poet*, 1949; *Seven Centuries of Poetry*, 1956; *A Commentary on the Collected Poems* (1958) and *Collected Plays* (1975) *of Yeats*. Editor of *Restoration Comedy*, 1974, and *Yeats · The Critical Heritage*, 1977. **Essays:** William Congreve; Richard Brinsley Sheridan.

KELLY, Gary. Member of the Department of English, University of Alberta, Edmonton. Author of *The English Jacobin Novel 1780–1805*, 1976. Editor of *Mary, and The Wrongs of Women* by Mary Wollstonecraft, 1976. **Essay:** Elizabeth Inchbald.

KUNZ, Don.   Associate Professor of English, University of Rhode Island, Kingston. Author of *The Drama of Thomas Shadwell*, 1972, and of articles on Shadwell in *Restoration and Eighteenth Century Theatre Research.* **Essay:** Thomas Shadwell.

LEWIS, Peter.   Lecturer in English, University of Durham. Author of *The Beggar's Opera* (critical study), 1976, and articles on Restoration and Augustan drama and modern poetry. Editor of *The Beggar's Opera* by John Gay, 1973, and *Poems '74* (anthology of Anglo-Welsh poetry), 1974. **Essays:** George Farquhar; John Gay; George Lillo; Sir John Vanbrugh; John Wilson.

LINK, Frederick M.   Professor of English, University of Nebraska, Lincoln. Author of *Aphra Behn*, 1968, and *English Drama 1660–1800 · A Guide to Information Sources*, 1976. Editor of *The Rover* by Behn, 1967, and *Aureng-Zebe* by John Dryden, 1971. **Essays:** Aphra Behn; Henry Carey; Hannah Cowley.

MACKERNESS, E. D.   Member of the Department of English Literature, University of Sheffield. Author of *The Heeded Voice · Studies in the Literary Status of the Anglican Sermon 1830–1900*, 1959, *A Social History of English Music*, 1964, and *Somewhere Further North · A History of Music in Sheffield*, 1974. Editor of *The Journals of George Sturt 1890–1927*, 1967. **Essay:** John Hughes.

MALEK, James S.   Professor of English and Associate Graduate Dean, University of Idaho, Moscow. Author of *The Arts Compared · An Aspect of Eighteenth-Century British Aesthetics*, 1974, and of articles in *Modern Philology, The Journal of Aesthetics and Art Criticism, Neuphilologische Mitteilungen, Texas Studies in Literature and Language*, and other periodicals. **Essays:** Sir George Etherege; John Home; Arthur Murphy.

MINER, Earl.   Townsend Martin Professor of English and Comparative Literature, Princeton University, New Jersey. Author of *Dryden's Poetry*, 1967; *An Introduction to Japanese Court Poetry*, 1968; *The Metaphysical Mode from Donne to Cowley*, 1969; *The Cavalier Mode from Jonson to Cotton*, 1971; *Seventeenth-Century Imagery*, 1971; *The Restoration Mode from Milton to Dryden*, 1974; *Japanese Linked Poetry*, 1978. **Essay:** John Dryden.

MORPURGO, J. E.   Professor of American Literature, University of Leeds. Author and editor of many books, including the *Pelican History of the United States*, 1955 (third edition, 1970), and volumes on Cooper, Lamb, Trelawny, Barnes Wallis, and on Venice, Athens, and rugby football. **Essay:** John Burgoyne.

OLIVER-MORDEN, B. C.   Teacher at the Open University and the University of Keele. Editor of the 18th-Century section of *The Year's Work in English 1973.* **Essay:** Oliver Goldsmith.

ROGERS, Pat.   Professor of English, University of Bristol. Author of *Grub Street · Studies in a Subculture*, 1972, and *The Augustan Vision*, 1974. Editor of *A Tour Through Great Britain* by Daniel Defoe, 1971, *Defoe · The Critical Heritage*, 1972, and *The Eighteenth Century*, 1978. **Essay:** Susanna Centlivre.

SCOUTEN, Arthur H.   Professor of English, University of Pennsylvania, Philadelphia. Author of articles on Swift, Defoe, and the London theatre in periodicals. Editor of *Ten English Farces* (with Leo Hughes), 1948, *The London Stage 3*, 2 vols., 1961, and *1*, 1965, and *A Bibliography of the Writings of Swift* by Teerink Herman, second edition, 1963. **Essays:** John Banks; Thomas D'Urfey; Sir Robert Howard; Nathaniel Lee.

SOLOMON, Harry M.   Associate Professor of English, Auburn University, Alabama. Author of *Sir Richard Blackmore* (forthcoming), and of articles on Shaftesbury, Swift, and others for *Southern Humanities Review, Keats-Shelley Journal, Studies in English Literature,* and other periodicals. **Essay:** Robert Dodsley.

SPENCER, Christopher.   Professor of English, University of North Carolina, Greensboro. Author of *Nahum Tate,* 1972. Editor of *Davenant's Macbeth from the Yale Manuscript,* 1961, and *Five Restoration Adaptations of Shakespeare,* 1965. **Essay:** Nahum Tate.

STAGG, Louis Charles.   Professor of English, Memphis State University, Tennessee; Member of the Executive Committee, Tennessee Philological Association. Author of *Index to Poe's Critical Vocabulary,* 1966; *Index to the Figurative Language in the Tragedies of Webster, Jonson, Heywood, Chapman, Marston, Tourneur,* and *Middleton,* 7 vols., 1967–70, revised edition, as *Index to the Figurative Language of the Tragedies of Shakespeare's Chief 17th-Century Contemporaries,* 1977. **Essay:** Nicholas Rowe.

STROUP, Thomas B.   Professor Emeritus, University of Kentucky, Lexington. Author of a book on composition, and of *Microcosmos · The Shape of the Elizabethan Play,* 1965, and *Religious Rite and Ceremony in Milton's Poetry,* 1968. Editor or Joint Editor of *Humanistic Scholarship in the South,* 1948; *South Atlantic Studies for Sturgis E. Leavitt,* 1953; *The Works of Nathaniel Lee,* 2 vols., 1954–55; *The Selected Poems of George Daniel of Beswick,* 1959; *The Cestus · A Mask,* 1962; *The University and the American Future,* 1965; *The Humanities and the Understanding of Reality,* 1966. **Essay:** Thomas Otway.

TASCH, Peter A.   Associate Professor of English, Temple University, Philadelphia; Co-Editor of *The Scriblerian.* Author of *The Dramatic Cobbler · The Life and Works of Isaac Bickerstaff,* 1971. Editor of *Fables by the Late Mr. Gay,* 1970. **Essays:** Isaac Bickerstaff; Charles Dibdin; David Garrick; Hugh Kelly.

THOMSON, Peter.   Professor of Drama, University of Exeter, Devon. Author of *Ideas in Action,* 1977. Editor of *Julius Caesar* by Shakespeare, 1970; *Essays on Nineteenth-Century British Theatre* (with Kenneth Richards), 1971; *The Eighteenth-Century English Stage,* 1973; *Lord Byron's Family,* 1975. **Essays:** George Colman, the Younger; Thomas Morton; John O'Keeffe.

THORNTON, Ralph R.   Associate Professor of English, La Salle College, Philadelphia. Editor of *The Wives' Excuse,* 1973, and *The Maid's Last Prayer,* 1978, both by Thomas Southerne. **Essay:** Thomas Southerne.

TRUSSLER, Simon.   Editor of *Theatre Quarterly.* Theatre Critic, *Tribune,* 1969–76. Author of several books on theatre and drama, including studies of John Osborne, Arnold Wesker, John Whiting, Harold Pinter, and Edward Bond, and of articles on theatre bibliography and classification. Editor of two collections of eighteenth-century plays and of *The Oxford Companion to the Theatre,* 1969. **Essays:** Richard Cumberland; Sir Richard Steele; George Villiers, Duke of Buckingham.

WEALES, Gerald.   Professor of English, University of Pennsylvania, Philadelphia; Drama Critic for *The Reporter* and *Commonweal.* Author of *Religion in Modern English Drama,* 1961; *American Drama since World War II,* 1962; *A Play and Its Parts,* 1964; *The Jumping-Off Place · American Drama in the 1960's,* 1969; *Clifford Odets,* 1971. Editor of *The Complete Plays of William Wycherley,* 1966, and, with Robert J. Nelson, of the collections *Enclosure,* 1975, and *Revolution,* 1975. **Essay:** William Wycherley.